FIGHT CHOREOGRAPHY

THE ART OF NON-VERBAL DIALOGUE

JOHN KRENG

Professional • Technical • Reference

Fight Choreography: The Art of Non-Verbal Dialogue
John Kreng

Publisher and General Manager, Cengage Learning PTR:
Stacy L. Hiquet

Associate Director of Marketing:
Sarah O'Donnell

Manager of Editorial Services:
Heather Talbot

Marketing Manager:
Mark Hughes

Executive Editor:
Kevin Harreld

Development Editor/Copyeditor:
Cathleen Snyder

Project Editor:
Jenny Davidson

Content Reviewer:
Jeremy Cantor

PTR Editorial Services Coordinator:
Erin Johnson

Interior Layout:
Shawn Morningstar

Cover Designer:
Mike Tanamachi

Indexer:
Kevin Broccoli

Proofreader:
Sara Gullion

Library of Congress Control Number: 2005924926

ISBN-13: 978-1-59200-679-3

ISBN-10: 1-59200-679-5

Cengage Learning PTR
20 Channel Center Street
Boston, MA 02210
USA

Cengage Learning is a leading provider of customized learning solutions with office locations around the globe, including Singapore, the United Kingdom, Australia, Mexico, Brazil, and Japan. Locate your local office at: **international.cengage.com/region**

Cengage Learning products are represented in Canada by Nelson Education, Ltd.

For your lifelong learning solutions, visit **cengageptr.com**

Visit our corporate website at **cengage.com**

Printed in the United States of America
2 3 4 5 11 10 9 8

This book is dedicated to my mother Phany,
for all the love and sacrifices
she has made for me throughout her life,
so I can have a better life in America.
I love you.

And to all the stunt professionals all over the world
(past, present, and future) who put their lives on the line
on a daily basis for the entertainment of others.

Acknowledgments

I'd like to thank the following people for their help in getting this book done. It is impossible to mention everyone who was helpful in making this book come to life, so I apologize—Robin Ritter, Daxing Zhang, Petra Jorgensen, Christian Voss, David Stein, Erika Bryce, Martin Blythe, Brian White, Bey Logan, Gary Lee Jackson, Ultimo Dragon, Rob Van Dam, Master Tom Meigs, Garrick Palumbo, Rick Stelow at www.DrunkenMaster.tv, James Lew, Anthony DeLongis, Dan Speaker, Greg Reifsteck, Mike Massa, Robert Lee, Yong Kim, Stephen Quadros "The Fight Professor", John Saxon, Cynthia Rothrock, Jeff Wolfe, Benny "The Jet" Urquidez, Mfundi Dennis Brown, Neil Ehrlich, Jeff Miller, Roger Yuan, Jeff Mulvin, Christian Voss, Garrick Palumbo, Rick, Anfrea Sea Namaste, Vic Armstrong, Brandon Shealy, Chad Stehelski, Chona Jason, Damion Portier, Dave Murphy, David Keats, Dean Ferradini, James Lew, Jeff Briggs, Jennifer Derkitt, Joey Carman, Karen Sheperd, Lisa Nemzo, Olga Alvarez, Greg Reifsteck, Dr. Craig Reid, Scott Levy, Linda Palmer, Tiger Chen, Richard Norton, and Chang Pei Pei.

Special thanks goes to Ron Strong for his undying support, advice, and help getting this book done. Jeremy Cantor for suggesting I write this book and being my 3rd eye. Keith Vitali—your friendship, support, and help over the years have been instrumental in me being where I am today. Jeff Imada—your friendship, support, and the many talks with me during the writing of this book. David Tadman—thanks for your friendship, support, and everything in helping me get this book done. Kevin Harreld—for his championing of this project in seeing this through and making this a reality—the only thing you are missing is a cape.

I'd also like to thank Risk Castinado for being instrumental in giving me my first break in starting my writing career and Martha Burr and Gigi Oh for being supportive of my writings over the years at Kung Fu Tai Chi magazine.

Thanks goes to some people who have been instrumental and influential in my life, and unfortunately, are no longer here but still live in my heart—Cheryl J. Miller, Catherine Farias, Mike Stahley, and Stuart Quan.

We never thank our teachers enough and I would like to thank the following who have been more than helpful and instrumental in my life and for me being able to write this book...

Mr. Andy Smith, my high school gymnastics coach, for teaching me much more than how to flip.

Mrs. Cosby, my 8th grade audio/visual teacher, for turning me onto Akira Kurosawa and for encouraging and teaching me the passion for film.

Mr. Charles Forsythe, my college art teacher, for teaching me art structure and visual dynamics.

Masters John Davis, Kim Bernhardt, and Mike Stahley for giving me my black belt and teaching me the warrior/artist spirit.

To Edwin Villa, Tang Nguyen, Jo Eric Mercado, Chris Blache, Tom Poorman, Cade Alvarez, Matthew Polino, Andre "Chyna" McCoy, Jeff Centauri, Jonathan Anderson, Geovanny Corvera, Marco Zaror, David Cordero, Geno Frazier, Van Ayasit, Chona Jason, Satoshi Nakagawa, Kenji Sato, Eiji I, and Todd Rex—you are all simply the best.

To the filmmakers who I have worked with over the years, my humblest of thanks for believing in me.

About the Author

John Kreng has been studying martial arts since 1973 and currently holds black belts in Tang Soo Do and Te Katana Jujitsu and has studied other various styles including Kali, Hung Gar, and Wing Chun Kung Fu. As a stuntman, screen fighter, fight choreographer, and/or stunt coordinator, he has worked with Jet Li, Tsui Hark, Yuen Cheung Yen, Roger Corman, and Steven Spielberg. He has written for *Inside Kung Fu, Impact, World of Martial Arts,* and *Kung Fu-Tai Chi* magazine, where he had his own movie review column. For the 25th Anniversary of the release of *Enter the Dragon,* John was the writer, coordinating editor, and project supervisor for the *Bruce Lee Tribute* issue published by TC Media. John was also a successful stand-up comedian, video game producer, and designer. He studied art at Montgomery College and Parsons School of Design and screenwriting at UCLA Extension.

Contents

Introduction . . . . *xix*

Chapter 1 Basic History of Fight Choreography and Fighting on Film 1

Basic Overview: The Evolution of Fight Choreography *2*
The Birth of Film in the United States *3*
Asian Martial Arts Influence on Western Films *35*
The Dawn and Influence of the Modern-Day Kung Fu Brawl *45*
East versus West *48*
The Chain of Command on a Set *51*
The Difference in Perception of Action: Seeing beyond the Physical *52*
Culture/Religion *55*
A True Art Form versus a Gimmick *57*
Ageism *58*
Code of Ethics/Conduct *59*
Mythology *59*
Emphasis of the Fight: Elaborate versus Brief *59*
Length of the Fight *62*
Editing *62*
Camera Angles *63*
Stuntmen *63*
Choreographers *64*
Sound *65*
Special Effects *65*
Room for Advancement versus Categorization *66*
Billing/Recognition *67*
Time and Preparation *67*
Film Genres *68*
Story *68*
Perceptions and Stereotypes of Foreigners in Film *68*
Asian Talent in Western Films *70*
Globalization of Asian Martial Arts Films *75*

What We Can Still Learn from Bruce Lee . . . 77
He Had No Noticeable Misses or Bad Takes in the Fight Scenes in Any of His Hong Kong Films . . . 77
He Had Simple Techniques but Rarely Repeated Himself . . . 78
He Had an Individualistic Screen Presence . . . 79
He Had a Learning Curve . . . 81
He Understood the Emotional Content and Impact behind Each Technique . . . 82
He Was Adept with Both Hands and Feet, and He Was Not Afraid to Mix It Up . . . 83
He Was Unafraid to Show His Vulnerability . . . 84
He Knew the Importance of Having Great Stuntmen around Him . . . 84
He Had Different and Unique Timing and Rhythm . . . 85
He Had Great Martial Acting Skills . . . 85
He Had Effective and Convincing Before and After Poses . . . 87
He Did Not Have a Trademark or Signature Move . . . 87
He Had a Physique That Everyone Envied . . . 88
He Understood the Difference between Cinematic and Real Fighting . . . 88
He Injected Philosophy and Fight Strategy into His Films . . . 88
He Fought Only When Necessary . . . 89
Watching Bruce Lee's Movies . . . 90
Way of the Dragon (aka Return of the Dragon) . . . 90

Chapter 2 The Differences between Sport, Art, and Self-Defense 93

Three Major Approaches to Combat: Art, Sport, and Self-Defense . . . 94
Common Ground among All Three Concepts . . . 94
Definition of a Martial Art . . . 95
Definition of a Combative Sport . . . 96
Definition of a Self-Defense/Combative System . . . 97
What Is a Martial Artist? . . . 97
The Root of Combative Sports . . . 98
Mixed Martial Arts . . . 98
The Birth of Brazilian Jiu-Jitsu and Vale Tudo . . . 100
Coming to America and the Birth of the UFC . . . 101
Why MMA Is Popular with Audiences . . . 102
The Different Ranges of Combat Involved . . . 103
Tournament/Point Fighting . . . 103
What Is Free Sparring? . . . 104

What Is Tournament Fighting? 104
Different Types of Tournaments 105
Different Eras of Tournament Fighting 105
Pro Wrestling 108
What Is Sports Entertainment? 109
What Is Fake? 110
Pro Wrestling Comparisons to Fight Choreography for Film and Television 111
A Brief History of Pro Wrestling 116
World Wrestling Entertainment (WWE) 121
Extreme Championship Wrestling (ECW) 122
Hooking the Audience 123
Pro Wrestling Outside America 126
Outside the Ring: Wrestling on Film and TV 133

Chapter 3 Definitions and Terminology 137

Empty-Handed Fighting Distance/Range 137
Different Types of Fighters 138
Offensive Fighters 138
Defensive Fighters 138
Counter-Attacker 139
Styles of Fighters 139
Technician 139
Brawler 140
Showman 141
Emotional 141
Intellectual 141
Definitions of Fighting Terms 141
Film Fighting and Stunt Terms 150
The Pulse of a Fight Scene 153

Chapter 4 Primer 157

Issues with Using a Real Martial Artist or Combative Athlete on Film 157
What Is a Screen Fighter? 167
The Importance of Rhythm in a Fight 168
Working with and Training Actors, Stunt Players, and Stunt Doubles 171
Differences between School Training and Film Training 172

Purpose . . . 172
Time Invested . . . 172
Learning Process . . . 173
Length of Classes . . . 173
Techniques Used . . . 174
Application of Skills . . . 174
The Actor's Role in the Film . . . 175
The Role of the Stuntman and Stunt Double . . . 175
The Script and What to Teach . . . 176
Collaboration with Other Creative Departments . . . 178
The Relationship between Trainer and Actor . . . 178
Assessing the Actor's Physical Skills . . . 179
Understanding the Actor You Are Training . . . 180
Possible Issues That Can Arise during Training . . . 181
Horror Stories . . . 183
Horror Story #1 . . . 183
Horror Story #2 . . . 184
What Is Strategy? . . . 185
Basic Types of Strategy . . . 187
Use of Technique with Strategy . . . 188
Showing Character and Personality through Strategy . . . 189
Issues That Can Nullify a Character's Strategy . . . 191
Ways for an Audience to See Strategy . . . 191
Real-Life Strategists . . . 192
Examples of Fight Strategy on Film . . . 194
The Difference between Violence and Action . . . 195
Justification for Actions Taken . . . 197
Five Basic Justifications . . . 198

Chapter 5 The Whole Structure 201

Introduction to the Process of Putting Together a Fight Scene . . . 201
The Balancing Game . . . 204
Relationship between Physical and Technical . . . 204
Problems That Can Arise on the Technical Side . . . 205
Compensating for One Another . . . 205
X Factors That Were Not Worked into This Equation . . . 205

Chapter 6 The Source 207

The Story . . . 207
Back Story . . . 208
Exposition . . . 209
Character Arcs . . . 209
Reveals . . . 211
Setups and Payoffs . . . 211
Justification of the Action and the Skills of the Characters . . . 214
The Characters . . . 215
The Role of the Hero . . . 215
Different Types of Heroes . . . 216
Justifying the Hero's Actions . . . 219
The Villain . . . 221
The Mentor . . . 223
The Buildup . . . 230
Training Sequences . . . 230
What Is a Form? . . . 244
Levels of Forms . . . 245
Use of Forms in Combat and Other Situations . . . 247
The Script . . . 248
The Three Acts of a Screenplay and the Types of Action Used in Each Act . . . 253
Questions . . . 262
Exercises . . . 263

Chapter 7 Extracting the Essence 265

Assembling the Character and Story Inventory . . . 266
Breaking Down the Script . . . 269
Creating Your Character Bible . . . 271
Putting Together Your Character Bible . . . 272
Creating the Fighter's IQ . . . 282
Number of Fights in Which the Character Participates . . . 284
Result of Each Fight . . . 284
Justification (Part 1): The Fighter's Skills . . . 284
Heightened Sense of Awareness . . . 285
Time Period . . . 287
Handicaps . . . 287

Traditional Fighter or Modern Eclectic . . . 287
Animal Representation . . . 288
Temperament . . . 289
Fighting Spirit . . . 289
Flashy or Effective Techniques . . . 290
Number of Different Styles, Disciplines, and Approaches to Enforcement 291
Character's Reaction/Response to New Places . . . 291
Uncomfortable Place or Environment for the Character . . . 291
Skills and How They Were Acquired . . . 291
Responsibility Due to Skills and Title/Position . . . 292
Direct Effect of Fights on the Character's Growth (Arc) throughout the Film . . . 293
Anger . . . 293
Conditioned or Unconditioned . . . 293
Reaction/Response . . . 300
The Caste System . . . 301
Fighting Distance . . . 302
Motivation to Fight . . . 302
Flaws, Weaknesses, and Strengths . . . 302
Learning Curve . . . 302
Physical, Emotional, Mental, and Spiritual Rituals . . . 303
Previous Physical Confrontations or Fights . . . 303
Street Sense . . . 304
Thinking Process . . . 304
Inventory of the Character's Mental, Physical, Spiritual, and Emotional Fighting Skills . . . 305
Things the Character Should Not Do in a Fight . . . 305
Morals or Code of Conduct in Battle . . . 305
Character's Actions during Events beyond His Control . . . 306
Ego . . . 306
Transcendence to Mental, Spiritual, or Mythical Aspects . . . 307
Personal Carriage When at Rest . . . 308
Actions in Uncomfortable Situations . . . 308
Character's Training . . . 308
Relationship to Mentor . . . 308
Respect for Authority Figures . . . 308
Character's Reaction to Lessons He Can't Understand . . . 309
Pre-Planned Fights . . . 309
Issues about Death . . . 310
Injury or Death at the Hands of the Character . . . 310
Signature Moves . . . 311

Distinct Signature Weapons . . . 312
Character's Level of Proficiency . . . 312
Interactions with More Highly Skilled Individuals . . . 314
Reputation . . . 314
External Symbols or Indications . . . 315
Fight Chart and Stats . . . 315
Your Fight Chart . . . 315
Stats . . . 316

Chapter 8 The Narrative Structure and Elements of a Fight Scene 323

Fight Scene Structure . . . 324
The Lead-Up . . . 326
The Physical Fight/Conflict . . . 336
Flexible Elements . . . 346
Overall Elements throughout the Fight . . . 358

Chapter 9 Physical Elements of the Fight Scene 361

The Framework . . . 361
Physical Elements Defined . . . 362
Intent and Choice of Techniques . . . 362
Beats and Pauses . . . 362
Rhythm . . . 363
Timing . . . 363
Cues . . . 363
Length . . . 365
Environment . . . 367
Stylization of Moves . . . 367
Body Language . . . 369
Centerline and the Centerline Theory . . . 369
Stances . . . 371
Combination of Approaches . . . 373
Camera Awareness . . . 375
Collective Rhythm of the Fight . . . 376
What Exactly Is Martial Acting? . . . 376
Good and Bad Martial Acting . . . 377
Martial Acting during a Fight . . . 378
Martial Acting before and after a Fight . . . 380

Reactions 383
Facial Expressions 384
Exercises 384

Chapter 10
The Technical Elements of a Fight 385

Cinematography 386
Rehearsing with the Cameraman 386
Effective Camera Angles 390
Distance from the Fight 390
Camera Height 392
Keeping It Visually Pure and Effective 393
Inserts and Close-Ups 394
Frame Composition 394
The Issue of Getting in Too Close 394
Showing Just Enough 398
Slowing Down or Speeding Up the Action 399
One Take: Continuous Action without Breaks 404
Editing 405
Different Styles of Editing 406
The Fight Choreographer's Dilemma 408
Solutions 410
Processing Information 410
The Pulse of a Fight Scene 411
Cinematography Exercises 415
Editing Exercises 415

Chapter 11
Developing a Choreographer's Eye 417

Developing an Eye for Action 418
See Films in a Theater First 418
Study Audience Reactions 420
Expand Your Tastes 420
Try Not to Prejudge a Movie 422
Be Selective about Whose Reviews You Read 423
Do Not Substitute Box-Office Gross for Aesthetics 424
Learn to Read Subtitles 425
Know What to Ask Yourself after Seeing a Movie 427

Know Your Action Film History and the Contributors . . . 429
Learn to Be Film Literate . . . 430
Know Whether the Film Was Made for You . . . 431
Too Much Information to Handle? . . . 433
Test Yourself . . . 433
Daydream about Fight Scenes . . . 434
Design a Fight Scene Every Day . . . 434
Learn, Observe, and Study Human Psychology . . . 435
Learn How the Human Body Moves and Works . . . 436
Compare and Contrast . . . 436
Learn and Hear about the Creative Process . . . 438
Go to the Creative Source . . . 440
Attend Live Sporting Events in Which Physical Contact or Body Rhythm Is Involved . . . 441
Learn Several Different Styles of Martial Arts . . . 441
Film Your Own Fights . . . 442
Learn to Take Criticism . . . 443
Starting a Video Reference Library . . . 446
A Filmmaker's Artistic Integrity . . . 446
Video Stores . . . 447
All DVDs Are Not the Same . . . 448
Do Not Limit Yourself to Viewing Only DVDs . . . 448
Why Look for Imported DVDs? . . . 448
How and Where to Find Rare, Obscure, and Imported DVDs . . . 450
Be Aware of "Dubtitles" . . . 453
TV Size . . . 454
PAL, NTSC, and SECAM . . . 454
Watch an Action Scene without Any Sound . . . 454
Keep Your Movies in a Database . . . 455
For Those on a Budget . . . 455
Be Aware of "Double-Dipping" . . . 456

Chapter 12 Recommended Reading, Viewing, and Other Resources 457

Further Reading . . . 457
Stunt Related . . . 457
Film Biography . . . 457
Filmmaking: The Process . . . 458

Producing 458
Film History 458
Screenwriting 458
Cinematography 459
Martial Arts 459
Artists and Creative Issues 459
Suggested Viewing 460
Fight/Stunt Related 460
Filmmaking 461
Screenwriting/Storytelling 461
Film Biography 461
Martial Arts 462
Combative Sports 462
Sports Entertainment 465
Other 466
Periodicals 468
Stunt-Related Periodicals 468
Screenwriting Periodicals 468
Filmmaking Periodicals 468
Daily Entertainment Business Periodicals 468
Action-Specific Entertainment Periodicals 468
General Film and Entertainment Reviews 472
Martial Arts Periodicals 472
Combative Sports Periodicals 472
Pop Culture Periodicals 472
Professional Wrestling Periodicals 472
The Major Studios 472
Additional Resources 473
DVD Distributors 473
Organizations and Unions 474
Independent DVD Dealers 475
Stunt Organizations 477
Women's Film Organizations 477
Film Conservatories and Institutes 477
Award Shows 478
Critics Societies 478
Online Resources 481
Books 481
Celebrity Sites 481
Daily Entertainment News (Subscription) 481

Screenwriting 481
Movie News 481
DVD Reviews and News 481
Martial Arts Online References 486
Boxing Online References 486
Mixed Martial Arts Online References 486
Pro Wrestling Online References 486
Sports Wrestling Online References 486
Conventions and Festivals 486
Festivals 488

Index **489**

Introduction

"Fight choreography is literally what Bruce Lee said in Enter the Dragon, *but taken in a different context, that it's 'the art of fighting—without fighting.'"*

—Jeff Imada, Martial Artist/Stunt Coordinator for *Rapid Fire, The Crow, L.A. Confidential, Daredevil,* and *Escape from L.A.*

Everyday audience members watching a movie or TV show usually cannot consciously describe the specific differences between a good or a bad fight scene they see, but subconsciously they do know the difference based on how they react to and feel about the sequence. When a fight scene is not done well, the audience member will feel disconnected from what they have just seen onscreen. One of the important things to the audience (whether or not they realize it) is the varying emotions they experience from an action scene depending on how effectively it is intertwined with the story. Audiences want to leave their lives for the moment and take an emotional ride with the hero as he defeats the villains who are in the way of peace, happiness, or justice—and viewers want to be with the hero when he wins the girl or the prize at the end. They admire and/or identify with the hero as he is fighting for his life, and they are emotionally behind every punch and kick. When a fight scene is done well, the audience takes that raw visceral energy they saw onscreen into their own lives, and they are rejuvenated, feeling they can take on the obstacles in their lives just as the hero did onscreen.

Even though the audience might not be able to verbalize what they like and don't like and what is real and fake about an action sequence, the filmmaker absolutely has to know the elements of what makes an action sequence effective. I'm sure you have seen films in which the story and acting are great, but the action sequences are not convincing enough, or terribly shot or edited so that you could not see anything, and/or do not integrate seamlessly into the story, calling unnecessary attention to their weaknesses and thereby rendering them ineffective, gratuitous, or worse yet, unintentionally humorous. This is because the audience watches movies two different ways. They process rational thoughts and actions in their head, and they experience the emotions that are being shown on the screen with their body. You can see it in people's body language when they are watching a movie, as their bodies react to what is happening on the screen. Have you ever gotten goose bumps, forgotten to breathe, or sat on the edge of your seat when seeing a movie? Such bodily reactions indicate the emotional power of filmmaking that should not be taken lightly.

What Is Fight Choreography?

Fight choreography is not just relegated to your standard action or martial arts, kung fu, or wu xia movies. Fight scenes can be seen in all categories of film with varying degrees of intensity and application. Consider comedies—Mongo punching out the horse in *Blazing Saddles*? Or the cat-and-mouse game between Kato and Inspector Clouseau in the *Pink Panther* series? King Arthur gradually lopping off the Black Knight's limbs, but still up for fighting him in *Monty Python and The Holy Grail*? Dramas (*Deliverance, L.A. Confidential, Good Fellas*), musicals (*West Side Story*), classics (*Romeo and Juliet, Cyrano de Bergerac, The Three Musketeers*), epics (*Braveheart, Spartacus, Saving Private Ryan*), critical award winners (*A Clockwork Orange, Rashomon, Rocky*), and foreign films (*La Femme Nikita, The Seven Samurai, Battle Royale*). Even something as mundane as an insulted woman slapping her boyfriend's cheek must be choreographed properly in order to look believable onscreen.

There are major differences between a fight scene you would see on film and a fight you would see at a live combative sporting event or even a real street fight. In a street fight, there is serious intent to do bodily harm to someone, usually caused by a misunderstanding and/or an issue of blinding ego or pride (often involving alcohol and/or drugs). There are no set rules in a street fight, especially when emotions get out of control, which can lead to serious injuries or death to the participants or even to innocent bystanders.

In a combative sporting event, such as boxing or a mixed martial arts (aka MMA) contest you would see in the UFC, Pride, or K-1,etc., the participants are focused on each other, strategizing about how to land a technique that will accumulate points or get their opponent to admit defeat. Even though the threat of serious injury or death could occur, there are rules in place to prevent this, and the combatants' main purpose is to win money or a trophy, or to advance to the next rank, level, or tournament position. Even though the combatants usually have a strategy in mind before they meet their opponents, what happens in the ring can cause a combatant to change his approach. This is considered a form of improvisation because it is a live event that cannot be repeated exactly the way it was originally done.

Fight choreography is the art of creating a staged and rehearsed physical conflict that is convincing to the audience for entertainment purposes. No one involved (or on the sidelines) gets hurt, and the participants know the outcome of the encounter before it ever happens, even though the audience does not. The magic of fight choreography is making the scene look as if it is happening right in front of the viewers' eyes and making the outcome unexpected by the audience.

Table I.1 displays a list of comparative issues that show the differences between a combative sporting event/real-life situation and a fight scene choreographed for entertainment purposes. However, note that the art of professional wrestling does not directly apply to the comparison in Table I.1; it will be discussed in much more detail later in this book.

Table I.1 Differences between Combative Sporting/Real-Life Events and Choreographed Fight Scenes

Live Competitive Sport Combat and Real-Life Confrontations	Fight Choreography for Entertainment Purposes
The combatants have a serious intent to restrain and/or do bodily harm to their opponent.	All the actors involved pretend as if they are doing bodily harm to each other. Altering the audience's perspective with effective camera angles, editing, props, sound effects, and visual special effects helps the actors make the audience think this is a real fight.
In a real-life fight situation, the combatants are usually emotionally overwhelmed and unaware of their specific actions because they are not physically and mentally conditioned. In drastic situations, the untrained fighter might black out and not remember anything or remember just glimpses about the fight and how he was involved. In combative sports, an athlete's goal and motivation are to (1) hit and not get hit, and (2) defeat his opponent within the rules of the contest to advance and/or win a coveted prize.	The actors involved in the fight understand the story and everyone's personal motivations for getting into the fight. They bring it to life for the audience with their theatrical combat skills, along with acting and miming. The fight serves the story/narrative that is for entertainment purposes.
No one knows the outcome of the encounter.	Everyone involved with the fight knows the eventual outcome of the encounter before filming begins. The fight scene is choreographed and rehearsed with all the actors before filming begins.
Combatants try not to think about the people around them who are observing the fight.	The actors involved are aware of where the camera is at all times and alter their techniques so that they will "read" well on camera.
Crafty, sneaky, or even "dirty" techniques are sometimes used on an opponent so that the opponent cannot see to restrain or subdue the combatant. In a competitive situation, the combatants try to use non-telegraphable techniques that their opponents will not see coming.	The actors use or alter techniques that telegraph their intentions so the audience can see and appreciate them. Performers also use techniques that look effective onscreen, even though these techniques might not be as effective in real life. Usually, wide, sweeping, circular techniques appear more effective on film than short, straight techniques that might be more powerful, and less telegraphed, in real life.
The encounter cannot be re-enacted exactly as it happened in real life and combative sport situations.	Combat is choreographed so it can be repeated multiple times for different camera angles, takes, and so on.
Combatants do not know what or when their opponent's next move will be.	Every actor involved in the staged fight knows what everyone's moves are, so each knows when it is his cue to become more involved in the fight.
Emotional stress is directed at bystanders, especially to those who have a vested interest of some kind (lover, friend, relative, gambler, spectator, fan, and so on) in any of the combatants involved.	When done well, a feeling of anxiety and excitement is achieved while getting the audience emotionally involved in the story.

Elements of Fight Choreography

Fight choreography should not be seen as simply using a martial art or a system or style of self-defense that has been altered for use in film. Rather, it should be looked at as a theatrical combative art form in and of itself because it is creating an illusion of a physical confrontation that combines the use of theatrics with martial arts to assist and enhance in telling the story of the film.

Broken down, the art of fight choreography for film, TV, and videogames is made up of a combination of several key elements—story, dance, acting, style of fight, props, camera, editing, audio, and technology. All these elements are combined to create a nonverbal narrative of conflict that assists in telling the story.

Story

For fight scenes to be effective, they have to be justified by the story, and motivation must exist for the combatants to get into physical engagements in the first place. Without justification in story and character motivation for the conflict, the fight scene becomes gratuitous. We remember the fight scenes from *The Matrix* and *Crouching Tiger, Hidden Dragon* long after the films have left the theaters because the characters' motivation and actions are justified, and because the outcomes of those encounters serve to move their respective stories forward. Action films that do not have a solid story and barely justify the characters' actions are not taken seriously as quality film-making and usually end up in the 99-cent bargain bin at the video store.

A fight scene is a story within a story, and as such the fight scene itself typically has a three-act structure of its own—there is a setup, a conflict, and a resolution. The three acts comprise a justified beginning, a conflicting middle, and a satisfying ending. Without any one of these elements, the fight will not be a believable part of any larger story.

Dance

In a choreographed fight, there are all the basic elements of dance—steps, rhythm, cooperation, and timing of a prearranged set of moves between agreed partners. I say "agreed partners" because everyone involved in the fight is willing, and each knows all the moves and cues their partner will do and will react accordingly when it is his turn. It should come as no surprise that the word "choreography" is used to describe the planning and arrangement of dance moves as well as fighting techniques.

There is also unsaid and unseen (by the audience) trust and agreement between the predetermined participants that they are cooperating with each other to create the illusion of a physical encounter onscreen that is usually repeated several times for the camera. It is no coincidence that Bruce Lee was the cha-cha champion of Hong Kong, while some of Jackie Chan's film influences are Gene Kelly and Fred Astaire. Jeff Imada (stunt coordinator for *Fight Club*, *Daredevil*, *The Crow*, and *Rapid Fire*, among others) was not a professional dancer, but a classically trained pianist and therefore understands rhythm. John McTiernan (director of *Die Hard* and *Predator*, among others) thinks of film as a musical structure. John Woo (director of *The Killer*, *Hard Boiled*, and *Face/Off*, among others) watches dance musicals before he choreographs an action scene to get inspiration. Such dance and music training provided these choreographers with an understanding of the timing and rhythm needed for film fights and action scenes that martial arts classes/training do not provide.

Acting

The partners in a filmed fight scene have to act by showing emotions (usually nonverbally through mime) that inform the audience about character motivations and attitudes as well as story details. Depending on what is required by the story and the actor's skill range, these emotions can vary from vulnerability to humor, rage, and everything between. Action stars such as Jackie Chan, Sammo Hung (*Prodigal Son*, *Warriors Two*, *The Iron-Fisted Monk*), Chow Yun Fat (*The Killer*, *Hard Boiled*, *A Better Tomorrow*), Bruce Willis, John Travolta, Sylvester Stallone, Tom Cruise, and Stephen Chow (*Shaolin Soccer*, *Kung Fu Hustle*) easily come to mind because of the wide range of emotions they are able to display during an onscreen physical encounter. This is what I define as Martial Acting and this will be explained later in detail. This skill brings emotional depth to the encounter and connects the audience emotionally to the scene because they are able to read the character's feelings without a break in the narrative of the action scene and the story.

Also, a good knowledge and understanding of human psychology and emotions is instrumental in adding life and individualizing each of your fight scenes. Many action films get a bad rap because of the terrible acting. This is why the actors just mentioned always get top dollar in the action film industry—they are all good actors. It's easy to see bad acting in an action film, but when acting is done well, we don't notice it because the actors are striking the right balance between truth and fantasy and are in synch with the other actors in the film during the action scenes.

Style of Fight

This element deals with choosing the right approach and style of fight for each character to express his distinctive personality within the story and within the genre. This does not necessarily mean all the actors involved and every character in the story needs to be a martial arts master or has to practice a certain style. However, the actors involved must be able to understand and perform the chosen arts and techniques empty-handed and/or with weapons (when required) convincingly, to the skill level of the character they are portraying. The actors should also show the proper martial intent when throwing the techniques against their opponents/partners, while showing emotional understanding of the outcome and ramifications of executing each technique.

It is crucial to have the fight suitable for the genre and rating of the film. Having a bloody and graphic fight like in *Braveheart* wouldn't be suitable in a film for kids like *The Chronicles of Narnia* series.

The fight should also show a strategy or agenda for each combatant that is unique to each character. Completely mismatched skill levels often make for predictable outcomes unless the inferior fighter gets a lucky break of some kind. But it is often a good idea to match up combatants with distinctly different, but potentially equivalent, fighting skills in order to keep the audience guessing. Popular examples include speed vs. power, contrast in size (Westley, the Man in Black, vs. Fezzik, the Giant, in *The Princess Bride*), contrast in styles, and tenacity vs. technique (Rocky Balboa vs. Apollo Creed in *Rocky 1, 2,* and *3*). Arranging a great fight scene requires the choreographer to have an extensive understanding of storytelling, different types of fight strategy, human psychology and emotions, human anatomy and how the body moves, acting, and teaching skills as well as knowledge of different ways (martial arts) of fighting. Films that easily come to mind as good examples of this skill are *The Matrix, Fight Club, Way of the Dragon* (aka *Return of the Dragon*), *Police Story, Odd Couple* (1979, Sammo Hung), *Heroes of the East,* and *Equilibrium.*

Sport/Spectacle

Pre-hype interviews on talk shows and entertainment-based programming, where the actors and the filmmakers talk about how long they practiced to prepare for the fight scenes of that particular film, create a buzz with the audience wanting to see them actually perform on screen. When you have someone like Jet Li, Jackie Chan, Bruce Lee, Donnie Yen, Sammo Hung, or Tony Jaa on screen you are expecting some kind of spectacle to unfold that is simply amazing, inspiring, and jaw dropping, that only a select few can do on the big screen. This is much like watching a highlight reel of the day's sporting events on the nightly news.

Props

Props are the physical equipment used to assist the actors in the illusion of the fight. These include mats, crash pads, trampolines, mini-tramps, air rams, wires, decelerators, and stunt doubles. This category also includes makeup, fake blood, prosthetics, furniture to trip over, and so on. If a prop is picked up and then swung or thrown at an opponent, it officially graduates to *weapon* status. This also includes the objects the stunt players fall or crash into. Props as weapons are masterfully done in many of Jackie Chan's films like *Rumble in the Bronx* and *Police Story.* Even the environment where the fight takes place can be considered a prop and become a unique part of the fight scene making each fight scene individual and unique.

Camera

Camera angles are extremely important in fight choreography and can be easily overlooked. If you have choreographed a great fight scene and captured the action using the wrong angles, you end up with an ineffective fight scene. The audience has to see what the actors are doing, or they will not understand what is happening. Camera angles must also be chosen carefully so that fake hits read as actual connecting strikes; otherwise, the illusion of reality will be broken.

Proper camera angles are an art when capturing action. The ability to capture the action is very important in telling a nonverbal story. Jan de Bont's camera work on *Die Hard* and *Robocop*, Peter Pau's on *Crouching Tiger, Hidden Dragon* and *The Killer*, Andrew Laszlo's on *The Warriors*, Lan Shan Ho's (aka Tadashi Nishimoto) in *Come Drink With Me*, Douglas Slocombe's on *Raiders of the Lost Ark*, and Christopher Doyle's on *Hero* easily come to mind when it comes to fight scenes that are well composed, artistically done, and easy for the audience to follow and understand. Many western filmmakers currently feel that they need to get up closer for a tighter shot on action so the audience can feel it. But how can you "feel" the action when you can't see what is happening in front of you?

Editing and Continuity

Cutting and assembling the raw footage into a cohesive visual narrative that makes sense is always one of the tougher endeavors in the filmmaking process. Editing an action sequence can drastically change the mood, tempo, and rhythm of what is being choreographed. When a film is edited well, we do not notice the editing and we get deeper into the story and characters onscreen. When a film is sloppily edited with poor timing and discontinuous cuts, the audience has a difficult time following the action on the screen and quickly loses interest.

Audio (Sound and Music)

A fight scene is enhanced with great sound foley. We have all experienced bad sound effects in the cheap chop-socky martial arts movies coming out of Asia during the '70s Kung Fu movie boom. All the hits sounded the same—as if they were smacking together two pieces of wood, even when a fighter would strike thin air. But great sound enhances a fight scene and we remember it well after we leave the theater. How many times have you imitated the sound of a light saber from *Star Wars*? That special sound the light saber makes was taken from a microphone that was too close to a speaker—it is now synonymously linked with the weapon.

Sound also includes music that accompanies the film or TV show. Music can greatly affect the mood of a fight scene. It can turn a lighthearted fight scene into a serious brooding combat sequence. A great example is with Jackie Chan's *Project A.* Compare the original Chinese version to the Miramax version, which has a new music soundtrack.

The music on both versions is completely different and alters the feeling of the action sequences. This is particularly true when you watch the foot-bicycle chase/fight scene between Jackie and the thugs that are after him, which ends with the famous clock tower fall in the middle of the film.

Special Effects Technology

The illusion of actual combat can be enhanced with the use of modern technology and/or equipment through special effects. Such technological enhancements may include CG stunt doubles or opponents (often motion captured), stop motion animated creatures, makeup effects (injuries), fake blood spurts, and various other special effects (explosions, CG limb removal, etc.). *The Incredibles, Jason and the Argonauts, King Kong, Spider-Man 2, Shaolin Soccer, Kung Fu Hustle, Storm Riders, Jurassic Park, Terminator* and *Terminator 2*, and the *Lord of the Rings* trilogy are excellent examples of technology assisting the fight choreography.

The last four elements (camera, editing, audio, and technology) are essentially anything that aids the performers with what they cannot do themselves and provides an enhanced narrative of the physical encounter for the audience that they could not reproduce by themselves, creating a heightened visual experience.

Camera, sound, and editing are not immediately associated as parts of the fight choreography process, but they are essential for making an action scene effective. You can spend months or years training the actors and choreographing them in the best fight scene since Bruce Lee was alive. Perhaps the director, producer, actors, and crew are all praising you because the fight scene is so exciting and they have never seen anything like it before. But if the action scene is not shot and/or edited well and does not capture the energy, mood, and feeling that you rehearsed, it will end up looking mediocre because the audience could not see what the actors were doing. Gratuitous blood spurts or inappropriate sound effects can similarly ruin the intended tone or overall effectiveness of an otherwise well choreographed fight scene.

Audiences and critics will then talk about how bad the fight scenes were and blame you, the fight choreographer, for the atrocity. You will try to explain to them that you choreographed this great fight scene that was beyond incredible but it was not filmed effectively and was edited backward with cheesy music and ineffective sound effects. But it's no use—it's your fight scene, so you'll take the fall for it.

This happens to almost every fight choreographer and stunt coordinator more often than I'd like to admit. Although it might seem like I'm biased toward the relative importance of fight choreography in filmmaking, that's not true at all. Every department of a film production is interrelated, but in martial arts or action films, it is often the fight scenes and stunt work that fill the theater seats, so the importance of effective choreography cannot be overlooked. Fight choreography requires all the departments discussed earlier to be in synch with each other during the production.

Why Do We Need a Book on Fight Choreography?

Some might say, "Who cares? Who needs a book on fight choreography? I wrote and directed the movie *Entrails of Vengeance*, which was number one at the box office last week, and I didn't follow any of the guidelines mentioned in this book! Heck, I just hired two black belts and told them to fight while I filmed it." What this person misses is a deeper connection that he could have made with the "silent character"—aka the audience. The film might've been number one that week due to celebrity awareness; a controversial, shocking, or taboo scene; and/or its part in a big media campaign, rather than for the actual quality of the film. Many fight scenes you see in film and TV are simply gratuitous and do not enhance the story. Instead, they simply call unnecessary attention to themselves.

Another argument is that if you have a great script, great characters, and top-notch actors to portray the characters, then who cares about how good the fight scenes are? Well-executed action scenes help to support and enhance the story, while heightening the audience's willing suspension of disbelief and making the film more memorable. When action scenes are done poorly, you take a big chance on losing your audience.

A great fight scene has the following elements:

- The fight scene advances and heightens the story and does not stall during the action sequences.
- The fight starts and ends with different emotions by furthering the dilemma or resolving it.
- The fight is justified and fits seamlessly into the story and character arcs.
- The fight scene keeps the emotions of the scene and enhances them.
- A gradual progression. The scene is better, more difficult and more exciting than the previous fight scene.
- The fight scenes do not recycle the same techniques continuously throughout the film.
- There are changes in emotion, timing, pace, and rhythm during the fight.
- The scene tells a nonverbal story.
- There are close-ups and inserts when necessary to let the audience know what the characters are feeling.
- The character's fighting skills are justified in the story.
- The scene uses the correct techniques for the current emotions and personalities of each character.
- The audience forgets they are seeing a movie and are emotionally drawn into the fight scene, rooting for a particular combatant.

- The audience is able to see and understand what is happening onscreen.
- The audience cannot predict the final outcome.
- The film stands the test of time. A great action film is still remembered and appreciated after repeated viewings and over the course of time, just like any classic film.

Performing a staged fight is as old as the art of acting itself and requires skills that acting classes or a martial arts school alone cannot teach. There is a gap between those two disciplines that this book will hopefully cover and bridge. When done well, a fight scene or action sequence on film conveys its feeling and message visually and non-verbally, like a masterful mime holding our imaginations with no exchange of words, but with all the thoughts, feelings, and emotions communicated through pantomimed expressions during the physical conflict. Hence, part of the title of this book—non-verbal dialogue.

The Current State of Fight and Action Choreography

In Asia, the award for Best Action Design is one of the highlights of the Hong Kong film awards. Ditto the Best Action Choreography for Taiwan's Golden Horse Awards. Both are considered the equivalent in Asia to the Oscars. There you will see some of the greatest names in action choreography. You might see Yuen Woo-Ping go up against his brother Yuen Cheung Yan, or Jackie Chan, Sammo Hung, and Ching Siu-Tung compete head to head for the coveted awards in any given year.

In Asia, fight choreographers spend more time developing and filming their action scenes than we do in the west. Jackie Chan spent three months choreographing and shooting the final 20-minute fight scene in *Drunken Master II*, making it arguably one of his most exciting finales ever captured on film. But in the west, most action films give the stunt coordinator sometimes an hour, a day, or a week at longest to prepare and shoot an action scene. With U.S. film productions, it is common for filmmakers to spend most of their time on dialogue and other shots, which get priority over the action sequences (even if it is an action film). And when the production is running out of time and money, the action sequences usually suffer first, even while shooting an action film!

There is also a reverse prejudice from producers and studio executives that occurs when a Hong Kong fight director comes to America to choreograph and shoot the action on a U.S. film. When a Hong Kong fight director comes here, he is given much more time to prepare, train the actors, and choreograph the fight scenes. However, a U.S. stunt coordinator is never given that much time to prepare, which makes comparison between the two unjust when you see the finished product. Also, a U.S. stunt coordinator does not have any type of control over how the angles are shot (unless they are the 2nd unit director) and is rarely given the opportunity to contribute to the editing process of the film, which is an absolutely crucial step in the creation of an exciting and effective action sequence. Imagine the disappointment when a qualified fight choreographer sees his carefully chosen techniques lose their clarity and entertainment value after a film editor (often with little or no martial arts training or choreography experience) cuts the sequence ineffectively. Hong Kong fight directors, on the other hand, are given much more control over the angles shot and how they are edited. When I have interviewed many people responsible for the choreography of fight scenes in the west, they have constantly voiced their frustrations about the end result of what they put together for their films.

In Hollywood, action has always been the bastard child in a dysfunctional relationship with the Hollywood studios and the unions that represent people in the stunt business. Action sells and brings in lots of money at the box office, but it is not very well respected by the inner circle of Hollywood.

Putting together an action scene is a combination of art and science. Unfortunately, up to this point in time, action/fight choreography is not taken seriously in America or in Europe. The Academy of Motion Picture Arts and Sciences (aka the Oscars), the SAG Awards (put on by the Screen Actors Guild, the union that represents stunt players and stunt coordinators), the César Awards (the French Academy Awards), and the British Academy of Film and Television (aka BAFTA) currently do not have a category for action choreography. Yet action films are in abundance as each summer rolls by, and they bring in a lot of box-office dollars. With the Oscars, all departments are represented in these prestigious award ceremonies—from producer to writer to special effects to sound to wardrobe to cinematography—except for stunts. There are several reasons why this might be, including the following:

- **The televised awards show is already long enough, and adding another category will make the show even longer.** This is a sorry excuse because there are two Academy Award shows. We only see one of them in its entirety—we see just the highlights of the other one (which takes place several days earlier), which highlights the technical achievements, where action/fight choreography could certainly be included.
- **Adding a Best Action category would open up a myth or illusion that Hollywood has been struggling to keep a secret since the days of silent films.** The "old Hollywood guard" wants to keep up the illusion that most actors are doing their own stunts or fights. In the early '80s there was a huge controversy about the movie *Flashdance* when Marine Jahan told the press that she was the one who did a majority of the dances, doubling for the film's star, Jennifer Beals. The myth continues with the PR, such as when *Rumble in the Bronx* was repackaged for U.S. audiences, claiming that Jackie Chan did all his own stunts. The truth of the matter is that Jackie will do all the hard stunts but leave the simpler ones to a double because he does not want to risk getting hurt on a simple stunt,

which would put him out of commission and halt production. Does this take away from the audience? No. This mentality belittles an audience's intelligence. By educating audiences about the intricacies of the action sequences, we can elevate the quality and approach to stunts and action.

- **Choreographing and setting up action on film is not considered seriously as an actual science and art.** This is by far the most ignorant statement and belief ever! Creating an effective action sequence with a high level of clarity and entertainment value is a very complicated endeavor, and the more intricate and dangerous the stunt, the more time it takes to set up and rehearse so no one gets hurt.

To be fair, there is one major awards show in the west that currently gives awards for best action. Since 2002, the Emmy Awards has given an award for Best Action in a TV Series to the stunt coordinator of the winning show. So there has been some progress made in getting recognition and prestige to the people who are in charge of putting together the action. This somewhat makes up for the fact that TV stunt coordinators have it the roughest because:

- They are usually not given assistants, although every other department has them.
- They do not receive residual payments for their work because they are considered the head of a department (even though they are represented by Screen Actors Guild). The only way a stunt coordinator gets residuals is if he puts himself into an action scene by being a stunt player or doubling for an actor.
- Their turnaround time is only eight hours when the production day stops, whereas the actors get 12 hours. This does not include the administrative paperwork and setup for the next day's action that a stunt coordinator has to do at the end of the day.
- Their pay is slightly above what a day-player stuntman receives. A stuntman usually gets paid more than a stunt coordinator does at the end of the day because the stunt player gets an adjustment or "bump" (for the specialized skill he was hired to do) on that day.

In Asia, in the opening credits at the beginning of a film, the fight director usually gets billing along with the actors and the director of the film. Fight directors are as popular as (or sometimes even more popular than) the director and/or stars of the film. In Asia, the audience is much more knowledgeable about action films and they know the work of various fight directors. They will take a chance and go see a film for which they do not know the director or actors as long as they know that the fight director's past work has been good. Ching Siu-Tung, Yuen Woo-Ping, Sammo Hung, and Yuen Cheung Yan all have this type of educated fan following.

In the U.S., the stunt coordinator (the person who is the head of the stunt department for the shoot) is usually credited because he is the head of a department at the end scroll of a film. But I've seen some films where in the end credits, the stunt coordinator gets his name listed after the caterer or not at all. And if you are a stuntman, it is always negotiable and up to the producer's discretion whether you will get credit and where. When you look at the end credits of an American film, know that usually a quarter to three-fourths of the stunt players who worked on the film did not get credit. It is also very rare for a fight choreographer to get credit at the beginning of an American film, even in the action or martial arts genres, where more often than not, the fights are the very selling points of the film itself!

Recently, in an attempt to make up for the lack of attention in Hollywood by the major award groups and their own union, the stunt industry formed their own awards ceremony, the Taurus Awards (aka the World Stunt Awards). In 2002, the American Choreography Awards (which focus on dance choreography for film and TV) added the category of Outstanding Fight Choreography for Film and TV. The committees for many of the major award shows fail to see what is involved in the skill, dedication, and craft of all the stunt players who take part in making action scenes work successfully and often risk their lives on a daily basis for the sake of entertainment.

Hollywood does not take stunts seriously enough to give them any accolades, and one myth is that stunts and fight choreography are not considered acting. Depending on which side you take on this, action is still much closer to acting than, say, special effects, musical scores, and producing (which all have their own categories at the Oscars). Action is an integral part of acting and the story. Where would *The French Connection* be without the famous car chase scene? Where would *Rocky* be without the final fight with Apollo? What if there was no chariot race in *Ben Hur*? What type of film would a James Bond movie be if he didn't have his trademark gadgets and action sequences? What would replace the battle sequences in the *Star Wars* films if you took those away? Every summer there are dozens of blockbuster films with good action scenes in them. Having a Best Action category would also raise the quality of action sequences in Hollywood because it would give the stunt coordinators a level of quality for which to aim.

Another issue is that many "old Hollywood guard" insiders don't want the audience to know about the tricks of the trade. As mentioned earlier, they want to keep the illusion that the actor is performing the action, rather than admitting that it is often done by a professional stuntman. This has been a secret since the birth of film in the silent era. PR continues to claim that "so and so is fearless and does all his own stunts." This is usually somewhat plausible until the DVD is released with its supplemental "making of" section, and you see another person who looks similar to the star and is wearing the exact same clothing as the star. Hmmm...I wonder who that could be.

Audiences today are getting more educated about angles and cuts and are able to tell when there is a stunt double. And, they are still able to enjoy the film and even appreciate it more. Another important point is that when audiences watch preview trailers for upcoming films, a good majority of the previews have action sequences in them to get the audience's interest. Producers use action to market a film because action is universal and transcends any language barrier, but studio executives continuously neglect to give credit where credit is due.

So far, the representatives of the Academy of Motion Picture Arts and Sciences has not provided a valid public response as to why a Best Action Scene category has been denied up to this point in time despite petitions and protests by the stunt community. The same issue applies for the SAG Awards but cuts on a much deeper level. The depressing point to reflect upon is, if the union who represents the stunt coordinators and stunt players (who pay annual dues) in film and TV won't take them seriously by giving them a category, then why should any other award show?

The Role of the Fight Choreographer

Filmmakers often think, "Why do I need someone to choreograph my fight scenes? I've got some world champion martial artists in this scene, and they can put a fight scene together and make it look good. They know what they are doing." But such attitudes completely miss the point of what makes a good fight scene.

The relationship between a fight choreographer and his screen fighters is equal to that of a film director and his actors. The fight choreographer might not have been the one who actually taught Jackie Chan how to do his acrobatic moves or his daring stunts, and often cannot perform such moves himself. But that's not his job—that's like expecting Steven Spielberg to be a better actor than Tom Hanks when he directed him in *Saving Private Ryan.* The fight choreographer's job is to know when to use and apply those acrobatic moves and daring stunts in the fight scene, and how to stage them in order to make Jackie look effective while telling a nonverbal story. He should see the overall picture of the fight and how it progresses throughout the film.

A good fight choreographer is much like the conductor of an orchestra. He might not be able to play every single instrument in the orchestra, but he should know how they all fit together in the big picture and be able to keep all the players (fighters) in sync with each other. Most importantly, he is the crucial third eye that is able to oversee how everyone works together as a whole. A fighter in the thick of the action cannot see the fight with a critical eye, or from the future audience's perspective, in order to make necessary adjustments for the sake of clarity and entertainment value. That is one of the roles expected of the fight choreographer.

What This Book Is About

In this book, I will focus on the craft of fight choreography to help you create your own style of fights for your projects, whether they are short films, TV shows, or feature films (low- to high-budget). When the audience gets deeply involved in your film for those two hours and forgets about their worries and lives, you have successfully done your job as a filmmaker. When done well, fight/action scenes will support and heighten your story and expand your characters.

It would be impossible for this book to show you everything involved in fight choreography, unless it was at least a couple thousand pages and took at least a decade out of my life to write. What I want this book to do is provide a foundation for the principles involved in making effective action sequences for all filmmakers.

I will also discuss the history of fight choreography and discuss some of the most influential choreographers in the history of film. If you are going to create a fight scene, you should know what is out there and what has been done before you entered the field. Why reinvent the wheel when you can learn from the past experiences of these innovators and contributors to the craft? If you don't consider the work of many of the principle innovators and contributors I will mention in the book, you will likely have a senseless fight/action sequence that might wow the audience initially but immediately be forgotten when the next over-hyped blockbuster is released. Worse yet, your film likely will not connect with the audience. Instead, it will simply be full of visuals that don't mean anything.

When an audience is watching a fight scene, they will respond positively to a good one and lose interest when viewing a bad one, but they cannot necessarily pinpoint the specific good or bad elements of each fight that caused their subsequent positive or negative reactions. For the filmgoer who wants to educate himself, this book can help shed light on what a good fight scene is and help you understand the subtle nuances and appreciate the action much better. In this book, I will dissect what makes a great fight scene—and what doesn't. Although the use of weapons has similar rules, they will be discussed in their own chapters about the similarities and differences and what makes a fulfilling a weapons fight.

This book is by no means meant to be *Fight Choreography in 10 Easy Steps* or a *Fight Choreography for Dummies* book. It is literally impossible and extremely dangerous to learn fight choreography only from a book. This book should instead help everyone involved in the process of making a fight scene get on the same page and understand what is important in making it a successful sequence. I strongly suggest that you have a trained professional on the set of your film at all times. If you are interested in learning fight choreography, I highly recommend you learn several different styles of martial arts and take stunt and theatrical combat classes. Hopefully, after that you can find a trained professional stuntman or coordinator who can show you the ropes on a live film set before you venture out on your own.

There is no clearly defined process to creating a fight scene. Ask 10 different stunt coordinators about their process and you will get 10 different answers and approaches. What I will attempt to do here is extract the essential ingredients that I feel are necessary to make a successful action scene so you can come up with your own approach to creating an effective fight scene. I will start by breaking down the script and how important it is to understand the story and build from there.

As a Chinese-American who began to discover and appreciate the rich heritage of my parents and ancestors through learning martial arts as a child, I feel I have a unique perspective on both eastern and western cultures that has not been expressed so far in other books of this genre. Also by having been an art major in college, a professional stand-up comedian for 11 years, and having taken two years of screenwriting classes at UCLA Extension, on top of working as a stuntman and/or stunt coordinator with both Hong Kong and American stunt crews, I feel I can bring to you a unique point of view to fight choreography that you might not have seen before. I will do my best to show you the best of both worlds by sharing the experiences of people who are in this business of the art of fighting without fighting.

What Is a Fight Choreographer?

The role of a fight choreographer in western filmmaking is not represented by any union in the U.S., but it really should be. It is usually up to the stunt coordinator to put together the sequences. However, the stunt coordinator has more duties on a film set than just choreographing fight scenes. They are the head of a department and have many duties (including administrative ones) while on and off the set, and putting together a fight scene is one of the more pleasant things the job has to offer. When a stunt coordinator is working on a film that is heavy on different types of action, he might employ a fight coordinator to take care of the fight scenes for that particular film.

To avoid confusion, I will use the term *fight choreography* to represent the creative process and responsibilities required for putting together the fight sequences. For this book, the term *fight choreographer* will include everyone involved in creating the fight scene, from writers to directors, actors, stunt actors, stunt coordinators, cameramen, editors, sound editors, composers, and so on. All of these people play an integral part in putting together a successful fight scene. If one of these departments drops the ball, it will directly affect how the fight scene will appear to the audience.

What Is the Difference between an Action and Fight Scene?

The difference between fight and action choreography is that action choreography has elements that are not immediately related to fight scenes. These elements include car and motorcycle chases, aerial dogfights, pyrotechnics, explosions, and high falls. If I included action elements in this book, it would be at least twice the size it is now and would take years longer to write, in fact requiring several volumes to cover every specialty. However, the general use of weapons will be included in this book, but I will not go into any detail because there are too many types of weapons out there to cover.

For example, in *True Lies*, the action sequence that begins in the men's room of the shopping center starts out as a gunfight between Harry Tasker (Schwarzenegger) and Salim's (Art Malik) thugs. It quickly turns into a brawl, then immediately becomes a spectacular and innovative chase scene between a motorcycle and a horse that ends atop a high-rise hotel. In discussing such a sequence in this book, I would only cover the gunfight leading into the brawl in the bathroom and would not discuss the remaining non-combat portions of the sequence.

But complex scenes, such as one in *Indiana Jones and the Last Crusade* that features a boat chase with a gunfight and fight sequence between Dr. Indiana Jones (Harrison Ford) and the Brotherhood of the Cruciform Sword, would be discussed because the actions are all interrelated and happening at the same time, making the scene impossible to dissect without discussing all elements. The same situation applies to the fight/chase scene atop a moving subway train between Spider-Man and Doc Ock in *Spider-Man 2*.

1

Basic History of Fight Choreography and Fighting on Film

There is no real way to track down all the information about the history of fight choreography because throughout the history of theater and film, the creators behind the scenes (except for the director and writer) usually would not get any type of formal credit. Unfortunately, it would take decades of research and at least twice the volume of this book to be completely thorough about the history of fight choreography, but even then, many conclusions would still be drawn from hypotheses. In this chapter, I will touch on important events in the evolution of fight choreography, some of the important movies, the performers, people behind the camera, and how it has evolved over centuries, decades, and years along with styles, trends, world events, new technology, and the changes in censorship that all affects fight choreography.

I will also stress the delicate relationship between creator (the choreographer) and audience and how the dynamics have changed in many ways, but yet in many ways have also stayed the same over the centuries. What is written here is meant to be taken in general because there are always exceptions to the rule.

Basic Overview: The Evolution of Fight Choreography

Arguably, fight choreography is as old as man's existence on Earth. But in the beginning, it had a different function. It probably happened after man's first physical conflict with a rival tribe or an animal explaining to his clan how he survived or defeated them, while serving as a precautionary warning to the others in the tribe. In prehistoric times, leaders, storytellers, and warriors would recount their exploits to their tribes by reenacting their experiences of the hunt, battles against other tribes, and the elements. Their experiences were retold so that the rest of the tribe could learn from their experiences and not make the same mistakes again. The emphasis was completely on survival and the passing on of knowledge, rather than on entertainment. But the storyteller had to be convincing and effective (and possibly somewhat entertaining) in how he passed on his knowledge.

This went on until mankind became a "civilized" society and no longer needed to fight the elements or animals for daily survival. The purpose of watching a fight changed from survival to entertaining the masses for fame, profit, honor, and prestige. It came to be about passing on stories and entertaining an audience that did not necessarily know (or care) about combat, but that was interested in seeing a dramatic conflict (real or theatrical) that could only be resolved by a physical altercation.

The ancient Greeks had dances, such as the *Pyrrachia*, in which a physical enactment of combat in mime-like movements served as an interpretive representation of physical combat for entertainment (not unlike martial arts kata). They would also stage dramatized plays in which slaves or captured criminals would perform and in the end would have to kill themselves and/or each other by the end of the play. If the audiences did not like the performance, they would jeer at the performers and encourage them to kill themselves and/or their stage partners sooner rather than later, all for the amusement and entertainment of the audience. In the Roman era, at the Coliseum, the promoter setting up and organizing the duels and battles would often create curiosity and stir up debates among the citizens (potential patrons) about the upcoming gladiator fights. They would also create a visual and strategic contrast by having the gladiators fight each other with different types of weapons of different lengths and effectiveness (such as a long spear versus a sword), creating an audience curiosity that would make them pay admission to witness the outcome of the deadly blood sport. This was the humble beginnings of using media hype, creating handicaps, and utilizing contrast in styles to create public interest in a fight. Still, fight choreography, as we know it today was a long way from developing.

It wasn't until the Elizabethan era and the reign of Queen Elizabeth I (1558–1603), at the height of the English Renaissance, that choreographed fight scenes in live theater would begin showing up in Europe. It has been speculated that Richard Tarleton (?–1588), a member of Shakespeare's acting company and the London Masters of Defence weapons guild, was one of the first fight choreographers for the stage. But Tarleton was more famous as a clown and the favorite jester of Queen Elizabeth I. It is also believed that Tarleton was the inspiration for the character Yorick in Shakespeare's *Hamlet.* At that time, fight choreography was more loosely structured than we know it today—the actors of the company would get together and loosely arrange moves right before the show would start.

From the late 1800s to the early 1900s, touring theatrical productions traveled throughout Europe and the United States. The choreographed fight scenes for these performances generally were composed of generic and simple combinations. Around this time, fencing masters in Europe started to explore, research, and experiment with "ancient" European weaponry (mostly bladed) that was no longer effective or efficient in the current day. They would hypothesize about their methods and approach to combat with the weapons, and then teach actors to use them onstage.

The Birth of Film in the United States

On June 17, 1894, Thomas Edison filmed the first fight recorded on film, which was between Mike Leonard and Jack Cushing. On September 7, 1894, World Champion Gentleman Jim Corbett fought Peter Courtney in six one-minute rounds. Both fights were filmed at Black Maria Studios in West Orange, New Jersey, widely known as "America's First Movie Studio", to display the uses of the Kinetograph camera to the public.

With the introduction of silent films in the United States, it was only a matter of time before a screen hero would rise from this new entertainment medium, enthralling and captivating audiences' imaginations all over the world. This person was Douglas Fairbanks Sr. (1883-1939), who starred in swashbuckling action classics in which he performed a good majority of his own stunts. Fairbanks would go to pro wrestling matches at night and come onto the set the next morning with his stuntmen, trying to figure out how to incorporate what he had seen the night before into his films. Fairbanks would make swashbucklers between 1920-1929, soon to be followed by Errol Flynn and Tyrone Power, to name a few.

Behind the scenes, fencing masters from Europe migrated to Hollywood to train the actors in cinematic fencing. Fred Cavens, Henry Uyttenhove, Jean Heremans, and Ralph Faulkner were the best of the Hollywood fencing masters who trained and choreographed the intricate sword fights while acting and performing stunts in the films, too. Cavens, Uyttenhove, and Heremans, all hailing from Belgium, were extremely accomplished fencers in their own right before working in Hollywood as fencing masters, trainers, and choreographers.

Fred Cavens (1882–1962) trained at the Military Institute of Physical Education and Fencing in Belgium. He took up the sword at age 15, graduated from the academy at 18, and became a fencing master at 21. Cavens' long and illustrious 40-year career in Hollywood started when he was the fencing master on Douglas Fairbanks Sr.'s *The Mark of Zorro*. He also worked on *The Black Pirate*, *The Adventures of Robin Hood*, *The Sea Hawk*, *The Black Swan*, and *The Robe*, as well as on the *Zorro* TV series (from 1957 to 1961).

Henry Uyttenhove was the first competitive fencing instructor at USC in 1926, training women's and men's teams that won 14 Pacific Coast Intercollegiate titles in his first 15 years of coaching. In 1920, Uyttenhove was hired by Douglas Fairbanks Sr. to train him in fencing for *The Mark of Zorro*. He also trained actor Ramon Novarro, among others, and continued as a fencing trainer through such films as *The Three Musketeers*, *The Prisoner of Zenda*, *Robin Hood*, *Monte Cristo*, *Rupert of Hentzauu*, and *Scaramouche*.

Jean Heremans (1914–1970), a five-time international fencing champion and an eight-time Belgian champion, succeeded Uyttenhove as USC fencing coach and continued their winning record. The 1949–50 team went undefeated in league competition. Heremans was hired by MGM in 1948 to supervise the swordplay in their remake of *The Three Musketeers*. He continued to work on *The Prisoner of Zenda*, *Scaramouche*, *Swordsman of Siena*, *Princess of the Nile*, *Demetrius and the Gladiators*, and *Prince Valiant*. His distinction was that two of the films he choreographed had some of the longest filmed screen duels at the time. *The Three Musketeers* had a five-minute duel and *Scaramouche* had a six-and-a-half-minute duel.

Ralph Faulkner (1891–1987) was already a working actor before he got into fencing. It was while working on the 1922 film *The Man from Glengarry* that he slipped, severely injuring his knee. During Faulkner's rehab, he found that fencing became a passion for him. It was so much of a passion, in fact, that he competed, winning the World Amateur Sabre Championships in 1928, making him a member of the U.S. Olympic team for that year and in 1932. He accomplished all this while still working on films as a stuntman and fight choreographer. His work on more than 100 movies and TV shows as actor, fencing double, and/or fight choreographer includes *The Three Musketeers*, *Captain Blood*, *The Prisoner of Zenda*, *The Sea Hawk*, *The Thief of Bagdad*, *The Court Jester*, *Jason and the Argonauts*, and *Clash of the Titans*.

The class, respect, and reputation these fencing masters carried with them from their previous accomplishments helped create the old-world majesty that adds to the grand and romantic dreamlike mystique that has always been associated with the art of cinematic sword fighting in Hollywood. Sword fights represent a distant time that we want to romanticize, where chivalry and honor were what motivated our day-to-day activities.

The Western Brawl

When it comes to choreographing and showing fist fights (aka brawls or Western brawls) on film, they are held in a much different regard than cinematic sword fighting that represents honor and chivalry in the minds of filmmakers and audiences. Keith Vitali comments, "The Chinese brought aesthetic beauty, a sense of rhythm and timing to their fight scenes. And Americans never had that. It was more brutal and ugly by just throwing one or a few techniques and the person just goes down."

With brawls, we get a different emotion, approach, and feel. There is not much romance (if any) in a Western-style fight, which is much more primitive and uncivil in emotion, with the visual emphasis on being simple and raw with only a handful of techniques in their repertoire, oftentimes repeating themselves within the same fight. The basic brawl is driven by emotion 99% of the time, which to an untrained or unconditioned fighter means their rational consciousness is blinded at the time from making choices on using different techniques, like what you might see in a Kung Fu movie.

A brawl is usually very short in length, emphasizing a character's power, seizing control over the opponent, and showing immediate decisiveness over the situation, similar to seeing two rams butting heads. Brawls are not "educated fights" where a combatant has schooled himself in a fighting art or combative sport using advanced footwork, blocks, and a wide variety of punches and combinations.

There are also unsaid rules in cinematic Western brawls, including:

Only punches are considered fair.

Open-handed techniques like slaps and chops are considered conscious choices but not as strong as a haymaker (a straight-armed looping punch).

Fakes, misleads, and light techniques to set up an opponent are rarely seen because the fighter is usually not emotionally balanced (not angry or mad) to set up his opponent.

Any other techniques like elbows, eye-gouging, and kicks, etc., are considered unmanly, cheating, or "dirty fighting."

Punches to the face do more damage than punches to the body (this is probably an aesthetics issue because a stuntman can easily sell a more spectacular reaction with a blow to the head than one to the body). Also, a disabling punch thrown to the body is not very dramatic when it comes to brawls.

The intent of each punch is to knock out or disable the opponent. Anything else is a waste of time and considered non-effective.

The timing and rhythm of most brawls are choreographed with the techniques at full beats. Half and quarter beats are a rarity. This is mainly because of the intent to knock out the opponent with each technique.

Grappling is acceptable, but usually does not finish the fight with something as subtle as a chokehold, wrist lock, or any type of submission (remember this is not a martial arts or "educated fight"). A brawl usually ends with an overpowering punch.

The ironic issue about showing one's power is usually measured by the strength of the punch or how quickly you can knock out your opponent. However, the ability to take a punch is not usually measured as a power, but is determined or gauged by one's size. The bigger a person is, the easier they are able to take a punch.

The philosophy of a brawl is that emotion, toughness, brawn, size, and power overrules any science of technique. This is demonstrated in *McLintok* (1963), when Devlin (Patrick Wayne), an educated fighter who was on the boxing team in college, fights Ben Sage (Edward Faulkner) at a town social gathering. Throughout the fight, Devlin is in complete control of the match as he is bobbing and weaving, utilizing superior footwork to get out of the way of Ben's attack, and countering with set up jabs and following through with right crosses to the face and uppercuts to the gut. But Uncle Fauntleroy Sage (Big John Hamilton), who is much older and twice Devlin's size, immediately comes to rescue young Ben's honor. Devlin throws a dozen boxing-style punches at Fauntleroy's face and it does not affect him. Then Fauntleroy gets angry and throws a single haymaker that sends Devlin flying onto a table and to the ground. This is a prime example of the brawl principle of power, size, and emotion over technique.

The brawl represents our brutal violent unrestrained emotion, manifesting itself into a physical expression. Traditionally, the primary emotion and code of conduct of the brawl is usually uncivil, unrefined, with an extremely macho-like attitude in a battle of wills.

An offshoot of the brawl is a slug-fest—an extremely macho mano e mano dogfight where the fighters are expected to:

Be able to take the punishment of the hit(s) without blocking or dodging the opponent's technique(s).

Never show the opponent(s) you are in any pain (even if hurt) or that it affected you.

Never back away from your opponent, because it shows submissiveness.

Have the strength to dish back the same or even more punishment at your opponent(s).

Be the last man standing.

Many think of the cinematic brawl as "real," (maybe in its rough and unclean execution and appearance), but there is not much strategy, common sense, or practicality involved. This is probably because at some point in everybody's life, they have been in a fight or altercation (and not a real swordfight), and what was remembered the most about the situation is how they felt during the experience and less about the techniques used during the fight.

Another point is we are accustomed to seeing similar looking brawls all around us, like in daily news reports, when a referee makes an unfavorable call during an important sporting event that can change the momentum of a game, a fight that oftentimes break out during a hockey game, between quarreling drunks at bars, during domestic violence situations, etc. All these situations are real-life examples of when our emotions dominate and cloud our rational thinking.

The principles and psychology behind the Western brawl in its approach and concept permeates into all types of empty-handed fighting for the screen with most filmmakers and their audiences in the West. The concept of what is thought of as "real" is attached to this but in actuality it is more of what Western audiences and filmmakers have been accustomed to (for more detail see East vs. West section in this chapter). The emphasis on the different faces of the Western brawl is more on the emotion of the scene and less on the choice of techniques used to create and support the scene. The filmmakers might not want to emphasize the actual violence of the technique, but instead experience the emotion without seeing it. The main reason for this probably stems from the limitations set by the Hays Commission (more on this later in the chapter) and their conservative and strict rules as to how action, acts of violence, sex, and criminality were to be portrayed in film. Unfortunately, these principles I have described are still in use today with fights filmed in the West. These principles also include a majority of Western-produced martial arts fights. It's not just a set of principles but an actual Western mindset that can be really limiting to what you might decide to choreograph.

Origin of the Brawl

Although the brawl is widely thought to have started with the cowboy western of the '40s and '50s with John Wayne's films, it actually started back in the early silent days of film. But in those days it had a different application and impact upon the audience. Since the performances were mainly mimed with limited dialogue (compared to talking films), the actors used their body language and facial expressions to help convey their feelings without any long cumbersome dialogue to halt the rhythm and flow of the scene. This is something Chinese fight choreographers like Jackie Chan and Sammo Hung have taken and applied to their fight scenes to this day. If we look at some of the silent film stars like Charlie Chaplin, Harold Lloyd, or Buster Keaton, when they got into a fight, we saw that the antagonist was much taller, bigger, and more powerful than them (a visual contrast). Usually it starts out with the hero getting hit with one big wide looping punch that knocks him down hard on his ass. This visually sets up and establishes the hero in the role of the underdog, a formidable villain, the audience's sympathy for the hero, and lays out the obstacle(s) the hero has to overcome, much like in a modern day video game. Usually we will see the hero gather himself, and after a couple of unsuccessful tries, he comes up with something smart and witty coupled with the physical advantages he has (like speed and agility from smaller size) that is surprising and entertaining for an unsuspecting audience.

Censorship and Morals in Film—The Hays Commission

In the 1920s, the American public was concerned about the amount of sex, violence, and lawlessness seen in movies, and this was supported by many civic, religious, and political organizations calling for the government to intervene. Hollywood looked like the new Babylon because it was full of scandals and immoral behavior, such as the trial of comedic superstar Roscoe "Fatty" Arbuckle accused of raping a younger actress. Banks began to repeal credit lines for movie companies. Fearing inevitable government intervention to censor their films, the Hollywood film industry decided to regulate themselves. In 1922, the movie moguls from the studios decided to form the Motion Picture Producers and Distributors of America, Inc. (MPPDA), and assigned Will Hays, former Postmaster General and former chair for the Republican National Committee, to chair the group. The MPPDA was soon known as the Hays Office or Hays Commission and quickly re-established good relations with banks so productions could have lines of credit. The MPPDA soon introduced "moral clauses" into actors' contracts, giving the studios the power to terminate their contracts if they were involved in scandals.

In 1934, Hays put into action the Production Code (aka, Hays Code), a rigid and complicated set of rules that described what was morally acceptable for a film that filmmakers would have to follow and implement into their films. This was because the newly formed Legion of Decency threatened to boycott all Hollywood films. They looked at all films to see if there would be anything offensive, including language, sexuality, nudity, violence, and how characters were portrayed on film. Producers were required to summarize their screenplays for approval from the Hays office. If a film did not meet the moral criteria set in the Production Code, the film would not be approved and therefore could not be released into theaters or instead experienced limited or restricted distribution. The filmmakers had to edit, delete, or re-shoot scenes in order for them to pass.

You can see why western-choreographed fight scenes placed more of an emphasis on the emotion and power of the fight, rather than highlighting or focusing more on the actual techniques, simply because they were not allowed to do so. However, filmmakers would continually fight with the Hays office on why their film was not certified. What also was unfair was that foreign films did not need to be certified in order to be screened in theaters.

Hays left office in 1950 and Eric Johnson took his place and changed the name of the organization to the Motion Picture Association of America (MPAA). The code would slowly lose its tight grip on what was accepted as the decades passed, and it stopped being utilized on November 1, 1968, when the present rating system was introduced placing no restrictions on the content of a film. However the debate still goes on about why certain films get a harsh rating when a previous film that had the same content got a softer rating.

However, in England, the BBFC was notorious for banning scenes of action and violence in movies, TV shows, and video games. An example of the banning was the nunchaku sequences in all of Bruce Lee's movies in theatrical and home video releases were deleted until 2003, because they thought it would be copied by local gangs.

Highlights of the Production Code

Some of the rules in the Production Code that affect fight choreography are as follows.

- No picture shall be produced that will lower the moral standards of those who see it. Hence, the sympathy of the audience should never be thrown to the side of crime, wrongdoing, evil, or sin.
- The technique of murder must be presented in a way that will not inspire imitation.
- Brutal killings are not to be presented in detail.
- Revenge in modern times shall not be justified. In lands and ages of less developed civilization and moral principles, revenge may sometimes be presented. This would be the case especially in places where no law exists to cover the crime because of which revenge is committed.

Crimes Against the Law

The treatment of crimes against the law must not:

1. Teach methods of crime.
2. Inspire potential criminals with a desire for imitation.
3. Make criminals seem heroic and justified.

The Brawl in Cliffhanger Serials

The brawl thrived and was the mainstay in the cliffhanger serials shown in theaters, starting in the silent era in 1912 and ending well into sound era around 1956, when the introduction of television drew audiences away from theaters. Each serial was about 12-15 episodes and ran 20-30 minutes in length and would usually end in a cliffhanger moment where the hero was left in a no-win situation, leaving the audience guessing as to what the fate of the hero would be, making them come back the following week to see what happened. Gunplay, stunts, and fights provided the action needed to keep audiences interested. Since the vocabulary of techniques used in the fights were basically straight punches, the surroundings, story, and/or other elements around the fight kept the fights fresh. *Flash Gordon, Commando Cody, The Perils of Pauline, Captain Marvel, Spy Smasher, Captain Midnight, Buck Rogers, Batman,* and *Superman* were examples of some of the successful serials that ran during that time. It was these cliffhanger serials that later inspired the *Indiana Jones* and *Star Wars* series.

The Barroom Brawl

Brawls also thrived in westerns (also known as horse operas) and oftentimes took place in the barroom where there were more disposable props to include in the fight (like glass to break and tables to throw people on) to add flavor and change the fight from one film to another. Usually, when you saw a barroom scene in a western, chances were a fight or some type of conflict was going to occur (especially when alcohol was present to impair a character's better judgment)—hence the term *barroom brawl.* Because using a gun against an opponent is so deadly and final, a barroom brawl is not as serious and can be used as an easy way to settle a difference that cannot be resolved civilly. The barroom in the western is a mainstay equivalent to the teahouse/restaurant fights often seen in Kung Fu or Wu Xia films in Asia.

John Wayne

When it comes to western-style brawls, the image of John Wayne (1907-1979) and his ham-fisted punches are usually one of the first things that come to mind, because of his worldwide fame as a movie star and American icon. Wayne represented conservative ideals of American democracy in his films by choosing roles and stories that represented the American ideals of freedom, self-righteousness, independence, and toughness. "The Duke's" approach to a fight was very similar to his straightforward ideals—to stand tall and proud, hit your opponent as hard as possible with a single punch, take a hit with dignity without cowering, and dish it right back when possible. Wayne made his fights look extremely easy.

What Wayne did with his punches was different from other actors and it stood out. He made his punches look much more powerful than many other actors. His punches started slow in his wind up and picked up speed and energy as he leaned his body towards his opponent, gaining momentum and speed in the pace of his punches. Coupled by his size—he was usually taller than most of his opponents—and long arms, he made the punch travel across the screen, looking that much more effective and powerful. Because of his long arms, he did not have to throw too many "looping punches" (a straight-armed punch thrown so the camera can see the punch). Over the years he was able to develop his own distinct style of cinematic fighting, by cocking back his arm (wind up) and throwing punches that were not as wide. He would lean or rock his body forward followed by his fist, which resembles something like a slingshot (pull back slow, accelerate forward fast). By doing this, Wayne created a nice rhythm with his fights, where the audience can see and recognize the punch coming (in his wind up) and respect the power and speed of the punch as he let the punch loose towards his opponent.

His wide punches telegraphed across the screen much slower than say Bruce Lee or Chuck Norris, but he was very convincing as a screen fighter for several reasons.

- He had great stuntmen who showed extremely effective reactions to the punches to sell Wayne's power.
- The sound effects added in post-production to his punches made his hits come across that much more authoritative and commanding—creating a much stronger impact.
- The calm confidence he had when throwing punches made us feel he has done this many times, giving the audience confidence in his character's skills.
- He had great reactions that said a lot when he got hit. This is something that has been very underappreciated about Wayne.
- His eye contact, facial emotions, and body language while facing his opponents before and after connecting, was very convincing. His choice in his many different emotions given as he follows through (martial acting) immediately afterwards is slightly different with each person he fights. "The Duke's" martial acting is much more internal and subtle compared to Jackie Chan or Sammo Hung (who are more extroverted), but it is still effective as the audience recognizes it subconsciously.
- He was much more "camera aware" than many other western screen fighters before him when it came to his fights. Usually when you saw a brawl, the screen fighters were framed either extremely close so you

could not see much action or from far away where the set would dominate the frame and the impact and emotion of the fight would be lost. With Wayne's fights it usually started with a mid shot (usually from the hip up) with him dead center and his opponent(s) just off to either side of him. Since Wayne usually towered over his opponent(s) and had long arms, he would use one side of the frame to wind up and as he hit his opponent, we would see the reaction throughout the rest of the frame. The audience was able to see everything from start to finish.

Wayne's fights are stereotypically known for being violent (in emotion), quick, serious, and to the point, much like the ending of *Red River* (1948) when he finally fights Matthew (Montgomery Clift). However, that is not always the case. In many of his fight scenes, there are light to broad touches of humor to them. Examples include:

- *The Quiet Man* (1952)—The seven-minute beer break he takes with his opponent, Red (Victor McLaglen) in the middle of the final fight.
- *The Sons of Katie Elder* (1965)—The disagreement at the dinner table about the youngest Elder going to school that leads to a family brawl between all four brothers (Dean Martin, Earl Holliman, Michael Anderson, Jr., and John Wayne).
- *McLintock!* (1963)—The two fights during the town social gathering and the mudslide brawl.

Comedic brawls did not stop with "The Duke" and are still seen in films today. They were "kid friendly" with the '60s *Batman* TV series and thrived in the '70s and early '80s when Clint Eastwood and Burt Reynolds ruled the box office. Also at that same time, Terrance Hill had his own twist with the comedic brawl with his *Trinity* films (for more examples, see the comedic fights section).

Brawls in Teen Films

The start of the 1950s was a time of conformity and middle class values, with the ideology of the Nuclear Family, where the father was the sole breadwinner, the mother was the homemaker, and the kids were well behaved, submissive, and obedient to their parents. With the booming economy, middle class white America flocked to the suburbs to their newly built tract homes in pursuit of their dreams. This was an extremely narrow view of the family structure, but the model was reinforced in TV shows like *The Adventures of Ozzie and Harriet* (1952-1966), while in real life, variations on that familial model (like single parents and having kids out of wedlock) were generally not accepted and looked down upon.

Meanwhile, racial segregation was about to change in 1955, when Rosa Parks would not move to the back of the bus and give up her chair, kick starting the civil rights movement. Also, the Red Scare and McCarthyism created a lot of paranoia and contributed to the underlying social unrest of the nation at the time.

The teen culture came about in the '50s when older kids began to spend more time with other kids their age, rather than their families, developing their own language, fashion, and values towards life. Teens became consumers in their own right by getting allowances from their parents or working jobs after school, buying their own clothes, cars, and music, eventually challenging the authority of the parents and the rules and ideals they had already established. This was because of the social changes that occurred during and after WWII when the father was busy fighting overseas and the mothers were doing their part by working in the local factories, giving the teens a lot of independence.

Knowing teens had more disposable income and more time on their hands, Hollywood decided to take a chance and make films starring young actors they could identify with, while exploiting their plight on the big screen. This was the emergence of the teen film—movies about teens for teens. A subgenre of the teen film was the teen rebel or juvenile delinquent (JD) films. These films reflected the emotional unrest of the nation's teens, reflecting the current times when teens were revolting against adults, struggling for acceptance while trying to find their identity as they grew out of adolescence into adulthood. Certain towns would ban the screening of teen films, fearing that seeing a switchblade fight on the screen would cause the kids in the audience to riot at the screenings.

The roughness of the brawls depicted in these JD films were well suited to express the uncontrolled raw emotions of the teen characters as they came into their own, rebelling against the adults and the rules they set for them, while also looking for acceptance, trying to find their way in society. Their symbols of rebellion are leather jackets, motorcycles, slang language, smoking cigarettes, and listening and dancing to rock music. The difference with the rebel teen film fights is that they added the weapon—a switchblade, into the mix of the brawl. The switchblade and brass knuckles (still illegal in many states today) symbolize their defiance to the adults and society, expressing their rage and rebellion, marking their territory and establishing their own rules in a world they never made. Brawls fit easily in this genre reflecting the rebellious teen angst films that were popular during the '50s to early '60s.

The first film of this genre starred the legendary Marlon Brando (1924-2004) in *The Wild One* (1953). The film did respectable business but was not a runaway success, and it serves more as a beginning of a film genre where the central character was a frustrated youth. The fight at the center of town between Johnny

(Brando) and rival gang member Chino (Lee Marvin) surprisingly mixed it up well with haymaker punches with judo type throws and wrestling moves. What sums up the situation perfectly is when a townsman asks, "What are they fighting about?" An old man replies while he intently watches the fight, "Don't know. Don't know themselves, probably."

One of the most famous JD films was *Rebel Without A Cause* (1955), starring the legendary James Dean (1931-1955). The famous switchblade fight atop Griffith Park between Jim Stark (Dean) and Buzz (Corey Allen) was choreographed by Frank Mazzola (who also played Crunch in the film), who served as a technical advisor because he was a member of a real life gang (the Athenians) and based the fight on a real switchblade fight he was in. The fight was very convincing, showing the contrast in emotions and intent between Buzz's aggressiveness against Stark's defensiveness and hesitancy, unsure of what was coming next, creating a live "in the moment" feeling to the fight. To prepare for the role, Dean would go to Athenian meetings to understand gang life. Dean's vivid portrayal of Jim Stark, as a confused, sensitive, and defiant teenager was the epitome of adolescent angst and pain in the process of self-discovery and finding their own identity, he summed up the feelings of many teens in America when he yelled at his squabbling and dysfunctional parents, "You're tearing me apart!"

Another standout film in the JD genre during this period was *The Blackboard Jungle* (1955), released seven months prior to *Rebel....* This was the first film to add real rock and roll music to the film, playing Bill Haley's "Rock Around The Clock." Post war veteran (and Navy middleweight boxing champ) Richard Dadier (Glenn Ford, 1916-2006) is a new teacher at an urban NYC high school where the kids are uncontrollable and the teachers are in fear of them. The film has two (three overall) well choreographed brawls that lead up to the tension filled final fight in the classroom at the end of the film between Dadier and gang leader, Artie (Vic Morrow). Although there were not many techniques thrown in the final skirmish, the tension and emotion of the confrontation was constant throughout, keeping the viewer guessing and on the edge of his seat. Glenn Ford handles himself very well in the fights with a confidence and presence that matches the screen fighting skills of John Wayne and Kirk Douglas.

There were many JD films throughout the '50s. Even rock star Elvis Presley starred in a few like *King Creole* (1958) and handled himself extremely well in his fight scenes throughout his film career. The JD film was countered by the "good teen" films and would eventually lose its popularity in the '60s, but we still see strains of it throughout the decades and even to this day. The difference between the JD films of the '50s and after is everything from the subject matter to the violence. This is because the Hays Code said depicting violent acts was only to be suggested and not shown. This is one of the reasons why a western fight emphasizes more on the emotion rather than impact of the technique.

Other films worth noting are Jerome Robbins' dance musical *West Side Story* (1961) and Jerry Lewis' first solo acting debut in *The Delicate Delinquent* (1957). These two films added rhythmical dance aesthetics to the brawl. The difference with these two films compared to previous musicals that had fight scenes (like in *The Bandwagon* starring Fred Astaire and Cyd Charisse) is that there is more of a dangerous edge and intent to many of the dance moves that could be used as actual techniques you would see in a brawl but not as stylized or purposefully rhythmical.

The teen rebel film is still alive and well because things have not changed that much emotionally for the teen. We saw them in *The Outsiders* (1983), *The Wanderers* (1979), *The Lords of Flatbush* (1974), *Massacre at Central High* (1976), and *The Principal* (1987).

One of the more memorable films that stands out in the post Hays Code of JD films is *Bad Boys* (1983), where Mick 'O Brien (Sean Penn) is sent to juvenile detention for vehicular manslaughter, accidentally killing the kid brother of Paco Moreno (Esai Morales), a rival gang leader, during a car chase with the police. Paco gets revenge by raping J.C. (Ally Sheedy), Mick's girlfriend, but gets caught by the police, sending him to the same detention center Mick is in, setting up the final showdown between both men. The many fights in the film were choreographed by the film's stunt coordinator, Chuck Waters. The two that stand out are when Mick establishes dominance in the detention center by brutally beating up Tweety (Robert Lee Rush) and Viking (Clancy Brown) by relentlessly clobbering them with a pillowcase stuffed with several soda cans. Mick's intention and execution shows his creativity and extreme street savvy over the two opponents who did not even have a chance. The final fight between Mick and Paco was well paced and constantly changed the type of fight from brawl to grappling, back to brawling then grappling, etc., while also changing the tempo and emphasis of the fight.

In the cult classic, *Class of 1984*, a modern reworking of *The Blackboard Jungle*, a high school gang led by Peter Stegman (Vince Van Patten) sells drugs to the other kids and intimidates and bullies anyone who gets in their way. Stegman constantly butts heads with an idealistic music teacher, Andy Norris (Perry King), when they blow up his car, a student overdoses on drugs, another is fatally stabbed, and they gang rape his pregnant wife. This all leads to a confrontation between Norris and the gang members, which leads to a final showdown between Norris and Stegman. Choreographed by Terry Leonard, each fight is very different with each gang member Norris meets in the end, using the environment of the different schoolrooms to his advantage. The fights are pretty savage, violent, and exploitative as each gang member gets his comeuppance for the things he has done throughout the film—like one gets his arm cut off and later gets impaled on a table saw.

JD films are not just limited to America. They are also evident in other parts of the world, like *Scum* (1979 Great Britain), *Attack the Gas Station* (1999), and *Once Upon a Time in High School* (2004). As a child actor in his teens in Hong Kong, Bruce Lee starred as a JD in the film *The Orphan* (1960).

The 1960s

President John F. Kennedy (1963), Malcolm X (1965), Martin Luther King (1968), and Robert Kennedy (1968) are assassinated. The US sends troops into the Vietnam war, resulting in many anti-war protests at home, and also the first time actual filmed footage from the Vietnam war is broadcast on television, bringing the war into the nation's living room for the first time. The introduction of the birth control pill helped to promote the free love movement. With Apollo 11 (1969), Neil Armstrong becomes the first man on the moon.

The '60s was a time of transition between old and new Hollywood. The studio contract system where actors, writers, and directors were bound to a specific studio was no longer. Movie audiences were declining due to the dominance of television. Because of the death of movie moguls and financial difficulties, studios were taken over by corporations and multi-national businesses. The first multiplex theater opened in Kansas City, MO in 1963. This was a sign of the eventual demise of the movie palaces.

Up until this point, stunts and action scenes were arranged by the Assistant Director. They would gather and arrange the necessary stuntmen, set up the stunt/fight with the help from the stuntmen, or hire specialized talent who would help choreograph the fight or action scene. It was around the 1960s when stunt and action scenes became more specialized and the title of *stunt coordinator* became an official title. It would be a decade or so before the stunt coordinator and stuntmen would get credit in the end scroll of the film for their work.

After WWII, England was in a time of terrible decline economically and socially, from the late '40s and '50s, going into the '60s. To reflect the sign of the times, the British film industry presented "Kitchen Sink" films with angry, bleak, everyday working class heroes with frank dialogue. Until that point, the spy genre was done before, but was not successfully exploited and generally ignored, except for Hitchcock's espionage films. Then in 1962, along comes *Dr. No*, the first James Bond film, based off of Ian Fleming's novels, where the film's alternate universe acts as if the British Empire was untarnished and England was still a thriving world power. And because of that, the film appealed to the audience as they embraced the character. The first two films, *Dr. No* and *From Russia With Love*, were very successful, but it was *Goldfinger* (1964) that had all the formulaic elements like the ingenious devices, the Bond girls, the cutting-edge action sequences, the super villain, that made the series a worldwide pop culture phenomenon.

Bob Simmons (1933-1988) was the stunt coordinator and fight choreographer on 12 of the James Bond films from *Dr. No* to *A View To A Kill.* Simmons was responsible for many of the memorable action and fight sequences (while also stunt doubling for Sean Connery) that the world has come to instantly associate and expect with the Bond franchise. Some of the standout moments are the fight in the train car between Donovan "Red" Grant (Robert Shaw) and Bond (Sean Connery), the catfight with the two gypsy women in *From Russia With Love* (1963), and the final fight scene in Fort Knox between Bond and Odd Job in *Goldfinger* (1964).

Arguably, one of the most underappreciated movies of the whole Bond series is *On Her Majesty's Secret Service* (1969). Because he was the Editor and 2nd Unit Director in the three previous Bond films, Director Peter Hunt was all too familiar with the style of action needed for the film and took it to another level. The film has seven brawls, choreographed by the film's stunt coordinator, George Leech, and the star George Lazenby (uncredited for his contributions to the choreography), who would later take the experience learned on this film and go to Hong Kong and star in several martial arts films. The difference in the fights compared to the previous Bond films was the rapid-fire editing (that was unique for the time), different camera angles, and at certain moments, lowering the film speed (f.p.s.), that gave it a hyper-kinetic pace and rhythm to the fights that we have never seen previously in any Bond film.

The spy films lit the imagination and fantasies of many youths and adults alike. The popularity of the Bond films would of course spawn imitators and parodies of the super spy genre. There were many spy-oriented TV shows and movies spawned by the success of Bond. One of the better parodies was with the two Derek Flint films starring James Coburn. In *Our Man Flint* (1966), the fight scenes were very well choreographed for the day, although they relied too much on the karate chops (something all shows and movies were doing at the time). But a clever fight in the film was when Flint goes into a smoky bar in France and meets Agent 008 (Robert Gunner) and gets into a fake brawl only to pass on information to each other. However, in the sequel, *In Like Flint* (1967), the choreography is much stronger and more detailed than the previous film. The stand out fight scene is when Flint fights General Carter's men in Miss Norton's spa grounds and into the gymnasium. What made this fight different from other stylized brawls of this time was that the film carefully balanced tongue in cheek parody while still keeping the serious intensity and purpose of the fight. The fight also had a subtext, showing a relationship between Flint and his opponents, displaying Flint's intelligence and superiority in the heat of battle, all while still keeping the audience entertained.

Having auditioned for the lead in the movie *Ben Hur* and losing it to Charlton Heston, actor Kirk Douglas decided to produce and star in his own epic, *Spartacus* (1960), based on the true story of a slave trained to be a gladiator for the entertainment of the privileged, only to lead a mass revolt to overthrow the Roman empire. The gladiator training sequences that are functional (in story and character development) build upon each other, eventually becoming treacherous, showing the audience the transformation from slaves to gladiators. We also understand their mindset and intent during their upcoming battles when their trainer, Marcellus (Charles McGraw), explains to them what different strikes to the body will do to their opponent by painting the strokes on Spartacus' (Kirk Douglas) body.

The training sequences leading up to the fights and battle scenes serve as a nonverbal narrative. One of the most memorable fight scenes in the film was between Spartacus and Draba (Woody Strode) because the senator's women wanted to see some people get killed because they were bored. There was no dialogue between Strode and Douglas before or during the fight. But their body language and facial expressions, along with how they interacted (subtle and obvious) with each other is masterfully performed and executed. The duel to the death has a classical three-act structure and visually uses a contrast in styles (long range trident and net vs. a short sword and mini shield) while successfully holding the emotional tension throughout the fight by changing its dynamics as the fight progresses. With all these elements working, the fight still holds its own after repeated viewings and remains a classic fight scene to this day. The stunt coordinator on this epic was none other than stunt pioneer Yakima Canutt (1895-1986), famous for doing the acting and stunts in western serials and on John Ford's *Stagecoach* (1939), among other notable films. He would later be given a special Oscar at the 1966 Academy Awards for helping to create the stunt profession and a variety of safety devices.

Some of the finer examples of brawls and bare-fisted fights in the '60s can be seen in the TV series, *The Wild Wild West* (1965 to 1969). The series' star, Robert Conrad, an ex-professional boxer, performed all his own fights on the show with technical precision, speed, grace, and power, while projecting a very confident and engaging screen presence. When watching the fight scenes, you get the feeling from Conrad's performance that he is extremely comfortable with his fighting abilities. The camera angles and editing were effective and did not call unnecessary attention or hinder the performances so the audience can fully take in and witness the action unfold right before their eyes. As a result, the fights are arguably still some of the most exciting and best-looking brawls on a TV series to this day.

1970s—The Birth of the Modern-Day Action-Adventure as a Film Genre

Because of the collapse of the studio system, the '70s marked one of the creative high points in American filmmaking. The counter-culture during this time influenced Hollywood to take more chances and experiment with younger filmmakers like George Lucas, Steven Spielberg, John Carpenter, Francis Ford Coppola, and Martin Scorsese to name a few. Restrictions on language, adult content, sexuality, and violence loosened up tremendously because of the freedom.

The birth of the modern day action-adventure was first started around the late 1960s to early 1970s, and is the accumulation of several film genres that were once thriving but no longer popular with audiences. The result is a combination of the following genres:

- **The western**—The moral code of the hero. The structure of the story and emotional build up/set up leading the hero to eventually confront the villain in the end.
- **The war film**—Overcoming group fears. The "Sacrificial Hero"—the character(s) who sacrifice their lives for the good of the group.
- **The film noir**—Dealing and exposing underlying secrets with the story and characters. Exploring the dark side of mankind and what propelled the character(s) away from humanity.
- **The swashbuckler**—Action set pieces throughout the film showing the skills of the characters. Setting up small action pieces that lead up to a big payoff at the end.
- **The detective/private eye film**—To show the hero's logic and procedures that eventually leads the hero to a showdown with the villain.
- **The thriller**—The dramatic tension and suspense. An action scene is in essence a thriller.
- **The gangster film**—The villain's search or quest for power and social and political metaphors.
- **The cliffhanger/serials**—Building up of and exploitation of anticipation and anxiety after the audience has (hopefully) invested emotional interest with the characters in the film.

The first films of the modern day action-adventure genre were *Bullitt* (1968) and *Dirty Harry* (1971).

Exploitation and Grindhouse Influences

One of the genres where the modern-day action-adventure genre "got its legs" is from the exploitation aka grindhouse films that started in the late '60s to mid '80s. They were sneered, snubbed, and overlooked by critics and the media at the time because of their exploitative nature with the sensationalist titles and subject matter. The term "grindhouse" meant it was a theater that played back-to-back films that exploited sex, violence, and other extreme subject matter and themes. The genres played in these grindhouse theaters were:

- **Sex exploitation**—Vehicles that show female nudity, known today as soft-core pornography.
- **Shock/taboo**—Films that are made simply to shock the audience using realistic looking graphic violence or forbidden sexual acts.
- **Outlaw biker films**—Typically lawless gangs of bandits who frequently act outside of the law and use drugs and alcohol, ready to commit violent acts and have sex.
- **Horror**—This includes the splatter (showing graphic scenes of excessive blood and guts), zombie, and cannibal film genre. An example of a film that had a good fight scene in this genre is *Grave of the Vampire* (1974), where vampire Caleb Croft (Michael Pataki) disrupts a couple making out in the graveyard and kills the man by breaking his back atop a tombstone, sucks his blood, and then rapes the woman in an open grave. The woman then gives birth to James (William Smith), who is half vampire/half human. James then grows up to find out who his father is and vows to kill him. They finally meet and have a lively brawl to the death. Another film is *Captain Kronos—Vampire Hunter*, one of the last films by Hammer Studios that combined elements of the swashbuckler in the horror film and was much different than other horror films.
- **Mondo**—Documentaries that are allegedly real, showing customs from around the world that are shocking, disgusting, or primitive to Western eyes.
- **Women in prison**—Films where women are in jail and tortured and humiliated, forced to have sexual relations by the guard staff. On top of all this, these films usually have your obligatory female nudity, lesbian love scenes, and cat fights. Films that had great catfights include *Bamboo House of Dolls* (1973) and *The Big Doll House* (1971).
- **Blaxploitation**—Starring black actors and made for a black audience, the story is usually about getting revenge against a Caucasian perpetrator usually known as "the man." These films also stereotypically depict urban living, drugs, and prostitution. The first blaxploitation film is credited to Melvin Van Pebble's *Sweet Sweetback's Baadasssss Song* (1971).
- **Martial arts**—Usually the importing of films from Hong Kong, Taiwan, and Japan (although some films were made domestically) that were usually poorly dubbed in English along with altering the story and/or scenes to appeal to a Western audience.

The common denominator with all these genres at the time was producing a film with an extremely low budget while still being shocking and exploitative. Usually fight scenes are aplenty in all these genres of film because they are very cheap to shoot and have a good shock value to them.

Lately, exploitation films have gained acceptance by the media, fans, musicians, and by a younger new breed of filmmakers who were weaned on those films growing up like Quentin Tarrantino and Robert Rodriguez, who both made their own homage to those films suitably titled *Grindhouse—Planet Terror/Death Proof* (2007). Audiences today are able to look back and appreciate the confines of working with an extremely low budget while being able to show the filmmaker's uniqueness, creativity, and originality. "The difference between the exploitation films of the '60s and '70s and the films today is that those earlier films were an unknown, meaning you as the audience did not know what you were in for. Films today hold no surprises. The old exploitation films were nothing but that!" states Ron Strong, film scholar.

The '70s was also a time of self-introspection and pointing out what was wrong with society in general. Here are some other films from the '70s with fight scenes of note:

A Clockwork Orange (1971)—Stanley Kubrick adapted and directed Anthony Burgess's novel that takes place in futuristic England where Alex (Malcolm McDowell) is a charismatic juvenile delinquent who brawls, steals, and rapes victims out of boredom with his "droogs" (gang). It has been widely debated to this day about the film's social message, and it has been banned in many countries. With Roy Scammell credited as the stunt arranger, the brawls are extremely lively and stylized, especially when Alex is front and center. The choreography of Alex's fight scenes are grandiose and celebratory (and at times phallic) as McDowell performs them with a wide-eyed and child-like zest and zeal, savoring each moment like a young tiger playing with its first kill. But the fights and acts of violence also come across as Alex's own form of artistic expression as the "ultra violence" is played against the classical musical score used as their own way to entertain themselves to escape from the emptiness of their dull and dreary dystopian society. The cinematography by John Alcott (1931-1986) was very subtle and unobtrusive, giving the viewer a voyeuristic feel to Alex's exploits.

All this leads up to the scene where Alex beats up a husband and rapes his wife, all while enthusiastically singing "Singing in the Rain," a contradiction to what is actually occurring on screen. The slow-motion sequence where Alex turns on his gang and suddenly beats them is poetic and graceful, yet sinister and cunning, but we cannot take our eyes off McDowell's performance as he emblazons the screen with much bravado and energy, making it a performance of a lifetime. This film was banned in many countries as well as the United Kingdom because of the extreme sexual violence, the threat of possible copycat crimes, and threats on director Kubrick and his family, and it was not released until after Kubrick's death in 1999.

Enter The Dragon (1973)—the first American martial arts film produced by a major Hollywood studio. The film was released in August 19, 1973, and was to showcase Bruce Lee in a film that was specially made with the Western audience in mind. It was the first US-Chinese co-production that many consider the *Gone With The Wind* of martial arts films. The story and Bruce Lee's choreography was tailored specifically for the Western audience (See East Vs. West for more detail) and was a key figure in ushering in the action-adventure film to the West.

Emperor of the North (1973)—An unusual subculture film that takes place during the great depression about two mythical characters—a legendary hobo, A- #1 (Lee Marvin) who meets Shack (Ernest Borgnine), an evil and sadistic train conductor, who prides himself on capturing hobos and will not let anyone ride his train for free. A- #1 is finally challenged to ride up to Portland on Shack's train, which leads to a brutal brawl between the two men.

The final showdown between A- #1 and Shack is arguably one of the most visceral and brutal brawls to ever be filmed. It is pure '70s machismo in its execution as both men use whatever they can get their hands on to beat each other with. The fight does not play up anything extremely bloody or grotesque, like what you might see in an exploitation grindhouse film. The feel of the fight is emotionally brutal, displaying and connecting to the savage animal instincts in all of us. What sets it apart from all the other fights you'll probably see on film is the physical and emotional commitment both actors give to the scene that only veteran actors like Borgnine and Marvin can deliver, which keeps you on the edge of your seat, hinged on every moment of the brawl.

Hard Times (1975)—Another story that takes place during the depression, Chaney (Charles Bronson), a drifter, comes into New Orleans and meets up with Speed (James Coburn), a hustler, who he teams up with to set up the illegal bare knuckle fighting in the docks and warehouses of the Big Easy. Charles Bronson was 53 years old at the time and was in great shape and very convincing as a bare knuckle brawler. The film's original title was *The Streetfighter*, which suited the style of the fight scenes well because they used rudimentary low kicks as well as grappling along with the brawls to keep them looking different from one another.

The Warriors (1979)—A modern-day urban comic book fable of a street gang, "The Warriors," are wrongly accused of the murder of a gang leader resulting in every gang in the city coming after them as they fight their way back home. The movie was based on the novel by Sol Yurick and the Greek non-fiction tale *Anabasis* written by Xenophon (431-355 B.C.). A patron in NYC got into a fight and was killed during a screening of the film, along with other outbursts of gang violence in different parts of the country, creating more of a buzz for the film. The fight scenes are visceral and stylish while still keeping its rough brawl type nature as a core theme. The best fight in the film was in the subway station men's restroom with The Warriors against The Punks. The film today is a cult favorite spawning a videogame and threats of a remake.

Rocky (1976)—An unknown boxer gets the chance of a lifetime to fight the world champion. *Rocky*, written by and starring a relatively unknown actor by the name of Sylvester Stallone, was inspired when he saw Muhammad Ali fight Chuck Wepner, a journeyman fighter who went the distance (15 rounds) with the World Champ. The film would get 10 Oscar nominations and win three Oscars (best director, best editing, and best picture) the following year, leading him to a prolific film career as an international action star, and five *Rocky* sequels. The film has great training sequences that gets the audience to sympathize and feel Rocky's pain, courage, and commitment like never before. The well-choreographed fight by Stallone in the end of the film with Rocky and Apollo Creed (Carl Weathers) was a contrast in styles (boxer vs. slugger) and told an extremely effective non-verbal story. This film was one of the first films to use the Steadicam camera manned by Garrett Brown, who also invented the revolutionary camera. The camera enables the cameraman to walk alongside the actors while holding the camera without the normal shaking and jarring of the camera. This camera was used during the training sequences and the famous run up the Philadelphia Art Museum steps.

The underdog journey of Rocky Balboa in and out of the ring captured the hearts of millions all over the world, as Stallone would make five sequels. The films in the Rocky series would easily access the inner psyche and manipulate the hearts of the audience by appealing to the fighter's spirit buried in everyone, no matter what the critics had to say about the films. The training sequences in each film continued to be more in depth and inspiring, changing his approach to the fight in each film. The cinematography and editing of the fight scenes as each film progressed got better and better. The boxing matches would eventually turn into unrealistic macho slug fests in sequels 3, 4, and 5, losing its base in reality. But in the final film, *Rocky Balboa*, inspired by the George Foreman match where he won the world title in his mid 40s, the final match looked the closest to what a real boxing match would look like. This is because of the new type of boxing gloves specially developed for film and first used in the bio-pic *Ali* (2001), where the screen fighters could throw punches and make actual contact with their opponent without hurting them because the air pump inside the glove absorbs the impact of the hit.

Star Wars Episode IV—A New Hope (1977)—Inspired by Kurosawa's *Hidden Fortress* (1958), writer/director George Lucas blends Joseph Campbell's concepts of world mythology into a science-fiction fantasy, along with revolutionary special effects, forever changing how the world will see films. The energy and pace of the film was driven by the cuts (edits), making it exhilarating and exciting, instead of letting the actors dictate the rhythm of the film. In the movie, Lucas created the mythology of the Jedi Knights—an ancient noble monastic group who are the keepers of peace and justice. The Jedis are known for their observance and practice of manipulating *the force*—a living energy force that permeates around all living things and binds the universe, a philosophy similar in principle to how a traditional martial artist practices and uses the concept of chi (or ki). The Jedi's main weapon of choice is the light saber—a sword whose blade is made of laser, created to be a defensive weapon in a futuristic world of ray guns, laser blasters, and laser cannons. The Jedi's actions are chivalric and honorable (much like the Japanese Samurai, Medieval Knights, and Chinese Knight Errants) and the light saber symbolized that. The fighting style used in Episodes 4-6 were based on Japanese kendo, European fencing, and Ching Gung (Chinese flying).

The film became a worldwide summer blockbuster (at the time) making more money than any movie in history, spawning two sequels: *Episode V–The Empire Strikes Back* (1980), and *Episode VI–Return of the Jedi* (1983). As each episode progressed, along with the Jedi training of the story's central character Luke Skywalker (Mark Hamill), the better the light saber duels became. The Star Wars saga is very much like a grand Western version of the Wu Xia Pian.

1980s—Muscle-Bound Gods, Buddies, Smart Ass One-Liners, and the One-Man Army

In the world of entertainment, the following changes occurred in the 1980s.

- Due to the escalating costs of producing films (special effects budgets, inflated salaries of name actors, etc.), corporations and multi-national conglomerates start to buy and take control of movie studios, and productions start to film overseas in order to save money. As a result, filmmakers are rewarded for cutting corners to save money and finishing their films ahead of time, even if the project lacks artistic content.

- The birth of the blockbuster/event film. Producers and studio executives have more of a "bottom line" frame of mind, creating "event" films that have wide mass appeal that everyone all over the world has to see. This is done by including amazing state of the art special effects and sound and paying high profile actors top dollar for their services. Then the movies are strategically marketed and blitzed to the public during the most opportune times to take advantage of maximum attendance periods (usually the summer months and holidays) to make the most money possible. Because of the worldwide success of the films *Jaws* and *Star Wars*, this approach is not only applied to US audiences, but also to markets worldwide.

- From this marketing process evolved the *high concept film*—a film easily described in two to three sentences or less so that everyone can understand the story or concept of the film. Another approach that evolved from marketing tactics and the corporate takeover of the film studios is the *formula film*—a film that has a compiled story and/or visual elements that have been tested to have positive ratings by audiences from previously successful films. By creating a film that has mass appeal they are also going for the lowest common denominator. Because of all these factors, studio films (especially action-adventure) are no longer a creative art form that can explore the human conscious and spirit, but more of a two-hour amusement park ride. Any types of emotional substance and/or action now become much more calculated and easily expected from the audience, while coming less organically from story and character.

- As a result, in general, '80s films are less daring and exploratory because studios are more financially conscious, wanting to sell the most tickets while causing the least amount of controversy and unexpected surprises that might turn away an audience. This affects action films and fight choreography specifically because creatively conservative decision makers usually do not want a fight choreographer to experiment with anything new, but rather stay with elements that have been done before.

- Home video market explodes. The birth of the secondary market with home video rental and cable TV gives the studios a second and third chance to recoup their initial investment of a film that might not have attracted audiences when released theatrically and begins to change the studio's film release and marketing practices. In 1988, over 15 million videotape copies of *E.T.* were sold to the public. This also makes the studios re-think certain films they felt might not have a good showing theatrically and take a lesser financial risk by releasing them *straight to video*. This gives the opportunity for unknown actors and martial artists (turned action stars) a chance to be seen by new audiences and develop a cult following of their own through the cable TV and video rental market.

- Cable TV programming takes off and offers the viewing audience more options than just programming options the three major networks have to offer. Studios begin to release films they feel would not fare well theatrically on cable making them "exclusive cable events." Between cable and home video, movie studios are given broader distribution choices with their titles, giving films a second chance at getting an audience that might not have found one when initially released in theaters.

- In 1980, Pioneer introduces the laserdisc player as another home video format option for consumers, which has a picture quality considerably better than VHS. The format attracts only hard-core cinephiles and karaoke enthusiasts. In 1984, The Voyager Company introduces The Criterion Collection, a line of high quality state of the art transfers in its original theatrical aspect ratio, with many supplemental extra features, director's cuts of the film, deleted scenes, outtakes, audio commentaries (often with the filmmakers), etc. These features become commonplace when DVD is introduced in 1997.

- In 1981, MTV starts to air music videos on cable TV and is an immediate hit. The advent of fast cutting style seen in music videos eventually seeps its way into film production as music video directors and editors are given the opportunity to direct and edit full-length features. Producer Jerry Bruckheimer is the first to take full advantage of this by using the same style of rapid fire cutting in his films to appeal to the younger crowd with films like *Flashdance, Top Gun, Beverly Hills Cop II,* and *Days of Thunder.*

  For good and for bad, the MTV style of rapid-fire editing eventually affects how fight and dance scenes are seen in Western films as a commonplace. When done well, it can accelerate the pace of the fight. When done poorly, we usually see the editing of the moves and techniques that does not make any type of sequential sense or logic, destroying what was choreographed and the performance of the actors.

- In 1982, while filming on the set of *Twilight: The Movie* (1983), actor Vic Morrow is carrying two child actors during a scene and a helicopter loses control and crashes killing all three of them. As a result, stricter rules in child labor laws and safety regulations during filming.

- In 1984, out of boredom while filming, actor Jon Erik Hexum takes a prop gun loaded with blanks and jokingly puts the barrel to his temple and fires. The wadding from the blank cartridge shatters his skull resulting in life-ending brain damage. Hexum's death made the film industry realize that even though only blanks are in the gun, it can still cause damage to an actor if they are too close to the discharge.

- During the filming of *City Heat* (1984), Burt Reynolds is hit in the face with a metal chair while filming a fight scene, breaking his jaw. Reynolds is restricted to a liquid diet for the rest of the filming and loses close to 30 pounds.
- In 1987, Sony abandons the Betamax because VHS dominates 95% of the market share, even though Beta was a smaller and superior quality format.
- The Bond series was in a period of transition. The last two films with Roger Moore, *Octopussy* (1983) and *A View to a Kill* (1985) were extremely far-fetched and on the verge of farcical and losing its dangerous spy- thriller image. The values of the world were changing, but Bond was not able to keep up with the social changes. Bond's amorous and not-so discretionary bed hopping with different sexual partners did not agree with the public's consciousness of the AIDS virus. Timothy Dalton succeeds Moore with *The Living Daylights* (1987) and *License to Kill* (1989), giving a darker side to Bond than ever before making him somewhat of a vigilante who was brooding, cruel, and methodical. We would not see another Bond film for six years.
- The '80s was also a time when Hollywood re-examined America's involvement in the Vietnam war and the Vietnam Vet becomes an exploited super hero in big to low budget films like *Rambo 2 and 3, Missing in Action 1-2-3,* and *Behind Enemy Lines (aka P.O.W.- The Escape).*
- *The Day After* (1983) was a TV movie that aired in two parts in successive nights. The film played into the fears of what would happen to us during a nuclear war. A year later in England, the BBC aired a docudrama titled *Threads* (1984) with a similar story about a nuclear bombing in the UK.

The American action hero of the '80s was definitely a reflection of the fears and fantasies of their audiences at that time. Western action stars like Sylvester Stallone, Arnold Schwarzenegger, and Dolph Lundgren were bigger than life action heroes, with glistening huge muscles. Displays of strength, power, and brawn usually ruled over brains, strategy, and logic. Big explosions (and the bigger the better) were the typical characteristics expected of action films of the '80s. If not, they had to have some martial arts or other types of fighting skills that did most of their talking for them—like Chuck Norris, Steven Seagal, and Jeff Speakman—or a hybrid of muscles and fighting skills like Jean Claude Van Damme and Steve James.

The '80s also brought us the concept of the "One-man army"—part superhero, part savior, part rescuer, part fighting machine, and part god. These heroes would be able to face an army of villains and be able to take all of them out easily with their bare hands, weapon, or firearm. They were also usually able to outsmart their opponents (especially the villain's thugs/henchmen), which is not saying much. This was typically seen in action films of this era, like *Invasion USA* and the *Rambo* sequels.

The fight choreography for the one-man army was usually (in retrospect) grandiose, impractical, maudlin, and self-absorbed, where their righteous cause for taking action/revenge gave them some kind of immunity. A typical example used often is when the hero is in a fit of emotional rage, he will suddenly stand up from where he was hiding and shoot away with his gun(s) or throw a series of techniques at his opponents, when nothing has really changed except for the emotional state of mind of the hero.

During the '80s, Sylvester Stallone and Arnold Schwarzenegger would battle it out for the king of the box office in action films making both of them international movie stars. In 1982, Schwarzenegger finally found his niche when he starred in the title role of *Conan the Barbarian*, making it a box office success.

The sword master for this film was martial artist Kiyoshi Yamazaki and the fight choreography was tailored specifically for the size and strengths (along with the type of swords) of the three leads—Conan (Schwarzenegger), Subotai (Gerry Lopez), and Valeriaa (Sandahl Bergman). The success of *Conan* made the sword and sorcery or heroic fantasy genre more viable, followed by many copycats, which had rudimentary and weak fight choreography that lacked any type of originality or creativity, including the sequel, *Conan—The Destroyer* (1984). Other Sword and Sorcery films that had good fight choreography around this time were *Hundra* (1983) and *Excalibur* (1981).

In 1982, Sylvester Stallone stars in *First Blood* as John Rambo, a decorated, ex-Green Beret/Vietnam vet, living on the fringe. While walking through a small Northwestern town trying to locate a friend, Rambo is harassed and wrongfully arrested by Sheriff Teasle (Brian Dennehy). In jail, Rambo is hosed down, harassed, and beaten by the sheriff's men, sparking traumatic flashbacks of his experiences in Vietnam, and then he fights and escapes. Rambo's empty-handed fight scene against multiple attackers as he escapes from jail is a brawl, self-defense, and grappling in a very well choreographed fight scene. Although a few of the moves and reactions in the fight were somewhat theatrically flashy, it still keeps the emotional core of the fight. What also made the fight/escape from jail so satisfying for the audience was the gradual set up that led up to the fight, so by the time Rambo emotionally explodes and fights back, the audience was already behind Stallone's character, and they are relieved of all the tension that was built up to that point.

After his escape from jail, he runs to the woods and single-handedly takes on all Sheriff Teasle's men along with the Reserve National Guard, where he sets up traps and is always one step ahead of his opponents, showing the ineptness and limitations of his opponents. Rambo's actions and character were not portrayed as if he was a superhero/comic book character (like in the sequels), but more towards a realistic and practical approach, as an experienced soldier who could easily kill his opponents, but rather chooses to hurt them enough as a warning to stop them from coming after him. The use of strategy, wit, and guile against his opponents throughout the film is an integral part of showing the audience Rambo's character, giving him a lot of depth. Stallone's portrayal of Rambo as a man of few words gives a very effective performance by using body and facial expressions to show emotion has generally gone unappreciated by audiences.

Stallone followed it up with two sequels, *Rambo First Blood Part II* (1985) and *Rambo III* (1988), which were more comic book in their approach to the action, losing the practical and effective styles to fighting, rather opting for the over the top one-man army approach. The budget in the third sequel was the most expensive film ever made at the time with a budget of $65 million dollars. Both of the sequels were more popular and profitable than the original, making the Rambo character into a film icon of the times.

The Wise-Crackin' Hero

Not only did the action hero have to kick ass, apprehend the bad guy, and get the girl in the end, he also had to be able to tell jokes too! Although this was done decades before, most notably with the James Bond series and a lot of Burt Reynolds films, it became more common in the '80s and on into the '90s. Schwarzenegger had his call back line, "I'll be back," that extended into almost all his films during this time. The audience would wait for him to say those lines and laugh knowing it was an inside joke for him and the audience. In many of Burt Reynold's action/comedies, he would look into the camera/audience with a knowing wink and nod letting the audience in on the joke like in *Hooper* (1978) and *Smokey and the Bandit* (1977). In *Beverly Hills Cop*, Axel Foley (Eddie Murphy) wise cracks his way much like a Taoist jester, showing the flaws of the Beverly Hills police department and how going by procedure can take too long and blind a police detective's street instincts. In *Die Hard*, Bruce Willis' character of John McClane would have a sharp one-liner to say to himself or his foes to break up the constant heavy tension.

The 1990s into 2000—The Everyday Man, Asian Invasion, and CGI

The following events occurred in the '90s that affected how we see films.

- In 1994, Brandon Lee was accidentally shot by a fragmented gun shell on the set of *The Crow* and died 24 hours later. One of the reasons attributed to Lee's death was the extremely (about 18 hours) long hours the cast and crew worked each day on a set, which severely impairs one's judgment and perception, especially when it comes to stuntwork. As a result, shorter working hours were finally implemented.
- In the beginning of the '90s, the VCR was the common popular home appliance in about 3/4 of all households. The purchase and rental of pre-recorded videotapes were overtaking ticket sales in theaters. This changed drastically in 1997 when DVD technology was introduced to consumers all over the world. Quickly, DVD becomes the fastest growing home video format ever.
- Reality TV was introduced on MTV with *The Real World* in 1992 and later becomes a popular commonplace on network television by the year 2000. This affects how a viewer sees stunts and fights because we see reality shows and news broadcasts of police car chases, domestic violence, assaults, etc.
- Pro wrestling becomes popular and is on TV several nights a week as two different companies, WCW (World Championship Wrestling owned by Ted Turner) and the WWF (World Wrestling Federation later changed to WWE-World Wrestling Entertainment owned by Vince McMahon), battle each other for supremacy in TV ratings and popularity of the fans.
- On November 12, 1993, a version of the Brazillian combative sport of Vale Tudo (Portuguese meaning "anything goes") is televised, changing the name to The Ultimate Fighting Championship (UFC) with a lot of controversy surrounding the event. The winner of the first two UFC events (and UFC 4) was Brazilian Jujitsu stylist Royce Gracie. Gracie's dominance in the first two UFC matches brings the grappling game into national awareness.
- In 2001, the UFC established legitimacy when purchased by Zuffa, LLC, they get sanctioned by the Nevada State Athletic Commission by adding rules and weight classes. The popularity of Mixed Martial Arts (MMA) starts to grow rapidly as Zuffa stages cable pay-per-view events every

three months as audiences become more aware of the sport and the competitors. The popularity rises with each event while professional boxing heads the opposite way because there are no consistently active fighters who have the firepower to draw in an audience.

- The emerging consciousness of women in film. Women are making their mark in film with groundbreaking, controversial, and defiant films like *Thelma and Louise* (1991). Kathryn Bigelow directs *Point Break* and *Strange Days*, while Penny Marshall directs *Big* and *A League Of Their Own.* Women are also more visible in the action genre (see Women in Action).
- Bond is back. There was a six-year gap between Bond films due to a litigation issue over character rights. This time Pierce Brosnan is James Bond with *Goldeneye* (1995), *Tomorrow Never Dies* (1997), *The World Is Not Enough* (1999), and *Die Another Day* (2002).
- The title of *fight coordinator* is created for someone who is responsible for all aspects of fighting for the film and reports to the stunt coordinator. This new title was created due to the specialized demands of a much more technical fight scene and higher expectations from audiences.

The "Every Day" Man Becomes an Action Hero

In the late '80s, the bodybuilder/Adonis hero in action films changed when well-respected, critically accepted, and award winning actors who had already proved themselves began to star in action films. This changed the face of the action-adventure films because the actor was able to bring a certain amount of legitimacy to action-adventure films by creating characters for the screen that have more emotional depth and realism (even though there was still a lot of exploitation elements in the films). Up until this point, many actors had a snobbish view of action-adventure films, because they felt the roles were one-dimensional and that the physical demands—jumping, running, fighting, and shooting—were not considered acting in their eyes (except maybe Shakespeare). However, this was all changed with two films.

In 1987, Mel Gibson starred with Danny Glover in *Lethal Weapon.* Although Gibson got his first starring role in the action classic George Miller's *Mad Max* (1979), he successfully displayed his acting skills and proved to be a solid leading man in dramatic roles that do not require action. Gibson played Detective Martin Riggs, a Vietnam vet with suicidal tendencies, who was a sharpshooter and experienced in different styles of martial arts. Gibson brought emotional depth, complexity, and a dark humor in his portrayal of Riggs, showing us his pain. A prime example of this is an extremely private moment near the beginning of the film, when Riggs is at his beach trailer home and feels he has emotionally reached his end and can't bear the loss of his recently deceased wife, Victoria. He plays with his gun, puts a bullet in it, and shoves the barrel into his mouth, but at the last second decides not to pull the trigger.

The final fight scene between Mr. Joshua (Gary Busey) and Riggs was a combination of different martial arts including Jailhouse Rock (a fighting style used by prison inmates), Capoeira, and Gracie jujitsu. The brawl finally ends when Riggs gets Mr. Joshua in a triangle chokehold, a move that had not been widely seen as of yet (but eventually commonplace in MMA events starting in the early '90s). It was rumored that the final fight scene was very difficult to perform; the actors and the stunt doubles were not able to perform the moves to the fight convincingly. So in order to distract the viewers from the unconvincing fight, they used a wobbly handheld camera, extreme close ups, shined a moving spotlight (from the helicopter), shot it at night, and edited the sequence very choppily so you only get a vague description of what was actually happening. Unfortunately, this is the beginning of a standard blanket practice with American fight scenes that actually diminishes what was originally choreographed, even though the screen fighters might have more than competent fighting skills.

The film that really changed the face of action-adventure films for years to come was released a year later: *Die Hard* (1988). New York Police Detective John McClane (Bruce Willis) is struggling with his marriage, gets trapped in an office building by a gang of terrorists led by Hans Gruber (Alan Rickman) who is holding all of the employees hostage, including his wife. With McClane still free, a chess game between McClane and Gruber starts, continually escalating the stakes.

What made this modern-day action-adventure film a classic was that there were no extraneous plot points or gratuitous action scenes during any point in the film. As the film progresses, each scene built upon the previous action by the main characters. The subplot with Sgt. Al Powell (Reginald Vel Johnson) being McClane's confidant did not complicate or dilute the story, but added emotional depth to McClane's character and supported the main story line. McClane typified the everyday man in action films because in the beginning he calls the police and fire departments to come for help as opposed to being a one-man army and taking Han's men from the start.

The critical and box office success of *Die Hard* made Bruce Willis an international action star, while firmly cementing the everyday man as the preferred action hero of the day. *Die Hard* also generated three successful sequels (*Die Hard II*, *Die Hard With A Vengeance*, and *Live Free Or Die Hard*), although they were not able to truly capture the lean story structure or uniqueness of the original. Because of the film's enormous success, countless producers would describe their upcoming action film as "*Die Hard* on a (fill your main location here)." For example, the movie

Speed was pitched to studio executives as "Die Hard on a bus," while *Under Seige* (1992) was pitched as "*Die Hard* on a boat."

Soon other A-list actors would jump on the action-adventure film gravy train, like Denzel Washington in *Richochet* (1991), Keanu Reeves in *Point Break* (1991), Wesley Snipes in *Passenger 57* (1992), Meryl Streep in *The River Wild* (1994), Nicholas Cage in *The Rock* (1996) and *Con Air* (1997), to name a few.

The impact of the common man as hero had a huge effect upon the one-man army and muscle-bound god movies and the actors who played them. Schwarzenegger and Stallone too had to change their screen personas with varying degrees of success. Stallone decided on more comedic films like *Oscar* (1991) and *Stop! Or My Mom Will Shoot* (1992), while also playing the flawed hero in *Cliffhanger*, and as a reserved, calculated, and cerebral hit man in *Assassins* (1995), which both had every-day man qualities. He then took a huge risk by trading in his trademark lean and chiseled physique by gaining 40 pounds to look overweight and play the lead in a non-action role in *Copland* (1997).

The Epic Returns

The '90s also marked the return of the epic film. In *Braveheart* (1995), Mel Gibson directed and starred as William Wallace, a real-life 13th century Scottish rebel, who unites the clans of Scotland and leads a medieval war against England's King Edward I, a.k.a., Longshanks (Edward Woodward), an obsessed ruler who wants to claim their country for his own.

Based on part myth and part fact about the exploits of William Wallace, the battle sequences were graphically violent, without the overuse of CGI, so the audience could fully grasp what would have happened during the time. Gibson hired actors who had missing limbs and gave them prosthetics, then had their opponent actually hack away at the false limb, looking like they were actually severing their limb. This practice was also used in the opening D-Day beach attack in *Saving Private Ryan.*

Before working on the fight scenes in his film, Gibson watched every battle film he could get his hands on to study what was previously done, so he would not rehash anything. The battle sequences were choreographed and shot to look graphically violent in order to give the audience the feeling of what it was like to have been in a medieval battle. The battle scenes on the films were so big in scale that two stunt coordinators (Mic Rogers and Simon Crane) were needed to do the job.

The biggest battle in the film was with The Battle of Sterling. Although not a true retelling of the battle, they decided to change the scenario in order to make the battle more cinematic and broader, taking full advantage of the anamorphic widescreen cameras to show the huge scale of the battle. The scene required eight cameras and took six weeks to film. The 2,000 extras who served as the Scottish and British warriors were all members of the Irish Army, and required three weeks to train them in the basics of cinematic screen fighting so no one would get hurt, yet look like they were killing each other on screen.

The Troubled Comic Book Hero

At the close of the decade, the release of *Batman* (1989) starring Michael Keaton as the dark knight and Jack Nicholson as the villainous Jack Napier/Joker, was a continuation from the *everyday hero*, where big stars would get involved in high profile action films/events. At first, comic book fans were appalled at the casting of Keaton in the dual role of Bruce Wayne/Batman and wanted a buff, chisel jawed actor to wear the cape. But, creator Bob Kane hit the comic book convention circuit and explained that Keaton was chosen for his versatility demonstrated in *Beetlejuice* and *Clean and Sober*. What made this different from other filmed versions of comic book heroes was that there is a duality/conflict with the heroes' purpose in life as a crimefighter yet wanting to return to belong like everyone else in society.

This was only done previously with Christopher Reeves, sensitive and multi-layered portrayal of the Man of Steel in *Superman: The Motion Picture* (1978) followed by *Superman II* (1980). The fight scene in the streets of Metropolis between Superman (Reeves) and General Zod (Terrance Stamp), Ursa (Sara Douglas), and Non was revolutionary for the time because they did not have the aid of computer graphics. They used piano wire to make the characters fly and made some of the sets using forced perspective to give it a sense of depth.

One of the reasons comic book heroes were not taken seriously was because of the camp and tongue in cheek humor that has been closely associated with the *Batman* TV series (1966-1968) starring Adam West and Burt Ward. The dialogue had humorous double entendres and was aimed for the adults; while the premise, action, colorful sets, and costumes were aimed for the kids. The fight scenes on this show were also taken very lightly and came across as a comedic romp that obscured most of the screen hits with on screen bubbles that read Pow! Zowie! Ouch!, etc. and were taken lightly as a result.

Although the Medieval warfare was extremely savage, bloody, and brutal, we were able to see Wallace's genius strategy unfold visually without having to be repetitive in the choreography, which is typical in these medieval epic films. The successful wedding of choreography, cinematography, and editing gave the fights a chaotic feeling without requiring cheap camera or editing gimmicks to create the emotion. It was also the edit points that Gibson chose and then edited together that really made the fight scenes effective.

Braveheart deservedly won many awards that year, including five Academy Awards for Best Picture, Cinematography, Directing, Sound Effects Editing, and Make-up.

Asian Martial Arts Influence on Western Films

The influence of Asian martial arts was proliferated when World War II soldiers came home telling of some "exotic" style of fighting they learned while stationed in Asia. The first arts to gain any popularity in the United States were the Japanese arts of Judo, Jiu-Jitsu, and Karate. During the Korean War, U.S. solders were exposed to the Korean arts, Tang Soo Do, Hapkido, and Tae Kwon Do (then known as Tae Kyon). However, the Chinese arts were still closely guarded in the Chinatown districts; the Chinese refused to teach their arts to Westerners. It wasn't until the late 1950s and the early 1960s that Chinese Kung Fu teachers such as Ark Wong and Bruce Lee broke the race barrier to teach to non-Chinese students.

The first Western film to include an Asian martial art/sport was 1945's *Blood on the Sun*. The film starred James Cagney as Nick Condon, a reporter working in Tokyo who uses Judo to subdue the imperialistic, anti-democratic villains. Because Cagney was a dancer, he was able to learn and perform the moves convincingly. However, the moves Cagney mainly used were basic hip and shoulder throws, but at that time something very new for the audience to witness.

During the 1950s and 1960s, fights using martial arts were rudimentary, using front kicks, hip and shoulder throws, and the oxymoronic term, the "Judo chop"—an open-handed hit with the blade of the hand usually applied to the side of the opponent's neck. You can typically see this on TV shows such as *The Avengers* (1961–1969) and movies such as *Goldfinger* and *The Manchurian Candidate*, although a brief exception and highlight during this time was the film *You Only Live Twice*. For the film, Donn Draeger (1922-1982) and Masaaki Hatsumi were called in as uncredited technical advisors for the martial arts and ninjitsu sequences in the middle of the film. Draeger was a U.S. Marine Captain/Major who started training in the martial arts at the age of seven in Chicago. As he grew older, he joined the Marines and spent over a decade stationed in Japan studying different styles of martial arts and then later living and studying in parts of China, Korea, Mongolia, and Indonesia.

Retooled Spies

Bourne

The *Jason Bourne* novel written by Robert Ludlum was adapted previously in the '70s but did not capture the audiences as much as it did when it was re-made with *The Bourne Identity* (2002). Jason Bourne (Matt Damon) is found floating unconscious in the middle of the Mediterranean Ocean with several bullet holes in his body and finally wakes up with amnesia not knowing anything about himself. As the story and each sequel progresses we discover that he is a CIA Operative Agent and he discovers/remembers the inhumane acts he was responsible for and tries to make an amends to his past. The series continues with *Bourne Supremacy* (2004), and *Bourne Ultimatum* (2007). What makes him more interesting than Bond is that Bourne has to improvise with what is available and use his wits and knowledge to get him out of trouble. Bourne is not co-dependent on technological gadgets to get him out of trouble like Bond traditionally was. This has a direct affect as to how the fight scenes are choreographed.

Bond Reboots

Brosnan's last Bond film *Die Another Day,* had a weak story and relied too much on cheesy and unconvincing CGI special effects rather than doing real stunts for which the series is known. It was void of any real excitement and turned into something of a self-parody. Although it was not Pierce Brosnan's fault, he was unfortunately jettisoned from the famed role of the British super spy.

In 2006, the Bond franchise decided to do something different and turned back the clock starting with Bond as a rookie when he gets his 0-0 status with MI-5. They hired a new Bond, Daniel Craig, who was blond and blue eyed and more rugged looking than the past actors. He played Bond in *Casino Royale* (2006). What they were doing was retrofitting Bond for today's audience, since other similar spy/action films like the *Jason Bourne* series, and TV shows like *24*, *Alias*, and *La Femme Nikita* in a post 9/11 world have become much grittier and cynical with complex plots that deal with a lot of political intrigue. Because of this, the fights have also changed emphasis and style.

The change starts immediately with the opening sequence where we are used to seeing a clever and spectacular action scene where Bond gets the best of his opponent(s) without breaking a sweat. But we are immediately introduced to something different. We see Bond in a messy brawl in the restroom that is brutal, relentless, and savage. Arguably, for the first time since Sean Connery, we saw a Bond who truly came across as extremely dangerous and volatile. To add more realism, the fights are no longer antiseptic. In the fight at the airport in the gas truck, Bond was cut and bleeding and we continued to see the cuts gradually heal on his face in the several scenes that followed. This also applies to the torture scene Bond takes from Le Chiffre (Mads Mikkelsen) that made men in the theaters cringe in their seats.

In 1966, ABC-TV premiered the series *The Green Hornet*, from the popular radio serial, which starred Van Williams as the crime-fighting hero and co-starred Bruce Lee as Kato, his lethal servant/butler. In this show, the West was introduced to something different—a cinematic interpretation of the art of Chinese Gung Fu (Cantonese for Kung Fu), and Lee got more fan mail than the star. The show only lasted for one season (26 episodes) before being cancelled. He got frustrated because he was only offered stereotypical Asian roles and he was not interested in playing what he calls a "Hop-Along Wong." So Lee went on to work occasionally as a technical advisor for fight scenes and took bit parts in TV shows and films such as *The Wrecking Crew*, *Walk in the Spring Rain*, and *Marlowe* before landing a guest-starring role on several episodes of the TV show *Longstreet*, starring James Franciscus as blind insurance detective Mike Longstreet. Lee played an antique dealer, Li Tsung, who teaches Longstreet to defend himself with the martial arts—more specifically his own art of Jeet Kune Do. In several episodes of the show Lee was able to show Longstreet and the audience his own personal philosophy with the martial arts.

However, Lee wanted more. He wanted to show Chinese philosophy and the martial arts to the American public. But with a nation that was at war in Vietnam, an Asian face was often viewed as the enemy. He was not easily able to earn a living as an actor. Along with Academy Award winning writer (for *In the Heat of the Night*) Stirling Silliphant (also Lee's student), he wrote the philosophical martial arts film titled, *The Silent Flute*, where Lee would star alongside another one of his students, American actor James Coburn. They had studio funding, but needed to film the movie in India, but could not find suitable locations to shoot the film. The film would later be rewritten and made after Lee's death, changing the title to *Circle of Iron*.

Lee created an idea for a TV series called "The Warrior" and was denied the lead role because the executives felt America was not ready for an Asian TV star, during the height of America's involvement in Vietnam. The role ended up going to David Carradine, a Caucasian actor portraying an Asian (later making the character Eurasian to justify the change). Shortly afterward, a disillusioned Lee left for Asia to star in a film for Raymond Chow's newly formed company, Golden Harvest, that would start the Kung Fu movie craze all over the world.

Around the same time, Hong Kong and Taiwan producers dubbed their martial arts films in English and sold them to American distributors, who released them in drive-ins, grindhouses, and urban theaters across the country. The first to come over in 1971 was *King Boxer*, retitled *Five Fingers of Death*. It was a huge hit. Soon after, *The Big Boss*, mistakenly titled *Fist of Fury*, starring Bruce Lee opened and was a hit in the United States and internationally.

In 1973, Warner Bros. filmed and released the first American-made martial arts film, titled *Enter the Dragon* and starring Lee. This film made Lee an international star and icon. Unfortunately, Lee passed away before the film was released and was not able to reap any of the fruits of his labor.

Also that year, independent filmmaker Tom Laughlin wrote, directed (under the name T.C. Frank), and starred with wife Delores Taylor in the movie *Billy Jack.* Although the film was not a "martial arts movie," it had elements of martial arts that made it a cult classic. The film did not do well during its initial release through Warner Bros. in 1971, but Laughlin was very smart about the selling of his films to theaters. Laughlin is also known as the "Father of Independent Film" because he would "4-wall" a theater (four-wall describes the process of renting out each theater himself and taking in the profits). The success of independently releasing *Billy Jack* spawned the sequels *The Trial of Billy Jack* (featuring "real" martial artist Bong Soo Han), *Billy Jack Goes to Washington* (unreleased theatrically), *The Master Gunfighter* (his Western remake of Goyokin), and the re-release of a prequel to the Billy Jack series, *The Born Losers.*

During this era, Black Exploitation films were very popular and extremely profitable showing at urban and grindhouse theaters, usually on a double bill with a martial arts film. The usual theme for these films was pretty simple, a black protagonist is suppressed in some way and eventually has their life threatened in some way by a Caucasian antagonist affectionately known as "The Man." So the marriage of martial arts and "Blaxploitation" was very easy and logical because it was just another way for the lead black character to beat "the man." Many of these films were forgettable because the actors lacked the skills to look effective on film and/or the choreography was not effective. Martial artist Jim Kelly found stardom in *Enter the Dragon* and went on to star in *Black Belt Jones, Hot Potato,* and *3 The Hard Way* (starring alongside Jim Brown and Fred Williamson). Even independent low-budget producer Roger Corman got involved with the genre by producing *TNT Jackson.* The studios took notice and found these films cheap to make, but extremely profitable. These films were responsible for getting them out of bankruptcy for some of the bigger mainstream films that were not profitable. It also made a star out of Pam Grier (see Women in Action).

Sydney Pollack directed *The Yakuza* in 1974. It starred Robert Mitchum and Ken Takakura. The movie did not do well. After this film, we didn't see an Asian talent star with incredible cinematic fighting skills in a major American film again until 1980 with *The Big Brawl,* starring Jackie Chan. Interestingly, 1974 also saw the first martial arts movie ever to get an X rating by the MPAA (see Figure 1.1). New Line Pictures bought a Japanese Karate movie titled *Sudden Attack! The Killing Fist,* which starred Shinichi "Sonny" Chiba and retitled it in the U.S. as *The Street Fighter.* The film was a cult favorite mentioned and partly shown in the

1993 movie *True Romance*, written by Quentin Tarantino, who is also a professed fan of the series. The several scenes that made the film so infamous have been "borrowed" by today's action filmmakers like the X-ray film sequence where you see Terry's (Chiba) fist crush the top of his opponents head and when he defeats an opponent by ripping out his throat where we see what looks to be pieces of chicken meat in his hands. The reason it got an "X" rating was for the portrayal of violence which looks tame today. The film's success caused New Line to import and dub the sequels that followed with *Return of the Street Fighter*, *The Street Fighter's Last Revenge*, and *Sister Street Fighter*.

Figure 1.1

The Street Fighter was the first martial arts movie given an X rating for its graphic violence (and not for the depiction of sex acts). However, it is rather tame compared to the violence depicted in films today.

In 1978, Chuck Norris starred in *Good Guys Wear Black*, in which the negative stigma of "martial arts movies" was retrofitted. Since the martial arts and Kung Fu films used unarmed combat to beat their opponents, Western (especially U.S.) audiences had a hard time giving up their willing suspension of disbelief because of the drastic differences in religion, beliefs, culture, and especially with the right to bear arms. The disarming or non-use of guns was addressed or had to be justified before an empty-handed fight progressed. Norris went on to star in films like *A Force of One*, *The Octagon*, *Silent Rage*, *Forced Vengeance*, *An Eye for an Eye*, and *Lone Wolf McQuade*, firmly establishing himself as an action hero, since he was also adept in the handling of firearms.

In 1980, Jackie Chan starred in his first American-made film, *The Big Brawl* (aka *Battlecreek Brawl*), to mixed reviews and poor box office returns. Even though Kung Fu comedies were sweeping Asia, the American audience had not embraced the genre yet. The few audience members who saw this film were amazed and had not seen anyone like him before. But for audiences who had first seen him in his Asian films, they were rather bored because the timing and rhythm was extremely slow and the moves were not as detailed or intricate compared to his Asian films. The main flaw was the use of Western wrestlers and stuntmen who were used to the simple rhythm of the wide haymakers and were too slow for Chan's style of screen fighting. You can see in certain scenes where Chan is waiting for an opponent to attack again. The film remains a sore spot for Chan and deservedly so because the fights did not compliment his style of screen fighting.

In *An Officer and a Gentleman* (1982), Zack Mayo (Richard Gere) learned to survive on the streets and acquired some basic martial arts as a kid in the streets of Asia. This is an integral part of the story as Mayo deals with his past and confronts Gunnery Sergeant Emil Foley, played by Louis Gossett Jr., who won a Best Supporting Oscar for his role in the film that year. The fight scenes were not very complex or even highly stylized in comparison to what you might see coming from Asia, but they were highly emotional.

In the early 1980s, Cannon Films released *Enter the Ninja*, starring Franco Nero, but the Ninja craze did not firmly take hold of the American public's imagination until Sho Kosugi starred in the U.S. film *Revenge of the Ninja* in 1983. A stream of American-made ninja films (usually made by Cannon) followed, such as *American Ninja 1-5*, starring Michael Dudikoff and later David Bradley. It even inspired a 1984 NBC series, *The Master*, starring Lee Van Cleef as John Peter McAllister, an aging ninja master trying to find his lost daughter while being pursued by the ninja clan he left.

In 1984, *The Karate Kid* (directed by John Avildson, who also directed *Rocky*) became a huge hit with the American public and spawned two successful sequels. The film was such a success that after its release, kids' enrollment in martial arts schools swelled! Here, for the first time in American martial arts films, we saw the multi-dimensioned relationship between student and mentor grow throughout the film. Again the fight scenes here were very simple and to the point. The screenwriter, Robert Mark Kamen, wrote all the sequels as well as *Kiss of the Dragon* and *The Transporter 1 & 2*.

In 1986, John Carpenter, known primarily for his horror films, directed *Big Trouble in Little China*, a big-budget comedy-action-adventure starring Kurt Russell and Dennis Dun. The film had heavy elements of Chinese mysticism and Wu Xia. The theatrical box office returns were poor, but the movie ended up being a huge cult favorite in the booming home video and cable markets.

In 1988, Steven Seagal made his movie debut with *Above the Law*, introducing the Japanese art of Aikido into cinematic fighting for the first time in a Western film. The film was directed by Andrew Davis, who also directed one of Chuck Norris' best efforts, *Code of Silence* (1985), and would later reunite with Seagal in 1992 to make *Under Seige*. The same year, Jean-Claude Van Damme made his starring debut in *Bloodsport*, based on the underground tournament fighting exploits of real martial artist Frank Dux. The success of the film legitimized tournament/kickboxing films as a subgenre of action films. Van Damme would soon follow it up with *Kickboxer*. It was also during this time real-life kickboxing champions would be given the opportunity to star in kickboxing/tournament genre films that usually went straight to video and/or cable. Some were very successful, but many others were not.

In 1993, Rob Cohen directed *Dragon: The Bruce Lee Story*. John Cheung, a former member of Jackie Chan's stunt team, was the fight choreographer. This film introduced the impact Bruce Lee made almost two decades earlier on a new generation of filmgoers. However, the infusion of exaggerated and unrealistic acrobatic moves did not capture the essence of Bruce's philosophy with the martial arts in the fight choreography, which had a drastic contrast to how he fought for the camera.

That same year, Hong Kong director John Woo came to direct his first American film, *Hard Target*, starring Jean-Claude Van Damme, introducing a tamed-down version of Woo's kinetic blood ballets to a mainstream American film. The original director's cut was much more of an anti-hero film focusing more on Emil Fouchon (Lance Hendrickson), but he had to go back and re-edit it and focus more on Chance Boudreaux (Van Damme's character). Van Damme would later go on to star in several action films directed by top Hong Kong directors, such as Tsui Hark and Ringo Lam, with mixed results.

In 1997, Phillip Kwok Chui was the fight choreographer for the James Bond film *Tomorrow Never Dies*. Hong Kong action star Michelle Yeoh costarred in the film and was portrayed as a contemporary to 007, not just a "Bond girl." The fight scene was choreographed in a Hong Kong fighting style, but unfortunately was shot and edited like a Western fight, losing the kinetic energy to the piece that Hong Kong action usually has.

In 1998, Hong Kong fights started to influence Hollywood as Hong Kong talent Jackie Chan starred with Chris Tucker in *Rush Hour*. This film finally established Chan as a bankable star in American films. This was also the first time in an American film where Jackie got to choreograph his own fights. But just because Chan was given the freedom to choreograph his fights did not mean everything was going to be smooth and easygoing. Chan could not get the cameraman to follow the action during the pool hall sequence and ended up shooting the scene himself.

That same year, Jet Li made his American film debut in *Lethal Weapon 4* and went on to star in several American films before moving back to China in 2005.

In 1999, the release of *The Matrix*, the first of a trilogy directed by the Wachowski brothers, elevated fight choreography to a respected art form by raising public awareness of the intricacies that are involved. Yuen Woo-Ping, responsible for the fight choreography and training of the actors, received international attention for his work on this film. What made this a ground-breaking film was the justification of the fights within the story and the seamless work of CGI in the story and the fights. It was also the first time we saw "A-List" Hollywood stars such as Keanu Reeves and Laurence Fishburne actually train before production and perform martial arts moves onscreen with a large degree of competency. Because of the success of the film, the excessive use of wires and of "bullet-timed" technology was copied in many films that followed for several years

Because of the success of *The Matrix*, the import of Hong Kong fight choreographers into American productions became the fad. For example, Yuen Cheung Yen was hired to work on *Charlie's Angels I & II* and *Daredevil*. Corey Yuen Kwai was hired for *The Transporter*, *Romeo Must Die*, and *Cradle 2 The Grave*, and Stephen Tung Wai was hired on *Bulletproof Monk*.

China/Hong Kong

In China, fight choreography got its roots from the Chinese opera. For those of you who aren't familiar with it, Chinese opera is not like the stereotypical European opera, in which overweight, Viking-costumed women sing classical tunes. Although there is singing, many of the Chinese opera themes depict old folktales and myths along with ancient battles that occurred hundreds to thousands of years ago. The Chinese opera has two distinct schools—northern and southern. The northern schools are more dynamic and involve more fighting and acrobatics. The southern opera relies more on drama and singing.

The Chinese film industry first started in Shanghai in 1896. One of the first martial arts films was 1928's *Burning of the Red Lotus Monastery*. The film was such an incredible success that two sequels were filmed immediately that year. The film industry lasted until 1945, at which time filmmakers moved to Hong Kong to set up shop because of the Japanese occupation.

Up to this point, the fights in Chinese films looked very staged, and the intention of the actors fighting looked more graceful than deadly because the performers were not martial artists—rather, they were trained to fight for film. This was all about to change.

WONG FEI HUNG

In 1949, Kwan Tak Hing (1905-1996), a Chinese Opera star turned film actor was tapped to portray the real-life Hung Gar Kung Fu master, Wong Fei Hung (1847-1924) in 99 black and white films that were made until 1970. For the fights, they used "real Kung Fu" that looked more like what you would see at a live demonstration with not much camera movement or editing. The choreography for each fight was pre-arranged by the actors themselves. The villains in the series were mainly played by Shek Kin (Mr. Han from *Enter the Dragon*) and Yuen Siu Tin (the old man in *Drunken Master*). The series was a breeding ground for future fight choreographers.

In 1971, fight choreography began to take a stronger place in the spotlight. Hong Kong child star (now an adult) Bruce Lee came to Asia for his first starring role in a martial arts film, *The Big Boss* (released in the United States as *Fist of Fury*). Up to this point, screen fighters in the Hong Kong film industry were not real martial artists. For example, before Bruce arrived on the scene, martial arts star Jimmy Wang Yu's background was as a competitive swimmer, and star David Chiang was a stuntman before both became fighters, where they trained to fight specifically for the screen. Jimmy Wang Yu ushered in the dawn of the Kung Fu movie with *Chinese Boxer* (1970), in which the simple story of revenge and Chinese patriotism over an oppressive Japanese sect stirred the emotions of the Chinese audience.

But Bruce Lee was different than the other screen fighters at the time. At the time, most screen fighters had limited, if any, actual martial arts experience and were trained only to fight for film, so they had no real emotional contact to what they were doing to their opponent. Their level of physical and mental commitment to a technique at the time was suspect and often their techniques appeared stiff, wobbly, and/or weak. Enter Bruce Lee, who was able to display physical grace, flow, animal magnetism, and a hypnotic screen presence like never seen before, revolutionizing how audiences saw action. Lee's fights were swift, fast, powerful, and to the point, as opposed to the extremely long, drawn-out screen fights of the time that used wide-looping straight-armed techniques that did not look effective. Above all, there were no wasted movements in Lee's screen fights.

In 1972, Lee took another step toward creative independence when he wanted to become equal partners with Raymond Chow instead of being just a hired hand.

Lee wanted to have more control over his films, so he decided to write, direct, star in, and choreograph the film *Way of the Dragon* (released in the United States in a truncated version and retitled *Return of the Dragon* after his death). In the film, the final fight scene takes place in the Coliseum in Rome, in a hand-to-hand death match between Lee and Chuck Norris. For the first time, here was a specifically detailed combative strategy in the fight displayed between the characters (and two real world class fighters) that was a part of the story that was still entertaining yet educational in the fundamentals of unarmed combat, whereas before it was not as pronounced or as gracefully displayed. This was also apparent in the two restored (John Little and Art Port-Japan) versions of *Game of Death.*

Because of Lee's influence and impact and longer fight scenes, the stories took more of a back seat and were reduced and became much simpler in order to give the fights more screen time. Fight choreography and fight choreographers got more attention from viewers and the media—sometimes more than the director of the film itself. This was good and bad. It was good because it gave fight choreographers a chance to move up to directing their own films, but it was bad because the stories suffered while there was an international demand for more and more movies. But the most damaging was that many fight choreographers did not know how to tell a non-verbal story with their longer fights.

Because of the shift in emphasis to fight over story, fight directors started getting their turn at directing feature films. In the late 1970s to mid 1980s, there was a period when the level of difficulty of the choreographed moves was at an exceptional high because of the proliferation of Chinese opera talent that had flooded the film industry. During this time, you would see fight scenes in which actors would perform 20, 30, or 40 moves without a camera cut.

With the cream of the crop fight directors finally getting their shot at directing their own films, they would have even more control over how the story and content would be incorporated with the fights. The directors would often do double duty as director and fight director (and in many cases triple duty by also starring or being featured in the film).

The major contributors in Hong Kong fight choreography during this time who were now directing their first films were

- Lau Kar Leung with *Spiritual Boxer* in 1975. Lau Kar Leung is mainly known for choreographing traditional Kung Fu movies.
- Sammo Hung with *Iron Fisted Monk* in 1977.
- Yuen Woo-Ping directing the pivotal *Snake In the Eagle's Shadow* (1978).
- Jackie Chan directed *Fearless Hyena* in 1979.
- Robert Tai helmed *Devil Killer* in 1980.

- Tang Chia directed *Shaolin Prince* in 1982.
- Ching Siu Tung directed *Duel to the Death* in 1982 and would go on to direct *Chinese Ghost Story.*
- Cory Yuen Kwai directed *Ninja in the Dragon's Den* in 1982.
- Yuen Cheung Yan directed *Taoism Drunkard* in 1983.

The art of fight choreography would now reach an elite level that would eventually influence the rest of the world and affect how they see this unique art form.

This point in time raised the difficulty level to an all time high giving Hong Kong films the world reputation it is known for. It was also during this time when stuntmen became more prominent actors and important behind the scenes innovators and Yuen Wah, Lam Ching Ying, and Yuen Tak, would train the actors and actresses.

The Dawn and Influence of the Modern-Day Kung Fu Brawl

Arguably, the birth of the Kung Fu brawl started in 1970 with Chang Cheh's *Vengeance* starring David Chiang and Ti Lung, with the fight scenes choreographed by Tang Chia and Yuen Cheung Yen. The story is very simple: David Chiang comes into town to get revenge for the death of his brother (Ti Lung) and kill everyone that was involved. The fights were purposefully messy, stressing more of the emotion than the technique. Because of the messiness of the fights, it effectively came across on screen as Chiang's fuming anger over the death of his brother and his disgust over the people who were responsible for it.

Then in 1975 came *The Man From Hong Kong* starring Jimmy Wang Yu and George Lazenby with choreography by Sammo Hung. Although it looked like Lazenby was not comfortable with highly stylized and intricate kung-fu style fights, the Kung Fu brawl was much better suited for him, making him look much more at ease with the fights in the film. Other modern day fight films also followed suit because getting into elaborate stances and stylized techniques did not look right in a modern day setting. A fine example of this is in *The Chinatown Kid* (1977) starring Fu Sheng, choreographed by Robert Tai.

In the early 1980s, starting with *Dragon Lord,* Jackie Chan took the choreography of the Kung Fu brawl to another level focusing on stunts no other filmmaker let alone stuntmen dare do. Both Jackie Chan and Sammo Hung were responsible for shepherding the growth and expansion of fight choreography in Hong Kong cinema that would eventually influence action filmmakers worldwide.

CHINA INTRODUCES THE WORLD TO JET LI AND WU SHU

In 1982, The People's Republic of China introduced the sport of Wu Shu to Asian cinema by making the first martial arts film since the beginning of the Communist regime: *The Shaolin Temple*.

The star of the film was already a legend before they ever shot one foot of film on him. Li Lian Je (later known to the non-Chinese speaking world as Jet Li), a member of the prestigious Beijing Wu Shu team, was the All-Around Men's National Wu Shu Champion five straight times (winning from the ages of 12 to 17). Because of Li's accomplishments and contributions to Wu Shu, he is considered one of China's living treasures.

Wu Shu is a contemporary sport and performance art that derives from a combination of traditional Kung Fu styles, gymnastics, and some elements of Chinese opera. When combined it creates a dramatic and visually drastic contrast between techniques. The main emphasis is focusing more on aesthetics and presentation of techniques in competition much like the sports of gymnastics or figure skating, where judges will evaluate a performance and give high points for presentation, level of difficulty, quality of technique, etc. At the time, Wu Shu was mainly practiced and seen in mainland China. The only way you could see Wu Shu outside of mainland China was by live demonstration by a touring company or seeing an occasional practitioner competing at an open martial arts tournament.

Although raw and somewhat primitive compared to Hong Kong productions, the film is still a marvel to watch because of the extremely high skill level of the performers involved. The international worldwide release of *The Shaolin Temple* (1982) was a groundbreaking film for several reasons:

- It was the first time the world got to see Wu Shu performed and applied to screen fighting.
- At the time, moviegoers were used to seeing traditional Kung Fu movies performed by actors who were taught cinematic martial arts for film. But, in *The Shaolin Temple,* EVERYONE that fought on screen was a world class Wu Shu athlete. As a result, every fight from the beginning to the end of the film was very good with high levels of difficulty, precision, and timing. One of the highlights from the film is the fight with Jet Li and Yu Cheng Hui in a drunken straight sword vs. drunken staff duel where the choreography, timing, and rhythm between the two screen fighters were hypnotic and captivating. But overall, because of the simple story, the fight choreography leaned more towards being an elaborate demonstration of the sport.
- It was the first time the world ever saw the real Shaolin Temple in Hunan. The beginning of the film contained a mini documentary explaining the history of the famous temple, and the movie was also filmed in the actual temple.

Li would star in the follow-up *Kids From Shaolin* (1983), showcasing adolescent and teenage Wu Shu talent. But it was the next film, *Martial Arts of Shaolin* (1986) that was the best of the bunch, directed and choreographed by famed Shaw Brothers fight choreographer Lau Kar Leung.

Having broken free from the detailed and intricate moves of the Kung Fu movies, Chan and Hung took it upon themselves to combine the look of wide looping, unclean, raw techniques (that are not as technically exact and precise as in a traditional Kung Fu movie) with the unrefined manic emotional energy of free-form brawls. They combined them with the rhythm and kinetic pace of a traditional Kung Fu fight, integrating and immersing each fight into the environment (using it as a weapon and/or obstacle), while adding jaw-dropping extreme stunts and acrobatics (falls, crashes, and so on), all designed to take the audience's breath away. The newer version of the Kung Fu brawl has modern sensibilities that anyone can appreciate, because the moves are not intricate and the fights do not carry any type of traditional, ritualistic feel.

The Kung Fu brawl style and approach works extremely well with modern-day fights and films and has more of an appeal to audiences outside of Asia, who rarely understand or appreciate the ritualistic and precise techniques used to make a Kung Fu movie (which also takes much more time to choreograph).

Chan continues to use Kung Fu brawls in his films in Asia and in the West, and has influenced Western-style fights. You can see the influence of Kung Fu brawls in films that have achieved different levels of success in the West, such as *Surf Ninjas, Teenage Mutant Ninja Turtles, Rapid Fire, The Transporter*, and *Spiderman 1 & 2*.

The Kung Fu brawl is very organic in nature (much like Cantonese, Hong Kong's native language) and continues to grow and expand today as other styles, arts, and competitive sports make their entrance into the world. A great example is with the movies *Sha Po Lang* aka *S.P.L.* (released in the US as *Kill Zone*) and *Fatal Contact* (2006), where they incorporate pro wrestling and MMA grappling moves into their repertoire.

The year 1997 proved to be rather tumultuous for Hong Kong cinema—a situation from which they would not recover. The economic recession that affected all of Asia, along with the handover of Hong Kong back to China from the British, made filmmakers unsure of their future. The introduction of digital media (DVD and VCD) made films that were hard to find now easily accessible. However, video piracy also became rampant and has undermined the financial returns and profits of the filmmakers, affecting their livelihood and slowly strangling the possible hope of future productions. Hong Kong could no longer crank out more than 300 movies a year, as they did in the late 1980s to the early 1990s. However, some good things came from this turbulent time. One of the benefits was that instead of quick production of many films in the hopes that one would be a hit, filmmakers consolidated their resourccs, and each would make one movie with better production value and story.

Also during this time, CGI made its debut in the Hong Kong film industry with Golden Harvest's production of *The Storm Riders*, based on a popular comic book. Here, Hong Kong did not imitate Hollywood—they made CGI their own, creating cosmic palm blasts like never seen before. The film was an instant box-office success. Over the years, Hong Kong and Chinese cinema have slowly incorporated CGI into their fight films with varying degrees of success, while still exploring the possibility of expressing their unique style of cinematic fighting along with it.

East versus West

When I was in grade school in Maryland, I was probably one of the few children who had immigrant parents in the neighborhood. I was very influenced by American culture and wanted to be and do things like all the other kids. However, my parents wanted me to carry on and preserve my Asian heritage, so we lived under Asian customs and traditions at home. I wanted to be accepted and not be different than all the other kids, but my life was much different than the other kids' lives, especially when I got home. I didn't understand why I had to speak another language in my house, or take off my shoes when I walked in the door, or eat with chopsticks instead of a fork and knife like everyone else.

I remember other kids would tell me that their parents would read them a bedtime story before they would go to bed. So one night, before I went to bed, I asked my Mom if she would read me a bedtime story. She was not familiar with that custom. I explained to her that all the other kids' parents read them a story before they went to sleep, so she grudgingly agreed to do so. I ran to my bookshelf, grabbed *Jack and the Beanstalk*, and gave it to my mother. She started reading. As she was reading, I started to feel as if I was not so different than the other kids at school. Then, she got to the part where Jack sold the only cows they had left for some "magic" beans. She leafed through the rest of the book with concern and worry on her face.

"What's wrong, Mom?"

She quickly skimmed through the book, and when she got to the end of it, she had a look of disapproval on her face. She took the book and tossed it in the trash.

"That's where that book belongs," she snorted.

I was heartbroken. "Why?"

"Three magic beans for a cow? Jack is not a good businessman! This story does not teach you good morals. It teaches you how to be irresponsible and immature!" exclaimed my mom.

She could tell that I was shocked and hurt. "Okay," she said, "let me tell you some stories my mother told me when I was growing up."

"Your mom told you stories?" I thought to myself.

"Let me tell you the story of the Monkey King!" beamed my mother.

"What's that?"

"Well, there once was a monkey who was born out from a rock and was the king of the kingdom. His name was Sun Wu Kong...."

My mother began to weave the tale of the Monkey King and the incredible things that he encountered in his journeys. Later, she told me stories about General Kwan Kung from *Romance of the Three Kingdoms* and other amazing stories about virtuous Chinese warriors who could fly through the air like Superman and could fight like Bruce Lee. For a while, I thought my Mom had the most vivid imagination, until she took me to a Chinese opera that was visiting town one day, and the story was about the Monkey King. I've been hooked on Chinese mythology and folktales ever since. I found out that these tales gave me examples of virtue, honor, and other qualities that she wanted instilled in me.

So what am I getting at? I have spent a lifetime straddling Eastern and Western points of view, and I have grown to realize that there is good and bad in both cultures and a lot of misunderstanding between the two. It's as if I have spent all my life standing in the middle, right between the two halves of the Yin-Yang circle, observing and sometimes taking different sides at different times of my life, with Asia on one side and the West on the other.

As I grew up, I would often bring my Caucasian friends to Chinese movie theaters to watch Kung Fu and Wu Xia films. They laughed at the things they did not understand or jeered at the screen when they did not buy what was occurring. The Chinese patrons would turn to us with nasty, disapproving looks that would make me want to sink down into my seat and disappear. This later affected me in my professional life as a stunt coordinator and fight choreographer when working with Western filmmakers who wanted a Hong Kong–style fight for their films. When it all was finished, the fights had the kinetic action and stylized moves of Hong Kong films, but with a Western perception of the action that ended up looking like a big jumbled mess because the filmmakers did not understand the reason behind the moves and were only interested in what looked dazzling and flashy to them.

With the success of films such as *The Matrix*, *Crouching Tiger, Hidden Dragon*, and *The Last Samurai*, there has been a newfound appreciation for Asian martial arts and culture by Western audiences. Unfortunately, with the good also comes the bad. In this case, the bad comes in the form of copycats hopping on the bandwagon by trying to capture the momentum created by the better films to sell a few more tickets. Some are successful escapist fantasies and a lot are financial and commercial flops. These films are as odd as going to a Western steakhouse and ordering sushi.

What I am suggesting here is that we try to understand what we are taking from Asian mythology, instead of just doing so because everyone else is putting it in their films in order to look cool. For a film to really last in a viewer's mind, there needs to be a healthy balance between style and substance, instead of one dominating the other.

In this section, I will try to explain some of the differences between Asian and Western thought which affect the way audiences see things and how that relates to film. I will also explore why the use of foreign talent in Western films usually misfires and is not as effective as these actors' work in their homelands. I will also explain how to watch an Asian martial arts movie, describing certain Asian mythology, the caste system, what certain symbols mean, and the myth of flying in Chinese movies. Also, a hot topic and an ongoing unresolved issue I will discuss is when Hollywood continues to belittle the Asians with its flawed interpretation and stereotypical treatment of the people and culture.

Throughout the centuries, there have been clashes between East and West in many areas, with both sides muttering that they do not understand why the other side is doing what they are. There have been several wars fought throughout the relatively recent decades—World War II, the Korean War, and the Vietnam War, for example—coupled with political and economic battles that continue to affect the general way Asians are perceived in the West. And in film, there are major differences in Asians' approach to filming fight scenes. The problem here lies with both sides; they need to look beyond the surface because we cannot understand anyone's beliefs when we do not look at the underlying foundation of culture and ethics that created those beliefs.

Even in film, there are different approaches to expression, and the approaches to a fight are very different when it comes to Asian and Western schools of thought. The rhythm and beats, as well as the characters intent, choice, and emphasis on techniques are drastically different. Even the choice of camera angles and style of editing differ. This is vital to understand when you want to bring elements of Hong Kong–style fights into your fight, or even if you simply want to put together an effective action sequence.

There are many differences between East and West in their approach to fight scenes.

> **Note**
>
> As a footnote, I'd like to add that if I'd had a copy of the nineteenth-century English version of *Jack and the Beanstalk*, my Mom would have liked it much more than the watered-down children's tale we know now. She probably would have been much more inclined to finish reading the story because it has a much more karmic and a virtuous Chinese knight errant theme to it: Jack's father was a knight who owned the castle and was killed by the giant, and Jack realized that it was his birthright to steal back the giant's possessions and reclaim the castle.

The Chain of Command on a Set

In order to know what it takes to put together a successful fight scene, we need to look at the chain of command in the process of shooting a film and the differences between East and West. But before we do that, let's define the different people and titles involved in the creative and technical decision making.

- **Producer**—A person who oversees the whole production of the film or TV series from initial concept to pre-production to post production to the actual distribution and releasing of the film. The producer also acquires and oversees the talent and heads of all departments involved in the project.
- **Director**—Usually hired by the producer, the director is usually the one who has the creative vision, much like the conductor of an orchestra. They carry out their vision of how they see the film (like costumes, casting, special effects, cinematography, set design, etc.) to help the director bring it to fruition. While having their creative vision, the director also has to keep in mind the interests of the production company, studio, and/or network.
- **Director of Photography**—In charge of every visual aspect (except special effects) of creatively and technically capturing the image onto film.
- **Editor**—Responsible for gathering all the raw footage shot by the D.P., 2nd unit director, sound effects, special effects (computer and traditional), and music, assembling it so it can make it a cohesive whole.
- **2nd Unit Director**—Responsible for shooting all the segments that involve action in the movie or TV show. Sometimes when a production is low budget, the D.P. will also be responsible for shooting the action.

- **Stunt Coordinator**—The head of the stunt department. The stunt coordinator is in charge of all aspects that involve the action and stunts on the project, including the hiring of all stunt players. The SC is also responsible for making all the stunts and actions as safe as possible.
- **Fight Coordinator**—This position is mostly used when a film or TV show has a lot of different types of action and the stunt coordinator needs someone who can just focus and specialize on training the actors, choreographing the fights, running rehearsals, and working on the fight scenes. This is a fairly new position that has emerged in Western filmmaking since each type of action has become more and more specialized.
- **Fight Director (Hong Kong/ China)**—The person in charge of choreographing and filming a fight scene, training the actors and stunt players, and supervising the final edit of the fight scene(s). The fight director is a very well respected and integral position in Hong Kong/China filmmaking.

The Difference in Perception of Action: Seeing beyond the Physical

Here's an example of a typical scene you might see when watching a Chinese martial arts film. The hero, with his straight sword in a scabbard slung over his back, immaculately dressed in white silk with a topknot, calmly and quietly walks into the crowded teahouse and sits down at an empty table without calling any attention to himself. Sitting across from the hero are a Gang of Bandits, looking for any reason to fight. Their presence is intimidating and menacing. They are ready to test out the hero because they think they have found the perfect prey due to his slim, scrawny build. They goad him and try to intimidate him at first with their imposing presence, but they get no response from the hero. They then taunt him with brash words, but even that cannot raise the hero's pulse as he calmly drinks his tea.

The customers surrounding them cannot handle the thick tension that is suddenly created in the room and can sense something is about to happen as they all flee to safety. The bandits surround the hero's table, wanting to get a better look at the "about to be deceased" man. The bandits continue to taunt the hero and make serious death threats to him. There is still no response. A couple of houseflies zip around in front of the hero's face. In the blink of an eye, the hero grabs a pair of chopsticks and effortlessly captures the two flies from the air in one clean swipe. The bandits look at the tip of the hero's chopsticks and see the two flies are caught by their wings, writhing to escape. This takes a few quick beats to register in their minds, and then they immediately dart out of the restaurant, running for their lives, leaving a trail of dust behind them. The hero lets the houseflies free as he smirks to himself about the encounter and finishes drinking his tea.

The Chain of Command

Western Filmmaking

When looking at the chain of command on a set in the West, it is usually the producer (sometimes executive producer) and director who have creative control of the film, with the director calling all the shots on the set, seeing the film through into post production to supervise the editing and sound mixing. The director usually takes responsibility and credit for the success or failure of the film (even though the action sequences are usually shot by the 2nd unit director).

After choreographing the fight scene and before shooting it, the fight choreographer has to show the director the fight and explain to him what is being done with the fight, move by move. Oftentimes when working with a director and a DP who do not know how to shoot action, you end up having to spend a lot of time "discussing" every shot choice.

The problem with the Western filmmaking chain of command is the choreographer (stunt coordinator or fight coordinator) of the fight scene(s) is usually not represented (or present) in the editing room because their work has not been documented in the script or the script supervisor's notes. Oftentimes a fight choreographer's work will end up looking different from what they originally choreographed and filmed. The reason for this is because all of the positions that are above the fight choreographer (stunt department) usually do not know anything about fight choreography. So during filming, they might not get the most effective angles during a fight or the shots they need to make the fight look effective when it goes into the editing room.

A common practice in the West is to shoot enough of the fight from several different angles to get coverage and let the editor piece it together in post-production. By doing this wide-sweeping coverage of the fight, they are not paying close attention to the techniques that make the fight effective and the special angles that make each move look dynamic. Because of this type of hierarchy, it leaves a lot of room for errors and often ends up looking like something else that usually misses a fighting logic and flow. Again, this usually happens when a DP, editor, and director do not know what the fight choreographer put together, let alone understand how to shoot and handle a fight scene.

The Chain of Command in Hong Kong/ China Filmmaking

In Hong Kong/China, the fight director works alongside the director of the film. The fight director has complete control of the set, knows and uses all the camera angles, adjusts the frame speed to shoot the fight, utilizes the actors and stunt actors, and goes into the editing room to assist the editor in piecing together the fight that they choreographed earlier.

The fight director usually gets credit at the beginning of the films along with the actors, screenwriter, producer, and director because it is a much more respected position in Asia than in the West.

They might be in awe of the hero's physical skill and his ability to do that feat. This is clearly apparent with many U.S.-made martial arts and action films, in which they use martial arts only as an exotic way to beat someone up and do not go any deeper to reflect the nature and evolution of the character. As a result, they see the mental and physical self as two separate entities within the character. However, we must look deeper, beyond the physical elements, to see what other elements are being conveyed.

Western audiences are still easily swayed by the flashiness of the way a martial arts or Hong Kong–style fight can look on film without knowing the subtext of the techniques and styles they are using. But there is no reasoning or logic behind the fights, making the action scenes appear disjointed and absurd. This also gives the audience the feeling they are watching two unrelated stories within a movie. This is very apparent in films such as *Ultraviolet*, *Aeon Flux*, *Lara Croft: Tomb Raider*, *Resident Evil: Apocalypse*, *Van Helsing*, and *Boondock Saints*, to name a few that demonstrate style over substance. Because the style of action is not justified and does not serve or complement the story and characters, the action appears gratuitous and illogical. On the other hand, the fight scenes in *The Matrix* all work because they are all within the context of the story and they leave the audience with a long-lasting and satisfactory experience. Another exception is the TV series, *Buffy, The Vampire Slayer*, in which all vampires inexplicably have martial arts skills, but because the show is intentionally campy and satirical, this otherwise illogical, just-for-the-fun-of-it usage of martial arts techniques is entirely acceptable.

Asian audiences understand the skill and presence of mind that the hero is able to bring with the mastery of his martial arts skills into everyday life. In the example I gave earlier, the hero's actions also serve as a warning (or an invitation, depending on the situation, the opponents' skills, and their motivation) because the hero is laying some of his cards on the table, showing the bandits his skills and what could happen to them if they choose to fight. The bandits are smart enough to realize that they are outclassed in almost every way. They imagine what could happen if they stay for the fight and they realize their fate, which is why they run for their lives.

The hero's capture of the two flies without killing them also shows the bandits that the hero's physical touch, sensitivity, and dexterity are probably beyond their skill level and that their cause of death at his hands would be beyond their comprehension, without the hero even raising his heart rate to complete the act. This also reveals the hero's passive Buddhist nature of respecting life and his surroundings by not hurting the flies, and then letting them go afterward. Also, by not drawing his sword, the hero tells the bandits that they are not worth his time and effort to even draw his sword, let alone get his silk clothes stained with blood. The straight sword also denotes that he belongs to a higher class of swordsman and is educated and possibly a scholar.

Culture/Religion

The belief in internal energy (aka *chi*) is often used in Eastern films. This is displayed by a screen fighter's conditioning and ability to absorb strong, heavy blows—empty-handed and with weapons—without getting hurt. Chi can also be used as a weapon when a screen fighter throws energy blasts (his chi) at his opponent, usually emanating from his palms. Also a person who has developed and stored up his chi can use it to shield himself from blows and weapons that might badly injure or kill someone who has not trained and refined his chi. It's also interesting to note that in Japanese films, screen fighters do not have as much of an outward physical manifestation and display of chi when they are fighting as Chinese screen fighters do.

Traditional Chinese medicine (TCM) believes in the concept of chi, and when one's chi is blocked or stagnant, it can cause illness. A fine example of how energy flow is applied to fighting is in the training sequences used in the movie *Executioners of Shaolin*, in which Hung Hsi Kuan (Chen Kuan Tai) practices his moves in preparation to fight against Pai Mei (Lo Lieh) by training against an elaborately designed metal dummy that has ingrained wells to show the flow of the meridians and little steel balls moving along the wells to represent the chi flow.

In the West, chi is not a part of fighting mythology, nor is it a part of the mainstream culture. Westerners in general are more pragmatic, believing, "If I can't see it, then it does not exist." But it is ironic that the concept of "the Force" used in the *Star Wars* films is widely accepted and embraced by Westerners, when its philosophy and approach is very Asian (and close to the definition and principles of chi). The *Star Wars* films also show characters throwing palm blasts and people flying in the air, defying gravity. Despite the audience's wonder and amazement, they do not question it. But why do these same audiences balk at an Asian film in which a character does the same exact thing?

The difference is that George Lucas introduced *Star Wars* and the Force to the Western audience and explained the concepts within the story. But with an Asian film, the filmmakers know that their initial audience has an idea about flying, chi, and palm blasts already because it's a part of the culture and their awareness. The Eastern audience is familiar with these conventions before sitting down in the theater, so there is no need for an explanation.

However, there is a recent awareness of alternative medicine in the West, such as acupuncture and TCM. Such treatments are beginning to be accepted by Western medical practitioners and some health insurance companies. Also, the concept of *feng shui* for home and business is being used by architects and interior designers and is gaining a foothold in the consciousness of Westerners. Both of these arts are based on improving the flow of energy—aka chi.

In the West, audiences and critics often ignore or choose not to acknowledge the subtle or heavy use of any form of Asian religious belief system that is integrated into a screenplay or subtext, such as Buddhism, Confucianism, Taoism, Zen, and so. Because of that, many films have been wrongly misjudged by Western critics and categorized as senseless action films, simply because critics were not aware of (and did not take into account) Asian beliefs, culture, and history, which usually play an integral part in the story. This is because Asian religion and spirituality are not a major part of Western mainstream society, culture, awareness, or consciousness—Christian values are much more predominant.

The Korean film *Shiri* broke box office records set by *Titanic* when it was first released in its home country. However, the film will probably not mean anything to a typical Westerner who might dismiss it as a formulaic action movie because he or she has no emotional connection to the film's story and underlying philosophies. All that person knows about North and South Korean relations might be gleaned from a 20-second news piece.

Another example is the movie *Ong-Bak*, in which Ting (Tony Jaa), an orphan from a small Thai farming village raised by the local monk, is asked to go into the big city to retrieve the head of a sacred Buddha (Ong-Bak) that the town prays to for its annual harvest. He volunteers to go into the seedy and corrupt areas of Bangkok to look for the Ong-Bak. If Ting is able to come back to the village with Ong-Bak, he will become a Buddhist monk.

Almost all of Ting's moves are defensive, waiting for the attacker to take the initiative (unless his action is justified, such as with the villain he confronts in the end). In one fight, Ting kneels and prays for one of his fallen opponents. Another spiritual/karmic issue in the film is when Ting wins his first match. His winnings are much more than the money George stole from him to bet on the fight, but Ting still wants his original money back because it also had the karmic energy of the hopes and prayers from the villagers who gave him that money. The cash prize he won for the fight had questionable karmic energy to the people in the bar.

The film resonated with a large audience in Asia and was Thailand's highest-grossing film ever. Unfortunately, when the movie was first released in the West, it was written off as a "no brainer," simply piecing one action scene to the next without any real story, only to showcase Jaa's amazing physical skills. I'm not saying that *Ong-Bak* is the Buddhist equivalent of *The Ten Commandments* or *The Passion of the Christ*, but it is not just a senseless action film. There is a reason for Ting's actions that requires further investigation.

A True Art Form versus a Gimmick

Because of the long history of martial arts in Asia, it has evolved from a way to defend oneself to a way to cultivate one's soul and spirit. As a result, it is looked upon as an art form. These principles make Asian film stories much more engaging because of the characters' inner struggles while dealing with antagonists. When looked at as an art form, martial arts has many commonalities with other arts and disciplines, in which a person has to understand and master himself (physically and emotionally), freeing himself from the bondage of his destructive ego, which blinds them from their true higher vision and purpose in life. As an artist, the practitioner's goal is to free himself of ego, to express and flow in his chosen medium. The belief is that once one understands and masters the concept of art and is able to express himself through one discipline, then he is able to express himself in any other discipline without having to completely start over again because he has mastered the common principles. Martial arts is often tied to the art of calligraphy in film because calligraphy similarly shows how one is able to flow and "be one" with the brush and paper while also showing that the artist is educated. Movies such as Zhang Yimou's *Hero*, *Magnificent Butcher*, and *Prodigal Son* are excellent examples of this principle at work.

In the West, martial arts in films are often seen and used as a gimmick—an exotic way to beat up someone—and used on a simpler physical and basic emotional level where the simple motivation is getting revenge and restoring honor either for the fighter or a loved one. Generally, using any type of martial arts or fight on film in the West is still looked upon and portrayed as something very external. Often the characters come across as extremely fabricated and one-dimensional, while the fighting skills and prowess are only justified on a superficial level. As a result, the fight and choreography end up looking weak and gratuitous and appear as only a shallow visual piece, having no real emotional resonance with the audience because of the narrow foundation upon which they rest.

There are only a few instances in which we see fighting depicted as an art or anything deeper in the West. A couple of these examples include:

- ***Fight Club.*** The participants in the club fight to liberate themselves from the trappings and expectations of society.
- ***A History of Violence.*** Tom Stall's past as a mob hit man comes back to haunt him and he has to wrestle with his violent past after he creates a new identity and family in a small town.

Ageism

Because the martial arts can be practiced by people of any age, the older one gets, the better he will be. This is because it is treated as an art form, not just a physical sport. As a result, you see older martial artists onscreen being able to handle younger opponents in Hong Kong films. Great examples are Cheng Pei-Pei, who starred in *Come Drink with Me* in 1966 and was still fighting more than three decades later in *Crouching Tiger, Hidden Dragon.* Often in Kung Fu movies, the villain is a much older person (or someone dressed up to look like a much older person) who has more power and experience than the hero and might need the assistance of another younger person to bring down and defeat the hero. This is demonstrated in *Secret Rivals, Clan of the White Lotus, Executioners of Shaolin,* and *Martial Arts of Shaolin,* to name a few. There are several reasons for this that are not common in Western culture:

- **The Confucian ideology of age.** One who is older has more life experiences and has a head start on a younger person. This applies to training in the martial arts, which is not just a physical exercise, but also a mental and spiritual discipline.

- **The concept of using internal power (aka chi) is much a part of traditional martial arts training.** The longer one trains and knows how to gather and cultivate his chi energy, the more powerful he is.

In Hollywood, age is a detriment to an actor (especially if the actor is a woman) because the marketing of a film is aimed at the youth who have more disposable income. The older an artist gets, the harder it is for him or her to get roles. However, Western audiences don't believe an older man can lick a younger person when it comes to fights because fights are thought of as physical things—Westerners do not delve into the mental or spiritual realm associated with Asian martial arts. It would seem ludicrous to have a scene in a Western movie in which a senior actor, such as Jack Nicholson, could easily take on younger actors, such as Tom Cruise and Nicholas Cage, at the same time, without any type of justification to the audience.

Then again, in real life, boxing champion George Foreman, who found religion and retired in 1977 to become a preacher, gave up boxing for good…or so he thought. Ten years later, Foreman got back into boxing to raise money to buy equipment for the community center he was building. He was considered an elderly man in the boxing world (at age 38) and somewhat of an oddity and novelty. He made fun of his weight and his eating habits before and after his fights as he moved up the world rankings. But on November 5, 1994, Foreman fought World Heavyweight Champion Michael Moorer for the World WBA and IBF titles.

Foreman was 45 and Moorer was 26, making Foreman almost 20 years his senior. At the time, Moorer was undefeated and was ahead in rounds on all cards throughout the fight, but in the tenth round Foreman connected a right cross to Moorer's chin, knocking him out. Foreman reclaimed the Heavyweight Championship after losing it 20 years prior to Muhammad Ali in 1974, making him the oldest person to win a boxing title. Foreman finally called it quits in 1997 at the age of 48, with a record of 76 wins, 5 losses, and 68 knockouts.

Code of Ethics/Conduct

The code of ethics in Asian films is based on the Chinese Knight Errant and the Japanese Samurai Bushido code, along with the caste system. The use of Taoist, Confucianist, and Buddhist principles is an internal and external guideline (depending on the character and story) that drives the character.

In the West, there is a code of conduct; however it is more internal as a duty or a deeper motivation driven by the character. It is not as outwardly obvious as the code in an Asian film. Often, a character's code of conduct is based on his career, such as a policeman, soldier, or hit man.

Mythology

In Chinese culture, martial arts, flying, and conflicts with warring states and other countries are a major part of the folklore. The reason one flies is the result of the mastery of the self and how one relates to the environment and universe. However, the newest reason one can fly is demonstrated in Zhang Yimou's *Hero*, where Nameless (Jet Li) fights Sky (Donnie Yen) in their minds. But the only reason someone can fly in Western mythology is if that person is a comic-book superhero or has supernatural powers that are justified in the story.

Emphasis of the Fight: Elaborate versus Brief

Structurally, Hong Kong fight choreographers have an advantage over Western fight choreographers. They use the three-act structure of a fight scene much more effectively than Western fight choreographers (also in part by being handicapped by not having creative control with camera angles and editing).

In Hong Kong films, the emphasis is on showing the character's power over an opponent by using finesse and execution of complex techniques with grace, power, speed, balance, precision, relative ease, and composure. One of the major differences and advantages Asian fight choreographers have is the wide variety of blocks available. Chinese Kung Fu styles have many different ways of blocking a technique within just one style, as opposed to a Karate or Tae Kwon Do style, in which the variety of blocks is much less. It is not the real-life effectiveness, but rather the variety that gives the choreographer more options and does not bore the audience as quickly because they always want to see something new and different. Their moves are much more intricate and because of that, they are able to tell a more varied story.

In Western fight scenes, there is still an external machismo-bravado type of approach. Western fight choreographers mainly emphasize the power of the technique and how it devastates the opponent with the least effort, showing the virility of the character throwing the technique as quickly as possible. If the hero has a ham-fisted one-punch knockout, he is better, more virile, and manlier. Whether one is conditioned does come into play, but not with any real depth. With films in the West, we are more accustomed to one-punch knockouts, thinking they are more real, when in reality they are not. Rather, we are just accustomed to seeing such punches all the time on film and in TV shows. If a one-punch knockout was real, then boxing matches would all end within seconds in the first round. As short as Mike Tyson's fights were (when he was in his prime), he never knocked anyone out with one punch.

Many blame John Wayne for the shortness of Western cinematic fisticuffs, but that is not the case. If we look at some of the old silent films with Buster Keaton, Charlie Chaplin, and Harold Lloyd, we see that when they faced the antagonist and got hit, they always fell down, which visually set up and established the role of the underdog hero, a formidable villain, and the obstacles the hero had to overcome. This practice has been handed down for generations, from the beginning of film in Western cinema, to the Three Stooges comedies, to the action-adventure serials of Tom Mix and Flash Gordon, to Tom and Jerry and Bugs Bunny cartoons, to westerns, and eventually to action films today. As a result, it is ingrained and conditioned into our psyches, so we think it is real. The problem with always showing power and having one-punch knockouts is that it can limit your character development and non-verbal storytelling. Jackie Chan comments, "I know one punch and you're out. But nobody wants to see one punch and out! We have to choreograph and make the real fighting like dancing. Like entertainment. Entertainment is not violent. I don't like violence. Violence of course is one punch, you're out, and the blood comes out. I don't like that. You can see in my movies I have a lot of punching and kicking and I show the audience and they say, 'Wow, that's difficult fighting!' It's not a violent thing."

However, one-punch knockouts are effective if you use them wisely. They work if you are trying to convey any of the following and you don't use them all the time:

- They work to establish that the character has a certain amount of superiority in fighting skills and knowledge over the recipient of the hit. For example, consider *Ong-Bak*. When Ting first walks into the bar and has to fight his first opponent, he knocks him out with one hit. Up to this point, we have only see him win a contest to grab a flag atop a huge tree and perform a kata of Muay Thai moves by himself to display his skills. But we still don't know whether he can take care of himself yet. We are also shown Ting's country-bumpkin innocence and naivety when he arrives in the big city and is deceived by George and led to the bar where the fighting matches occur. Then we see his first opponent brutally beating up an adversary. This is how the filmmakers set up the viewers by stacking the odds against Ting, contrasting what is about to occur when Ting throws only one shot—a knee to his opponent's head—and knocks him out. The audience's dead silence and awe is exactly what the viewers are thinking also. What also sells Ting's abilities to the audience are his physical prowess and his resolve, his composure, and the relative ease with which he throws the technique.

- They also work if the situation involves the center of the fight versus multiple opponents. A character's superiority can be shown by pitting him against multiple inferior opponents, as in *Enter the Dragon*, in the fight in the underground caverns between Lee and Han's guards. Another example of this is in *Fist of Legend*, when Chen Zhen (Jet Li) comes into the Japanese Karate school and takes on the whole class. The key to making these army-versus-one fights visually effective is using different techniques and approaches and not repeating combinations or highlighting the same techniques over and over again. Using the same technique repeatedly during this type of fight will prove to be monotonous for the audience.

- They work to show that the recipient of the hit has not had previous experience, is overwhelmed by the impact, or did not have the proper conditioning to take a blow. Often the reaction to a hit by a person who is unconditioned looks awkward and can provide a comedic break. An excellent example occurs in *Above the Law*. After Nico (Steven Seagal) chases down and beats up a thug, a friend of the fallen bad-guy approaches Nico and insists on fighting. After trying unsuccessfully to walk away, Nico finally turns around and knocks out his new opponent with a single solar-plexus punch. That one-hit knockdown is both impressive and comedic at the same time, mainly because of the surprised reactions and amusing dialogue coming from the other thugs in the background after their friend drops like a sack of dirt.

- They work to show that that the recipient was caught off guard or unready. A good example of this is in *Blazing Saddles*, when Mongo throws a punch and knocks out the horse.

- They work as a setup in the story. For example, in *Midnight Run*, Jack Walsh diverts Marvin Dorfler's attention so he can sucker-punch and knock him out to get what he needs from him several times throughout the film. But in the third act, at the Las Vegas airport, Marvin does not fall for it and only complicates the final conflict between Serrano, Jack, and the FBI. But the fact that Marvin constantly falls for Walsh's diversion for most of the movie tells us a lot about his intelligence compared to Walsh's.

Remember that it gets pretty boring for the audience when you have one-hit knockouts constantly throughout a film because you do not pose any type of challenge to the hero. It is best to sprinkle these throughout the fights in the story.

Length of the Fight

Asian films tend to have longer fights. This is especially true for films coming from Hong Kong and China. A 20-minute fight scene in the West is practically unheard of, but it is more common in Asia, especially in the final fight scene. Good examples are in *Drunken Master III* or *The Young Master*. The fights are longer because of the fighter's conditioning and inner chi power, along with his will to overcome the odds no matter what. Asian film fights usually last longer than a couple techniques and are much more like a strategic chess match.

The strategy and approach to fights in the West is much more immediate and quick. The only types of lengthy fights that a Western audience will tolerate are boxing matches and swordfights or duels, such as the ones you might see in *The Three Musketeers*, *Zorro*, or the *Star Wars* series. Interestingly, the principles of an extended sword fight are similar to the archetype of a Kung Fu movie. Perhaps audiences tolerate these longer duels because the use and impact of a weapon such as a sword is fatal and final once a combatant is struck with the bladed weapon (besides a flesh wound), so they want the fight to play out longer.

Editing

In Hong Kong films, the editing of a fight is usually between beats (or techniques), which enhances the timing and rhythm of the fight. The cuts make logical sense with the continuity and flow of the fight. You do not notice the editing of the fights just for editing's sake, because the cuts are not arbitrary.

But in the West, the cuts are much more haphazard and unnatural in rhythm—they don't make any logical sense to the progression of the physical conflict. Often, a fight will look like a brief highlight reel of the conflict. As a result, this takes the audience emotionally out of the picture because you are asking them to put the pieces together in their own minds. Film scholar Ron Strong comments, "What bothers me about a lot of the American action films that come out today is that they are cutting for 'eye candy,' just to be cool. They cut for the sake of cutting, when they should be cutting for story and emotion. It's as if they are afraid of having a scene where the camera does not move." Western filmmakers use rapid cutting to create the emotion of the fight for the audience, but it does not work because the cuts are much too rapid and often do not make sense.

Unfortunately, for the actors involved in the fight, you cannot see their work and the time that they spent in training beforehand to prepare for their fight onscreen—that is all lost. Even though the audience might not be consciously aware of this, they are subconsciously aware of it and are emotionally removed from the cinematic conflict. Too often, when you see a fight that is badly cut, you have to watch the "behind the scenes" segment on the DVD (if they are included) to see how the fight was choreographed before they cut it so you can make sense of what happened.

Camera Angles

In the West, the current trend is to get in very close to the action to give the audience an up-close, almost paranoiac feel. Originally, this was done for actors who could not really fight. But this practice has extended to screen fighters who can handle themselves well on screen. The documentary style of up-close handheld camera use creates for the audience an emotional duress and a harried feeling that is involved with the physical conflict, which is sometimes appropriate when used sparingly. But unfortunately, this often diminishes the actor's performance, especially if he spent months preparing for his role, because you do not get to see any of the fruits of his labor.

Asian filmmakers like to pull back much further and show the beauty and aesthetics of the fight and let the fight create the emotion, instead of using technical tricks. With Hong Kong style, the audience bears witness to the fight, actually watching it unfold in front of their eyes, which makes them appreciate the performance more. The chances of catching a "miss" on a Hong Kong film are pretty rare, but you will often find them in Western films. This is because it is not a priority to Western filmmakers, who think the audience will neither know nor care.

Stuntmen

One of the major differences between East and West is the risks the stuntmen will take for a fight scene. Generally, Hong Kong stuntmen will take more daring risks than United States stuntmen. They will actually take real hits for the camera. "The major difference between Hong Kong stunts and what we do here in the West is that in Hong Kong, they are doing the actual stunt. But here in America, we are creating an illusion of doing the stunt," explains U.S. stunt coordinator and fight choreographer Jeff Imada. The daredevil approach and mentality of the Hong Kong stuntmen gives the audience a certain feeling, knowing that they are witnessing something real that is unfolding on film. I am not saying that stuntmen in the United States are wimps–not at all. But union rules and safety commissions prohibit those types of stunts from being done on U.S. union films and, as a result, a U.S. stuntman's career can last much longer than that of a Hong Kong stuntman.

Choreographers

In Asia, film is still a director's medium, and the fight choreographers (aka the fight directors) have a lot of creative freedom to craft their fight scenes. Fight director is a highly respected position in the pecking order of Hong Kong filmmaking. They are often parallel to the director of the film, with as much creative freedom and control.

Fight directors are also able to go into the editing room and assist the editor in piecing together the intricate fight scenes they previously shot. A fight director has a team of dedicated stuntmen who follow him from project to project. These stuntmen also can be actors; be stunt doubles; or assist in helping choreograph the fight scenes, wire pulling, and whatever else the fight director needs to get the job done in front of and behind the camera. A well-respected fight director will have a dedicated following of an audience who will see his films, no matter who is starring in or directing the film. Prime examples of fight directors who have this kind of following even though they might not make an appearance onscreen are Yuen Woo-Ping, Sammo Hung, Ching Siu-Tung, and Lau Kar Leung.

In the West, (non independent) film is more of a producers' and studio executives' medium, in which they have final control over the creative content. The fight choreographer has to answer to the director and producer, who might not know anything about the logic or subtleties of a fight scene and who can drastically affect how the fight scene is put together. I've heard stories and have seen many instances when a fancy move is demanded by the director just because he thinks it's cool. Typically, directors can only suggest effective angles to the director of photography; they cannot direct the scene (unless they are the second-unit director and are shooting it themselves). The fight choreographer in the West does not have any assistants (but oddly enough, every other department head on a film project does) or a consistent team of supporting stunt players who go with him from project to project, as their Hong Kong counterparts do. Even though fight choreographers might be able to control what was shot on the set, they have no creative control in the editing room, and often what they choreographed will end up looking completely different after it's edited. It's often very frustrating for a fight choreographer to work in Western films because of the chain of command and how a fight can get muddled along the way. Along with the predominant mentality of showing the power of a technique in the West, this also limits the range of creativity and the emotional range for the fight choreographer to play with.

But the presence and influence of Hong Kong fight choreographers have raised the awareness of the importance of fight choreography in film and TV in the West with the success of films such as *The Matrix* and *Rush Hour.* However, just getting a knowledgeable fight choreographer or importing someone from Hong Kong on your project is not enough. It's very easy to see why—just watch the work of a Hong Kong fight choreographer in a film made and produced over in Asia, then watch how diluted, toned down, and often illogical his work is here in the United States.

Sound

Sound is where Asia is weak. In Hong Kong, the sound quality is known for the cheesy, loud clap noise that has been used for the sound of hits over the decades. This is because most of their films are shot without sound, and the sounds are added in later. However, they are slowly catching up with sound technology.

In the West, we do not have the cheesy slap sound that Hong Kong films have. Chuck Norris' film *The Octagon* was the first film to break away from "canned hits" and provided a more natural thud when someone got hit.

Special Effects

Special effects in Asia are still behind those in the United States as far as technology, quality of resolution, and believability for the audience. However, Asian filmmakers have taken the technology and made it their own without having to copy what was done in the West. A perfect example is with some of the CGI-enhanced fight scenes in 1998's *The Storm Riders.* This movie brought to life and added more dimensions to the cosmic palm blasts and flying. But then there are special effects on some Asian films that are not even up to par with higher-end PC videogames. An example of one such film is 2005's *The Promise.*

In the West, CGI is much better than in Asia, but it's not very consistent across the board. When we think of computer special effects, we think of the incredible dinosaurs created in *Jurassic Park.* But when it comes to fights created or assisted by CGI—for example, in *Blade II*—some were poorly done and unconvincing to the audience because the simple laws of gravity and body dynamics did not make any sense, nor were the moves justified.

Room for Advancement versus Categorization

In Hong Kong, there are opportunities to move up the filmmaking ladder. It is very common in Hong Kong films to see stuntmen also as supporting actors in the films, with dialogue and characters to portray. This gives the director immense creative freedom because he does not have to cut away and substitute a stunt double for the actor. Instead, he can keep it in one shot and go straight from dialogue to action.

Prime examples of people who have advanced up the filmmaking ladder are Jackie Chan, Sammo Hung, Yuen Woo-Ping, and Lam Ching-Ying. Jackie was one of Bruce Lee's stuntmen in the early 1970s and has been an international action star, producer, and director for almost 30 years. In most of Jackie's Hong Kong films, his supporting players are his stuntmen who are also actors. Sammo Hung also started out as a stuntman, and then became a fight director in the 1970s with films such as *Lady Kung Fu.* Hung has become an influential filmmaker and fight choreographer. He also won the Golden Horse award for acting in the non-action movie *Eight Tales of Gold.* Yuen Woo-Ping also started out as a stuntman in the black and white Wong Fei Hung films starring Kwan Tak Hing and has gone on to revolutionize the art of fight choreography, directing and choreographing classic films such as *Iron Monkey, Snake in the Eagle's Shadow,* and *Drunken Master.* He was also instrumental in reintroducing the importance of the fight choreographer in the West with *The Matrix* trilogy. The late Lam Ching-Ying was Shek Kin's stunt double in *Enter the Dragon* and trained screen fighters such as Michelle Yeoh and Michiko Nishiwaki. He was always a popular supporting player in many Hong Kong action films and starred in the ever-popular *Mr. Vampire* films. It was the role of the Taoist exorcist for which audiences fondly remember him, not for his work as a stuntman.

The way that stuntmen are treated in Asia hardly happens here in the West. In general, Hollywood likes to categorize and label people and their skills sets in all departments, especially stunts. If you are an actor, you have a stuntman "double you" on the much harder and riskier stunts. If you are a stuntman, you do not act. The prevailing mentality is "that's what an actor is for." But what is a stuntman doing when he is performing his skills onscreen? He is *acting* in a specific physical manner according to the scene and stunt to make it convincing (aka "selling a gag").

However, there are a few exceptions. Hal Needham was a stuntman and stunt coordinator before he directed such popular and successful drive-in classics as *Smokey and the Bandit, Hooper,* and *Cannonball Run*; actor/singer Branscombe Richmond, who started out originally doing stunts (and whose dad was a stuntman); and most recently, Zoe Bell was Lucy Lawless' stunt double in the *Xena* TV series and doubled Uma Thurman in *Kill Bill 1 & 2* and starred in *Grindhouse*—

Death Proof (2007). But once you are a stuntman, you are pretty much linked to being a stuntman for the rest of your film career. The highest position you would probably get to is eventually a second-unit director. There are exceptions (like those mentioned above), but they are very few and far between. It is very rare that a stunt coordinator gets a chance to direct a feature film. And when he does get a chance to do so, it's usually with the odds stacked against him because he is given a B-grade script without much of a plot or any character development, but heavy on the action. (Producers tend to think that's what stuntmen are only good at.) But the project does not have much of a chance of doing well from the onset, which discourages the fledgling director and forces him back to stunt coordinating.

Billing/Recognition

In Hong Kong films, the fight director usually gets title billing before the movie starts, along with the stars and the director. In the West, this happens occasionally, but not consistently at all. The stunt coordinator and fight choreographer are billed at the end of the film (at the producer's discretion), creating the illusion that the director was responsible for everything in the film, including the action. However, if the fight choreographer has somewhat of a following or the producer feels that his name will lend a certain amount of credibility to the film, the choreographer will get billing in the opening credits.

Time and Preparation

In Hong Kong, choreographers are given a lot of time to prepare a fight scene. Jackie Chan took three months to choreograph and shoot the final fight scene alone in *Drunken Master II*. It took him the same amount of time to shoot the underwater fight sequence in *First Strike*. And as a result, the craftsmanship of the fight shows.

In the West, you are not given much time to prepare for a fight scene. Action scenes (let alone fight scenes) are not given much time for preparation and shooting, even if the movie is an action-adventure film. As a result, this lack of preparation time shows in the final product. No U.S. production will give a film production three months to shoot a final fight scene, no matter how good the end product is. Unfortunately, it is not a creative choice; it is more of a financial decision.

There has been an unfortunate backlash with the influence of Hong Kong fight directors working in the United States. Producers and filmmakers give their imported talent more time to prepare action sequences than they give their American counterparts. They think an American choreographer cannot do what a Hong Kong choreographer can, so why bother giving them the extra time? In reality, the general reason American choreographers come across as inferior to Hong Kong choreographers is because of the short amount of time they are given to put together a fight scene and the limited creative control they are given to shoot and edit the scenes on which they worked. With these handicaps, it's easy to see how Western fight choreographers can pale in comparison to Asian fight directors...but it's not the choreographer's fault.

Film Genres

Kung Fu and Wu Xia movies are in distinctly different genres that are legitimate and thriving in Asia, not just on TV and film, but in great works of Chinese literature over the centuries, such as *Journey to the West*, *Water Margin*, *Romance of the Three Kingdoms*, and *Outlaws of the Marsh*, to name a few. These are much like the classic tales we have in the West, such as *Robin Hood*, *The Three Musketeers*, *The Count of Monte Cristo*, and so on. Not only are these genres in film, they are also serial TV shows (much like soap operas here).

In the West, the action genre is simply labeled as action-adventure, which is a very broad definition that includes all types of action. Some might consider that there are subcategories in the action genre, such as westerns, swashbucklers, and so on. But if we look at some of these genres closely, not necessarily every film in each subgenre will always have action elements in it. Kung Fu and Wu Xia are not considered genres in the West because they are not a native part of the mythology and folklore of our culture, but they are something to admire from the outside looking in without fully understanding the genres.

We've seen crossovers in which the hero comes to a foreign land not knowing the ways of the place, and we watch him stumble and we laugh at his expense. We live through the experiences of the journey with the hero, seeing whether he adapts or assimilates to the new land and culture. Films such as *Iron & Silk*, *Rush Hour*, *The Challenge*, *The Last Samurai*, and *Shanghai Noon* are cross-cultural examples of this.

Story

The stories in Asian films with fights and martial arts are much richer and have much more emotional depth than Western films do. This is because of the long history of martial arts in Asian history and in novels. However, there are always exceptions on both sides.

Perceptions and Stereotypes of Foreigners in Film

In Asia, Caucasians in film are usually looked upon as foreign devils and barbarians invading the land. This is especially true in historical films. However, blackface has been used as recently as 1995, in the movie *Don't Give a Damn*. In action films, Cynthia Rothrock is the only example of a Caucasian starring as the hero in a series of Asian-produced films.

In the United States, it gets much more complex because the U.S. is a melting pot of many different cultures that make up the masses. The population is extremely diverse, but apparently not so when it comes to getting lead parts in Hollywood or being in the position to make creative decisions. People of different races have been struggling with this over the decades in Hollywood.

One of the most obvious "creative choices" in a lead role was in the early 1970s, when Warner Brothers asked Bruce Lee to help develop a movie that would introduce Asian martial arts and philosophy to Western viewers. It was to be called *The Warrior*. This movie ended up turning into a TV show that was then retitled *Kung Fu*, and Lee lost the lead role to David Carradine, a Caucasian actor. The studio justified this decision by making the lead role (Kwai Chang Caine) a man of mixed Chinese-American ancestry.

The "reasoning" for this decision was that the powers-that-be came to the conclusion that America was not ready to invite an Asian in a lead role into their living rooms every week. We can only imagine what type of impact the series would have made if Lee was cast in the lead role. But based on the incredible fan response Lee got on the 1966 TV show *The Green Hornet* and the 1970 show *Longstreet*—in which he was able to explain the philosophy of martial arts as he trained his student, Mike Longstreet—we can only imagine how much stronger of an impact *Kung Fu* would have made upon audiences with much better choreographed action, Lee's magnetic onscreen presence, and the strong philosophy already integrated into the story.

But the stereotype of Asian males (whether they are Asian-American or imported talent, such as Jackie Chan or Jet Li) is that they typically never get the girl, they are asexual, and they are geeks. This is somewhat of a contradiction in many action films, in which Asian males have the self-confidence, self-awareness, and bravado to be competent or masterful martial artists. Jet Li's character never got to kiss Aaliyaha at the end of *Romeo Must Die*. In *Enter the Dragon,* Bruce Lee's character was a Shaolin monk, while all the other competitors on Han's island had their share of the action at night. However, there have been a few exceptions in Hollywood where an Asian man has coveted a Caucasian woman, such as Samuel Fuller's *The Crimson Kimono* and *The Big Brawl* (aka *Battle Creek Brawl*), in which Jerry Kwan (Jackie Chan) has a white girlfriend, Jenny (Kristine DeBell).

However, Hollywood has had a history of stereotyping and racism since the dawn of film. The film industry is probably the only place where discrimination based on one's looks and race is allowed and plays a part in the creative and marketing decisions for a film. The perception of Asians and the culture is very stereotypical and unfair. Asian women are constantly objectified and coveted by the storming Caucasian hero of the story, and the perception and interpretation of Asian culture is flawed and demeaning.

The history of Caucasian actors who have portrayed Asian actors in "yellowface" is long, from Warner Oland and Sidney Toler portraying Charlie Chan, to Marlon Brando in *The Teahouse of the August Moon*, to Mickey Rooney in *Breakfast at Tiffany's*, to John Wayne as Genghis Khan in *The Conqueror*, to Joel Grey as a Korean martial arts master in *Remo Williams: The Adventure Begins*, to Jonathan Pryce in the Broadway production of *Miss Saigon*. The reasoning behind which producers usually hide is that they searched for an Asian for the role but could not find anyone suitable and had to resort to a Caucasian using prosthetic makeup. Unfortunately, "yellowface" still exists today. A current example is in *Norbit* (2007) in which Eddie Murphy plays a series of roles, including an Asian man with a stereotypical accent and glasses. The fact that yellowface still exists in Hollywood shows the world a very sad commentary on how far we have to come in understanding each other and looking past the color of one's skin.

Asian Talent in Western Films

Overseas Asian action talent did not start with Jet Li or Jackie Chan in the 1980s and 1990s. On TV, it was Bruce Lee in 1966, when he co-starred with Van Williams in the TV series *The Green Hornet*, where he introduced Kung Fu to the American audience. In film, it was Toshiroô Mifune in 1968's *Hell in the Pacific*, starring opposite Lee Marvin and directed by John Boorman. Mifune later starred with Charles Bronson and Alain Delon in 1971's *Red Sun*.

Note

Even though Bruce Lee was born in the United States in 1940 and is officially considered an American citizen, his formative years and martial arts training were while he was living in Hong Kong. He did not truly live in the United States until 1957.

In 1968, acclaimed director Akira Kurosawa was asked to direct the Japanese sequences of *Tora! Tora! Tora!* but that only lasted for three weeks, and none of his footage made it in the final cut of the film. This was because Western and Japanese filming practices were drastically different and Kurosawa lost his trust and faith in the studio when they said he would be directing opposite David Lean, but instead he got Richard Fleischer as the director. Japanese directors Kinji Fukasaku (*Battle Royale*) and Toshio Masuda (*Shadow Hunters*) were hired to replace Kurosawa for filming the Japanese sequences.

In 1973, Bruce Lee starred in the first American-made martial arts film, *Enter the Dragon*. The film was a great success everywhere except for Asia because Asian audiences felt Bruce stylized the movie for American audiences. In comparison to the intricacies of the fights in his earlier films, the fights in *Enter the Dragon* are much simpler, comprised of one-hit shots. Certain camera angles were much too close and at times did not make any sense. For example, there are certain sequences in which Lee is fighting Oharra, and all you see are the foot movements, not the actual technique he used to hit Oharra. There is another scene in which you see only the tops of their heads. Artistic freedom?! Also, notice that the camera is in much too close for no real reason when Roper fights his opponent at Han's tournament. Story-wise, with the buildup of the conflict, we never feel Lee's character is in over his head or overwhelmed at any moment, nor does he have anything to overcome or learn during the film. That factor alone does not make it a Kung Fu movie—it was more of a showcase film for Lee's talents.

Shortly after Lee's death, Sydney Pollack directed Robert Mitchum and Japanese star Ken Takakura in 1974's *The Yakuza*. The film failed to gather any box office heat, but it is rumored that the film was re-edited for Western tastes and there is a completely different cut that director Pollack submitted to the producers. With no one else in the sidelines ready to emerge, Asian talent starring in U.S. action films laid dormant until the beginning of the next decade.

In 1980, Jackie Chan starred in *The Big Brawl* (aka *Battle Creek Brawl*) to mixed reviews and dissatisfaction from fans who had followed him in his Asian films shown in the Chinatown theaters. Unfortunately, the filmmakers were not able to capture the ingenuity, creativity, humor, and intricacy of the fight scenes that made Chan stand out in his Hong Kong films because of *The Big Brawl*'s emphasis on brute strength, power, and size. This was the emphasis for the stuntmen, and that style of fight was not a good match for Chan's speed, agility, and acrobatics. The problem was that pretty much everything from the story justified the type of macho fight that did not accommodate Chan's comedic fighting style. And the stuntmen were too slow to react to his techniques. You could see Chan waiting for the stunt fighters to react so he could throw his next move. Also, the fights were still using the one-punch-knockout mentality. The cues were too much like one-step sparring, where everyone was reacting to a right-handed lunge punch, which also slowed down the pace and narrowed down the possibility of what could be done.

Golden Harvest tried several more times to break Jackie into the American market with *Cannonball Run I* and *II* (1981 and 1984, respectively). They had him star with an assortment of established Hollywood celebrities, but they still could not break Jackie into mainstream America. Then there was 1985's *The Protector*, an ill fated attempt at making Chan a serious no-nonsense Dirty Harry cop character. Unfortunately, this type of character was not a good match for Chan's brand of comedic fighting, which was lighter and more comical at the time. Not only that, the filmmakers did not understand Chan's appeal to his fans, which didn't help matters.

In 1996, New Line Cinema bought the rights to the modern-day action Hong Kong film *Rumble in the Bronx.* They re-edited, dubbed, and marketed the film extremely well. In the beginning, the marketing poster for the movie did not show Jackie's face; it showed a silhouette of the NYC skyline with a fist ripping through the image, making audiences curious. This marketing even appealed to conservative areas in the country that might not have immediately appreciated foreign talent, thinking "Another cheap Kung Fu movie?" It was only later that New Line added Chan's face to posters, claiming that he did all his own stunts. As a result, Jackie was finally able to break into the American film market after 15 years. Along with the release of his older titles into theaters and home video, Jackie starred in his first American film with comedian Chris Tucker in *Rush Hour.* The odd pairing proved to be a big box office success in the United States and worldwide. However, the fight scenes lacked the visual energy that Chan's Hong Kong fights provided, and the ending was very anti-climactic—Chan's character finally meets the villain, who proves to be no real challenge.

After the success of *Rush Hour*, Hollywood decided to invest in Chan and his charming comedic appeal to children and adults (of both sexes) by cutting, dubbing, releasing, and saturating the market with his older film library in theaters and on home video, along with producing U.S. films. But the problem with Chan's later U.S. efforts is that he is always teamed up with filmmakers who have much less experience than he does. Add to that flimsy storylines that barely justify his comedic style of action. This problem is also evident in many of Chan's later Hong Kong films, in which the story is written to accommodate the fights and stunts. However, in his Hong Kong films you at least always get solid, well-constructed fight and stunt sequences, whereas in his Western films, you get neither.

Jet Li was the five-time all-China Wu Shus champion from the ages of 12 to 17 (from 1974 to 1978). He performed his Wu Shu for President Nixon on the White House lawn as a child. He starred in the 1982 movie *The Shaolin Temple*, the first martial arts film produced by the People's Republic of China. This movie introduced the sport/art of Wu Shu to the world as a cinematic fighting form. Even though today, looking back at *The Shaolin Temple* along with the two sequels that followed (*Shaolin Temple 2: Kids from Shaolin* and *Martial Arts of Shaolin*), they might look simple and primitive, these films were able to show the athletic dynamics of the sport at a level never before witnessed onscreen.

Li then moved to Hong Kong and starred in 20 films from 1986 to 1997, establishing himself as an international action film star. In 1998, he was introduced in America as the villain in *Lethal Weapon 4*, along with Cory Yuen Kwai to help choreograph the fight scenes. Li went on to make forgettable films in the United States such as *Romeo Must Die*, *The One*, and *Cradle 2 the Grave*. These films received mixed reviews and a lukewarm public acceptance, despite the huge media push. The films were trying to put Li into the mold of the Western definition of an action hero that is outwardly tough and macho, one-dimensional, almost comic book-ish, and it seemed as if he was not comfortable portraying that role onscreen. Further, the roles really did not seem to fit the stories nor the characters he was portraying compared to his Hong Kong efforts.

The fight scenes for Li's U.S. films generally lacked any type of non-verbal dialogue with the fight choreography. The style or type of fights also did not correlate to the world in which the story took place. He was just another Asian guy who could kick serious ass and nothing more.

In between his U.S. films, Jet made two films in Europe for Luc Besson, who produced *Kiss of the Dragon* and *Danny the Dog* (released in the United States as *Unleashed*). These were more suited to Li's screen range and showcased his talents much better than his U.S. efforts did. His U.S. films felt as if he was miscast and the stories did not match his persona. However, he did make a huge acting leap with a great performance in *Unleashed*.

The problem with Li's U.S. films is the same as with Chan's—the decision makers do not understand the actor's persona and they try to fit the actor into a pre-existing mold of how they conceive action, without giving any consideration to what the actor is able to bring to the table. A prime example is *The One*, which was originally written for ex-pro-wrestling star Dwayne "The Rock" Johnson. The Rock is an extremely extroverted and in-your-face personality, whereas Li is pretty much the opposite. Li came on board when Johnson dropped out of the film, and the filmmakers did not bother to change the dialogue or character to suit Li's screen presence and persona, which is quite different from the Rock's.

This also applies to the creative people behind the camera, such as the directors and fight choreographers. The first people who come to mind when it comes to choreographers are Yuen Woo-Ping and Yuen Cheung Yan, who worked on *The Matrix* trilogy. Cheung Yan went to work on *Charlie's Angels* and *Charlie's Angels: Full Throttle* to mixed/lukewarm response. After the success of *The Matrix*, producers thought that if they could get a Hong Kong choreographer on a film, it would bolster interest in the film. Besides, everyone else was doing it.

Because of their work in Hollywood, Western filmmakers and producers have given more attention to the stunts and fight choreographers in the minds of audiences. On the negative side, the fad of using wires was exploited by Hollywood filmmakers to the fullest for a couple years, in unjustifiable action scenes that reached a point where audiences were no longer mystified or enthralled by the use of wires. Some were successful, but many were not. This is much like an artist wanting to use the color lavender in his painting because the artist next to him had a successful painting with the color lavender. The artist may have blindly forgotten that the composition of his piece does not need that color.

It's heartbreaking to see this happening to artists and filmmakers who have developed a following for their unique style and vision in their homeland. They bring their talent to the world of action cinema to the attention of fans who are looking for something different. But when they come to the United States hoping to have more people see their work and wanting to appeal to a larger audience, unfortunately they end up with their creativity neutered because their hands are tied. They are unable to get their own expression of action onscreen—instead, their work looks like everything else that comes out of Hollywood.

One reason for this is because Hollywood has turned into a machine, where film is now considered a disposable product—the first week of box office receipts determines the life of a film. As a result, filmmakers do not take chances on an artistic vision and instead go by a "formula" that they know the audience wants. Unless the filmmaker goes independent, film is no longer a creative medium because films are now made by corporations that only care about the bottom line of their accounting books. Film studios are not run by creative executives who know how to run a studio, as they were in the 1960s and 1970s.

In Asia, the filmmakers come up with generic blockbusters, but there is somewhat of a healthy balance in which they still have creative freedom to express themselves—they don't have to resort to being extremely predictable. This does not happen only to Asian talent, such as John Woo, Chow Yun Fat, and Tsui Hark, but to any foreign talent coming to work for the major studios. Guillermo Del Toro, Gérard Depardieu, Antonio Banderas, Cantinflas, Sophia Loren, Marcello Mastroianni, and Alain Delon are some other examples, just to name a few. It is much like trying to fit a square peg into a round hole. Their work in their homeland is much more interesting to watch than their generic efforts for the studios.

But U.S. movie studios are buying up intellectual properties from other countries and adapting them for the palates of Western audiences. The mentality is that it's been proven and done before. Because the studios know what was a proven success somewhere else, they don't want to take a risk on something new, groundbreaking, and different that might not appeal to the masses and make a ton of money for them. Having studio executives make the decision to put the audience in the driver's seat, trying to guess what they want, is suffocating any type of cinematic creativity out there. As a result, after the audience leaves the theater, they are not elated because they know what they are getting when they buy their tickets. It is much like a rollercoaster without any thrills or chills. The studios also think the audience is not flexible in their preferences because you cannot show that on a linear spreadsheet. There needs to be a balance in knowing what the audience wants, but taking them on a journey that provides emotional satisfaction by giving them something that is not predictable.

Globalization of Asian Martial Arts Films

The globalization of Asian martial arts films really exploded with 2000's *Crouching Tiger, Hidden Dragon.* The film won numerous awards from all over the world and had 10 Academy Award nominations (the most for a foreign film), winning four awards for Best Foreign Film (Taiwan), Best Art-Set Decoration (Timmy Yip), Best Cinematography (Peter Pau), and Best Original Score (Tan Dun). The film did many different things than its predecessors to open itself up for Western palates. Here are some examples of what the filmmakers did that was different from their Wu Xia predecessors, forever changing the way Wu Xia films are seen, for better or worse:

- **Reduction of characters.** Most Chinese novels like this have a ton of characters, and for the American audience, it can get very daunting to remember who everyone is, especially if they are not used to foreign names. Like an organic painting, many secondary characters don't have an arc throughout the story and are there to deliver a message or enhance another more prominent character.

- **Simpler story.** Because of the reduction of characters, the story became much simpler, making it easier for the audience to remember all the characters that came onscreen. The critics were right when they described *Crouching Tiger, Hidden Dragon* as a cross between *Sense and Sensibility* and *The Matrix.* It grounded the Western audience with the dramatic sit-down dialogue sequences, but took them through the fairytale with the fight scenes.

- **No overacting.** Typically, in most Hong Kong films from the 1970s to the early 1990s, the audience would see a proliferation of Chinese opera–trained and/or inspired actors who tried to perform to the back row, which ended up looking on film like overacting (similar to what we see when we watch professional wrestling on TV). This was not the case in *Crouching Tiger, Hidden Dragon.*

- **No comic book heroic posturing.** Most Hong Kong films that were imported overseas and to the United States had actors who would overact and end or break a fight with a comic book type of heroic pose. *Crouching Tiger, Hidden Dragon* reduced that to a minimum, which made the fights appear more natural to Western audiences.

- **Absence of Taoist, Confucianist, or Buddhist philosophy or concepts.** Most Wu Xia stories have some type of philosophy or moral code based on the main three ways of belief in China. *Crouching Tiger, Hidden Dragon* was pretty much void of any of those systems of belief. This could be one of the reasons why this movie did so well in the West. Most Westerners are not familiar with Asian culture, religion, or spirituality, and therefore they can get bogged down by it. To make a film about a culture in a well-established genre without one of the major pillars—the moral code—would essentially be considered "Wu Xia light" to longtime fans of the genre.

- **Choreography.** The fight choreography of Yuen Woo-Ping is more subtle and understated compared to his other work. The toning down of the impact of the fights complemented the dramatic non-action pieces. The fights were not done over the top—superhero-like—but with more subtle beats to them. Each fight varied in its tone and mood to complement the environment in which the fight took place.

- **Production value.** The set pieces and locations were not confined to the inside of a studio, as with many other Wu Xia films. The cinematic palate used here was much bigger, and the artistic composition was richer than previously done.

- **Effective media attention.** Because Ang Lee was a media darling and an art-house favorite, it was relatively easy for him to get critics to see this film. That would not be the case for a director who already had a track record with action films.

- **Use of subtitles.** The filmmakers were bold enough to retain the film's integrity by keeping it in its original language instead of hiring actors to dub over the voices in English. This practice of overdubbing has a bad stigma associated with the poorly dubbed "chop-socky" martial arts films that came out in the 1970s and showed in grindhouse theaters all over the United States. At the time of *Crouching Tiger, Hidden Dragon*'s release, subtitled films were mainly relegated to art houses that would show foreign films in limited release. Mainstream Western audiences at the time were quite apprehensive about having to work for their entertainment by reading subtitles for a popular film; many would avoid it at all costs.

Now, subtitles in foreign films have been more widely accepted and are preferred to dubbing, which can take away from an actor's performance when it is not done right. As a result, subtitled Asian martial arts films that followed *Crouching Tiger, Hidden Dragon*'s release were released into mainstream theaters. Examples include *House of Flying Daggers, Kung Fu Hustle*, and even the Russian action-horror-adventure film *Night Watch.* These films were able to profit by keeping the artistic integrity of their work. And because public acceptance of subtitles is becoming more widespread, filmmakers are beginning to integrate subtitles into their films in creative and entertaining ways, such as in Tony Scott's *Man on Fire.*

What We Can Still Learn from Bruce Lee

There have been countless books and documentaries on the legendary martial artist and action film star, Bruce Lee, but hardly any touch on what made him so special on film or deal with his style of choreography. Sure, they talk about his films, the events that occurred around them, and the people involved, but they do not ever analyze why his fight scenes were so special and different and still remain a high mark to which other screen fighters are compared more than 30 years after his death. Know that everything did not come easy for Lee and that he persevered to get what he dreamed and desired. Because of his death at the early age of 32, Lee is now seen by the public as a flawless legend of mythic proportions. Lee had all the right skills to make his name and films legendary. He could act and fight and he had incredible screen presence.

In this section, I will present some of the elements that still make Lee the screen fighter to whom all other screen fighters are automatically compared. If you cannot clearly see the significance of any of the examples that I am pointing out in this section, watch a Bruce Lee movie, and then watch a movie starring a Bruce Lee impersonator, and you'll immediately see what I'm talking about.

He Had No Noticeable Misses or Bad Takes in the Fight Scenes in Any of His Hong Kong Films

The fact that there were no noticeable misses or bad takes in his Hong Kong film fight scenes does not necessarily mean that Lee never had any bloopers or misses, but we never saw them in the final cut of any of his films. He had a certain amount of control over the action after *The Big Boss* and he knew what he needed to do to make the action sell correctly to the audience. You still see that many fight scenes today have obvious misses and bad takes in the final release of the film.

Note

When I speak of the movie *Game of Death,* I am not referring to the 1978 theatrical release, but two of the more recent versions, in which the missing footage was edited to the specifications of Bruce's original script to form the fight scenes up the pagoda, where James Tien, Chieh Yuan, and Bruce go up the steps to face Dan Inosanto, Chi Hon Tsoi, and Kareem Abdul-Jabbar. There are two different versions available. The first is the John Little version showcased in the documentary *The Warriors Journey.* The second is a Japanese version made by Art Port, also available in the UK Bruce Lee box set. Both of these versions have the fights unlike you've seen them before; they show his fighting strategy and philosophy as a cinematic art form. Both are slightly different in editing and each has its flaws.

This is a sign of the filmmakers being lazy or not knowing or being aware of what a good take is. There is simply no good excuse for this today; it is pretty much unforgivable because you have a video playback of the scene you just shot. But sure enough, it still happens...and it happens often. Bruce Lee and the filmmakers who worked with him back then did not have the luxury of a video playback monitor, but they always knew whether they had a good take.

It's important to know where the camera is for each technique and whether it makes each technique look effective. You should know whether you have a good take before moving on to the next scene.

He Had Simple Techniques but Rarely Repeated Himself

When you look closer and break down Lee's techniques, they were simple and not very extreme by today's standards. In fact, any proficient martial artist today could perform them. *But,* this proves the point that it's not what you do, but how you do it that really matters. It's not the techniques Lee threw that made him a legend. Instead, it was how he executed each technique with incredible grace, speed, and power, coupled with his commanding stage presence (see next section) and intense explosive emotion behind them. These elements would captivate audiences all over the world. The physical and emotional commitment he made to his techniques (martial acting) is cinematically engaging and hypnotic to this day. To keep things fresh, Lee would also change camera angles and the order of combinations of techniques, giving each scene a different emotional emphasis to make it look and feel different.

Lee also varied each fight scene through the timing and added something a little different or new to each film. However, there are some sequences that he repeated, such as the barrage of punches he did against Robert Baker in *Fist of Fury*—that was the exact same barrage he did against Chuck Norris in *Way of the Dragon*. Even though Lee made four-and-a-half films, he was able to keep it new each time. We can only speculate on how he would have evolved with his fight choreography had he lived longer.

If you read Lee's book *Tao of Jeet Kune Do* or see his interview with Pierre Berton, you will see that he has a deep knowledge and understanding of the martial arts and its application to real-life combat. Lee also had an understanding of human psychology and emotions in combat and he used that knowledge, along with his understanding of techniques and the effects and repercussions of them to apply to his expression when he fought onscreen. This was not done before him as effectively because previous martial artists' understandings of the techniques were superficial in comparison.

He Had an Individualistic Screen Presence

After Bruce Lee's death, his onscreen style was often imitated (usually unsuccessfully) by many screen fighters, including Jackie Chan. (Although it should be mentioned that this was not Chan's fault—director Lo Wei tried to force Chan into that persona.)

It's great to be influenced and inspired by Bruce Lee, but to imitate him or anyone else will only lead you down an infertile path of ridicule and fruitless inspiration for future projects. Some say that imitation is the best form of flattery. I can see that theory working when you are doing it as a parody, such as the "Fistful of Yen" episode in *The Kentucky Fried Movie*, but copying or mimicking someone is not being true to the character or to yourself as an artist, especially if you want to have any type of longevity in the business. We are all as unique and individual as our fingerprints. It's important to find your own screen presence, your own personal truth while fighting onscreen as a non-verbal narrative, and your own style of how you want your techniques to look onscreen. Don't be afraid to find your own path.

In the entertainment and performance aspect of fighting, whether it's a real combative competition or pure show, a character or competitor's presence is very important in being seen by the masses and gaining popularity, making that person a bigger draw. Muhammad Ali had an incredible stage presence that drew people to come see him fight, regardless of whether they liked him. Professional wrestlers are always working, developing and honing their stage presence to gain popularity (or scorn if they are a heel) with the audience. Screen fighters such as

Jackie Chan, Sammo Hung, and Jet Li also have incredible screen presence, but notice that it is uniquely theirs—it is not imitated or borrowed from someone else. And there is no denying that Bruce Lee had an incredibly strong presence that blazed the screen; his impact is still felt to this day. The audience can tell what is true and fake with a performer's stage or screen presence, which is why these performers have lasted this long.

Stage and screen presence are essential in the livelihood of a screen fighter or combative performer in terms of how they communicate to their audience. Many think stage presence is an unattainable magic——a magnetism or charisma that radiates from the performer. This magic is so hypnotic that you cannot take your eyes off the person. This is true and it is the result of a lot of working of their craft. But many think that you are either born with this magic or you're not. This is far from the truth—let's break it down.

First, there is a difference between stage and screen presence. *Stage presence* is the energy a performer gives to the performance in a live setting, whether it is staged (such as pro wrestling) or real (such as a boxing or MMA match). *Screen presence* is the energy the actor gives in his performance to the camera. The difference is in how one chooses to project his lines, techniques, and personality to his prospective audience. Live performances tend to be bigger and broad in their expression of action because they have to convince everyone in the room about what they are doing. On the other hand, performances onscreen are toned down (in comparison), intimate, and play to a camera that is often only a few feet away from the person. Pro wrestlers often have a hard time adjusting to screen performances and oversell to the camera because their training is geared to a live venue. Likewise, screen fighters often undersell their performance to a live audience because they are used to selling only to a nearby camera.

Screen presence is not a skill that someone can teach you, but it is something you can acquire through time and experience. On the other hand, to have screen presence, you have to be comfortable with who you are and what you are doing, and you have to understand that the character you are portraying is an extension of who you are. Often you will hear an actor say that he has turned down a role because he did not relate to the character in the story. This is because the performer did not feel he could find or bring any truth and believability to the character. Actors such as Jack Nicholson, John Cusack, Marlon Brando, and Sir Laurence Olivier command high dollars for portraying characters who are actually extensions of themselves, even when playing villains. I'm not saying that actors have to find the killer thug in them, but they must find some aspect of the character they can identify with and bring it to life.

The same principles apply to screen fighting, in which all of your previous training and experiences are now an extension of the character while you are fighting for the camera. If you can effectively portray this, you will not look like you are pretending to fight. Screen persona also depends on how much of himself one is willing to emotionally commit to his performance, while losing his consciousness (but not his awareness) of the camera and/or the audience and giving himself the freedom to lose himself in the performance while immersing himself in the character.

Unfortunately, this is where a lot of martial artists who attempt to be screen fighters fail miserably. They strived hard to get to the top of their field of expertise, but mentally and emotionally, they cannot let go of who they really are and what got them there. They end up looking too rigid or stiff and unconvincing with their performance. The mistake lies in the perception that acting is fake and that the actor is just putting on a mask, pretending to be someone else. Truth be told, it's actually the opposite. Acting is being able to open up and perform without the mask and without any flashiness that distracts from one's performance, while bringing one's inner soul and spirit to the performance. You can have incredible stage presence but not be able to technically fight well onscreen, and the audience will forgive you. But if you can technically fight well and you have no screen presence, you will not have much of a future in the business.

The fact that Bruce Lee and Jackie Chan both have strong screen presences and incredible technical fighting skills makes them rare and special.

He Had a Learning Curve

If you look at Lee's fights from *The Green Hornet*, to his guest appearance on *Ironside*, to *Marlowe*, to *Longstreet*, to his martial arts movies, you will notice that his understanding of angles and using the right techniques grew each time he performed in front of the camera. Notice his kicks got more varied, elongated, wider, more detailed, and more elaborate from *The Green Hornet* to *Enter the Dragon*. His kicks in the beginning were mainly snapping-type kicks (which recoil fast), with no overextension of the hips that shows speed, but he had no real driving power or any spin-type kicks to display on film. Then look at Lee's later films, especially *Way of the Dragon* and *Enter the Dragon*, in which he was able to display more powerful sidekicks and a variety of spin kicks that visually swept across the theater screen. His choice and application of techniques expanded too. He was much more comfortable with the action as he went further along in his filmmaking, making it look much more natural as time went by.

Rumor has it that when Lee made his first TV appearance in the United States in 1966, co-starring as Kato on *The Green Hornet*, he actually hit and hurt the stuntmen, knocking out several of them, and as a result they did not want to return to the show. Plus, Lee was not aware of where the camera was and how his techniques worked onscreen, so Van Williams (the series' star) snuck Lee into a screening of the dailies (a screening of the raw footage that was shot the previous day) for the executives. Lee heard the executives laughing at his fight scenes because he was too fast for the camera to follow and the camera was in much too close for anyone to see any of the techniques. Because Lee took his martial arts seriously, it was offensive to him that anyone would laugh at what he was doing. He went to the stunt coordinator of the show, Bennie Dobbins (also Williams' stunt double on the show) and showed him that he could look effective without having to hit anyone by understanding camera angles.

The moral is, don't be so hard on yourself when you are first starting. Know that the more you practice fighting onscreen, the better you will become if you are able to look objectively at your work. Learn to be critical of your work but never damning toward yourself, which will only hinder your growth. Be prepared and do your homework by getting a video camera, practicing constantly, and learning about effective and convincing angles that give the audience the most impact.

He Understood the Emotional Content and Impact behind Each Technique

Lee understood what each technique could do and applied this knowledge to his martial acting skills. This also holds true for Lee's emotional intensity. He was living in the moment when he fought and he was able to show it to the audience. His emotions and intensity differed with each of his techniques, as well as whether he snapped the technique or followed through with it. He hardly ever had the same type of emotions follow one another. Compare his emotions and emphasis when he threw a circular snapping technique, such as a roundhouse kick, to a straight follow-through type of technique, such as a sidekick.

If you train at a martial arts studio, you will understand easily the impact of each technique, how it affects the person getting hit, and the person who is throwing the technique. This is especially true if the school's emphasis is heavily on fighting. By being around it and carefully observing people, you slowly develop a sense of the emotions and motivations involved with the different personalities that come into the school. Then get a video camera and re-create the feeling of the impact by using camera angles (so you are not actually hitting your partner) that look convincing and, more importantly, dramatic.

He Was Adept with Both Hands and Feet, and He Was Not Afraid to Mix It Up

Even though Lee started out in Wing Chun (a predominately in-close hand trapping and punching style), he had very effective-looking kicks that evolved and improved throughout his short career. Compare his kicks when he was in *The Green Hornet* to his kicks in *Enter the Dragon.* In *The Green Hornet,* his kicks were snappy, without much hip extension, and very compact. In *Enter the Dragon,* he had more of a repertoire and his kicks were elongated by the extension of his hips. This is a huge leap in growth. Lee was dangerous because he was well balanced with his hands and feet. He did not really have a trademark technique that overshadowed any of his other techniques.

Also, Lee was not happy just striking his opponent. He varied the ranges of the fights and even went into grappling or wrestling (in some form), as exhibited in most of his final fight scenes. He mixed the different ranges of fighting in all of his movies, which added a sense of realism to his fights. He knew that in real fights, eventually you go to the ground. This is very evident in *Game of Death,* when he is able to finish off Chi Hon Tsoi and Kareem Abdul-Jabbar. Also, watch his fight in the courtyard against the Russian fighter Petrov (Robert Baker) in *Fist of Fury.*

In Hollywood, there was a time when if you knew only one style of fighting, you could get work as a fight choreographer. That's not so true today. The film industry now requires a wider knowledge of different ways to fight onscreen. Besides, audiences will get bored if you don't have anything new to show them.

Thinking your style is all encompassing is a huge fallacy, and you should get your money back from your instructor for selling you a bad bill of goods. Each individual style has flaws and weaknesses. For every strength, there is a weakness because for every attack, we leave ourselves exposed somehow. The ingenuity of the human mind along with man's will for survival means we are always looking for a defense to protect ourselves from an attack. This instinct has been alive since the dawn of man. Unless we have an advantage over another man, there will always be a flaw to every particular style or system of fighting.

This is why it is completely absurd and ego-stroking to say that one practices a perfect or flawless style. If an instructor *does* make that claim, my advice is to get your money back and run away as fast as you can. A perfect example of this is with the introduction of Gracie Jiu-Jitsu with the birth of the UFC in 1993. Royce Gracie was able to easily defeat his opponents in the first several competitions because none of the opponents were ever exposed to that way of fighting, so his style seemed invincible. But other fighters, such as Kazushi Sakuraba, started analyzing what the Gracies were doing and were able to expose the style's flaws and capitalize on their knowledge to defeat the Gracies. This earned Sakuraba the nickname "Gracie Hunter," for being the only fighter to ever defeat four members of the Gracie family in professional competition. And on May 27, 2006 UFC Welterweight Champion Matt Hughes defeated Royce Gracie at UFC 60 by technical knockout with strikes in the first round.

He Was Unafraid to Show His Vulnerability

In the Chinese version of *Way of the Dragon*, Lee was able to show vulnerability and humor. In the version retitled in the United States as *Return of the Dragon*, the comedic scenes were cut when it was originally released in 1974. This was because the distributors at the time felt an action hero such as Lee should not show that type of vulnerability. Even though Jackie Chan has broken that mold with his comedic action films, he is still seen as an exception to the rule. Action films are still generally seen in the West as testosterone-laden explosion fests with no real substance.

People seem to forget that Bruce Lee came from an acting family. His father was a famous Chinese Opera star and film actor. And Lee was an accomplished child-teen actor, starring in several non-action roles in Hong Kong, so he already had a lot of camera acting experience before he came to the States.

The fact that Lee came from an acting family helped him to understand elements of dramatic performance, psychology, and dynamics of the martial arts at an early age. However, he never had the chance to combine the two art forms until he was hired as Kato on *The Green Hornet.* Lee proved to be a consummate actor; he was able to land a guest-starring non-action role in the first season of the TV show *Here Come the Brides.*

Most martial artists are afraid to show any vulnerability because they have been trained to keep in their emotions or be very conservative about expressing them, and many want to create the illusion of invincibility. But acting is the opposite of this—you are asked to express your emotions. By being vulnerable and opening up to the audience, you are inviting them into the character you are portraying. This has to be done genuinely and sincerely from the story and the character to get the audience on your side. An audience can tell quickly when you are insincere and faking something.

He Knew the Importance of Having Great Stuntmen around Him

When Lee worked in the United States, he worked with legends in the stunt business, such as Bennie Dobbins and Gene LeBell on *The Green Hornet.* In his Hong Kong films, he worked closely with Sammo Hung, Jackie Chan, Yuen Biao, Lam

Ching Ying, Yuen Wah, Mang Hoi, and Mars as his stuntmen. These guys would all find success as some of the best stunt coordinators, directors, actors, and producers in the Hong Kong action genre several years after Lee's passing. Was this a coincidence? Not likely at all. Lee knew he had to have great stuntmen in order to make him look great.

You could be the greatest martial artist in the world, but if you don't have great stuntmen to take the proper reactions to your techniques, the fight scene will not look effective and you will not look good. The stuntman taking the reactions for you is responsible for how good you look. If you find good ones who can make your hits look convincing, hold onto them.

He Had Different and Unique Timing and Rhythm

Bruce Lee did not have the typical timing of most Chinese screen fighters in the 1970s, when a continuous barrage of techniques would go on for a long time without a break, often with extremely metronomic timing and rhythm. After a while it got overwhelming and monotonous for the audience. Lee had long fight scenes too, but they were made up of little spurts of action pieced together with breaks in between, so the audience could mentally catch up and take in what he had just done. This was more like the fights you would see in Japanese samurai films. Lee understood that the audience had to be emotionally and visually with him in order to be on his side.

You could be the fastest or most powerful martial artist out there, but if you are not able to let the audience take in what you have just done, how are they going to be impressed by your skills? Timing and rhythm is much like music: It's not the notes that make the music, but rather the breaks in between. The same applies to how the audience sees and appreciates a fight scene.

He Had Great Martial Acting Skills

Bruce Lee was easily able to express his emotions through his fighting, which drew the audience into the conflict regardless of whether they understood the nuances of the fight. His martial acting was very complex, private, intimate, sometimes conflicted, and often intense for his action scenes, so the audience was compelled to get emotionally involved in his fight scenes. His inner process always came from a genuine and truthful point for his character. Lee had extremely convincing and effective martial acting skills that he used to convey his emotions and thoughts without use of dialogue (notice how few lines he actually has in *Enter the Dragon*). This ability allowed Lee to transcend the language barrier more than any other Hong Kong screen fighter who came before him and is one of the many reasons why he became an international icon and is still loved and respected all over the world, even 30 years after his death.

For a great example of Lee's martial acting skills, range, and depth, take a closer look at his performance in *Enter the Dragon*, when he crushes Oharra's chest. Look at the emotional complexity, depth, and personal truth Lee expresses on his face. What made this scene much harder (performance-wise for Lee) was that it was an extreme closeup (only his face was onscreen) and it was shot in slow motion. This is difficult because your face is more than 20 feet tall on the big screen, and the audience can see every nuance. Because the scene was shot in slow motion, Lee could not emotionally hide or just pretend to act because the audience would immediately pick up on it and would know he was not emotionally committed to the scene. This means Lee made a deep, truthful, and emotionally genuine commitment to honestly express himself in that specific scene without any false airs. In some way, he had to emotionally draw it from his psyche to make it real and believable for himself (without killing or hurting anyone in real life—no method acting here, please!) in order for it to be believable for the audience.

Although we do not see the physical impact of what Lee did to Oharra, we see how it affected Lee because we see the personal and intimate conflict of the complex emotions he is processing. This makes it feel as if we are almost intruding on a deeply personal and intimate moment, which can make some people feel uncomfortable or uneasy in their seats. This is probably much more effective and emotionally moving for the audience (seeing the effect of this act of violence on Lee's emotions through his facial expressions) than showing the physical act itself because the audience has to fill in the gaps themselves.

Another martial acting principle Lee used better than the majority of screen fighters out there was that he was emotionally "in the moment" with each and every fight. Because it was real in his mind, he made it real for the audience. You can easily notice this by watching the intensity of his eyes as he follows his opponent to the ground after he hits him.

Over the years, I've seen many screen fighters and actors since Lee who have tried to recreate this type of intensity for themselves, but they lacked the sincerity or emotional honesty for the given scene and tried to overcompensate by overacting or putting on an emotion that was not at all truthful. Or, they simply didn't want to do the work and took the shortcut by asking themselves, WWBLD? (*What Would Bruce Lee Do?*)They would then imitate his mannerisms and actions. Either choice is being insincere and false to your audience, depriving them of the emotional truth of the character you are portraying.

Understanding the emotional content of your moves and giving them the right amount of emphasis without underselling or overselling is one of the most difficult things about martial acting. It's easy to see bad martial acting because it's so obvious that the emotion or degree of emphasis does not fit the scene properly.

Good martial acting always goes unnoticed and takes the audience on an emotional journey. They forget that they are watching a movie. Being good at martial acting is part understanding the emotional and cinematic impact of your techniques, and part being genuinely in that moment and conveying it to the audience.

The more you practice this in front of the mirror and on camera, the better and more natural you will be at it. Make your mistakes and learn from them in your own home or on your own video, so when it comes to be your time to fight onscreen, you will not waste the time of your fellow castmates and crewmembers. Learn to be constructive and not demeaning with your criticism so you can learn from your mistakes and improve more quickly. Start with just yourself, and then work with a partner to match and contrast emotions. Also, this is a time when you should find your screen-fighting persona. It's easy to imitate Bruce Lee or Jackie Chan's poses and expressions, but they are truly not yours, and that will resonate with the audience as not being genuine. Learn to express *yourself* through the moves. You will be surprised at what you will discover.

He Had Effective and Convincing Before and After Poses

Between the action scenes in Lee's fights were breaks where he would have his before and after poses to let you know the emotion or disposition of the character at the time.

Lee's martial acting in his before and after poses communicated to the audience the emotions of his character, so they could sympathize with and root for the character. The poses were simple, but extremely genuine and powerful for the moment of the scene at hand, which made them all the more convincing.

He Did Not Have a Trademark or Signature Move

Bruce Lee had fast and powerful hands and feet and also grappled when needed. He did not favor one or the other, which kept the audience guessing what he would do next.

By having a signature move, you are bound or burdened by your ego, and this actually limits your potential as a screen fighter because you have to integrate that move into each film you are in. This also means you are not into the character you are portraying—you are more involved with the celebrity you are.

He Had a Physique That Everyone Envied

Lee had an incredible physique that a lot of athletes wished they could have. There's no doubt that Lee worked very hard on developing his hard physique, but he had "functional" muscles for the martial arts and looked good in a suit, and you could not tell that he was really buff underneath.

He Understood the Difference between Cinematic and Real Fighting

Bruce Lee was a real martial artist who understood which techniques were convincing on film and what angles were the most effective in making a strong impact for the audience. Lee's experience as a real martial artist was a help as opposed to a hindrance to his screen fighting because his ego was not caught up in the doctrines, dogma, and politics of the martial arts community.

There are principles and techniques in the martial arts that do not work well onscreen and will make your performance look wooden and not at all natural. Lee was able to make a clear distinction between screen fighting and real fighting. Because he was a real martial artist, he was able to bring those real experiences and emotions onto the screen without being tied down to what a martial artist usually thinks of as "real and not real." Effective cinematic fighting is much different than effective fighting in the dojo, on the street, or in a tournament.

Most martial artists starting out in film usually don't understand that what they are doing is for entertainment, not educational purposes. A lot of other martial artists who came after Bruce Lee are arguably equal to or better than him in martial arts skill and ability, but they were not able to look natural on film simply because they could not act or did not know which techniques look effective onscreen.

He Injected Philosophy and Fight Strategy into His Films

Bruce Lee added martial arts philosophy in his films in such a way that an educated martial artist could learn from it, but it was still enjoyable to the layman because it was part of the story. This is evident in *Way of the Dragon* when Lee explained the approach to Chinese boxing to one of the waiters, then had to show it to another one. Then he proved his case when the karate that Jimmy unsuccessfully used on the Italian thug (which was incorrectly mocked and labeled as Chinese boxing) got him knocked out. In *Enter the Dragon* (the 25thth anniversary version), we see that he is still learning lessons when he talks to his Master and is able to impart his wisdom to his student. And in *Game of Death*, when Lee faces off with Dan Inosanto, he passes lessons on to us disguised as taunts to Inosanto. Rumor has it that Lee's fight with Oharra in *Enter the Dragon* had dialogue between exchanges where Lee taunted Oharra and ridiculed his training.

Also, Lee had a different strategic approach to each opponent that was very entertaining, even though the layman in the audience might not understand the nuances of this. This is very apparent in the opponents Lee fought in *Way of the Dragon* and his version of *Game of Death*. Showing a strategy that unfolds became a form of entertainment before the audience's eyes. This is much like letting the audience in on a joke because there is a premise (situation), a setup (in which you are leading the opponent and the audience), and the punch line (which you will hit the opponent with, unbeknownst to the audience and the opponent).

He Fought Only When Necessary

Bruce's characters in film fought only when necessary. There always had to be a reason for him to fight; nothing was gratuitous or senseless in any of his fight scenes. Doing this builds up the tension because the audience is anticipating when he is going to fight. Recall the scene on the boat in *Enter the Dragon* where Lee accepts the invitation to fight the taunting thug, but then effectively defeats him by utilizing the "art of fighting without fighting." Another great example is in *The Big Boss*—his first real fight did not come until nearly 40 minutes into the movie. In *Fist of Fury*, the fight scene in which he goes to the Japanese school to challenge everyone comes much sooner, but it made sense in that movie because the motivation, anticipation, and emotion was built up much more quickly than in *The Big Boss*.

In *Way of the Dragon*, Tang does not fight until the second time the Italian thugs show up to break up the restaurant, because the first time he is in the restroom while it all occurs. So by the time Bruce is ready to fight, the tension has built so that the audience is more than ready to see him fight. And when he does fight, the audience is ready to explode with emotion from the anticipation that has built up.

It's important to tease the audience and not always give them what they want, when they want it. You should play and tease them a little and build up their anticipation as if you were Mrs. Robinson and the audience was Dustin Hoffman in *The Graduate*. Having an effective story that emotionally engages the audience and can build up to the fights is necessary in getting the audience emotionally behind the fight. I'm sure you've seen films that have a nice set piece for a fight with incredible, spectacular moves, but you are not emotionally behind it. That's because these films are giving the audience a fight when they have not given them a proper emotional buildup that leads into it.

Watching Bruce Lee's Movies

To further explore Bruce Lee's contributions to screen fighting, I suggest you watch his movies to dissect what he contributed and come up with some of your own conclusions. In this next section, I break down the final fight scenes of *Way of the Dragon* so you can start to get an idea of what to look for.

Way of the Dragon (aka *Return of the Dragon*)

The reason I chose this film is because it's the only finished film in which Lee had complete creative control. For several reasons, I suggest you track down the original Chinese version of the film with English subtitles. The U.S. version (released here as *Return of the Dragon*) is lacking four cut scenes that show us Tang Lung's predicament, naivety, and vulnerability about being in a new country and not knowing the language. These deleted sequences all add up to his dilemma in a new and strange land and show how Tang deals with it. The scenes also add humor and much-needed logic to the movie.

The cut scenes are as follows:

- At the airport, Tang Lung tries to motion to a kid that he wants to get something to eat, but he ends up scaring the kid, who runs off crying for his mother.
- The next scene immediately follows. Lee goes into a restaurant inside the airport and cannot read the menu, so he ends up ordering several bowls of soup.
- The next scene is right after Chen is scolding Tang in the outside plaza, telling him to lighten up and reciprocate to people when they do something nice for him. A hooker escorts Tang to a room. The deleted scene is when the hooker takes Tang to the hotel room, and he shadow boxes in the mirror until the hooker comes out in the nude. Tang freaks out and immediately darts out of the room.
- The last deleted scene is of Tang using a Western as a squatter, and a customer comes in and looks at him baffled as he closes the stall door.
- In the English dub of the movie, the effectiveness and logic of the film are reduced because everyone is speaking English—the major obstacle that Tang Lung has to overcome in the film is no longer there. This is especially true in the following situations:
    - Tang gets on the phone to talk to the operator, trying to give him the phone number of the restaurant in English.

- Tang asks his friend to tell the Italian thugs, "This is Chinese boxing." The impact of the scene is completely lost, it does not make sense, and it is completely unnecessary in the English dub.
- All the scenes in which Tang communicates with the Boss are lost when everyone speaks English. There is no real reason for the miming and body gestures. This also lessens the role of the effeminate translator for the Boss.
- Colt (Chuck Norris) meets Tang. The reason they do not exchange any words is that they do not speak a common language. The translator is the one who sets up the exposition for Tang, and the audience wonders why Colt is there.

I feel Bruce was calling the shots because the fights are more dynamic than in his previous efforts. There is a certain strategy and a lesson to the audience that is different and distinct with each fight scene, more than in his previous films. This is especially true of the fights toward the end of the film, with Fred (Bob Wall), the Japanese fighter (Whang In Sik), and Colt (Chuck Norris).

Tang Fights Robert

Tang gets Fred winded and takes note that he is a right-leg-dominant fighter. He taunts him and "trains his mind" with the crescent kick that hits his lead hand guard, and then once Fred is used to that kick, thinking that it's the furthest extension Tang's lead leg can make, make Tang fakes, as if he's going to throw it again, then changes it in midstream to a round kick by turning over his hip, giving him more distance to cover the gap and hit Fred in the face.

Tang Fights the Japanese Fighter

With the Japanese fighter (Whang Ing-Sik), we see that Tang is able to predict his moves because of his traditional wide stance—the fighter is not very mobile and he has to step up and have a foot under him to kick. And that is enough time for Tang to hit the fighter before he can complete a technique. We see that Tang is faster in recognition (mind) to execution (body) of technique.

The Final Showdown: Colt versus Tang

In the beginning of the fight with Colt (Chuck Norris), Colt has the advantage and beats Tang to the punch. Nothing Tang has used before works on Colt. Tang changes his rhythm and game plan by starting to become more fluid. He does this by being lighter on his feet and using a broken rhythm to even out the playing field. Eventually, Tang takes control of the fight, while Colt is still fighting flat-footed and has to depend on his initial hand and foot speed from a dead stop.

When Colt finds himself on the losing end of the fight, he changes his rhythm by being light on his feet also, but it's much too late. A possible interpretation of this could be that Colt was too immersed in his ego and did not notice the change in momentum until it was way too late. Or, perhaps he thought he could still fight the same way he did to change the momentum his way until Tang caved in. The fight has many different changes in rhythm and flow throughout that were not done previously onscreen. This fight is the most serious of the whole film because Tang consciously has to take Colt's life in the end. He then grows up to be a man, no longer a kid.

When watching this film in its original form (in Cantonese with English subtitles and deleted scenes), I have noticed the character arc of Tang Lung is very subtle underneath all the action, but still very effective. All the fights that lead up to the fight with Colt in the Coliseum gradually get more and more serious, especially when Tang meets up with Fred, the Japanese fighter, and Colt. Up to that point it was fun and ego-gratifying for Tang and the audience because no one posed a serious threat to him. But the fight with Colt is no longer fun—it is deadly serious in the execution of technique and mood of the fight. Look at the expression on Tang's face when he realizes he has to kill Colt. He has now lost his innocence and life is no longer a game.

Because this was Bruce Lee's directorial debut (he also starred, wrote, and choreographed), the original Chinese version is an underestimated classic.

2

The Differences between Sport, Art, and Self-Defense

When putting together a fight, it is important for the choreographer to know the specific differences between a combative sport, a martial art, and a self-defense/combat system. This is because certain applications, emphases, and specific uses of techniques are different for each combative form. These applications or uses need to make logical, applicable, and practical sense with the fight you are choreographing. Plus, if the fight choreographer was trained in a style or system that heavily emphasized one application, then he might put the wrong emphasis on a fight if he is not adept at the way that particular fight should be expressed. This is much like asking a classically trained ballet dancer to put together an interpretive modern jazz performance. Depending on the dancer's background and training experience, he or she might be able to put together something reasonable, but will undoubtedly be unable to support it fully.

A couple reasons why the fight choreographer needs to understand the difference between a combative sport, a martial art, and a self-defense/combat system apply behind the scenes as well as in front of the camera.

- Use of the correct style or the correct application of the art, sport, or combat training to match the situation and emotion of the scene are critical.
- Also crucial is the use of screen fighters who are experienced, have trained extensively, and/or feel comfortable with the chosen approach or style of fight. For example, you would not want to hire a screen fighter who is strictly an Olympic fencer (art) to perform in a duel to the death in sixteenth-century England (combative sport). The expression and dynamics of techniques are different today than they were in sixteenth-century England, to say the least.

Here's another example: Two equally skilled combatants are in a serious street fight over something very emotional to them. In such a scenario, it would not look right or be effective to use American tournament point-fighting techniques and principles in which the combatants bounce around and fall over each other just to make light or moderate contact. Nor would it be appropriate for a fighter to pepper his opponent with fast but light flippy-looking kicks that make no strong impact. Nor would you use a street-effective fighting style, such as Krav Maga, or fully apply a technique such as an eye gouge in a friendly classroom sparring session or a modern-day tournament fight. The principles of the concepts for fighting are taken out of context in these situations. If not corrected, this can possibly damage the emotion of the scene.

These are, of course, rather obvious examples. But, often when you look at a fight scene, you feel or sense that something is not right, but you can't put your finger on it. When this happens, look at the emphasis on the technique first and see whether it needs to be altered for the scene to get across the intended emotion.

Three Major Approaches to Combat: Art, Sport, and Self-Defense

There are differences between the three approaches to fighting. They are interrelated in certain ways and they have things in common, but their application and emphasis on technique creates differences between the three.

Someone who doesn't know anything about martial arts probably cannot differentiate between a combative sport, an art, and a self-defense system. Even people who have been practicing for a while still wouldn't know the difference unless they were able to step back and take a look at what they're doing.

It is important to know what aspect of the specific martial art you are using to choreograph for your fight.

Common Ground among All Three Concepts

As mentioned earlier, all three techniques share some common ground:

- All use techniques that can hurt or damage an opponent.
- All train the student to see physical situations differently.
- In all three, the better the student gets, the better he is able to apply his skills to more difficult situations.
- All depend on razor-sharp timing to make contact with a live opponent.
- All teach and develop self-confidence and self-awareness.

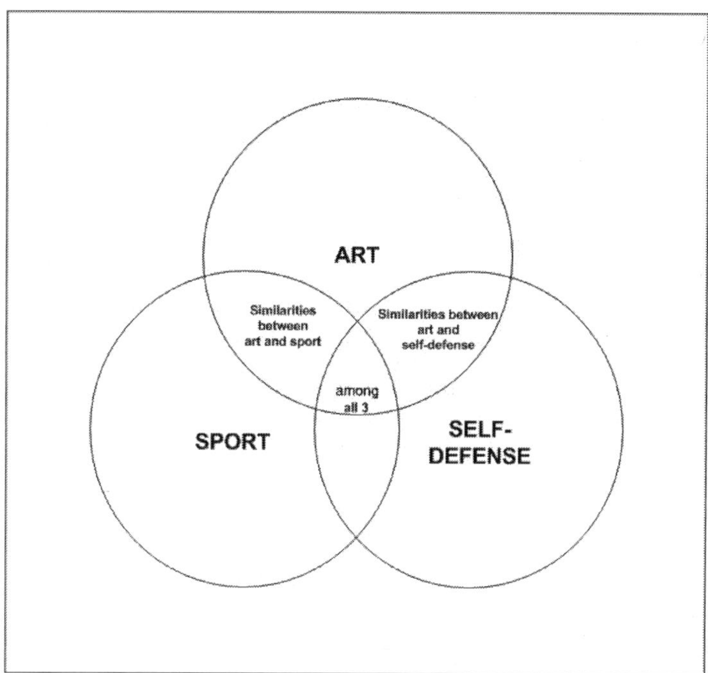

Figure 2.1

Even though the emphases of the three major approaches to combat are different, there are certain similarities in each approach. This is best described by the circles for each approach in this diagram. The part of the circle that intertwines with each approach represents the commonalities between each one. But as we leave the center of the diagram, the parts of the circle that are not touching represent the differences in each approach.

Definition of a Martial Art

A martial art focuses on the growth and cultivation of the student. This is something that has been carried over from Asia, where it has been in practice for centuries. The purpose is for the student to understand himself—his thoughts and actions—while training the mind and conditioning the body. Without the philosophy, morals, and spirituality (not religion) taught in the art, it would deteriorate to just a sophisticated and stylized form of street fighting.

A martial artist is better-rounded in his training than a combative sportsman or a student of a self-defense system. A martial art takes longer to master—often it takes a lifetime to grasp the concept of just one art. The emphasis is on the everyday person who is interested in getting into shape, having more control over his body, and learning more about himself and how he relates to others. Classroom sparring, self-defense, and learning the basics are emphasized here. However, many schools and instructors today do not heavily emphasize character growth, discipline, and spirituality because they are more focused on casual students who take classes purely for recreation and pleasure.

The techniques used in a true martial art are tempered with morals, respect for life, and self-restraint—even when a practitioner might feel like lashing out at an opponent. Emphasis of these principles can be found in feature films such as *The Karate Kid* and *The Shaolin Temple,* as well as in the 1970s' television show, *Kung Fu.*

Definition of a Combative Sport

A combative sport has rules, demands sportsmanlike conduct from competitors, requires protective equipment to be worn, and has safety guidelines that protect the well-being of the athletes involved in the combative event. The emphasis on the techniques is to earn points by landing clean techniques that are acknowledged by the judges. The combatant who accumulates the most points by the end of the match is declared the winner. However, a combatant can also advance by landing a technique that will immobilize an opponent to a point where he cannot continue the match—the combatant who threw the technique is then declared the winner.

Depending on the sport and the time in history, certain techniques are outlawed in order to protect the athlete. Just because it is a sporting event, that does not mean the athletes have to hate their opponents inside and outside the ring...but this *can* provide good drama. However, in real life the opposite is usually true. Respect for each other's skills results in a bond and/or friendship that is common among combatants.

What differs in combative sports as opposed to the other two disciplines is that the competitor is not out to kill or maim his opponent with his techniques, as he would in a self-defense situation. He is not expected to carry himself or throw techniques in a highly ritualized and controlled manner, as he would in a martial art.

I'm not saying that if you surprised someone such as George Foreman or Mike Tyson in the middle of a dark street, you would have a good chance of beating him. Chances are Foreman or Tyson would still beat you like a red-headed stepchild. The point I am making here is that the main emphasis of the training and the types of techniques used is for in the ring, where the rules protect the fighter from serious injury. (Although this is not to say that serious injury and death haven't occurred in the ring—indeed they have.)

Also, if commonsense practicality in fighting is not emphasized in training, then it is considered a sport. A good example is a combative sport in which the rules state that it is forbidden to punch to the head, but you are able to kick to the head. The rule effectively nullifies this as a practical self-defense system because you have to be prepared for everything in a street situation (including getting punched to the head).

Another example that would separate a martial art or self-defense system from a sport is whether the combatants practice defending themselves against multiple opponents. If not, then it's pretty much a sport. In most combative sports, combatants do not train to fight multiple opponents and will fight only in their own weight classes. On the other hand, a martial art or a self-defense system will train and teach combatants to fight opponents of different heights, weights, and numbers.

A combative sport also does not train in techniques and tactics that would be considered illegal in the sport, such as groin kicks or eye gouges, but the same illegal maneuver might be effective and save the combatant's life in a self-defense situation.

Definition of a Self-Defense/Combative System

Combative or self-defense training is a way of training that uses techniques to quickly disable, cripple, kill, or escape from an opponent. This type of training is used in military combat or personal survival classes. Self-defense is not really considered a martial art because cultivation of the student and his spirituality are not the primary emphasis. Techniques used with extreme control in a classroom setting or that are considered banned, dangerous, or illegal in a sport are the bread and butter here. The primary goal with the techniques is to defend oneself, take control of the enemy, or kill the opponent as a means of self-protection. Depending on the self-defense system, there are probably many techniques that would not be considered legal or gentlemanly in a sport or a friendly sparring situation. Usually a fight ends quickly due to the type of technique used, such as open-handed or clawing-hand techniques to vital organs or sensitive parts of the body, or perhaps breaking techniques to a knee or elbow joint that can certainly incapacitate or kill the opponent if done correctly.

A self-defense system does not require years and years of training. It's constructed for the practitioner to remember moves in a short amount of time while using body leverage, pressure points, and simple but effective techniques to escape to safety. An apprenticeship is not usually required in a self-defense system.

What Is a Martial Artist?

The term "martial artist" is often thrown around rather loosely these days. Just because someone practices a combative sport, or a self-defense system does not necessarily make that person a martial artist, just like someone who takes a few piano lessons is not necessarily (or at least not yet) a musician. Being a martial artist has to do with applying the philosophy, morals, and principles learned in the style outside of the place where one trains or competes. This includes creating and maintaining a positive and constructive influence with your students and others around you inside the school, in a ring, and outside in everyday situations in the community around you. In other words, a true martial artist takes and applies his training wherever he goes.

Many combative athletes claim to be martial artists, but few truly satisfy the criteria of that classification. Just because someone has a certain level of proficiency or has won titles or championships, that does not mean the person is a martial artist—he is a combative athlete. Sure, the person has excelled to a certain level of physical and mental proficiency—more so than your average student who walks in from the street—but unless he truly understands and constantly practices the underlying philosophies of martial arts training, the label simply does not apply. This is certainly not to say that a martial artist is a superior individual to, or necessarily a better fighter than a combative sportsman, but it is important to understand the difference.

The Root of Combative Sports

The history of combative sports is arguably as old as man. They were used to solve disputes between warring tribes or even within a tribe in many ancient civilizations. They were also used to train warriors and soldiers, giving the combatants practical experience they could apply on the battlefield. And, they were rites of passage.

The most famous recorded combative sporting event in ancient times was the Greek Olympic games held every four years in Olympia. The ancient Olympic games first started in 776 B.C. and lasted almost 1,200 years, to 393 A.D. They were later resurrected as what we currently know as the modern games in 1896. There are many differences between the ancient games and the modern games as we know them today.

The ancient games were a religious pagan celebration to honor Zeus, the god of sky and thunder, ruler of Mount Olympus, and king of all gods. When we think of the spirit of the Olympic games today, what comes to mind are a moral force and the human spirit, which demonstrate the elevation of the human potential, equality between races and nations, the spirit of friendship and fair play, the pursuit of excellence, and the respect and admiration for the valiant loser and the disadvantaged, beyond manmade borders, human prejudices, and politics. But in the ancient games, winning meant the athlete was closest to the divine, that he was greater than human and was to be worshipped. It was an honor and shame society. Only the winner was celebrated, praised, and considered divinely favored, while the loser was mocked and embarrassed even by his own family. There were no team sports because it was all about personal fame and glory, and it did not matter how ruthless an athlete was in the pursuit of this. Three combative sports from the ancient Olympics are still with us today–wrestling, boxing, and Pankration (known today as mixed martial arts).

Mixed Martial Arts

Many people think mixed martial arts (MMA) matches got started recently, with the Ultimate Fighting Championships (UFC) in 1993. The truth is that MMA got its start in the Olympics in 648 B.C. as a sport called Pankration (although historians argue that it was created in Egypt in 2600 B.C.). Pankration was not only a sport, but also a basis for the combat training for Greek soldiers, the Spartan Hoplite warriors, and Alexander the Great's Macedonian army.

Although Pankration was not the first sport introduced into the Olympics, it was the most popular. In Greek, "pan" means all and "kratos" means strength or power. Pankration was created as a result of combining two other sports that were in the Olympics prior to that time—wrestling (introduced in 708 B.C.) and pugilism or boxing (introduced in 688 B.C.)—over the debate of who would be the better fighter. There were two types of Pankration—Ano, which allowed the fighters to stand and was used during training, and Kato, which was used in the games where the fights went to the ground. Essentially, the word "Pankration" in modern terms means "no holds barred" (NHB).

Pankration matches would take place in a square arena or ring that was 12 to 14 feet across and filled with sand and dirt. The combatants would fight naked, their bodies doused in olive oil and sand, so they could get a grip on their opponents. They did not wear any gloves. The only rules were no eye gouging and no biting (although the Spartans would allow it), and serious and permanent injuries were common. If any competitor violated the rules, an umpire was nearby to flog them. Standing strikes using the hands, feet, knees, and elbows to any and all parts of the body were common, but most fights would end on the ground, where submission holds, takedowns, joint locks, and strikes would occur. There were no weight divisions or time limits. Matches would often go on for hours and would end when a combatant surrendered, fell unconscious from a strike or stranglehold, passed out from exhaustion, or died. If there was no winner declared by sunset, the fighters would have to alternate throwing undefended blows at each other until one was defeated. This was known as a "klimax."

The spirit of good sportsmanship and goodwill through competition was not the reason to fight back then. No medals were awarded, and only the winner was celebrated. It was for personal achievement, entertainment value, and to celebrate the god Zeus. Wrestlers and boxers did not want to have anything to do with Pankration because of its violent nature. But the Greeks placed it above boxing and wrestling because it was a combination of both sports, and therefore a Pankration champion could easily best a fighter who possessed only one of those two skills.

Dioxippus was one of the most famous Pankration fighters. He won several Olympic games and had such a great reputation that no one would dare challenge him. As a result, he was crowned Olympic champion by default in 336 B.C. During a banquet thrown by the Macedonian emperor, the Athenian fighter was challenged by Coragus, a celebrated warrior of the Macedonian army and a close friend of Alexander the Great. Dioxippus accepted the duel. Coragus attended the duel in full armor, armed with a javelin, spears, and a sword. Dioxippus showed up unarmored with only a club. Dioxippus dodged the javelin and broke Coragus' spear. Before Coragus could draw his sword, Dioxippus applied his Pankration techniques to throw down the warrior, ending the fight with his foot on Coragus' neck, sparing his life. Dioxippus was announced the winner of the duel. The Greeks celebrated the victory, while the Macedonians were humiliated and shamed.

The popularity of Pankration died out with the rise of the Roman Empire, where other combative sports would take its place.

The Birth of Brazilian Jiu-Jitsu and Vale Tudo

Mitsuyo Maeda came to northeastern Brazil in the early 1900s as a representative of the Japanese government. Maeda had plans to build a colony whereby Gastão Gracie, a political figure in the area, would assist him in establishing the colony. Maeda was not only known for being a politician and businessman; he was also a Judo champion. Maeda taught Gastão's son, Carlos, from age 15 until 21, when Maeda returned to Japan. Carlos taught his brothers, Helio, Jorge, Osvaldo, and Gastão, Jr., what Maeda had taught him. However, they were not bound by the rigid traditions and rituals the Japanese practitioners were, so they modified and adapted the art to their needs, making it more practical for them.

In 1925, Carlos took his younger brother, Helio, to Rio de Janeiro to open up a Jiu-Jitsu academy while continuing to modify and make the art specifically theirs. To bring attention to the fledgling academy, they would take out ads in the local newspapers. In what began as the famous "Gracie Challenge," the caption for an ad with a photo of Carlos would read, "If you want a broken arm or rib, call Carlos Gracie." This would usher in the re-emergence of mixed martial arts contests in the Western world because local karate schools, boxers, capoeira practitioners, and other various martial artists wanted to show that they were better than the Gracies.

The first of these matches was between Brazilian lightweight champion, Antonio Portugal, and Carlos' younger brother, Helio, who was much smaller than the boxer. Despite his size, Helio won the match within 30 seconds. Soon word spread about these matches throughout Rio, with the public wanting to see more of them. Because of the intense public demand for these matches, they were held at soccer arenas. This also marked the birth of the sport of Vale Tudo (Portuguese for "anything goes"), which consisted of competitions of unarmed combat with minimal rules.

Eventually, word spread to Japan about what the Gracies were doing, and many Japanese practitioners flocked to Rio to challenge the Gracies, feeling they had dishonored and desecrated the Japanese art. Helio (who was usually outweighed and outsized, often by 100 pounds or more) would accept the challenges, and he defeated many opponents between 1935 and 1951, participating in more than 1,000 fights. Years later, Carlos' son Carlson and Helio's sons Rolls, Rickson, and Rorian would continue the family tradition of upholding the "Gracie Challenge."

Coming to America and the Birth of the UFC

In the early '80s, Rorian Gracie came to the United States to teach Brazilian or Gracie Jiu-Jitsu. He continued the "Gracie Challenge" in America, but added a twist to it, making the stakes higher. Rorian offered $100,000 to anyone who could defeat him or any of his brothers in a Vale Tudo match. It was Rorian's dream to make Vale Tudo popular in the United States.

Note

The Gracie style was first briefly shown in *Lethal Weapon*, in the final fight scene between Martin Riggs and Mr. Joshua in Sgt. Murtaugh's front yard. Riggs finally finishes the fight by getting Mr. Joshua to submit using a Gracie Jiu-Jitsu move.

Rorian then met Art Davie, an advertising executive who was interested in recreating the Vale Tudo matches seen in Brazil. Davie set up a meeting with Rorian, himself, and Bob Meyrowitz, president of Semaphore Entertainment Group (SEG), a corporation that put on Pay-Per-View events on cable television. The three men created the Ultimate Fighting Championships, in which challengers from other martial arts styles could come into the ring and fight each other. However, this was not a new concept. Wrestler/Judoka Gene LeBell fought and defeated boxer Milo Savage on December 2, 1963, in Salt Lake City, Utah. And in June, 1976, Muhammad Ali fought Japanese wrestler Antonio Inoki in a "worked" match in Tokyo, Japan.

In 1993, Rorian and his partners had their first Pay-Per-View event, from which Rorian's younger brother, Royce, emerged as the winner. The first six Pay-Per-View events had very few rules and no weight classes, time limits, rounds, or mandatory safety equipment. The only rules were no eye gouges or "fish hooks", and the fight could only end by the referee stopping it; by a knockout; by submission, which could be signified verbally; or by "tap out," where the fighter taps three times on the mat or on his opponent's body with his hand or foot.

The matches took place in an eight-sided cage called "the Octagon," in single elimination matches that would advance each winner to the finals. The fighters in the first several contests had not seen that type of fighting before and were not able to adjust with a suitable counter or defense. As a result, Royce won 11 matches by submission and won UFC I, II, and IV. To many, it was an infomercial for Brazilian Jiu-Jitsu because a majority of the fighters were not reputable or of equal caliber. However, fighters began analyzing the Gracies' tactics and started studying and incorporating ground fighting as a part of their training, which was evident in UFC IV because the matches lasted longer and ran over the allotted time in the Pay-Per-View event. This culminated in UFC V (in 1995), when Royce faced Ken Shamrock in the finals. Shamrock was the first opponent to withstand the Gracie submission attacks, which ended in a draw with Royce's right eye swollen shut. The fans were outraged by the results of the match, so from then on judges were used to determine the outcome if a match went longer than the time allotted.

The SEG marketing team who promoted the event as a blood sport with no rules attracted curious viewers to pay to watch the event, but they also attracted lawmakers. Arizona Senator John McCain launched a campaign against the UFC, and as a result, the major Pay-Per-View carriers dropped the event from their lineup in 1997. The event was banned from a majority of states for several years. During this time (between UFC XII and UFC XV), they still held events. Weight classes were introduced and gloves became mandatory, while strikes to the back of the head and neck, small joint manipulation, and pressure-point strikes were banned. Finally, five-minute rounds were introduced in UFC XXI. While the UFC was restructuring their format, other mixed martial arts leagues and federations were getting sanctioned and being shown on television.

In 2001, when the UFC was about to declare bankruptcy, they were purchased by Zuffa, LLC. A month later, they secured sanctioning in Nevada, and UFC XXXIII returned to the Pay-Per-View lineup. The UFC began to rise in popularity due to effective advertising and marketing, corporate sponsorship, events held at high-profile casinos, and television broadcasting deals.

Concurrently, other MMA leagues and organizations have sprung up, such as Pancrase, Pride, and the IFL, to name a few.

Why MMA Is Popular with Audiences

MMA matches are currently popular for several reasons:

- The popularity of boxing is on the decline because there are currently no champions who are captivating or charismatic enough to consistently capture an audience.
- In a combative sport where only striking is involved, when the competitors get into a clinch (where both arms of a fighter are tied up by the opponent so he cannot punch), the referee breaks up the fight so the competitors can move to punching distance to restart. Therefore, it feels so much more like a controlled sport rather than an actual fight. In an MMA fight, on the other hand, when the competitors are in a clinch, the grappling and submission game starts and the fighters are not separated (unless they are at a stalemate for too long).

- The concept of MMA is more "real," as opposed to being controlled by too many rules, as in other combative sports such as boxing or kickboxing. The reality is that the MMA fighter has more ranges of combat to address in his matches, as opposed to one range. To many viewers, this is much more exciting, because the loosened restrictions make an MMA fight look a lot more like the real thing.

The Different Ranges of Combat Involved

The sport of MMA requires the fighters to be adept at a variety of different "games" or ranges of fighting, where only a singular subset thereof is often the only emphasis in another combative sport (i.e., boxers can only punch, and only with the front of their gloves). For MMA fights, the fighter needs to have the following styles and ranges of combat managed in order to be successful:

- **Striking.** This involves long-range (kicks and punches) to medium-range (knees and elbows) strikes. Strikes are used to hurt or knock out the opponent. This is the typical range a boxer or kickboxer is comfortable with and trains for, although all of the above strikes are not necessarily legal in those sports.
- **Grappling.** This involves close-range skills for gripping and controlling an opponent without striking, usually through holds, counters, and throws. Grappling is used in both the standup and ground games.
- **Submission.** This involves getting an opponent to submit due to a hold that can be a choke, a compression, or a joint lock. The fighter establishes the dominant position and gets an opponent in a submission hold that causes extreme pain, causing the opponent to submit before he dislocates a limb, tears a ligament, breaks a bone, falls unconscious, or dies.
- **Ground and pound.** This is a part of ground fighting in which a fighter brings his opponent to the ground with a takedown or throw (grappling), then establishes a dominant position and strikes his opponent repeatedly until he is knocked out or submits, or until the fight is stopped by the referee.

Tournament/Point Fighting

Tournament fighting as we know it today has its origins in Japanese karate, where it is called Kumite, which literally means "meeting of hands." The original idea was to have a friendly meeting of martial artists to try out their skills in an unrehearsed manner (such as one-step sparring), where they could see whether their techniques and strategic theories would work. Pulling techniques just short of contact was the best solution so that no one would suffer any serious damage and all would learn from the experience. The other martial artists observing would make comments about who would've made contact first and who landed the single blow to the correct area that appeared strong enough to stop, injure, or kill the opponent.

What Is Free Sparring?

Free sparring can be defined as a friendly match between two or more opponents, although it is usually done with two people, generally in a martial arts school with supervision by a person of higher ranking.

The purpose of free sparring in a classroom setting is to learn about one's own weaknesses mentally and physically. In many traditional martial arts systems, free sparring is one of the only times when you are confronted with a live opponent not throwing a predetermined or arranged technique at you. Rules are imposed to protect the students in the match from suffering any serious damage or injuries. In your typical "striking type" school today, students are asked to wear safety equipment (usually foam padded gear on the hands, feet, and head) and protective gear (mouthpiece, groin cup, and soft flexible body armor).

The rules in free sparring vary from system to system and even from school to school. But in general, the rules of good sportsmanship and conduct apply to free sparring. For beginners, hitting their partner is not stressed—instead, they are taught to use control with the techniques they are learning and to throw them with power, speed, and correct timing and form. Essentially, the student tries to apply what is learned in class in a more uncontrolled—but still safe—atmosphere.

What Is Tournament Fighting?

In the free-sparring section of a tournament, there are five judges in each ring. There is one for each corner, and a center judge who starts and stops the fight and pretty much runs the action. When a judge sees a fighter make contact with his opponent, he can stop the match and ask whether the other judges saw the technique and felt that it was thrown with balance and poise. Three out of five judges have to agree that the fighter was in control of the technique when he threw it and that contact was made. In other words, the fighter must have his composure and balance when throwing his technique and he must not throw anything wild or out of control. Even if a valid point was scored, and the majority of the judges do not see it or call it as a point, it will not count.

The other way of judging a fight is by rounds, where the judges award the win to the fighter who dominates the fight, without stopping the fight whenever a point is scored. Olympic-rules Tae Kwon Do fighting currently subscribes to this style of judging a match.

Different Types of Tournaments

There are two types of tournaments—open and close.

Open Tournaments

An open tournament is one in which anyone using any style can choose to compete against competitors in other styles and systems that are primarily striking arts. There are uniform rules that protect the fighters and do not handicap a certain striking style.

Closed Tournaments

A closed tournament is held by an organization, school, and/or specific style. It is open to competitors who are part of that organization or who practice the same style. The tournament is closed to competitors who do not belong to the organization or school or who do not practice that specific style. Or, sometimes the tournament is by invitation only.

There are many reasons someone might choose to hold a closed tournament. For instance, it could be because of organizational, political, or compatibility issues with other styles. Within these tournaments, the specific rules might not apply to certain other styles or systems. For example, a Judoka (Judo practitioner) would not know how to score a point and might be at an extreme disadvantage (with the tools he was given within his art) if he competed against a Tae Kwon Do black belt in an Olympic-style Tae Kwon Do tournament, and vice versa. Also, sometimes these tournaments are closed for political reasons—to see who is the best within that certain style, organization, or school.

Closed tournaments are usually created to highlight the sport or art that is being emphasized. Another reason for a closed tournament is for closer scrutiny of details, because the judges are also trained in that style.

Different Eras of Tournament Fighting

The following sections detail the three important eras in point-tournament fighting.

The Blood and Guts Era

In the early '60s, tournament fighting had few standardized rules. Hard and heavy contact was allowed and expected, safety equipment was not required of the competitors (nor did it exist), and a fighter was never penalized for drawing blood. A lack of movement was common among fighters during this era. Fighters during this era were known for being tough as nails. This earned the distinction as the "blood and guts" era of point fighting.

Also during this era, at Ed Parker's Long Beach Internationals tournament in 1964, an unknown martial artist performed a demonstration that eventually got him noticed by Hollywood producers. That man's name was Bruce Lee.

The Renaissance Era

Because of the void left by superstar point fighters such as Bill Wallace, Jeff Smith, Benny Urquidez, and Joe Lewis, who left the tournament circuit and went into kickboxing, there was a hole left in the sport. But in the mid to late '70s, the rules for point fighting changed for the better.

Foam-dipped safety equipment created by Jhoon Rhee was now being used by point fighters and in tournaments all over the country. Now fighters were able to make solid contact with their opponents in order to score points, without risking major injury.

In the black-belt division, solid contact was required to score a point. In theory, it was moderate contact to the body and light contact to the head, but in real life it was all-out contact to the body and moderate-to-heavy contact to the head. Groin kicks were now allowed. Sweeps and takedowns were also allowed, and fighters were given three seconds to hit an opponent while he was on the ground. This would really hurt, especially if the tournament was held at a place where the floor was concrete or hardwood. "I've knocked people out and never got disqualified. I've also seen people get their teeth knocked out, and [the person knocking their teeth out] never got disqualified," notes Keith Vitali.

A ratings system was run by both *Karate Illustrated* and *Inside Kung-Fu* magazines. And a national tournament circuit rated the top ten fighters, forms, and weapons competitors—nationally and regionally. Tournament attendance in America was at an all-time high as competitors showed up to earn points and spectators showed up to watch. Each month, somewhere in the country, there was a national tournament to which all the nation's best competitors would travel to compete to earn valuable ratings points. Previously, there was a top 10 list of national competitors listed alphabetically. Now there was a pecking order, a king of the hill, something to shoot for.

For three years between 1979 and 1981, Keith Vitali either won or placed in every major U.S. tournament and was the number-one fighter in the country (see Figures 2.2 and 2.3). He was an intellectual fighter and a technician who studied and analyzed his opponents. He always had his trusty sidekick, a lightning fast backfist, and fluid movement that frustrated and baffled his opponents and got him out of trouble when he needed it. And when Vitali beat you, he beat you with class, grace, and style. In and out of the ring, Vitali was gracious, charismatic, and articulate. He was a positive role model for upcoming black belts and a great representative of the sport. Glenn Keeney described Vitali as "someone who could beat you with just his brains alone."

Figure 2.2

Keith Vitali (right), number-one tournament fighter, 1979–1981.

Figure 2.3

Here Keith Vitali gets Steve "Nasty" Anderson with his trademark sidekick to the face.

Other famous point fighters of the era included "Super" Dan Anderson, Steve "Nasty" Anderson, Billy Blanks, Harold "Scorpion" Burrage, David Deaton, Mike Genova, Robert Harris, Larry Kelley, John Longstreet, Ray McCallum, Alvin Prouder, Bobby Tucker, and women's fighters Linda Denley and Arlene Limas.

After Vitali's era, different organizations had their own ratings and number-one fighters. Tournament organizers decided to also bar fighters from fighting the winners in different weight divisions in order to be a grand champion.

Pro Wrestling

Professional wrestling is not listed in the types or styles of fights or described as a sport or art because it is actually in an arena of its own. It is described as "sports entertainment" and is very similar to the elements of fight choreography. Pro wrestling gathers elements of acting, fight choreography, martial acting, live theater, showmanship, and simulated reality—all dealt within and around the ring. The shows are performed differently and in a different town each time.

Professional wrestling has gotten a bad rap over the decades as being cheesy, having larger-than-life dramatics in the storyline, being "too staged," using over-the-top theatrics, and not being a real "sport" because the outcomes are predetermined. I don't deny any of these allegations at all. But I would like to point out that there are similarities in the elements involved in pro wrestling and in choreographing fights for film and TV. We can learn a lot from this.

Pro wrestling is still popular and is a big business all over the world. Why is this? The general consensus is it's all fake, but millions tune in each week to watch anyway! For many fans, pro wrestling is a guilty pleasure that people only admit to their closest friends and loved ones.

Some things about pro wrestling definitely come across as "cheesy," like many of the unbelievable larger-than-life characters, the over-the-top acting, and the outrageous soap-opera-like dramas that exist in and around the ring. Then again, many action films made over the decades are equally as cheesy. But from a choreographer's perspective, I ask you to look beyond the "cheese factor" and take a closer look at what these guys are doing to entertain the crowds. Since the carnival days, pro wrestling has used a shroud of misleading information to fool the audience about what is the truth and what is fiction, much like a magician does.

We can learn a lot from watching pro wrestlers and we can apply some of their skills to film—both psychologically and physically. The techniques pro wrestlers use in the ring are designed to tell their story in a very visual way—they are geared to elicit a strong emotional response from the audience. What I am suggesting is nothing new. Borrowing ideas and moves from professional wrestling has been done since the early days of silent film, when Douglas Fairbanks Sr. would go to wrestling matches to study the moves, and then go to the set of his film and figure out how to apply what he saw to his films. This practice still continues to this day. And because of the relevance of their experience, many professional wrestlers have eventually found themselves being similarly choreographed in films and TV shows.

What Is Sports Entertainment?

Today, pro wrestling is a blend of live theatrics and competitive physical combat "exhibition." It is part of a larger narrative that leaves the viewer hanging each week with some type of emotional and/or physical cliffhanger. It hooks viewers so they tune in the next week to see what will happen to a certain character. Pro wrestling has had several monikers in the past, including "thespians in tights" and "men's soap operas."

In addition to the issue of predetermined outcomes, several other factors explain why pro wrestling is not considered a real sport, but is looked upon as sports entertainment.

- Results of the matches are not covered in the daily sports pages.
- Pro wrestling shows on television end exactly at the end of their allotted time slot. However, other sporting events, such as boxing matches, baseball games, or basketball games, can end earlier than expected or be extended beyond their time slot, depending on how the game is played.
- There are no official standings for viewers to see. You do not see a top-10 standing of pro wrestlers, like you would see for other competitive sports. You never hear an announcer tell you the next fight will be with the number-five-ranked wrestler fighting the number-one-ranked wrestler to move up in the standings. That's too boring, and there is not enough at stake. In pro wrestling, there needs to be something immediately at stake, even though the combatants who are wrestling do not hold any type of championship belt. This is where a compelling back story comes into play to emotionally lure in viewers. This back story is usually something that takes place backstage between the wrestlers, and something personal is at stake, usually pride.
- There is no official win-loss record and tale of the tape giving the stats for each wrestler when he enters the ring. However, this is standard for any type of combative sports competition.
- There are commercial breaks taken while the fight is in progress.

What Is Fake?

Wrestling has always gotten the bad rap of being "fake," but to be perfectly honest, that's not exactly a fair assessment. The wrestling term "worked" means a match has a predetermined outcome. The opposite of a worked match is a "shoot," a legitimate match between opponents. I hardly ever hear anyone say that what Bruce Lee, Jackie Chan, Chuck Norris, and their counterparts do on films is "worked," because isn't that what fight choreography is? Maybe these actors proved themselves in real life before being on film. Even if that's the case, it's not always the truth with everyone, and what does that have to do with being entertaining onscreen anyway? Many real martial artists have proven themselves through competition or have exemplary skills, but their attempts to become screen fighters have failed miserably because they do not have the screen presence or acting skills to carry a scene.

In professional wrestling, there are times when you'll see really bad matches containing bad acting, terrible storylines, and wrestlers out of sync with each other in their reactions to hits (aka bumps). For whatever reason, the match just does not come across as convincing. But if you have seen and/or been in real fights, you can tell when it's real and when it's fake. When a trained martial artist watches a wrestling match in which an opponent is caught in a simple hold that the artist learned to get out of as a beginner, it breaks the illusion for the martial artist. Or perhaps he has developed a discerning eye and he knows that the hold or move might not really have the power to match the opponent's reaction. Or maybe he knows that the stranglehold is not being applied correctly and would not have that type of effect upon the opponent. But a normal audience member without martial arts training will often be completely convinced, and of course, thoroughly entertained.

What we do in the film stunt industry is also fake or "worked," but that does not take away the element of danger involved each time we prepare for a stunt or fight. The only people who balk about what is real are staunch traditionalists or purists who don't believe that what they see in martial arts films is proper, ethical, or shows the martial art in a positive light. I feel this is very selfish and shows severe tunnel vision and self-aggrandizement of one's own stature in the martial arts community.

Watching a martial arts master demonstrate his skills in an exhibition for an audience is also "worked," because the master is not actually killing or maiming his students with his moves. He is exhibiting control, and the attacker taking the fall (usually one of his students who is not equal in skill) is also cooperating (to a certain degree) with the master so the master will not hurt him. So does that constitute being "worked?" You're damn right it does. In a real situation, the attacker would not attack in a smooth and controlled manner, using rigidly prescribed techniques, and he would not give up so easily. And in a real situation, the defender knows his life is in danger and might do something much simpler to stay alive than what his style might have officially trained him to do.

On film, a screen fighter is also displaying his skills, but for the purpose of a story or tale being told. If we break things down and look at what we see on film, it's not only the fight that is fake. The dialogue the actors speak is not natural when you really look at it. The actors' interpretation gives the words life. If we wanted films to be more representative of life, we wouldn't see movies because they are too long and slow. A movie shows the highlights of a person's life (cutting out the boring parts) and moves along to keep the general audience entertained.

The Hollywood film industry is much like the pro wrestling industry, in which hype and illusion are used to sell the product. I highly encourage you to go see a live professional wrestling match because you will see the competitors actually making solid contact on many of their moves, while "selling" the reactions to the audience live and on television. It is an entirely different experience to watch a match live as opposed to watching it on TV. At a live match, you do not have the announcers feeding you the hype of the story; you have to rely on the wrestlers to tell the story for you. Often, when you watch a match on TV, they craftily cut away to another angle when the wrestlers make contact with each other, so you do not see contact being made. This is probably so that the match can be shown on television without drawing any negative attention from conservative groups who are concerned about violence on TV.

So, yes, in terms of predetermined outcomes, professional wrestling can indeed be officially labeled as a "fake" sport, but that does not diminish the training and athleticism of the performers or the real dangers involved. Even a fake fall can end with very real impact and pain.

Pro Wrestling Comparisons to Fight Choreography for Film and Television

These next sections discuss the similarities in story and choreography between pro wrestling and fight choreography for film and TV.

Similarities in Story

Following are some of the common story elements of both forms of entertainment:

- **A willing suspension of disbelief is required.** This is probably the most important factor in both wrestling and film/TV fighting. Pro wrestling and feature film and TV fight scenes are built around a story. Proper buildup to a fight is a key in getting audiences into the fight. This helps create a willing suspension of disbelief with the audience. The better the storyline that is created around the fight, the more the audience will dismiss any flaws in the story or presentation because their emotions will override their sense of logic.

- **Injuries and deaths are faked for dramatic purposes.** The objective of faking an injury or death (mostly for film) is for dramatic story purposes and to "get over" or establish a fighter's skills for the audience. I hardly ever hear people say that what Bruce Lee or Jackie Chan did on film was fake. Bruce was not a method actor and he did not snap Chuck Norris' neck in *Way of the Dragon* for the sake of getting the shot. But we believe it is happening (to the character, but not to the actor) because we come to be entertained and we are immersed in the story and what the character is doing. Injuries and deaths are indeed faked in both fields, but this is not to say that real injuries do not occur during matches and fights. Unfortunately, serious injuries and deaths do occur in both fields.
- **Each fight has a cause and an effect and revolves around a bigger story.** There is a reason why each fight happens. And the result of the fight is woven into a bigger tapestry that is the script in film or TV and the ever-evolving story in pro wrestling.
- **There is a predetermined outcome.** A predetermined outcome has been established to serve the story that is being told. This is shown in the script for film or TV and culminates at the end of the fight or story.
- **Hype is generated.** Audience anticipation is an important tool in engaging an audience. This can be done through story development, character motivation and behavior, and media promotion.
- **Established rules are meant to be broken.** In pro wrestling, a wrestler hits his opponent with a steel chair while the referee is not looking or cheats to get the advantage. In TV and film, rules are set up and broken as well. Luke Skywalker promises Yoda he will stay on Dagobah to finish his training, but he leaves to rescue Han, Chewbacca, and Princess Leia shortly thereafter.

  In *The Transporter*, Frank Martin promises his client that he will not look in the trunk of his car to see what is inside as he makes his delivery. But shortly thereafter, Martin hears a noise in the trunk and breaks his promise.

Similarities in Choreography

Following are the similarities in how fights are put together in pro wrestling and in fight choreography for television and film.

- **A choreographed fight tells a story for entertainment purposes.** The fights have to support a story, character arcs, and fight strategy to entertain the audience. A well-staged or well-choreographed fight tells a story about the characters and the reasons why they are fighting. Both pro wrestling and fight choreography for TV and film tell non-verbal stories with their fights. In film, this is also supported by the reasons that led up to the conflict. In pro wrestling, the same applies, but it's more with the backstage drama than with what the wrestlers bring into the ring.

- **Certain techniques require the cooperation or assistance of their opponents (or others) to successfully sell the move to the audience.** There are certain techniques that need assistance or cooperation from the opponent to look effective in the wrestling ring. A perfect example is a suplex. You need the opponent's assistance to make that technique work. You also need the opponent to react properly in order to sell the technique. In fight choreography, the same principles apply. An example is the use of wires to sell a big reaction to a hit that the screen fighter cannot do himself. You need the assistance of wire pullers off-screen, as well as a convincing strike from your attacker, to help make the move look effective onscreen.
- **Performers have gotten badly injured and have died.** Unfortunately, this is one of the dangers of both businesses. You don't hear much about it in the news when it happens in the film industry, but it does happen.
- **They live again to fight another day.** Even though a wrestler has been leveled by his opponent, he is able to get back up and fight again in another town the next day. The same goes for the screen fighter on a film or TV show. He might have to do the same fight scene several times because of bad takes and coverage from different angles. There is an art to making a fighter *look as if* he has taken a beating, as opposed to *really* taking a beating. Losing a fight in real life, on the other hand, can incapacitate a fighter for several minutes, days, months, or in some cases, even permanently.
- **There are trademark or signature moves.** Each wrestler has some kind of trademark move that is part of his personality and separates and individualizes him from the other wrestlers. Rey Mysterio Jr. has his 619. RVD has his spin kicks and five-star frog splash. Screen fighters have the same types of trademarks, signature moves, or favorite weapons. James Braddock has his left hook punch. Indiana Jones has his bull whip. James Bond has his PPK Walther gun. Luke Skywalker has the Force and his light saber. Captain Hook has a hook to replace his hand.
- **Each participant and match has an individual and a collective rhythm, respectively.** The style, skill, and motivation to fight creates each wrestler's individual rhythm. That individual rhythm, combined with an opponent's individual rhythm, makes the collective rhythm of the match. The same applies to screen fighters.
- **There are different styles of fights, and they are not just relegated to the ring.** In pro wrestling, there are many different types of matches to keep things exciting for the audience, such as ladder matches, battle royals, steel cage matches, extreme hardcore matches, and so on.

- **Some wrestlers/screen fighters cannot fight or lack wrestling or fighting skills.** In pro wrestling, some characters are great at hyping up a fight with pre-fight interviews, playing to the crowd, and getting an audience on their side and into a frenzy with their stage presence. But when it comes down to reality, some wrestlers do not have any physical fighting skills or are very limited in what they can do. Some might not know the difference between a headlock and a head of lettuce. But audiences want to see these wrestlers because they are captivating.

  Believe it or not, the same applies on film and TV. Some actors closely associated with action and martial arts lack the skill and understanding to fight and practice in real life, or they fight onscreen by using a stunt double. And when these actors are onscreen, they rely on up-close camera angles and editing to obscure their moves and tune up their speed and timing to give the audience the illusion that they are able to fight. But in reality, these actors are not agile or well-coordinated and they cannot put together a simple combination and make it look convincing. Or, sometimes they are simply too slow. And unfortunately, some of these actors end up believing their own hype, thinking they are some type of bad ass in real life.

The Differences

Following are some of the issues that make a pro wrestler's job more difficult than working on film.

- **There is only one take in wrestling.** The wrestler is playing in front of a live audience and is given only one take to get it right. However, a good, seasoned wrestler can cover up his mistakes without the audience knowing. But some audiences are very well aware of when a pro wrestler misses a cue or makes a mistake. In the ECW, the legendary faithful and hardcore audience will uniformly chant "You f---ed up!" when a wrestler messes up a move. The luxury with TV and film is that the fighter has several takes to get the stunt right, as well as to get coverage from different angles of the stunt.
- **A wrestler is playing to and selling moves to two different audiences.** A wrestler has to be aware of the live audience and the TV cameras, playing to both of them. This creates a dilemma for the wrestler and affects primarily the TV audience. When you see the event live, the wrestlers take the stage and play it "big" for the audience, projecting their performance all the way up into the nosebleed seats of the huge arena to get everyone involved. This is the same as watching a live theatrical performance of any type involving actors in a large venue. However, when a performance is being taped by a camera only a few feet away from the wrestlers, live theatrical performance appears over the top or is perceived by the TV viewers as overacting. On film the stunt

fighter plays to a camera (or sometimes to several cameras) and projects in a manner that is effective only to the camera. This is probably why you don't see many live Broadway shows and performances sold on home video—the acting for a live audience seems overdone on camera.

- **There is no stunt double in wrestling.** There is no such thing as a stunt double for a pro wrestler. Wrestlers are required to do everything from giving their pre-fight interviews, to choreographing their matches, to performing the matches for the audience. But in film or TV, an actor has the option of having several stunt doubles—each one for a specific skill that is needed. It's often possible that an actor does not raise a finger to do anything physical on a TV show or film; he may leave it up to his stunt doubles to do all the action. This is because the production cannot take a chance on the actor getting injured; they risk losing insurance coverage or precious shooting time and money each day the actor is out.
- **For wrestling there are a limited number of locations.** Usually a majority of the fight takes place in and around the ring (in the arena) for the live audience to respond and react. Because locations are very limited, wrestlers have gotten very creative over the years. The audience always wants to see something new, and it is up to the individuality, imagination, character persona, and contrasting styles of each wrestler to make each fight exciting and as new as possible given the weekly situation. Wrestlers have had fights outside the ring and in other places, such as alleys, locker rooms, offices, and so on. But this is still limited in comparison to film and TV. In film, you can shoot anywhere in the world—and, through the magic of CGI, even in places that don't exist.
- **Wrestlers are required to perform and stage their own fights.** Even though wrestlers are told the outcome of the match beforehand, they are responsible for putting together the physical moves with their opponent/partner and leading the audience to the predetermined ending. In film and TV, the choreography is left up to the stunt coordinator or the fight choreographer. The actor does have to give his input on the fight, but he is not responsible for preparing and preventing dangerous situations. Also, in professional wrestling, certain performers will occasionally improvise moves, which almost never happens in TV or film fight choreography.
- **In wrestling, the timing and rhythm of the fight are based on fighters' skills.** In film or TV, the timing and rhythm are greatly affected by editing, special effects, stunt doubles, and camera angles. In pro wrestling, the timing and rhythm of the match are based on the efforts put together by the wrestlers involved. Editing and camera angles assist the wrestlers, but they cannot drastically change what is happening live (experienced by the audience) at that moment.

- **Wrestling matches are shorter than filming a fight scene.** Wrestling matches are performed much like a stage play because when they start, there is no stopping the match because a wrestler messes up or gets hurt. There are no mulligans in professional wrestling because there is a live audience to whom the wrestlers are playing. The longest match could be about an hour. But with film, the whole fight scene is usually never shot from beginning to end in one shot. Rather, it is shot in segments. A fight scene could take 90 days to shoot depending on its length and complexity.

The point I am making is that fight choreography in film and TV is probably more "fake" than what we see in pro wrestling. Pro wrestling dances on a fine line each time it airs on TV and can fall on the side of great dramatic spectacle/physical exhibition or onto the side of cheesy, implausible, and unrealistic grandstanding. The same goes for film, but it is not as easily noticeable because in film there are more smoke and mirrors, such as editing and CGI, to divert the audience's attention. Also, when watching a film or TV show, audience members agree to suspend their disbelief for the sake of entertainment, but in the professional wrestling world, many fans actually believe (or have managed to convince themselves) that what they are seeing is entirely real, and will defend that claim with tooth and nail.

A Brief History of Pro Wrestling

Believe it or not, professional wrestling started out as a legitimate sport in the United States. Irish immigrants would actually wrestle to resolve many of their differences. During the nineteenth century, Irish settlers came to the United States and settled in the Vermont area, bringing wrestling along with them. Presidents George Washington, Zachary Taylor, and William Howard Taft were all wrestlers. But the one who stands out the most is Abraham Lincoln, who reportedly had 300 matches to his credit. During the Civil War, wrestling was a way to pass the time between battles for both sides.

It was during the post–Civil War era that professional wrestling got its start here in America, because when the veterans who learned to wrestle came home, they would wrestle at county fairs and have matches in small towns for money. At the turn of the twentieth century, wrestling became an established international sport with the help of newspapers and magazines. Other sports, such as baseball, were just beginning to make themselves known, while football and basketball had not yet caught on with a national audience. Each country had its wrestling champions, and promoters wanted to establish a champion in America, dreaming of the money they would rake in.

In 1901, Estonia-born George Hackenschmidt (aka the Russian Lion) was considered unbeatable, even though he had only one move—a bear hug and an inside trip. He was so strong that he won every weight-lifting tournament in Europe and Russia, did strongman exhibitions, and had the same agent as actress Sarah Bernhardt. Needless to say, Hackenschmidt reigned supreme all across Europe and was considered unbeatable by everyone. He came to the United States in 1908 to wrestle with Frank Gotch, the American champion. The match between Gotch and Hackenschmidt was considered a high point of professional wrestling as a competitive sport. The first match, which lasted for two hours and three minutes, ended when Gotch applied his step over toe hold, forcing Hackenschmidt to surrender his world title belt to Gotch. After the match, Hackenschmidt told the media Gotch won the match by oiling his body so he could easily slip out of his holds.

In 1911, 33,000 people showed up at Chicago's newly built Comiskey Park to see the rematch between Gotch and Hackenschmidt. At the time, it was the largest crowd ever to attend a sporting event (other than horse racing) in America. To improve his chances of winning, Gotch gave $5,000 to Ad Santel, a fierce German wrestler (known as a "hooker"), to seriously injure Hackenschmidt in a training match before the fight was to take place. Santel got Hackenschmidt into a step over toe hold and ruined his knee. Needless to say, the fight between Gotch and Hackenschmidt was just a formality and ended pretty quickly—within 20 minutes, to the disappointment of the audience. Gotch's actions to secure the fight were soon discovered by newspapers and magazines, which quickly expressed their disillusionment with "the fix" to their readers. As a result, professional wrestling's popularity started to decline.

However, this decline wasn't all because of Gotch's underhanded actions; it was also because the matches were too slow and scientific and they went on too long. A single match would last for more than five hours! Gotch retired four years later, undefeated as world champion; however, newspapers were no longer interested in covering pro wrestling, and it was considered a dead sport.

The concept of professional wrestling as a form of entertainment got its start from the carnivals that traveled across the country just after the Civil War ended. These carnivals would have athletic shows in which wrestling was a popular part of the program. These carnivals were run and operated by showmen and often conmen, who were much more interested in making money from the audience than in promoting a legitimate competitive sport. The organizers of the athletic shows created colorful costumes and made up fictional biographies for the wrestlers in order to generate publicity and get the audience interested in coming to see the show.

In the athletic shows, the wrestlers would stage exhibition bouts with each other for entertainment. As a part of the show the wrestlers would accept challenges from anyone in the audience, taking on all comers. But every once in a while, they would encounter a local in the audience who could really wrestle. To avoid losing their established false credibility and, more importantly, their money, the organizers would have what is known as a "hooker" in their troupe.

In the athletic show wrestling hierarchy, at the top of the heap was a hooker—an experienced pro wrestler who could easily tie up or cripple an opponent with legal or illegal techniques. Hookers were the most feared and respected men in the troupe—they would take on any and all challengers. Below the hooker was the "shooter"—a competent wrestler who usually came from amateur wrestling and could hold his own in a real competitive contest, but who was still learning the performance aspects of the business. Often a hooker was mistaken for a shooter. A hooker could be a shooter, but a shooter could not be a hooker because of his lack of experience. Underneath the shooters were the "journeymen"—the ones who had little or no real wrestling experience. Journeymen were usually ex-football players or sideshow strongmen. They would perform as the fool or strongman in matches with the more experienced shooters.

By the beginning of the twentieth century, these showmen started opening up offices, calling themselves promoters, establishing territories, and booking wrestling exhibitions, much like they would a vaudeville show. The first two things a promoter would do when he opened a territory were to declare a champion and rent out an office space. Because of the control and monopoly the promoters had over pro wrestling, the competitive aspect of the sport no longer existed, although the audience still could not tell whether it was real or fake. But to get the audiences to go to their shows, the promoters knew that something had to be at stake, and that was usually a title belt.

Ed "Strangler" Lewis, born Robert Julius Friedrich, a carnie wrestler from Nekoosa, Wisconsin, toured Europe from 1910 to 1915. He was nicknamed by the press in France as *L 'Estrangleur* for the sleeper hold he would put on his opponents to look like he was strangling them. When he came home to the United States in 1915, Lewis was already an established international celebrity. His reputation from Europe as a dangerous hooker easily preceded him and, as a result, the East Coast wrestling promoters took Lewis as a threat to their business and did not want to work with him. This was because Lewis could easily beat any of their wrestlers and could take over and completely dominate any territory in which he wrestled.

As a result, Lewis went to Chicago to team up with manager Billy Sandow and Joseph Raymond "Toots" Mondt to form the Gold Dust Trio. Sandow was a shrewd negotiator and businessman. Mondt, a wrestler, was an innovator who revolutionized how wrestling was seen by the audience. He felt the audience could not appreciate scientific wrestling and the matches needed to be shorter and more exciting, so he introduced time limits and developed a series of spectacular, flashy, crowd-pleasing moves that are still used in pro wrestling today. He called this "Slam-Bang Western-Style Wrestling."

The threesome also developed the first storylines, creating "worked" feuds between the wrestlers. And they initiated several matches as the undercards before the main event, as opposed to having just one long match. They also packaged a stable of wrestlers that would travel from town to town in their territory. At their peak during the 1920s, the team had 500 wrestlers under contract.

In 1921, "Strangler" Lewis wrestled and defeated Joe Stecher in a legitimate contest to win the world heavyweight title. Lewis, Sandow, and Mondt knew that audiences would get fickle and eventually bored if Lewis held his title for too long. So, in order to keep the patrons interested, they kept the title belt moving between promoters or territories as a device to garner more interest in their matches. The promoters could afford to do this because they knew Lewis could win back the title belt whenever he felt like it.

During this era, "Handsome" Jim Londos, an average but popular wrestler, could draw a crowd by his handsome looks alone. Londos came to America from Greece as a teenager and started work as a vaudeville strongman before he became a wrestler. Londos was one of the first wrestling personalities to create a wrestler's gimmick—a unique trait that defines the wrestler's identity and persona to separate him from other wrestlers. Londos handpicked the ugliest wrestlers to go up against, creating a visual contrast and using the "Beauty and the Beast" concept. As a result, Londos' gimmick would almost single-handedly draw women audience members into the wrestling arena.

The '30s proved to be difficult economically for America, and wrestling suffered along with the country. To make matters worse, New York promoter Jack Pfefer was edged out by the other promoters in his territory. Enraged and vengeful, wanting to get back at the promoters, Pfefer went to the New York sports writers and exposed all of pro wrestling's secrets. The sports writers revealed what Pfefer had to say and, as a result, the box office gate dropped to next to nothing. With the Depression about to begin, the final nail in professional wrestling's coffin was hammered in when a drunken press agent sent to the newspapers the results of a wrestling match that would take place the next day!

In 1936, "Strangler" Lewis wrestled a workout match in St. Louis with a young man by the name of Aloysius Martin Thesz (a.k.a. Lou Thesz), who made his professional debut at the age of 16 and first trained under George Tragos, then Ad Santel. Lewis felt Thesz had the ring savvy and the charisma to be a champion and decided to manage his career. In 1937, Thesz went on to win the world heavyweight title at the young age of 21 (still a record to this day).

Even with a wrestler of Lou Thesz's caliber, professional wrestling was at an all-time low. In 1938, a wrestling show at Madison Square Garden drew less than 5,000 people, and it would be a long while before wrestling would come back there. However, Lewis's instincts were right about Thesz, who went on to hold more than 19 world titles with 936 consecutive wins throughout his career. He continued wrestling consistently into the 1960s and occasionally into the '70s and '80s. Thesz's last match was on December 26, 1990, in Japan, at the age of 74, where he wrestled and lost to his own student, Masahiro Chono.

By the 1940s, no one wanted to see pro wrestling anymore, and the matches took place in half-empty clubs and beer halls. Unfortunately, radio is not a medium made for wrestling, so other sports such as baseball and football took precedence with the public. After World War II, with the introduction of the television for mass public consumption, professional wrestling was resurrected. But in the late 1940s, not everyone had a TV set. It averaged out that one person for each block had a TV set. And, stores would have a TV set turned on in their display windows, where people would gather around in the streets to watch. So watching TV was very much a communal experience, and people would gather around the set and watch wrestling.

At the time, TV and wrestling made great partners because wrestling was cheap, easy, and inexpensive programming. Because of TV, wrestling made major changes. Before television, it took a good six months to introduce a new character to the audience, but with TV it took only two weeks. Characters became much more outrageous and flamboyant to get the audience's attention. Another way that TV changed pro wrestling was with on-camera interviews with the wrestlers. Now TV viewers could get to know the wrestlers up close and personal, as the wrestlers told their stories right to the viewers before and after the matches. Interviews continue to be an integral part of a wrestler's repertoire in promoting his matches and personality. They also added another dimension to the entertainment aspect of a wrestler's performance. Interestingly, with the inception of television, world champion Lou Thesz was the most watched man on TV.

At this time, the lines between heroes (aka "baby faces" or "faces") and villains (aka "heels") in the ring became more played up with theatrics and outrageous characters that were larger than life. The first and biggest superstar from the early television era was with George Wagner, a psychiatrist and journeyman wrestler who bleached his hair blonde and went by the name of Gorgeous George. He was a vain and villainous character audiences loved to hate. He would enter the ring, tossing gold hairpins at the audience, acting like a prima donna to his opponent and the audience. He didn't want to be touched by anyone before the match. If you touched him, he'd scream out loud for the whole audience to hear, "Get your filthy hands off of me!" Wagner was an expert emotional manipulator at bringing the audience into the match—or "getting over." Gorgeous George also inspired and influenced a young up-and-coming boxer who started imitating his outrageous behavior by saying things like, "I'm so pretty, I deserve to be champion." This earned the boxer the nickname the "Louisville Lip." That athlete was none other than Muhammad Ali.

In the 1950s, most wrestlers primarily stayed on their feet and grappled. But Antonio "Argentine" Rocca was one of the first "high-flyers," using aerial techniques to show speed and agility. High-flying techniques were generally used by smaller wrestlers who were not able to do power moves. Rocca used them to capture the imagination of the fans. He would taunt his opponents by slapping them with the side of his foot. Rocca's appearance pretty much guaranteed a sellout because of his flamboyant acrobatic style of wrestling.

World Wrestling Entertainment (WWE)

After the dissolution of the Gold Dust Trio over issues of power, Toots Mondt booked matches in NYC with several other bookers, including Roderick James "Jess" McMahon, a boxing promoter whose past achievements included co-promotion of the Jack Johnson versus Jess Willard fight in 1915. Together, the men formed Capitol Wrestling Corporation (CWC) and joined the National Wrestling Alliance (NWA) in 1953 to cover the Northwest part of the country, while bringing in Vincent J. McMahon, Sr. to replace his father.

The team of Mondt and McMahon proved to be such a success that within a short time they controlled 70 percent of NWA's bookings. However a dispute between NWA and CWC occurred when they let the NWA Champion "Nature Boy" Buddy Rogers travel out of CWC's territory, only to lose his title belt to Lou Thez on January 24, 1963 in Toronto. Leaving the NWA in protest, Mondt and McMahon created the World Wide Wrestling Federation (WWWF). In March of 1979, they changed the name to the World Wrestling Federation (WWF) for cosmetic reasons.

In 1980, McMahon Sr.'s son, Vincent K. McMahon, Jr., bought the business from his father. The younger McMahon fundamentally changed the sport by expanding operations and breaking the unwritten law of regionalism, which had been a foundation for more than 50 years, by distributing and selling videotapes (for home video and to television stations) across the country and using the profits to attract the best wrestlers from other territories. His first acquisition was AWA champion Hulk Hogan, and then Roddy Piper as Hogan's nemesis to establish national notoriety. He also acquired other popular wrestlers, such as Jesse Ventura, Ricky Steamboat, Jimmy Snuka, the Iron Sheik, and Andre "the Giant," to name a few.

McMahon wanted to bring the WWF into the nation's consciousness by targeting the mainstream audience who were not currently wrestling fans. He got celebrities involved with WrestleMania on March 31, 1985, at Madison Square Garden. This so-called "Super Bowl" of pro wrestling was a huge success and was broadcast on Pay-Per-View and closed-circuit TV. It is now a yearly event that follows the Hall of Fame induction ceremony for legendary wrestlers. In 2002, the company finally changed its name to World Wrestling Entertainment (WWE) after losing a legal battle with the World Wildlife Fund (WWF) over the acronym.

McMahon Jr.'s dream of making his company a nationally recognized brand did not stop there. The WWE is now a globally recognized sports entertainment company. Their wrestlers travel to put on events all over the world, are as popular as rock stars, and are seen on TV several times a week, with monthly Pay-Per-View events that lead up to the annual crown jewel of wrestling—WrestleMania. Up-and-coming wrestlers aspire to be on the WWE roster, knowing that if they are offered a WWE contract, they are considered the best of the best.

Extreme Championship Wrestling (ECW)

This organization was started by Tod Gordon in 1992 as Eastern Championship Wrestling, but it legally changed to Extreme Championship Wrestling when they broke off as an affiliate of NWA. ECW changed its format when booker Paul Heyman came to it and created extreme hardcore matches that essentially had no rules. They were "anything goes" matches, in which the referee was essentially there to count out a pinfall or submission.

Heyman was also responsible for bringing back more technical matches. He introduced Lucha Libre to America (outside of the smaller independent leagues) with Rey Mysterio, Konnan, and Psychosis, and bloody, violent, hardcore matches that included barbed wire matches and flaming table matches. He also hired wrestlers who were deemed "too dangerous" by the two multimillion-dollar companies—WWF (now WWE) and WCW—and made them stars. Older wrestlers and purists felt the extreme hardcore approach was not true wrestling and that it was just a gimmick. Whatever stance one takes, ECW has definitely raised the level of expectations with audiences.

As a result, ECW developed an extremely devoted and rowdy audience that was very educated about their wrestling and would be quite vocal if a wrestler attempted to "get over" the audience with a gimmick to hide his lack of skills in the ring. The audience also had specific and distinctive chants, such as "You f---ed up!" when a wrestler had a "blown spot" (a maneuver that did not go as planned). The audience would also taunt a wrestler of whom they didn't approve. For example, they chanted, "You still suck" and "You can't wrestle" to WWE champion John

Cena when he wrestled longtime ECW fan favorite Rob Van Dam in *ECW: One-Night Stand 2006.* (They also posted banners all over the arena saying, "If Cena wins, we riot!") The popularity of these chants has carried over to other wrestling venues outside of WWE and ECW.

Heyman compared ECW in wrestling to the grunge movement in music: He considered old-school traditional wrestling passé, much like the "hair bands" of the 1980s, while ECW was like the cutting-edge grunge movement. He definitely shook up the old-school mentality and created a cult following for ECW by bringing in a more extreme, hardcore, physical style of wrestling to his shows, where the wrestlers performed dangerous and spectacular moves that other organizations would not allow. The wrestlers were also given the freedom to be creative and express themselves and their characters in their matches, no matter how extreme or violent they chose to be, without the imposition of rigid time limits, as in the bigger organizations. Rob Van Dam was the TV champion for an astonishing 23 months and constantly had to find ways to come up with new moves to keep his audience interested every time he would enter the ring. As a result, the extremely athletic wrestler has arguably more signature and finishing moves than any other wrestler working today. Some of the other wrestlers who were popular with ECW were Sabu, Tommy Dreamer, Sandman, Al Snow, Taz, and Raven.

ECW went bankrupt in 2001, and their assets were bought by the WWE in 2003. WWE resurrected the brand in 2006 to complement the *Raw!* and *SmackDown* weekly shows.

Hooking the Audience

Pro wrestling has elements that psychologically hook the audience into the drama of the fight in the ring.

Good versus Evil

Watching pro wrestling is much like watching a morality play in which we see the battle between good and evil unfold and we witness its results. We don't get tired of it because it is something we want to see happen. We want to see the bad guy (heel) get his comeuppance for taking advantage of the honest wrestler (face) who plays by the rules. The heel might not get his payback right away, but it can build up over a series of matches to get the audience "over" until the villain finally gets what he truly deserves. This is why we see many parents bringing their kids to see Lucha Libre events (where good vs evil is the central theme)—they feel there are lessons their children can learn while being entertained.

Replicating Life Events

As the stories evolve, one of the keys to why pro wrestling has been so successful is that it is a reflection of the events of our everyday lives played out in the ring. But in real life, many things happen that we do not have control over, and we don't always get to see people get retribution the way we feel it should happen. But often with pro wrestling, we get to see justice served for things we know are not right in the world. It is like a morality play because we are able to see events unfold the way we desperately want them to happen.

Guy LaRose, a wrestler from Quebec, became one of the most hated heels in the '50s and wrestled by the name of Hans Schmidt—a German who hated Americans right after WWII and would insult the American audience as he walked into the ring. The same happened around the Iran hostage crisis. Sgt. Slaughter fought the Iron Sheik three years after the end of the crisis, in 1984.

Corporate takeover of companies and upper management's arrogance and insensitivity toward their employees have also been replicated in pro wrestling, when Vince McMahon, the owner of the WWE, got into the picture by playing the heel after the collapse of the rival company WCW. He started the "Kiss My Ass" club, in which wrestlers and other company members literally had to kiss his rear in the middle of the ring to keep their jobs.

Building Up the Audience's Anticipation

A good wrestler and booker can create anticipation with an audience and finally give them what they want...and then some. A great wrestler can get the audience's emotions in the palm of his hand and play them like a world-class concert violinist. This is called *ring psychology*. This can also be accomplished by having the impatient audience wait for the wrestler to execute his signature move on his opponents. Eddie Guerrero, Hulk Hogan, and Gorgeous George are examples of wrestlers who have good ring psychology.

Blurring the Lines of Reality and Entertainment

Ever since the carnie days, pro wrestling has blurred the lines between what is real, what is fake, and the events between with varying levels of effectiveness. And this practice continues to this day, with a more skeptical audience questioning whether something is true, requiring bookers to continually find creative ways to manipulate the audience's emotions so they will tune in each week or come down to the nearest auditorium to see the matches. It's not the fact that someone won or lost—the more important underlying question here is, "Were we entertained?"

A great example of blurring the lines between entertainment and reality is late Hollywood actor/comedian Andy Kaufman, who had a real dislike for telling jokes as traditionally understood and agreed between performer and the audience. He was more interested in evoking a real emotional reaction from the audience than making them laugh. A huge wrestling fan since childhood, Kaufman extrapolated his comedic perceptions into the wrestling arena by playing the ultimate heel, acting like a pompous and elitist Hollywood male chauvinist, and the self-proclaimed "Inter-gender Wrestling Champion of the World." He challenged any woman to wrestle him and would give the woman $1,000 and a wedding proposal if she could pin him. He would also enrage the audience by telling them how dumb they were and that he was smarter than them because he was from Hollywood and could make people believe that he was that lovable foreign character Latka Gravas on the TV show, "Taxi."

This eventually led to the year-long "feud" between Kaufman and pro wrestler Jerry "The King" Lawler, who was sick of seeing women humiliated by Kaufman. This hit the proverbial fan when Kaufman beat Foxy, a woman wrestler who was trained by Lawler. Kaufman continued humiliating her after the match. Lawler had enough and came to her rescue, pushing Kaufman off her. Lawler challenged Kaufman, who threatened to sue, but later accepted Lawler's challenge.

On April 5, 1982, in the Mid-South Coliseum in Memphis, Tennessee, Lawler was finally able to get Kaufman in the ring. After about five minutes of Kaufman's incessant taunting of Lawler and the audience, Lawler let Kaufman into the ring to apply a headlock on him, which Lawler immediately reversed on Kaufman, getting him into a suplex, followed by two pile-drivers. Lawler broke Kaufman's neck; Kaufman was taken out of the arena on a stretcher and rushed to the hospital. Kaufman won the fight by DQ (disqualification) because the pile-driver is considered an illegal technique.

On July 28, 1982, Kaufman and Lawler appeared on *Late Night with David Letterman* to settle their differences. Kaufman appeared in a neck brace and apologized for his actions, asking for an apology from Lawler in return. Lawler refused, which sent Kaufman on a tirade about how he could have sued him for millions of dollars, but did not. Lawler stood up from his chair and slapped Kaufman so hard that it knocked him off his chair. Kaufman got angry and cursed him, but most of the tirade had to be censored. Kaufman threw a cup of coffee on Lawler and ran away. NBC threatened to ban Kaufman from ever appearing on the station again. Kaufman threatened to sue NBC for $200 million, then buy the network and turn it into a 24-hour wrestling network. This event caused such a controversy and gathered so much heat that it made the front page of the *New York Times.* The angle between the two continued as Kaufman offered a $5,000 bounty to any wrestler who could administer a pile-driver to Lawler.

Other celebrities much more famous than Kaufman would later get involved in the world of wrestling, but none were as intriguing and unconventional. Kaufman went on to take part in a parody of *My Dinner with Andre* titled *My Breakfast with*

Blassie, in which Andy had breakfast with wrestler "Classy" Freddie Blassie and they talked about wrestling and life.

Kaufman died of cancer on May 16, 1984. Lawler continued his wrestling career and has been the commentator for the WWF (and later WWE) since the mid '90s. The Kaufman-Lawler feud was later recreated in *Man on the Moon*, with Jim Carrey portraying Andy and Lawler as himself, exposing the feud between the two as a put-on.

There are other examples of real events that blur reality and made up "high concept" drama. One good, stranger-than-fiction example is Tonya Harding's attempts to derail rival Nancy Kerrigan at the 1994 U.S. Figure Skating Championships by allegedly conspiring to break her kneecaps. Another example is Dennis Rodman's outrageous off-court behavior (such as wearing a wedding dress to his own book signing). Then there's pro basketball player Ron Artest going into the stands and brawling with spectators. And who can forget Mike Tyson biting off part of Evander Holyfield's ear in the middle of their second fight? These are some examples of real events that continue to blur reality and make up "high concept" drama. These types of events make the public scratch their heads, not knowing what to think—is it real or made up? It really makes the drama that is written into pro wresting seem somewhat tame compared to what is happing in real life, doesn't it? Is art imitating life, or vice versa?

Pro Wrestling Outside America

Pro wrestling is popular worldwide. But wrestling varies in its approach because of the culture and the time it was brought to the public's awareness. Following is a basic history and the people who have made wrestling popular in Mexico and Japan.

Lucha Libre

Although wrestling already existed in Mexico, it really did not take off until 1933, when Salvador Lutteroth created Empresa Mexicana de Lucha Libre (EMLL). Lutteroth created EMLL because he was sick and tired of chasing down payments from clients for his furniture store in Mexico City. He wanted a business that would have immediate profits and one in which he would not have to lend any type of goods to anyone. The former paymaster in General Álvaro Obregón's army remembered that when he was on assignment in Texas, he was very impressed by a wrestling match.

Lutteroth started by renting out the Arena Modelo, a rundown and abandoned arena where boxing matches used to be held. At first the matches drew small crowds. But when he hired wrestler Ray Ryan from the United States; Lutteroth's business really took off. He immediately started to book wrestlers from the United States, Italy, and Japan for his shows while developing Mexican idols from local talent.

He constantly packed in crowds for each show, so he decided to open a bigger arena. The Arena Coliseo was inaugurated on April 2, 1943, when Tarzan Lopez beat El Santo for the world middleweight championship. Now, homegrown Mexican Luchadores have become popular throughout the country, and smaller arenas have popped up everywhere. By the time Arena Coliseo's tenth anniversary came around, a bigger venue was needed, and Lutteroth built Arena Mexico.

As its own unique form of sports entertainment, Lucha Libre has evolved over the years with its own style, intricately woven into the Hispanic culture, myth, and folklore. It is now known for being very fast-paced and for its high-flying, daredevil, acrobatic maneuvers coupled with intricate and complex moves compared to its American counterpart. Because of the acrobatic and extremely agile nature required of Lucha Libre, the wrestlers are not as physically big as American wrestlers. The battle between good and evil is usually the theme of the matches, while national pride (especially when battling foreign opponents) and a wrestler's personal honor are the underlying subtext of many of the matches.

Over the years, many American wrestlers, such as Dean Malenko and Chris Benoit, have journeyed south of the border to pay their dues and hone their craft before coming back to the United States. The style of Lucha Libre and the Luchadores have also expanded into American wrestling and influenced the style. Although El Santo and the Blue Demon have made appearances in the States, Lucha Libre made a huge impact on American wrestling fans when it was introduced in ECW (and later WCW), eventually making its way into WWE. Luchadores such as Rey Mysterio, Jr. and the late Eddie Guerrero have gained immense popularity in the United States, with both winning WWE world heavyweight championship titles at separate times, opening the door for other Luchadores to be seen by a wider audience.

Lucha Libre was highlighted on a TV episode of *Angel* titled "The Cautionary Tale of Numero Cinco" and has even spawned a kids' cartoon called *Mucha Lucha.*

What's with the Masks?

The masks worn by the Luchadores in the early days were simple, with different colors to distinguish between the different wrestlers. But as Lucha Libre progressed, the masks got more elaborate and creative, representing animals, gods, ancient heroes, and other archetypes. They were usually somewhat based on modern or ancient folklore, such as a comic-book superhero or a warrior or hero drawn from Aztec, Mayan, or Christian legends that the Luchador represents and personifies during his matches to help create his character.

It is an incredible dishonor for a wrestler to lose his mask and show his identity in the ring. During his career, a masked Luchador is extremely protective and secretive about his identity under his mask—only his family can see him without his mask. This usually means that wherever the Luchador goes outside of his house, he still dons his mask—even if he's going to a family wedding. Only when the Luchador is about to retire will he be unmasked, signifying the Luchador's loss of identity with that character. There are "Máscara Contra Máscara" (mask versus mask) matches in which two masked Luchadores battle in the ring, and the loser has to take off his mask and expose his true identity to the audience. If a Luchador does not wear a mask, he has to shave the hair off his head. Naturally, the Luchador who is able to keep his mask on (or keep his hair) the longest gains popularity and establishes prestige among the class of wrestlers.

Figure 2.4

Dealers sell replica masks of their favorite Luchadores in front of the Olympic Auditorium in Los Angeles, California, before a Lucha Libre event.

The only exception was El Santo, a much-revered, legendary wrestler who continued to wear his mask after retirement, only revealing his face to the public in old age. When El Santo died, he was buried with his mask on—a great example of the character transcending the person. The enigma of El Santo was so popular that his son now wears the famed silver mask.

The Luchadores

This section describes a few of the legendary and colorful Luchadores in Lucha Libre history.

Figure 2.5

Two kids wearing masks of their favorite Luchadores before going in to cheer them on.

El Santo (The Saint)

Following in the footsteps of his three brothers, Rodolfo Guzmán Huerta (1917–1984) started training in Jiu-Jitsu and Greco-Roman wrestling and made his pro wrestling debut at age 16 on June 28, 1934. He was not very successful in the beginning. He tried out several aliases before settling on "El Santo" (the Saint) eight years later.

El Santo did several things that made him a cultural icon. He changed from being a "Rudo" to a "Technico" in the early '60s, before finally retiring in 1982. He starred in 52 action movies that were popular in almost every Spanish-speaking nation, and he was the central character of a weekly comic book series that lasted 35 years. No one knew his real identity until he unmasked himself on TV in 1984 and died a week later of a heart attack. Because of his career that lasted more than 40 years, El Santo was more than just a Luchador. He is a cultural icon, a folk hero, and a symbol of truth and justice for the everyday man.

El Demonio Azul (The Blue Demon)

Alejandro Muñoz Moreno (1922–2000) was trained by Mexican wrestler Roland Vega, who created the character of the Blue Demon for his student. Starting off as a Rudo in 1948, the Blue Demon then turned Technico in 1952, when El Santo beat and unmasked the Black Shadow in a mask versus mask match, sparking a legendary feud and arguably one of the most important and well-publicized matches in Lucha Libre history between the Blue Demon and El Santo. In 1953, the Blue Demon won the NWA world welterweight title from El Santo and kept the title until 1958. From 1964 to 1977, the Blue Demon starred in 25 sci-fi/horror/action films; nine of those films co-starred El Santo. The Blue Demon was arguably as popular El Santo and was his greatest rival.

Mil Máscaras (The Man of a Thousand Masks)

The character of Mil Máscaras, created by film producer Enrique Vergara, was the first Luchador created especially for the movies. The reason Vergara created the character was because El Santo walked out after a contract dispute, and Blue Demon was injured and unable to work.

Aaron Rodriguez, born in 1949, was a young, athletic man who was going to represent the Mexican Judo team at the 1964 Olympics, but backed out because he needed to make money to survive. Around that time, he heard about the character of Mil Máscaras. He auditioned and won the role, making his debut in 1965.

Blessed with the build of a bodybuilder, Mil Máscaras was the first Luchador to rule the heavyweight ranks, which was previously completely dominated by foreign wrestlers. He is truly an international superstar, having wrestled all over the world many times, winning the American heavyweight title four times between 1968 and 1971 and the IWA (U.S.) world championship in 1976. Mil Máscaras also introduced the high-flying aspects of Lucha Libre to Japanese fans and inspired future Japanese wrestlers. In Japan, he is known as Kamen Kizoku—"The Masked Noble." Mil Máscaras starred in more than 30 Mexican horror/wrestling films and was the only Luchador to star along with El Santo and his son, El Hijo del Santo.

Fray Tormenta (Friar Storm)

In 1973, Father Sergio Gutierrez Benitez found inspiration while watching the film *El Señor Tormenta*, starring Júlio Aldama as a priest who becomes a Luchador in order to save an orphanage. But Father Sergio was far from a passive pushover and transformed into a Hercules motif. He had previously earned the respect of the people of Veracruz by fighting El Pilon, the gang leader responsible for vandalizing Father Sergio's first parish.

In 1974, after 18 months of rigorous training, he made his debut as Fray Tormenta (Friar Storm), hiding his identity under a gold mask accented with scarlet-red lightning bolts alongside the face. By 1986, the sacred warrior priest had an estimated 1,000 fights under his belt. His efforts in the ring brought in enough money for him to build La Ciudad de los Niños (the City of Children), a home and sanctuary for more than 3,000 homeless children. He was even able to build his own arena, where he would wrestle opponents and hold Mass. Ironically, Fray Tormenta's life inside and out of the ring, which was inspired by a film, in turn loosely inspired the American slapstick comedy *Nacho Libre*, starring Jack Black.

Puroresu: Pro Wrestling in Japan

Pro wrestling in Japan did not become popular until after World War II. Kim Sin-Nak, a Korean who went by the name of Mitsuhiro Momota, traveled to Japan at age 15 with aspirations of becoming a Sumo wrestler. But unfortunately, the discrimination he encountered in his dojo and in his matches, along with the back-breaking demands of the sport and the constant hazing of the senior members, made him leave after 10 years of training, after finally achieving the rank of Sekiwake (two ranks below Yokozuna—meaning "wide rope"—the highest rank in Sumo).

After leaving Sumo, Sin-Nak trained in Kyokushin-kai karate under founder Mas Oyama. During this time, he was discovered by Bobby Bruns, an American wrestler touring Japan with a group of American and Japanese wrestlers. Bruns also discovered another talented wrestler, Rikidozan, and wrestled him at his professional debut on October 28, 1951 to a draw. Bruns immediately signed him up and took him to Hawaii. Rikidozan wrestled more than 260 matches, losing only five. He returned to Japan two years later and formed the Japan Pro Wrestling Alliance (JWA).

The opening of the JWA took place in February, 1954. Rikidozan and Masahiko Kimura, Japan's greatest Judoka, teamed up to wrestle against the Sharpe brothers—International Tag Team champions. The event was broadcast live all over Japan. Thousands of Japanese swarmed anywhere a TV set was working to see the event. Playing the heel, the Sharpe brothers kicked and bit Rikidozan whenever the referee was not looking. In anger, Rikidozan let loose on them with karate chops, beating them with a three-count pin. The crowd was ecstatic because for the first time, a Japanese technique and tactic was used to defeat an American. The nation could not believe what had happened. The whole country was in pandemonium as a result of the match. The country and its people gained back confidence. Later that year, Rikidozan went up against his Tag Team partner, Masahiko Kimura, for the Japanese heavyweight championship. The fight was billed as pro wrestling against judo, and Rikidozan shocked audiences by knocking out the Judo champ in a bloody match.

In October 1957, Rikidozan took on Lou Thesz for the JWA and NWA world title, to a draw. The event was the most watched wrestling event in history at the time, sending droves of Japanese to the stores to buy television sets, just so they could watch the event. Rikidozan went to Los Angeles to fight Thesz again and brought back the title belt. He continued to promote Puroresu and also had a stable of wrestlers, including Giant Baba and Antonio Inoki, whom he met while touring Brazil and whom he brought back to Japan to take under his wing and train. In December of 1963, Rikidozan was at a club in Tokyo and got into an altercation. He was stabbed and he died a week later at the age of 39.

What makes Puroresu different than American wrestling and Lucha Libre is that the matches are portrayed as legitimate with no blatant cheating or interference. Puroresu fighters use very intricate and complex submission techniques, along with high-flying aerial maneuvers. The audience treats them more like legitimate athletes than as larger-than-life entertainers. Their mic skills are not as flamboyant as Western wrestlers; Puroresu fighters use a more natural or normal tone of voice and approach. They do not employ the character structure of "heel" and "face" in their matches—matches are presented as more legitimate competitions. This also gives the promoter the freedom to match every wrestler in the lineup against one another, as opposed to the heel-versus-face theme. The wrestlers are also known to work their matches "stiff"—they do not pull their punches and kicks.

Many American wrestlers have gained valuable experience by wrestling in Japan. These foreign wrestlers (now superstars) have included Chris Benoit, Rob Van Dam, Mick Foley, Hulk Hogan, and Andre the Giant, to name a few. The longest foreigner to spend time wrestling in Japan was Tiger Jeet Singh, from India, who spent a total of 22 years there. The influence of Lucha Libre has also brought some of Mexico's top wrestlers to the Land of the Rising Sun.

The Wrestlers

Following are some of the more interesting wrestlers in Puroresu.

Kazushi Sakuraba

As a child, Kazushi Sakuraba dreamed of emulating the famous Japanese pro wrestler, Tiger Mask. He joined the UWFI, a pro wrestling league known for its highly technical and realistic-looking matches. Under the tutelage of Billy Robinson, Sakuraba was taught catch wrestling. Sakuraba had to work his way up the company ladder, "working" matches as a mid-card wrestler. It wasn't until they had an inter-promotional feud with New Japan Pro Wrestling that Sakuraba wrestled in high-profile matches and was able to display his ring psychology and technical skills, which impressed the management and finally elevated him to main-event status. The hope was that the feud would get more people interested in UWFI, but the opposite happened, and they closed in December 1996. For the final show, Sakuraba was the headliner, defeating Yoji Anjoh by submission.

Sakuraba then joined Kingdom Pro Wrestling, which had the same theme as UWFI. He had a hard time drawing a healthy crowd from the onset because MMA contests were capturing the attention of the audience. Hoping to establish credibility, two wrestlers from Kingdom participated in UFC's Ultimate Japan tournament. As fate would have it, one of the fighters was injured while training, and Sakuraba was a last-minute replacement. However, the tournament was for heavyweights (200 pounds and over), and Sakuraba weighed only 183 pounds.

To enter the tournament, he reported to officials that he weighed in at 203 pounds. He ended up winning the tournament against Marcus Silveira (who was 243 pounds, a BBJ black belt, and an extreme fighting champ) by getting him to submit with an armbar.

Kingdom Pro Wrestling finally closed its doors in March of 1998, but it gave birth to one of the most electrifying and captivating fighters in MMA history. Because of his brilliance and adeptness in catch and freestyle wrestling and his intellectual approach to fighting, Sakuraba has been nicknamed "The IQ Wrestler." However, he is more noted for his surprisingly consistent and dominating victories over the famed Gracie family (with wins over Royler, Royce, Renzo, and Ryan Gracie), earning the nickname "Gracie Hunter."

Antonio Inoki

Kanji Inoki adopted the stage name Antonio because it was similar to Antonio Rocca (the flamboyant acrobat of the 1950s). Inoki was a protégé of Rikidozan, who along with Giant Baba carried the torch of Puroresu after the passage of their influential mentor. In 1972, he formed New Japan Pro Wrestling (NJPW). His first match was with Karl Gotch, who taught him and several other wrestlers the art of hooking and shooting, the roots of pro wrestling.

Inoki would stage mixed martial arts (MMA) matches against fighters from other styles and disciplines, such as Judo and karate. The most famous match of all was when he fought world heavyweight boxing champion Muhammad Ali, which ended in a draw. There is continued debate about whether those matches were "worked." Many of Inoki's disciples have been very successful in Puroresu and MMA because NJPW would promote wrestling and MMA in the same program. Inoki's wrestling career lasted 35 years, and because of his combination of using martial arts techniques with catch wrestling, he is a strong influence in the sport of shoot wrestling.

Outside the Ring: Wrestling on Film and TV

Pro wrestling has had a long history of coming across as cheesy when portrayed on TV or film. However, a number of films and TV shows were effective in making pro wrestling look good "outside the ring."

Wrestling-Themed Movies and TV Shows

Following is a list of some films and TV shows that have wrestling as their central theme.

- ***A Titan in the Ring.*** In this 2002 Ecuadorian film, the people in a small South American village live with their heads hung low because the village is being run by a corrupt gangster. However, when a masked wrestler comes into town and defeats the town Rudo in the ring, the spirit of people starts to rise, and they become more optimistic about their future.
- ***...All the Marbles.*** In this 1981 movie, Iris and Molly are a women's pro wrestling tag team called "The California Dolls." They travel across the country with their manager, Harry, wrestling at arenas to get a shot at the title belt. Real-life pioneer wrestling champion Mildred Burke trained and choreographed the wrestling sequences. This was Robert Aldrich's last film, and it is an under-appreciated classic.
- **"The Cautionary Tale of Numero Cinco."** In this television episode of the series *Angel*, Tezcatcatl, an ancient Aztec warrior, is brutally killing select people by cutting out their hearts. Angel consults Numero Cinco (#5), an old man, who was able to battle and kill Tezcatcatl previously. But Angel finds out Numero Cinco has lost the thrill of the battle because Tezcatcatl killed his four brothers the first time around. This is a humorous and loving homage to Lucha Libre and the El Santo films, in which Luchadores are detectives or spies between wrestling matches. It was written and directed by executive producer Jeffrey Bell, who is a Lucha Libre fan.
- ***The Foul King.*** In this 2000 Korean film, Dae-Ho, a meek bank clerk, is constantly harassed by his boss because of his frequent tardiness and slumping commissions. He has a crush on a fellow worker, but is too shy to do anything about it. His father scolds him as if he is still a child. And to make matters worse, Dae-Ho's boss physically harasses and embarrasses him by constantly getting him in a headlock. Dae-Ho goes to a friend's Tae Kwon Do school for his help, but his friend is unable to help him with grappling techniques. Dae-Ho walks by a pro wrestling school on the way home and decides to enroll in classes. As his confidence grows, he starts to take chances in his life and becomes a masked heel in the ring who has to cheat to win, thus he is known as "the Foul King."
- ***Rikidozan.*** This 2004 Korean film is a biopic about the godfather of Puroresu.
- ***Paradise Alley.*** This 1978 film was Sylvester Stallone's directorial debut about two brothers trying to get out of Hell's Kitchen by being wrestling managers. Many pro wrestlers played parts as well as fought in the film.

Movies and TV shows with Wrestling Elements

Following is a list of some films and TV shows that have effective wrestling elements in their stories.

- ***Rocky III.*** Rocky participates in what he thinks is an exhibition MMA match for charity with pro wrestler Thunderlips (played by Hulk Hogan). Rocky quickly realizes he has gotten more than he bargained for, and the match ends up being a free-for-all between the two.
- ***Rocky V.*** In the final fight scene, we get to see the "street" side of Balboa in a brawl between Rocky and Tommy Gunn. The brawl was choreographed with the assistance of pro wrestling legend Terry Funk.
- ***They Live.*** Nada (wrestler Roddy Piper) tries to get Frank to put on the special sunglasses, and they end up brawling in the alley. Choreographed by Jeff Imada, the fight in the alley was one of the longest fights in Western film history.
- ***Sha Po Lang.*** This film is also known as *S.P.L.* and was released as *Kill Zone* in the United States. Star and fight director Donnie Yen fuses MMA and pro wrestling techniques into Hong Kong action. In the movie, Yen applies suplexes and the hurracarana (from Lucha Libre) in the fight scenes.
- ***Black Mask 2: City of Masks.*** In this Hong Kong action film, pro wrestler Rob Van Dam costars with Yuen Woo Ping serving as fight director.
- ***Tom Yoong Gong.*** In this movie, released as *The Protector* in the United States, Tony Jaa fights a group of professional wrestlers in the final fight scene.
- ***Ultraman.*** A kaiju TV show in which Ultraman battles the creatures at the end of the show. The techniques they used in the fight choreography are a combination of martial arts and pro wrestling moves.
- ***The Princess Bride.*** Andre the Giant (as Fezzik) costars in this romantic comedy. The fight between Fezzik and Pirate Robert was simple but effective and convincing.
- ***Huo Yun Chia.*** Also known as *Fearless*, this movie features Ho Yuanjia fighting Hercules O'Brien, an American wrestler, in a duel.

3

Definitions and Terminology

This chapter provides definitions of the basic terminology of fighting and fight choreography, broken down into categories.

Empty-Handed Fighting Distance/Range

This range is not a set definite standard because it changes with the opponent's height. What might be long range to a person of short stature might be mid-range to an opponent taller than him. These range definitions should be used on an individual basis, depending on the situation, unless the combatants are close to the same height.

The person with the longest reach and height will establish the three distance ranges according to his size. A great example of this is in *Game of Death*, where Bruce Lee (5'7") fights Kareem Abdul-Jabbar (7'2"). I recommend you see the documentary entitled *The Warrior Within* to see the choreographed fight in its entirety along with the other fights. *City Hunter* presents a comedic parody of the fight, with Jackie Chan against a security guard that is as tall as Abdul-Jabbar. The strategy used in both fights is worth studying.

The three ranges are:

- **Long range.** These are fights that use kicks delivered by the lower part of the leg (shin and foot) to keep an opponent away. Weapons fights with staffs, spears, and swords are also considered long-range fights.

- **Mid-range.** These are fights that use the hands, short kicks (Japanese-style kicks with no hip extension), and the knees as weapons to strike. Kicks are not as effective because of the distance. Nunchaku are popular mid-range weapons.
- **Close range.** These are fights that use elbow jabs, head butts, knee strikes, and grappling. Kicks are generally not effective because of the close range. Close range weapons include knives and brass knuckles.

When weapons are involved, no matter what the outcome of the fight is, the combatant who has the longest weapon will dictate the three distance ranges. For example, consider a fight between someone who has a long staff and someone who has a knife.

Different Types of Fighters

Generally, there are three different types of fighters—offensive fighters, defensive fighters, and counter-attackers. Please note that there are combinations of different attributes that make up a fighter, and you should not classify a fighter as simply one of these three types. There will always be characteristics and situations that might turn a defensive fighter into an offensive fighter (after turning the tables with a particularly successful defensive technique), or an offensive fighter into a defensive fighter (after an injury or a loss of confidence).

Offensive Fighters

Offensive fighters take an aggressive posture and try to dictate the fight by taking the initiative or staying in control of the opponent. Being an offensive fighter does not always mean that the fighter is aggressive in his approach or nature. It simply means he dictates the fight by controlling his opponent.

Offensive fighters can control the space in the ring with their footwork or psychologically "train" an opponent by using body language, or even verbal taunts, to fake out the opponent. Offensive fighters also can blitz their opponents using techniques of varying speed and power to throw opponents off and stay in control of the fight.

Defensive Fighters

Defensive fighters are just the opposite of offensive fighters. Defensive fighters wait for an opening when the fighter attacking them makes a mistake. They wait for the opening, which is very elusive and somewhat of a passive/aggressive approach. The opponent might get cocky, thinking he is taking control of the fight, but the defensive fighter has a very tight defense and doesn't open up anything for the other fighter to attack.

Offensive fighters keep attacking, hoping to expose a flaw in the defensive fighter's defense. The defensive fighter looks for an opening while being attacked. When defensive fighters find an opening, they throw their technique quickly, hoping it will put a wrench in their opponent's attack. When this strategy is successful, it will cause the attacker to question his approach, and it will undermine his confidence.

Counter-Attacker

A counter-attacker creates an opening without making an aggressive attack. He usually draws his opponent or waits for the opponent to attack him. The counter-attacker will typically throw his technique *during* his opponent's attack, rather than after, as would a defensive fighter. Incredible timing and knowledge of the opponent's traits are crucial to allow the successful counter-attacker to pick the right technique.

Styles of Fighters

In addition to different *types* of fighters, there are also different *styles* of fighters.

Technician

This type of fighter has crisp, clean techniques similar to those you would see illustrated in a textbook, but the technician is able to actually use his clean techniques against a live, moving opponent. The technician's understanding of fighting techniques is deep, and he is able to apply the techniques in a real situation whenever he wants. Technicians are usually students of their sport/art, so they are always learning and applying their skills to their trade. Technicians have highly developed timing instincts and are very effective counter-attackers.

Some examples of real-life technicians include

- Muhammad Ali, the three-time heavyweight boxing champ of the world.
- Sugar Ray Leonard.
- Marvin Hagler.
- Roy Jones, Jr.
- Joe Louis.
- Chuck Norris, who had such command over his techniques that he could hit you at will with his spin kick.

- Bill "Superfoot" Wallace, who could only kick with his left leg, but who threw his kicks at 60 mph. Wallace was the undefeated world middleweight kick-boxing champ.
- Keith Vitali, a diverse tournament fighter who won every major tournament in the country. Vitali was the number-one black-belt fighter for three years.
- Mike Tyson, the two-time undisputed heavyweight boxing champ. Tyson was a triple threat because he was not only a technician, but he also had incredible power and aggression. Tyson broke Rocky Marciano's record by having 19 straight knockouts at the start of his career.

Some examples of technicians on film include

- Bruce Lee
- Jackie Chan
- Tony Jaa
- Sammo Hung
- Donnie Yen
- Lam Ching Ying
- Yuen Biao

Some examples of technicians in fight choreography include

- Yuen Woo Ping
- Ching Siu Tung
- Bruce Lee
- Jeff Imada

Brawler

A brawler is a fighter who does not have clean technique, but who gets the job done. A brawler's fight looks ugly when compared to a technician's fight. Brawlers often use things such as body leverage to get the upper hand in a fight. Brawlers are difficult to figure out because they are usually unorthodox in their approach and do not have a set approach to attack or defend.

A few brawlers would be

- Leon Spinks
- George Foreman

Showman

A showman is flashy and flamboyant in his style and/or approach to fighting. The showman sometimes plays to the audience and manipulates their emotions. Jean Claude Van Damme is an example of a showman.

Emotional

This fighter is driven emotionally in a fight. Joe Frazier is a good example of this type of fighter.

Intellectual

This type of fighter is intellectual, analytical, and scientific in his approach to fighting. Jet Li is a good example of an intellectual fighter.

Definitions of Fighting Terms

This section contains definitions of many common fighting terms. For ease of use, I have included several helpful abbreviations in this section. See the key in Table 3.1 for an explanation of these abbreviations.

Table 3.1 Abbreviations Key

Abbreviation	Description
MA	This denotes a general martial arts term.
T	This denotes a technical fighting term that applies in all martial arts and film.
GRP	This denotes grappling arts, which includes mixed martial arts (MMA), Jujitsu, and all types of wrestling.
BX	This denotes a boxing term.

Bob (T). The act of moving your head and shoulders up and down so your opponent cannot hit you. Mike Tyson and Joe Frazier were great at this. Bobbing is similar to ducking, but a duck is a direct response to a technique. Also see *weave.*

Broken rhythm (T). Creating a rhythm of attack that is not predictable and telegraphing to an opponent. This is a flow of moves and techniques that do not evenly follow each other, creating a stutter-like flow. This creates an attack in which the opponent does not know when he is being attacked or faked. This in turn causes the unsure opponent to leave himself open. The main approach of the Chinese drunken styles of martial arts to an attack is a broken rhythm, which looks like a drunken man or animal (depending on the style).

Centerline (MA). An imaginary vertical line that goes down the middle of a fighter. If a fighter's centerline is straight up and down, this usually shows he is centered, ready to attack, defend, or counter. If the centerline leans away from the opponent, it shows the fighter is in more of a defensive posture, ready to counter with a lead leg kick or more when the opponent attacks. If the fighter's centerline is more forward, this tells his opponent that he is in more of an aggressive/offensive stance. All these different types of positions can change in an instant, depending on the situation.

Centerline theory is also used when a trained fighter connects with a blow to his opponent. If you hit a person straight on the shoulder, it won't do much damage. Chances are, the opponent will still be coming at you. But if you hit your opponent in the shoulder and aim the impact of the blow toward his centerline, it will make much more of a jarring impact that will be felt throughout the opponent's body. This is because you are disrupting his physical centerline (which consists of his internal organs and central nervous system, which is connected to the entire body). By aiming the impact of the blow toward your opponent's centerline, you can stop him much more effectively and quickly than by just using glancing blows.

Chamber (MA). Bringing your leg/knee up to position when you are about to throw your kick. Chambering his leg gives the fighter the opportunity to throw more than one kick before putting his leg down.

Check (T). To jam an opponent's technique with a technique of your own before the opponent's move reaches its full power and speed.

Clean technique (T). A technique that is technically perfect, similar to what you would see described in a textbook. A clean technique is also aesthetically pleasing. However, having a clean technique does not necessarily mean you are a technician.

Closed stances (T). This is when both combatants are squaring off against each other, and their chests face in opposite directions. Opposite of *open stances.*

Closing the gap (aka bridging the gap) (T). When a fighter steps into the *neutral zone* to attempt to land a technique on his opponent.

Combination (T). A series of two or more techniques that quickly or directly follow one another. One of the reasons to throw a combination is to create an opening with an initial strike so the fighter can hit his opponent with a follow up technique.

Cross (T). A punch that is thrown with the hand that is furthest away from the fighter's opponent. Usually this is the hand opposite the foot that is in the lead. In martial arts this is generally known as a *reverse punch.*

Disengage (T). To mentally and/or physically not be actively engaged in a fight. In the middle of a fight of length (such as in a combative sport), a fighter can concentrate for only so long before he temporarily "goes to sleep." By disengaging, the fighter is out of range of his opponent and can regroup for a few seconds.

Draw (T). An act of luring your opponent to attack or come into range in a certain way, so you can counter with a technique.

Duck (T). To avoid a strike by moving your head downward to go under an opponent's strike.

Fake (T). A technique used to distract an opponent so the fighter can then connect with another technique. A fake needs to be thrown as convincingly as if the fighter were throwing a real technique, otherwise the opponent will not react as intended and the fake will be ineffective.

Fakes are designed to get an opponent to lose his fighting composure and to create an opening. A fake is usually thrown in the opposite direction of where the fighter wants to throw the actual technique. For example, the fighter might fake with a low punch to get the opponent to react and lower his hands. Then, the fighter might immediately throw a high kick to the head.

Fakes are usually done in sets of three. For the first fake, the fighter throwing the fake notices the unconditioned reaction of his opponent and begins to think of a technique to take advantage of the opening. The second fake is to make sure the opponent will react the same way to the same fake. If it is so, the third fake will be thrown partially while flowing into a follow up technique that is suitable for the opening that was created. If the fighter is fast, sharp, and confident enough, he can sometimes succeed in throwing the final strike after the second fake.

Falling asleep (aka being caught sleeping). A fight takes a lot of concentration and requires a fighter to be aware of many things all at once. The fighter can keep that high level of concentration for only so long before he temporarily "zones out" or "falls asleep." A "sleeping" fighter will usually get out of range to disengage and gather his senses before he goes back to fight.

Fighter's composure (T). An emotionally cool state of mind that a fighter tries to maintain during the fight so he can properly make the changes and adjustments necessary during the encounter. A fighter's composure shows his experience in handling the situation at hand.

Typically, we are used to seeing a composed fighter who is relaxed physically and mentally enough to respond to whatever stimulus comes his way. The mind-body connection usually works hand in hand. When composed the fighter uses his peripheral vision to see what is coming his way, he has almost a sixth sense about what is about to happen. He is ready to respond to whatever comes his way. The fighter's opponent does what he can to get the fighter to lose his composure so he will be more susceptible to making mistakes and wrong judgments.

Fighting composure is attained through fighting experience and training. This is not to be mistaken with a fighter being cocky or overly sure of himself. A person fighting for the first time usually does not have fighting composure, and usually reacts the opposite of what was described here.

Another term often used to describe a fighter with this state of body and mind is *centered.*

Fighting stance (T). A fighter's posture for a fight. The stance can be aggressive, passive, or anywhere in between. It shows in the fighter's body language, centerline, leg posture, and hand placement.

Finishing technique (T). A technique used to finish off an opponent, usually to knock him out.

Follow-through (T). To throw a technique that goes through the target the fighter intends to hit. The same principles are used in martial arts to break a board. *Snapping* a technique is the opposite of following through.

Follow-up (T). A technique that directly follows another. This is similar to putting together a combination, but following up requires the combatant to be quickly aware of openings in the opponent's guard and to follow up with an appropriate technique when such an opening presents itself.

Whereas a combination might be thrown as a series of moves to create an opening and/or overwhelm the opponent, a follow-up is more instinctual than a combination. Combinations are more of a rehearsed and practiced series of techniques. A series of follow-ups might look like a combination to an outsider who does not know the combatant's intentions, style, or skill level.

Footwork (T). The way a combatant uses his legs to attack, evade, or counter. Footwork gets you to or away from your opponent. Muhammad Ali and Roy Jones, Jr. had evasive and graceful footwork. In film, footwork can also be used to show the character's emotions when in combat.

Form [aka *kata* (Jp.), *kuen* (Ch.), *Hyung/Palgue* (Kr.)] (MA). A set of prearranged moves to teach a student the rhythm and flow of specific techniques and how they flow into subsequent moves, which makes the style the student is learning unique unto itself. Almost every style has a set of forms. This was how techniques were passed on from teacher to students when the martial arts were outlawed by other countries or tribes that were occupying the territories in question at different times in history.

There is a practical application to each form that teaches something different to the student. Each form has its own distinct personality, rhythm, timing, and application that the student needs to apply to his skill set.

Forms are done both empty-handed and with weapons. Many Chinese martial arts have two-man forms, in which the practitioners fight each other in a prearranged fashion.

Form could be considered a distant relative of *shadow boxing*.

When a form is done well, a person viewing the performer can actually see what the move is doing to the imaginary opponent. The practitioner applies the same amount of effort and commitment to the technique as if he was executing the move on an opponent, but he can alter the technique for aesthetic reasons.

In films, performing forms is an easy way to show how the character is comfortable with the skills that are being taught to him. Usually, the hero learns the form and is forced to practice it over and over with no end in sight. He does not understand how to apply the moves while fighting and, as a result, he is easily discouraged. It isn't until the hero is in a near-death situation that he sees things differently and understands what he has learned. The hero masters what was taught to him and makes what he learned his own way of expression by adding his distinct personality to the style. He is no longer a slave to the art; he is now a master as he faces the villain who almost killed him earlier.

Following are some examples of great forms in movies, as well as some you might never have considered.

- Jackie Chan in the opening credits of *Snake & Crane: Arts of Shaolin*, *Drunken Master*, *Snake in the Eagle's Shadow*, and *The Fearless Hyena*.
- Sammo Hung in *Magnificent Butcher* and *Odd Couple*.
- Jet Li in *Shaolin Temple*, *Martial Arts of Shaolin*, and *Fist of Legend* (with a group in unison).
- Bruce Lee in *Way of the Dragon* (1966 20th Century Fox audition reel).
- Tony Jaa in *Ong-Bak*.

- Ralph Macchio in *The Karate Kid*, practicing the Crane technique on the beach atop a stump and then applying it when he faces off against William Zabka (Johnny Lawrence).
- Ti Lung in *The Kung Fu Instructor*, teaching a student part of a form but never completing it because he is afraid that someone will discover the secret and defeat him.
- Robert DeNiro in *Taxi Driver*—the famous scene when DeNiro stands in front of the mirror and practices taking out his gun as he says, "You talking to me?" This is considered a form because he was practicing a response to a scenario in a physical manner.
- Tony Curtis in *The Boston Strangler*. At the end of this film, Curtis (as Albert DeSalvo) is finally arrested for the murder of 13 women. At his interrogation, he undergoes hypnosis and reenacts a scene in which he killed a woman by himself.

Form (T). This term also refers to when someone throws a technique, and the quality of the execution of a technique. This does not necessarily mean the person has a complete understanding of the technique or is able to apply it in a real situation.

Going to sleep. When an opponent is not fully aware or living in the moment with the fight. This is normal when fighting for any length of time because a fighter can only hold this level of concentration and awareness (mentally and physically) for so long before his brain blanks out for a short amount of time. The fighter has to be aware of when this is happening to him; otherwise, he might be in striking range of his opponent while asleep, in which case he would be vulnerable and could get hit.

Hard fake (T). A fake thrown as if it was a finishing technique to knock your opponent out. Hard fakes are thrown with much more commitment and emphasis than regular fakes. Hard fakes are thrown when an opponent does not react to or respond to a normal fake.

Highly stylized (FF). See *stylized* in the "Film Fighting and Stunt Terms" section later in this chapter.

In range (T). This means a fighter is within striking range of his opponent without having to take a step toward him.

Jab (T). A lead hand technique. A jab is usually a speedy technique that keeps an opponent occupied while the fighter prepares to immediately follow up with a cross—a stronger technique that can knock the opponent out. Muhammad Ali, Roy Jones, Jr., and Larry Holmes had great jabs that helped set up their opponents to get hit with other techniques. Also see *stiff jab*.

Jam (aka *crowd*) (T). Throwing your body or a part of yourself at an opponent so he cannot complete his technique. This does not, however, immobilize the opponent like a *trap* would. To get out of a jam, the opponent needs to step back to reset the distance range.

Leg sweep (T). The act of taking an opponent down to the ground by *sweeping* his leg(s) with your leg(s). This appears more like a strike than a grappling style of takedown.

Neutral zone (T). The free space that is between opponents. This neutral zone varies depending on a person's height, reach, and size and style of fighting. When an opponent enters the neutral zone, he is taking a chance of being hit.

Non-telegraphing. Throwing a technique that does not give the opponent any clues that it is coming. The opposite of *telegraphing.* Quick jabs are good examples.

Open stances (T). This is when both combatants are squaring off against each other, and their chests are both facing the same direction. This stance usually limits the types of techniques that can hit the opponent.

Opening (T). A part of an opponent's body that is susceptible to getting hit and is not protected by his current fighting guard.

Out of range (T). When a fighter is a safe distance away from his opponent and he cannot get hit.

Pace (T). A rhythm established between two opponents. A combatant who is in charge of that rhythm through experience, superior technique, and/or power "controls the pace" of the fight.

Primal conditioned response (T). An initial reaction from a trained/conditioned fighter. When a fighter throws a convincing fake to his opponent, the opponent (also a trained/conditioned fighter) will respond (without thinking) with an appropriate defense to the fake or technique. The difference between a primal conditioned response and *reacting* is that the primal fighter's skill level is higher than that of an opponent who merely *reacts.* A response from a fighter in a primal conditioned response is to counter, defend, or move away without having to think.

React (T). The opposite of *respond.* A combatant's untrained response to a technique (stimulus). This usually occurs when a combatant reacts to a technique that is faster or that they cannot handle or keep control of. Such a *reaction* usually occurs when the combatant is inexperienced or has lost his fighting composure. If the opponent is aware of this, he can easily take advantage of the situation. To get a trained opponent to *react,* a fighter has to throw a technique or fake that is faster than what his opponent is trained and conditioned for. If the attack is not fast enough, the fighter will get a primal conditioned response from his opponent.

Respond (T). The opposite of *react.* A combatant who is able to keep in control of himself (physically and mentally) responds with the proper counter to the opponent's stimulus. This is a more conscious response than the last two.

Reverse (GRP). When a fighter is taken down to the mat or the ground, and then is able to get out of the takedown, hold, and/or lock and get his opponent on the ground. A successful *reverse* steals the upper hand from an opponent.

Reverse punch (MA). See *cross.*

Shadow boxing (BX). A distant relative to *form.* A boxing term in which a fighter goes through a series of moves as if he were sparring with an opponent in front of him. This requires the boxer to visualize an opponent in front of him and move according to what he imagines his faux partner is doing.

Signature move (T). A technique for which a fighter is known. A signature move is also a technique a fighter uses frequently with success, often hitting his opponents at will with it. Mike Tyson's uppercut and Bennie "The Jet" Urquidez's spinning back kick are good examples.

Sleeper hold (GRP). An immobilizing choke hold that cuts off the supply of oxygen to the opponent's head and makes him pass out. When the opponent passes out, he loses bodily control, making it look like he has fallen asleep.

Southpaw (BX). In boxing, where the boxer's power hand is his left hand, so he fights with his right hand forward.

Square off (T). To face off against an opponent in a fighting stance, ready to fight.

Stiff jab (T). A powerful jab that stops an oncoming opponent or sends him backward. Body alignment is crucial in a stiff jab. The fighter must torque and shift his body so his whole body weight is behind the jab. This is slightly slower than a regular jab because the fighter is throwing the technique in order to make solid contact, to stop the opponent with power, as opposed to blitzing the opponent with the speed of a regular jab that typically does little or no actual damage. Also see *jab.*

Structure (T). Proper body alignment when executing a technique to generate maximum power. When throwing a technique that has proper body structure, the fighter does not get hurt and does not absorb any energy from the technique back into himself while giving it to the opponent.

Submission hold (GRP). A hold or lock that puts the opponent in severe pain and makes him want to tap out and quit the fight. Submission holds are typically applied to limb joints, rather than to the neck, as in the case of a *sleeper hold.*

Takedown (GRP). The act of taking an opponent down to the floor without a strike. You can use any part of your body to execute a takedown by using proper body mechanics and leveraging. Judo and Jujitsu are in-close styles that primarily use throws and takedowns.

Tap out (aka *tapping out*) (GRP). Used in grappling events usually where a fighter is in a hold and cannot bear any more pain and/or pressure or is about to be choked out. The fighter taps his free hand on the mat or someplace where the referee can see that he is obviously giving up. This is much like *throwing in the towel*, but done by the fighter in the ring.

Taunt (T). A close relative to a fake, but more of a bullying or intimidating type of tactic in which the fighter threatens to hit the opponent. This can be done through physical or verbal intimidation. This is an overbearing technique that is used to psychologically infect an opponent. Taunts often make the aggressor appear obnoxious or "cocky," but in appropriate situations, experienced fighters will use them as effective weapons in their overall strategy. Some great examples of taunts include:

- **Liston vs. Clay I.** Muhammad Ali's (then Cassius Clay's) verbal and psychological warfare on Sonny Liston before their first fight in 1961.
- **Duran vs. Leonard II.** Sugar Ray Leonard taunts Roberto Duran by sticking his head in Duran's range and then quickly backs off. Later, Leonard winds up with one hand as if he is going to hit Duran with it, and then hits him with a stiff jab of his opposite hand. All this led Duran to give up and say, "No mas."
- ***The Rundown.*** Travis (Seann William Scott) verbally taunts Beck (The Rock) "Afraid of thunder? How about his friend, lightning?" before a fight.
- ***Rocky III.*** Clubber Lang (Mr. T) constantly launches verbal assaults on Rocky Balboa (Sylvester Stallone) and physically harasses him in the ring.
- **The Three Stooges.** Curly does many taunting motions and makes noises as he reacts to Moe's actions in many of the Three Stooges films.

Telegraphing (T). Throwing a technique in a way that the opponent will see it coming. For instance, reaching back too far, too slowly, or too obviously with a fist before throwing a punch. Telegraphing can be due to technical flaws in the execution of the technique or physical habits a combatant is unaware he exhibits before he throws a technique. Also see *non-telegraphing*.

Throwing in the towel (T). A term for a judgment and actual act used in boxing when the corner man and/or coach think their fighter has had enough and feel it is unnecessary to continue the fight. This often occurs because the corner man and/or coach don't want their fighter hurt. Usually the coach or corner man takes a white towel (for surrendering) and throws it into the ring to signify that he no longer wants the fight to continue because he feels the safety and health of his boxer is at stake.

Throw (aka *throw down*) (GRP). A specific type of *takedown* where a fighter uses his body leverage to throw down an opponent. This is a grappling move.

Thrust (T). To throw a technique that does not snap back and goes past the object or body part the fighter is hitting. This technique looks powerful.

Timing (T). The ability to throw a technique in defensive, offensive, and/or countering mode that connects in the opening of the opponent's defense. This requires quick coordination from eye to mind to physical execution. The fighter creates or recognizes an opening, chooses a proper technique, throws it, and hits his opponent with it at his chosen spot before the opponent can close the opening and possibly counter with his own technique.

Trap (T). The fighter immobilizes, shuts down, and collapses an opponent's limbs so he cannot use them against the fighter. The Wing Chun Kung Fu system made popular in the West by Bruce Lee is famous for their hand trapping.

Weave (T). To move back and forth and from side to side to avoid a strike and not get set up by an opponent. Also see *bob* and *duck.*

Film Fighting and Stunt Terms

Bump (aka *adjustment*). A stunt term referring to the monetary adjustment for a fighter performing his specified skills.

Crossing the line. A strike passing an imaginary line that starts at the camera lens and goes to the targeted area where a strike is to land. When a strike goes past the target, it crosses the line, and on the screen it looks like a *hit.* When a technique does not cross the line and there is a gap or space between the target and the full extension of the technique, then it is considered a *miss.*

Exchange. A series of techniques thrown between combatants without an extended break or pause. A fight scene is usually made up of several exchanges between opponents.

Exclamation point. The final move and/or reaction in an *exchange* that ends in a spectacular way. This is also used when the *front and center* character is fighting multiple opponents, and the final person who he is fighting reacts more flamboyantly than the other attackers to end the exchange sequence. Exclamation points are made famous and more obvious by Hong Kong fight choreographers.

Example of a Sparring Match (Using Definitions)

1. Fighter A meets Fighter B in the center of the ring.
2. They bow in respect for each other and for good will and sportsmanship.
3. They square off and face each other in fighting stances.
4. The distance between them is far enough so that they cannot hit each other without having to take at least one step.
5. The space between them is called the neutral zone.
6. This gives each combatant time to react or respond when someone decides to attack, depending on each person's respective skill level.
7. Fighter A throws a low hand fake that diverts the attention of Fighter B.
8. Fighter A quickly shuffles (using footwork) into the neutral zone, gets within a long-distance striking range, and throws a rear-leg front kick to Fighter B's head.
9. Fighter B recognizes the kick coming at him, side-steps the kick (45 degrees), takes another step, and crowds Fighter A, getting into grappling range and nullifying the kick.
10. Fighter B slips his leg behind Fighter A's plant leg (the kick is still in the air) and throws a straight arm across Fighter A's neck, creating a clothesline.
11. Fighter B hits Fighter A with the clothesline across the neck and sweeps his support foot with his leg.
12. Fighter A falls to the ground.
13. Fighter B immediately follows up with a controlled snap kick to Fighter A's head to finish him off.

All this would take place in only a few seconds.

Front and center (aka *hero of the piece*). The main character around whom the fight scene is centered. Essentially, which character is this fight scene about? A fight scene can have several characters who are front and center (either fighting together or against each other), often found in the midst of a larger battle. The term *hero of the piece* is not restricted to only a hero; it can also refer to an antagonist, a protagonist, or the supporting characters. It denotes who the fight scene is centering on for that moment. Being front and center or the hero of the piece does not mean that the character will survive.

Hero of the piece. See *front and center.*

Hit. When a technique at full extension hits the target and has no gap or space by crossing the line.

Miss. When a technique at full extension does not hit the target because there is a gap or the strike does not cross the line.

Sell (aka *selling, selling a move, sold*). Making a technique look effective on the screen. Selling a technique is a threefold process that includes a person throwing a technique, an opponent receiving the technique, and the proper camera angle to display the technique with utmost clarity and impact.

Sticking/nailing a move (stick/nail it). A term borrowed from gymnastics that refers to the performer executing a move (usually a complex technique) with strong authority, presence, and technical precision, showing the judges he or she is in command of the move. The same applies to fight choreography, but the judges are the audience. When performing a kata, a martial artist will often stick a punch or kick by holding its extension longer than would be appropriate in an actual fight, in order to ensure that the judges don't miss the technique's flawless execution.

Stylizing. Changing a style or fight to make it more appealing on screen. Essentially, all styles and systems are stylized by varying degrees, depending on the fight choreographer. The techniques need to be performed wider and telegraphed so the camera can pick up the technique and the audience can see it.

A similar use of the term *stylized* is for the style of martial art that is used for a film. A great example is the *Once Upon a Time in China* series. In the film, the hero, Wong Fei Hung, actually uses classical Chinese martial arts techniques, but his technique is stylized with a large sprinkling of Wu Shu, which did not exist at that time period. But because Wu Shu is still from the same family and is a direct product of traditional Chinese martial arts, the film is effective.

The term *highly stylized* describes a fight that focuses on an actor's physical showmanship skills to a high degree. To make a highly stylized fight effective in a movie, the characters and story must support the extreme stylizing of the fights. Examples of films that are highly stylized include *Ong Bak, Once Upon a Time in China I, II,* and *III, Equilibrium,* and *Kung Fu Hustle.*

Wide (aka going wide). (1) Making and adjusting a technique so that it can be more readable by the camera. This usually involves throwing the technique with a wide, sweeping arc, beyond what would be appropriate (and otherwise non-telegraphed) in a real fight.

The Pulse of a Fight Scene

Now that we've explored all the aspects of a fight scene from narrative, physical, and technical elements, hopefully you can start to dissect such a scene and find the strengths, weaknesses, and what will make the fight scene better.

When looking at a fight scene, you might think something is amiss, but not be able to put your finger on what is missing or wrong. This section includes general descriptions of what you might encounter when putting together a fight scene. You can also use these definitions while watching films that are currently out in theaters or on home video.

Carried or carrying the actor. A fight scene (or a section of it) in which it is obvious that the attacker is catering to the hero and adjusting his approach to make up for the hero's shortcomings in a valiant attempt to make the scene work. This might occur because the actor that is *front and center* is too slow, too uncoordinated, or not skilled enough for the choreographed fight scene. As a result, the audience is far ahead of the film, having already anticipated the attack by the time it arrives. When the attack does come, it is no longer exciting to the viewer. Another example of *carrying the actor* is when a group of opponents unrealistically and ineffectively attack one at a time, patiently waiting their turn after each predecessor is vanquished by the hero.

Clash or bad fit. When an incorporated style or technique does not complement or work with the situation, character, and/or story.

Coolmoveitis (cool-move-it is, pronounced *kool-moov-eye-tiss*). A serious (but curable) disease that impairs or blinds the fight choreographer's judgment and critical eye. The disease manifests itself by the choreographer putting in a "cool" move—a technique, style, or approach to fighting—that is not justified by the mood, theme, character background and/or motivation, or story. This also can occur more noticeably when a martial artist turns into an actor and feels the fight scene is all about his moment to shine in the spotlight and display his skills, while ignoring the principles of story and character development. The result of coolmoveitis is that the audience can be taken out of the scene emotionally. They may lose their faith and belief in the character's skills or, even worse, they may lose the complete movie-going experience.

Flashy. When a series of visually spectacular moves are combined in a fight scene. A fight scene that has only the visual thrill and ignores the story can be called "all flash and no substance." (See *no substance.*)

Gratuitous. A fight scene or move that is used cheaply as a device to get a rise from the audience. For example, the inclusion of excessive blood or gore to get a rise from the audience would be gratuitous in a film in which other fight scenes were not similarly gory. A fight scene can also be considered gratuitous if it is not motivated by the story and seems to exist only to show off the choreographer or actor's favorite flashy techniques in the hopes of impressing other filmmakers, rather than actually contributing to the plot progression.

Implausible or no steam. A fight scene that has no credibility or loses credibility right before or during the fight. As a result, the audience loses interest. The typical symptoms of this can be any combination of the following criteria:

- Martial acting that is unbelievable, false, or does not match the emotion of the character and/or fight scene
- Flaws or weaknesses in the story or character development so that the character has no real justification for fighting skills
- Choice of style, skill level, and/or technique that does not match the story or personality of the character
- Obvious technical flaws, such as misses, unflattering angles, off edits, poor lighting, and so on

Lean (aka *no fat*). A fight scene that moves very quickly, yet still has all the non-verbal story elements in place. This type of scene helps the fight choreographer achieve a believable and convincing fight scene, something he or she should always strive for.

No resonance. A fight scene that is emotionally false in martial acting and provides no emotional buildup and/or release. There is no real spirit or energy behind the actors' physical performance that resonates with the audience.

No substance. A fight scene that has no real meaning or purpose behind it and/or is not connected to the story at all. The techniques used have no real meaning behind them.

Off. When the timing of techniques and cues between actors is not accurate and throws off the entire rhythm of the fight scene. Being "off" can also occur when the martial acting does not match the moment of the conflict.

Oversold or too much. When a fight scene (or part of it) has too much energy (over the top) and does not fit into the story and/or characters. In martial acting, this is easily noticeable by audiences because the scene or parts of it do not come across as genuine, honest, or sincere; rather, they call for and attract unnecessary attention.

Perfect, on, or alive. The fight is technically exact and clean, has energy, has timing and cues in synch, and holds a convincing emotion throughout the conflict. Visually, there are no misses, and cinematic composition and edits are such that the audience knows what is happening with each beat of the fight. The audience feels as if the fight is naturally unfolding right in front of their eyes because the martial acting is very convincing, supported by a solid story that justifies the action and the character's skill level.

Posing. When an actor is conscious of himself at any moment during the fight and/or poses in a fighting stance or in a before or after pose for the camera. An actor can also be called a *poser*, which means he is only there to fight to make himself look good for vanity and ego purposes.

Repetitious. When a fight scene has the same repetitive rhythm throughout the fight. This also applies to repeating the same technique in a single fight or throughout other fights in a single film. There are several problems with being repetitive with a technique and rhythm:

- Strategically, it does not make any sense.
- Mentally, the audience is already expecting the techniques, and they are already ahead of the fight.
- Visually, it gets boring and lacks variety on the choreographer's part.
- Rhythmically, you can lull the audience to sleep, and it gets especially boring if the fight scene is long.

A fight scene is much like dialogue in the script—it needs to progress at a steady pace. Much like in real life, dialogue can get very tedious and cover the same issue over and over, not really leading anywhere specific. A fight can easily be the same way if you are not aware of the different types of repetition. Also, each successive fight in an action film should be more difficult and exciting than most of the ones that came before, otherwise the overall progression of the film's intensity will likewise be flat and repetitive.

Rooted or having substance. A fight scene that is strongly based on the story and character background and development. The actions are justified, and it makes sense why the characters are fighting as they are.

Stale or flat. There is no life or energy to the fight scene because the actors are not in the moment with the fight. A fight can also become stale or flat by having the same continuous rhythm, beat, and techniques throughout, offering no real variety.

Stiff. When the actors in the fight are too rigid or appear conscious that they are in a choreographed fight, as demonstrated by their anticipation of the next move. Sometimes the actors know what move is coming and are not able to act/react/respond in a realistic fashion as if they do not know what's ahead. As a result, the fight looks rehearsed and has no real spontaneous energy to it because everyone is too conscious of the choreography. This is comparable to a dramatic actor who appears to be simply reading his lines out loud.

Tight. A fight scene that has it all. Following are all the elements that make a tight fight scene.

- Believable cause and motivation for all characters involved in the fight
- Nonverbal narrative (solid reasons with a well-crafted three-act structure)
- Visual resonance that leaves the audience speechless
- Effective and believable martial acting by the actors and stunt players
- Proper and effective choice of styles and techniques that are believable extensions of the characters involved in the fight and time period
- Effective camera angles so the audience can comprehend and believe the move the actors are performing on screen
- Believable and convincing sound effects that will draw the audience deeper into the choreographed physical conflict
- Music that reinforces and enhances the mood of the fight
- Editing that heightens and enhances the rhythm of the fight and has a logical continuity, showing a fight strategy the audience can easily understand without destroying the integrity of the fight

Too aware. Similar to *posing*. When an actor breaks character and is too much aware that he is in a fight scene. The actor might appear just a little too excited to be in a fight scene, calling unnecessary attention to himself because of it. His expression might read, "Hey, everyone! Look at me—I'm in a fight scene! Ain't it cool?" Or, just the opposite might occur—an actor might break character by feeling uncomfortable or afraid of being in a fight scene for personal reasons that he cannot shake.

Too staged. The fight scene has a rehearsed and premeditated feel to it and does not come across as organic or natural. In this case, the viewer does not get the feeling of the fight unfolding right before his or her eyes.

4

Primer

This chapter is designed to present some things you might need to know before starting to break down the script and train your actors.

Issues with Using a Real Martial Artist or Combative Athlete on Film

Imagine you are attending a live sporting event where two world-class boxers are fighting each other for the world championship title. The reigning champion has defended his title consistently and spectacularly for a couple years, has a devoted following, uses flashy yet effective techniques, is charismatic, and is a media darling and a crowd-pleasing fighter. His opponent is the top-rated challenger in the division—at one time a world champion himself. He is a no-nonsense, powerful fighter who punishes his opponents and knocks them out, leaving the audience in fear and awe. In short, he is a real bruiser.

These opponents have fought each other twice in their careers, each winning one match, and this fight will be the tie-breaker between the two fierce competitors. The contrast in style, personality, and approach to the fight has the media drooling over the match, sparking constant debates on TV and in print predicting who will win and why. The media is split down the middle because the competitors are evenly matched. You cannot ignore this match because everyone has been talking incessantly about it as one of the best matches in a long time, and this fight will provide you with excellent research material for the boxing film you've always wanted to make. What makes this match even more special for you is that you've got awesome tickets to witness it in person.

So you're there in the arena, and the fight is very exciting and evenly matched so far. For once, the media hype is correct about the fight being a barn burner. The challenger is giving the champ a run for his money. The crowd is on its feet throughout most of the fight, cheering and gasping as they watch this unforgettable match. There is electricity and a buzz in the air as the match teeters in dominance from one competitor to the other. The combatants and the audience are one collective emotional body as the audience reacts to every move and hit as if they were in the ring with the fighters, experiencing each hit themselves. So far, the fight has been a war. Each fighter has been unloading bombs that would have stopped anyone of lesser character and spirit. The evenly matched opponents are not fighting for the money, because someone would have tossed in the towel by now; they are fighting for respect and pride. It's amazing how the spirit and essence of these two athletes can captivate 80,000 people in the arena, who hang on every move the competitors make in a 20-square-foot ring.

The bell for the final round rings. So far it has been even, and anyone can take the fight. The challenger lands a devastating shot to the champ's head that resonates throughout the arena and is felt by everyone…even all the way up in the cheap seats. With wobbly knees, the champ is dazed and stunned. Literally and figuratively, he is on the ropes. The challenger comes in for the kill. The crowd can't believe what they are seeing as they hold their collective breath. The champ is hit with a vicious blow to his ribs that bends him in half, followed up by a ferocious shot to his head that pops out his mouthpiece and sprays his sweat far into the third row, giving you a personal souvenir. The champ crashes heavily to the mat. The referee starts his count. The crowd is torn. Half stand up and cheer for the challenger. The other half are also up, trying their best to collectively will the champ to his feet. But the champ does not know where he is. The challenger is battered and tired, but anxiously waits for the champ in a neutral corner, keeping his eye on the fallen man, knowing the fight is not over until the final bell rings.

Struggling to get up, the champ valiantly claws his way up using the ropes. "Four, five, six…" counts the referee. The crowd feels the champ's undying spirit and start to cheer him on as he finally stands before the referee has finished the count. He's somewhat conscious and breathing through his mouth. The referee looks in the champ's eyes. The champ nods that he's okay and ready to fight. The referee cautiously watches him, ready at any moment to jump in and stop the fight.

The challenger smells a wounded animal ready to be put out of its misery. He senses the title belt is ripe for the taking, knowing the champ is out of gas. The champ leans against the corner of the ring to save what energy he's got left—he's dead on his feet. In an act of defiance he waves, inviting the challenger to come and get him. With an obliging grin, the challenger quickly rushes in and puts everything behind a finishing shot that would knock over an elephant. The crowd holds their collective breath. But at the very last second, the champion sidesteps and dodges the punch, leaving the challenger vulnerable, off balance, and open.

The champ immediately counters before the challenger can recover, landing a crushing blow on the challenger's chin, putting every ounce of energy he has left into it. The challenger's legs instantly buckle as he crumples to the mat. The referee starts his count. The champ leans up against a neutral corner—it's the only thing keeping him up. The crowd goes wild over the champ's display of fortitude. "...8, 9, 10. You're out!" The referee waves his arms, signaling the fight is over. The crowd erupts with cheers and hoots in reaction to the euphoric high they are feeling, and for the incredible battle they just witnessed between two warriors whose will and desire went above and beyond their physical skills and the audience's expectations.

The champ raises his glove in the air in a hard-fought but well-earned victory. The challenger is up, and they hug each other over a well-fought fight. After he is announced the winner, the champ proclaims to the still-standing crowd that he is retiring and wants to do something a little safer, such as becoming an actor. The crowd sadly cheers his decision, knowing this is the end of an incredible era in combative sports history. But your heart is racing faster. You can't believe that he wants to be an actor. This is the perfect opportunity for you!

Meanwhile, you are three rows back, completely exhilarated and in awe from what you just experienced, and you want everyone to feel the same thing you experienced, but on a larger scale...in your film! You are fortunate because you know the security folks who work at the arena and you have been given a backstage pass to meet the champ in his dressing room.

Drunk with the euphoria you have just experienced, you finally meet the champ to congratulate him on his incredible victory. You pitch your story idea to him, and he thinks it's a great story and agrees to do it. You are both elated that what you just witnessed will happen on the big screen so the world can experience what you saw in the live arena...but on a larger scale because the action is going to be more than 40 to 60 feet wide on the big screen. Given your feeling when experiencing this fight in the arena from three rows back, think how the audience will feel when the camera gives them this same intimate experience from inside the ring. This is a no-lose situation. You will get a lot of media press about your upcoming film with the champ, which will help settle the investors' worries for now.

The champ confides in you and lets you know his true feelings: "You know, I've seen all those fight films out there. But what bothers me about a lot of them is that they don't even attempt to be real. They lack anything that's convincing and they don't make any sense at all with what they do inside the ring. Heck, if I did *any* of the moves that I saw in a movie in the fight tonight, I'd be the one on the mat getting counted out! Trust me, I've been doing this fight game all my life, and I know I can do a better job of putting together a fight than any of those hacks in Hollywood, because none of them have the experience of being a champion!"

You agree with the champ's thoughts and decide to let him choreograph the fight scenes because you want the fight to look and feel authentic. Besides, it looks impressive in the credit roll—the audience will feel assured that a real pro was behind the scenes, giving an authentic feel to the action sequences. And, your decision also makes for good PR. To make it even better, the challenger agrees to play the champ's opponent in the film. All three of you agree that the real fight you saw tonight will be recreated and captured on film.

You are simply elated. This will take your career as a filmmaker to another level. You all agree that your film is going to be better than any fight film out there because you are using seasoned world-class professional athletes on the big screen, and therefore, the audience is going to feel every blow. You're not worried about the champ's acting skills because he is so captivating and charismatic that whenever the press shoves a camera and mic in front of him, he's able to turn a boring interview into the highlight of the night on ESPN by making colorful statements and predictions that the press eats up.

A few months later, you are on the set filming the movie. The media is covering the shoot almost daily, interviewing the champ whenever they can. You are getting exposure and being touted as a new up-and-coming young action filmmaker right on the verge of greatness.

But the champ is stiff during the dialogue scenes. He's not as natural onscreen, for some odd reason. You notice that when he does not have to recite dialogue from a script, he's back to his normal boisterous self—and even more so when he's hanging out with his friends in his trailer, but it's quite another story when he's scripted. You think to yourself, "No worries. The fight scenes the champ will choreograph will more than make up for it."

A couple weeks later, it's time to shoot the climactic fight scene with the champ and the challenger, and it is nothing close to what you experienced when you saw them fight in the arena that night. The dailies of the raw footage of the fight do not have any of the same chemistry, raw energy, or impact that you originally felt and experienced in the live arena—that energy you wanted the whole world to experience. The flow and techniques don't have the same feeling as when you saw it live, and for some odd reason, it does not have the same effect on film. There is no real electricity or vibrant energy between the two fighters. You cannot see any of the techniques, even though the camera was closer to the action than you were at the live event. For most of the shots, all you see are the fighters' backs and shoulders. You don't understand why these two world-class professional fighters look sloppy, lifeless, rehearsed, and dull. The editor cannot piece the footage together successfully because the choreographed fight scene was missing some key shots that kept the flow.

Unfortunately, the champ is now overseas. Due to financial reasons and a recent divorce, he went back on his word and is fighting professionally again. At the current time, he is preparing for his upcoming fight and cannot come back to reshoot the fight scene. You use a stunt double who matches the champ's physique and looks somewhat like him. When you do the reshoots, you don't focus much on the stunt double's face. But even with editing, the fight still looks lifeless and the timing does not make any real sense after it is pieced together, and worse yet, the stunt double doesn't move like the champ so the substitution is visually obvious.

You finally have the film cut together and you show it at a private screening to get the audience's opinion. They feel that it's like every boxing film out there, but the fights and acting are lifeless. As a result, the producers release the movie straight to DVD in the hope of recouping their losses. When it comes out on DVD, you only get lukewarm reviews, and the champ gets skewered for his "acting" abilities. He receives a Golden Turkey Award later that year for his contributions to the cardboard acting school. Other critics say the champ's acting skills make them yearn for an old Pauly Shore movie. Meanwhile, you are again working in the back room at the video store, afraid to show your face to the customers for fear that they'll laugh at you or ask for their money back for renting such an awful film. And word on the street is that the champ now wants to fight *you* for making him look so bad onscreen!

Believe it or not, I have seen and heard many stories like this—they happen all the time. Look at the video store shelves and the bargain bins, and you will see the screen fighters on the DVD cover along with their world titles. Some of these films are good, decent, or above average, but a majority of them are not—they end up in the two-for-one clearance bin or the 99-cent rental section. But why does this happen?

Let's break down the mistakes and assumptions that this filmmaker made.

1. There are differences between a real fight and a staged fight for film. The filmmaker thought there was no difference between a real fight and a film fight. Even though he is in the business of filmmaking and knows some of the smoke and mirrors you can use to create illusions in filmmaking, he was still baffled over the process of what makes an effective fight scene for film.

As discussed previously, there are big differences between live fights and staged and rehearsed fights for film. A fight for film is used to tell a story of its own in the midst of the plot progression of a larger story. In a prize fight, the competitor's goal is to advance and win the purse while the announcer tells the back story of each fighter and creates the needed tension to pull you into the fight and fill in the gaps during lulls in the fight (if you are watching the fight on TV). Rumor has it that while casting for Rocky III, Sylvester Stallone auditioned heavyweight boxing champion Earnie Shavers for the part of the villain, Clubber Lang. When they got in the ring to feel each other out, Shavers' boxing instincts took over and he ended up roughing up Stallone instead of just getting a feel for Stallone's rhythm and seeing whether they could "dance."

Also, in the traditional martial arts, a practitioner carries a great deal of honor and self-pride as he trains. He also carries a certain code of ethics within the style, which might have transformed him from a misguided delinquent into an upstanding leader in his community. I have experienced martial artists auditioning as stunt fighters who will only have their art portrayed in a certain, positive light. Or, sometimes they will not stylize their moves in order for the technique to be readable on film because that is not how they throw the technique in real life, or because they feel that doing so will dishonor their art and their masters, or they simply cannot consciously change it because of all the years of throwing it a certain way.

A real fight cannot be reproduced exactly the way it was done for film—not only technically, but also emotionally. The human eyes see differently than a camera does. The camera has a limited scope and does not interpret depth perception like the human eye does, nor can it change its point of view based on individual preference, as an actual viewer can do by moving around.

Martial artists and combative athletes often judge a choreographed fight by saying, "What the #@&* was that? That wouldn't happen in real life!" For instance, single techniques often land successfully in film fights, while combinations are usually necessary to score a hit in real life. Of course such things wouldn't happen in real life, but we are telling a story in which the aesthetics of the fight are at times more important than its realism, practicality, and effectiveness. The reverse is also true—it would not be fair for a fight choreographer to watch a real-life competition and judge the competitors for the lack of aesthetics in the fight by saying, "I would have believed it more when the guy got hit in the stomach if he would have reacted a little bigger to sell the hit!" If a fighter showed his emotions in real-life competition, the opponent would take advantage of his vulnerability.

In short, a staged fight is specifically geared for entertainment purposes, and a real-life fight is geared for competition and self-improvement. It is illogical to make a judgment about one kind based on the other, even though both sides make valid points in their criticism. Neither criticism can stand on solid ground because the comments are out of context.

2. A real fighter does not always make a good screen fighter or actor. Unfortunately, this is a common mistake made by filmmakers who do not know the difference between a real fight and a fight for film. They commonly think a real fight can be captured on film easily and will have more of an impact on film than a choreographed fight will. This is much like having a very lively conversation with an individual about something that person feels passionately about, and then coming to the conclusion that the person would make a successful actor. In both cases, you are taking the person's skills out of context.

   Just because you see a great martial artist perform extraordinary feats at a school, a tournament, or a demo, that does not necessarily mean the artist will be able to do the same thing on film. The performance aspect is taken completely out of context and placed into a medium that cannot be compared.

   A typical martial arts school or boxing gym does not teach their students the following film specific concepts, and thus a filmmaker should not assume the fighter would know these things.

   - **Techniques.** What works in competition or in a class situation might not work well on camera. The fighter trains himself not to telegraph his techniques so his opponent cannot anticipate them. But in film, how can the audience be entertained if they can't see the techniques that will be thrown? Telegraphing is necessary for entertainment value in a fight choreographed for a film scene, because the audience often needs to be told "don't blink, something cool is about to happen."

     In competition or in class, techniques usually are short, concealed, and not too flashy. In film, the techniques that usually work best are circular techniques that naturally loop or arc and the camera picks those up much better than short, concealed techniques.

- **Timing.** The timing in a real fight changes constantly depending on the fighters. Timing is crucial in a fight to throw an opponent off so the fighter can take advantage. In film, there is an "agreed timing" between the two opponents—the opponent getting hit knows about it beforehand. A real-life fight is much like a live chess match, in which the players constantly have to adjust and set their timing to react to what is currently happening. This is not the case on film, where the timing is created with both the actors cooperating to make the illusion of the fight.

- **Control.** Fighters are taught to hit someone with maximum effect and to make contact. So control might be an issue depending on the fighter's philosophy and type of training. Often real fighters are also taught control over techniques by "pulling" them just short of hitting an opponent. Screen fighters are taught to pull their techniques as well, but they also have "camera awareness," meaning that they know which camera angles will make pulled techniques look like they actually made contact.

- **Martial acting.** If a real fighter shows his emotions while fighting, he can easily be taken advantage of and eventually defeated by his opponent. A fighter spends years learning not to show emotion or any type of intention that might telegraph to his opponent his state of mind or what is coming (however, martial artists are taught to show emotions when performing kata routines). Unfortunately, this creates a major roadblock for a martial-artist-turned-fledgling-screen-fighter because he has to display emotions with his face and body language during combat in order to tell the story. He needs to telegraph his emotions to the audience to get them emotionally into the fight scene. These emotions also include "selling" reactions when getting hit, to show that the fighter has been hurt by the opponent. Hong Kong screen fighters such as Jackie Chan and Sammo Hung have been doing this for most of their lives because of their backgrounds in the Chinese Opera, where they had to perform choreographed fights while showing emotions onstage for a live audience.

- **Vulnerability/ego.** A fighter spends a majority of his training developing a certain amount of prowess with his skills. For many fighters, this defines who they are. You may encounter a fighter who might not want to do something because his martial principles have told him not to do so because it does not make sense to them. I've been in many situations in which a martial artist is hired to play an opponent who fights the hero, but the martial artist is not capable of taking direction because he feels that he would not be susceptible in real life to something like the events in the scene.

Also, a fighter trains throughout his career *not* to show vulnerability or weakness when he is fighting because an opponent can take advantage of that weakness. But on film, a flaw or a certain amount of vulnerability needs to be conveyed to the audience so they can sympathize with the fighter, knowing what he is feeling.

In other situations, the martial artist may be used to being treated as the star at a tournament or the prized pupil at his school, but on a film set, he might be hired as Thug #10—even if in reality he can easily beat the hero, who is often a famous actor with little or no combat training. In this case, the martial artist may not understand why he is not the star of the film. He might demand more pay or want more screen time simply because of his past achievements outside of the film world. Martial artist and film star Keith Vitali comments, "How many tournaments or world titles you've won; no one cares and none of that helps. But if you have the confidence and poise of a champion, then you're able to transfer that onto the screen with that image along with the story. Then the way you carry yourself, the way you deliver your lines—that's how you can use all that experience in the ring and transfer it onto film. But you have to remember that a white or gold belt can convey the same feelings, thoughts, and emotions as a tenth-degree black belt...and sometimes even better."

- **Frame of mind.** A real fighter is self-preserving in nature and is conditioned to survive an attack, take punishment, and defeat his opponent. The fighter knows that he has to rely on his skills, conditioning, and guts to defeat his opponent. A screen fighter knows he is usually not the star of the film and his main purpose is to make the star look good by "selling" convincing and at times incredible reactions to the hero's hits, no matter how impractical or weak the technique might be. If the screen fighter is the star of the film, he also knows that his opponent is not out to kill him, but that he must act as if the opponent is and respond using what has been previously choreographed.

A fighter and martial artist is trained through repetition over many years to learn effective, practical techniques and combinations. But when working on a film, an actor has to learn and remember the series of techniques much more quickly. Mike Massa, stunt coordinator on the TV series *Angel*, comments, "I took jazz dance classes for two semesters back in college. It taught me to memorize things quickly. It really forced me to learn things fast. In a martial arts class, everything is drilled into you over a longer timeframe. Well, if you ever go to a dance audition, they teach the moves to you fast. Your trick is to learn how to memorize fast. Well, I learned how to memorize the moves fast because that's what they taught you in these classes, along with how to move more gracefully. Every day you came into class, they would teach you something new—and it was not the same routine as yesterday. You had to learn something new every single day. It teaches you to tie 1, 2, 3, 4, 5, 6, 15, 20 moves to music. With fights, we do that every day. We tie in 20, 30, 40 fight moves together. And you've gotta know how to pick it up and repeat exactly what you just saw. So in that case, I think it really helped a lot."

2. Being a trained professional fighter does not automatically qualify someone to be a fight choreographer. Just because a professional fighter can throw techniques in succession, know when to throw them, and look impressive in real life, that does not make the fighter qualified to be a fight choreographer. A fighter or martial artist who has not worked on a film and who is asked to choreograph a fight scene definitely has an uphill climb ahead of him because he not only has to know how to choreograph a fight, he has to be aware of the following things:

   - **Camera angles.** A trained fighter does not know techniques for what camera angles work best. A real fighter knows what is effective in a street situation or competition, but he is not trained to find the best angles to shoot the action and make it look effective. He is more concerned with effectiveness than the visual aesthetics of the fight. However, an experienced tournament fighter will have some understanding of the importance of camera angles, because he has learned to throw techniques from positions that the majority of the judges will see in order to ensure that his points will be awarded.

- **Story.** Most fighters' knowledge and skills are more important than the story because usually their knowledge and skills *are* the story... which does not always mean they can tell a story with a fight. Practicality, self-preservation, effectiveness, and not telegraphing a fighter's moves overrides telling a story with the fight.
- **Camera effectiveness and stylizing of techniques.** A fighter does not know what works on film—rather, he knows what is more effective for his own survival in the situation at hand. The techniques used on film have to telegraph and "sell" in order to be effectively read on camera and seen by the audience. This means the technique has to be changed and usually "telegraphed" in order to be seen as effective by the audience. When a technique is not stylized to read for the screen, the audience might miss it because they didn't know it was coming, and therefore they are emotionally left out of the conflict of the fight.

Only a small number of professional fighters have been able to make the leap to being effective screen fighters, simply because the conditioning and instincts taught in professional fighting and screen fighting are contradictory to each other. The transition from professional fighter to screen fighter is not impossible, but it requires a martial artist to unlearn many of the things he has been taught.

I am not saying that a trained professional fighter or martial artist cannot acquire these skills, but their combative training does not include cinematic fights as a part of their black-belt curriculum. It's not practical and functional to learn effective screen-fighting techniques unless you plan to make a film.

The prospective screen fighter coming from any real fighting background has to make a major shift in his thinking and focus in order to succeed as an action star or filmmaker.

What Is a Screen Fighter?

A screen fighter is a person who makes an onscreen fight look convincing to the audience, as if it was actually happening and the audience was witness to it. A screen fighter in the film is anyone who is physically involved in a fight. This can be the star, the villain, a supporting player, a stunt player, a stunt double, and so on.

The objective of a screen fighter is to make the fight look convincing through physical action, acting, and the non-verbal narrative established for that particular fight. The second and third attributes are often ignored in Western film these days because many filmmakers think physical action is all that is needed to sell the emotion of the scene. But this is not true. As an example, if you watch Bruce Lee or Jackie Chan when they hit an opponent who falls down, their eyes follow the opponent as he falls. Their eyes show an emotion—they are ready for the opponent to get back up again, even though in real life the actors know the stunt player is not going to attack again. Their minds are still in the fight, and they act as if they do not know the outcome, even though they do.

An inexperienced or poorly trained screen fighter is usually noticeable and draws unnecessary attention to himself or his actions (or inaction) by being out of sync with the rest of the fighters. This breaks the illusion at that point, taking the audience emotionally out of the picture. Even though the screen fighter might not be fighting at that very moment, he has to act as if he is present and in the fight, looking for the right time to get into the scuffle. Many martial artists who get into film with no screen fighting and martial acting experience make this mistake, as do inexperienced actors who aren't comfortable with action or don't know what to do with themselves while between opponents. This is much like a dramatic actor who doesn't know how to act in between his lines.

A good screen fighter fully understands the story of the conflict and his own character's motivations. He will convincingly sell the fight scene, using his actions, facial expressions, and body language to communicate his emotions. Good screen fighters are able to do this because the fight is so real to them in their minds. They make it look natural and easy, making the audience think that they could do it too. But a good screen fighter usually goes unappreciated until you see a really bad one perform.

A screen fighter knows what everyone involved in the fight will be doing and moves along with the other screen fighters as if they are a well-oiled machine. It's much like a choreographed dance that has to be repeated several times for camera coverage.

The Importance of Rhythm in a Fight

Bruce Lee was the cha-cha champion of Hong Kong. Cheng Pei-Pei was a trained ballerina. Jeff Imada is a classically trained pianist. Some of Jackie Chan's influences are American dancers Gene Kelly, Ginger Rogers, and Fred Astaire. John Woo watches dance musicals for inspiration before he choreographs his action sequences. Oscar-nominated film editor Frank Urioste (*Robocop*) was a music major in college, with aspirations of becoming a music composer. Director John McTiernan (*Die Hard*) sees the script as a lyrical form.

What is my point, you ask? Does this mean I have to have a music degree to choreograph a fight scene? No, not at all. What these people all have in common is an innate sense and understanding of grace and rhythm that they apply when they work on action scenes in front of the camera and behind it. Whether or not we realize it, everything we do has a rhythm and a flow. The same applies to putting together an action sequence.

Jackie Chan had an amusing story when describing the timing and rhythm of a part of the mall fight at the end of *Police Story*, where he sends one of his screen fighters through a glass display in slow motion. The screen fighter reacts to Jackie's hit by doing a full twisting butterfly into the big four-sided glass display. Regarding this scene, Jackie jokingly states, "When I write down my choreography, I don't write down the punches or the kicks. I write bum bum bum...bum bum bup bup bum bup...bum bup bum bum! So this way you can see in my movie it's like...ta da ta da ta da! Then music! [He sings.] Ha da ta data duh duh duh ta da! Then breathe! Then the feet! [Jackie makes a shuffling of feet noise.] Sha sha sha sha! Then I come up. In slow motion, glass breaking! Bwaaang! Daaang daaaang daaaang! They come at me! [Hits.] Da da tung ta ta dung dung. The whole thing comes up just like dancing. I shouldn't tell you that. This is my secret." To Jackie Chan, the underlying rhythm of the fight is more important that the individual techniques therein.

Each fight scene in a movie should have its own individual rhythm that is different than the rhythm of the rest of the fights in the film. I'm not suggesting that you go out of your way to create a fight with a manic rhythm just because the previous fight was more subtle or low key, but variety is crucial. The rhythm of a fight also has to take into account the number of people in the fight, as well as their emotions and intent.

Having the same rhythm throughout a fight can actually lull the audience to sleep. But an even worse scenario is having the same type of rhythm in all the fights in the film. This can easily happen to you if you are not aware of it. This is much like listening to a musician who plays almost the exact same beat for every song on his CD. After the second or third song, the listener's attention has dulled or they've tuned out, even though the lyrics to each song might be different. Great examples of different rhythms in each fight throughout a film are *The Matrix* and *Police Story*. Both films use different situations and camera tricks, such as slow motion, to play with the rhythm of each fight.

When asked what is missing in most American fight scenes, Jackie Chan commented, "They are missing the tempo and rhythm. Sometimes if they have a good fighter, they don't have a good stunt coordinator to choreograph. I know there are a lot of American movies that learn from me. They learn what Jackie Chan choreographs. But the actor doesn't know how to do it. I know how to choreograph by myself. I know what I'm doing, and I have my own stunt team. Like right now, a lot of American movies are hiring Hong Kong stunt guys. But if you hire them, you have to know how to use them. But they just don't know how to use them. They still use American rules.... The rules of rehearsal are set before filming, and you can't change it on the set. Two days to fight and two days to finish."

Rhythm is not easily noticed by the general movie-going audience, but they are definitely moved and affected by it. If you really look at it, there are many different rhythms in a film. The editing has its rhythm. The story has a certain rhythm. Even the dialogue has a certain rhythm interpreted by the actors. That's what makes actors such as Jack Nicholson, Gary Oldman, and Christopher Walken so compelling to watch. It's the cadence of their dialogue and the emotions they put behind it that collectively become the rhythm of their dialogue and make their performances so interesting. Directors and screenwriters like Martin Scorsese, Woody Allen, David Mamet, Quentin Tarantino, and the Coen Brothers similarly understand the importance of dynamic and interesting dialogue rhythm. The same principles are applied to the rhythm of a fight.

Chan continues the conversation and describes his process of rhythm as he puts together his fight scenes: "On the set we've got our stuntmen, cameraman, lighting, and everybody else. I tell them, 'Let's do this... [imitates the rhythm of the fight] dah...dah...dah...dah.' Everyone says, 'Ah, good!' Then we have to gather a lot of energy. Energy, energy, energy, energy! Then all the energy comes. And maybe this guy gives me a kick and makes me angry. Okay, let's do it! Wham... wham...wham. Then one take. Everyone likes one take. Then we feel tired because you've already done it 20 or 30 times! Then you go home. When Kenneth Lo was kicking me in *Drunken Master II*, he just keeps kicking me...quick kicks. After 20 takes he cannot kick anymore. He was shaking. He was very tired. I said, 'Go home.' We make sure the shot is good. Timing and rhythm is very important."

When constructing a fight scene, the rhythm of the fight should have a life of its own and not feel forced or false, or else it becomes contrived. Even though a fight on film might look like a rough, gritty fight to the audience, in reality it is more of a dance with its own set of timing and rhythm for all the participants involved. It might look as if it's chaotic, but in reality, to the participants involved, it is a prearranged, rehearsed, set piece. Remember, even though the fights in a film might all have a serious tone to them, the rhythm for each fight scene has to have its own specific timing and flow.

Here's an exercise for you: Put on a DVD of a film that has several fight scenes. Skip to all the action scenes, close your eyes, and listen and feel the collective rhythm of each fight scene by clapping your hands or tapping your foot to each hit. Compare and contrast the rhythm of each fight scene with fights in similar genres from different decades. When watching films from different decades and genres, you will notice the difference in the rhythm for each film because of what the filmmakers are creating for the audience. Then do the same thing with a Hong Kong fight scene and a Western fight scene to get a sense of the differences in rhythm. Then compare the rhythm of a fight scene to that of a dance sequence in a film. While doing this, pay close attention and observe how different rhythms affect you differently.

Now, when you are choreographing a fight, be aware of the intended rhythm of the fight scene you are putting together. Should it be fast or slow? Chaotic or melodic? Metronomic or sporadic? In the beginning, you will be very aware of the rhythm—maybe too conscious. But eventually the rhythm will become a natural part of the fight if you continue to be aware of it.

Working with and Training Actors, Stunt Players, and Stunt Doubles

The art of training actors for combat on film is a delicate balance that requires the trainer to be many things—parent, guide, disciplinarian, therapist, coach, supporter, and so on. It is important to keep in mind that working on a film is about creating an illusion. You have to know the difference between having an actor *appear* as if he knows what he is doing and having him actually *be* proficient—they are two completely separate things. The first can take a few sessions or months to achieve, and the latter usually takes a few years to accomplish. Unfortunately, you do not have the luxury of a few years, and it is impossible to cram everything into the amount of time you are given.

If the actor is able to perform a difficult move with the right amount of confidence and control, then that's great. But if he cannot, don't fret. There are options for making an actor look as if he is performing the technique, such as using a stunt double or piecing the scene together from different takes. These are just some of the options you have at your disposal.

It is also important to note that you are not any less of a trainer if you cannot teach the actor to do a certain technique or fight at a certain level by the given time. And, it's important not to get stuck working on just one technique or concept the actor is unable to perfect. If you know this, your training sessions will go much more smoothly.

Differences between School Training and Film Training

There are many differences between training students in the classroom and training an actor for an upcoming role.

Purpose

A person might train in a martial arts school for health, self-improvement, self-protection, recreation, a serious hobby, or for many other personal reasons. But for film, the purpose of training is to make the character the actor is portraying look convincing onscreen. If the actor is able to be a better person because of the training, that's great. But self-cultivation is not the primary purpose of the training, although it can be of great use for the actor to express himself in a healthy way.

Time Invested

At a regular school, the teacher can spend several years of training and guidance to make the student become proficient in his style. The teacher can be extremely thorough about passing on his skills and expertise. But if you've got four weeks to make an actor look like a black belt, you cannot take him through the entire belt system in that short amount of time. You have to teach him only what is described in the script and make him look as if he knows what he is doing. This is where an actor's skills come into play. This type of quick training is much different than having several years to get to know the student and to guide and mold him into someone who is extremely proficient and capable.

The first obvious obstacle when training an actor for a film is typically beyond your control—that factor is time. This is your greatest enemy because you have to get the actor ready in a short amount of time—ready enough that he carries himself like a professional combative athlete or a seasoned master. But if you know what you need to teach the actor in an efficient manner, you will be able to pull it off.

You need to know how much time you have to train the actors. Yuen Woo-Ping had the luxury of training the cast of *The Matrix* for three months before production started and continuing the training while they were filming, so their training lasted almost a whole year. It took Tony Jaa four years to prepare for *Ong-Bak*, and the time spent really showed and paid off. But if you are just starting out, chances are you will not have the clout to be given sufficient time to make an untrained actor come across like a black belt. You'll have to learn how to juggle all the actors' training times to get enough time with each one of them to teach them what they need to learn.

So do you teach the actors everything in hopes that they will know it all? No. That would be completely fruitless, frustrating, and disappointing for all parties involved. Just because an actor speaks a foreign language in a film does not mean he is completely fluent in that language. Actors basically know their lines of dialogue in that language and not much outside of that. The same goes for training an actor in the moves for a film. It is always best to teach the actor the techniques that you know he will use in the film so you do not waste time. Teach him basic techniques that can be applied easily, are similar, and can easily flow into other techniques. You have to be selective about what you teach the actor because time is your enemy. Making him appear proficient is key—the rest is up to the actor's skills. He must add emotions to the techniques to create an illusion of believability for the audience.

Learning Process

In a typical martial arts class, the teacher passes on the tools and lessons to the student through years and years of repetitious drills, so they are ingrained in the student's psyche and eventually he no longer has to consciously think about every technique in order to throw it. Instead, he responds instinctively and makes the moves his own.

You cannot do this when training an actor simply because of the time allotted. Instead, you have to tell the actor the "answers" for what they need to do. In the time allotted, you need to tell them what the moves might mean and their applications. There are many characteristics and qualities that cannot be taught in the time allotted, so you have to describe and show them to the actor so he can incorporate them into his martial acting. Between the actor's interpretation of the character and your guidance on what is effective and convincing, you are collaborating with the actor and molding and giving life to that character. But you can do a shorthand version by giving the actor select techniques that he will practice constantly and make automatic.

Length of Classes

Usually a martial arts class will last anywhere from 45 minutes to 90 minutes. After several years, the student has learned the required black-belt skills through repetition. But the school is usually training students who have careers and families, so martial arts training is treated as a serious hobby for most students.

The allotted time and the actor's availability and physical condition determine the length of classes for screen-fight training. The sessions should last as long as the actors can stand. Start short, and then constantly add more time to the sessions as the actor gets stronger, more confident, and more proficient. When Yuen Woo-Ping trained the principal actors for *The Matrix*, they worked for three to four hours in up to two daily sessions. When I have trained actors for their parts, I trained them whenever I could find time, such as between camera setups, for an hour before they were supposed to show up on the set, or any other time they were free to train, even if it was just for a few minutes.

Techniques Used

In a martial arts school, students not only learn tournament-appropriate techniques, but also practical techniques that can be used on the street for self defense. This is a gradual process, and it takes a while for the student to gain confidence. Eventually, the goal is to have the student be able to defend himself at any given time and in any given situation.

But in film, you cannot teach an actor to improvise a fight scene or fight naturally because it may very well not look cinematically effective. There are too many factors outside of the fight that you have to take into consideration, such as camera position, lighting, and so on. The fight scenes are choreographed, and it's up to the actor to make it look as if the action is happening right then and there. You cannot teach an actor every technique you feel he might need; you have to be selective about what you teach him by knowing how the actor plans to portray his character. You need to teach him the techniques specific to the story, the character, and the type of fight. Anything that does not have a direct application to what the actor is doing onscreen is a waste of time.

Application of Skills

Usually a student coming into a martial arts school does not have any aspirations of being a movie star. (At least the majority of them don't.) Sure students might be influenced by seeing Jet Li or Jackie Chan onscreen kicking ass—maybe that's what got them to sign up for martial arts and to stick with it, but that's usually as far as it goes. The techniques taught in an everyday class are taught for a class, a tournament, and/or a self-defense situation. The techniques are designed not to telegraph, so an opponent cannot see them coming. And a teacher in a martial arts school is not qualified to teach screen fighting just because he has his own school, he has won *x* amount of tournaments, he has been featured on the covers of various magazines, or he has starred in commercials promoting his school. Unfortunately, this is where the lines of reality and entertainment are blurred by the student and/or the instructor.

There are many real-life practical techniques that simply do not look effective onscreen, like quick jabs and knee kicks. Such techniques need to be altered so they can be read by the camera and seen by the audience. This alteration of techniques may make them impractical and able to be telegraphed, but they are more entertaining to an audience.

When teaching actors screen-fighting techniques, you have to help instill the meaning, confidence, and authority behind the techniques, but then show how to alter or exaggerate them for the sake of cinematic clarity and entertainment value. Your personal experience as a martial artist and your knowledge of acting must come across when you teach a crash course or a shorthand version of what you've learned and experienced throughout your martial arts life.

The Actor's Role in the Film

For the film, the actor is responsible for transforming the character depicted in the screenplay into a living being who is convincing enough for the audience to believe what is happening onscreen. The actor is in many ways the x factor in the equation of the actual film production because if the script has clunky dialogue or lots of exposition, the actor (depending on his skill and experience) can convincingly sell the character and the dialogue by bringing it to life despite the flaws.

Actors are usually first in line to draw criticism or praise from the critics, the media, and the public because they are usually much more visible than the director, producer, or screenwriter. The more popular an actor is with the audience and media, the more attention or heat he will attract to a project. A popular actor can become a draw—just by being in the film, he can attract more funding and other actors of his caliber to the project. This means a certain amount of attention will be paid to the project, which translates to a profit/return in the financial investment. That said, such an actor faces a lot of pressure to make the project a success. And because you are training the actor so his performance will be believable, this translates to pressure on *you.*

The Role of the Stuntman and Stunt Double

If you ask an actor whether he wants to perform a stunt or fight, chances are he will say yes. Whether he can safely do it is another issue. You need to know when to let an actor do a stunt, even though it might seem perfectly safe. The problem is that you risk the actor getting injured, which would result in downtime for the actor and could possibly jeopardize the production of the film. This is why you must think about having experienced and well-trained stuntmen and stunt doubles perform action sequences. Besides, an actor might not be able to sell a fight or stunt as convincingly as a stunt player could, and the production company's insurance policy might not even allow your actors to perform stunts.

When a stunt player is fighting an actor, the stunt player should be aware of any potential danger that might occur and should make the actor aware of it. Even though the actor might look like as if he is in control of the fight, it is actually the stunt player who controls the rhythm and pacing of the fight because the stunt player has more experience in the situation. Also, the stunt player is usually the one doing the attacking (which is the point of control), and the actor is the one responding in defense to the attack.

When choosing a stunt double, it is important to choose someone who is close to the same height and body type as the actor. Audiences are more educated than ever before and they are aware of stunt doubles, especially since they have access to DVD special features and "pause" buttons.. The movie *I'm Gonna Git You Sucka* spoofed poor stunt doubles in the scene where Jack Spade's mother, Ma Bell, does a series of somersaults and fights an attacker in a diner. She is doubled by a Caucasian male with a mustache who is nowhere near her body type. Unless comedy is the intent, your use of stunt doubles should be as transparent as possible.

An experienced stunt player and double can get your action sequence done much faster and more efficiently than if you trained an actor from scratch. However, it is best if you have the stunt double as a backup, to perform the more difficult scenes and techniques that the actor cannot safely do. It is also important to have the stunt double train along with the actor whenever possible, so the stunt double can get used to the actor's rhythm and cadence when executing techniques. The stunt double's job is also to look after the actor he is doubling, while assisting the actor with training and giving the actor help and pointers when he is doing a stunt or fight. With the stunt crew, it is always a good rule of thumb to take the time to make sure everything is as safe as possible for everyone involved.

The Script and What to Teach

When reading the script, do not get overwhelmed if the character description looks something like this:

> *"CHRISTIAN VOSS, thirty-something, unassuming meek appearance, master of disguise, and lethal assassin who is a master of numerous fighting styles from all over the world, enters the room, looks around casually, and surveys the layout of the space."*

Upon reading that, you might start to panic, thinking you need to teach the actor portraying this character all those different styles within a certain amount of time. Don't panic...yet. It is important not to get psyched out by the hyperbole of the writer. You must read the whole script and see how the fight scenes will unfold to support the character's description.

You could read further and find a scene like this:

> *"The lights go on, and Voss is caught. It was a setup. He is confronted by a group of thugs. They come at him. He fights them off easily with single strikes to each thug, immobilizing them as he escapes into the night."*

And then you might continue reading to see that the fights are pretty similar throughout the screenplay. After reading the script, do you need to immerse the actor in many different arts with only weeks before principle photography begins, with the definite possibility that you will overwhelm him? No. Just because the character has a rich background in mastering different arts, that does not mean you have to do the same with the actor. But by reading the description of the fight scene, you get the idea that the character has evolved as a martial artist to the point where efficiency is key and he is no longer attached to the intricacies or ritual involved with most arts. So it would seem more practical and feasible to just teach the actor the techniques, along with the attitude that an experienced martial artist and assassin would have.

This is how you begin to formulate the techniques you are going to teach the actor. At this point, it is best to imagine how the character would carry himself in the situations described in the script. What techniques would he use? How would he throw them? What type of composure would he have? Imagine the fight scenes as they would unravel and write them down.

If you have time, teach the actor basic kicks, punches, and stances so he has a fundamental understanding of what he is doing and a foundation on which to build his additional training. This is something you can always revert to before launching into a new technique or concept.

Read the script and know the characters who will be fighting so when you meet the actors, you can start working toward what they need to be able to perform in the script. The writer might not have had that particular actor in mind when he wrote the scene. You need to know what can be changed and what cannot so you can help the actor look effective and good onscreen.

But before you train with the actors, you will need to read the script to get a roadmap of what each actor needs to be trained in. Here is the start of a checklist of things you will need to look for:

- **Character arc.** What specific events happen to a character throughout the story and how do these affect each fight scene? The character and his skills might progress and grow throughout the story, which may change how the character carries himself and how he fights.
- **Number of fights.** How many fights are in the story? How many fights scenes is each character in? What story and/or character elements are revealed in each fight?
- **Techniques.** Do the characters have to learn any specific techniques that are pertinent to the story and characters? What do you have to teach them?

Collaboration with Other Creative Departments

As a fight choreographer, you should have a general idea of how each fight should look and feel before you start to train the actors. However, this plan should not be set in stone for various reasons:

- The actors might not be comfortable or capable of doing what you're choreographing. If this is the case, you should consider a stunt double for that particular technique.
- An actor might have a different interpretation of the character than what you originally had in mind, and the fight you had in mind might not match the actor's interpretation of the character.
- The director might have a different point of view about that scene or the whole movie in general, and the fight scenes you have planned might not support this point of view.
- The fight might not match the proposed rating of the film.

The Relationship between Trainer and Actor

The trainer needs to develop a relationship of complete safety. The atmosphere must be non-judgmental, and trust needs to be established quickly between the trainer and the actors—from the first meeting throughout the training process. Actors have a lot on their minds and a lot of pressure during the pre-production of the film, and it is important to help them with the development of their character and with their training, instead of being a burden on them.

The trainer also has to know what and how to teach, while having excellent communication skills. The trainer also has to know how to instill confidence while motivating and inspiring actors to learn more, all within a short amount of time. It is best to create a private and safe atmosphere for actors, one where they are not gawked at by others while they are learning.

Poor trainers are those with big egos who are always demanding that attention be focused on them. These trainers run their classes like courses at a military academy, and they expect respect and subservience from their students. For these trainers, the priorities of the instructor come first, and they do not actively guide actors with a hands-on approach. Instead, they bark out orders, which is an ineffective approach. Don't be that guy!

You cannot expect the actor to be as proficient at martial arts as the character is in the story. So you need to train the actor to a point where he looks proficient enough, and then let his acting skills in emotional aspects make up for any lack of proficiency. Putting authority, confidence, and emotional content behind a technique can hide any type of technical flaw the actor might have, depending on his range and depth.

It is also important to train the actors in a place where they can let their guard down and are able to learn and make mistakes without any curious onlookers (and possible paparazzi if they are high-profile celebrities). Actors don't need to be open to unnecessary criticism, judgment, ridicule, or commentary by others. This can make them too conscious of their actions and hinder their learning process. Making mistakes in training is a natural part of learning, and you have to create a positive setting by finding a private place where the actors are able to make mistakes without any external elements that can hinder their progress.

The actor also has to be proactive about preparing for his action scenes. Apart from training and learning how to screen fight, this means going to the gym to sculpt his physique and increase his endurance. Doing this will allow the actor to endure longer training sessions.

Assessing the Actor's Physical Skills

It is important to make an assessment of the actor's skills within the first three sessions. This will also give the actor time to get used to your approach and cadence to teaching. Within these first three sessions with the actor, the trainer has to learn the following things to help the actor look good and proficient onscreen:

- The actor's ability to take direction regarding fight choreography.
- The actor's ability to take constructive criticism and the speed with which he can make the necessary corrections.
- Whether the actor "lives" in his mind or body. This might be a little difficult to detect in the beginning. Is the actor in tune with his body and his actions? Or does he live in his mind? Sometimes people live in their mind when they have suffered some type of trauma that makes them emotionally retreat into their mind. In these cases, their speech and expressions do not involve the body much, and they speak more of intellectual ideas and facts than about how things are executed.
- How the actor's inner dialogue is.
- Whether the actor is athletically inclined.
- The actor's mind-body connection.
- The actor's basic balancing skills.

- The actor's other natural skills. Does the actor have any physical skills or hobbies outside of the martial arts or fighting? If so, you can use his skills and apply them to his fighting skills. For example, if the actor loves baseball, you can take his bat swing and apply it to a right cross or a reverse punch.

When you know the answers to all these questions, you will know where you need to start and where you can go within the time allotted.

If the actor has already had martial arts training or screen-fighting experience, there are several other things you should also look for, including:

- The actor's blinded martial pride and/or his limitations from his previous training. This can hinder an actor because he might not be open to new ideas.
- The actor's ability with simple to complex hand and foot combinations and basic footwork.
- The actor's ability to adapt and change while performing a series of choreographed moves (simple and complex). This shows how open-minded and flexible the actor can be, which is important because you might have to change a fight that you have been working on for a while
- The actor's martial acting range.
- The actor's basic and advanced reactions to hits of different velocities.
- The actor's tumbling and falling skills.
- The actor's use of weapons (if applicable). Test the actor's control and accuracy with each weapon.
- How the actor relates to and works with another partner in a choreographed fight situation.

By assessing the actor's skill level, you will be able to see where he is at and determine what you will need to do to prepare him for his part.

Understanding the Actor You Are Training

When teaching actors, you must immediately connect with them in a positive and motivating way. Their agenda is very obvious compared to a regular student in a martial arts class—they want to look and perform their best when the cameras roll. As a result, there is more cooperation to reach a common goal between you and the actors, even though they might not fully understand all the elements involved.

As the trainer, you need to connect with an actor as soon as possible while still respecting his personal space and private life. I am not suggesting that you hang out with the actor before or after training sessions to be his new buddy—in fact, doing so would not be professional. However, you should have an active rapport and connection with the actor *during* training sessions.

Each person has three learning styles, and you must find out which learning style is dominant for each actor. If you know an actor's thought-processing skills, your training sessions can move much more quickly and will be much more productive. These three learning styles are:

- **Visual.** The actor learns by seeing the technique performed.
- **Auditory.** The actor learns by hearing the technique described.
- **Kinesthetic.** The actor learns by experiencing the technique himself.

You might come across a situation in which an actor you are training is "not living in his body." This means the actor is not emotionally and spiritually connected to the moment. This can be caused by an actor being overwhelmed, or it might be triggered by past personal issues the actor associates with the session. Clues to such a disconnect include

- The actor constantly bumping into things
- The actor not being observant of his surroundings
- The actor using catch-all phrases to tell you his feelings
- The actor constantly asking you to repeat things
- The actor's body language contradicting what he is telling you verbally

It is important for you to be connected with yourself to help keep the actor emotionally connected as well. When you don't connect with an actor, it is important to be aware of this and change your approach to create a rapport with him.

Possible Issues That Can Arise during Training

There are many problems you might encounter during training. Here are some of the possibilities:

- The actor is not very physically inclined, coordinated, or active.
- The actor has an inflated opinion of his own skills.
- The actor has previous issues with physical abuse or domestic violence and might have some emotional blocks toward the training session.

- The actor has a different perception of the training than you do.
- The actor has had a previous bad training experience.
- The actor thinks it's macho to muscle everything he does.
- The actor is not conditioned to having blows come so close to his face.
- The actor is severely dominant in his left or right hand.
- The actor doesn't take training seriously or respect the trainer.
- The actor perceives what he is doing as something against his nature.
- Despite your best efforts and the actor's desire to learn, he is simply unable to execute a particular technique.

Some actors might want to treat the training session much like going to an academic, trade, or correspondence school, where they learn the techniques from you and then go home to practice by themselves. This theory is flawed in many ways and has proven to be ineffective and much more time-consuming in the long run. The reasons for this are as follows:

- The actor can easily pick up bad habits while training by himself, and you will have to correct those habits the next time you see him.
- There is a lot involved in the techniques, and the actor does not know how to correct his mistakes.
- If the actor is training alone, he might hurt himself.

An actor's desire to train alone might come from his insecurity about looking inept, bad, or vulnerable, or he might just not be a social type. The actor might make an excuse that he doesn't want to waste your time or that he has other things to do with the production. This might be true, but he is still neglecting the actual training. Therefore, it is best to hold all training sessions in enclosed and secure areas, where curious onlookers cannot watch, make comments, or simply make the actor feel uncomfortable.

The key is to be structured in the training sessions and have the actors understand that it is their job to work on the techniques because the techniques are as important as the lines of dialogue the actors are delivering. If a situation becomes extremely problematic and an actor cannot or will not learn a particular move, you will need to alter or cut that technique or scene, or rely on a stunt double and some effective camera work and editing in order to succeed.

On-Set Injuries

Injuries can also happen when you have worked too many hours on a set, your brain is no longer sharp, and you cannot make clear and concise safety judgments. Another risk of injuries arises when you are rushed by other departments to get a stunt set up much more quickly than usual, for one reason or another. When someone *does* get hurt, everyone on the set (including the producer) gets a wakeup call about what can happen if anyone is negligent. Hopefully, this does not occur at the price of someone being severely injured or killed.

Horror Stories

The following two sections relate horror stories and experiences of some stunt coordinators (who shall remain nameless).

Horror Story #1

The stunt coordinator for the film was not on the set one day—the producer told him he was not needed because no action sequences were going to be filmed that day. But naturally, the director came up with an idea to spice up the scene and asked the lead actor to take a running start and do a simple butt slide across a desk. The director demonstrated the move the best he could. The actor told the director that he felt uncomfortable doing the scene. The director then pressured the actor: "Aw, come on! If I can do it, you can. Jeez! Anyone can do this!" After more whining and pressuring by the director, the actor finally gave in and did the stunt. On the first take, the actor ended up injuring his leg when he landed wrong. The actor was hauled to the hospital for a checkup. Fortunately, the injury was nothing crippling or debilitating, but it was a severe sprain, and the doctor ordered the actor to stay off the leg for several days. As a result, production was delayed because the actor was in almost every scene in the film. Unfortunately, the director and producer did this constantly throughout the production behind the stunt coordinator's back, just to save money.

There are several lessons to be learned from this horror story. First, when an actor or stunt player tells you he doesn't feel comfortable doing something, there's probably a good reason why. Respect the actor's wishes, move on, and find another way to cover the shot if you need it so badly. Pressuring and bullying the actor is extremely unprofessional and juvenile.

When trying to save money, the primary goal of the producer is to get the production under budget by cutting corners here and there...until something wrong happens and someone gets hurt as result. When a stunt coordinator is not on a set and someone gets hurt, the coordinator is not responsible for what occurred, but the director and producer are—their primary concern is generally not safety when shooting a scene (and often they just don't realize that a stunt may be dangerous).

Regretfully, these types of situations happen more often than people are aware of, and they usually are not reported in trade papers or television reports. Unfortunately, the only time the public hears about this type of accident is when a high-profile person dies. Prime examples of this are actor/model Jon-Erik Hexum, who shot himself in the head with a prop gun loaded with blanks on the set of a CBS series; Vic Morrow, who was killed along with two small children when a helicopter crashed into them on the set of *Twilight Zone: The Movie*; and Brandon Lee, who was killed in a tragic shooting mishap while filming a scene for *The Crow*.

Unless you work in the stunt industry, you won't hear about it when a stunt actor gets severely hurt or dies on a set because stunt actors do not have high-profile names that would be recognized by the general public. Further, disclosing reports of such accidents will bring unwanted attention to the production, so most reports are kept quiet.

Often we struggle to get things done and we are pressured by people above us who might not be aware of the day-to-day stress of trying to come in under budget and on time. I understand that this is all part of show business and making a profit, but I cannot begin to emphasize enough how much more important a human life is than getting a shot or two to save money. At the end of the day, when you look back at what you have accomplished, it's not finding a cure for AIDS or cancer, ending world famine, stopping countries from fighting, or solving other issues that plague the world. You're making pop commercial art for entertainment, and that really needs to be placed in perspective. Ask yourself, "Is it worth the risk of severely injuring or losing a human life, just to capture an image on film or tape?"

Horror Story #2

A fight choreographer was asked to train the lead actor for a film. The actor did not have any previous training in any martial art or combative sport. The actor was also the co-director and the screenwriter, and it was his first film. The actor was in every scene, and fighting onscreen was three quarters of the film's content. Stunt fighters were hired, and fight scenes were choreographed with the actor.

The choreographer attempted several times to get the actor to train with him on the basic kicks, punches, and stances, but the actor made excuses about being too busy to train and said that there were other important things for him to do. The actor thought that being an active member of the choreography blocking was enough training for him. But at this stage, the moves are shown only at half or three-quarters speed, at best. The actor/director tried to show the moves he wanted in the choreography from several films he had seen. But the choreographer merely saw the actor/director flopping his arms around like a lifeless squid. He asked, "What does that mean to you?" The actor/director replied, "I don't know. I saw it in a movie. It looks cool and I want to do it."

The fight choreographer was only able to train the actor for two 30-minute sessions because the actor did not have the strength and endurance to go any longer. The choreographer warned the actor that if he wanted to look good on film, they needed to get together more often as filming got closer. The choreographer also reminded the actor that he needed to get in shape. The actor agreed; however, he did nothing to get in shape. He was essentially all talk and no action.

Filming took place at the end of summer, during some of the hottest days of the year in the San Fernando Valley. The heat sapped the actor's energy quickly. The takes were not as crisp and clean as everyone wanted them to be. Several takes were done for each segment, until they were done right, to the best ability of the actor. After a couple hours of filming, the lead actor collapsed on the floor, complaining about how hard the techniques were to do. The crew was forced to take an hour break so the actor could regain his stamina. The screen fighters ended up padding the fight because, as the filming progressed, there were obvious and severe lag times between fighters as the actor got ready for the next opponent. This affected the timing and rhythm of the fight in a negative way, and the movie ended up looking comical in parts when it should not have.

What Is Strategy?

> *"If the opponent truly knows himself, then he needs not worry about the result of 100 battles. If the warrior knows himself and his opponent, he needs not fear the result of 1,000 battles."*
>
> —**Sun Tzu,** *The Art of War*

Put simply, a strategy is the result of a decision by the characters to resolve, deal with, or handle a physical conflict. The above famous line from Sun Tzu's *The Art of War* has been directly applied to the story arc of a film. A strategy is a game plan—a conscious or unconscious approach (depending on the character's training and disposition at the moment) that is a combination of mental, physical, emotional, and/or psychological approaches designed and implemented to overcome, divert, and/or defeat an opponent.

Question #1

If I have to train an actor with no experience and make him look like a black belt, a master, or a seasoned fighter, do I have to teach him everything that a real person with that type of experience and knowledge would know?

Of course not. That would be impossible due to the time you are given to get the actor ready. And it is also completely unnecessary to teach the actor everything. It will only bring on frustration from you and the actor, and you'll get a very angry producer and director because the actor might know a bunch of moves but not be good at any of them.

To train an actor successfully for film, you must understand that it's partially real and partially acting and attitude. The solution is to find out what the actor is good at doing or what he is physically inclined to do best. Train him in those few techniques so he is good at them. Then, teach him the attitude he needs to have when he is using that certain technique. You have to train him in the basics so he gets used to the moves and is comfortable with what he is doing, while he gains self-confidence.

This does not by any means translate to having easy, laidback sessions. You really have to know what the actor needs to learn and be a taskmaster when it comes to teaching and drilling him about new techniques and how to utilize them. It is best to have the actor be really good at a few moves, as opposed to him knowing a lot of techniques and being really bad at them.

The actor's acting skills also aid in the illusion that he knows what he is doing. And this is where you come into play. You have to tell the actor the reasons behind and the emotional ramifications of each technique he is learning. Some techniques are simple and do not need much explaining. But there might be complex or esoteric moves that the actor might not fully understand. In a regular martial arts class, the teacher lets the student figure out for himself correct application of the technique. But when training an actor, you must give him answers about application of the techniques, along with the emotions and motivation behind the techniques. This is the only way to make the actor look effective onscreen.

In film, even though a character might not have any formal training or any type of official strategy against his opponent, he is still considered to have a strategy because the action is still a form of narrative storytelling that needs to be planned out by the fight choreographer.

An important backbone element in the Chinese Kung Fu movie genre is the use of strategy in combat. Although the audience knows what is going to happen in the end because the hero usually wins, they are nonetheless intrigued by the hero's journey and intense training, which develop the strategy the character uses and how he implements what he has learned when he finally faces the villain. As in any film genre, there are many examples of poorly executed elements (in this case, strategy). However, there are also some standout classics, such as Yuen Woo-Ping's *Snake in the Eagle's Shadow*, Lau Kar Leung's *36th Chamber of Shaolin*, Sammo Hung's *Prodigal Son*, Joseph Kuo's *7 Grandmasters*, Ng See Yuen's *Secret Rivals*, and Chang Cheh's *Five Deadly Venoms*. These films use strategy in creative and ingenious ways while being completely entertaining to the audience, who might not be practicing martial artists.

A well thought-out strategy by the fight choreographer will show the character's thought process and is an extension of the character's personality. A strategy in a film exists for the following main reasons:

- To advance the story
- To display a character's motivation, character arc/development, and approach to self-preservation, even though he might die
- To serve as an extension of the character's personality and show how he would express himself in a physical conflict
- To show the character's intelligence in a physical and non-verbal expression

Basic Types of Strategy

There are two types of character strategy that a choreographer needs to be aware of. They are:

- **Planned.** This type of strategy is premeditated in thought, training, and preparation before the physical encounter occurs. The time to prepare can be seconds, hours, days, or years before the conflict starts. Of course, the more time given before the battle, the more elaborate the strategy scheme will be. This type of strategy gives the combatant an offensive state of mind even if he doesn't throw the first blow because he has had time to think it over.

- **Organic.** This type of strategy is thought up and/or developed while the physical conflict is occurring. An organic strategy often occurs because the combatant did not expect the situation to escalate into a physical confrontation. Sometimes an organic strategy is used when a planned strategy did not work out as expected. Quick thinking, improvisational skills, and the ability to immediately respond are required for the combatant to get out of the situation with minimal damage. If the combatant does not have any training, he will almost certainly react out of haste. He will not be able to quickly assess the situation and respond accordingly or get himself out of danger because he has no previously conditioned responses or reflexes.

The two types of fight strategies can be combined to become more effective in storytelling. For example, sometimes a fighter prepares for an opponent to approach him in a certain way, and then when the fight actually occurs, the opponent comes at him in an unexpected way for which the fighter is not prepared. To survive, the fighter has to adapt to a new way to fight.

Strategy can be difficult to see in a one-on-one situation. It's much easier to see a strategy when a large group of fighters is involved because the combatants in the group have a similar purpose.

Use of Technique with Strategy

The character's choice of techniques has to serve the strategy in order for him to be successful. Keep in mind that the technique and how it is applied reveals the strategy and personality of the character. When a strategy is played out between people of equal skill and power, it can be very complex, like a physical chess match.

In chess, there is a general strategy that a player thinks several moves ahead. In fighting, the same rule of strategy applies. The fighter has a strategy in mind (depending on how much he knows about his opponent) before he starts fighting. This can all change when the opponent does not react or respond in the way the fighter originally projected. The fighter has to think of another way to defeat his opponent. Although he might not have the correct strategy, the opponent might give him an opening that he can take advantage of.

Also in chess, you have pieces that can only move a certain way. You have to play so that the pieces all work together and can back each other up. In fighting, the same rules apply. Each technique has a specific angle, purpose, and direction, but they all must work together in order to be effective.

Now, the questions to ask are:

- How comfortable and adept is the character with his techniques?
- Is there a character arc where the character understands the techniques better than he did before?
- How physically intelligent is the character? And how do you display it?

Showing Character and Personality through Strategy

A strategy is a proposed hypothetical solution based on what a fighter knows of the opposition, coupled with his creative and cognitive thinking skills. This solution is designed to protect the fighter, an object sacred to him, or someone he loves. The hero usually does not know whether a strategy will definitely work, but he devises the strategy to the best of his knowledge and experience. Often the hero's initial strategy does not work against the villain, and then the stakes are raised and he has to come up with another strategy—planned, organic, or a combination of the two.

A character's strategy for a fight on film is based on the following components:

- **Purpose and motivation for getting into the physical conflict.** The character's purpose is the key foundation in the strategy and his approach to confronting his opponent. There are big differences in purpose between a person who wants to fight for revenge and a pacifist who does not want to fight, but is forced to, for example, to rescue his daughter. The character's purpose gives you the parameters for how the character will manage and approach the confrontation. What motivates the character to get into the fight? A character's motivation is very important in developing your fight strategy.
- **Desired outcome.** Similarly important to why the fight began in the first place is how the character wants it to end. Is his intention to outscore, immobilize, embarrass, kill, or escape from his opponent? Knowing this will influence the character's strategy. But his strategy needs to be flexible because his desired outcome might change during the course of the fight. At first he might plan on knocking out his opponent, but after taking a few too many good hits, he might change his mind and make survival and escape his goals instead.
- **Choice of technique.** The choice of technique is a reflection of the character. Imagine this as a game of chess. What pieces does the character have on the board? How does he use them? Sparingly? Conservatively? Or aggressively? What is his knowledge and savvy in being able to use the pieces to his advantage?

- **State of mind.** Is the character able to think and carry out the strategy while under pressure? Can he adapt and change when an initial strategy does not work? Does he have a backup strategy?
- **Will.** Does the character have the guts, courage, and passion to follow through with the strategy? What obstacles will threaten his courage?
- **Assets and handicaps.** What are the character's assets and handicaps going into the confrontation? This includes mental, physical, and emotional handicaps. Depending on the story, a handicap can turn into an asset and vice versa.
- **Sacrifice.** What is the character willing to give up in order to be successful? Does he fully understand what he is giving up to follow through with the strategy?
- **Preparation.** What type of preparation did the character have before the confrontation? This includes physical, emotional, and mental preparation. If the character is only prepared in one way (physically, mentally, or emotionally), the strategy might very well fail.
- **Self-knowledge.** How well does the character know himself? Self-knowledge is very important in a confrontational situation because the character might place impractical expectations upon himself.
- **Knowledge of opponent(s).** How well does the character know the opponent? This gives the character a way to prepare his strategy to confront the opponent. If he does not know his opponent, he would have to be thorough in his training and preparation and be ready for anything. But in film, there is always something for which the character is unprepared.
- **Surroundings.** The physical environment where the fight takes place has a great effect on strategy. What does the character know about the surroundings where the fight takes place? Can he use what he knows to his advantage? Or are the surroundings a disadvantage for him? Can he adjust his strategy accordingly? Are there any unforeseen elements in the environment for which the character was not ready?

  A good example of the effect of surroundings on a character's strategy is in *The Seven Samurai*, when the leader shows the terrain of the village and its surroundings, and then discusses what they plan to do to protect the village. Another good example is in *Star Wars: Episode IV*, when they use the holographic image to show the Death Star and how it can be destroyed.
- **Tenacity.** Does the character have the guts and tenacity to follow through with the strategy, even though it might seem like a seemingly impossible task?

Can the character handle the actual physical, psychological, and emotional pressures of the conflict? Do others balk at the character's strategy? And does the character have the tenacity to defy skeptics and his own self-doubt?

Issues That Can Nullify a Character's Strategy

Several issues can nullify a character's strategy. These include the following:

- The opponent is able to foresee what is coming because he knows the character well, because he has been informed by an ally of the character's strategy, or because the character is telegraphing his strategy through intention or emotion.
- Unforeseen issues were not worked out beforehand when the character planned the strategy.
- The opponent is much greater than the hero expected.
- The hero is faced with unexpected events that he did not anticipate in his strategy.
- The hero does not have enough confidence in himself and/or the strategy to follow through with it.
- The strategy is weakly constructed.
- Acts of nature occur that alter the terrain.
- The strategy is too complex for the combatant to remember while in the throes of combat.
- The combatant is not skilled enough to execute the strategy.

Ways for an Audience to See Strategy

It's really good for the choreographer to have the audience piece together the strategy. To do this, the choreographer has to lead the audience by the hand, giving them subtle clues. The object is to make the audience think they discovered the strategy themselves. Strategy can be revealed with dialogue, but this is a bad practice and can seem campy if it is poorly executed and too much is exposed to the audience. Instead, the strategy should unfold as the action starts and be revealed through the choice of techniques as the action progresses.

The audience can see strategy in the film when you:

- Make the strategy an integral part of the story

- Contrast the styles and approaches between different fighters and different fights
- Make sure they know the terrain of the environment before or during the conflict
- Ensure that they understand the agenda of the people involved in the physical conflict
- Show a premeditated preparation of a strategy unfolding before their eyes
- Show techniques used in a training sequence to get the audience used to seeing these techniques practiced, and then show their strategic and practical application in a "real" situation in the film

Often you will see a strategy applied and there is no real tension because the strategy is too sound or easily applied without any resistance from the opposition. Thematically, the gray area that a filmmaker needs to understand is creating a strategy that will:

- Produce doubt in the audience. The audience has to have a certain amount of doubt, thinking to themselves, "Will this idea work? Are they able to do this? How is this going to work against the antagonist?" If they do not ask themselves these types of questions, then the strategy could be much too sound.
- Not be so simple that the audience will be a step ahead of the story. This is lazy storytelling and choreography.
- Not be so complex or convoluted that the audience cannot follow or understand it.

Real-Life Strategists

Following are examples of some real-life strategists that we can watch and learn from:

- **Muhammad Ali.** Ali is a three-time world heavyweight boxing champion. He is a master strategist in and out of the boxing ring. He played with his opponents mentally and physically before and during the fight. When he fought Sonny Liston, Ali would mentally throw off Liston before the fight with strategic taunting. Another example is when Ali fought George Foreman, then the heavyweight champion of the world. Ali, the challenger, played psychological games with George Foreman's head during their only fight in Zaire. Everyone thought Foreman was going to destroy Ali with his powerful punches, as he did with all his previous opponents. But Ali talked to Foreman during the fight, telling him things such as, "Is that all you've got?" Ali leaned on the ropes while Foreman pummeled away at him. This "rope-a-dope" technique is probably the most recognizable strategy phrase in boxing history. And to counter Foreman, Ali would throw and connect solidly with right crosses (the furthest hand from Foreman) without throwing a punch with his closest hand. This is considered a great insult to a fighter because Ali did not have a lead punch to set Foreman up, and he was able to hit Foreman with the hand furthest away from him. Eventually, Foreman got physically tired and started questioning his skills and having doubts about his power. Soon, Ali was able to knock out Foreman in the seventh round to become the new heavyweight champion.

A very similar strategy was used by the hero in the final fight in *Rocky III*, when Clubber Lang fought Rocky for the second time.

- **Phil Jackson.** Jackson is an NBA coach, winning nine world titles as a coach and one as a player. He is also known as the "Zen Master" for his holistic approach to coaching his players and his Eastern philosophy influence. Jackson is noted for modernizing Tex Winter's triangle offense, which stresses selfless team play, as well as for his handling of difficult players on the team. Jackson is known as a master strategist for motivating and getting the most out of his star players, as well as for his approach against opposing teams.
- **Miyamoto Musashi (1584–1645).** Musashi was one of Japan's most famous swordsmen and the author of *The Book of Five Rings*, originally a series of letters to one of his students explaining his strategy and philosophy for why he lived beyond the lifespan of several swordsmen. (Most swordsmen did not live past the age of 18.) Instead of dying on the battlefield, Musashi eventually died of natural causes. He fought 60 duels, created the two-sword Kenjutsu technique known as "two heavens as one" or "two swords as one." Musashi's life story has been recreated numerous times for film, episodic TV, and novels.
- **Dennis Rodman.** Rodman is a former NBA player. His outrageous clothes, hairstyle, and wild personal life off the court took attention away from his ferocious style of play that intimidated opposing players. He is noted for his aggressive defensive style of playing and his being unafraid of anyone he posted up against, even if that person was bigger or stronger than him. To give you an idea of the power Rodman had over some of his opponents, the flamboyant forward was once called on a technical foul during a playoff game against the Dallas Mavericks, because he was staring at an opponent to intimidate him while taking a foul shot. That's a great example of using mental, emotional, and physical warfare.

- **Sun Tzu (544–496 BC).** Tzu was a Chinese strategist who wrote the classic book of Chinese literature, *The Art of War*. It is said that Mao Tse-Tung and Joseph Stalin read the book to help them with their war campaigns.

Examples of Fight Strategy on Film

Here is a list of some films that use and display strategy as part of the story:

- ***Home Alone.*** Kevin's approach to the burglars as he booby traps the house shows his intelligence over the bumbling adult burglars.
- ***Saving Private Ryan.*** Strategy is shown in the opening assault as the U.S. soldiers approach the beach.
- ***Rocky II.*** The second fight and rematch with Apollo shows strategy when Rocky learns to be an orthodox fighter and switches back to southpaw.
- ***The Seven Samurai.*** This film shows strategy involving the terrain. Kurosawa gives you the feel and space of the village's terrain throughout the film.
- ***Die Hard.*** This movie demonstrates a cat-and-mouse game of strategy between Hans and John McClane throughout the film.
- ***A Nightmare on Elm Street.*** A nice example of a planned strategy is how Heather plans to catch Freddy Krueger.
- ***Way of the Dragon.*** An excellent example of strategy is present in the final fight scene in the Roman Colosseum with Colt (Chuck Norris). Tang Lung (Bruce Lee) changes his strategy with broken rhythm and defeats Colt.
- ***Yojimbo.*** A good example is Toshirô Mifune's mental and psychological strategy with the warring clans, pitting them against each other.
- ***Fistful of Dollars.*** This film is full of little strategies that all add up to the finale.
- ***Once Upon a Time in the West.*** The opening scene, with the gunfighter waiting for the train to arrive, is a great example of setup and payoff. Another good example of strategy is the scene in which Cheyenne (Jason Robards) is atop the moving train and ingeniously uses a boot to hide his gun.
- ***High Noon, Gunfight at the O.K. Corral,* and *Open Range.*** The final gunfights in these movies are excellent examples of strategy.

The Difference between Violence and Action

The ongoing argument in the media regarding the difference between action and violence is a very touchy and individual issue. What might be considered action to one person might be violence to another, simply because of that person's upbringing and values.

But for the purposes of this book, the distinctions between action and violence for entertainment purposes are defined by what you want to show (graphic), the type of fight (context of action in relation to the story), reaction and intent of the performers involved, and the type of sound or musical accompaniment involved. Willing suspension of disbelief also plays a vital part in what can be interpreted as action or violence.

In real life, striking someone is considered a form of violence, whether it was done for real or in jest. The differences between action and violence are the intent and purpose of the characters; the mood, feel, and emotion of the scene in relation to the story; and the emotion they are trying to elicit from the audience.

Following are the definitions of action and violence within a choreographed fight scene for TV and film. Note that there are gray areas in which a fight scene will have a heavy emphasis on action but can have a pinch of violence or vice versa—or the scene can be somewhere right down the middle, with elements of both violence and action.

- **Action.** The purpose and intent are to show a character's (often exceptional) skills in relation to his opponent's. The fight scene is designed to celebrate, focus on, and highlight the character's physical grace and skills. Elation, wonder, and euphoria are the general emotions elicited from the audience. For a comedic fight, the technique is sold by the deliverer and/or the recipient with an emphasis on farce or absurdity to elicit laughter from the audience. Examples of such fights can be found in *Rumble in the Bronx*, *The Three Stooges* episodes, and the *Mighty Morphin Power Rangers* TV show.
- **Violence.** The purpose and intent are to show the impact and repercussions (emotional and physical) of a technique on an opponent, displaying the raw emotions and intent of a physical encounter in a graphic/gory manner (in other words, showing bone breaking, excessive blood, loss of body parts, or death). The reaction from the audience is usually shock and terror at the effects of the encounter. Examples of such fights are in *A History of Violence*, *Vengeance*, the *Friday the 13th* series, and *Raging Bull*.

When putting together your action scene, the difference between action and violence rests on the following elements:

- The scenario and theme that were set up at the beginning of the film and follow through to the end of the film.
- The motivation and intent of the characters involved that gets them into the fight. Do they want to simply outscore or perhaps kill? How you portray a fighter's state of mind and purpose is crucial.
- Any dialogue and/or non-verbal martial acting to convey emotions and thoughts to the audience before, during, and after the fight. These are clues as to how the scene might play out.
- The mood, feel, and emotion of the fight scene in relation to the rest of the story. The fight is intricately linked to the other scenes. Choosing the wrong emphasis in a fight can throw the whole picture off balance.
- A character's intent behind the technique and the types of techniques used in the fight. How do you want to show the character's intent in the fight?
- The reactions of the characters when getting hit. The reaction to a hit can be anywhere from comedic to dramatic to graphic. Consider the reaction to a strike when it is used in different scenarios in different situations, genres, and moods. Think about the reaction when Curly from the Three Stooges reacts in disbelief and taunts Moe when he gets his eyes poked. In contrast, Yu Lou (Ti Lung) reacts and convulses in severe pain and anger when he is blinded right before he dies in *Vengeance.*
- The feeling and emotion of the outcome of the fight. Emphasizing action or violence in the fight has a direct effect on the scene that follows it, along with the rest of the story.
- Sound effects used to create either a comedic or serious effect. The use of a crunching noise as opposed to a "Three Stooges" pop noise can drastically affect the perception and believability of your fight.
- The overall emotional tone of the fight. This affects whether the fight should emphasize violence, action, or something in between. A fight can still be emotionally violent without showing any physical violence on the screen.

Justification for Actions Taken

The choreographer has to convey a lot of unspoken rules to the audience. The type of action is key to either connecting or disengaging the audience from what you are doing. The audience has a vested interest in the characters and what will happen to them, and that must be respected.

For example, suppose the hero is about to fight the main villain of the story, who raped and killed his wife, murdered his kids, and burned down his house. The audience expects retribution for the hero, so they give him a license to do what was done to him back to the villain. In this case, you are allowed to break the villain's legs, poke out his eyes, crush his skull, and stab him repeatedly with a knife until he is dead.

Now, suppose the main villain didn't murder the hero's wife and children. Suppose he was simply drunk and tried to kiss the hero's wife, but the wife slapped him. If the hero reacted as he did in the previous example, it would certainly be considered overkill and you would lose the audience—they would no longer like the hero.

Following are some examples of films in which action or violence was justified by the events that occurred:

- ***Man on Fire.*** Creasy (Denzel Washington) is justified in killing the members of La Hermanidad (The Brotherhood) because they kidnapped, and allegedly murdered Pita (Dakota Fanning). Creasy's job is to protect her at all costs and, on a deeper level, she restored his faith in life and gave him a reason to live. If Creasy merely gave the members of La Hermanidad flesh wounds and then let them go, the hero would feel off balance and out of character.
- ***The Princess Bride.*** We want to see Montoya kill Count Tyrone Rugen because the Count killed his father, and we have gotten to know Montoya throughout the film. We know Montoya is a righteous character who helped Westley get back to health, so we sympathize and root for him.
- ***Rocky III.*** We want to see Rocky win back his title from Clubber Lang to erase the doubt that Mickey, his deceased trainer, did not need to carry him. Rocky does not take Clubber's life because he was not responsible for the death of Mickey—doing so would have been out of line with the plot of the movie, and out of character for Rocky Balboa.
- ***First Blood.*** We want to see John Rambo give Sheriff Teasle his comeuppance because of Teasle's wrongful abuse of power.
- ***The Karate Kid.*** We want to see Daniel finally beat Johnny Lawrence at the tournament. But if Daniel decided to kill Lawrence for all his tormenting throughout the movie, it would be out of place.

- ***The Killer.*** Seeing Johnny Weng get arrested by the police is not enough retribution for the audience. Only when Inspector Li kills Johnny do we feel that he finally gets his comeuppance.
- ***The Chinese Connection.*** We feel relieved when Chen Zhen finally gets his revenge by killing Suzuki, who was responsible for poisoning his teacher and wreaking havoc on his school. Seeing Suzuki hit by Chen's flying kick and sent through the screen and out into the middle of the yard to die is a great ending exclamation point to a fight.
- ***Billy Jack.*** We want to see Billy Jack "put his right foot on Old Man Posner's face" because of all the atrocities Posner has gotten away with up to that point. We also want to see Billy kill Posner and his son, Bernard, because of the evil actions that they have committed throughout the film.

Five Basic Justifications

You need to be aware of the five types of justification in a fight scene.

- **Justification for the fight.** The fight needs to be justified by the story. There needs to be a reason why the fight is taking place and a motivation for the characters to be in the encounter. This also includes how the fight starts and ends. Without this justification, the fight becomes gratuitous. Lack of justification for the fight was a problem with many of the cheaply made Kung Fu movies that invaded grindhouse theaters in the '70s.
- **Justification for the type and style of fight.** The type and style of fight are essential because they should match the tone and mood of the story as well as the skills and training of the combatants. If a character is a Mob enforcer who collects protection money from his clients and has to beat them up if they won't pay, you should not have him flying around on wires or doing anything flamboyant because it would not match the style and timeframe of the film. It would look really odd to have Jason Bourne (*The Bourne Identity* and *The Bourne Supremacy*) perform acrobatics and extremely flashy techniques like Tony Jaa or Jackie Chan because the reality level of the fight is not that extreme.
- **Justification of the character's skills.** Are the character's skills justified in the story or is the audience expected to instinctively know the justification? People can fly in *The Matrix* because it was established and justified in the film with the "jump" from one building to the next. Most Western audiences emotionally leave the film when watching Asian films in which there is a lot of flying. The flying is not justified in the story, but it is a part of the culture's mythology so it does not need to be explained to the core audience.

- **Justification of the character's limits.** If a hero is fighting, he must have limitations; otherwise, he will lose the audience because he has no Achilles heel. Having weaknesses make the character more realistic and also helps with making the outcome of each fight less predictable. If a character has no weaknesses, he'll win every fight, which can quickly become boring for the audience.
- **Justification for the level of violence or action by the character.** You have to know the level of action or violence the character is going to take. The type of action the hero takes has to fit the actions that were taken upon him. This includes physical, mental, and emotional torment and anguish. This is much like the law of physics. For every action, there is an equal and opposite reaction.

5

The Whole Structure

A choreographed fight scene that is used for entertainment purposes in film and TV is ruled overall by a narrative structure. The fight has to serve a narrative purpose in order to get the audience emotionally involved. The physical choreography and technical aspects of putting together the fight scene also serve the narrative of the film. If a fight scene does not fit into the narrative structure of the film, then it will not serve a purpose except maybe for the choreographer or the fighting artist in front of the camera. If you do not have a story, motivation, and justification for the fight scene, you end up with a gratuitous fight scene to which an audience will not emotionally connect.

Introduction to the Process of Putting Together a Fight Scene

The structure of a fight scene is supported by the story and script from which everyone works. The script needs to be evenhanded and well-rounded to support and balance the fight scenes. From the story and script, we are able to extract the narrative of the fight scene, where the non-verbal dialogue of the fight is established and presented with a three act structure of its own. The narrative of the fight scene supports both the physical and technical elements of the scene. The physical elements are the actual choreography and assembly of the fight. The technical elements are the cinematography, editing, sound, and lighting of the fight scene. Both the physical and technical elements work hand in hand and balance each other out. With these three elements, we get the final product of the fight scene, which fits seamlessly into the script and story of the film (see Figure 5.1).

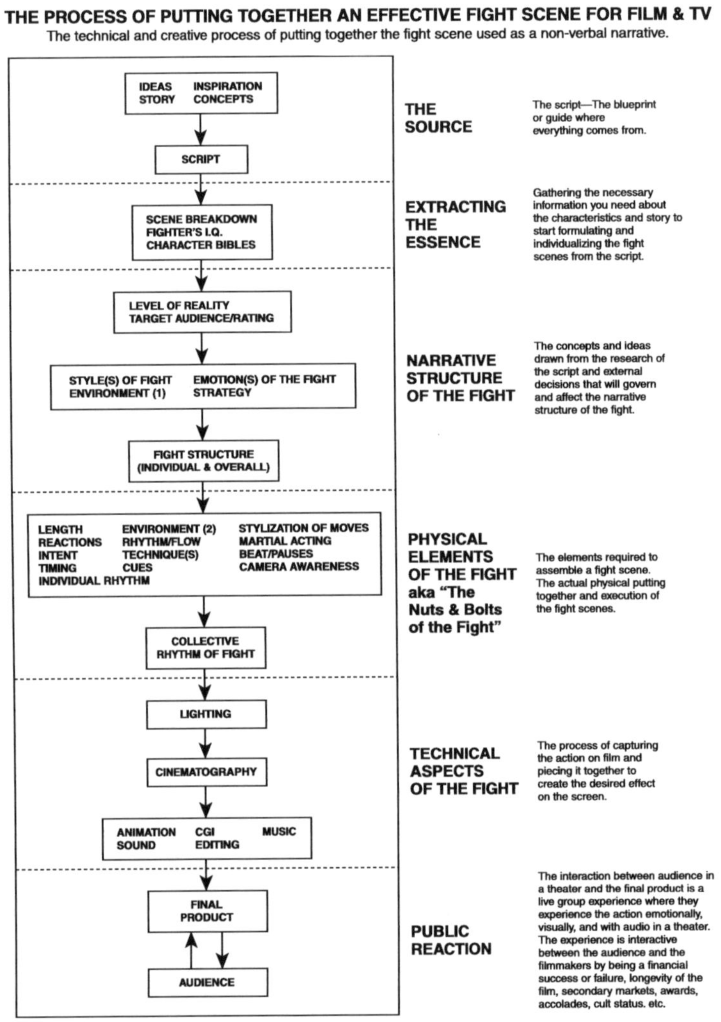

THE PROCESS OF PUTTING TOGETHER AN EFFECTIVE FIGHT SCENE FOR FILM & TV

The technical and creative process of putting together the fight scene used as a non-verbal narrative.

IDEAS INSPIRATION STORY CONCEPTS → SCRIPT

THE SOURCE — The script—The blueprint or guide where everything comes from.

SCENE BREAKDOWN FIGHTER'S I.Q. CHARACTER BIBLES

EXTRACTING THE ESSENCE — Gathering the necessary information you need about the characteristics and story to start formulating and individualizing the fight scenes from the script.

LEVEL OF REALITY TARGET AUDIENCE/RATING → STYLE(S) OF FIGHT ENVIRONMENT (1) EMOTION(S) OF THE FIGHT STRATEGY → FIGHT STRUCTURE (INDIVIDUAL & OVERALL)

NARRATIVE STRUCTURE OF THE FIGHT — The concepts and ideas drawn from the research of the script and external decisions that will govern and affect the narrative structure of the fight.

LENGTH REACTIONS INTENT TIMING INDIVIDUAL RHYTHM ENVIRONMENT (2) RHYTHM/FLOW TECHNIQUE(S) CUES STYLIZATION OF MOVES MARTIAL ACTING BEAT/PAUSES CAMERA AWARENESS → COLLECTIVE RHYTHM OF FIGHT

PHYSICAL ELEMENTS OF THE FIGHT aka "The Nuts & Bolts of the Fight" — The elements required to assemble a fight scene. The actual physical putting together and execution of the fight scenes.

LIGHTING → CINEMATOGRAPHY → ANIMATION SOUND CGI EDITING MUSIC

TECHNICAL ASPECTS OF THE FIGHT — The process of capturing the action on film and piecing it together to create the desired effect on the screen.

FINAL PRODUCT ⇄ AUDIENCE

PUBLIC REACTION — The interaction between audience in a theater and the final product is a live group experience where they experience the action emotionally, visually, and with audio in a theater. The experience is interactive between the audience and the filmmakers by being a financial success or failure, longevity of the film, secondary markets, awards, accolades, cult status. etc.

Figure 5.1
The whole process.

The diagram in Figure 5.2 shows the delicate balance between physical, technical, and narrative elements. The most active and crucial part of this chart is the balance between physical and technical elements involved in the fight that is being supported by the narrative story of the fight.

Here is a brief explanation of each element in Figure 5.2:

- **Story and script.** These are the foundations that support everything the film is based on; they are the blueprint. The well-rounded and balanced script that everyone works from is represented by a ball. When the story is unbalanced, it cannot properly hold nor support the action.

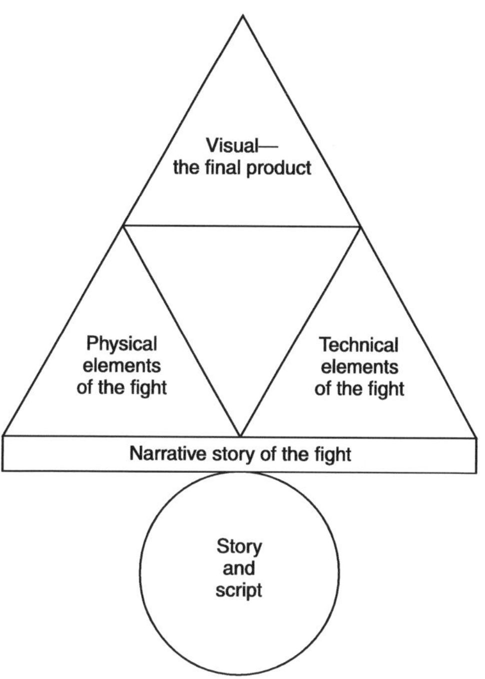

Figure 5.2

The balancing act.

- **Narrative story of the fight.** This is the story based off the script that the fight will tell in a non-verbal way. This serves the script and provides a base for the other elements to balance themselves and work from.
- **Physical elements of the fight.** This represents the actual physical choreography of the fight, using actors, stuntmen, and so on.
- **Technical elements of the fight.** This represents cinematography, lighting, editing, sound, and special effects (traditional and CGI). A majority of this process is done after the physical production of shooting the fight scene.

Note

There are people and departments who straddle the physical and technical realms, such as the director, stunt coordinator, fight choreographer, and sound engineers, who provide a very important balance between the two disciplines.

- **Visual elements.** This represents the end product of both technical and physical elements.

The Balancing Game

The balance between all departments is crucial in creating an effective and successful fight scene. If one area is off balance, other parts have to compensate for that part's weakness.

The model in Figure 5.2 shows a perfectly balanced relationship between physical, technical, and narrative elements that is supported by the story and script.

Relationship between Physical and Technical

The crucial part of the balancing game here lies between the physical and technical elements, where both sides need an equal balance and each side must understand what the other side is doing. Both sides need to stay balanced and lean on each other when necessary. There are often times when the technical comes into play and can overcompensate when the physical is weak (such as when an actor cannot do the stunt or fight or when the fight might be too long, requiring editing fixes to improve the pacing). However, the balance can get disrupted even when you have a well-choreographed fight scene involving capable actors. Poor choices in camera angles and/or choppy, illogical editing decisions can disrupt the natural flow of the fight, which in turn takes the audience's emotions and viewing experience out of the picture.

For an example of an unbalanced scale, suppose you were filming Jackie Chan and Jet Li battling against each other in what should result in one of the greatest film fights of all time. You've got them for three days only and you cannot go back for any reshoots after those three days. But the Director of Photography (DP) is used to filming messy barroom brawls where the action is not as detailed and intricate as what is about to be filmed between these two elite, world-class screen fighters. He gets in too close when he should be much wider to show the action better, and he gets angles that do not highlight the two actors to the best advantage. Or maybe the DP comes from the highly stylized world of music videos and commercials, and he uses exciting angles and swish pans, but is not able to capture the relationship between the actors or the essence of the fight because the camera moves are way too flashy. Or, maybe you have a great DP who captures everything beautifully on film, and then you have an editor who unnecessarily messes with the timing and rhythm between Jackie and Jet, using quick cuts that don't give you any idea of what they are doing onscreen. As result, you don't see much of anything from these two great film fighters.

Problems That Can Arise on the Technical Side

Several potential problems on the technical side can throw the scale off balance. For example, the DP might not get the shot and may have to do it over several times. This tires out the actors and stunt players, and the fight starts to look sloppy. The DP might finally capture the fight properly after several takes, but perhaps he captures the sloppier of the fights.

The technical side has an edge that the physical does not have, and that's time allotted for editing the action, as opposed to time allotted for shooting the fight. The actors and stunt players can perform a fight only so many times before they get tired; also, the shooting schedule is more limited and costlier compared to an editing schedule.

Compensating for One Another

Nothing will ever be perfect in the technical and physical relationship. Often when the physical side is lacking, the technical side can compensate, and vice versa. But there has never been a film where physical has overpowered technical, just because of the way a film schedule is structured, works, and operates.

X Factors That Were Not Worked into This Equation

I've discussed the main factors of this delicate balancing act, but there are also some other factors that can affect the balance. These factors include:

- Studio head and executive producer decisions that can override everything (including the story)
- MPAA movie rating
- An actor's interpretation of the scene

6

The Source

What is the source? The source is a place where you get all the information you need to know about the characters, the story, everyone's motives, and most importantly for the fight choreographer, each character's reason to fight. You're probably thinking to yourself, "I don't need to know and understand the story. I just wanna put together the fight scene," and to be perfectly honest, anybody can put together an incredible fight scene that looks cool and will dazzle the audience visually. But these choreographers understand only part of what it takes to put together an effective fight scene, and don't realize that the difference between a good fight scene and a great fight scene often lies in how effectively that scene is incorporated into the overall film story. A great fight choreographer can create great fight scenes because he understands the story and is able to emotionally suck the audience into the conflicts by specifically tailoring every fight to enhance the story and individualize the moves for each character and their emotions for those scenes. So do you want to take the steps to being a great fight choreographer? If so, let's start with the story.

The Story

Story is the raw elements of inspiration and creativity that eventually grow into a script. People who are not writers assume that a screenwriter just sits in front of the computer and pecks away at a screenplay until he finishes it. But that's not true at all. There's a process to it that is different for everyone. Often if you're given a script, someone will ask, "What's the story about?" I've seen people (who were not the writers) shrug their shoulders and wave the script in the air in front of the person's face, suggesting that they're holding "the story" in their hands. No, that's the script you are holding. What is the story about?

The story is the core of what the script is trying to get across. It is the main thread throughout the script that holds everything together; it is the foundation from which the script is written.

Some stories can be very complex and hard to describe in a few sentences. There are a few things to note when you are trying to describe an action story.

- Action has to be expressed in a physical manner; otherwise, it wouldn't be called *action*. So certain scenarios and characters have to be written and created to express action in a creative and entertaining manner.
- Action is a visual experience that needs to be described in terms that start with one emotion and end with a different emotion.
- Unfortunately, a lot of action films get banal because of a very predictable story that does not push the envelope and challenge the audience.

The following sections describe some of the story elements that specifically make an action film. By knowing these elements, you'll be able to understand the type of action and what is needed for each character that is involved in an action sequence.

Back Story

Back story is an event or something that happened to a character in the past, before the point in time at which the screenplay starts. This adds depth to the character and usually results in a payoff in the end (but not necessarily). Examples of back story include:

- ***Dirty Harry.*** We realize that Harry Callahan was married and was a different person in the past than he is now, when he visits his fallen partner at the hospital. There is no real payoff here, but we realize Callahan has a history, and this adds emotional depth to the scene.
- ***Star Wars.*** We are led to believe by Obi Wan Kenobi that Luke's father, Anakin Skywalker, was killed by Darth Vader. The payoff is when Luke goes to destroy the Death Star, providing the audience with the feeling that justice has been served. This back story is revisited in *The Empire Strikes Back*, when Luke discovers that Anakin became Vader, making Vader Luke's real father.

- ***The Karate Kid.*** Daniel finds Miyagi drunk and passed out in his old U.S. army uniform. He reads that while Miyagi fought for his country, his wife was in an internment camp and died while giving birth. There is no real payoff, but the scene adds a lot depth to the characters involved.

Exposition

Exposition is the art of passing on necessary information to the audience to advance the story. The most difficult thing about exposition is expressing the details in a natural way so they become part of the story and dialogue without calling unnecessary attention to the information.

Bad exposition is when the character says exactly what he is going to do, and then goes out and does exactly what he just said. This does not provide any excitement or suspense to the story. Director Martin Campbell comments,

> *I always contend that if you believe in the characters and you believe in what they are saying and you're involved, then of course you can get away with it. One of the problems always is that with a convoluted/complicated plot, there are times when your back is against the wall and you have to tell people what is happening and what the intentions are. So it becomes expository. Well, I'm afraid that's a necessity and there's no getting away from it, so you'll have to do it as elegantly and as convincingly as possible.*

Character Arcs

A *character arc* is the growth of a character from the beginning to the end of a film. What does the hero learn about himself? How does he change? What are the events and characters that make that character change? Is the character in a better place than when he first started?

For example, in *The Long Kiss Goodnight*, Samantha Caine is a schoolteacher with amnesia who does not remember anything from her life starting from six years ago. She desperately wants to find out who she was and what she did before the amnesia. Each time someone from her past appears, things happen to her that make her question what she did in her past. In the second act, she discovers that her real name is Charly Baltimore and that she was a trained assassin for the government who went deep undercover while posing as a schoolteacher. When Samantha/Charly finally accepts who she really is, she does not want to accept her feminine/passive side along with her daughter, Caitlin, and she does everything she can to forget that side of her. It isn't until Caitlin is kidnapped that she reconciles her passive and loving side and is able to embrace who she wanted to be and who she was (her feminine and masculine sides) in order to go after the villain and rescue Caitlin.

In other instances, the hero does not change or have much of a character arc, but the situations and people around the hero do. With these types of characters, their skill set encompasses their world, and we see it unfold. We see the character adapt as the story advances. Inspector "Dirty" Harry Callahan is a self-righteous loner who constantly struggles to operate in a flawed justice system. Dr. Indiana Jones is driven by his all-consuming quest to find ancient artifacts, despite all the odds set against him. James Bond is a self-assured master of espionage who single-handedly saves the world and gets the girl in the end—all with a certain sense of style, panache, and grace. Jack Ryan is much smarter and more resourceful than the people around him, whose high morals force him to correct the worldly injustices that come his way. In the *Once Upon a Time in China* trilogy, Wong Fei Hung is a Chinese patriot who takes action when his Confucian morals and high ideologies are threatened. In the TV series *Kung Fu*, Kwai Chang Caine is a Shaolin monk, a man of peace who does everything passive to avoid physical confrontation. But, he is forced to fight when he is cornered and has no other options.

To increase their depth, characters usually will have some type of a flaw, yearning, phobia, or expectation that is satisfactorily dealt with and/or resolved by the end of the film. How the character responds and takes on his limitations gives him depth. However, you cannot create a flaw just to have a flaw. It needs to be integrated into the story; it must be a working part of the story and somehow pay off later.

As an example, in *Rocky*, Balboa is proud that in his entire career, no one has broken his nose in a match—that is, until Apollo Creed easily breaks it in the first round of the fight. In *Raiders of the Lost Ark*, Indiana Jones is afraid of snakes. This later becomes an obstacle when he has to enter the Well of Souls to find the location of the Lost Ark of the Covenant. Unfortunately, the floor is covered with snakes. In *Midnight Run*, Jack Walsh still wears an old, broken watch that his ex-wife Gail gave him when they were married. When he finally sees her and finds out that her current husband is being promoted to captain of the police force and is still on the take, he realizes that she is not coming back to him, and he is finally able to let the watch go and move on with his life.

Why do we watch these films when we know that the hero is going to come out alive in the end, ready for another sequel? These heroes are much larger than life, so we are willing to suspend our disbelief when the story and action are well-executed. When a story is expertly told, the audience is more concerned about the journey and the quality of it than the eventual destination. If the story is told well, the audience wants to get on that ride again.

We also see something in these characters that we admire or wish we could do in real life, and we want to see how the characters will deal with the situations that surround them. We live vicariously through them, emotionally going through every step in their journey with them, which creates an emotional bond.

Sequels, however, can get dicey and boring if the creators have already exhausted every possible situation for that character. The creators have to stay one step ahead of the audience. This also includes the choreography of the action scenes. If the audience can guess what the character's next action is, you are in big trouble. The tension the action holds is no longer there. With action, it is important to know the characters' arcs because there will be fight scenes sprinkled throughout the film. The fight choreographer needs to know where the characters are in the character arc to create an effective fight scene and not give anything away regarding what will happen further on in the story.

Reveals

A *reveal* is a moment in a film when an issue or something about a character is unexpectedly brought to the character. It is important for the choreographer to know when to reveal personality traits, habits, and skills. Think about this: How would the story change if Jenny knew John was the hit man who accidentally blinded her when they first reconnected in *The Killer*? In *True Lies*, what if Harry's wife or daughter found out that he was a spy earlier in the movie because he got a severe cut or injury that could not be easily explained or hidden from them? In *Rocky*, Rocky is proud that he's never had his nose broken in a fight. What if Spider Rico broke Rocky's nose as the film opened, as opposed to Apollo breaking it later on? It would not have been a big issue when Apollo broke it, if Spider had broken it first. As it stands, we immediately understand that Rocky is outclassed and over his head when Apollo breaks his nose in the first round. If made at inopportune times, these revelations would change the dynamics of the story, let alone the action. As a fight choreographer, you have to protect these revelations by knowing when to reveal them in your fight scenes.

Setups and Payoffs

It is crucial for a fight choreographer to pay attention to the setups and payoffs in a script. A *setup* is an event, situation, trait, and/or flaw in the character about which you show or tell the audience in the story. The *payoff* is an event, situation, or revelation as a direct result of the setup that the audience hopefully does not expect. There can be multiple setups and payoffs in a film. When well done, there are sometimes several setups that can all lead to one big payoff in the end. The setup does not necessarily have to be in the first act, nor does the payoff have to be in the end. In some cases, the payoff can immediately follow the setup, depending on the story.

It is important for a fight choreographer to know whether there is a setup and payoff associated with a particular fight scene. If there is, he must be careful not to tip off the audience by making it obvious that the payoff is coming, which might deflate its impact. Setups and payoffs can have different types of emotions, from melodramatic to humorous. Setups and payoffs are an integral part of the story and should not be separate, nor should they call unnecessary attention to themselves.

Following are several examples of setups and payoffs on film.

- ***The Killer.*** John finds out he's being framed by Sydney, his contact. After John disposes of the assassins who were out to kill him, he tells Sydney that he always saves the last bullet in his gun for either himself or his enemy. The payoff is near the end of the film, when Sydney finally delivers to John the money owed to him from the ruthless gangster, Johnny Weng. Sydney, close to death, does not want to die at the hands of a less-than-honorable gangster, and he asks John to kill him with the last bullet in his gun so he can die a respectable death. John fulfills Sydney's wish for an honorable death by shooting him. Another payoff is in the beginning, when John tosses Sydney a can of beer and he can't catch it because of his bad trigger hand. But the real payoff is in the third act, when Sidney shows up at Johnny Weng's house to retrieve the money that is still owed to John. He is still able to shoot Johnny's men with his bad hand.

- ***Rocky.*** Balboa has never broken his nose. As a result, Mickey questions his heart and commitment to the sport and kicks him out of his gym. The payoff is when Apollo breaks Rocky's nose in the first round, showing the audience that Rocky is way over his head and that Apollo is not a typical fighter he's encountered before.

- ***Raiders of the Lost Ark.*** In the beginning, Indiana Jones escapes in a plane from the South American natives and finds a snake in his seat. He tells Jock, the copilot, that he is afraid of snakes. The final payoff is an obstacle, when Indy finds the entrance into the Well of Souls to retrieve the Lost Ark of the Covenant with his nemesis, Belloq, close by, but the floor is full of snakes.

- ***Enter the Dragon.*** Before Lee goes to Han's tournament, Lee is told the truth about how his sister, Su Lin, really died. She had to either commit suicide or suffer deep moral dishonor at the hands of Han's men, lead by Oharra. The first payoff occurs late, at the tournament, when Lee's first opponent is Oharra. Lee easily defeats and outclasses Oharra to the point of humiliation.

But Lee is forced to kill Oharra when Oharra's ego gets the best of him, and he attacks Lee with a pair of broken bottles. It's a complex scene when Oharra is killed because it all focuses on Lee's face as he stomps on Oharra, crushing his chest. On Lee's face, we see the anger and revenge he is able to take for the death of his sister, mixed with sorrow that he has contradicted the philosophies of his passive Buddhist teachings as a Shaolin monk, which consider all life precious. The second payoff occurs in the final fight scene, when Lee finally faces Han. We are reminded of Lee's motivation when he faces Han and tells him before they fight, "You have offended my family and the Shaolin temple."

- ***Die Hard.*** The second act of Die Hard is full of intricate setups and payoffs that turn into new setups. One setup occurs when McClane hears gunfire and runs for cover before he is able to put on his socks and shoes. The first payoff is a humorous one where, after fighting and killing one of Hans' henchmen, McClane takes his shoes, only to find out that the henchman has feet smaller than McClane does. This payoff then turns into a setup, because the guy McClane killed was Karl's brother. Karl then loses control and vows to get revenge by killing McClane himself.

  The setup to the second payoff is when Hans first comes face to face with McClane, disguised as a hostage, and notices that he is barefoot. The payoff is that McClane escapes but is cornered; Hans gets his men to shoot and break the glass partitions, causing broken glass shards to sprinkle all over the floor. The only way for McClane to escape is to run through the broken glass in his bare feet. This shows how crafty, strategic, and ruthless Hans can be and also how gutsy McClane is when his back is to the wall. This also creates another payoff with Karl, who wants to get revenge for the death of his brother. Like a carefully set-up line of dominoes in which each one falls exactly where it needs to fall, *Die Hard* is made up of extremely well-crafted setups and payoffs that are intricately and expertly woven into a series of cause and effect situations from beginning to end, which is one reason why the film is considered a classic.

It is important for screenwriters and fight choreographers to understand that the relationship between a setup and a payoff must be delivered with an appropriate balance of anticipation and uncertainty. The setup must be satisfied at some point, but the payoff cannot be too obvious or too telegraphed. If, early in the story, Q shows James Bond an amazing new weapon, the audience will come away disappointed if they never see it in action. But if Bond practices with his new weapon too many times before using it to resolve the final conflict, the audience will have been prematurely informed of the impending payoff and the impact will be lost.

Justification of the Action and the Skills of the Characters

Now that you have a basic understanding of some of the fundamental elements of a story and a script, it's important to note that two of the most misunderstood and neglected elements in many action films are the justification of an action scene and the skills of the characters. The script should explain in a narrative form the reasons why the characters are fighting and the types of skills they have (if any). The action sequences need to be justified so the audience or reader can stay emotionally involved in the movie or script.

What elements logically and emotionally lead the story to an action scene? When reading a script you are going to choreograph or watching a film for the first time, think about how the audience is emotionally and logically led to the action scenes. If there is no reason or no solid justification, then the action scene is gratuitous and will lose the audience. The more reasoning behind the action, the better it is. Does the character's skill match his background and how he got that skill? If he has a military background, would he fight as if he was trained in Wushu?

Following are some examples of justification for action scenes.

- **Justification for when to fight.** In *Fist of Fury*, there is no real reason for Chen to fight until he loses the necklace that represents the promise he made to his mother to not fight. That, added to watching the immoral practices of the Boss and the physical abuse his henchmen are dishing out on Chen's fellow workers, leads Chen to take physical action to stop the injustices. The first time he fights is 40 minutes into the movie. That is a very long time, but the tension is built with the audience and their anticipation of seeing him fight. The buildup in story and character development that leads up to the fight is the foundation of what makes a great fight scene.
- **Justification for the character's type of fighting skills.** In *Die Hard*, John McClane's background is as a New York police detective. His process of deduction, his approach, and his fighting style are practical and streetwise, not flamboyant or extremely stylish or flashy. It would seem out of place for him to fight like Jet Li unless it was justified by his background or because in the world of that film, everyone fights like that (as in the *Once Upon a Time in China* series).
- **Justification for a mental and emotional connection with the character's fighting skills and special powers.** Does the script show how the characters relate to their fighting skills and/or special powers? Acquiring martial arts or fighting skills not only transforms the physical skills of the character, but also changes his outlook and how he sees things around him. This is especially true

when it comes to special powers that are newly acquired, such as in the birth of a superhero. Without an emotional connection to his skills/powers, the character will appear to be shallow and one-dimensional.

- **Justification for what the character should or should not do to his opponents.** This gives the parameters of what the characters can get away with without losing the audience. For example, suppose the hero of the film is a professional fighter, and he is being confronted by a minor character in the story, an unarmed, snot-nosed teen who does not know any better and forcibly asks the hero for his money. The hero savagely kicks him on the side of the leg and shatters his kneecap, and then gouges out the teen's eyes with the tips of his fingers. That would be considered overkill, really unnecessary and unjustified, and would probably turn off much of the audience. Now, if the villain of the story burned down the hero's house and killed his family, then that would justify the hero shattering the villain's kneecap and gouging out his eyes.

The Characters

When choreographing a fight scene, a choreographer needs to know the strengths and limitations of each main character, along with his traits that are specific to each story.

The Role of the Hero

The hero is usually the lead character and is the most active character in the story because his will and desire to overcome the odds propels the action. Typically, the hero is associated with self-sacrifice—he usually sacrifices his own needs on behalf of others. Sometimes the hero is reluctant to sacrifice himself because of ego, peer pressure, ignorance, fear, or insecurity. There can also be more than one hero in the story, such as the hero characters in *The Avengers, The Three Musketeers, Fantastic Four, X-Men, The Seven Samurai*, or *Ten Tigers of Kwangtung*.

Often, the hero is asked, forced, required, or decides to take a journey in pursuit of something or someone. This journey forces the hero to take action when he normally would not do so. The journey is usually a separation from a tribe, a group, a family, or a community. Although the hero might be reluctant to take the journey in the beginning, certain situations arise, forcing the hero to realize there is no turning back, and that he must take the journey. This is much like cutting the hero's umbilical cord—he is no longer spoon-fed, his daily, mundane routine no longer exists, and he has to rely on himself and his instincts for the answers.

Usually, the hero does not know what really lies ahead in the journey. This challenges the hero physically, mentally, and emotionally, making him more worldly, mature, and aware than when he first started, thanks to the obstacles, encounters, mentors, allies, and enemies he has encountered along the journey. The hero usually leaves emotionally as a boy and comes back a man. Even though his journey might only be a few days, the life experiences and challenges mature the hero.

Generally, the audience looks up to and follows the hero throughout the story. This is because the hero portrays or acquires a set of ethics, values, skills, or powers that we wish we could have. Heroes also have admirable qualities that we wish we could have, such as an ability to fight or to attract any woman in the room. Perhaps we envy the hero's self-confidence, swagger, and charisma, as with Bruce Lee or James Bond. Or, we might admire the underdog qualities of Rocky Balboa or Zatoichi, or the righteous doings of Wong Fei Hung or Marshall Matt Dillon from *Gunsmoke.*

The hero has to have personality traits that are universal, so the audience can identify with him, but he also has to be original. A healthy balance has to be struck between originality and universality. I'm sure you've seen films in which the hero's qualities are too universal. This ends up being generic and leaves little or no room for originality. By identifying with the hero in some way, the audience's personal identity is ingrained with the character of the hero on screen.

Usually, the driving forces that propel the story are the hero's will and desire. We are able to watch the hero grow and find his identity, and we see how the hero integrates with his part of the world. As we see the hero grow, we identify him with our own growth and our place in society because the hero on screen has universal qualities, emotions, and motivations we have experienced at one time or another. This is why underdog films are constantly told over and over—subconsciously, they empower the audience when they're well-executed.

The hero also represents the human spirit who takes positive action in life. He can also show the consequences of weakness and not taking decisive action. In the beginning, we might see the hero with the dark or negative side dominating his thoughts and actions. But as he is eventually exposed to and made aware of his flaws, he starts to shed the ones that are obstructing the path to his destination. Eventually, a part of the hero has to symbolically die (whether the part is physical, mental, emotional, or spiritual) in order for him to move on, complete his journey, and succeed.

Different Types of Heroes

The type of hero determines the type of story you want to tell. Generally, there are two types of heroes. The first type is the hero who is willing, self-motivated, and proactive, committing himself to action bravely and without any doubts. The second type is the hero who is reluctant and unwilling to take action. This type of hero is initially too passive to be proactive about taking action. He needs to be motivated or pushed into action by some external force.

The following sections contain descriptions of the basic types of heroes you'll find in a story. Often you'll find that certain hero types are combined, depending on the type of story that is being told.

The Underdog

The underdog is the type of hero who has all the odds stacked against him. There is nowhere for him to go but up. Usually this type of hero is so downtrodden and rejected by society, family (if he has any), and his peers that he finds or is given some small sliver of hope that propels his life and draws him into an adventure beyond the expectations of the people around him. Often, this adventure is even beyond the hero's own expectations. What makes the hero truly unique is how he seizes the opportunity given to him. It is the hero's determination, indomitable spirit, and willpower to overcome the odds while shedding his old internal thought patterns and traits that makes the story compelling and emotionally engaging for the audience.

Examples of the underdog include Rocky Balboa (Sylvester Stallone) in the *Rocky* series, Daniel LaRusso (Ralph Macchio) in *The Karate Kid*, and Chien Fu (Jackie Chan) in *Snake in the Eagle's Shadow*.

The Antihero

An antihero is seen as an outlaw or villain by the majority of the characters in the story, but the antihero has at least one trait with which the audience sympathizes. The antihero is the central character around whom the story revolves. Somehow we identify with the antihero because the character appeals to our common sense of loneliness, isolation, or rejection by society at some point in our lives.

There are basically two types of antiheroes.

- **The cynical/wounded antihero.** This might be the heroic knight with tarnished armor or a loner who has rejected society or was rejected by society. These heroes are outcasts, rogues, or bandits who have the sympathy of the audience throughout the story, but are considered outcasts by society. These heroes are usually honorable people who have withdrawn from the codependency of society, disillusioned for one reason or another, and they are usually doing something to rebel against it. They often do the wrong thing for the right reasons. We admire these types because they are able to turn their noses up to the very thing we all wish we could. Examples of this type of hero in action films include Robin Hood and Han Solo.

- **The tragic/unlikable type.** This is a central character who the audience does not admire. The audience sees this character's actions as immoral or unethical. These types of heroes are flawed, and they are not able to overcome their inner demons. Their flaws eventually win out, and the hero is destroyed by them. These are much like morality tales, warning us about what would happen if we took the easy route in life or sacrificed our humanity and respect for our fellow man for personal gain. Audiences like this type of hero (despite their distaste for his actions) because he brings out the curious voyeur in all of us. The audience wants to see this antihero get his comeuppance for his actions. Examples of this type of antihero in action films include Tony Montana (Al Pacino) in *Scarface* and Ryunosuke Tsukue (Tatsuya Nakadai) in *Sword of Doom.*

The Loner

The loner is the type of hero who is not connected or dependent on a community or group on a daily basis. His natural habitat is somewhere in the wilderness—a sanctuary where he is in his element and he feels safe and secure. At some point in the story, the loner has to go back into the group or society and interact to resolve or take action on an issue or conflict. Usually, the loner either later reconnects with the group or community or goes back to his sanctuary, away from everybody. An example of a loner is Dirty Harry.

Catalyst Heroes

This is the only type of hero who does not change throughout the story. The primary function of this type of hero is to bring change and transformation to the characters around him. Catalyst heroes are very useful and often used in episodic TV shows and continuing sequels for film. Examples of catalyst heroes include James Bond, Zatoichi, Dirty Harry, Yojimbo, and Wong Fei Hung.

Superhero

A superhero is one who is noted for acts of bravery, courage, and nobility beyond anything a normal human is capable of. His heroic acts are usually done in a costume to disguise his identity, so he can observe life without having attention called to him when he is not acting as a superhero.

Typically, a superhero is immediately associated with having superhuman skills, such as the ability to fly, run faster than a normal human, and/or use other incredibly heightened senses and skills beyond human capacity. However, that is not always the case. Superheroes such as Batman, the Punisher, Iron Man, and Shang-Chi are not bestowed with any superhuman skills. Batman has the skills of a master detective and strategist, he has technical knowledge and understanding, and he has mastered several different styles of martial arts. The Punisher has a Marine background, incredible fighting skills, and an extensive knowledge of weapons and explosives. Iron Man (alias Tony Stark) has his suit to protect him; this gives him the ability to fly and shoot beams of energy from the suit. And Shang-Chi has been trained in Kung Fu since his birth to become a living weapon.

The other type of superheroes includes the ones who have supernatural skills and powers. Generally, there are two types of superheroes with supernatural skills.

- Those that are given their super powers at birth. These are usually aliens from other planets and dimensions that come to Earth (or wherever the story takes place) for a reason or by accident. Superman is perhaps the most obvious example. The supernatural skills might be normal to people of their species from their planet, but these same skills make them stand out here on Earth because no one has their abilities. These characters have the point of view of an observer; they do their best to adapt and blend in with human Earth society. These types of characters give us a godlike perspective and show the frailties, ignorance, and blind spots we have as a species.
- Those humans who were transformed and given supernatural powers. This usually occurs from freak accidents in which the hero is exposed to dangerous unknown elements that have transformed him, giving him his supernatural skills and powers. The Hulk and Spiderman are fine examples. This type of superhero is interesting because of how he incorporates his supernatural traits while trying to live a normal life, all the while knowing deep down that his life has changed and there's no turning back. It can become a double-edged sword, in which the superhero accepts his skills and responsibilities, but he also knows he cannot live a normal life any longer, while they still have to deal with everyday human struggles.

Usually superheroes have a strong moral code that, combined with their own inner motivation, makes their desire to battle crime border on compulsive. They often reach a point of inner turmoil and conflict that can torment the lifestyle of their alter ego.

Comic-book superheroes generally appeal to teens because teens are struggling to find their identity and how they fit into society. This struggle parallels the feelings, growth, and eventual self-acceptance of the superhero.

Justifying the Hero's Actions

Unlike the villain who (depending on the story) can do whatever he feels is appropriate without any real moral boundaries, the hero's actions are bound by justification of the type of action he can take. The justification for the hero's actions is set and established by the villain. The villain's actions enable the hero to take action and violate the villain and his cohorts.

The level of action taken by the villain sets the parameters to which the hero responds. If the hero's action doesn't fit within the cause for the action set by the villain, it will be considered overkill and the audience may lose attention and emotional investment in the hero. There is an unspoken rule for the hero that the punishment must fit the crime because of what the hero represents to the audience. You cannot make the hero look as bad as (or worse than) the villain because you will lose the audience.

For example, consider these two scenarios:

- **Scenario #1.** The bad guy engages and taunts the hero by throwing a rock into his house. The rock hits the hero in the head, leaving a slight bruise. Mad, the hero walks outside and gouges the villain's eyes out for no other reason than because he was hit with the rock. This action would be considered overkill, and chances are the audience would lose the emotional investment they had made so far in the hero.
- **Scenario #2.** Now, if the bad guy takes a grenade, tosses it into the hero's house, and kills his wife and daughter, then it would seem more than appropriate for the hero to poke out the bad guy's eyes. In fact, the hero could justifiably do much more without losing the audience emotionally. This would not be considered overkill.

Now consider some examples in film:

- ***Man on Fire.*** John Creasy (Denzel Washington), just a shell of a man, living on the edge with no real reason to go on, develops a bonding relationship with Pita (Dakota Fanning), the nine-year-old girl he's assigned to bodyguard. This relationship gives Creasy a new lease on life and a reason to live. When Pita is kidnapped, it forces Creasy back into his old line of work, as a government assassin, as he attempts to rescue Pita and kill the people who are responsible for her abduction (and possible murder). Creasy's motive for revenge is a combination of the deep emotional bond he has developed with Pita and his code of ethics for his line of work.
- ***Enter the Dragon.*** Lee (Bruce Lee) easily defeats Oharra (Bob Wall) at Han's tournament, to the point of humiliating his opponent in front of everybody. With his pride devastated, Oharra grabs a pair of bottles and breaks them. By doing this he has breached the conduct of good sportsmanship and truly shows his colors. The fight has changed. It is no longer a tournament fight; it has turned into a duel because of Oharra's actions. Lee kills Oharra because

of his intent to do serious harm with the broken bottles. Lee's actions are further justified because Oharra was responsible for the death of Lee's sister, Su Lin (Angela Mao Ying).

- ***The Princess Bride.*** We initially see Inigo Montoya (Mandy Patinkin) as an antagonist because he assisted in the kidnapping of Princess Buttercup and had a duel with "the man in black." He tells us he was scarred as a child (physically and emotionally) when Count Tyrone Rugen (Christopher Guest) murdered his father, and then scarred the side of Inigo's cheeks with his sword. As the story progresses, we see how evil the Count truly is and how sincere, virtuous, dedicated, and chivalrous Inigo is when he rescues the man in black and assists in bringing him back to life. By the time he finally faces the evil Count, we want to see Inigo serve his revenge to the Count with his sword.

However, there are some exceptions to the rule about not making the hero look worse than the villain. Sometimes the hero starts out as less than heroic, or misguided, or somewhat immoral in his actions, and then changes his ways, such as Wyatt Earp or Huo Yuan Jia in the movie *Fearless.* The hero balances himself with virtuous action in the latter half of the story, sort of like an active redemption for the previous ill-willed actions. Or, if the hero of the film is an antihero, the audience follows his exploits, which serve more as a moral lesson to the audience about what happens when you drop your morals for personal gain.

Also keep in mind that a character's actions reveal who he is, and his actions are often much more telling than his words. That's because a character can say something he doesn't really mean, and it can be easily forgiven or ignored. But if the character consciously set out and struck someone with a blow to his body or head, and then explained to everyone that he didn't mean to do that, it would be very difficult for everyone around him to forget, forgive, or ignore him, because he physically violated someone's personal space.

The Villain

A good villain is what makes a good action/fight film. Without a great villain, the hero has nothing to rise above. Also, a great villain sees himself as a hero and has just motivations for doing his deeds. Often, the villain is a character who initiates the action, while the hero reacts to the actions of the villain, much like competitors in a chess game. A good example of this is in the movie *Die Hard.* New York detective John McClane is a flawed character who flies to Los Angeles to reconcile his relationship with his wife, Holly. But when Hans Gruber decides to rob the vault in the building, McClane's skills as a New York police detective and his flaws as a family man work perfectly to foil Hans' attempts to escape.

To have a good, effective villain, he or she must be extremely crafty, deceitful, sneaky, resourceful, and intelligent. In addition, he or she must be an effective leader. In the beginning, the villain's actions usually appear much bigger than the villain. All-encompassing, threatening, and deadly in their purpose, the villain's actions make the hero look diminutive in comparison, like Goliath compared to David. By doing this, the villain has laid a path out for the hero to follow—one that's set with booby traps that await him. As the hero takes this path that the villain laid out, we get to understand and see the hero's skills of deduction, savvy, and survival, and his ability to quickly think on his feet. The further the hero progresses, the smaller the villain appears. But to keep the suspense going with the audience, the villain shouldn't appear smaller than the hero unless he is extremely resourceful.

The villain's persona should be as rich and important as the hero's because the more we know about the villain and his motives, the more we worry about and sympathize with the hero. What you're asking the audience to do (without actually doing it for them) is to compare and contrast the hero to the villain as they are watching the movie. If you effectively stack the odds against the hero, the audience will be curious to see how the story will end.

The Yin/Yang Relationship between Hero and Villain

Almost everything the hero does is in reaction to the strategy, traps, and motives set up by the villain. We look at this from a bird's-eye view of the story—it is the villain who sets up and constructs the maze. And the hero, who's the most active person in the story, is the lab rat who has to successfully maneuver through the maze and make it out alive. Without the villain initiating an action, such as a robbery, kidnapping, murder, and so on, the hero has nothing to respond to.

Even though the hero is proactive with his actions, what sends him on his journey is the inciting action of the villain. The hero takes action in response to what the villain has done. If Darth Vader did not kidnap Princess Leia in *Star Wars*, how would Luke Skywalker have been able to find Obi-Wan Kenobi and leave Tatooine? James Bond would be doing pretty much nothing (except maybe drinking shaken martinis and sleeping with women, possibly providing us a different type of "action") if there was no evil villain trying to take over and control the world. Would Chien Fu have been able to learn the snake fist and create the cat-claw style if Pai Chang Tien was not on the run from Shang, the Eagle claw master? Imagine how boring it would be to see Indiana Jones teaching an archaeology class, and not partaking in an adventure.

A Villain's Skill

The villain's skill and prowess should be intimidating and should instill fear in the audience. If you show the audience what the villain can do, the audience immediately will compare that to the skills of the hero. Initially, a good villain is usually equal to or better than the hero. It is the hero's quick wit and his ability to think on his toes that keeps him alive. Using this strategy, you can not only keep the audience on the edge of their seats, you also can get them emotionally involved in the conflict and more willing to suspend their disbelief. A well-constructed villain gets the audience to think, "How is the hero going to overcome the villain this time?"

The villain's skills are often introduced first, and the hero has to eventually rise above to beat the villain. The villain usually thrives in the beginning of the film. In a fight scene at the beginning of the film, the villain usually has the upper hand if he faces the hero. Why is that? Because the hero needs a hill to climb that could be personal, an insult to the hero's pride, or a threat to the community or the hero's family and loved ones. The villain sets the parameters for the hero to react heroically, while also giving him a motivation and a reason to fight. Without the villain's actions, the hero would have nothing to respond to. Essentially, he would have no fire to put out. The villain's actions at the beginning of the film are what gets the hero to become proactive in getting involved. It also helps when the villain does not think that he is doing anything wrong, and that his actions benefit him and everyone around him.

The Mentor

The key function of the mentor is the teaching and training of the hero. Besides teaching and training the hero, the mentor can also pass on a gift that will eventually be a key to the hero becoming his own person. This could be a rite of passage or a key to open the door to an adventure. A good example is in *Star Wars*, when Obi-Wan Kenobi gives Luke Skywalker his father's light saber. Another example is in *Snake in the Eagle's Shadow*, when Pai Chang Tien gives Chien Fu a set of detailed foot patterns so he will no longer be beaten up by the bullies at the Kung Fu school.

Mentors often speak in the voice of God, a higher power, divine inspiration, or higher wisdom. Good mentors teach with enthusiasm, which affects the student, much like transferring of energy. The mentor acts as a higher conscience that guides the hero down the road of life and is there to protect the hero when he makes a mistake. The mentor also represents the highest aspirations or ultimate bliss for the hero. Usually, mentors themselves are former heroes who have survived their trials in life and are now able to pass on their gifts of knowledge and wisdom to the hero of the story.

Some mentors perform a special function as a conscience for the hero. They can introduce to the hero and reinforce a moral code. Another important function the mentor provides to the hero is motivating him and helping him overcome his fears. Often the hero might not be willing to overcome his fears, or he might be ignorant of them. It is up to the mentor to find a way to motivate the hero with what usually amounts to an unconventional kick in the butt. An example of this is in *Warriors Two,* when Sifu Tsang (Leung Ka Yan) teaches Hua (Casanova Wong) the art of Wing Chun Kung Fu and explains the theory of how recognition from eye to brain to hand takes too long and how Hua must act on instinct and not think by pricking his side with a needle while training to get him to respond by punching without thinking.

Another function of the mentor is sometimes to plant information or a prop that will become important later. The weapons master and designer "Q" in the James Bond films is a typical example of this. In the beginning of the film, Q shows Bond certain props, gadgets, and weaponry that he will use later on. When Bond is in trouble, he uses them to get out of the predicament.

The use of a mentor is a great way to show the transformation of the hero, and it's also a great way to show an intimate relationship and bond that is forged between student and teacher. For thousands of years, the role of mentor to student basically has not changed. This is especially true when it involves a specific trade or craft that takes a considerable amount of time to master because the specifics of the craft demand years and years of mentored practice to make it presentable to the public. In a fighting style or an approach to combat, the mentor's main objective is to make sure the student is ready to apply the skills passed to him in a "real" situation, outside of the safe and nurturing confines of the training arena. In a film, because the training sequence and development of the hero usually do not take up the entire run time, the mentor knows in the back of his mind that he must pass on a considerable amount of potentially incomplete information in the hopes that the student will understand, grasp, apply, and make those skills his own by the time the student leaves the training arena.

Sometimes mentors are sly, manipulative, and tricky and have to teach the hero lessons the hard way when they don't listen to the conventional way. A prime example of this is in *Drunken Master* where Beggar So (Simon Yuen Siu Tin) is trying to train a stubborn, rebellious, wiseass, Wong Fei Hung (Jackie Chan), who doesn't want to learn and keeps finding shortcuts or ways to avoid training. With each exercise, they keep trying to top each other. One example is when Wong is performing sit-ups while taking small cups in each hand and filling a bucket into another. Thinking his sifu is asleep (when he really isn't), Wong gets down and fills the empty bucket. Then Wong pretends to be tired and sweaty, telling his sifu he's finished. His sifu gives him a smaller set of cups to bring the water down to the lower bucket while continuing to do the sit-ups.

The mentor-student relationship is very much a part of our psyche, but it has fallen by the wayside since the industrialization of the world. Trades and crafts passed down from generation to generation have drastically fallen, and we have become more of a disposable workforce mentality.

What a mentor does is expand the student beyond his capabilities, understanding, and sight. The mentor knows things well ahead of the student. Sometimes they operate in ways that are unorthodox and that the student and audience might not understand.

In the Chinese language there is a separation between the words *teacher* and *mentor.* In Cantonese, *Sing sang* is what you would call a teacher who teaches you something in school that is not personal or requires you to express yourself in a deeper level than what you would expect in school, such as math, a language, and so forth. It is also how you would address a man—it is equivalent to *Mister* or *Sir.* A sifu is someone who teaches you a craft, trade, or art. A sifu knows his students on a deeper, more intimate level. The sifu probably knows the student more than the student knows himself because the sifu has been on the same path to self-discovery and knows the trials and expectations he puts on his students are the same that were expected of him when he was in the same position. The mentor essentially sees the student as a lump of clay that needs to get trained and molded, and he changes the student's untrained will and spirit to focus and channel his thoughts, efforts, and energy in a focused, positive direction for the better and for the art he is passing on.

Before accepting the student, the mentor studies and observes the prospective student in his natural habitat or everyday life to see whether he is a worthy candidate of the mentor's teaching. All the while, the student is unaware that he is being observed and scrutinized. The mentor looks at the student's temperance, level of humility, and demeanor in terms of how he handles everyday issues and how he treats others who are above and beneath him (if applicable). The mentor does this to get a clear picture of the prospective student to see whether he can handle the responsibilities and power that will be passed on to him. Essentially, the mentor asks himself, "Will this prospective student eventually be able to represent the art, style, or clan respectfully and honorably?"

The mentor-student relationship is very deep and intense. Much like a marriage, it brings out the best and the worst in both parties. We see the struggles of the mentor, trying to teach, inspire, and enforce his unique, personal ideology, philosophy, approach, strategy, and techniques to a student who does not understand the whole picture. The mentor is asked to stoop lower than he initially really wants to in order to pass understandable information on to the student. As a result, the mentor extends himself further than he expected and gets more emotionally invested in the student. Seeing that the mentor has flaws, such as impatience and intolerance toward a student, makes him more human, yet also shows the student that there is a level of proficiency and understanding he has not achieved yet.

There are different types of mentors. Sometimes mentors are able to teach despite their shortcomings, but other mentors teach through bad examples they are going through themselves. Mentors can also be an inner code of behavior that the hero has internalized to guide him along his journey.

Depending on the story, the mentor does not have to appear at all. The mentor could be mentioned as back story describing how the hero became who he is. An example of this is the transformation of Wesley (Cary Elwes) into the Man in Black (aka Dread Pirate Robert) in *The Princess Bride*, where we learn that the Pirate title had been handed down for generations whenever the current Pirate Robert retired.

Agreements Made

During some point in the training (usually at the beginning), the mentor makes an agreement with the student that he is expected to keep. Unfortunately, due to the student's brashness, ego, and inexperience, the student usually ends up breaking the promise. This is much like telling a child not to do something—the child will inevitably end up doing it anyway and getting in trouble. And then, like an errant child, the hero will have to get out of his predicament somehow, occasionally requiring assistance from the mentor.

Following are some examples of such promises between hero and mentor:

- ***The Empire Strikes Back.*** Luke promises Yoda he will not leave Dagobah until he has completed his training, but he leaves in haste when he uses the Force and senses his friends are in danger. Little does Luke know, Darth Vader has set this up as a trap to lure him out of Dagobah.
- ***Snake In The Eagle's Shadow.*** Chien Fu promises the Old Man to never use the snake-fist style that the Old Man has taught to him in public, even when he is in trouble. But when the Master Hung is in a vulnerable position while dueling the Three Provinces Champion, who is about to take advantage of him, Chien Fu tosses his shoe and hits him in the face to distract him. The champion comes at Chien Fu, and Chien Fu is forced to defend himself by using the snake-fist style. Shang, the villain, sees the fight and recognizes the distinct style he has been out to destroy.

There are times when the mentor is known within the circles in which the hero is currently involved. When the mentor tosses his hat into the circle to train the student, his reputation and name are on the line. This adds more pressure to both the student and the mentor during the training sequence because the student is now representing the mentor. The mentor does not want to tarnish his reputation, even though he might have a love-hate relationship within that circle.

A mentor is someone who passes on knowledge and skills that are uniquely his and teaches an apprentice/student a certain specific mindset and approach to survival and success. This requires the mentor to mold the student's body, mind, and spirit for the student to survive. This is not as easy as it might seem, even if the student is willing.

Relationship Dynamics

The student often has to comply blindly with the mentor while trying not to out-guess or out-think the mentor about what lies ahead. The whole development process is much more complicated than the student imagines and cannot be second-guessed. The X factor is how open the student is to accepting the mentor's teachings and point of view about things (aka his style of expression), as well as the concepts and training regimen. Learning to fight does not just require the student to remember and execute the moves during a training session; it requires him to be able to apply the moves in a real situation with an opponent with a serious intent.

The mentor's responsibility to the student is to:

- Pass on not only his skills, but also his past experiences and what he has learned so the student does not make the same mistakes he did. The mentor's past experiences give a certain weight, resonance, and truth to what he is trying to get across in his teachings.
- See some potential in the student that the student and others around him (including the audience) might not even see.
- Be firm-handed and know when to be a disciplinarian to the student. The mentor knows how harsh it will be when the student will have to defend himself against someone outside of the training area. The mentor also knows the student will test the mentor's beliefs, teaching structure, character, and skills, just like a child will test the boundaries of his or her parent.
- Teach the student to be self-sufficient and find the answers to his own problems when they arise. The mentor gives the hero part of the answer and encourages him to find out the rest of the equation for himself. This way, the student is not dependent on the mentor.

- Establish rules and agreements by which the student must abide.
- Maintain extremely high standards and accept nothing less than excellence from his student.
- Always present obstacles or difficult training regimens to advance the student and keep him humble.
- Pass on training and lessons to the student. These also serve as exposition for the audience. They can also serve as a setup that pays off when the student finally meets the villain and uses what he had learned.
- Always challenge the student, never allowing him to become complacent.
- Have some type of reason or motivation to teach the student.
- Be somewhat of an extension of the student.
- Teach the student an ideology that will elevate him to a higher, more noble and respectful position in the caste system.
- Treat the student as if he was the mentor's own child.
- Warn the student about what lies ahead and what the student will need for his journey. The mentor is usually aware of what the student will encounter when he leaves the safe nest that is the training arena. But like a rebellious child, the student usually does not listen to the mentor, thinking he knows better than his teacher.

Asian martial arts films are famous for their mentor/student relationships. The Chinese movie-going audience pretty much knows the hero will endure arduous training sessions to transform himself into a supreme fighter to finish off the bad guy in the end and get his revenge. The audience knows the basic story before they even sit down in the theater, but what they feel is important to their interpretation of the journey and the twists and turns that set it apart from other movies.

One thing many scriptwriters and filmmakers tend to ignore is the actual emotional bond established between the student and the teacher. The teacher is also human and has quirks, a particular temperament, and idiosyncrasies; he is never perfect. You will sometimes see the mentor get impatient or short-tempered with the student. This is a flaw of all humans—one that even a mentor might have.

When watching a well-crafted mentor-student relationship, the audience is emotionally involved because they want to feel taken care of and that someone out there really wants to take them under their wing and teach them everything to be a better person. They want to feel as if there is someone who has all the answers.

The audience lives vicariously through the characters when a movie is done well—they share the experience without having to go through any of the hero's hardships and emotional, physical, and mental pain. Most audience members probably have never had a student-mentor relationship, but they've yearned to have something similar.

Limitations of the Mentor

The mentor's primary responsibility is to prepare the hero for combat physically, emotionally, and mentally. The mentor generally should not fight the hero's battles for him. However, the mentor might fight the hero's battles for him before the training, as Mr. Miyagi did in *The Karate Kid*, coming to his future student's rescue. But it is imperative that the mentor does not fight the hero's battles after training because it will impede the hero's journey. If that happens, the mentor gets in the way of the hero's growth, and the hero will then require additional training.

Often the mentor is either incapacitated or dies once he imparts the necessary information and skills to the hero, so the hero can no longer lean on or depend on the mentor for help.

When the Mentor Is Also the Villain

The mentor can also turn into a villain. For example, sometimes the mentor teaches the hero all the skills he knows, but in the final reel of the movie, the two confront each other and fight, where the hero often learns that the mentor had kept a few secret techniques to himself. This is an emotionally complex setup between the hero and the mentor/villain. Because the mentor has taught the hero most everything he knows, the hero has to rely on his wits and interpretation of the strategy taught to him by the mentor, but in a unique way that the mentor would not suspect. While the hero confronts the mentor, a couple things must be taken into account:

- The hero's unique thinking will be put to the test—he must outwit the mentor at his own game. This also shows the hero taking the art that was passed onto him by the mentor/villain and making it his own. This is much like cutting the umbilical cord—the hero can no longer depend on the mentor for all the answers. This is very painful for the hero because his identity is a direct result of the mentor's teachings, yet it is a step toward the hero's own individualism and self-identity.
- The hero may have had an experience or encounter without the mentor that might give him a unique perspective, making him think outside the box. In other words, this experience might cause the hero to think outside of the locked and conventional concepts and theories that were taught to him by the mentor.

Some examples of the mentor turning into the villain and confronting the hero include:

- ***Young Sherlock Holmes.*** Professor Rathe (Anthony Higgins) is Holmes' (Nicholas Rowe) fencing instructor and turns out to be the villain who Holmes eventually has duel to the death in the end.
- ***Batman Begins.*** Bruce Wayne (Christian Bale) joins Ra's Al Ghul's League of Shadows and is taught the art of stealth and combat by Ducard (Liam Neeson). But Wayne leaves the group and finally confronts Ducard in the end when he finds out Ducard plans to destroy Gotham City.

More examples of mentors in films and TV include:

- Obi Wan Kenobi (Alec Guinness) and Yoda (Frank Oz) in the *Star Wars* (Episodes IV through VI) series
- Pai Chang-Tien (Siu Tien Yuen) in *Snake in the Eagle's Shadow*
- Sam Seed (Siu Tien Yuen) in *Drunken Master*
- Mr. Miyagi (Pat Morita) in *The Karate Kid* series
- Master Po (Keye Luke) in the *Kung Fu* TV series
- Mickey Goldmill (Burgess Meredith) in *Rocky I, II, III,* and *V*
- Apollo Creed (Carl Weathers) in *Rocky III*
- Bruce Wayne (voice of Kevin Conway) mentoring Terry McGinnis in *Batman Beyond* TV series
- Lee Tsung (Bruce Lee) in *Longstreet* TV series episode of "The Way of the Intercepting Fist"

The Buildup

The buildup includes scenes and situations in which characters are involved with one another to move the story along, building up to the finale, when the hero meets the villain. Proper buildup is key to getting an audience frothing at the mouth and on the edge of their seats in anticipation. Training sequences serve as buildup in many fight films.

Training Sequences

A training sequence develops a character by enhancing his sense and scope of awareness. It also improves the character or gives him a physical skill set he did not have before the training sequence. Although a training sequence is not necessary in every instance, it justifies the character's newfound skills to the audience.

To the audience, a training sequence might initially appear to be an action sequence or fight scene in which the conflict between characters is shown and expressed. But actually, training sequences are more complex than that, and they resonate on a deeper level with the audience than you might think. A training sequence shows the character's inner conflict expressed outwardly in a physical and visual manner. When done well, the audience is given an intimate look at the psyche of the character—blemishes, flaws, and all.

Training sequences are a great way of getting the audience emotionally behind the character. When we think of training sequences, the ones that instantly come to mind are the sequences in the *Rocky* series and in *The Empire Strikes Back*, in which Luke travels to Dagobah to train in the ways of the Jedi under Master Yoda. Intense, torturous, and grueling training sequences are also the backbone of many Kung Fu movie classics, such as *Drunken Master* and *36th Chamber of Shaolin*. The training sequences in films such as these are able to get audiences intimately and emotionally involved with the characters, feeling every step, action, and emotion that the characters are going through.

In the story, the hero will usually be in one of three types of categories with his skills. First is the hero who already has the skills necessary to overcome his obstacles, such as James Bond or Indiana Jones. These heroes don't really need training because of their unique ability to recognize, assess, and respond accordingly. Second is the hero who doesn't have any type of fighting skills and needs to acquire them to overcome his obstacles. The third hero is a combination of the first two—the hero already had a certain amount of skills before the story started, but he needs to alter or acquire an additional skill set, philosophy, or strategy to complement or enhance what he already has.

There are three basic types of training sequences, as described in the following sections.

Apprentice Training Sequences

In this type of training sequence, the hero is acquiring skills from a mentor in order to overcome personal obstacles and eventually confront an antagonist. Usually, in the apprentice type of training sequences, a mentor in some way molds, teaches, inspires, and assists in the evolvement and maturation of the hero. This is probably the most common type of training sequence used to tell a story.

Some examples of apprentice training sequences include

- ***Star Wars.*** In Episodes IV and V, Luke learns about the Force and the ways of the Jedi from Obi Wan Kenobi and Yoda.

- ***The Karate Kid.*** Daniel learns karate from Mr. Miyagi.
- ***Drunken Master.*** A mischievous Wong Fei-Hung (Jackie Chan) is disciplined and trained in the drunken-fist style by his Uncle Beggar So.

Recall Training Sequences

In these types of training sequences, a hero with skills lets them lie dormant for a while, until he is asked to use those skills again. Although this might not be considered a training sequence in the classic sense, the common denominator involved with other types of training is a state of transformation and transition.

The factor that separates this type of training sequence from the other two types is the experience of the character. The interesting thing about this type of training sequence is how the character recalls and conjures up his past experience, but has to retrofit and modify his skills with regard to the things he has experienced and how he views the world, now that he is a bit older and sees the world differently.

Recall is not training in the traditional sense; it is more of a reintroduction or getting used to an old habit for the hero. While recalling, heroes use an active meditation in which they try to relive the experience by visualization or by acting out in a controlled situation by practicing old moves, rituals, a certain mindset, and demeanor to get reacquainted with a part of themselves again. The mind and body do not forget things that we do, especially when we do them repetitiously or they present a major trauma to the body. When it comes to a certain move or techniques that have been practiced repetitively, such as moves in any martial art or combative sport, they become more and more a part of you the longer you practice. They become a part of muscle memory—where you trained the body to do a specific action repetitiously and you no longer have to consciously think to execute the technique.

The more the character trains to recall his skills, the more that part of himself begins to wake up. The interesting thing about recall training is that the character gets to compare and contrast his actions with those same actions when he was younger. Now, he is obviously much older and wiser. This is when the character chooses to continue with that old self, completely discard it, or pick and choose qualities and traits he likes and dislikes.

Some examples of recall training sequences include:

- ***Unforgiven.*** William Munny (Clint Eastwood) is told about a bounty that could help his current living conditions on his farm considerably. Having been an outlaw when he was younger, he tries to recall his shooting skills with some target practice.

- ***The Long Kiss Goodnight.*** Samantha Caine (Geena Davis), a schoolteacher, suffers from full retrograde amnesia and cannot remember anything in her life before eight years ago. Up to this point, she's been given clues about her past but has refused to accept them. But when she is caught, tied to a waterwheel, and dunked several times into freezing-cold winter water by Luke (aka Daedalus), she is forced to realize that she is actually a U.S. government assassin whose real name is Charly Baltimore. This might be considered a "forced rebirth" that makes her recall all her dormant assassin senses and survival skills that are immediately summoned when she realizes her life is at stake. This is not classically considered a training sequence, but it achieves all elements involved in a recall training sequence—forcing the hero to summon her skills or die.

Restructure Training Sequences

In these training sequences, the hero is already proficient in skill, but he cannot beat the antagonist for various reasons that are explored in the story. Through the help of a mentor, an experience, an observation, and/or a fellow peer, the hero is able to restructure and acquire new skills so he can defeat the antagonist. Even though the hero might be learning a new skill set or strategy, he already has a foundation with a certain amount of practical experience and understanding.

Some examples of restructure training sequences include:

- ***Rocky III.*** Rocky (Sylvester Stallone) decides to have Apollo Creed (Carl Weathers) be his new coach. Rocky learns to be more mobile and learns a different approach to fighting so he can win back his title from Clubber Lang (Mr. T), because his old fighting style was ineffective against Lang.
- ***The One Armed Swordsman.*** Fang Gang, already a proficient swordsman, loses his right arm during a senseless duel and has to learn how to use a shorter sword to keep his balance.

Depending on the story, training sequences serve many purposes concerning the story and can accomplish the following goals:

- They can show the character emotionally vulnerable or "naked." Other scenes often do not provide the opportunity to do so.
- They can establish and provide a deep emotional bond and trust between the hero and the mentor.
- They can change the character's perspective on life and the obstacles set in front of him.

- They can give the hero a completely new or improved skill set.
- They can show a gradual improvement in the hero's skills and attitude.
- They can show techniques that will be used after the hero completes his training.
- They can get the audience to sympathize with the hero.
- They can get the hero to understand that part of the battle also lies inside of himself. If the hero cannot withstand training, chances are he will not last a moment in real combat outside of the training arena. This needs to be resolved because the hero will sabotage himself on the battlefield if he cannot withstand training.
- They can provide the audience with a healthy doubt in the hero as he prepares to finally meet the villain.
- They can show character development.
- They can help the audience understand the hero's growth and journey on a more intimate level.
- When the hero is practicing alone, they can allow the audience to see the character's thought process, drive to succeed, and personality come through in a physical manner—especially if the hero is doing a kata or shadow boxing.
- They can show inner dialogue and the hero's inner struggle.
- They can directly affect any action sequences that follow.

In relation to the script, the training sequence usually takes place somewhere in the second act. Before that, we see the hero getting by with what he has from the beginning of the story. Through some event (usually with the antagonist), the hero is forced to go into training in order to protect, preserve, or defend himself or somebody close to him. Usually the hero is in a situation in which there's nothing for him to do except retreat for training while licking his wounds. The training sequence transforms the hero into a person with stronger convictions who is ready to confront the antagonist.

Training sequences can be looked upon as emotional, physical, spiritual, and mental defragmenting and rebuilding of one's own inner hard drive. Without the training sequence or anything where the hero changes his approach, it would be senseless, fruitless, and unjustified to meet the antagonist for a second time because nothing has changed with the hero. It would simply be redundant.

Let's break down what is involved in the training sequence. Basically, a training sequence provides the character involved with physical, mental, and emotional skill sets for him to believe in himself and deal with the obstacles set in front of him. However, the training sequence is not simple and basic. If it was, it would be very boring, and the audience would already know the outcome of the encounter. Deep down inside, they might know that the hero is going to make it out alive, but you have to pull the audience into the moment so they can focus and enjoy the journey and not be so concerned about the eventual destination of the hero.

The other factors involved in the mix are the character's level of understanding and practical application of what the mentor taught him. Adding another layer to the equation is the character's emotional state. Can the character accept the teachings of the mentor? Is the character his own worst enemy? Of course. Usually this is what creates a compelling dramatic scene in the training sequence.

A great training sequence should be extremely grueling and painful for the hero on all levels—emotionally, physically, and mentally. The audience should sympathize, groan, and feel for the character every step of the way. But it has to be done with a purpose that leads to a confrontation with the antagonist who forced our hero to go into physical and emotional seclusion to train. The techniques learned and used in training should finally be realized, applied, and executed outside of the incubating boundaries of training and in a real-life situation for the character, where an antagonist intends to do actual harm to the hero.

A training sequence also has to strike somewhat of an incomplete balance. By this I mean that all the questions (conscious and unconscious) the character has cannot be completely answered and resolved during the training sequence, but will be completely answered once the hero leaves training. You have to leave the audience with a certain amount of hesitation and doubt in the character as he finally leaves the training scene, which occasionally happens prematurely because an emergency comes up that the hero cannot ignore. The audience has to say to themselves, "Sure, the hero is really good now, but the villain is much better. I don't know how he's going to beat the villain, but I can't wait to see what he'll do." Creating a certain amount of doubt and worry for the audience generates some healthy tension and anticipation leading up to the confrontation. Then it's up to the hero to show how much he is in command of the skills he has learned during the training session, but this time in a real-life situation.

Examples of effective training sequences include:

- ***Spartacus.*** As Spartacus (Kirk Douglas) is being trained as a gladiator in the training school, we are given the lay of the land.

- ***La Femme Nikita.*** Nikita (Anne Parillaud) trains to be an assassin. At first she is reluctant, but when she realizes she will die if she does not pass her training sequence, she thinks twice about her rebellious ways.
- ***Drunken Master.*** Beggar So trains a rebellious Wong Fei-Hung in drunken boxing. Wong Fei-Hung does not want to learn the last form, Miss Ho, because he feels it is unnecessary and not masculine enough.
- ***The Empire Strikes Back.*** Yoda picks up where Obi Wan Kenobi left off in teaching Luke the ways of the Force. Luke learns to look deeper inside himself and unlearn what he had learned previously.
- ***Rocky III.*** In the beginning of the sequence with Apollo training Rocky, notice the rhythm and flow is sluggish. It's more of a beating than a training sequence. Rocky's mind is not in it. This comes to a head when they run on the beach against each other. Notice the use of slow motion with Rocky, yet the camera is at normal speed on Apollo while they are running the same race. This is effective use of slow motion as an emotion or feeling. Then there is the moment between Adrian and Rocky when he admits to her and to himself that he is scared—he turns himself around at the end of the scene, which changes the emotional tide. The second half of the training sequence picks up the pace. Notice the symmetry in the moves between Rocky and Apollo as they mirror each other—it feels as if they are in tune with each other.

When and Why a Training Sequence Might Occur

The training sequence usually serves as the hero's slow ascent back or his rebirth. It usually comes after the hero experiences an emotional, psychological, and/or physical low point in the story. Typically it occurs after the hero was in a heavy conflict and has exhausted all his resources and skills, but still could not defeat the antagonist.

The training sequence is a way to remold the hero so he can defeat the villain, but it is also a place to introduce new ideas, theories, concepts, and techniques. And, it is a place for the hero to change his life for the better. It is also a place where the character can restructure his thinking and approach to all things related to his life that he might not be aware of when he first comes back to training.

Another story element that is important to establishing a training sequence is a reason why the villain can't find the hero or is preoccupied or busy with another pressing issue. The villain's preoccupation causes him to forget about the hero, which gives the hero time to recover, train, and transform himself. This scenario creates a temporary sanctuary for the hero to lick his wounds, reassess what happened in the past, make the necessary changes, regain his strength and confidence, and go out and reclaim what was lost with the villain.

When it is effectively integrated into the story, a training sequence (depending on its purpose) has an effect on not just the action scenes, but the rest of the story as well. This is much like a ripple effect because it affects the direction of the story, the characters and their relations, and the hero's new outlook due to his newly gained wisdom and improved inner relations within himself—all as a result of what the character learned and experienced in training.

What Is Passed On, Learned, and Applied

The techniques taught in the training sequence should be difficult for the character to grasp and master. This requires the character to grow and expand mentally, physically, and emotionally. This way, the hero has a stronger command of techniques, a stable and broader foundation, a greater understanding of himself and his surroundings, and most importantly, a stronger conviction and commitment when confronting the antagonist.

The major problem with a lot of unsuccessful training sequences is that they dwell only on the grueling physical aspects and forget about character growth, making the training sequence impersonal and gratuitous. They forget to connect with the audience on an emotional level; instead, they connect with the audience on a spectacular level, creating distance instead of bringing the audience into the story. The training sequences that really affect the audience most are the ones that change and improve the characters in all aspects—emotionally and mentally, not just physically.

It is important that what is being taught to the hero be applied afterward. The tricky part is to be discreet about it. If at all possible, have the application of the skills learned come when the audience least expects it, once the hero is outside of the training sequence.

It is also good to keep in mind that the character's emotional maturity—how he feels about himself and others—is reflected in his physical actions, especially in training because of its introspective nature. The more intimate and in depth the training session is (while still applicable to story and what will happen afterward, but not overstaying its welcome), the more effective it will be in emotionally hooking the audience.

Physically, the hero should learn and acquire skills that are not easily attained. The hero has to earn everything that is given to him. Mentally, the hero should be challenged with theories and strategies in combat and life that he will grow into. Emotionally, the hero should be stronger than he was before entering training, as well as more centered, wise, confident, and determined now that he has a new outlook on life.

Some examples of what is learned and applied in training sequences include:

- ***Star Wars.*** Obi Wan Kenobi teaches Luke Skywalker the ways of the Force while Luke trains without much success against a remote droid. Obi Wan gets Luke to put on a blast shield helmet so he cannot see and must trust his instincts rather than his eyes and his conscious self. To Luke's amazement, he takes Kenobi's advice and is able to deflect the shots from the droid. This lesson and skill learned are applied in the third act, when Luke is in his X-wing fighter flying low in the Death Star trench. He does not use the aid of the targeting computer and trusts his own instincts and the Force to shoot his proton torpedo into the thermal exhaust port to destroy the Death Star.
- ***The Karate Kid.*** Mr. Miyagi promises to teach Daniel karate. But all he does is make him do household chores in a specific manner from which Daniel must not stray. Later in the training, we realize that Miyagi was actually training while conditioning Daniel because the specific movements for the chores ("Wax on, wax off") resemble the blocking techniques in his method of karate.
- ***Snake in the Eagle's Shadow.*** Pai Chang-Tien plays a game with Chien Fu as he tries to take a bowl away from him. Little does Chien Fu know that when he is doing this, he is learning defensive footwork so he will no longer be beaten up easily.

The Hero in Training

The hero is being molded during the training sequence and is usually at his lowest emotional point in the film, essentially emotionally naked, with all his flaws and shortcomings exposed to the mentor. This is a chance for the character to express an inner monologue to the mentor (and himself) and work out whatever problems and issues made him go into training. This is also a moment when the character can have a greater understanding of himself, excise his negative traits, and replace those negative traits with healthier ones through reinforcement and practice in the training process. Due to the events leading up to the training, the character has no choice but to truly show the mentor who he truly is deep down inside, without any pretense—he is emotionally unarmed and naked. The sincerity, courage, strength, and desire it took for the hero to take this step are directly felt by the audience, who admire the hero for being that honest and sincere in asking for help. By being the student, the hero has to take a passive role and have an open mind in order to learn and absorb the lessons, while his impatient ego wants to fly the coop early and kick some ass. This causes contradiction, depth, and inner struggle in the character as he goes through his changes.

The mental, emotional, and physical transformation of the hero is much like a caterpillar turning into a butterfly. Even though the hero might decide to go back to where he was before he began his journey, he has changed. This means that he'll see the place much differently even though it hasn't changed because he has transformed into a different person, and he'll see things with different eyes because of the experiences he went through.

An issue with training sequences that prove ineffective is how quickly the hero changes without any type of inner conflict, understanding, or process of change. I'm sure you've seen films in which the hero goes into training and quickly learns the lessons, with no real transformation in character, and then goes out and kicks the villain's butt to save the day and trots off into the sunset with the girl. The problem is that there is no change in the character and he has not gone out on a limb or risked his life physically or emotionally. As a result, the audience is left with a flat response or feeling that translates to a poor box office. If there is no challenge or conflict as to how the hero changes in training, then there is no conflict or drama. Lessons and gifts given to the hero need to be earned. If they are not earned, then the hero does not truly know the worth of the lessons and the gifts that were given to him and cannot truly savor them.

The hero has to go through emotional growing pains as he sheds his old self and transforms into a newer, stronger, and more effective hero who hasn't changed so much that the audience won't emotionally recognize him by the end of the film. They're called growing pains for a reason. The term "growing pleasures" doesn't really make sense and is somewhat of an oxymoron. Personal transformation is painful because you're shedding past issues, memories, patterns, and ideologies that might be no longer useful, but you've held onto them from either fear or ignorance of the unknown. Humans are complex individuals. We're not computers, where you can simply delete or add things onto the hard drive and move on. The training sequence has to show human complexity in the midst of change.

The Mentor in the Training Sequence

Also in the training sequence, a bond is forged between mentor and student. Here the characters are able to be sensitive, caring, and open with each other, whereas in other scenes, they might not have been afforded this type of situation. The role of the mentor is to guide and teach the impatient hero who wants to leave as soon as he can to kick some butt. The mentor tempers the hero's impatience by imparting valuable lessons and strategies that need to be practiced continuously until they become ingrained in the hero's subconscious.

By being slow and methodical, the mentor is water to the hero's impatient fire. Usually the mentor knows much more than the hero and has fought the same battles the hero is now facing. Because of this, the mentor is now able to pass on his past experiences to the hero. The mentor is like a swordsmith and the hero is like the raw material—the clump of metal that needs to be bent and made into a sword. It is the swordsmith's bending that turns the raw, unrealized metal into a sword. The mentor passes on lessons from his own past experiences, always testing the hero and asking and demanding more from him than what the hero feels he is able to give. The hero sees his own limitations, but the mentor sees endless potential that needs to be mined in the heart and spirit of the hero.

The audience can relate to these types of mentor/student relationships because they are learning about empowerment in confronting obstacles while living vicariously through the student, feeling as if they've learned or realized something as they leave the theater.

Dynamics between the Hero and the Mentor

Typically, the relationship between the hero and the mentor should not always be easygoing and simple when it comes to imparting knowledge and skills. The hero should be resistant, and the mentor should constantly doubt the hero's skills. This causes friction, drama, and struggle between the two characters. Also, if it was too easy to impart the mentor's skills to the hero, the sequence would be pretty boring.

The hero is the voice of the audience's cynicism in the beginning, whereas the mentor's voice comes from one's higher self, experience, and wisdom. The friction between these two different frames of mind—a push/pull relationship—ends in a resolution. It is not a perfect resolution, mind you, but it is some sort of resolution that the hero needs to take with him in order to deal with the villain. The audience also needs to be convinced, and between the wisdom of the mentor and the cynicism of the hero is where the audience sits emotionally. When the audience is convinced by the ways of the mentor and the eventual concession of the hero, they begin to emotionally back the hero.

It is normal for the hero to rebel against the mentor's training methods, philosophies, and tactics. This is not just because the hero is challenging the mentor—on a deeper level it is the hero's inner conflict. The hero might also be eager to return to battle and therefore respond to his training with impatience. If there is no type of friction and personal strife within the hero, it is too easy for him to move on, and the story will lack conflict and drama. In addition, the hero will not appreciate his newfound skills. Showing strife and sacrifice within the hero can provide character arc and depth, as well as explain the concepts and training methods more clearly. This is a normal part of human nature because we appreciate the things we get through hard work, persistence, and sacrifice more than the things that are easily given to us.

The mentor can only do so much; it is up to the hero to fully see it through. In the end, the hero has to deal with the encounter and resolve the conflict. It would be wrong for the mentor to take over and fight the hero's fight for him because the story is not about the mentor's journey; it is about the hero's. The mentor is essentially passing the baton or transferring energy from one person to the next.

The mentor can also be flawed by having an unresolved past, which gives the character depth and dimension. The mentor and hero can exchange energy by helping each other out. For example, the mentor might have gotten through issues that the hero has not yet resolved. The mentor would be energized and motivated when this situation occurs. By assisting the hero, the mentor is able to redeem his past while helping the hero not make the same mistakes he did.

The Villain in Training

The villain in the story is traditionally the one who establishes the high mark that the hero has to rise above and go beyond. As with the hero's training, the villain's training shows the intimate and internal processes that result from the intensity of his workout. When the audience sees the villain in training, they immediately compare it to how the hero is training and preparing. In these instances, it is best to show contrast and possibly contradictions in the conditions, style, approach, and strategy of the training.

Rocky III is a great example of the villain in training. When Rocky trains to fight Clubber Lang for the first time, we see a contrast in their approaches, styles, intensities, and personalities in training. Lang is hungry and angry, with no luxuries surrounding him. Rocky is the complete opposite. His intensity and hunger are gone; he's much too aware of his surroundings and he's too much of an accommodating celebrity. Essentially, he has become a civilized human, seduced by and enjoying the luxuries of life—he has stopped being a fighting machine.

Self-Seclusion/Training Alone

The hero does not often train alone in films. Usually when the hero trains alone, it is because he was extremely damaged by some incident in society or he was cast away by others. This forces the hero to retreat into seclusion, becoming a loner with no one to trust but himself and no one to look to for answers but himself. This is a very macho attitude, yet it is also an introspective approach.

Usually when the hero goes into self-seclusion, he already has somewhat of a foundation—albeit one that is incomplete or needs to be revised and/or strengthened. The hero builds upon this foundation and comes up with his own unique theories and perspective on his chosen method of combat. The hero has to be self-driven or be forced into a situation in which self-seclusion is the only option to make this type of scenario convincing to the audience.

Examples of heroes training alone in film include:

- ***Fighter in the Wind.*** Choi Bae-dal goes into the snowy, freezing mountains of Korea to rough it with nature while he trains. He conditions his body, mind, and spirit and reads Miyamoto Musashi's *The Book of Five Rings.*
- ***The One Armed Swordsman.*** After being caught off guard and losing his right arm in a duel, Fang Gang is nursed back to health by Xiaoman, but he cannot defend her honor when two ruffians attack them. Before his injury, he probably would've easily disposed of them, so he realizes he must train to gain his self-respect and pride. Even though Xiaoman wants him to quit and live off the land with her, he is in a mental state of self-seclusion with his training. The same situation applies in Tsui Hark's remake of this film, *Blade* (1997, Hong Kong).
- ***Unforgiven.*** William Munny shoots a tin container with his pistol but misses with every shot. But then he takes out his rifle and knocks off the container with one shot. Munny is dusting off his rusty skills and recalling everything that came with them as far as poise, outlook, and frame of mind when he was an outlaw in his younger days. This is a wakeup call for him that summoned all the past experiences (and demons) he needed in order to perform the bounty.
- ***Snake in the Eagle's Shadow.*** As he is already trained in the foundation of the snake fist, Chien Fu is struck with an epiphany when he sees his cat in a deadly duel with a cobra. And as a result, with a newfound zeal and inspiration, Chien Fu goes to the beach to train alone and incorporate what he's learned so far by coming up with his own style, called "Cat's Claw." He incorporates it into what he has already learned with the snake-fist style to unexpectedly surprise his opponents while fighting them. By now Chien Fu's self-esteem and confidence are at the highest level in the film so far, which easily justifies his character to train by himself, so the audience doesn't question it. It also shows another step in his evolution as a self-actualizing martial artist.
- ***Oldboy.*** Dae-su Oh (Min-sik Choi) is in a hotel/prison for 15 years and does not know why. In his solitude, he starts training by kicking and punching an outline of a human on the wall to get out his frustrations as he tries to figure out who imprisoned him and why. Although he has had no previous training, Dae-su Oh is in an introspective frame of mind when in the hotel/prison and is conditioning himself as he self-trains for 15 years.
- ***Rocky.*** Notice when Rocky first starts training, he does it alone and in solitude. When he turns on the radio, the DJ tells us how cold it is and begins to rant and rave about the 20-degree weather at 4am. Later, Rocky goes to the

meat locker to punch on the side of beef. Combine this with his apprentice training with his coach, Mickey, and it shows the hero's self-determination and his ability to surrender his ego to take direction, learn, and take in someone else's perspective. This balance shows individualism and teamwork.

Fighting While in Training

Fights in a training sequence are usually the free-sparring type, where the purpose is to prepare the hero for the antagonist. But the intensity of the training and free-sparring can get dangerous, bordering on deadly, which can (and often should) raise the bar in intensity and skill level so the hero will be used to this level of fighting later. This can be gradual, to push the hero along, or it can happen suddenly, to wake up the character so he can immediately grasp how serious the situation is.

Free-sparring for film is a personal expression of how a character is able to express himself in a controlled conflict situation (in training—this would be uncontrolled in a fight). Free-sparring for training provides the controlled atmosphere of prearranged combinations and responses; in an uncontrolled fight situation, there would be more nonverbal combative improvisation and free-flow of techniques exchanged between characters.

Things to Pass On during Training Sequences

There are several elements that should be passed on during a training session. Following are some suggestions of several such elements:

- **Gifts.** These are given to the hero by the mentor and should be justly earned by the hero through learning, sacrifice, and commitment. A gift does not always have to be a physical present you get for a birthday or special occasion, like a weapon—it can also be a perspective, a technique, or an outlook to make the hero's life a littler easier.
- **A new or revised code of conduct.** Sometimes the hero might need a newer, revised, or higher code of conduct that gives greater meaning to his training so he can be a better warrior and possibly more respected in his community.
- **Techniques and strategies.** Another element could be different techniques, strategies, and approaches to the antagonist than what the hero has tried to use in the past.
- **Self-confidence.** This element concerns restoring the hero's self-confidence that was lost before he came into the training session. The confidence gained this time should be much stronger than the hero had before because the antagonist will test the hero again.

- **Change in perspective.** Usually a change in perspective changes everything else around the hero because of his actions, which also affect his life choices. Typically after a training session, the hero will have a greater perspective on life, and he will have an even greater, more enhanced life once he has successfully dealt with the antagonist.

Healthy Questions from the Audience

After a training session, the audience has to ask healthy questions such as, "He has gotten better, but is it enough to defeat the villain?" The training sequence might even out the playing field between hero and villain, but is the hero able to beat the villain in the end?

Bad Training Sequences

Just as there are good training sequences, there are also bad ones. This section details the elements of what usually makes a bad training sequence.

- The actor does not deliver a convincing performance in terms of struggling and looking awkward while learning a new technique.
- The obstacles and resolutions presented in the training sequence do not have a direct application to the fights that occur after training is over.
- The training sequence is purely physical, with no emotional or psychological change in the character at all.
- Obstacles in the training sequence are too simple for the hero to overcome.
- The hero does not stay ahead of the audience. In this case, the audience is able to easily deduce how the hero will defeat the villain during the training sequence. Having a training sequence that is too predictable, without any creative twists, indicates poor planning and execution on the part of the writer.
- Poorly constructed codes of conduct appear shallow and manipulative and do not add depth and substance to the world that is being created in the film.

Effective training sequences can help further a film's plot immensely, but ineffective training sequences can quickly ruin a film. Now that you have a strong understanding of training sequences, let's move on to forms.

What Is a Form?

A *form* is a set of prearranged moves that is distinct within a particular style of martial arts. In Chinese, forms are called *kuen*. In Japanese, they are called *kata*. In Korean, forms are called *plague*. In the West, the closest thing to forms is *shadow boxing* in the sport of boxing. There are forms for different skill levels, from beginner to advanced.

The use of forms is unique within each style and showcases that particular style's unique techniques of timing and application. However, there are common principles that apply to all forms no matter what the style. One of the beliefs behind practicing forms is that if you can't do the move with full commitment, speed, and power by yourself, then chances are, you probably can't execute it with a live opponent in front of you with proper poise, control, balance, power, speed, clarity of technique, and composure.

When forms are performed by someone proficient or highly skilled, you feel as if you would not want to be on the receiving end of that person's technique because of the emotional intensity, timing, speed, balance, and power, along with commanding presence, that the practitioner is putting behind the performance.

Performing forms in the martial arts is much like performing a monologue in acting. Executing a form on film is a combination of both disciplines, in which practicality, speed, and precision are as important as character, emotion, motivation, and purpose.

Levels of Forms

This section includes a basic description of what a student learns at different levels while doing forms for his or her level of competence.

Beginner Forms

With a beginning student, emphasis is mainly on the physical aspects of the form. The student has to learn to be "in his body"—that is, to be more aware of his movements and more in sync with his body and mind than a normal person is. The student must accomplish this before he is able to express himself freely with more advanced, intricate moves.

Following is a general list of all the qualities and expectations required from the student when he is learning beginning forms.

- The student must learn basic stances, blocks, and strikes.
- The student must get used to the rhythm and patterns in the style, how basic techniques and stances are put together, and how to move with them.
- The student must learn balance and hand/foot coordination.
- The student must learn basic conditioning of muscles and the body for the specific demands of the particular style.
- The student must demonstrate a general understanding of the system and his approach.

Advanced Forms

As an advanced practitioner, the student no longer has to consciously think about each move or struggle physically to find his way around the system. The advanced student is more consciously living in his bodies. With the advanced student, emphasis is placed on individual artistic expression and how he interprets the style.

Following is a general list of all the qualities and expectations required from the student when he is learning advanced forms.

- The student should not have to consciously think about each technique and should move effortlessly.
- The student should be able to apply the form to practical situations.
- The student should demonstrate composure, balance, and self-control while performing the moves.
- The student should apply a fighting spirit and intensity to the form (called *bunkai* in Japanese).
- The student should be able to perform more intricate movements, combined with realistic timing and application of each move.
- The student should demonstrate a certain level showmanship in his presentation of the form.
- The student should practice a realistic timing to the moves, as if he were fighting an imaginary opponent.
- The student should integrate more complex combinations and stances into the form.
- The student should demonstrate a higher understanding of the technique.
- The student should express himself and his spirit through the technique and make it his own expression of the moves as he has interpreted them.
- The student should make the form and art his method of expression, as opposed to being a slave to the principles.

Great examples of forms performance in film include:

- Jackie Chan in *Snake in the Eagle's Shadow*, *Drunken Master I* and *II*, and *Snake & Crane Arts of Shaolin* (in the opening credits)
- Sammo Hung in *Magnificent Butcher*, *Odd Couple*, and *Prodigal Son*
- Biao Yuen in *Dreadnaught*
- Gordon Liu in *36th Chamber of Shaolin* and *Eight Diagram Pole Fighter*

- Lau Kar Leung in *Mad Monkey Kung Fu* and *Legendary Weapons of China*
- Ching-Ying Lam in Prodigal Son and *Mr. Vampire*
- Bruce Lee in *Way of the Dragon* (when he taunts the gangsters to attack him), *Enter the Dragon* (when he is practicing in his own room right before the tournament begins), and his filmed 1964 audition for 20th Century Fox
- Jet Li in *Shaolin Temple, Martial Arts of Shaolin,* and *Fist of Legend*
- Master Pan in *Iron & Silk*
- The gun *kata* in *Equilibrium*
- Eddie Murphy in *Trading Places*
- Robert DeNiro in *Taxi Driver*
- Tony Curtis in *The Boston Strangler*

The last two films might seem out of place, but they do show great examples of how a *kata* is used outside of a conventional action film. In *Taxi Driver,* it is the famous scene in which Travis Bickle (DeNiro) stands in front of the mirror, rehearsing the scenario of what would happen if he was to be harassed by someone. He says to the mirror, "Are you talking to me?" In *The Boston Strangler,* DeSalvo (Tony Curtis) is hypnotized in a cell and recreates one of his killings when he chokes a woman to death.

Use of Forms in Combat and Other Situations

Forms can also be used in combat. Traditionally in Chinese films you might see the hero be confronted by a gang of bandits. The hero does a short form in front of the bandits, who then assess the character's skills from seeing the form. They decide to either take him on or run away. This was also shown in the West with great comic effect in the movie *Trading Places,* as well as in a number of other films:

- ***The Boston Strangler.*** Serial killer Albert DeSalvo is caught and put under hypnosis and acts out one of his killings.
- ***Trading Places.*** In a jail cell, Billy Ray Valentine (Eddie Murphy) is trying to bluff, brag, intimidate, and taunt his cellmates by performing a *kata* he describes as the "quart of blood technique." He bluffs that when you do these moves, a quart of blood will fall out of your opponent.

- ***Way of the Dragon.*** Tang Lung (Bruce Lee) faces a group of Italian thugs in the back alley of a restaurant. Because Tang does not speak English, he does part of a form and finishes it by taunting the thugs to attack him.
- ***Fight Club.*** Edward Norton beats himself up, throws himself all over his boss's office, destroys the office while he reacts to each hit and throw as if his boss was beating him up. This is the opposite of what we traditionally see in forms because the performer is not usually the one to administer the punishment.
- ***Spooky Encounters.*** Cheung (Sammo Hung) is at a restaurant, while a Mao San (Taoist magician/priest) casts a spell and possesses his hand. Cheung's hand causes havoc in the restaurant and gets him into a fight. The form in the fight is when Cheung battles his own hand. This is also similar to *Evil Dead II*, in which Ash (Bruce Campbell) has his hand possessed and fights himself in the kitchen.

The use of forms is very beneficial when you are having actors perform in front of a blue or green screen for digital effects. The same principals of performing a kata definitely come into play when an actor fights against creatures that are not visibly in front of them, but will be inserted digitally through CGI later.

Even though what they are battling is not in front of them, the actor still has to perform his moves as if the enemy were there. The actor has to find a way to bring to life the performance by understanding what he's doing with the techniques he is performing. He also has to have an organic or natural rhythm and flow to what he's doing (just like he would do with his dialogue), even though nobody is in front of him. Often you will see an actor perform with blue screen and CGI, and he doesn't know what he's doing. He might be performing the moves correctly, but you can see in his eyes that there is no comprehension of what he's doing. The actor looks lost, which makes an unconvincing performance.

Another issue common to blue-screen performances is when the spirit and energy of the actor's physical performance does not match the scene and what we eventually see onscreen.

The Script

If the story is what justifies your action, then a script is a rough blueprint for the action that is more descriptive than what was written in the story treatment or synopsis. If you work without a script, it is much like trying to build a house without a solid foundation. You can only hope and pray that it will all fit together, hold up properly, and not fall apart. Many times you'll see a film that has a flimsy, mechanical story to get you from point A to point B to justify the action in between. Unfortunately, those films are not very memorable unless the action is truly exceptional—which is a very rare instance these days.

Reading a script is much different than reading a novel. Unlike in a novel, in a script there is no room for an extensive back story, descriptions of internal thought processes, or inner dialogue. A script is a blueprint for everyone involved, from the nuts-and-bolts budget and production planning to the artistic interpretation by all the artists. Almost everything written in the script will appear onscreen. To the uninitiated, a script might at first appear flat, cold, and matter of fact. It also might not appear as rich and full of colorful expressions as a novel, but rather as if it was written in coded shorthand only James Bond could decipher.

So why tackle the script? You're probably thinking, "Heck, I'm not a writer, nor do I want to be. I'm the fight choreographer. I just want to create great kick-ass fight scenes. Why do I need to know about the story and script?" You need to know about these elements because, while anyone can put together a series of moves that looks cool and impressive, the difficulty lies in creating an effective fight scene that fits into a story that will emotionally hook the viewer. The audience might not be able to tell you why they like the fight scenes in *The Matrix*, but they are able to recount the experience and euphoria they felt when watching the scenes because they believed the story and characters.

Any stunt coordinator/fight choreographer worth his weight in the film industry might not know story elements as well as a writer, but he will innately know the important story elements that are involved in the script and what is being emotionally set up for the audience when putting together an action scene from the pages of the script. It is the fight choreographer's responsibility to interpret the script and bring to life the appropriate action scenes that have the proper emotion for the audience to feel while moving the story along. Relying solely on the director or producer to tell you about the upcoming action scene is irresponsible as an artistic collaborator. Further, it is dysfunctional and codependent to lean on a director or producer who already has enough work on his plate.

Everyone working on the film, from the producer down to the production assistant, is in one form or another dependent on what is written in the script. Without the script, the actor has no dialogue to act out. The director has no scenes to direct. The set designer has no scenery to create. The producer cannot begin to forecast a film budget. The same goes for the fight choreographer because he needs to know what type of action scene to put together to support the story.

Depending on how it is written, a script might leave a lot of things loose for interpretation and/or improvisation. This is especially true when it comes to action sequences. However, this does not give you a license to choreograph anything you want. Whatever you stage has to be true to the vision and tone of the story. For example, suppose you're choreographing a mixed martial arts match for a film in which the hero is a flat-footed brawler type. All the fights so far have been in close, realistic, rough, and gritty. For the final fight scene, in which the hero faces the antagonist in the film, you decide to end the fight scene by having the hero throw a series of spectacular acrobatic highflying Chinese Wushu-style techniques to knock out the villain! You're thinking this will look really cool onscreen and the audience will gasp with a collective "Wow!"

However, by doing this, you called unnecessary attention to the fight scene by being irresponsible to the story and characters. There was never a scene in the script in which the hero practiced or learned the skill, so you can't justify the style or techniques. The character is a big brawler in style and body type, and he looks like a moose in a tutu trying to do ballet. Then suddenly you gave him intricate, flowery acrobatic skills, and he became a technician? The Wushu techniques you chose are not as practical and suitable to the character's body type as the other techniques previously used. You unjustifiably broke the flow and continuity of the style and feel that were already established.

This also shatters the illusion and continuity that has been set up for the audience up until that point. The audience will collectively scratch their heads, thinking to themselves, "What the hell was that?" And all this was done by making one unjustified decision in your fight choreography. This is much like watching Shakespeare's *Othello* performed by an entire cast speaking Old English with thick Southern accents while wearing feudal Japanese armor! It does not blend well. Unfortunately, you see examples like this occur in films, TV, and videogames all the time.

A good fight choreographer understands the script and is able to design a fight scene that enhances the story and the characters. The choreographer understands the story, theme, and characters from reading the script, and they extract the necessary information from the script to make the action scene work into the framework of the film.

As a fight choreographer, it is your job to make this film come to life by understanding the story, interpreting it the best you can, and turning it into reality on film. It is also important to understand that you are serving the story, not the other way around. If that happens, the story will be weak and the audience will not be emotionally involved in the stunts. Always remember that you will get a lot of information about your characters and the action involved simply by reading the script.

If the script is loosely written and you are not able to interpret it into your action scenes or you have too many questions regarding the story, characters, and/or script, get together with the director, producers, and/or actors to see how they interpreted the script.

The rule of thumb with screenplays is that one page of the script is equal to one minute of screen time. This is why most movie screenplays are usually fewer than 120 pages. TV shows average about 40 to 50 seconds of screen time per page. Action scenes are the one exception to this rule. In the script, a fight scene might read something like what you see here:

```
                    (Name of Project)

                           by
                 (Name of First Writer)


                   (Based on, If Any)



                      Revisions by
              (Names of Subsequent Writers
               in Order of Work Performed)


                  Current Revisions by
                 (Current Writer, date)




Name (of company, if applicable)
Address
Phone Number
```

```
INT. PSYCHOBABBLE CAFE- LOS FELIZ- SOMEWHERE IN L.A.- DAY

The hip cafe is busy with interesting artist types- chatting
with one another.  Others surf the internet on their wi-fi
laptops.

JOHN enters and notices JEREMY, his Technical Editor, 40-
something, seated in the middle of the cafe.  They greet each
other as John sits across from him.  John seems uneasy and
tries his best to hide his nervousness.  Jeremy does not seem
to notice or care.

                    JEREMY
          So where are we at with the book?

                    JOHN
          The hardest part was defining the
          process on how to put together a
          fight scene.  There is so much
          involved, I keep revising and
          adding stuff.  Also the film
          research- breaking down the films
          for examples and tracking down
          people for interviews is taking up
          a lot of my time.

                    JEREMY
          Of course, that makes some sense.

John breathes a sigh of relief.

                    JOHN
          So what do you think of the book so
          far?  Mind you this is a first
          draft.

                    JEREMY
          I think it's very special…

John is pleasantly surprised and finally drops his guard.

                    JEREMY
          As in the Special Olympics!  A
          first grader writes better than
          this.  I'm surprised you didn't
          write it with a crayon!

Aghast, John chucks the cream dispenser in the Jeremy's face.
Appalled, Jeremy responds by throwing his drink in John's
face.  As they fight, they destroy the place while the crowd
runs for cover, as they grab and protect their precious
laptops.

The MANAGER, small, petite, woman, 50 something, manages to
rush in and break up the fight.  John and Jeremy cannot
believe the Manager broke up the fight.
```

Not much of a description, huh? No description of the type of fight or the techniques used. This scene takes up almost an entire page of the script. But the sentence "They fight and destroy the place" only takes a part of one line on the page. Does that mean you make the fight last less than five seconds on film? Chances are, no. What type of fight scene do you choreograph? In what act does this fight scene take place? How was the manager able to break up the fight? Did this fight scene take place in the first, second, or third act?

If the choreographer read the script, he would find out that in the first act it was mentioned earlier that John and Jeremy have known each other since high school, went to the same college, and got their black belts together, and that the manager was a police officer for a good part of her life. From the scene alone, the patrons in the café using Wi-Fi-enabled laptops to surf the Internet clues you into the fact that it is a modern-day scenario, not a period piece. Knowing that John and Jeremy have a background of being black belts gives you wider options in terms of the type of fight you can choreograph.

Depending on who wrote the script, an action scene can be as simple as a one-line sentence (as in this example) or it might describe the fight blow by blow. (However, chances are the fight won't be described blow by blow because it takes up too much precious space on the page.) That's why you need to understand the story, extract all the necessary information from the script, and collaborate with the director and actors to make this fight scene come to life.

Chances are the screenwriter is not an experienced fight choreographer and might not know what is technically involved in making the stunt. And depending on your film's stunt budget, you might not be able to make it come to life exactly as it was written. But from the script you usually can get the proper motivating factors and emotions that carry the fight scene to keep the story's integrity.

Sometimes, if the story is really elaborate, or hard to grasp at first (as with *The Matrix*), or if it has big set pieces that will have major stunts (such as in the *Indiana Jones* trilogy), the stunts will be storyboarded. A great example is the film *The Matrix.* The concept of the film was difficult for everyone to conceptualize, and the written word was just not enough, so elaborate storyboards had to be made so others could get a visual reference and understanding of what they would be filming. But a good majority of films will not have anything storyboarded, and you will have to rely on interpreting the script and collaborating with the director and the actors. Your job as a fight choreographer is to extract each character's essence from the script and apply it to each action sequence.

The Three Acts of a Screenplay and the Types of Action Used in Each Act

It is important to know the three acts of a typical script because each act dictates the types of action scenes you will be putting together. Basically, the three-act structure includes the setup (first act), conflict (second act), and resolution (third act). A good way to learn this structure is to watch films and look for the act breaks. After some practice, you will notice that most films have three distinct acts.

The following sections describe the basic breakdown of the three-act structure and give a description of each act, along with the different types of action found in each one.

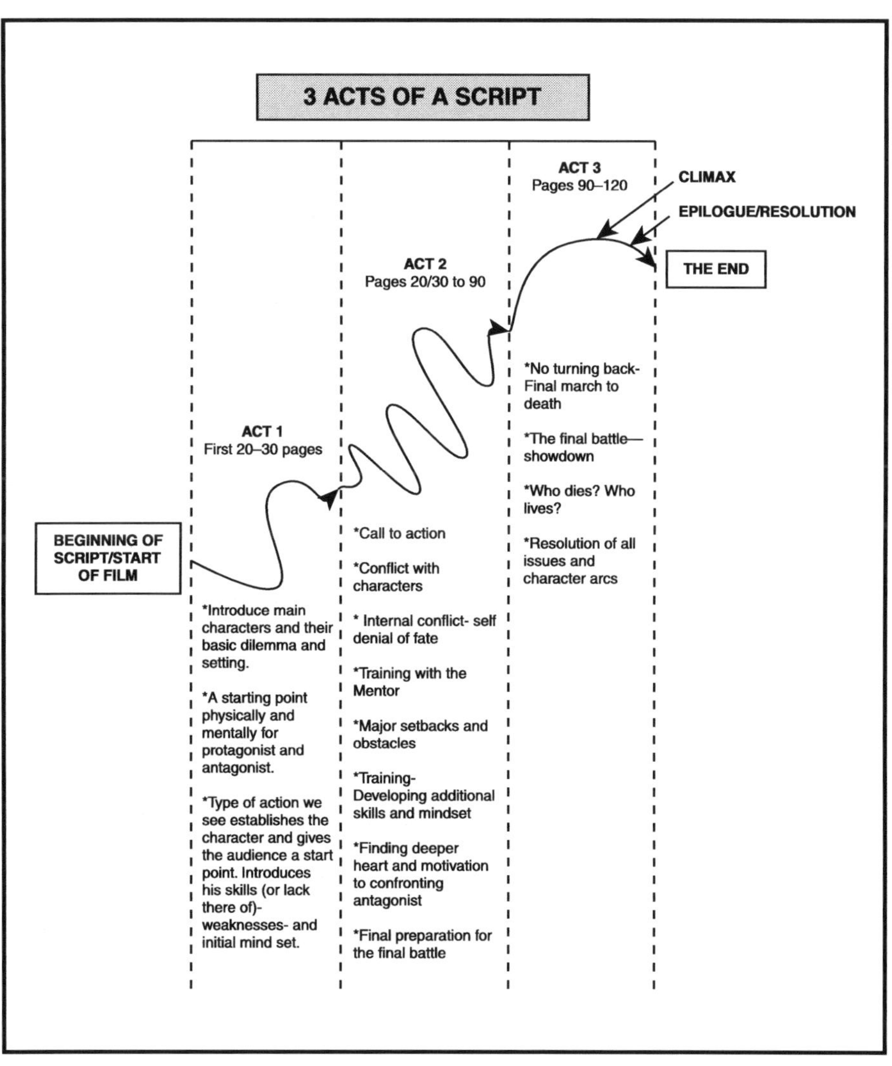

ACT I

The first act comprises the first 20 to 30 pages of a screenplay, which roughly equals about the first 20 to 30 minutes of the film. In the first act, we are introduced to all the main characters involved in the story, the world they live in, their agendas, and their issues.

The first act is also known as the *setup* of the story. You wouldn't kill off the hero of the story in the first act because you wouldn't have a story to tell (unless the rest of the story is told in flashbacks, or the hero turns out to be someone else). Typically, the types of action you would see in the first act would introduce the characters and show their prowess/skills (if they have any at first) and where they stand in the world. You can look at the first act as a starting point of change or transformation for the characters that gives the audience all the information necessary to follow the character's journey. The first act is essentially a starting point for everyone involved.

Here are some examples of what we see in the first act:

- ***Rocky.*** In this film, Rocky Balboa is a low-rate club boxer earning a measly $30 a fight for his efforts as he works to be a "leg breaker" for a local mob boss to get by. His hardened coach, Mickey, cleaned out Rocky's locker after six years at the gym because he thinks Rocky is fighting bums and going nowhere, and he questions Rocky's lifestyle. Mickey also questions Rocky's commitment to the sport because he has never broken his nose; Mickey tells him he has the heart of a champion but fights like an ape.

  The only action we see in the first act takes place as the film opens, with Rocky fighting in the ring with Spider Rico. It's an ugly brawl. No one is really dominating or in control of the fight. But Rocky lets his emotions overcome his rational ring sense when he gets an illegal head-butt from Spider. He throws a series of hard punches that Spider cannot trade with or defend against and knocks him out. Rocky is still out of control as he continues to pound on Spider after he has hit the mat. This shows us that Rocky did not dig deep enough inside himself to get the willpower and desire to dominate his opponent. It took an outside stimulus to make him go to that place buried deep within him to overcome his opponent. He's not very health-conscious either, which shows he placed limitations on himself, because right after he leaves the ring, he bums a cigarette from a patron.

  How Rocky carries himself inside the ring and outside of it tells us everything we need to know about him. Physically, he does not care too much about his conditioning—just enough to do the job. Emotionally, he is not able to find the will to take himself to the next level of proficiency and is dependent on external factors, such as Spider Rico's head-butt, to take him there, but his advancement is short-lived because he was not able to take the steps to do it by himself. This establishes a starting point and the transformation (physically and emotionally) he goes through in order to go the distance with World Champion Apollo Creed. All this is reinforced verbally by Mickey's speech when Rocky is kicked out of his gym after six years.

- ***The Karate Kid.*** In this movie, Daniel LaRusso, a recent L.A. transplant from New Jersey, is trying to fit in at his new high school. He learns karate out of a book, training by himself and learning from an instructor at the YMCA. Daniel meets a girl named Ali, and there is an attraction between them. But John, her ex-boyfriend and a black belt, still has feelings for Ali and will not let her go. He constantly bullies Daniel with his gang of fellow black belts, making Daniel's life miserable. All this occurs while Mr. Miyagi silently observes from the background, although Daniel thinks Mr. Miyagi is only the maintenance man for the apartment building.

  The action in the first act establishes the bullish personality of John and his friends at the karate school. This also shows the audience the obstacles that Daniel has to overcome. Daniel's martial arts skills learned from books and the YMCA are pretty much nonexistent; he lacks the proper instruction he needs to effectively defend himself, let alone to truly believe in himself. Daniel is clearly no match for John because he is not able to get in a single blow. But Daniel does have persistence and tries to get John back in other ways when given the opportunity, and that gets him further into trouble. Meanwhile, Mr. Miyagi is the silent observer.

- ***The Killer.*** In this film, John is a lone hit man who only takes jobs assassinating people he feels deserve to die. We see he has a conscious and a sympathetic heart when his gunfire blinds Jennie, the singer at the nightclub who is accidentally caught in the middle of the gunfight. He even throws himself in the middle of the gunfire to save Jennie's life. John asks Sydney, his middleman, to get him one final job so he can pay for Jennie's cornea transplant. Meanwhile, Inspector Li is a police detective who does not fit in with the bureaucratic police system where his superiors care more about the public image of the department and their next promotion than about upholding the law.

  The gunfight at the nightclub and what immediately follows in the first act tells us a lot about John's character. We see how proficient, graceful, and resourceful an assassin John is even when he is outnumbered and at times without a gun. And it's all done without John losing his cool. He is only out to kill those who are contracted to die. But when Jennie is caught in the middle of the gunfight, John is willing to use his own body as a shield to protect her. This type of moral, self-righteous action is repeated throughout the film in different ways, which endears the character to the audience. This affects the audience more immediately afterward, when they see that John is not superhuman and he is in a vulnerable and painful place with the suffering and pain he experiences as he gets the bullets taken out of his back.

However, the first act does not always have to have an action scene to define the lead characters.

- ***Die Hard.*** In this film, NYPD Detective John McClane has just flown into Los Angeles from New York to visit his estranged wife, Holly, for Christmas. He hopes to patch up their strained relationship. We are also led to believe that Hans Gruber and his gang are international terrorists about to seize the Nakatomi Plaza building where Holly works.

  In the first act, we see how Hans' men work together like a well-oiled machine as they quickly take over the building's security system and any connection to the outside world, scare the employees into thinking they are terrorists, and kidnap Joe Takagi, president of the Nakatomi Corporation. McClane reacts to what is happening by using his police detective skills to stay alive. We also realize that McClane's treatment of Holly is not great, but his behavior is effective in dealing with Hans and his men. The action in this film is set up like a carefully crafted puzzle in which the characters' motivations and actions interlock in each scene. This creates a cause and effect we see on the screen that makes this film a classic. This sets up the physical chess match between Hans and McClane in the second act.

- ***Star Wars.*** In this movie, the opening scene does not involve Luke Skywalker, but sets up the world, the people, and the type of action he will be thrust into later. When we fist see Luke, he's just a farm boy who dreams of flying jets in space.

- ***The Terminator.*** In this film, Sarah Conner is living a simple and sultry life as a waitress in 1984 Los Angeles. A robot from the future has been sent back in time to kill her and alter the events of future history. But Kyle Reese, a human resistance soldier also from the future, has been sent back to stop the robot from fulfilling his mission.

  In the first act, the action is all happening around Sarah as the Terminator hunts down and kills anyone in Los Angeles named Sarah Connor. Meanwhile, Reese runs away from the police and tries to find Sarah before the Terminator can get to her. Sarah does not do any action herself, but she is in the eye of the hurricane of action, which all finally comes to a head in the second act.

As you can see, the action in the first act is generally used to establish the character and what his world is like, and to give the audience and the character an introduction and starting point for the journey the character will make in the film. It is important to keep in mind that when you are establishing the action sequence in the first act, you are setting up the audience for the initial starting point of the action. You are showing them how this character takes to action and/or his thought processes, logic, and how he sees the world. Usually the first act shows the hero in a low, vulnerable, and/or weak position from which he will move on as the story progresses.

After the first act, every action scene you stage should become progressively more complex (in story, emotionally, and physically) and better designed than what was seen in the first act. When creating an action scene in the first act, show just enough action to get the audience's attention, making them ask for more and leading them into the second act. When planning out your action scenes in the first act, take them as an introduction, with every successive action scene being better. If you start off strong in the first act and the following action scenes do not get better than the first act, you are deflating the expectations of the audience and you will lose their attention. It is best to build the action to better and better scenes as the story progresses.

Think of the action in the first act as an appetizer course (usually one or two action scenes to establish each of the main characters involved). The action in the first act should be substantial enough to whet the audience's appetite for what they will be "eating" in the second act, making them want more. Giving the audience too much here will spoil their meal, which will be the second act. Ask yourself how many courses (fight scenes) you will serve and whether they will complement each other, gradually getting better with each dish, while staying different from the previous dish. The third act is the dessert course (what happens to the characters in a physical way). This caps off the first two courses (acts).

If the scene that follows in the second act is not as strong as what you did in the first act, you will deflate the expectations of the audience and stand a good chance of losing their attention. Once you take the audience to a certain level, you need to match it or, better yet, elevate the action to the next level. This does not mean that you have to make each progressive action scene bigger and more expensive. Each progressive scene should delve deeper into the character's personality and/or make the situations worse. Most action films are set up much like puzzles that are eventually solved. If the characters could talk to the creators, they'd probably say something like, "You've gotten me into this mess, so now how do you plan to get me out of it?" And for the fight choreographer, you have to ask yourself the same question for each action scene, but slightly modified: "How do you plan to get me out of this mess, but not in the same way you have done it in previous scenes?

Remember, you still have to stay within the framework of the story and characters!" These are the parameters within which you have to work.

Be aware of the audience's first impressions of the characters in the action scene because this establishes who they are (or who we want them to think they are) in the first act. Imagine the audience meeting the characters for the first time. Ask yourself, "How do I want the characters to come across in the first act in an action scene?" This is all about first impressions—how do you want to manipulate the audience's thoughts and feelings with the actions in the first act? How do you want them to feel about the characters through action? It's not just about whether the audience will like the character. What type of reaction do you want the audience to have after seeing your character in action? Remember that all action in the first act sets up and is the foundation for everything that will follow in the second act.

ACT II

The second act is usually the longest section of the screenplay and film. It usually takes place between pages 30 to 90 in the script. That's about 60 minutes of screen time in a 120-minute film. This is where a good majority of the confrontation, conflict, and action takes place.

The second act begins after the main characters are all introduced and the conflict begins. An *inciting incident* usually (but not always) marks the beginning of the second act of a script and film. The inciting incident also kicks the story and action to the next level. The inciting incident is not always restricted to a physical act. It can be subtle. An inciting incident is when something unexpected happens to the hero. The inciting incident is something that radically shakes up the balance of the character's world. The character has ups and downs, but always comes back to normal. But an inciting incident shakes up his world so badly that there is no real turning back, whether or not the character realizes it.

Examples of inciting incidents that launch the story into the second act include:

- ***The Killer.*** The second act begins when John realizes he's been framed. The exact moment occurs when he sees the glare reflected off the sniper's scope from his sunglasses. Right before this, we see mob boss Johnny Weng in a car overseeing the setup.
- ***The Karate Kid.*** In the second act of this film, Mr. Miyagi decides to teach Daniel karate so he can protect himself from John and his gang. Note: The second act in *The Karate Kid* starts close to 45 minutes into the film, which is a rarity. Even though it takes that long to start the second act, the movie is still effective in its storytelling. This is a rare exception.
- ***Die Hard.*** In this film, Takagi is killed because he does not give Hans the combination to the vault. This causes Hans and his men to drill the vault, so

it takes more time to crack the safe and get the German bearer bonds. This plot device creates more tension and obstacles for Hans and his men. If Takagi gave Hans the combination to the vault, the film would have ended much more quickly and would not have had much of a conflict—they'd be out of the place in 10 minutes.

- ***Rocky.*** In this film, World Heavyweight Champion Apollo Creed is scheduled to fight Mac Lee Green in Philadelphia, but the challenger cancels the match when he breaks his hand. Other ranked fighters are not available to fight Creed on such short notice. To salvage all the time and money Apollo has already invested, he decides to create a "novelty event." Because America is the land of opportunity and is celebrating its Bicentennial, he wants to give a local unknown fighter the chance of a lifetime to fight for the title. This subtle lead into the second act does not have a physical action to break into the second act, but effectively incites it nonetheless.

After the inciting incident ushers in the second act, the story usually escalates physically and/or emotionally and puts the lead character in some sort of danger. The character feels a need to act urgently, beyond his usual comfort zone (or ordinary world). For a successful second act, the hero should be challenged somehow physically, emotionally, spiritually, and morally. The conflicts can be internal as well as external. Here, the hero can lose everything, come close to dying, actually die (physically, emotionally, and/or spiritually, but somehow be resurrected), learn things about himself that will make the audience think he will not succeed, and so on. This is the meat of the film. Without a proper setup that does not insult the audience in the first act, the second act will struggle to keep the audience's faith.

Following are some examples of the action that occurs during the second act:

- ***Rocky.*** In this movie, we see the sacrifices Rocky is going through to fight Apollo, such as getting up at 4:00 a.m. to do his running when it is only 28 degrees outside. The radio deejay complaining about how cold it is outside adds to the feeling we get. We also see Rocky training in unorthodox ways, such as using a side of raw beef as a punching bag and breaking the ribs, drinking down a glassful of raw eggs as soon as he gets up, tying his ankles together so he can get good footwork, and so on.

  His transformation is gradual. In the beginning, he barely makes it up the steps of City Hall. In the first act, Rocky is set up as an underdog. He is so low on the totem pole in all aspects of his life that he has nowhere to go but up. We see this unfold in the second act. The training session also gets the audience emotionally invested in the character's development, as well as other characters and elements that were set up in the first act.

Rocky faces not only his own expectations, but those of the characters surrounding him, who are riding on his coattails and hoping he succeeds. For 50 years, Mickey has been waiting, but he has never gotten the chance to pass on all he knows about boxing to a pupil with a chance at fighting the champ. Paulie feels the world owes him and is looking for respect and an easier life—and he wants Rocky to help him. Adrian is a meek woman who, by being with Rocky, gets to believe she is much more than what others have been telling her she is. In return, she gives Rocky a reason to believe in himself.

- ***The Killer.*** In the second act, all the characters' lives intertwine, elevating the tension as Jennie slowly loses her eyesight. The relationship between Inspector Li and John heightens as they play a game of cat and mouse. But as Inspector Li gets closer to John, he respects and admires him more than his promotion-hungry colleagues in the police department.

  Sydney is ordered to set up John, but fails and ends up siding up with John because of their longstanding friendship and code of ethics, which is no longer respected by the new leaders in the Triad underworld. The action we see in the second act is cause and effect, which leads to deeper conflict. Like pieces in a chess game, certain characters are suddenly vulnerable and others become powerful. Sydney's failed setup of John leads to his excommunication of Johnny Weng's gang, and he is now a target himself as a young, opportunistic hit man is hired to kill John and Sydney at all costs.

  Each action scene we see in the second act is compounded by several different emotions. For example, consider the emotional dissonance between Li and John when they first meet in Jennie's apartment and point their guns at each other. Yet they pretend they are old school buddies when blind Jennie comes into the room. Their tones of voice are friendly, but their intentions, with the guns still pointed at each other, are deadly.

ACT III

The third act begins with the resolution of the story. This is usually the shortest part of the story. While watching a film, you will notice that all the issues and conflicts created will come to a head in the third act. All conflicts introduced in the first and second acts are finally resolved here. It is the last and final stand the hero will make against the antagonist. Does the hero live or die? What happens to the supporting characters? And how does it happen?

Essentially, the third act is when the protagonist is no longer in critical danger and/or issues are resolved with the antagonist. The third act consists of the final resolution, the climax, and the epilogue. Basically, this is the point where there is no turning back. It can also be seen as a final death march to war, and there is no turning back.

The end of the third act ties up all the issues and character arcs for all the important characters in the script. It also resolves all the action that took place in the second act and shows what happens to the hero after the climax.

Here are some examples of how the third act starts:

- ***Star Wars.*** In this film, the third act starts when the Rebel Alliance gets together to plan to destroy the Death Star.
- ***The Killer.*** In this movie, the third act starts when Sydney shows up at Johnny Weng's place to get the money that was due to John, so he and Jennie can get her cornea transplant.
- ***Die Hard.*** In this movie, the third act begins when Hans' men finally get the treasure, pack the truck, and begin to leave.

Climax

The climax is the moment of final resolution to the story. Everything that was set up from the beginning of the script is finally resolved at this moment in the film. Do they complete the mission or not? These questions are finally answered at the climax.

Examples of climaxes in the third act include:

- ***Star Wars.*** This movie climaxes with the explosion of the Death Star.
- ***The Killer.*** In this movie, the climax occurs when John is killed in a gunfight with Triad boss Johnny Weng.
- ***Die Hard.*** In this movie, the climax occurs when Hans Gruber falls to his death.
- ***Saving Private Ryan.*** This movie climaxes with the death of Captain Miller knowing that Private Ryan is safe from any danger as the U.S. planes fly over.
- ***Rocky.*** This film climaxes when Rocky is still standing after the final bell in his fight against Apollo. He has accomplished one of his only goals. As a result, he redeems himself and others around him.
- ***The Karate Kid.*** In this movie, the climax occurs when Danny knocks out Johnny Lawrence, his nemesis throughout the film, with a kick to win the Valley Karate tournament.
- ***The Terminator.*** In this movie, the climax occurs with the crushing death of the robot sent from the future to kill Sarah Connor.

Resolution

After the climax, when all conflicts are settled, the resolution shows what happens to all the characters.

- ***Rocky.*** In this movie, a battered Apollo tells Rocky there will be no rematch.
- ***The Killer.*** In this film, Detective Li kills Johnny Weng, knowing that he will get off easily if he is not killed and that John, his best friend, is now dead.
- ***Terminator 2: Judgment Day.*** In *Terminator 2*, the Terminator (Schwarzenegger) kills himself by lowering himself into the molten steel pit because he contains a chip that can be used to create future generations of Terminators.
- ***Star Wars: Episode IV—A New Hope.*** In this film, Luke Skywalker, Han Solo, and Chewbacca are rewarded with medals and a ceremony by Princess Leia.

Most importantly, the action has to be justified by the story to keep the audience emotionally involved. If you decide to place a fight scene in the film that does not have a purpose, you will run a very serious risk of diluting the story.

Questions

As an architect of the action scenes in the film, you will have to be as exact as a screenwriter with the orchestration of your action sequences. As a result, the action for each act has its own specific needs individual to each story.

Here are some questions to ask yourself when you are putting together a fight scene for the first act:

1. What are you telling the audience about the character?
2. What flaws are you exposing for each character?
3. Will you be exposing something prematurely that might need to be exposed later? Be careful to not reveal anything that needs to be revealed in following fight scenes. If you reveal something too soon, you will destroy the structure of the story and deflate the audience's expectations.
4. How do the action scenes in the first act relate to the second and third acts?
5. What skills does the character have in the beginning of the story?
6. What skills will the character acquire later in the story?

7. Does the character acquire his skills during a fight or training sequence?
8. How does the character's acquisition of skills affect the fight scenes that follow?
9. What are the character's thoughts and feelings about his skills? Do his feelings change? If so, how?
10. What is the character's relationship to his weapon (if he has one) in the beginning? Does the weapon become a part of him as the story progresses, or is it a part of him from the beginning of the film? If the weapon *is* a part of the character from the beginning, what is the back story?

Exercises

Watch a movie and/or read a movie script and ask yourself the following questions:

1. When does the first act end?
2. What incident incites the second act?
3. When does the third act begin?
4. Can you spot a setup and a payoff?
5. Can you trail the arc of a character?
6. Can you find the justification in the story for an action scene?
7. What are the important scenes and elements in the story that build up to an action scene?

The more you think about these things when you read a script or watch a film, the better you will be at this. This applies to the projects you are working on as well. Eventually, you will find yourself doing these things without having to think about them.

Does this take the magic out of your movie-going experience? Yes and no. Your analysis may distract you from the film's entertainment value, but you will eventually be able to spot a good story from a bad one much more quickly than before, which will help you to further appreciate good films and therefore enjoy them even more. You will also learn to spot when a film is leaning heavily on the action so the audience will not focus too much on the story.

7

Extracting the Essence

Gone are the days when the fight choreographer would not even read the script and would only have a general idea what the story was about. The fight choreographer basically depended heavily on the director to guide him through each action sequence. Stunts, action sequences, and fight scenes are now getting more and more highly specialized, requiring much more input, experience, and knowledge from the fight choreographer to add sufficient depth and impact to the scene.

Once you're given the script, you have to know what the story is about; what the function, arc, and resolution of each character is; what type of hero you are working with; and so on. I recommend you read the script several times in the following ways:

- **First reading.** Use this reading simply to get the feel of the story, the mood and flow of the script, where it's going, what happens to all the characters, and so on. Reading the script the first time, I would not make any particular notes or observations, but rather just read it without having too much of a critical view or asking too many questions yet. It's helpful to find a quiet place where you won't be interrupted to read the script from beginning to end. Also, try to immerse yourself into the script as if you're reading a novel for enjoyment. This way you're able to capture and recreate or enhance the emotion of the action scene when it comes time to choreograph and film your fight scenes.

When reading the script for the first time, try to visualize each scene in your mind. Also be "the observer," noting your emotions and thoughts as you read the script. You either can do this while reading the script or you can take mental notes and write down your observations and notes after finishing it.

- **Second reading.** Dog-ear, highlight, and/or mark up the script with whatever unanswered questions you might have and bring these questions to the attention of other cast and crew members. When reading the script this time, you will know the twists and turns that occur in the script so you will see them coming. Take note of this, because you will need to take action on these items in the next reading.
- **Third reading.** By now, you will have a pretty good idea of the nuances of the script. Mark and count how many fight scenes are in the script. Then research the script and find the justifications in the plot and story, character motivations, and other reasons for the fights to occur. Also, look at how each action and non-action scene builds up to a fight scene and try to think of the elements from the story that need to be added into the fight. This is also the time to start studying and dissecting how each fight scene elevates (in emotion, intensity, and complexity) and is different from the previous fight scenes.

  To do this well takes a little bit of time and experience. You should give yourself at least several days in order to get this done in the beginning. You will notice with each script you read that each fight scene is set up and paced differently. Some are well written and some are not. Depending on how the script is written and formatted, some scripts are easy to read and break down, while other scripts are much harder to do. And the page count has nothing to do with it—rather, it is more about how the script is written and laid out. You will glide through some scripts easily and smoothly, like a hot knife through butter, while others will be like trudging through molasses.

  Because of these issues, it is best not to try to get all this stuff done the night before a cast and crew meeting, especially when you're first starting out. Because you are now an "architect of the action scenes," you will need to know how the foundation is built so you can erect the proper architecture for the story.

Assembling the Character and Story Inventory

Now that you've read the script, what do you do? Go out right away and start putting together the fight scenes! Yeah! Yippee! Hold it—not quite yet.

Once you have read the script over several times, you are now ready to put together your character and story inventory, which consists of the following steps:

1. Break down the script for a basic understanding of the story and how it affects each fight scene.

2. Create a character bible to thoroughly understand each character in the film.

3. Create a fighter's IQ based on what you read in the script and what you can extrapolate from what was not written, but can be assumed or might be used as back story. Do this to get a better gauge or estimation of the character's fighting skills, aptitude, attitude, strengths, weaknesses, and blind sides.

4. Create a fight chart to line up all the fight scenes that you are going to do in each of the three acts of the script so you can start to think about how to escalate the level of progression and intensity with each fight. The fight chart also lines up important reveals and developments with the story and characters. A separate sheet that accompanies the chart describes in detail story and character elements that you need specifically for each fight scene.

Essentially, this is the beginning of your research and development for putting together your fight scenes. The simple reason for this is that you have to understand the character and intention in each scene to tailor the fighter's specific approach to combat. If you don't know where the character is coming from, then odds are you won't know where the character is going.

These four lists put together will comprise your character and story inventory. By having this information, you will have a working in-depth knowledge of the script while using the information you have gathered as a template for consistency and continuity in your fight scenes—all the while holding the willing suspension of disbelief high enough that the film is believable throughout for the audience.

Also, the collaboration process can get difficult when working with people who don't understand non-verbal dialogue or who might simply want to make a fight scene that is "just cool" or visually attractive, with no logical base behind it. Like the script, your character and story inventory are never to be written in stone. Often, throughout the production process (pre-production, shooting, and post-production), you can get many script changes in the arc of the story and its characters. You might get a completely different rewrite on the day you're shooting that scene, or the fate of a certain character might change. This is why it helps to thoroughly know the story and the purpose of each scene and yet be very flexible with each change that occurs. So it is always best to see a script as something organic and ever-changing even through the production process, as opposed to something that is written in stone and inflexible. Also in the mix is working with acting and stunt talent who might have another interpretation of how the characters and scenes should be played out.

By having the script breakdown, character bible, fighter's IQ, and fight chart, you'll be able to begin mapping out and thinking with confidence about choreographing fight scenes that are individual and unique to each scene and to the film overall. Consider these four lists as your foundation so you can build upon them and make changes on the fly.

If you have never taken these steps before, I recommend you not wait for your first gig to try it. You should practice doing this on published scripts you might find at a bookstore, a collectors' convention, a Hollywood memorabilia store, or somewhere online. It's best to work with a script that you have not read before and one for which you have not seen the big-screen or TV interpretation. This is because if you break down a script for a TV show or movie that you're familiar with, what the filmmakers and choreographers already have done could influence and cloud your own interpretation of the script. It is important to begin to trust your creative instincts on how you interpret a script and see the action. I also suggest that you get scripts of different genres (action adventure, martial arts, science fiction, espionage, fantasy, historical drama, comedy) that have action in them to develop your four lists.

Also, while watching movies, think about these four lists and put them together in your mind. This is another way of slowly getting yourself to instinctually think about how the fight scenes integrate with the story and the characters.

I urge you not to give one-word or simple answers to each inventory topic. Hopefully, you'll delve deeper into the characters and breathe life into them.

Note

You will notice that each script you read and break down as you create your lists for your story and character inventory will contain character traits and story issues that might not be covered in the questions asked here. Each script has an individual personality, pulse, and rhythm to it. The questions asked here are not to be used as a "catch all" or "end all"; rather, they should act as a general broad template that you will modify, refine, and add to where you find it necessary. I also hope that these questions will spark more specific questions you might need answered in order to assist you with the particular story and characters for your project.

Making the characters three-dimensional, living, breathing people should be the result of the writer's creation and you adding more life to that creation by answering the questions that are involved in the action as you create your fight scenes. Instead of putting together a fight scene on a superficial level, you need to understand the characters on a deeper level because you are also a creator. The depth of your creation will be reflected in the audience's response.

Breaking Down the Script

Breaking down the script requires you to analyze each scene and cull for information about each character. Essentially, you're playing detective here and learning about the characters—understanding their motivations and why they're doing what they're doing in the script. While reading the script, it is also important to understand that not everything is spelled out for you. While reading, it pays to observe what the characters ***do not*** say and/or do. Often, a character's non-action or lack of response to something says a lot about him—for instance, if he walks away instead of engaging in a fight he knows he can win. While breaking down the script, it is important to keep in mind that you're transforming something literal into something visual, which leaves plenty of room for interpretation.

It is important to see the script as a source for answers about the characters and the story. With each scene, you have to ask yourself:

- What is the purpose of this scene? And what emotion and information does it pass on to the audience (the reader)? What is revealed to you in this scene?
- What did you learn about the characters in this scene?
- Is there anything you need to know about these characters (backgrounds, traits, personalities, motivations, and so on) and the situation? Anything you need to take note of and bring into the fight scenes?
- How does each fight scene progress as the story moves along?
- What is revealed about the character and story before or during each fight scene?

While reading scripts, you will come across a wide variety of stories that range from extremely intelligent to very simple and everything in between. But what is very important, regardless of the budget or how the story is written, is the emotion of each scene. It is necessary to find the motivation and emotion of each scene because the action sequences that you are putting together will have to complement and be in sync with the non-action scenes that lead up to them.

There are often times when a scene that is written might no longer work (due to various reasons, such as the actor's interpretation or location, time, or budget constraints), and you might have to help the director come up with a new action scene that will work better. You do not want to look ignorant if and when this situation occurs. And believe me it will happen to you, so make sure you've adequately broken down the script so you can do your job effectively.

Knowing your story inside and out will also prepare you for many unknown issues that can arise during production and that you might have to help solve quickly (or in some instances, immediately). That's why it always pays to do your homework by not just reading the script, but knowing and understanding all the elements that make up the script. If for some reason you feel overwhelmed or that this is a very daunting task, I recommend and sincerely hope that you take the opportunity to take a screenwriting class or seminar or read books on the elements of screenwriting. This will definitely help you feel more at ease with it.

You should also start thinking about the practical issues of putting together each fight scene. Consider the following:

- How and what you are going to do to make the fight look dangerous, yet keep all the actors involved in the fight safe and out of danger. And what will you need to accomplish this? This is the most important thing you have to keep first and foremost in your mind every time you put together any type of action or fight scene.
- What props, supplies, and equipment will you need to make each fight come to life? This varies depending on the type of fight, the situation, the actors involved, and the location.
- How and where to hire the most qualified screen fighters based on their ability, experience, and availability, in order to make your fights believable and effective.
- How to be practical and realistic with what you have to work with. In other words, think about putting together a fight within the confines of what is given to you. Working on a film, you are usually given a very short amount of time to prepare. It is an incredible luxury to have three months to train the actors before principle filming begins (and an additional three during production), like Yuen Woo-Ping and his team had on *The Matrix*. Those conditions were very much the exception to the rule. It is extremely rare and costly for the production company to have the actors and stunt talent committed for so long. Here are some issues you should think about as soon as possible to deal with actual production:
    - The restrictions you might have at the location where you're shooting at, such as time, place, availability, and so on.

- The budget. You can't plan an elaborate fight scene with expensive props to destroy, two dozen people on wires, explosions, and so on with only a bare bones stunt budget. You have to work within your means. Often in film, the miracle is making something out of nothing when you know how to get away with camera angles and how to shoot the scene so it looks like something that it actually isn't.
- The amount of time you are given to shoot the fights.
- The limitations of the performers. Everyone has limitations, as well as strengths and weaknesses. It is important to know what everybody can and cannot do and to highlight and emphasize their strengths.
- The amount of time it will take to prepare each fight scene to be filmed. This includes the training and rehearsal of the actors and stunt players.

Creating Your Character Bible

After breaking down the script and getting a feel for the story structure and how it flows, now it's time to take it a little further by putting together a character bible from all the information you have gathered while breaking down the script.

What's a character bible, you ask? A character bible is an extensive description of each of the major and supporting characters in the script. It gives you the background of each character and all the events that led them up to the point where the film begins. TV shows usually have this readily available for new writers on their staff because the new writers have to get up to date with each character so they do not write a scene that contradicts something a character might have done before they joined the staff. However, for a film, you will have to draw one up for yourself. The reason a fight choreographer has to do this is to help draw up the emotion and style of fighting for each character. You must know your characters as well as (or sometimes even better than) the actor who is portraying them because you are putting together moves that need to suit the character.

A character bible is a list of character traits and mannerisms that you work from to create the specific fight scenes in which the character is involved. Understanding the character's traits and motivations will help you individualize each fight scene specific to each character and story. Putting together a character bible makes you start thinking logically about your characters and how they interact physically, verbally, and emotionally.

When putting together a character bible, you are getting to know the characters and you can analyze their history and actions that make them come to life from the page. Notice we have not yet begun to choreograph a single move. By putting together the character bible, you are getting to know and understand the characters on a deeper and more intimate level. You need to do this because you need to know the character so well that, to you, he is an actual living being. Only when you know this character that well can you begin to start choreographing a fight scene for him.

If you are choreographing fights on a recurring TV series, having a character bible and the fighter's IQ is considered essential because the characters can change drastically from episode to episode and from season to season, and you will need to stay up to date with the progress of each character. After all, you don't want to add any character traits or story elements into a fight scene that might no longer be relevant. For example, suppose you were brought in to choreograph fight scenes for the TV show *Alias* and the only episodes you saw were in the first season, but you're now working on the fifth season. You can't simply make assumptions and put together fights from what you saw in the first season because Sydney (Jennifer Garner) was not pregnant in the first season, but she is in the fifth, which will drastically affect her mobility, choice of techniques, and willingness to take risks. You would need to get briefed and up to date with all the essentials of where all the characters are at.

Putting Together Your Character Bible

Think of creating a character bible as digging in the script for information about each character in order to put together fight scenes that can blend seamlessly into the story.

The following sections list some of the questions you should ask yourself and think about for each character.

Character's Name

Rather obviously, this is the name of the character you are entering in the character bible.

Nickname

Does the character have any nicknames? Using nicknames is usually a type of shorthand to indicate to the audience a person's skills or reputation prior to the start of the film. If a character was given the nickname "Rough and Tumble," I would imagine grace and finesse would not be a primary trait, unless the nickname is used as a humorous contradiction of the character's reputation and skill.

Does the Character Like His Name?

In *Indiana Jones and the Last Crusade*, we learn that Indiana Jones' real name is Henry and that he was named after his father, who throughout the movie refers to Indy as "Junior." We also learn that Indiana was the name of their dog. What does that say about Indiana Jones' character and how he feels? He wants to be his own person, which is a refection on the character and his actions throughout the film series.

James Bond is actually cock-sure of his name, as is evident when he announces it: "Bond. James Bond." In Chinese movies, names are a representation of character or something the character might aspire to become. In *Way of the Dragon*, Tang Lung means "Chinese Dragon." Often filmmakers give them nicknames and do not use their formal names.

In *Yojimbo* and *Sanjuro*, Toshirô Mifune's character never tells anyone his real name; he makes one up. The same applies for Clint Eastwood's character in Sergio Leone's *Man with No Name* trilogy. In *The Fastest Sword*, Ding Meng-Hao changes his name to Zhang Xin when he moves to another village and decides to quit fighting and become a stone sculptor. He does this because his real name is well known and he knows he will attract other swordsmen who want to challenge him.

Age (or Age Range throughout the Film)

The age or age range is important to know because as a person ages, he will move and perform his actions differently. In *Raging Bull* we see a young Jake LaMotta as a contender and champion. Then we see him as an older and heavier man once he has retired from the ring.

Physical Appearance

Some of the questions you should ask about physical appearance are:

- What body type does the character have? Ectomorph, mesomorph, or endomorph?
- Are there any physical traits, such as a limp or scar, that set him apart from everyone else?
- What does his physical appearance say about him?
- Does the character have any physical limitations?
- Does the character's body limit how he can express himself physically? (This is not reserved to physical conflicts.)

For this section, you will need to collaborate with the actor playing this role and discuss how he plans to approach the character.

Emotional Relationships with Family Members

Does the character get along with other people in his family? Does the character react differently when his family is around? Do they affect him physically and/or mentally? These factors can affect the character when he is in a fight scene with a family member.

For example, in *The War of the Roses*, the relationship between husband and wife Oliver and Barbara Rose slowly disintegrates into an all-out war between the two of them.

Social Position with the Family and in Society (Wealth, Rank, Occupation, and So On)

This question affects how the character sees the world during his formative years. This in turn also affects how he sees others. For example, the character might have grown up in a poor, low-class blue-collar neighborhood and might have an axe to grind against white-collar people who have better living conditions. He might feel he cannot get out of his neighborhood and living conditions. This directly affects the character's personality, drive, and perception of the world.

Social position and wealth affect the character's attitude and thus affect the character while in a fight. These factors have an effect on how the character carries himself in a fight and how he might relate to the opponent.

A couple examples include:

- ***The Karate Kid, Part III***. We see that Terry Silver, the millionaire entrepreneur, is a pompous, arrogant, and vindictive person, which reflects his wealth.
- ***Million Dollar Baby***. Maggie Fitzgerald comes from a poor family; she manages to get by as a waitress.

Occupation

Occupation can affect the character's self-esteem and how he carries himself when mingling with others who are more or less successful than he is. The character's occupation affects him in a fight because of how he sees the world, the immediate resources available to him, and how he fits or doesn't fit into the grand scheme of things in the world of the story. A character's occupation can greatly affect his thought-processing skills in a fight because it affects his approach to what he does every day. This is especially true if the possibility of conflict is an everyday issue to the character.

Some examples include:

- ***Rocky***. In the beginning of the film, Rocky started off as a "collector" for a small-time loan shark.

- **The *Indiana Jones* films.** Dr. Indiana Jones teaches anthropology between adventures.
- **The *Die Hard* films.** John McClane is a New York police detective.
- **The James Bond films.** James Bond is an secret agent who works for MI5 in England.
- ***Lone Wolf and Cub: Sword of Vengeance.*** Ogami Itto is Ronin (a roving master-less swordsman for hire).
- ***Zatôichi.*** Zatôichi is a masseuse by trade.

Education

Higher learning also affects a character's thought-processing skills and is not to be mistaken as street smarts or common sense. There are many people out there who have a college education and have a great job, but who are not street savvy or who have no common sense in real life outside of their chosen profession. Is your character street smart or is he blind to the world around him? Does he have any common sense besides the knowledge gained from his education? James Bond and Indiana Jones are perfect blends of characters that are well educated and also have common sense. Also see the "Street Sense" section later in this chapter, when we talk about the fighter's IQ.

Where the Character Lives or Has Lived

Where the character lives affects his view of the world and how he sees life. Where the character came from can affect his outlook on life and everyday situations.

Some examples of this include:

- ***Way of the Dragon.*** Tang Lung lives in the country in the New Territories outside of Hong Kong. He's a country hick, not wise to the ways of the city.
- ***Shanghai Noon.*** Chon Wang is an imperial Chinese guard in the United States during the 1800s. Even though he speaks and understands English, he is not familiar with Western customs and ideology.
- **Zatôichi and Yojimbo.** These characters do not live in any set place, but they wander throughout medieval Japan.

What the Character Believes or Is Interested In

How does the character see life? What does the character like to do as a hobby? What would this character be doing if he was at rest?

Some examples of this include:

- Zatôichi loves to gamble and see whether anyone wants to take advantage of him because of his blindness.
- Indiana Jones loves archaeology.
- Luke Skywalker dreams of someday of flying jets.

Primary Emotional Traits

This is simply how the character basically reacts and responds to everyday situations.

History of Experiences, Feelings, and Thoughts about Other Characters in the Story

Make a list of how the character interacted with other characters before the script starts. This is considered the back story of the relationship between the characters, which may affect how they approach one another in a combat situation. In the case of sequels, the history between characters in the film that occurred before the current one would also be considered back story.

Ambitions or Desires

Does the character have any ambitions or desires in his life? How far is the character willing to go and sacrifice to achieve them? This also is a measure of the character's will and spirit.

Some examples of this include:

- ***Midnight Run.***- Jack Walsh is fed up with being a bounty hunter and wants to open a coffee shop. He also wears a broken watch as a symbol that he is hoping to get back with Gail, his ex-wife.
- ***Rocky.*** Rocky knows he cannot defeat the world heavyweight boxing champion, Apollo Creed, in his upcoming match with him. All he wants to do is still be standing once the final round ends.

Back Story

Are there any important events that occurred in the character's life before the story begins? Discovering this requires you to thoroughly read the script and see whether there is any back story that the character carries into the story. Sometimes the character might not even be consciously aware of it. This back story can be shown as a flashback, implied by behavior, mentioned in passing, or just discussed. A character's back story can be very obvious or just mentioned in passing and can easily be overlooked.

Some examples of this include:

- ***Enter the Dragon.*** There are flashbacks to what happened right before Williams and Roper came to Han's tournament. And Lee's sister, Su Lin was forced to kill herself in front of Oharra and his men.
- ***The Karate Kid.*** Daniel reads an old telegram to Mr. Miyagi, informing him of the death of his wife and child while she gave birth in a Japanese internment camp while he was serving in the U.S. Army in World War II.
- ***Star Wars.*** Obi Wan Kenobi tells Luke Skywalker that his father was "killed" by Darth Vader.
- ***Lethal Weapon.*** Martin Riggs has not gotten over the death of his wife, Victoria, and he feels he has no real reason to live, but he cannot get himself to commit suicide. So he takes dangerous risks while doing his job, hoping to die in the line of duty.

Character Arc

Is the character going to change/develop in the story? If so, how? This question makes sure you know the development of the character, the lessons he learned, and the changes and growth he experienced during the film. You would not want to choreograph a fight scene in which the hero was making the same type of mistake that he learned to correct in an earlier scene.

Some examples of this include:

- ***The Fastest Sword.*** Ding Meng-Hao (Ping Liu), the hero, is an egotistical, self-centered swordsman who (when egged on) will fight anyone at the drop of a hat with little or no regard for the opponent's life. His skill and reputation have earned him the title of "South Sword"—the best swordsman in all of Southern China. But he loses a duel to an 80-year-old Taoist master. For losing, Meng-Hao is the master's servant for three years. What he learns in those three years is essentially a seed that is planted in his psyche and grows as he leaves the master. He soon has compassion and respect for life, along with a new vocation as a stone sculptor. After he accidentally kills a young challenger, he decides to change his name and go to another village as a stone sculptor. But his real identity is soon found out and he is put into situations that before would immediately cause him to draw his sword, but now he has no desire to do so. He no longer wants to live his life by the sword. But his reputation follows him even though he no longer wants to fight. When he meets Qiu Yi-Xing (a.k.a. "Northern Sword"), he is forced to have a duel with him to see who is the best swordsman.

- ***Snake in the Eagle's Shadow.*** Chien Fu starts out as a lowly janitor and a walking target on whom the instructors can demonstrate their deadly techniques. When he rescues an old man, Pai Cheng-Tien, the old man befriends and teaches him the snake fist style. His confidence and self-esteem grows. As the story progresses we see that Chien Fu displays a good aptitude for quickly understanding and applying martial arts concepts and does not have to accept the beatings from the teachers and the students of the school. We also discover that he is not as dumb as the instructors of the school perceive him to be—he is just naïve. Also as his confidence grows, he is able to stand up for himself. This is accompanied by a sarcastic sense of humor that also functions as a voice cutting to the truth of the situation. Finally, he is also astute enough to create the cat fist style to patch up the weaknesses of the snake fist style that were exploited by the villain and he is able defeat him in the end using what he created.

Gestalt Therapy

Imagine meeting a particular character at a party. What would be your thoughts and reactions? This is a question to help you to breathe life into the character by mentally projecting and visualizing what type of character you will be helping to develop along with the other creative artists (actor, director, and so on) on the film. Depending on how clear and astute your imagination is, this can help you visualize the character better and give him depth by seeing how he would interact with a large group of people. Would he be more attracted and open to a certain type of person as opposed to another? Would he be cocky and arrogant toward one person and be humble and respectful to another? What type of person at the party would make that character be shy or reluctant? By playing this mental game, you are visualizing the character and giving him life beyond the words on the script.

Self-Worth and Self-Esteem

What is the level of the character's self-worth and self-esteem? What does the character do to determine his self-worth and self-esteem? What does this character do to feel good about himself? This can change throughout the script, especially if the hero transforms throughout the script. It is important to know at what point the character changes and what elements and situations make him change because the fight scene needs to match his state of composure at that moment in the story.

Mental/Mind Games

Does the character play mental games with himself and/or with others? Does this person like to manipulate others mentally or emotionally for his own purposes? Is the person cruel with this type of behavior? Or is he doing it to get the truth out of someone, as an inquisitive detective might?

Some examples of this include:

- ***Midnight Run.*** Jonathan "The Duke" Mardukas mentally plays with stubborn Jack Walsh by asking him questions and commenting on his thoughts and actions. He does not give up until Walsh is finally able to see things his way.
- ***Star Wars.*** Obi Wan Kenobi uses the Jedi mind trick to get past a couple of curious Imperial Stormtroopers. "These aren't the droids you're looking for."
- ***Moonraker.*** James Bond is snooping around in a room when Corrine Dufour walks in on him and asks what he is doing. Bond asks her whether there is a hidden safe in the room. She says there is none, but reacts to the question by looking in the direction of the hidden safe. Bond is astute enough to be aware of her reactions and finds the hidden safe right where she was looking.
- ***Bull Durham.*** When Ebby Calvin "Nuke" LaLoosh challenges Crash Davis to a fight in the back alley of a bar after vying for the affections of Annie Savoy, Davis plays mind games with Nuke. Davis stalls Nuke's emotional momentum by getting him to think as he challenges Nuke to hit him in the chest with a baseball at full speed. Davis adds fuel to the fire by taunting Nuke, telling him the truth—that even though he has a million-dollar arm, he has got a ten-cent head. This gets Nuke to questioning himself. The taunting also gets a rise and response from the rest of the teammates, which adds peer pressure. Nuke finally reacts by throwing the ball. It misses Davis, who does not even flinch, as it breaks the window next to him.

Note

This part of a character's personality can and often should be shown in a non-verbal way by the character taunting, misleading, and/or faking out an opponent if the story calls for it.

Body Image

Often a person's physical appearance is tied into his self-esteem and how he carries himself in a physical way. What is it that the character does not like about his body? Is he doing anything to change his appearance? If the character likes his body, does he do anything to express this? Does the character see his body as simply a vehicle that houses his brain? Or is it something he respects and works at? While forming the answers to these questions, look at the character's strengths and weaknesses physically and whether these affect the character mentally, socially, and emotionally.

As an example consider *The Long Kiss Goodnight.* When Samantha Caine finally turns into Charly Baltimore, she hates that she let her body go to waste during the seven years she lived a normal suburban life as a schoolteacher.

Self-Sabotage

What is it exactly that holds a character back from realizing his ambitions or goals? Could a mental, emotional, or physical drawback be holding him back? Usually, what holds a person back is belief systems, patterns, and habits that were passed on by others or that were formed from life experiences. These no longer serve the character and are now holding him back. The role of the hero is to overcome these obstacles.

Often the character might surround himself with like-minded people in the beginning of the story. But when the character wants to make a change in his life, those like-minded people either don't understand what the character is doing, feel that what he is doing is unsafe, or feel the risk he is taking is not a healthy one. In reality, it is these people's fears, inhibitions, and limitations that they project onto the character. By having the character break through taboos, he is forced to see the limitations that he chooses to make as his doctrines and dogma. Ultimately, the hero has to somehow give himself permission to follow his dreams, or else he will sabotage himself on his journey.

As an example, consider *Rocky.* In the beginning, we see Rocky Balboa sabotaging himself by smoking right after a fight, going against fighters who are going nowhere, and working as a "collector" for a loan shark. Rocky does not really see these problems until Mickey, his coach, cleans out his locker.

Introvert/Extrovert

Is the character an introvert or an extrovert? Or both? What situation would make him become one or the other? Showing this demonstrates that the character has limitations, as well as what he might do to slam on the brakes or push forward with his life. When used well, this information also gives the character depth and something to which the audience can relate. Often the change from introvert to extrovert or vice versa is brought on by an internal emotional conflict, usually caused by an external stimulus.

Some examples of this include:

- ***Superman* and *Superman II.*** Superman and his alter ego, Clark Kent, are a good example of these personality traits. Notice the characters act differently when they are around Lois Lane (especially) and the rest of the people they see on a regular basis at the *Daily Planet.*

- ***Spider-Man* and *Spider-Man 2.*** Peter Parker acts shy and introverted in front of Mary Jane Watson. But when he turns into Spider-Man, he is much more virtuous and confident when he is around her.
- ***Face/Off.*** As they assume each other's identities, Sean Archer and Castor Troy demonstrate these personality traits, along with their responsibilities, which conflict with who they are.
- ***Unleashed.*** The dual personality of Danny is a good example. He is quiet and submissive when wearing the collar around his neck, and then he turns into an animalistic fighting machine when the collar is off.

Senses

Senses are thinking, feeling, or physical sensations. Which sense does the character trust the most? This refers to the deduction process upon which people rely to make decisions. When we are in situations that are unusual, uncomfortable, or different to us, our senses are heightened. We rely on these feelings and sensations to inform us about the situation. Sometimes people say, "Something does not feel right about this" or, "I have a sneaking suspicion that something isn't right." However, our emotions can cloud these senses if we let them get in our way.

Character Interactions

Does the character have any insecurities or phobias, even on the slightest of levels, that might affect him or could be exploited by his opponent in a physical conflict? With this question, we are trying to breathe life into the development of the character and find out his limitations, weaknesses, or blind spots.

Inner Conflicts or Contradictions

Inner conflicts and contradictions affect the character's psyche and how he might react to things. These could be elements that can trigger him to fight (or not fight).

For example, in *The Twilight Samurai*, Zenemon Yogo, one of the clan's best swordsmen, defied his Lord's orders by not committing ritual suicide when asked to do so, telling the leaders of his clan that if they wanted him dead, they would need to come and do it themselves. But when Seibei Iguchi comes into his house and announces he has been ordered to kill Yogo, they have a very open conversation talking about the flaws of the feudal caste system. By how the conversation is going, we are led to believe it will not end in conflict and that Yogo plans to somehow escape and be a Ronin at a nearby village, out of the Lord's territory. But Yogo is deeply offended when Seibei tells him that he sold his sword in order to feed his family and has a piece of bamboo in place of his blade, even though he plans to fight him with a shorter sword (that has a blade). Thus the fight begins.

Comfort with Surroundings

A character's level of comfort with his surroundings can tell you a lot about him. It shows his life experiences and the effects. Someone who is not as experienced might not be as comfortable in his surroundings and might overreact at times, leaving himself vulnerable to the enemy. Is the character passively at one with his surroundings? Or does he seize his surroundings?

Some examples of this include:

- ***Seven Samurai.*** The samurai Kyuzo stays cool, calm, centered, and in control throughout the whole film, no matter what the situation. He has the same level of composure during a mock duel with bamboo sticks as swords as during a live duel with real swords. Yet Kikuchiyo overcompensates with his oversized sword and by making his presence known at the village for not being a true samurai, but in actuality the son of a farmer.
- ***Lethal Weapon.*** Martin Riggs is fearless on the job and uses unorthodox methods to get the job done by risking his life. He does this because he wants to die in the line of duty.

So you're thinking to yourself, "How does this all work into choreographing a fight scene?" Easy. Notice we have not yet put down a single piece of choreography. We need to know the characters and story very well before we start to choreograph anything. Just like writing lines of dialogue for characters, for choreographing a fight you must have an idea who your characters are and what their motivations are. By creating a character bible, you are taking the steps to know your characters and make each fight scene unique to the film and to the specific scene.

Creating the Fighter's IQ

Before you begin to think about putting together a fight scene, it is important to have your character bible written and especially to have a solid grasp about your character's fighting IQ. The fighter's IQ is an extensive physical, mental, emotional, and sometimes spiritual study of the character in physical combat. This also includes the preparation for the fight, what happens during the fight, and how the character accepts the results.

The character bible and fighter's IQ for each character in the story work together hand in hand. By understanding each character's fighting IQ, you will be able to provide a foundation to make the fights unique and different for each character. The character's fighting IQ and skill level are based on the following criteria:

- Training background, such as military, law enforcement, martial arts, and combative sports

- Actual experience
- Ability to learn, understand, and apply the principles taught
- Ability to think, handle emotions, and perform under stress in a fight
- Ability to change strategy in the middle of a fight
- Skills to seize control of the situation
- Overall skill level
- Motivation
- Emotional, mental, and physical manipulation of the opponent
- Cognitive skills in a strategic mode
- Conscious awareness of emotions and ability to not let them get in the way
- Emotional ability to handle the stress and pressure leading up to the fight (if it is pre-planned)
- Time period during which the fight is taking place
- Level of conditioning

To make things a little easier, the fighter's skills, instincts, and intuition can be lumped into the following categories when it comes to the story and how the character acquired these things:

- **Empty cup.** The character does not have any fighting skills whatsoever at the beginning of the film and acquires the knowledge and skills throughout the story. Essentially, he is a white belt in physical combat. His experiences are usually on the receiving end of the fist. This does not mean he cannot handle himself, but chances are that the character will lose in a fight. This also represents someone who is not aware of his surroundings. A good example is Daniel LaRusso in *The Karate Kid.*
- **Half full.** The character already has some knowledge, skills, and experience, but he needs to acquire and develop more in order to fulfill his goals. Examples include Chien Fu in *Snake in the Eagle's Shadow* and Louden Swain in *Vision Quest.*
- **Fully loaded.** The character already has the full inventory of knowledge, skills, and experience when the story begins. However, he might have to make slight to major adjustments and/or pick up new techniques/weapons to add to his arsenal when confronting different opponents. Essentially, he is a self-maintaining character. Examples include James Bond, Indiana Jones, Tang Lung in *Way of the Dragon,* and Jason Bourne in *The Bourne Identity.*

By answering the questions in the following sections, you can begin to formulate the character's strengths, weaknesses, and specific approach to a fight in the script. Some of these qualities, skills, tolerances, and preferences might apply to any or all of your characters.

Number of Fights in Which the Character Participates

How many fights does the character have in this script? This also includes training sequences.

Result of Each Fight

How does the result of each fight affect this character physically, mentally, and emotionally?

Justification (Part 1): The Fighter's Skills

Justification is a twofold process. We need to justify the character's fighting skills through the story and also justify the fight within the story. These two issues work hand in hand and need to be justified to sustain the audience's willing suspension of disbelief. Part 2 of the justification of the fight in the story will be discussed later in this chapter, when we talk about the fight chart. This joins character motivation and background with the story and the cause for the fight.

I'm sure you've seen many films in which a character's fighting skills are never justified in any way and he simply fights. This could occur for many reasons, which could include any or all of the following:

- It is a weak script in which the writers or filmmakers expect the audience to automatically assume, without any type of narrative justification, that the characters can fight.
- The scene in which the justification appeared was edited out of the film because of constraints on running time.
- The decision makers didn't feel that the justification scene was important enough to keep in, so it was cut.
- The justification scene was cut because it slowed down the pace of the film.

Keep in mind that if you are just choreographing the fight scenes, these issues are beyond your control.

Justifying a fighter's skills can be done by any or all of the following:

- **Dialogue.** The fighter's skills might be mentioned in passing, in the context of training, vocation, hobby, reputation, desire, or experience. This can be done either subtly or obviously.
- **Training sequences.** Such sequences might show the character practicing his combative skills through mentions in dialogue, flashbacks, or in the present tense of the story.
- **Character's occupation.** If the character is a law-enforcement official, soldier, professional fighter, martial arts instructor, or the like, in which combat is a part of his daily life in some way, the audience will already know he is able to defend himself to some degree that will unfold in the film. Some examples of this include John Rambo (from the *Rambo* trilogy), who was an ex–Vietnam vet; John McClane (from the *Die Hard* series), who is an NYPD detective; and Yojimbo, who is a Ronin (a samurai with no master to serve). However, remember that the fighter's occupation should match his skills and his approach to combat.
- **Character's desires and dreams he has put into action.** The character's intent in his daily actions can say a lot about his expertise and what he aspires to become. A good example is Louden Swain, the high-school wrestler in *Vision Quest.*
- **Reputation or legend that follows the character.** Does the character have a reputation as a fighting legend that precedes him?
- **Past experiences/back story.** The character's training and/or experiences can happen before the time when the script actually begins.
- **Props or weapons.** Props can either be an extension of the character or a "mask" or "façade" to protect or hide who he truly is. How a character carries his weapon can say a lot about him. A good example is Zatôichi—even though he is a masseuse by trade, he carries a sword to defend himself.

Heightened Sense of Awareness

As a result of the character's training and experience in situations outside training, he can develop a certain sixth sense and spot things that might seem volatile—even if a layman or rookie might interpret a situation as calm. But due to a combination of training, experience, and understanding of human emotions, the fighter can be sensitive to and aware of these situations. As a result, he can sense a volatile situation right before it erupts into physical violence. Or, he can see a technique coming by understanding its subtleties. Or, he might be aware of how he may be set up for a technique before it physically happens, just by knowing his opponent's intentions.

This sixth sense or heightened intuition is a combination of training, practical experience, understanding of human emotions, awareness, and extreme clear-mindedness to assess the situation at hand, and then take proper action to defend oneself or get out of the situation safely. This can get tough because the mind and emotions can cloud one's judgment.

Certain characters can develop this sixth sense because they have trained and practiced with partners to be aware, to detect, and to be sensitive of certain techniques and an opponent's intent. Coupled with real-life experience in combat, the character is able to develop a feeling and instinct. What might be subtle or undetectable to a layman might be obvious to someone who has trained for that exact situation. This can also be applied to a character's past experiences that he is using in his deduction as he assesses a current situation that he has experienced in the past.

In some films, a character's sixth sense or sense of awareness goes into the extremely paranormal-psychic or mystical sense that you might see in fantasy, sci-fi, or horror film. This all depends on the film genre and, more importantly, on how the character acquired his skills.

Some examples of this include:

- ***The Seven Samurai.*** The samurais knows there is someone waiting on the other side of the door, ready to hit them with a stick—except for Kikuchiyo. The reasoning for this practice is that they do not have time to test every prospective samurai's skills because he will be doing battle with the bandits very soon. Plus, this is also a device that moves the story quickly, while justifying their experience and skill level.
- ***Zatôichi.*** Zatôichi is blind but has highly heightened senses of hearing and feeling and a good sense of someone's true intention and emotion. He can sense many things based on a person's voice. By using an underhanded grip with his sword, his distance and range of motion are in closer; they are not as long and wide as a your typical overhanded grip with a samurai sword. However, having his opponents closer for him to strike at is better because he is blind. He is able to feel and sense his opponents when they are close to him, and thus swing his sword in their direction.
- ***Star Wars - Episodes IV and V.*** Obi Wan Kenobi, Yoda, and Luke Skywalker tap into the Force to sense events that are happening around them and to their friends.
- ***Billy Jack.*** Billy Jack, a Native American and Vietnam vet, senses when one of Posner's men has tampered with his car.

Time Period

It's important to know the time period the fight takes place, along with the type of fight. This is critical because if the time period is in the past, you must make sure the character is using a fight technique that has already been developed by that point.

But there are exceptions. Using a martial art that is in the same family would be one such exception. For example, historically Wong Fei Hung's style of martial art that he practices is Hung Gar Kung Fu. But in the movies *Once Upon a Time in China I, II,* and *III,* the moves and techniques used are partly traditional Kung Fu but mainly the modern martial sport of Wushu—a modern-day interpretation of traditional Chinese martial arts that is still within the same family.

Handicaps

What physical and mental handicaps does the character have that affect him when he is fighting? Physical handicaps can include temporary or permanent injuries that hinder the character from fighting at his maximum potential. Mental or psychological handicaps can include past unresolved issues, such as the death of a loved one or maybe a fight with someone the character respects and loves—perhaps he didn't want to fight this person, but was forced to. Can the character overcome his physical, mental, and/or emotional handicaps? If so, what elements and actions must the character take to overcome these?

Another type of handicap can occur when a fighter holds back, giving himself a handicap, to show their superiority while fighting his opponent. For example, think about the superior fighter who either acts bored or fights with one hand while his opponent attacks him with everything he has got.

As an example, consider *Snake in the Eagle's Shadow,* when Sheng fights Chien Fu. Even though Sheng has a deep hatred toward any practitioner of the snake fist style and is close to wiping out the whole clan, he does not kill Chien Fu. The challenge/training session is controlled by Sheng as he toys with Chien Fu to find out where Pai Cheng-Tien is hiding by handicapping himself.

Traditional Fighter or Modern Eclectic

Does the character practice and use only one style or system of combat? Or does he absorb other systems and approaches to combat? This factor is also affected by the time period and the character's personality type.

A traditionalist lives, exists, and operates within the style of his choice and does not find any reason or purpose to explore, learn, or absorb other systems. The traditionalist also believes that it takes a lifetime to understand and master just one system. For someone to leave and study another system would mean that person's education was incomplete. A traditionalist is not limited to being in a period piece. Mr. Miyagi in *The Karate Kid* trilogy would be considered a traditionalist in his approach to the martial arts, even though the story takes place during the present day.

A modern eclectic is a martial artist who might have a base martial arts system that he uses as a home base, but who will go out and study other systems and add them into his repertoire. A modern eclectic stylist is not concerned about thoroughly mastering one system; rather, he learns and absorbs what he feels will accommodate his needs and how he wants to express himself in the martial arts.

Even though a modern eclectic is easily associated with a modern-day fighter, it can still be applied to period pieces.

An example is with *Snake in the Eagle's Shadow*, a classic period piece Kung Fu movie in which the snake fist style is close to extinction at the hands of Sheng, an eagle claw stylist. Chien Fu, an unofficial student of the snake fist style, realizes there are flaws to the system when he first fights Sheng and creates the cat claw style to complement the snake fist after seeing his cat kill a live snake. By doing this, Chien Fu is able to defeat Sheng because he is able to throw techniques with which Sheng is not familiar.

Animal Representation

There is an old acting exercise in which you match the character's personality to the closest species he resembles in the animal kingdom. Even though we are civilized people, as humans we still have an animalistic nature within us. We use terms in relation to things in everyday life to describe the attitude or state of affairs of a certain situation and many times don't realize it. The financial stock climate can at times be called a "bull" or "bear" type of market. When someone is tricky, we say they are "sly as a fox." Or when talking about someone's lack of intelligence, we say he is as "dumb as an ox." The same type of correlation to a character in combat can be used, but in a deeper, more in-depth way.

This is very helpful when you're having a hard time trying to figure out how this character would act in a fight. You can learn a lot about fighting and approaches to it by watching nature videos of the animal kingdom. When watching these videos, study the animals' composure, patience, and preparation for a fight or attack. Also study how animals defend themselves, their pack, and their infants. What is beautiful about studying these nature films is that there is no dialogue (at least not in a language we understand), and you can sense the animals' intentions and feelings through their body language and facial expressions. Much like humans in a physical conflict, not much is said.

Temperament

What is the character's frame of mind or natural disposition when he is in a fight? Is he in control of himself? Is he easily agitated?

A fighter's temperament says a lot about the character when he is in a pressure situation because it shows how the character can handle stress and pressure when confronted, cornered, and forced to take physical action. His emotional, psychological, and physical changes right before the physical confrontation are very telling about that character.

Fighting Spirit

A fighting spirit is something we see in many films in which the main character has to overcome insurmountable odds in order to succeed.

A character's fighting spirit is made up of several things:

- **Will.** This is the character's drive to overcome all the obstacles placed in front of him and succeed, even though the odds are stacked against him. It's a "never say die" attitude. However, a "never say die" attitude needs to go hand in hand with a clever and strategic mind for the character to survive. If the character has a "never say die" attitude and is not smart about his approach, he will not survive. A character's will must come from a proper motivation that is in sync with the character's personality and background—his personal inner motives —and the task at hand. It is mind over matter.

- **Commitment.** This is the character's commitment to the conflict when a normal person would have backed down or given up much sooner. Usually a commitment is made emotionally and mentally before it happens physically. The stronger the cause and motivation for the character, the stronger the commitment to putting himself in combat is.

- **Self-discipline.** This is the ability to focus and concentrate in order to get the job done and ignore all distractions that can take away from the character's all-important mission.

- **Foundation/background.** The foundation and background are developed through training to give the character tools to work with in order to succeed. This aspect is physical as well as mental.

- **Practical experience.** This is applied through experiences the character encounters in life—usually through setbacks and failed attempts—and can be considered a dress rehearsal for the character's eventual success. The character also needs to know when to quit so he can fight another day.

- **Attitude.** The character's feelings toward the conflict are physical, mental, and emotional connections and expressions of his beliefs that are shown in his posture, mood, opinion, and feelings.

Some questions to ask about this character include:

- Where is this character's fighting spirit?
- Does his fighting spirit change at different stages of the fight, or between fights?
- What will get this character to commit to a conflict?
- What will make this character back away from a conflict?

Flashy or Effective Techniques

This issue affects the film both visually and in terms of narrative storytelling. The choreographer needs to know what techniques are flashy and/or effective and which are suitable for the character and the story.

Employing a *flashy technique* is using a move that uses or alters techniques so they appear fancy, dynamic, flamboyant, visually attractive, and aesthetic. An *effective technique* uses or alters techniques so the audience knows and feels the move would have been practical and also would have hurt. This type of effect is aided visually by the reactions of the person taking the hit and/or through a bone-crunching sound effect. The audience is either familiar with the effectiveness of the technique or sees the windup and delivery of the technique, which shows a certain amount of power onscreen.

Not only is this a visual aesthetic quality, but it is also something that affects the personality of the character and the mood of the film. It would not have been a great fit to see Tom Stall, an ex- Philly mobster in *A History of Violence*, fight with a flashy high-kicking Tae Kwon Do style or something as elaborate as Wushu unless it was somehow justified in the story. An effective hard-hitting street-fighting style is more befitting of the character and the story. To see Wong Fei-Hung (from the *Once Upon a Time in China* series) get into rough and dirty brawls that are ugly, vicious, and raw would also not befit the character's mythology—he is righteous, dignified, a patriot, and a martial arts master whose superior fighting skills are legendary.

A technique or fight can, however, be both flashy and effective by having a healthy balance of both elements. The choreographer needs to select techniques that can balance the scale between flashy and effectiveness. This is done by selecting and altering techniques so they are just flashy enough while maintaining effectiveness, or by mixing techniques that are flashy along with ones that are effective to create visual and emotional contrast.

Number of Different Styles, Disciplines, and Approaches to Enforcement

In a story, you will have to do detective work to find out whether the character has been exposed to or trained in other disciplines and different modes of law or military enforcement. This can add depth, variety, and justification to the character's actions.

Character's Reaction/Response to New Places

The character's level of awareness is the question here. Being aware of one's surroundings is something that is trained and practiced. But don't mistake being aware of one's surroundings for being paranoid—there is a great difference between the two.

Uncomfortable Place or Environment for the Character

By considering this issue, you are finding the limitations and vulnerabilities of the character. Finding a place or environment where the character feels uncomfortable can also even the playing field or change the odds during a fight.

Skills and How They Were Acquired

How does the character feel about his acquired skills, natural gifts, and/or place of authority? What are his thoughts and feelings about the people and/or events that got him to where he is? Is the character happy or content with himself and the events that brought him to where he is now? Does the character have a love/hate relationship with his power? Was he given his skills or gifts begrudgingly? Or did he struggle through personal obstacles and issues to get to where he is now? Was his training or induction so grueling that he longs for the life he had before his change or transformation? Or is he grateful for his skills and the gifts taught or given to him?

Some characters struggle to develop and achieve a certain skill level; others are forced to develop it in order to survive. And some already have powers and skills bestowed upon them, regardless of whether they agreed to these powers. The different ways that characters have acquired their skills create different sets of issues for them because of their acceptance of the skills, their temperament, and how they choose to live with their skills.

As discussed in other sections of this book, a person who gave a character his skills is considered a mentor. Sometimes the character might not like the person who gave him his skills. The character may feel he is damned because of his powers. Perhaps the character is an unwilling or unaware candidate who would not have accepted the "gift" of his skills if he had known what would happen.

What makes this interesting is the love-hate relationship the character might have with the skills bestowed on him and with the person who gave him his skills. This can get even more complex when the character has to use the skills for purposes of good. This can help lead to the character's self-acceptance of who he has become.

Some examples of this include:

- ***X-Men* and *X-Men 2*.** Wolverine has a painful and traumatic past of being a government experiment with adamantium (an indestructible metal) laced around a skeletal structure. This makes him fearless, ornery, and a loner-type personality.
- ***Unleashed*.** There is a love/hate relationship between Danny and Bart, who treats Danny like a caged animal. However, Danny gets to express his anger when Bart undoes his collar.

Responsibility Due to Skills and Title/Position

Is the character able to handle (or be comfortable with) his acquired skills, natural gifts, and/or position of authority? Usually, this issue comes up when the character first comes into his skills, leaving his normal, everyday lifestyle and stepping up to the heroic, superhuman, and/or supernatural role. This is also when the character realizes that with the power he has comes a certain amount of responsibility. This can prove to be a double-edged sword and can provide extreme conflict for one who is coming into his power as he sheds his past and comes into his own.

Some examples of this include:

- ***Lethal Weapon*.** Martin Riggs is considered a "lethal weapon" by the superiors in the police department for ignoring proper procedure and unnecessarily putting his life on the line while apprehending criminals and suspects. His suicidal tendencies and reckless attitude in his professional life stem from his personal life, in which he is still mourning the loss of his wife, Victoria, who died in a car accident.
- ***Spider-Man*.** Peter Parker is given spider powers by the bite of a genetically enhanced spider. He tries to find a way to make quick money with his newfound powers. But when his Uncle Ben dies at the hands of a hoodlum and Peter realizes he could have prevented the act, he realizes that with his power and skills comes an equal amount of responsibility.

- ***Once Upon a Time in China.*** Wong Fei-Hung, a local doctor/healer and righteous martial artist, rises to the occasion when his Confucianist ideals are challenged by corrupt and immoral people.
- ***The Fastest Sword.*** Ding Meng Dao has a reputation for being the best swordsman in all of Southern China and is dubbed the "Southern Sword." This is a title he proudly and arrogantly carries until he takes a young swordsman's life because he does not want to have a duel with him.

Direct Effect of Fights on the Character's Growth (Arc) throughout the Film

Do the character's skills change and adapt as the story progresses due to an incident or conflict in the story? By knowing the character's growth spurts along with his level of maturity and understanding throughout the film, we know what type of fight to choreograph, what elements to put into it, what skills and techniques to display, and how the character's growth will affect him throughout the story.

Anger

There's a difference between getting a person mad and getting him to fight. Essentially, when a person is mad, he loses control of all his senses and rational thinking, which is important to consider when choreographing, because an angry character will typically choose bigger and sloppier techniques, and the intensity and pace of the fight will likely be significantly higher. Anger does not always result in a fight, but it definitely can lead to one. What will get the character to this emotional point? And how quickly is the character able to recover, gather his senses, and regain his composure?

Conditioned or Unconditioned

Is the character a conditioned or an unconditioned fighter? Are there areas in which the fighter is conditioned and others in which he is unconditioned?

Whether a character is conditioned or unconditioned with his skills depends on his background, training, awareness, and—most importantly—the given situation in the story.

A *conditioned fighter* is the result of the union of body and mind working as one unit. A conditioned fighter has practiced various situations and how to get out of them alive until it has become second nature to him. Depending on the situation, he is able to disassociate with his emotions so he can think about the best options and adapt when necessary in combat.

An *unconditioned fighter* is one for whom the body and mind do not work together and are probably in conflict when needed. This fighter has not trained or practiced in any style or method of combat. He does not have all his logical senses to assess his options and he is often clouded by his emotions and cannot think clearly in combat.

Why is this distinction important? It all has to do with the character and his level of awareness, experience, training, and, above all, his ability to seize and control the moment. But there are always moments when the character can be caught off guard and have an unconditioned reaction, even though he is trained and conditioned.

To illustrate, the following sections present some situations broken down to what might actually happen in the same scenario with a conditioned and an unconditioned person. All these situations usually happen within seconds.

While putting together your fight scene with your character's conditioning in mind, you should not consider the fact that he is either conditioned or unconditioned as an absolute. The character might be still in training and might not be fully conditioned in certain areas. Or the character's style or approach to fighting might have a weakness, an aspect, or a blind side that he has not practiced, leaving him unconditioned in that area. A conditioned character can also have unconditioned responses depending on the situation and/or location. He might not be accustomed to a site or he might be in an altered mental/psychological state at the time (due to alcohol, drugs, emotional duress, and so on).

Falls

Before discussing falls, consider the dynamics of a walk. A walk is a constant shift of weight that is shuffled and exchanged from one leg to the other. A walk can also be looked at as a controlled fall. The person has to lean forward slightly and put a foot out in front of him in order to avoid falling flat on his face. This continues when he leans slightly and the other foot steps forward to catch him again. Given this explanation, I can go on to explain the anatomy of a fall from unconditioned and conditioned points of view.

Unconditioned Fall

It tells a non-verbal story when we are able to dissect what is actually happening. This is what happens when a person falls and he is not conditioned to do so.

1. The person is balanced and in control of most of his mental and physical facilities that keep him walking, but he does not notice the bump on the floor just in front of him.

2. He trips over a bump and suddenly loses his balance.

3. As he falls, a look of surprise or shock registers on his face. Panic sets in. This limits his thinking because he is in a state of fear.
4. The ground stops his fall. Usually the body hits the ground evenly, with nowhere for the energy or momentum created from the fall to disburse. As a result, the body absorbs the shock from the impact.
5. The impact of his body hitting the ground usually hurts him as he lands on areas of his body that are sensitive or vulnerable to impact. Usually when the character is unaware and cannot control the fall, he falls on a part of his body that is not covered by muscle.
6. Reality finally sets in that he has fallen, if this has not happened already. Sometimes he might be unable to accept what has just occurred.
7. Varying degrees of self-directed anger or denial occur because he fell.
8. Depending on how hard the fall was, varying degrees of pain start to register.
9. He eventually gets up and shakes himself off.
10. He looks at what tripped him, and then either blames the bump or how shortsighted he was not to have noticed the bump.
11. This often happens so quickly that he does not know what happened until he hits the ground. But if he is aware of the fall happening, he might tighten up his body out of fear to brace himself upon impact. However, he will probably end up getting more hurt because of his tenseness, which results in the impact of the fall not disbursing through him, possibly bruising his muscles or bones. He might also forget to exhale right before he hits the ground, and thus he gets the wind knocked out of him. Or he might place an arm out to stop the momentum or to break the fall. Usually in such cases, the impact is taken on the arm, and the person ends up with his arm/shoulder very sore, bruised, or broken.

Conditioned Fall

This is what happens when a person falls and he *is* conditioned to do so.

1. The conditioned individual is balanced and in control of most of his mental and physical facilities that keep him walking, but he does not notice the bump on the floor in front of him.
2. He trips over the bump and suddenly loses his balance.

3. Depending on the extent of the individual's conditioning, the first flag raised in his mind is when he feels his foot trip because the natural feeling is different. The individual's momentum of the walk is still falling forward, but without a foot to stop the forward momentum of the controlled fall, it now becomes an uncontrolled fall.

4. The individual disburses the fall by angling his body so that it does not hit the floor all at the same time. Preferably, the first body part that hits will be one for which there is not just bone under skin, but also some extra padding, such as more clothes or muscle. A slight arch of the body is created—it looks a lot like the semicircular bottom of a wooden rocking horse as it touches the ground.

5. As the body hits the ground part by part, the energy created from the fall is channeled to flow through the body gradually because the whole body is not hitting the ground all at once.

6. The last part of the body that hits the ground feels the sting of the inertia created by the fall, but the individual does not injure himself badly because of the way he changed his body positioning right before he made contact with the floor, steadily and gradually decreasing the momentum of the fall, thereby softening the final impact.

Hits

Getting hit can be very painful, especially if you are not used to it. The conditioning for getting hit is physical and mental training. To an untrained person who gets hit, it can be pretty traumatic, especially if he lives a sedentary type of lifestyle, because the mind can easily make the hit a bigger deal than it actually is.

Unconditioned Person Taking a Hit

1. The person is tense and nervous about the situation. Physically, his body is now so tense and stiff that if he did do something, he would be much slower than if his muscles were relaxed.

2. The opponent throws a punch at the person's head.

3. The person does not see it coming. Or if the person does see it coming, he might not have the conditioned reflexes to do anything constructive about it and he might end up overreacting, leaving himself more vulnerable to an attack.

4. If the person sees it coming and there is nothing he can do about it, chances are the first thing he will do is tense up and brace for the worst. But tensing his muscles to resist the punch is the worst thing he can do because he will absorb the energy of the entire punch.

5. The person gets hit on the side of the head and does not know how to react because of the shock of the impact of the blow to the side of the head. He is neither physically nor mentally conditioned to know how to respond to the hit.

6. The impact of the blow is probably more than the person can handle. Mentally, he makes the impact of the hit greater than it actually is because his definition and threshold of pain is different than a conditioned person's would be.

This is much like a passenger in a car bracing himself right before a head-on collision. He ends up getting the brunt of the shock upon impact because he is frozen and tense, as opposed to being relaxed and flexible.

Conditioned Person Taking a Hit

1. The fighter's body is relaxed even in a tense situation because he knows that being tense or uptight will make matters worse for him.

2. The strike comes from the opponent toward the fighter's head. The conditioned fighter might or might not see it coming, depending on how telegraphed the strike is thrown.

3. The punch hits the fighter on the side of the head.

4. The fighter relaxes the appropriate muscles surrounding the strike so he does not absorb the full impact of the strike. He is not tense and fighting against the punch with his body as the punch follows through, even though the opponent did make solid contact.

5. The opponent follows through on the punch as the fighter rolls with it.

6. After the punch is finished, the fighter quickly snaps his head back to face his opponent, ready for anything to happen next.

This is not to say that the fighter did not feel the impact of the opponent's punch; rather, he let it go through him, by rolling with it instead of absorbing the full energy of the punch if he was rigid against it.

Strikes

Usually if someone who is not conditioned throws a forced, deliberate strike at someone else, it is based on an emotion of fear or anger. An unconditioned person usually is blinded by emotion and does not see the other options that might be available to him. The conditioned fighter is able to take stock of his surroundings and the opponent while repressing the emotions that might cloud his thinking (depending on the situation).

Unconditioned Strike

1. The person is driven by an emotion (fear or anger) to hit his opponent.
2. The person makes a fist, tenses his body, winds up, and throws the punch as if he were pitching a baseball.
3. The person does not think about what type of punch to throw at his opponent—all he cares about is punishing the person by making hard contact with a general vicinity on his opponent's body.
4. The person makes contact with the opponent's shoulder when he was actually aiming for the opponent's chin. The impact is lessened because he did not know which surface of his fist to hit the opponent with—as a result, he hit him with the palm side of his fist. A person can hurt himself more than his opponent by not knowing how to hit correctly.
5. This angers the opponent, and the unconditioned fighter is now facing a serious beating.

Conditioned Strike

A conditioned person is usually in control of his emotions when throwing a strike (depending on the situation and experience). Usually he knows that fighting motivated by an overwhelming emotion will get him hurt more than it will do him any good.

1. The fighter sizes up his opponent and does his best to stay calm and not tense.
2. The fighter throws a non-telegraphing punch.
3. As the fighter throws the punch, he slightly leans his body toward the opponent to give extra leverage to the punch while also exhaling to add more power.

4. With blinding speed and ferocious power, the fighter buries the two biggest knuckles of his fist in the opponent's solar plexus—a vulnerable spot on the body.

5. The opponent instantly collapses in pain and shock.

Using a Stick

A weapon should be considered an extension of the character who is using it. This applies to the unconditioned and conditioned skills, mentality, and experience of the character.

Unconditioned Person with a Stick

1. The unconditioned person sees his attacker coming at him with a sword.

2. Out of desperation to even the playing field, the person grabs a long stick from a pile behind him to protect himself.

3. The opponent attacks him with his sword.

4. The person blocks the sword strike with his stick by meeting it with the blade. Naturally, the stick snaps in two.

5. The opponent points the tip of his sword against the person's throat.

6. The unconditioned fighter surrenders.

Conditioned Person with a Stick

1. The fighter is empty-handed and is on the defensive as his opponent presses him with his aggressive sword attack. To even the playing field, the fighter grabs a stick from the pile behind him to protect himself. Instinctively, he holds the stick and feels the weight of it, then throws it back into the pile. He then grabs a sturdier one that has more weight to it.

2. The opponent attacks with his sword.

3. The fighter keeps just out of range of the sword, which barely misses him.

4. The fighter waits and finally finds an opening when the opponent over-commits with a sword strike and leaves himself open and vulnerable to a counter attack.

5. The opponent strikes back because the fighter is in range. The fighter is able to deflect the strike with his stick by hitting the flat edge of the sword.

6. The fighter swings down to smack the opponent's sword hand, dropping his sword.
7. The fighter points the sharp end of his stick a fraction of an inch from his opponent's throat, with the intent of doing serious damage, while backing him up against a wall.
8. The opponent quickly assesses the situation. His hand is by his side and he cannot redirect the stick so he will be safe. Body movement is restricted because his back is against the wall, so sidestepping is out of the question. A diversion of any type to distract the fighter's mind from the stick might work. But is it worth taking the risk, especially if there's a stick a fraction of an inch from his throat, ready to pierce his soft flesh?
9. The opponent surrenders.

Reaction/Response

When the character is in a situation in which he feels he might be harmed or struck, he usually will do one of two things—either react or respond. The quality and effectiveness of the response or reaction depends on the conditioning, training, awareness, speed, and timing of the technique. Also, the element of surprise when the opponent's guard is down (depending on how quick his assessment skills are) can elicit a reaction—even if he is trained and conditioned. There is a difference between a character who reacts or responds in terms of what he does with an attack or defense and whether he is able to protect himself.

Conditioned Response

Taking action (defensive or offensive) in a way that he has trained and prepared for is a conscious or unconscious part of a character's being. He is in control of himself and always at a point of taking any type of action in response to whatever comes at him. At times, because of his training, the fighter is able to assess and seize the moment—his sense of time feels as if it actually slows down, but his cognitive thinking is still in real time. He has already made his decision about what to do and he is essentially waiting for his opponent to get there (as if the opponent was coming at him in slow motion).

Conditioned Reaction

A conditioned reaction occurs when one responds to a stimulus without having to consciously think about it. This means that a character's training is very deep and very much a part of his psyche. To get a conditioned fighter to consciously react, the opponent will need to throw a stimulus that is beyond the top speed to which the fighter is conditioned or used to reacting. Essentially, he needs to face an opponent that is much better than he is—in other words, he needs to be outclassed. This is the easiest way to get a fighter to make mistakes and overreact. However, if the fighter's processing skills are quick enough, he has a good strategic solution against which the opponent cannot defend himself, and his emotions are not clouding his cognitive thinking, then he can recover and possibly find a way to survive or defend himself against the superior opponent.

Unconditioned Reaction

In an unconditioned reaction, the fighter is not in conscious control of his actions when attacked or surprised. This presents the possibility of the fighter leaving himself open when reacting to a technique. An unconditioned response leaves the person in a vulnerable position because he is not aware of his actions and his emotions with regard to the stimulus, nor is he able to control them. A typical example of an unconditioned reaction is when you sneak up on an unconditioned person to scare him, and he uncontrollably reacts by jumping out of his chair and screaming. His emotions overwhelm, overload, or take control of the rational skills and thinking that govern his usual composure and cool behavior/state of being.

The Caste System

In what regard does the character hold his opponent, emotionally and socially? Even though the fight might not take place in medieval times, the caste system is still in effect. Unfortunately, it is a human trait to typecast, pigeonhole, or cast judgment upon others. Even though your character might not be a samurai or a knight, we tend to judge people in other ways and put them above, below, or alongside of us. Our opinions of people are based on how much money they make, their job title, the school they went to, where they live, their personal beliefs, and so on.

When putting together a fight scene, it is important to know what the character thinks about his opponent and in what regard he holds the opponent. This matters because it gives the audience an emotional perspective of the fight. For example, suppose the character is fighting his boss. Chances are we see this as an act of rebellion because the character is no longer respecting his boss' title and position. But if the character is fighting someone *he sees* as below him, such as a farmer fighting against a gang of cattle rustlers who stole his livestock, the emotional perspective is different. This perspective may also affect how the character approaches the fight. If a fighter sees his opponent as beneath him, he may fight with arrogance, not taking his opponent's attacks seriously and perhaps not even bothering to block them. Of course, this is often a costly error.

Fighting Distance

This element is directly related to the character's training. Each character has a weakness when it comes to style, art, sport, or approach and prefers to fight in a manner that accentuates his strengths.

A great example of this is in *UFC 59: Reality Check*, where Tito Ortiz fought Forrest Griffin to a split decision in favor of Ortiz. The fight went back and forth, with each fighter trying to draw his opponent to play into his range and strengths.

Motivation to Fight

Usually you can't just have a person fight for any simple reason at the drop of a hat. There has to be a certain level of restraint established. By finding out what makes this character fight, you'll know the limit that his opponent will have to go past to force a fight. You are creating the fuse and how long it needs to burn before the character will explode (fight). The character's fuse can also grow throughout the story, as is the case with Ding Meng-Hao in *The Fastest Sword* when he learns compassion, respect, patience, and understanding toward others.

Flaws, Weaknesses, and Strengths

Is the character aware of his flaws and strengths? While forming the answer to this question, look at the character's physical, mental, social, and emotional strengths and weaknesses.

For example, consider *Snake in the Eagle's Shadow*. Chien Fu develops a smart mouth and wants to stick it to others who are arrogant, but he is still naive. This gets Pai Cheng-Tien and Chien Fu into trouble when Sheng watches him fight using the snake fist style.

Learning Curve

Does the character already have fighting skills before the story starts? Or are they acquired in the script? Or is the reality somewhere in the middle, where the fighter has enough skills to survive, but he needs to acquire more skills to achieve his goals? As a fighter, does the character change and learn to adapt throughout the story? If so, how? When? Why? If there is a learning curve, what will he need to learn in order to succeed? Are the concepts, skills, theories, strategies, and philosophy taught to him beyond his scope and understanding at first?

For example, consider *The Fastest Sword*. Ding Meng-Hao learns compassion and understanding. He finally learns that he does not have to draw his sword every time he is challenged.

Physical, Emotional, Mental, and Spiritual Rituals

People are creatures of habit. Showing a ritual before a fight demonstrates that the character is superstitious and/or knows that he is not the only entity that exists in this world.

Some examples of this include:

- ***Rocky.*** Rocky Balboa gets on one knee to pray before each fight.
- ***Saving Private Ryan.*** Private Daniel Jackson, the sharp-shooting sniper of the group, says a line of prayer before he shoots someone.
- ***Lone Wolf and Cub* series.** Ogami Itto needs to know why they want someone killed before he will accept any assignment.
- Before they fight, traditional Muay Thai kickboxers perform a "Wai Khru"—an elaborate dance/prayer—to pay respects to their masters who taught them the art.
- Muhammad Ali said a silent prayer in his corner before the start of his matches.

Previous Physical Confrontations or Fights

If the character has been in a previous physical confrontation or fight, what primary emotions motivate the character? If the fighter is trained (depending on his experience), he can rationally and/or instinctually run through the encounter depending on the opponent's experience. If not, what drives the character to get into this physical confrontation?

Many times in films you'll see a character who has no real experience in a fight be able to take a hit and defeat the experienced opponent just on pure emotion. This is not practical and it throws the audience's willing suspension of disbelief out the door. Even though the audience might not make a conscious note of it, they will definitely feel something is not right and walk away from the theater feeling unsatisfied.

Sometimes you'll see the character will have a lot of training, but not a lot of practical experience—but the character will still be able to take care of himself easily in a real fight situation. Many films do this, as if training is some magic pill a fighter takes and then *poof*—he can kick anybody's butt! Unfortunately, in real life it does not work this way. Being good in training does not automatically guarantee that you will be successful in a real-life situation. The difference is that training gives a fighter the time to get used to techniques in a controlled situation where the training partner is giving him something—a stimulus for the character to defend against, counter, nullify, evade, and so on, without risking any serious injury.

When the character is in a real fight, the training will help him; however, there are no do-overs if you make a mistake. Also, the opponent's intent is not friendly or understanding (as it is in training); rather, it is emotional, heated, and with harmful intent behind the techniques. If the character has not had any type of practical experience, the techniques he has learned in training will not be practical to him yet. When he is able to apply the techniques he has learned in training in a real situation, *then* the techniques become practical.

The jump between the hypothetical incubator of training with techniques and using techniques in a real-life situation requires the practitioner to have self-confidence, timing, awareness, and a certain amount of speed with a technique (that does not telegraph). It also requires him not to overanalyze the situation because it will be too late for him to do anything and he might get hurt. Often, the techniques thrown in training are much cleaner and precise than those in a real-life situation. This is because the opponent might not have any type of formal training, and usually the situation is emotionally charged, which changes the intent behind the techniques thrown.

The most important thing the character needs to have initially is the courage to take action in the face of fear and to apply his hypothetical skills in a real situation.

Street Sense

Can the character detect trouble or a volatile situation before it happens? And if caught in the middle of a volatile situation, does the character have the experience, sense, courage, and confidence to get himself out of the situation? Street sense can be acquired in two different ways. First, it can be acquired by training in a selected field, such as law enforcement, the military, a practical-based martial arts system, and so on. Second, it can be acquired as a result of one's environment and what he is exposed to. If a character grew up sheltered, living in a gated community where crime is usually low, chances are his level of street sense for a volatile situation would be pretty low, bordering on naïveté. If he grew up in a war zone of gang-related incidents or simply a place where crime occurred on a daily basis and he constantly had to look over his shoulder, over time he automatically would develop street sense because it is a matter of survival and now part of his psyche. The common denominator between these two ways of developing street sense is experience.

Thinking Process

Using cognitive thinking (reasoning skills) under stress is an important skill to have in order to survive in a combative situation. This comes with training and experience. It requires the character to multitask—he must keep a somewhat cool head (as well as possible given the situation) while staying alive as his opponent is about to pounce on him and do some serious damage.

Questions to ask include:

- Does this person have adequate processing skills when confronted?
- Does his thinking process change throughout the film? If so, what are the major points at which he makes changes?
- Can you pinpoint exact scenes where he acquires tools so that he is not his own worst enemy?

Inventory of the Character's Mental, Physical, Spiritual, and Emotional Fighting Skills

Physically, mentally, spiritually, morally, and emotionally, how much in control of himself is the character when he is in a physical encounter? At what point does he reach his breaking point, when he will lose control? What happens when he loses control? What primary emotions take over when he loses control?

Things the Character Should Not Do in a Fight

If you are dealing with a hero, you cannot do things that will cause the audience to be unable to identify with him. This is different with each character, story, and motivation. With the villain, you have more freedom to do more and be more vicious simply because he is the bad guy, and the audience is supposed to hate him. This is also an issue to investigate in order to find out the limitations of the character.

Morals or Code of Conduct in Battle

Does the character have any specific morals or a code of conduct under which he performs? Is there anything the character will not do because of his moral ethics or cultural, religious, or spiritual beliefs? Does he have a certain protocol when he is in combat that he was trained in and taught to enforce?

Some examples of this include:

- ***Kung Fu* (original 1970s TV series).** Kwai Chang Caine is a Buddhist monk, a man of peace, who avoids confrontation until he has no way of avoiding it.
- ***The Big Boss.*** Cheng Chao-An promised his mother that he would not fight and is constantly reminded of this promise by the jade pendent he wears around his neck.
- ***Once Upon a Time in China I–III.*** Wong Fei-Hung is a staunch Confucianist and behaves according to the Confucianist doctrines in terms of how he should act and carry himself at all times.

- Usually a samurai acts accordingly and does not stray from the Bushido code.
- A police officer has a certain code of ethics and protocol under which he has to operate when he is on duty and when he approaches a suspect or someone who has broken the law.
- A soldier has a code of conduct under which he has to operate when he is stationed in foreign countries.
- Even though a bounty hunter is able to cross state and sometimes international borders, he has a certain set of rules under which he must operate when pursuing a wanted criminal.

Character's Actions during Events beyond His Control

Is the character able to use what he has learned in training and apply it to his personal life? Is the character able to fight when he has psychological, mental, and/or emotional hurdles in his way? Are these issues self-imposed or a result of something external ? What personal issues does the character have to work through in order to free himself from the bondage of his past? Essentially, this question asks you, "What are the character's emotional flaws?" No one is perfect. If you have a character with no flaws, he will not have much of a connection to the audience—there is nothing for them to sympathize with.

Some examples of this are

- ***Rocky III.*** Rocky mourns the death of his coach, Mickey, and questions his own self-worth when he finds out that Mickey carried him by matching him up with fighters who did not pose a threat to him.
- ***First Blood.*** John Rambo has flashbacks to Vietnam when he is beaten and tortured by the police.
- ***Raiders of the Lost Ark.*** Indiana Jones must go down the Well of Souls, but there are snakes all over the floor of the place, and he hates snakes.

Ego

Does the character have a healthy or destructive ego? Is the character's skill physically bound to his ego? Does he have to go around always proving it to everyone? Does he know how to apply the lessons learned outside the ring or school? Usually if the character is trapped in his ego, it will cloud his thinking in everything he does. A character's insecurity about himself and where he stands usually lets his ego rise and take control, blinding him to his own principles of moral conduct.

A destructive ego is not just relegated to the villain of the story; it can also apply to the hero of the story. A good example is in *Jet Li's Fearless*, in which Huo Yuanjia is a cocky, self-serving street brawler. When he kills Master Qin in a fight, his life takes an about face, he loses his sanity, and he eventually learns compassion and cultivation of the body, mind, and spirit.

Examples of destructive egos include:

- Tommy Gunn in *Rocky V*
- Sensei John Kreese, owner of the Cobra Kai school, in *The Karate Kid* and *The Karate Kid III*
- Clubber Lang in *Rocky III*

Examples of healthy egos include:

- Indiana Jones
- James Bond

Transcendence to Mental, Spiritual, or Mythical Aspects

If one is fortunate enough, as he gets older, he is able to look back at his mistakes and learn from them, being wiser and seasoned for it. Because of this, his words carry more weight and resonate much deeper with his students because of what he has gone through and the fact that he has lived to tell the story. To him, the fight is no longer physical, as it was when he was younger.

This does not mean that he is above experiencing all human experiences. He is simply a flesh-and-blood character who feels he is more of a spiritual being having a human experience. Usually in the Western world, this is associated with a character who is about to die. But in Asia, this is just a part of the evolution process of the human spirit—it is not always associated with death.

Adding frailties and vulnerabilities gives the character dimension and weight. The audience can accept, relate to, and admire when the character has overcome something.

Some examples of this include

- ***Remo Williams: The Adventure Begins.*** Master Chiun is a great example.
- ***Snake in the Eagle's Shadow.*** Master Pai Cheng-Tien is another good example.
- ***The Karate Kid I, II, and III.*** Mr. Miyagi is also a good example.
- ***Star Wars – Episodes IV, V, and VI.*** Yoda and Obi Wan Kenobi are both excellent examples.

Personal Carriage When at Rest

How does the character walk and carry himself with people who are not physically intimidating or threatening? Does he walk with confidence? Does he appear bored when he is not in action? Does he look for trouble?

Actions in Uncomfortable Situations

How does the character act in a life-or-death situation? Is this different than the way he acts in a practice or friendly sparring session? If so, how do his actions change in a non-verbal way? The problem with a lot of fight films is that the fight scenes are the same in serious and training situations.

Character's Training

The character's training can either take place during the film or be a back story before the film begins. Was the training for recreational purposes? Was it military training? Was it for law enforcement (such as John McClane in *Die Hard*)? Was it for sports competition purposes? Or was it for self-defense reasons? Did the character learn on streets (like Zack Mayo in *An Officer and a Gentleman*)? What was the teacher's training and approach to the character when teaching? The type of training defines the type of approach the character will have toward a physical confrontation. The purpose of the training and the personality of the instructor heavily influence the way the character breaks down and assesses the situation and the action he will take during potential physical confrontation.

Relationship to Mentor

Does the character's demeanor change when he is around his mentor? What are his thoughts when he is around the mentor? Is the mentor's influence apparent even when he is not around? What are the limitations of what the mentor can pass on to the character and why?

Respect for Authority Figures

Does the character fit in with society and get along well with the people who have authority over him? Or does he have a hard time respecting authority figures who can tell him what to do? Or is he somewhere in the middle?

Often in the beginning of the film, the hero fits into society well, including his peers and those over him. Then there is a break somewhere in the story and the hero breaks off all his connections and travels to the beat of his own drum.

Character's Reaction to Lessons He Can't Understand

The character's reaction to lessons he can't understand shows his limitations and the fact that he still has a lot to learn.

Some examples of this include:

- ***Drunken Master.*** A young Wong Fei-Hung is reluctant to learn a form named "Miss Ho" that is patterned after a woman's movements because he feels it is not a manly thing to do.
- ***The Karate Kid.*** Daniel does not understand why Mr. Miyagi is making him paint the fence, sand the floor, and wax his car. In reality, these actions are similar to martial arts techniques that Mr. Miyagi wants to teach Daniel.

Pre-Planned Fights

Pre-planned fights affect a character differently than a fight that suddenly happens. With a fight that suddenly happens, you are given no time to gather your senses and figure out what is causing the fight. Your self-preservation instincts kick in, and you have to ask questions later.

With a pre-planned fight—which can be a combative sports competition, a duel, a blood sport, or a tribal ritual, among other things—you are generally given time to prepare mentally, physically, psychologically, and emotionally. A predetermined conflict can also wreak havoc on the combatant's emotions, making him question what he is doing and the consequences of what could happen if he wins or loses.

Questions to ask during a pre-planned fight include:

- What issues are getting in the way of the fighter preparing for the fight?
- Does the fighter's idle mind play mental games with him?
- What skills does he need to acquire in order to win or survive?
- How do the other characters around him feel about the fight? Are they projecting their fears and expectations onto the combatant?

Examples of pre-planned fights can be seen in the following films:

- ***Three 'O Clock High***
- ***The Duelists***
- ***Braveheart***
- ***The Karate Kid***
- ***The Quick and the Dead***
- ***Vision Quest***

Issues about Death

How does the character handle issues about death in general? How does this character feel about dying? Is he afraid of dying? Has he accepted that he might die if he goes into combat?

Usually, when a person frees himself from the fear of dying by accepting that he will die, he is actually liberated and is able to commit more of himself to the fight/cause. This psychological, emotional, and mental shift changes the stance or point of view of the character, making him more committed to his cause.

Some examples of this include:

- ***Snake in the Eagle's Shadow.*** Before fighting Sheng, the snake fist master salutes his ancestor, knowing his life will not be taken in vain.
- ***Million Dollar Baby.*** Maggie feels she has lived a good life as a professional boxer and does not want to be confined to a hospital bed for the rest of her life after a catastrophic injury sustained during a fight.

Injury or Death at the Hands of the Character

Often when a character (especially the hero) takes the life of another human being, whether deliberately or not, it affects his psyche regardless of whether he chooses to acknowledge it. He may do whatever he can to repent for his actions, withdraw from society, or go further down the dark side by turning off his conscious self and continuing to hurt and/or kill.

The character can also justify in his mind why he killed people, such as for noble causes. Also, a character might have a comic-book attitude toward killing someone. For a character to kill someone, he really has to justify it in his mind that his opponent:

- Defied a rigid moral code of honor and conduct that the character stands behind
- Deserves to die as punishment for actions that the character deems immoral or threatening to society
- Threatened, abused, and/or killed the character's life, family, and/or the people he loves
- Broke the law in a way that is punishable by death

Different examples of how characters have treated death include:

- ***Die Hard.*** Sgt. Al Powell accidentally killed a youth. His regret now keeps him stationed to a desk job, pushing papers.

- ***The Killer.*** John admits to Jennie that he has killed people for money, but says he never took on an assignment where the target did not deserve to die. The same belief system holds true for Ogami Itto (in the *Lone Wolf and Cub* series), Harry Tasker in *True Lies*, and Martin Blank in *Grosse Pointe Blank.*
- ***Harakiri.*** Before he takes on the whole Iyi clan, Hanshiro Tsugumo, an elder samurai, explains to them that he lost his daughter, son-in-law, and grandson due to the totalitarian-esque samurai code, which he feels is a façade. He feels that they should have had mercy on his son-in-law and should not have forced him to commit ritual suicide (hara-kiri or *seppuku*) with a dull bamboo blade.
- ***The Princess Bride.*** Inigo Montoya has a quest for revenge to kill the six-fingered man who killed his father and scarred his face.

Signature Moves

Signature moves are techniques that are usually specific to one character. The character's signature moves separate him from the rest the characters in the story. Often it's something that was passed onto him from a mentor or colleague he met or spent time with along the way.

Professional wrestlers are noted for their signature moves in the ring. Almost every wrestler has some kind of signature move. Some have more than one. When it comes to signature moves, we can all learn a lot from these sports-entertainment athletes. The story told in a pro wrestling match is much shorter than the story in a film—wrestling matches usually average between three and ten minutes. But pro wrestlers know how to milk an audience during the fight and build them up to a point where the crowd is clamoring, wanting their favorite wrestler to finish off his opponent with his signature move.

Film and TV have a similar way of setting up an audience and delivering a payoff, but they have longer timeframes (30 to 60 minutes for TV and 120 minutes for movies) to build up anticipation and more ways of telling the story at their disposal. For example, they can use camera angles, editing, locations, and CGI, and they can take their time getting perfect takes.

Kung Fu movies are more noted for developing signature moves and are more obvious and specific about it in their stories, compared to Western action films.

Examples of signature moves include:

- ***The Karate Kid.*** A good example is the crane stance Daniel takes when he faces Johnny Lawrence at the end of their fight at the tournament to win.
- ***Once Upon a Time in China.*** Wong Fei-Hung has his "shadowless kick."

Distinct Signature Weapons

Much like a signature move, a character's distinct weapon also separates him from the rest of the characters in the story. A distinct weapon can be very simple, complex, or extremely elaborate. But whatever the weapon is, it needs to be an extension of the character.

Questions to ask include:

- In the story is the weapon already an extension of the character?
- Is the character learning to make the weapon a part of himself?

Examples of characters with distinct signature weapons are

- The Monkey King and his magical staff in *Journey to the West*
- Indiana Jones and his bullwhip
- A Jedi knight and his light saber
- Bruce Lee and his nunchaku
- Jane Smith and her knife in *Mr. & Mrs. Smith*
- David and his sling when he fights Goliath
- Robin Hood and his bow and arrow
- Dirty Harry and his .44 Magnum
- El Mariachi and his guitar case full of weapons
- James Bond and his gadgets
- General Kwan Kung and his 500-pound Halberd (aka Kwan-Do) from *Romance of Three Kingdoms*

Character's Level of Proficiency

Does the character's level of proficiency change or stay the same throughout the film? How do the character's skills change throughout the story? Do the character's skills get better or worse? During what act and scene do the character's skills change? A character's level of proficiency can be:

- Beginner
- Intermediate
- Advanced
- Proficient
- Master

Beginner

A beginner is someone who still has to fight for and find his balance when executing techniques and must consciously think about each move. Chances are extremely great that the practitioner will get his butt kicked if he tries to use what he knows in a real-life situation and might end up hurting himself before his opponent hits him. He is probably not really aware of his actions at this point. In a fight situation, he probably would not know how to hide his emotions so the opponent can easily take advantage of him. He might easily get mad and frustrated during practice. The beginner does not know real-life applications of techniques taught to him. His focus is not clean—it is scattered. He is probably easily overwhelmed. Beginners usually muscle all their moves and get tired more quickly than more advanced students do.

Intermediate

The intermediate knows enough to hurt somebody if he is able to land a lucky shot. He is beginning to understand the body-mind-spirit connection.

Advanced

An advanced practitioner starts to assist in teaching students under him. The student is not a great instructor, but he learns much about himself while teaching.

Proficient

The proficient student is a black belt. However, just because he has a black belt, that does not mean he is the "master of his domain." It simply means that he understood the basics taught to him and now he is really ready to learn the principles of the martial arts. What occurred up to this point? Put it this way: Up to this point, he has been learning the alphabet, how to put letters into words, and what those words mean. Now he will learn how to put these words into sentences. The proficient student does not have to think about the basics.

Master

Between proficient and master, you are no longer a slave to your art and you are able to express yourself fully through the art as if it was second nature. The pitfalls that come with this position are usually ego-related—a master can get complacent because he feels there is no more to learn.

The variable here is the mentality and outlook of the practitioner. He might have had a rough time in the beginning with the obstacles set in front of him.

The first three levels are still considered slaves to the art they are studying because they have not yet been able to fully express themselves without limitations.

Interactions with More Highly Skilled Individuals

How comfortable is the character within the limits of his skills? Is he insecure around others who are more skilled than he is? Or is he okay with himself and where he is at? How realistic are the character's ideas about where he is at?

Reputation

Usually, the fighter's reputation is earned, witnessed, and agreed upon by a group or community that agrees on the fighter's skills and the way he handles his opponents in combat. This could be a one-time situation or something the character has done several or countless times. A reputation can either be positive or negative toward the character. A character's reputation might be positive if he demonstrated heroics at a time when everyone was helpless and he came to the rescue. His reputation might be negative if he has a sour attitude, trigger points, or weak fighting skills. Sometimes a fighter's reputation can fall into mythic proportions because of people spreading false rumors and/or embellishing the truth.

Does this character have a reputation for his fighting skills? If so:

- Was it earned? If so, how did he earn it? If not, how did he acquire his reputation?
- Is the reputation accurate for the character's skills?
- Does the character's nickname reflect his reputation?
- What does the character feel about his reputation?
- Does the character put on a façade when he is around others?
- What do the other characters think about the character's reputation?
- How does the character use his reputation when not fighting? And when fighting?
- Is the fighter's reputation only within that community or does it go beyond that community?

Examples of characters with reputations include:

- ***Drunken Master.*** The King of Bamboo goes to Su Hua Chi to challenge him to a fight. When Su Hua Chi mentions his name, the King of Bamboo walks away, knowing of his reputation. But he stops when he sees Su's shaky hand (due to alcohol withdrawal) and decides to fight him, thinking he might not be who he says he is.
- ***Dirty Harry.*** Harry Callahan has a reputation for equally hating all races and also for taking jobs that no other detective would take.

External Symbols or Indications

Does the character wear or show anything of his rank and/or previous experience? This can be from the very obvious to the very subtle. Some examples include:

- **Uniform.** This might be a police, SWAT officer, or armed forces uniform.
- **Rank.** Even with a uniform there are ascending ranks to show who is in charge and his primary function.
- **Weapons.** Weapons may be scratched, scraped, dinged, and damaged from experiences on the battlefield, but still functional.
- **Physical indications.** These may be scars, handicaps, or habits.

By showing these things, you can reveal a lot about the character without having to use verbal exposition to inform the audience. But you have to back it up with the character's actions because you have set the audience up with certain expectations for that character.

Fight Chart and Stats

A fight chart helps you plan out all your fights throughout the story. The fight chart can also help you plan your fight scenes if you look at it to get a general overall bird's-eye view of how each fight leads to the next, on to the final fight scene. This can also help you not be repetitive with the motivations and emotions of your fights, but it cannot help with the potential redundancy of techniques and rhythm. You must remember and be aware of that fact each time you physically choreograph the fights.

Your Fight Chart

When breaking down your fight chart, you should have a graph basically describing each fight scene and which act it is in, as well as a worksheet that supports the graph.

The only thing you can't do here is show the timing and rhythm of each fight. But it is still something you should think about in order to make sure each fight is unique.

Figure 7.1 shows a sample fight chart.

When assembling your fight chart, it is helpful to start asking yourself the following questions.

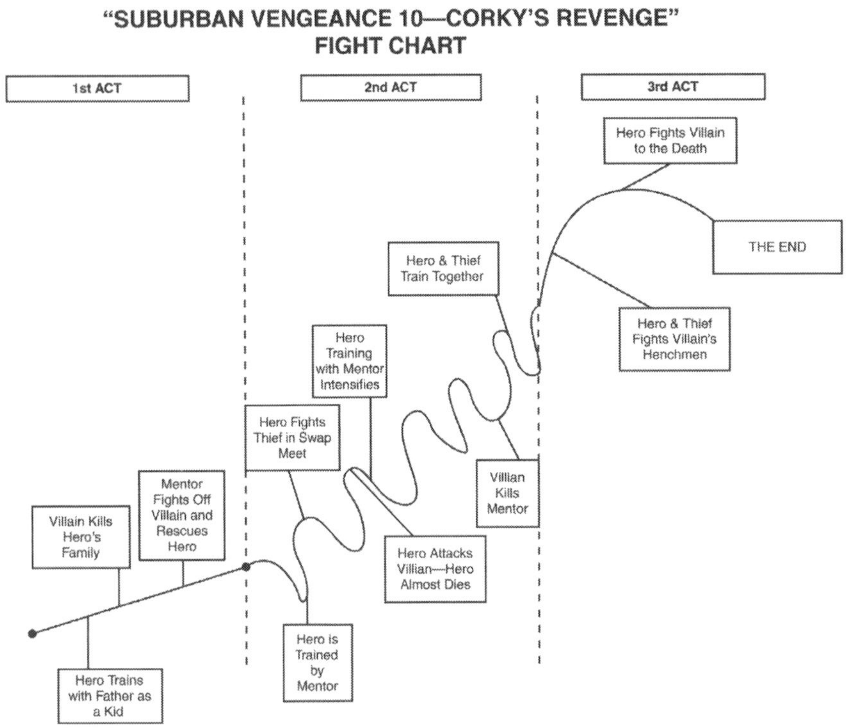

Figure 7.1
Sample fight chart.

How Many Fights Are in the Script?

This includes training sequences and anything you might have to choreograph. Once you count how many fights are in the script, you start to find out the next piece.

How Many Fights Are in the First, Second, and Third Acts?

By breaking down all the fights into each act, you can begin (if you haven't already) to think about how and why each fight is integrated into the story of the film.

Stats

The stats comprise the info that accompanies each fight. The fight info is a detailed information report on each fight. It should include the information discussed in the following sections.

Classify Each Fight in the Script

Classify each style of fight so you can figure out what the emotions, reasons, and rules or protocol will be in the fight. Also know that a fight scene can be a combination of several different styles of fights.

Characters Involved in Each Fight

While reading the script, the fight scene should tell you how many characters are involved in the narrative. However, usually the script only mentions the main characters involved, rather than any minor characters in any sort of detail. You might get a script that reads like this:

```
(Name of Project)

by
(Name of First Writer)

(Based on, If Any)

Revisions by
(Names of Subsequent Writers
in Order of Work Performed)

Current Revisions by
(Current Writer, date)

Name (of company, if applicable)
Address
Phone Number
```

```
INT. GUIDO'S WAREHOUSE- DAY

Holding a flashlight in his mouth, Ron frantically searches
through the files- looking- looking. Suddenly, the
houselights come on. It's too late for him to hide.

Spadero stands by the entrance with his Thugs behind him. He
looks at Ron with total disgust. Ron acts as if nothing is
wrong as nervous sweat starts to drop down his face.

                    RON
          Hi, Boss!

                    SPADERO
          Boss? Do I look like the Police
          Commissioner...Detective Strong?

                    RON
          Huh? I don't know what you're
          taking about, Boss.

                    SPADERO
          I brought you up as if you were my
          own blood and you still play this
          charade?
               (To his thugs)
          Make him experience pain like never
          before. Make him beg to be killed.
          Beat him again. Then kill him.

Spadero's Thugs all wear evil grins as they take out baseball
bats, chains, knives, and other weapons.

                    RON
          You're not gonna get away with
          this!

                    SPADERO
          Send my regards to Jimmy Hoffa.

Spadero leaves the room to let his men do his dirty work.
The Thugs attack Ron as he valiantly fights back as he takes
some lumps himself but is able to dispose of all of them.
```

You know Ron is the main character in the fight and he is front and center. Spadero is another main character, but he has left the room and is not involved in the fight. So the question is how many people comprise "Spadero's Thugs?" That is what you will need to find out as the shooting of that scene gets near. So for this particular fight, you would complete the fight list as follows:

Spadero's Warehouse Fight

- Type of fight: assassination, brawl
- Main characters: 1 (Ron)
- Other characters: Spadero's Thugs (TBD)
- Props: Bats, chains, knives, various weapons (TBD)
- Reveals: Ron is an undercover cop

Justification (Part 2): How and Why Does Each Fight Start?

In the fighter's IQ, we had the first part of the justification of the fighter's skills in the story. In Part 2 of the justification, we need to understand the justification of the fight scene within the story in terms of how and why each fight starts.

With an unjustified or just lightly justified fight scene, one immediately thinks of the low-budget "chop socky" Kung Fu movies of the 1970s, imported from Asia, or many of the U.S.-made ninja or kickboxing films of the late 1980s to mid-1990s that would go straight to video or cable. These types of movies are the ones in which there is no justification for fighting crafted into the story. As a result, these types of films only attract a limited audience. For unjustified action, the audience should just watch a combative sport live or on television. Movies or TV shows with fights that are unjustified might attract an audience initially, but are usually forgotten after a short while. This is a product of lazy writing, and, as a result, everyone has to up the ante in other departments to try to salvage the project, making other things stand out so the audience does not focus too much on the weaknesses of the story.

The stronger and deeper the justification for the fight in the story and the character's motivations, the more memorable each scene will be and the more engaged the audience will be. When done well, the scene can immediately hook an audience, even if they don't like action scenes. A good fight scene is much like a well-written dramatic sequence: It starts with one emotion and ends with a different emotion. This is a good way to measure whether a fight scene is gratuitous. If the story and/or characters do not change as a result of the fight, then chances are it is gratuitous.

Keep in mind that the fight does not have to be justified beforehand; it can also be justified afterward, especially if there is a reveal or some back story told as a flashback.

Result of Each Fight

For each fight, what happens to the characters who are involved? Are they physically, emotionally, and/or mentally injured as a result of it? Also, what happens to the peripheral characters who were not physically involved in the fight? Does the hero learn anything about himself from the fight that he can correct or improve upon next time? Do any of the characters learn anything about their opponent that they can take advantage of the next time they meet?

Differences That Separate Each Fight

What makes a fight scene different than the others? This question asks you how each fight scene will be different than the others in theme, rhythm, visuals, techniques, and personality. Each fight scene should have its own identity—a personality of its own—because each fight has different scenes, characters, and motivations that lead up to each conflict.

What the Audience Learns about the Characters from Each Fight

A fight scene is much like any other scene in a well-written script. It is supposed to advance the story by telling you something about the characters or the situation.

Some examples of this include:

- ***Enter the Dragon.*** Roper fights at Han's tournament. The fight is an extension of Roper's character as a gambler when he initially throws a fight to up the ante on a bet by Williams.
- ***Spider-Man.*** When Peter Parker fights Flash Thompson in school after he is bitten by a genetically enhanced spider, we discover along with him that he has incredible reactions, reflexes, and powers and he is able to think quicker than before in a pressure situation.

Physical and Emotional Continuity Changes

Knowing what reveals are in the story will help you know what to put together for each fight scene as the story progresses. This also assists with the continuity of each fight. This is especially helpful in production because most films do not shoot in sequence order.

Following are some examples of reveals and issues of continuity throughout a story you might encounter if you were not aware of what fight scene you were shooting:

- **Physical continuity changes.** The hero has four fights; he gets a minor injury in the second fight and a major physical injury in the fourth fight. As a result of the injury, the hero fights differently each time. If the fights are not shot in sequence order, you might have him fight with the major injury in the third fight instead of the fourth. That would be a major continuity error.
- **Emotional continuity changes.** The hero, a champion boxer, is a calm and reserved character when he fights. He is very cool, efficient, and composed in the first fight, easily beating his opponent and retaining his title. In the second fight, he kills an opponent (and good friend) in the ring by accident. He decides to retire, but is forced to fight again because of contractual and financial obligations. In the third fight, he is just a shell of a man and he takes a beating because the fight in him is gone. As a result, he loses his title. But a local mobster kidnaps his wife and kid and forces him to win back his title or else his family will die. In the fourth fight, the hero is deeply emotionally distraught. He does not want to fight, but he has to fight to win back his title, or else his family will be killed. He finally overcomes his emotions and is able to lay his friend's death to rest. He wins back the title, saving his family. This is a little tougher because the actor's interpretation and emotional range come into play and they are more subtle. But the choreography has to reflect the character's state of mind and emotion to tell the story.

To a layman, the fights might appear like any other fight in the film, but if you look deeper you will see that each fight is specific to the psychological and emotional stage the character is at. The choreography has to be in sync with the progression of the story and why the character is fighting. The choreography has to reflect the physical, mental, and psychological state of the character with each successive fight. If you are not aware of where the fight takes place in the story, you can commit some very grave continuity errors that can contribute to the failure of the film.

Effects of the Fight on Each Character

A fight is a conflict that cannot be resolved civilly by one or all parties involved in the conflict. A fight affects the people on both sides of the conflict. This is pretty obvious, especially if they are on the losing end of the conflict. But what price did the victor pay in order to win? Was the victory for the character worth the price of the conflict? Did the character lose anything in order to win?

Does the fight also affect characters not involved in the fight? Like a domino effect, a fight can also indirectly affect peripheral characters who were not physically involved because of the different types of investments they might have in the character involved in the conflict.

Some examples of this are

- ***A History of Violence.*** Two robbers hold up Tom Stall's café and then kill his employees. Tom fights off and kills both of the killers and becomes a local hero on TV and in the newspapers. However, the news of this event attracts the attention of Carl Fogarty, a Philly mobster who exposes Tom's dark hidden past, putting his wife and children in jeopardy.
- ***Jet Li's Fearless.*** Huo Yuanjia fights Master Qin because one of his students was beaten up by him. Huo makes a public challenge by kneeling in front of him. A fight in a restaurant ensues, and Huo beats and fatally injures Qin. Huo comes home to find his family has been killed by one of Qin's men in retaliation, and he finds out that it was his apprentice's fault because he slept with one of Master Qin's concubines and was punished for it.

Physical Elements Involved in the Story of the Fight

Other than the actors, what things are involved in the story of the fight? Can they affect the outcome of the fight? This can include reveals, time bombs, props, environment, locations, and so on. This aspect might or might not be written into the script. As the fight choreographer, you are responsible for bringing ideas to the film (within budget) and making it work within those parameters.

8

The Narrative Structure and Elements of a Fight Scene

As discussed throughout this book, a great fight scene has to follow the narrative structure of the film or TV show. The script gives the fight choreographer the rules for how, when, and why the fight will take place. The script can also be looked at as a set of guidelines that are loosely or tightly (depending on the script) interpreted and made into a live or filmed experience for the audience to witness and enjoy. The guidelines are the rules and conditions that need to be extracted from the script and applied to the fight scenes you are choreographing.

The truth of the matter is that almost anyone can choreograph a fight scene that is dazzling, spectacular, and amazing to the eye and get a "Wow! That was awesome!" reaction from someone viewing the choreographed fight. All you need are some very gifted performers and a camera to shoot the action. The difference that separates a memorable and exciting fight scene from one that is forgettable and gratuitous comes from the choreographer's understanding of the narrative structure and purpose of the scene in relation to the rest of the script and applying it to the fight scene as a non-verbal, physical form of character expression and storytelling. To become a great fight choreographer and to engage an audience emotionally, a person must have a working knowledge of fight choreography, understanding the emotional content and visual ramifications of the techniques used, storytelling, and acting, as well as the technical aspects of filmmaking.

Fight Scene Structure

Amid all the chaos and frenzied action that a fight scene brings, there is an underlying structure. To understand the narrative elements that are in a fight scene, the fight choreographer needs to have a basic understanding of the three-act structure of a script. This is because the three-act structure in a fight is almost the same as the typical three-act structure of a script. And by understanding the three acts of a script, the fight choreographer will also know what types of fight scenes will work and not work in each act because a fight scene in one act will have a different tone, effect, and purpose from a fight scene in another act. As a fight choreographer, you are essentially telling an integral, non-verbal, mini-story with a definite cause and effect all told within a bigger story.

Understanding the three acts of a fight scene will help the fight choreographer much more easily conceive of his action scenes, simply because he will have a clear framework of the story around which the fight revolves. It will also be easier for the fight choreographer to explain to other members of the cast and crew what he will be choreographing and how everyone fits into the intricately choreographed puzzle. This structure can also help the choreographer easily deduce and assess what type of mood and feel the fight should deliver for that section of the story.

When you look for the three-act structure in many fight scenes from films and shows of the past, you will find that many do not follow this type of structure; but this does not necessarily mean that those fights are less interesting, logical, or exciting. The three-act structure of a fight scene is certainly a recommended and time-tested formula, but it should not be seen as an inflexible set of rules that imprisons the fight choreographer. Rather, it should be seen as a flexible tool to be used and altered, as you feel appropriate to your fight scene, to enhance your film.

Following are a couple similarities between the script and the narrative structure of a fight scene:

- A fight scene can be broken into three separate acts—beginning, middle, and end—just like the screenplay that the fight scene is serving.
- A fight scene functions as a narrative form of expression to the story.

And here is a list of differences between the script and the narrative structure of a fight scene:

- A fight scene may last only a few seconds or several minutes instead of running 90 to 120 pages, as a script does.
- A fight scene can be told using just one technique. (For example, in *Ong-Bak*, consider Ting's first fight in the fight bar.)

- A fight scene serves a different function and purpose and has a different effect on the story and characters depending on when it takes place—whether it is in the first, second, or third act of the script.
- When characters meet to fight, the basic three-act structure still applies because the characters' dynamics are different each time they get together given that emotions and motivations, which have been building up to that point, need to be expressed and/or released.

A fight scene is broken down as follows (see also Figure 8.1):

- **Lead-up.** This is a very important scene that occurs right before the fight starts. It gathers previous issues in the story while setting up and justifying the fight.
- **The physical conflict.** This is the actual fight itself, broken down into three acts:

  Act 1 introduces the characters' initial intent and how they integrate with each other.

  Act 2 presents the heightened conflict, perhaps a change of strategy or increasing emotional intensity.

  Act 3 gives the outcome, explaining what happens to the characters.

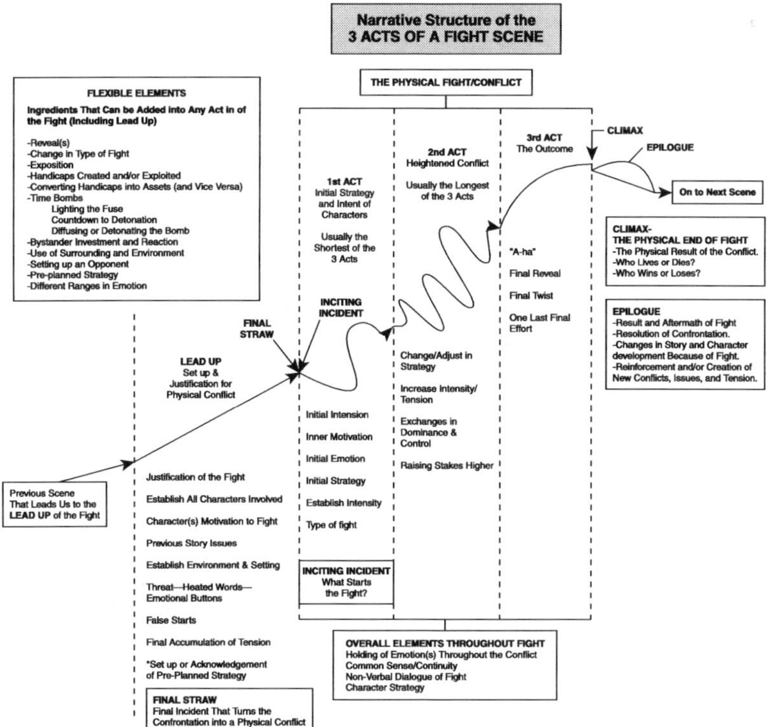

Figure 8.1

Narrative structure of the three acts of a fight scene.

The Lead-Up

The lead-up is the scene that occurs right before the physical conflict starts with the inciting incident. It can be looked at as the calm before the storm. Here is where the justification of the fight occurs, answering these essential questions: Who is fighting? Why are they fighting? Where are they fighting?

Setting Up the Physical Conflict

The lead-up is an accumulation of unresolved conflicts, issues, and differences from previous scenes that cannot be civilly resolved up to this point in time of the storyline. Characters are therefore forced to deal with the conflict on a physical level. The lead-up is a place where the tension builds between the characters with their conflicting motivations and reasons that boil, percolate, and eventually explode into the physical conflict. The lead-up also sets up the mental and physical state of the characters involved in the fight. Characters' mental and physical states can greatly affect the tone of the fight. Taunts, dares, and strikes to the hero that go unanswered usually take place here.

It is up to the writer to create a situation in which there is no turning back (motivationally, emotionally, and/or physically), forcing the characters to engage in a physical conflict. If a lead-up is not strong, convincing, or effective enough to justify the fight, then the scenes, motivations, and issues that have accumulated need to be reevaluated and possibly rewritten to be more effective and justified. If not, there is a good possibility you will end up with a fight scene that appears gratuitous. This happens when the justification of a physical conflict does not properly support the cause and motivations of the story and characters. However, there are some instances when the screenwriter will alter the timeline of the story and have a fight scene first and then have the lead-up after the fight, perhaps even much later in the story.

The diagram in Figure 8.1 shows the lead-up as a straight ascending line. This is to symbolize the buildup (emotional, mental, and physical) from previous scenes that justifies and leads up to the actual physical encounter. Even though emotionally it might appear to be haphazard and crazy right before the fight, in reality this is a premeditated emotional tinkering with the audience in the story that is planned by the writers and filmmakers, which is why we also call it a *setup.* Tension and reasons to fight can build on top of each other either slowly, quickly, or somewhere between, depending on the story.

A well-constructed lead-up is absolutely essential in making a great fight scene that will hook an audience emotionally and be much more memorable to the viewers well after they have left the theater or turned off their TV sets.

The justification for physical conflict typically needs to be established in the lead-up or during earlier scenes, but in rare cases, it can be presented after the fact.

Justifying the Physical Conflict

The story has to justify why the characters are fighting. The writer has to pit the characters in a corner where there is no possible way to get out of the predicament other than resorting to physical conflict. Ask yourself questions like these: What elements are causing this fight to occur? Are there any other possible ways of avoiding this physical conflict? What is at stake for each character? Is a character's mental state causing the conflict? What would the characters lose if they did not fight? If there are easier ways out of this fight, then the fight is not justified and is therefore gratuitous.

Examples of justifications for a fight include:

- ***Pedicab Driver.*** As the film opens, there is a heated discussion at a restaurant between the Coolies and Pedicab drivers over how each group is cutting into the other's business. Then we are given a setup in the kitchen, where a cook is setting up a trap to catch a cat, who has been stealing his food. Next we are given a false start when a waiter walks past the Coolies and Pedicab drivers, asking if anyone wants any BBQ pork buns. Several Coolies think the waiter is insulting them and quickly beat him up. This shows that everyone is on edge and that this is a volatile and sensitive issue they are trying to settle. A few minutes later, the Coolies and the Pedicab drivers hastily settle on an agreement but are still emotionally raw and not really satisfied with the outcome. Right at that moment we are given the payoff, as the cook runs out of the kitchen armed with a butcher knife and yells, "Bastard, I will kill you!" Both sides, being already mentally on the edge, immediately assume the cook is a member of the opposing side out to kill them and do not see that he is instead chasing after the thieving cat, which prompts the inciting incident—and the fight between the Coolies and Pedicab drivers starts.
- ***The Chinese Connection* (aka *Fist of Fury*).** Before the fight in the kitchen between Chen Zhen, Feng, and Tien, we learn that Chen Zhen (Bruce Lee) cannot contain his anger and is not a passive type of individual. When he returns to the Japanese Bushido school, the insulting and disrespectful sign says that his Ching Wu school were "Sick Men of Asia," and Chen Zhen single-handedly beats up the whole school. He then beats up a group of Japanese men who try to degrade him by making him get on his hands and knees and act like a dog in order to get into a park he is not allowed to go into because of his race. When he gets back to his school, he finds the place in a shambles because the Japanese came and destroyed the place and beat up everyone because of Chen's actions. The Japanese demand that Chen be turned into

them in three days. Chen is chastised by the senior instructor of the school and is asked to leave before the whole school gets in trouble because of his actions; he agrees to leave the next morning. That night, Chen overhears Feng (the housekeeper) and Tien (the cook) talking together about how they poisoned his master and are about to make a run for it. To further add fuel to the fire, Tien is an arrogant Japanese racist who is not afraid of Chen and wants to fight him.

The audience is emotionally on Chen Zhen's side from the beginning of the film because of all the injustices he and the members of his school have suffered at the hands of the Japanese school using the police and the law to their advantage. Chen Zhen is the classic antihero acting outside the law by taking matters into his own hands, while the other members of the Ching Wu school are passive and act only when it is morally right. Unfortunately, this comes too late. When Tien and Feng boast to Chen Zhen that they poisoned his teacher, Chen's previous actions (although not morally and legally correct) are immediately emotionally justified in the mind of the audience. The audience is emotionally hooked because we have all experienced some kind of injustice or been taken advantage of at some point in our lives and would like to get some kind of instant gratification and deliver the justice we wish the perpetrator would receive.

◉ ***Project A.*** The fight is between the Coast Guard and police in the bar. Before the fight we are shown a lot of tension between both departments, stressed about the capture of the dreaded Pirate Lo. Most of the pressure lies on the Coast Guard, which is blamed for not doing its job and capturing him. The pressure starts from the highest rank and is felt all the way down to the enlisted officers. At the bar, a group of Coast Guard officers are having a final night out before they sail off the next morning. At a table nearby, a group of police officers notice their loud, boisterous behavior and make comments to them about how inept they are since they've been unable to capture Pirate Lo. One thing leads to another, and the tension escalates between the two groups as verbal taunts are tossed back and forth. After Ma (Jackie Chan) temporarily calms things between both parties, he walks away, is tripped, and accidentally spills his beer on Tzu (Yuen Biao), who gets insulted and in turn pours his drink on Ma's head. Ma asks for an apology, but Tzu replies with a punch that incites the fight.

Establishing All Characters Involved

Which characters are involved in the fight? How many are involved? It is important for the sake of the audience to show all the characters involved in the fight.

You don't want opponents coming out of nowhere for no reason, like a cheap "Chop Socky" film. The audience feels nervous anticipation when they know the hero has his back up against the wall and is facing 15 opponents. You don't need to show all the opponents unless you plan to use the characters that show up as a reveal.

Following are some examples of establishing characters:

- ***Billy Jack.*** Billy fights Posner's men in the park. We see how many men he is up against when he walks into the park and meets up with "Old Man" Posner.
- ***Enter the Dragon.*** Lee has an underground fight with Han's guards. Even though there is an unknown number of guards coming after Lee, they are established by (1) the phone call by a guard to send more guards, (2) off-screen sounds of more guards coming and Lee, acknowledging their eventual arrival, getting ready for them to come, and (3) the countless number of guards shown practicing in the various courtyards when the contestants first arrive on Han's island and during the morning ritual before the tournament begins.
- ***The Chinese Connection.*** This fight takes place when Chen Zhen enters the Japanese Bushido school for the third and final time. When Chen goes to the Bushido school to eventually confront Suzuki, he is met by a small group of Japanese students cleaning up the training area. Chen asks them to leave, saying that this fight has nothing to do with them. The students defiantly stand their ground, ready to fight him. This scene is visually similar to the opening gunfight at the train station in Sergio Leone's *Once Upon a Time in the West.*

Establishing the Characters' Motivations to Fight

Why are these characters forced to fight? Why are these characters there? And what issues drove the characters to be there? Do the characters know they are about to get into a physical conflict? The more complex the motivation and issues, the better. If you let the audience discover the reasons for the fight by putting the pieces together themselves instead of hitting them over the head with the answers, they will appreciate it. Let them think they discovered the reasons firsthand. A character's motivation to fight is usually set up through one or several scenes prior to the lead-up. Character motivation can also be revealed after the fight has occurred and can serve as a reveal.

Think about what would push a person to resort to violence to stop a heated situation or conflict. One motivation might be a direct threat to one's life. Or, if the characters know each other well, you could use the character's weakness as an emotional button an opponent can push to initiate a fight. A fight has to start for a reason, or else the audience will not be emotionally involved and the fight will appear gratuitous.

Some examples of establishing motivation for a character to fight include:

- ***Star Wars: Episode VI - Return of the Jedi.*** Remember the final duel between Luke Skywalker and Darth Vader on the Death Star? Emperor Palpatine, Lord of the Sith, has captured Luke on his new Death Star (which is still under construction), tempting Luke to join him on the dark side of the force alongside Luke's father, Darth Vader, to rule the entire galaxy. All Luke has to do is let his anger take over and strike down the emperor with his light saber, and his education will be complete. Luke does not comply. Then the emperor shows him that the Death Star really is not still under construction, but is fully operable. He does this by destroying a Rebellion battleship, showing that Luke's friends have walked into a trap and will surely die. Luke's emotions get the best of him as he gets his light saber and attempts to strike the emperor down, but he is met by Darth Vader's saber. And the fight between father and son begins as Luke's anger seeps through his veins, completing what we think is his journey over to the dark side.
- ***Ong-Bak.*** Ting fights Big Bear at the fight club. Ting, Muay, and George go back into the nightclub for a second time to find Don, who stole the sacred Buddha head statue, Ong-Bak. Big Bear taunts Ting to get into the ring and fight him. Big Bear beats up a waiter who challenges him but is not good enough to compete with him. Ting does not respond because the waiter went into the fight with his blind pride and ego and walked in to challenge him of his own free will. As Big Bear is about to finish off the waiter, a waitress stops Big Bear by pushing him away. Big Bear then slaps the helpless waitress and is about to beat her up. Hurting a harmless woman violates Ting's Buddhist ethics, so he finally steps into the ring and answers Big Bear's challenge to fight. This is the first of a series of three fights that Ting has at the club.
- ***Spider-Man.*** Peter Parker defends himself against Flash (the school bully) in the school hallway. Peter is not fully aware of (nor can he control or understand) his newfound powers of strength, speed, and precognitive thinking/feeling or how he is able to shoot webs from his wrist. In the cafeteria, Peter accidentally slings a plate of food with his web all over Flash, who comes after Peter in the hallway to punish him for what he did. Peter discovers his powers more clearly as Flash attacks him. He realizes he cannot escape the encounter without having to defend himself in the end, or else Flash will still come after him.

A character in a fight scene can also have multiple motivations for getting involved in the fight. Often the reasons can conflict each other, which can make the fight much more interesting and complex.

Examples of multiple motivations for fight scenes include:

- ***Police Story.*** Consider the "fake baby stroller" fight. Selina Fong (Brigitte Lin) is forced to confess in court against Chu Tu, her boss, about his illegal drug dealings. Ka Kui (Jackie Chan), a Hong Kong police detective, is on 24-hour duty to protect Selina and escort her to court the next day. They are driving to Ka Kui's apartment after he convinces her that it is a safer place to hide. He makes a turn, and suddenly, between the parked cars, a man pushing a baby carriage pops out in front of him. Ka Kui slams on the brakes, but it's too late—he slams into the stroller. He gets out of the car to see whether the baby is okay, but finds out it is only a doll—and he immediately realizes he is being ambushed by Chu's thugs. Ka Kui is kicked in the face and immediately put in a defensive state of mind. Chu's thugs' motives are to "take care" of Selina and Ka Kui. Meanwhile, Ka Kui does not have any assistance with Chu's thugs and has to protect Selina from them and tell her to give him the gun that is in his jacket, which she is wearing—all while fending off all of Chu's thugs. But Selina is frightened by the attackers, which affects her rational thinking, and she stays inside the car, which she feels is safer because everyone else is outside fighting. But she kicks and screams and does her best to fight off the thugs, when they finally get in the car, while she tries to get the gun out of Ka Kui's jacket pocket.

Addressing Previous Story Issues

What past events in the story are being brought forth and used in the fight? Previous story issues can also include events that occurred before the movie started and are a part of the history between the characters. Previous story issues can conflict with a character's motivation to fight or not to fight, which can create character depth and make a more compelling fight. Previous story issues can also double as a character's motivation to fight. These issues have a direct effect on the character's approach to a fight and how he sees the world.

Examples of previous story issues include:

- ***Star Wars: Episode V - The Empire Strikes Back.*** Before they meet in the final duel of the movie, Luke's perception of Darth Vader was that he is the embodiment of pure evil, as well as the one who killed Obi Wan Kenobi and Luke's father, Anakin.
- ***Man on Fire.*** Creasy's past as a high-level government assassin still haunts him, even though he tries to bury it with his constant drinking.
- ***Enter the Dragon.*** Oharra was responsible for the death of Lee's sister, Su Lin.

- ***The Bourne Identity.*** Jason Bourne does not know why he was floating in the middle of the ocean, left for dead, but he slowly realizes he was a lethal secret agent before he lost his memory. When attacked, he's able to defend himself with ease.

- ***The Seven Samurai.*** A woman farmer is fatally hit by an arrow, but before she dies, she gives Kikuchiyo her baby to take care of. Kikuchiyo breaks down and finally admits to the rest of the samurai that he was a farmer's son, not a samurai, and this was exactly what happened to his parents when he was the baby's age.

Establishing Environment and Setting

You'll want to show the place where the physical conflict will take place so the audience can get a sense of familiarity with the surroundings. This way, when the action happens, the audience will already have a sense of where things are. Establishing the environment and setting can be done in scenes before the fight begins that take place in the same place and should also be a part of the story. The environment itself can also build up tension and anticipation for an upcoming fight, like when a character is walking down a dark alley, the possibility and fear of a mugging will enter the audience's mind. When well planned, the environment is a vital part of the fight scene that cannot be repeated in another situation because each environment and story is different. This also works hand in hand with using the environment as part of the fight.

Some examples of environment and setting in movies include:

- ***Police Story.*** Watch each fight and stunt in this film, and notice the quick establishing shots that show you the terrain of the area before a fight or stunt begins. This is especially true with the final fight scene in the mall, starting when Selina goes into Cho Tu's office in the mall to get important papers to convict him. The audience doesn't have to know every single nook and cranny of the area, but a general idea of where the fight will occur is a good establishing shot. This way the audience gets a scope of the hero in relation to the size and terrain of the environment. Depending on the fight, the audience sees the "natural obstacle" (which is the environment) and what the hero has to conquer on top of also dealing with the villain.

- ***Raising Arizona.*** The audience gets an idea of the size and space of H.I. and Edwina's modest low-income trailer home from the scenes already established that lead up to the point when Evelle and Gale kidnap Nathan Jr. H.I. catches them before they can get away and fights Gale in the living room. We realize how small and cramped the place actually is when H.I. scrapes his knuckles on the ceiling as he winds up to take a swing at Gale, who then puts holes in the walls with missed punches. The fight is much bigger than the living room where the fight first starts.

Using Threats, Heated Words, and Emotional Buttons

Words and threats get an opponent to fight when he is reluctant to go to that emotional state.

Some examples of the use of threats and words include:

- ***Star Wars: Episode VI - Return of the Jedi.*** Emperor Palpatine does some emotional button pushing with Luke Skywalker to get him angry enough to go to the dark side of the force.
- ***Rocky III.*** Clubber Lang taunts Rocky Balboa at the unveiling of the statue in honor of Rocky for not giving him a shot at his title, accusing him of ducking and fighting has-been fighters. Notice how the emotions change when Lang starts attacking Rocky's emotional center (his wife, Adrian) and in a knee-jerk reaction gives him a shot at the title. This continues when they first meet in the ring, where Lang constantly taunts Balboa.

False Starts

A false start occurs when an opponent taunts another opponent with a physical strike or something verbal, and the opponent does not fight back or lash out physically. A false start can create a motivation for a character to actually fight. False starts are often mistaken as inciting incidents, which are what engage the combatants to exchange techniques. With false starts, there usually is a slight break before the inciting incident is made to create a dramatic pause and to give the audience a chance to catch up with everything that has led up to this point before the fight begins. The false start can also create instant tension and anticipation, with the audience waiting anxiously to find out what will happen next.

Some examples of false starts include:

- ***Bridget Jones's Diary.*** Mark (Colin Firth) and Daniel (Hugh Grant) are jockeying for the affection of Bridget (Renée Zellweger), when Mark tells Daniel to "step outside" of Bridget's apartment. Once outside, Mark tells Daniel that he wishes he had done this several years ago and throws the first punch, which connects hard to Daniel's nose (a false start). Daniel bends over and holds his nose, not believing what just happened. Then Mark punches Daniel again (a final straw). At first Daniel does not retaliate; instead, he takes a slight pause and leans against a trashcan to gather his senses. (Unbeknownst to us, he is gathering his inner motivation to fight back—a slow fuse.) There is a short beat before the inciting incident occurs when Daniel takes the trashcan lid and hits Mark with it. This begins the actual fight.

- ***The Princess Bride.*** Inigo Montoya (Mandy Patinkin) finally gets his chance to fight Count Tyrone Rugen (Christopher Guest), who was responsible for killing Montoya's father when he was a child. Inigo recites the "prepare to die" speech that he has prepared, rehearsed, and waited all his life to say. There is a slight pause as they both get set to fight, then the count runs away, and a chase with Inigo throughout the castle ensues. All the elements are there to set up for a fight, but it did not happen, so this is a false start—a comedic one at that, because we do not expect it. Another false start occurs soon thereafter, when Inigo rushes into a room down the hall, only to be suddenly stabbed by Rugen, which seemingly ends the duel before it begins. But Inigo slowly recovers and the actual fight eventually gets underway.

Setting Up or Acknowledging Preplanned Strategy (Optional)

There are times when you need to let the audience know there is a preplanned strategy before the fight begins. This typically happens with the final fight, which takes place in the third act of a film, when the all-consuming villain has defeated the hero to a point where the audience does not have too much faith that the hero will make it out alive if they are to meet again. Usually, before the final fight starts, the audience sees the hero thinking, planning, and/or trying out his new strategy. This, of course, does not mean you have to color the picture completely for the audience by hitting them over the head. Somehow, though, you have to let the audience in on the character's motivation and why the character is setting it up—but don't show them the application.

The acknowledgment of a preplanned strategy is very dependent on the structure of the story and should be sensitive to the development of the story and how vital story elements are revealed.

Examples of preplanned strategy include:

- ***A Nightmare on Elm Street.*** Nancy plans how to bring Freddy Krueger out from the dream world into the real world by falling asleep for 30 minutes and going into the dream world where Freddy lives. Once there, she'll wake up while tussling with him, and then she'll bring him back into the real world with her. Back in the real world, she has booby traps set up for him all over the house. Notice when she sets them up, we are just observers and we are not let into all the hows and whys. We are left to experience what happens right as the traps unload on Freddy. The same type of setup is also used in the comedy *Home Alone.*

- ***The Warriors.*** Swan conceals a knife in the back of his pants when he meets Luther at the beach for a final showdown. When they face off in the next scene, Swan appears unarmed while Luther has a gun.
- ***The Karate Kid.*** Mr. Miyagi promises Daniel that he will teach him karate, but instead he gets Daniel to paint the fence, sand the floor, and wax the cars for weeks. Daniel wonders when he will learn karate because the tournament is coming up soon. Little does he know that he's actually learning the basic building blocks of how to defend himself.
- ***Die Hard.*** McClane has to give himself up to Hans, who is holding McClane's wife hostage. Before he does, McClane sees a roll of tape, and we have to figure out for ourselves what he is going to do with that. At the very last moment, we see that McClane has a gun taped to his back. The audience appreciates it when they are given puzzles to figure out, and that in turn makes them more active and reactive, resulting in the film being a more memorable experience.
- ***The Seven Samurai.*** The preplanning is in the changing of the terrain of the village so the bandits will be trapped once they run into the village. Preplanning is also in place with the training of the farmers so they can assist the seven samurai in defeating the bandits.

Final Straw

The final straw is the last incident that pushes the confrontation in the lead-up and sparks the first act of the fight with an inciting incident. The final straw can be any element already defined in the lead-up; it can be something subtle and quiet or big and obvious. The final straw can be looked at as the boiling point, where the character cannot contain his emotions and thoughts any longer and has no other way to channel that energy but to erupt physically.

A good example of the final straw is in the following:

- ***Star Wars: Episode VI - Return of the Jedi.*** Emperor Palpatine shows that the Rebel Alliance is doomed with nowhere to go and tells Luke that his friends on Endor will be dead also. The emperor asks Luke to strike him down with his light saber, which will make his education complete. Luke tries to contain his anger and frustration, but his emotions finally win over as he draws his light saber, only to be met by Darth Vader's sword.

The Physical Fight/Conflict

The actual fight/conflict is broken down into three sections: the first, second, and third acts. In each of these three acts, some specific story elements are usually presented non-verbally with martial acting elements that push the conflict and story forward while still keeping the audience's attention. In the beginning it is very hard to tell which act you are in while watching a fight, but after repeated viewings you will begin to notice the differences. Each act has specific story elements represented in a physical and visual way, making each act of the fight different. What you should think about is what type of a story you want to tell with your fight scene. Simply saying that you want the hero to beat up the bad guy and win the girl is not detailed enough. Do you want a fight where the "upper hand" changes several times? Or a fight where the hero takes a beating the whole time but ultimately wins with a desperation strike at the very end. Or perhaps a fight where one character dominates the whole time and systematically destroys his opponent without ever losing the upper hand, like when Sonny Corleone mercilessly beats up his sister's husband in *The Godfather*. There are narrative beats in the fight scene that need to be fleshed out by the fight choreographer; these are usually not described in the script. To avoid becoming overwhelmed, it is good to know how the fight scene starts and ends and to begin to fill in the blanks in the middle.

First Act of the Fight Scene: Initial Intent and Strategy of Characters

The first act introduces the character's intentions translated into a non-verbal physical expression of conflict with his opponents that has escalated as a result of the lead-up—previous scenes and events that have gone unresolved up to this point. A character's initial intent toward his opponents in a physical strategy, which might or might not be successful, is shown here in the first act. Opposing character chemistry as well as contrasting physical, strategic, and mental approaches and styles between opponents during the conflict are introduced here, though they can change during the second and third acts. Depending on the character's experience and familiarity with the opponents, there is usually a certain awkwardness or feeling out when first engaging, much like how a couple dancing together for the first time gets used to each other's rhythm and flow.

Between closely matched opponents, the first act can be used to test each other out, and their strategies will generally end at a stalemate. But the first act is much shorter when a fighter meets a more skilled opponent—showing the weaker fighter's initial intent immediately being smothered by the superior fighter's overmatched skills.

In Figure 8.1 earlier in this chapter, the line in the first act of the fight is curvy to indicate the introduction of the intent of the characters involved in the fight and how they begin to integrate with each other in the physical conflict.

As the first act of the fight starts, the elements discussed in the following sections make the first act distinct by establishing the characters' initial intent.

Inciting Incident

A fight always starts with an inciting incident, which happens when the first person throws a punch or uses any other technique intended to inflict harm or damage on another person's body. If a main or supporting character is the cause of the inciting incident, the how and why of the incident should be justified and should be a part of the character's personality, story arc, and makeup. Usually, a character who feels uncomfortable emotionally, morally, and/or physically with the opposing character and/or with the events that have culminated in the lead-up initiates an inciting incident. Otherwise, if a character throws a punch as the inciting incident for no justified reason, you will have audiences scratching their heads, wondering why that happened and what it had to do with the story, and you could very well end up with a gratuitous fight (unless you explain the reason for the seemingly unwarranted attack later in the story). The inciting incident does not have to result in contact being made; the reasoning and emotion behind that intention matter more.

Following are some examples of inciting incidents:

- ***Billy Jack.*** The inciting incident that starts the fight with Posner's men in the park is when Billy Jack finally knocks down Old Man Posner with a crescent kick to his head. The reason that Billy Jack knocked him down with the kick was because of all the corrupt and illegal things Posner had been doing along with his son, Bernard, up to that point—things to which the law had been turning a blind eye.
- ***Enter the Dragon.*** Lee's underground fight against Han's guards is an example of an inciting incident. When the alarm sounds, signaling that there is an intruder, Lee tries his best to escape without being seen, which would blow his cover. But when he's unable to escape, an incredibly well choreographed fight scene unfolds. When you look at the fight carefully and break down the series of fights, notice that Han's guards are the ones to initiate the fight (inciting incident), which puts Lee in a defensive position and frame of mind, adjusting to each attack that comes at him differently. This shows his superiority in skill above all the guards.

Initial Intention (or Outer Motivation)

What is the intention of the character while in the fight? Does he want to injure, kill, embarrass, outscore, or merely escape from his opponent? Certain issues will arise and can change the character's intention throughout the fight, differing or intensifying the initial intention, thereby making the fight more emotionally deep and complex.

Inner Motivation

What are the emotions of each person involved in the fight? Even though the fighter might fight for a cause, inwardly he might feel scared, overconfident, or unsure. This can be a direct contradiction of his initial intention (or outer motivation).

A good example of inner motivation is the following:

- ***Enter the Dragon.*** The relationship between Oharra and Lee shows inner motivation. Externally, Han tells Bolo to begin the fight. But Lee remembers the time his sister was forced to take her own life in front of Oharra. This is his inner motivation to throw the first punch, which immediately knocks Oharra down to one knee.

Initial Emotion

Showing the characters' emotions throughout the fight is key to communicating to the audience the story of the fight and what the characters are feeling during the fight. The characters' initial emotions can change throughout the fight due to physical and emotional changes that might occur. This is a part of what is described as *martial acting*. A great fight scene starts with one emotion and ends with a different emotion.

Initial Strategy

Initial strategy is different from other strategies used in a staged fight because it is heavily based on the person's assumption or deduction (or a varying degree of both) of what he has assessed will work against his opponent when they first meet to fight. This is followed through and applied strategically in a physical manner to accomplish the person's desired goal. When effectively set up, this can create a lot of dramatic tension as the fight begins. The external purpose of the initial strategy is to establish immediate dominance over the opponent in order to achieve a goal.

Assumption is based on what the character thinks are his best skills from training and past experiences that have led up to this point and how they will affect his opponent. When a fighter is overconfident or does not know what skills his opponent has, he relies heavily on skills of assumption.

Deduction is more of a fact-based thinking process that requires the hero to assess a villain from past fights and/or training sessions, observations, and knowledge gathered from other opponents who have fought the villain. The hero then matches the villain's skills against his own past experiences with the villain, his confidence, and a personal inventory of his own strengths and weaknesses, to sift for the best possible solution to his advantage.

Other factors that also have an effect on one's initial strategy depend on the character's emotions or processing skills at that moment (the character might be injured, scared, inexperienced, or too tired to think clearly) or the amount of time the character has to strategize. The initial strategy can be preconceived, responding, or reactionary (or a combination of all three) in approach, depending on the character and situation.

Typically in a Kung Fu movie, the initial strategy the hero comes up with is usually not good enough to hold up against the villain, so he ends up losing the fight. The villain at first might seem to have an impenetrable defense, an easy counterattack to the hero's strategy, and/or a signature technique or skills for which the hero initially feels he has no defense or counter. But the hero might go away, train by himself, and discover a defense or he might encounter a mentor or an equal who passes a skill on to him, so he can make adjustments to his strategy when he meets the villain next.

Creating an initial strategy varies with each character's personality and depends on the goals he wants to accomplish in the fight, followed by his skill and experience level in actual combat, developed into a workable strategy suited to his skill set for the goal he wishes to accomplish. If the character fighting does not have any previous training, then the initial strategy would probably be predominantly emotion driven, where the character might not be aware of his physical actions as much as the emotions that are overriding his rational thought. This is still considered an initial strategy because it is an approach taken in reaction to a physical affront (stimulus) by the character's opponents.

Examples of initial strategies include:

- ***Way of the Dragon.*** Tang Lung fights Colt in the Roman Colosseum. The fight starts out with Tang and Colt fighting flat-footed, throwing hard techniques at each other, but to Colt's advantage as he is able to dominate the fight. Tang's initial strategy does not work to his advantage, so needs to change his approach before Colt kills him.
- ***Indiana Jones and the Temple of Doom.*** Indy is confronted by two of Mola Ram's swordsmen. They twirl their swords. Like in the first film, Indy reaches for his gun. But this time he does not have a gun in his holster. He must have another strategy to deal with them.

Emotional Intensity

Establishing emotional intensity is showing a combination of the initial strategy, the character's intent, the type of fight, and the physical timing between the combatants. Emotional intensity is the glue that holds the non-verbal narrative of the fight together. The emotional intensity can change throughout the fight, but it is important to know what emotions are used during the fight, how they change the dynamics of the fight, and what corresponding techniques should be used to match the different emotions. A great fight scene has depth, just like any other scene in the story; it starts with one emotion and ends with a different emotion.

Type of Fight

What type of a fight is it? Establish the type of fight to match the story and characters. Once you choose the type of fight, you can jump around to different types of choreography that you think can tell the non-verbal story of the fight depending on the time period for which you are choreographing. When choreographing a historical piece, the type and style of fight should match the time period, or at least be in the same family. A good example of this is found in the *Once Upon a Time in China* trilogy, where the style of fight is not exactly how everyone fought at that time. Wong Fei-hung (Jet Li) used stylized Wushu moves, which did not exist at that time. But Wushu is a modernized derivative of Kung Fu, Chinese opera, and gymnastics that was turned from an art into a sport. So Wushu is still considered a part of the same family and is therefore justified, despite being from a different time period. It would not make sense to use modern combat systems, such as Krav Maga or Brazilian Jiu-Jitsu, in that time period in China because in addition to being from a different time period, those systems are not in the same family tree of styles. See different types of fight charts and descriptions for more information.

Second Act of the Fight Scene: Heightened Conflict

Now that the first act of the fight has established the character's intent and prowess, the second act of the fight uses what has been established in the first act to heighten the conflict in story, emotion, and choreography. The second act displays the struggle to achieve the goals set out by the combatants and should play out to full bloom in all its physical and emotional complexity. Anything can happen here in the second act. The hero can die physically, emotionally, and/or spiritually and can be resurrected—and it is justified. In the first act, the fighters gathered necessary and vital information about their opponents while trying to feel each other out. The second act shows the applied or altered—sometimes completely different—strategies, as the characters are much more familiar with each other's presence, making the fight more intense and full.

In the diagram in Figure 8.1, the line in the second act is much more wavy and turbulent than in the first act to represent the exchanges and level of intensity that ascends and moves along to the third act.

The following sections deal with the integral elements that make up the second act. Note that these elements all work hand in hand with each other.

Changing and/or Adjusting Strategy

After the initial strategy in the first act, adjustments in a character's approach toward his opponent and goals are to be expected in the second act of the fight in order for the character to survive the encounter. Adjustments and/or change in strategy can be emotional, physical, and/or mental. Emotionally, the characters can change after enduring the pain given and taken during the fight so far. Physically, the character's approach can change toward an opponent after learning about a weakness or trait the fighter might be able to take advantage of. Mentally, the character might have a different thought about the goal at hand and change his approach to it, which in turn affects him physically and emotionally. If things are working well for the characters in the initial strategy, then think about what the characters need to do to seal the deal and move on to the next scene. Also think about what other obstacles might pop up to prolong the conflict.

By the second act, the combatants might have different motives or feelings about following through with the conflict because of the physical and/or emotional pain that might have occurred up to this point. How a character tolerates that pain is also an important facet to a change or adjustment in his approach. Because this is still a narrative, think about the character's goals and what adjustments he might need to make to fulfill those goals.

Whatever adjustments and changes in strategy you make in the second act, always have that character in mind and ask yourself, "What would this character do in this situation if the initial approach/strategy did not work or to stay in control of his opponent?"

If a character is dominating the fight, often very little attention is paid to the person who is in the submissive position. But the person who is getting beaten is as important as the one dominating during the conflict. You can learn a lot about a character by the way he reacts to a hit—and also a lot about the person administering the technique.

Increasing Intensity and Tension

By increasing the intensity and tension of the fight, you get the audience emotionally involved. You can do this internally, between the combatants as their emotions run higher and higher, or by using something external to the fight that will raise the stakes.

Exchanges in Dominance and Control

The opponents usually have conflicting goals, which is why they are in the fight in the first place. Having exchanges in dominance and control causes the audience to wonder whether the hero will make it out of this conflict. This cannot be done just to be done, as we see in a lot of movies. The exchange in dominance and control needs to be justified and set up properly in order to make this work effectively.

We've seen so many fight scenes in films in which the characters are struggling to dominate or control an opponent, but we're not emotionally involved because we don't believe it. Exchanges in dominance and control have gotten to be very cliché in films lately, and audiences over the years have come to expect that they already know the outcome, where the hero ultimately prevails, despite the fact that he appeared to be losing for the majority of the fight. Filmmakers are no longer a step ahead of the audience.

Exchanges in dominance and control often aren't believable to the audience for the following reasons:

- The audience doesn't know enough about the characters to be emotionally invested in them.
- The characters were poorly introduced and set up, and their physical skills were introduced as a second thought.
- The fight choreography is not convincing enough to hold the emotional tension of the scene.
- The actors are not convincing enough in their martial acting.
- The audience can't see the struggle because of the use of obscure camera angles, which takes away from the emotion of the scene. Often the camera is too close, trying to get the audience intimately into the action, but it does not really work because due to the closeness, we do not get all the information needed to get emotionally involved in the struggle.
- Fast-paced editing takes away from the emotion of the scene.

Raising Stakes

Raising the stakes higher than initially anticipated changes the fight scene by changing the narrative rhythm and flow to the fight scene. As a result, the fight scene becomes more complicated and intense. You can raise the stakes by giving the character an even greater reason to fight than he originally anticipated, for instance, in the midst of the fight, the villain might say something like, "I'm the one who killed your father." Other ways to raise the stakes can include the adding of time bombs (see "Flexible Elements" a little later in this chapter) or reveals, exploiting or creating handicaps, and so on.

Third Act of the Fight Scene: The Outcome

The third act of the fight scene is where the fight ends. Depending on the fight scene, the third act usually takes a more serious and heavier tone than the first two acts. Previous issues in the story come to a head here, and in the end are resolved, elevate the current situation, and/or further complicate character and story issues by creating more issues and problems, making the drama even more complex.

The third act is when everything is resolved or more problems are created so the opponents can meet at a later time in the story. The third act is usually looked upon as a do-or-die situation or a last-ditch effort to defeat the opponent. The major difference between the third act of a fight scene and the first two acts is that in the third act the combatants' actions convey a sense of immediacy to end the fight. Although this might seem organic, natural, and eventual when it appears, it is preplanned by the screenwriters and/or the fight choreographer (depending on the depth of the script).

The arc in the third act (see Figure 8.1) is different from the wavy lines of the first two acts. In the third act, the arc shows that the fight reaches its emotional crescendo and then plunges into the climax, where the fight ends. The third act is probably the most emotionally intense of all three acts because there is an impending doom instigated by the characters in the story or a payoff of a time bomb that will take place in the climax. The third act of the fight scene will often show new problems created from the conflict and/or resolve issues that led up to the fight.

The elements that make up the third act are discussed in the following sections.

Aha!

An "aha!" is an inner awakening that happens to someone who is in the thick of the battle. It is a brief moment of clarity amid all the chaos. It is like a mind shift within a character when he is hit by a lightning bolt of inspiration that makes him realize what he has to do in order to defeat the opponent. The approach to the fight afterward usually makes a big change in momentum that leans in favor of the hero. This is used often and is a major story ingredient with Kung Fu and Wu Xia films. However, it is interesting to point out that with most Western films, this either does not exist or is very understated, unless it is a functioning story element of the script. An "aha!" moment usually is a major turn in the fight, generally for the hero.

Examples of "aha!" moments include the following:

- ***Ong-Bak.*** In the final fight scene, Ting is about to be choked by Saming. As he is about to black out, Ting sees the head of the Buddha, which reawakens his spirit, helping him to come to his senses and defeat Saming.

- ***Magnificent Butcher.*** Lam Sai-wing fights Wildcat. In the beginning of the fight, Wildcat, an animal stylist, is getting the best of Lam by jumping from pillars and beams to attack him. In the middle of the fight, Lam accidentally dips his hand in oil and has a moment of realization (an "aha!"). Just as Wildcat is about to jump onto a pillar to attack, Lam tosses oil on the pole, causing Wildcat to slide down it. Lam is able to take advantage of this and turns the fight around to finally defeat Wildcat.

Final Reveal

A great fight scene usually has some sort of final reveal that will twist the story and send it into another direction the audience has not anticipated.

An example of a final reveal is in the following:

- ***Star Wars: Episode V - The Empire Strikes Back.*** One of the greatest final reveals in a fight scene is in the final duel between Darth Vader and Luke Skywalker, when Darth Vader tells Luke that he is his father.

Final Twist

A final twist is a turn near or during the climax of the fight that the audience does not expect but that is completely plausible.

Examples of final twists include:

- ***Star Wars: Episode V - The Empire Strikes Back.*** Luke loses his hand in battle.
- ***Face/Off.*** In the final fight between Sean Archer and Castor Troy (both played by John Travolta and Nicholas Cage), Sean/Castor takes a knife and cuts his own face, knowing that Castor is stuck with the face he is currently wearing.

One Final Effort

In a fight where the hero tastes defeat, usually at some point he will realize that he's down and his opponent has got the best of him, and he will give it one final effort before he calls it quits and goes home to lick his wounds.

Climax

The climax of a fight scene is the action that finally stops the fight. The climax is a final visual and emotional release of what was built up in the story to that point. Unfortunately, many fight scenes have an anticlimactic ending, which leaves the audience unsatisfied.

Examples of climaxes include:

- ***Enter the Dragon.*** Lee kicks Han into the spear and impales him, leaving him for dead.
- ***Star Wars: Episode VI - Return of the Jedi.*** Darth Vader throws Emperor Palpatine down the shaft of the Death Star to kill him.
- ***Way of the Dragon.*** Tang Lung breaks Colt's neck and kills him.

Epilogue

The epilogue takes place immediately after the fight scene. This scene, which is the emotional postscript to or conclusion of the fight scene, starts to explore how the fight directly affected all the characters involved.

An example of an epilogue is:

- ***Way of the Dragon.*** Tang Lung kills Colt. All the fights that led up to this were just child's play. This is the first time Tang has ever taken a human life. No longer the innocent country bumpkin, he has grown up emotionally to be an aware adult. In respect for Colt as a martial artist and a person who was responsible for being a part of this sobering and somber lesson, Tang places his karate gi top and black belt over Colt's face. Compare this fight scene with the first fight scene, where Tang shows the Italian thugs Chinese boxing. The tone, approach, and emotion to the earlier fight scene were light and uplifting compared to the fight with Colt. The ending climax is much different in tone also.

On to the Next Scene

How does the fight scene affect the scenes that follow? Does it bring up other issues with the characters involved?

An example of how a fight scene affects the scene that follows it can be found in:

- ***An Officer and a Gentleman.*** Remember the scene in the motel with Zack and Paula that takes place right after he beat up Troy, a local guy who was harassing him outside of the bar? Paula casually talks to Zack about how she really does not know him and asks him how he learned to fight like that. However, Zack does not want to open up and be vulnerable to her and talk about his rough and traumatic past. This fight scene opens up other problems in the relationship that are explored and resolved by the end of the film.

Flexible Elements

The following sections discuss various elements you can put into the different acts of your fight as you see fit. These elements in different combinations introduce randomness and unpredictability, creating individuality and making each of your fight scenes different in theme.

Reveals

Reveals are elements in the story or character that need to be revealed during the fight. They can get the audience more emotionally involved and can be used to keep ahead of the audience and keep them guessing. A reveal can change the emotion and the type of fight. Reveals are usually done with (but are not limited to) dialogue. A reveal can change the emotion, intensity, and purpose of the fight.

Examples of reveals include:

- ***Star Wars: Episode V - The Empire Strikes Back.*** An example of a reveal in dialogue and story comes during the final fight between Darth Vader and Luke Skywalker, when Darth Vader tells Luke that he is Luke's father, which significantly alters the tone of the fight.
- ***Star Wars: Episode III - Revenge of the Sith.*** An example of a physical reveal comes in the fight between General Grievous and Obi Wan Kenobi. Grievous reveals that his two arms are actually four as he wields four light sabers, creating an almost impossible obstacle for Obi Wan to overcome.
- ***The Princess Bride.*** An example of verbal and physical reveal is when Dread Pirate Roberts is in a sword duel with Inigo Montoya atop of the Cliffs of Insanity. Before the fight begins, Inigo tells his boss, Vizzini, that he will fight Roberts with his bad hand, his left, because if he uses his right hand, the fight will be over too quickly. Inigo and Roberts both start the fight with swords in their left hands and are pretty even. In the middle of the fight, Inigo informs Roberts that he is actually right-handed, switches hands, and thinks he now has the upper hand of the fight. Then shortly after the switch, Roberts informs Inigo that he, too, is really right-handed (the reveal), switches hands, truly gains the upper hand, and eventually knocks Inigo out with the butt of his sword.

Changes in Type of Fight

Often the type of fight will change between opponents in the middle of the conflict. This is because either the purpose of the fight has changed or the emotional intensity of the fight has elevated to a level such that the previous type of fight is no longer suitable.

Examples of changes in the type of fight include:

- ***The Seven Samurai.*** What starts out as a friendly match turns into a duel. When we first meet Kyuzo, he is having a friendly match using bamboo sticks with another samurai to see who is better. After the match, the other samurai says he beat Kyuzo. But Kyuzo tells him he hit him first and if it was done with real swords the samurai would be dead. The samurai's ego gets in the way of his clear thinking; he feels insulted and challenges Kyuzo to a real duel with their swords. Kyuzo is reluctant, but finally accepts and easily kills his challenger in the duel.
- ***Enter the Dragon.*** The fight between Lee and Oharra starts out as a tournament fight where there are rules and general ring etiquette. The tournament fight ends when Lee knocks Oharra out of the ring with a lunging side-kick. But Oharra's pride and ego are shattered, so he grabs a pair of bottles and breaks them. At this moment, the tournament fight turns into a life or death challenge. Lee answers the challenge, knocks the broken bottles away, snaps Oharra's neck with a kick, stomps on his chest, and kills him. Notice that the mood turns much more intense with the choice of techniques along with the intent, while Oharra's reaction to the techniques changes as well.

Exposition

During a fight scene you might have to pass on information to the audience to justify the action that will follow. Exposition is a necessary element in cinematic storytelling. Everyone notices badly told and poorly executed exposition, and the audience will also hate you for it because you were not slick enough to slip the information to them subtly. The best way is to do it so it feels as if they were eavesdropping. The key is being able to tell the audience the necessary information without making it look obvious.

Handicaps Created and/or Exploited

Especially if a fight is in the beginning or middle of a film, a handicap that is created for the hero during a fight should be treated like an obstacle the character needs to overcome in order to defeat the villain in the end. In between the fights, the hero learns more about himself and often figures out how to convert his handicap into an asset. The villain usually compensates for a handicap with some part of his arsenal. It is interesting that in Western movies, heroes who have handicaps usually end up overcompensating for them. But in Asia, handicap themes are often used in the Kung Fu film genre with a hero's strategy of overcoming the handicap mentally, emotionally, and physically before he is able to confront the enemy.

Heroes with Handicaps

There are many movies that use the theme of a hero with a handicap. Some examples of this theme include:

- **The *Zatôichi* films.** The blind swordsman, Zatôichi, uses his blindness to his advantage, especially in the gambling dens when others want to take advantage of him. But Zatôichi has very clear hearing skills that compensate for his loss of sight, as well as amazing swordsmanship to serve as a backup.
- ***The Fearless Hyena.*** Shing Lung loses his voice while training to get revenge for the death of his grandfather and unexpectedly bumps into Yen Ting Hua, the man who killed his grandfather. Shing Lung attacks him with reckless abandon. Thinking he is just a harmless insane person, Yen has mercy on Shing Lung before Shing's master saves him and whisks him away. But if he was able to speak, Shing would surely have died in the fight.
- ***Rocky III.*** Emotionally and mentally, Rocky Balboa is a wreck. His only coach and mentor, Mickey, dies of a heart attack right before his fight with Lang. And as a result, he goes into the ring mentally unprepared and loses his title to Lang. Before Mickey passes away, he tells Rocky that he had been setting him up with fighters who he felt were easy for Rocky to beat. Rocky then gets together with his former foe, Apollo Creed, who takes Rocky on as his new coach.

Villains with Handicaps

Notice that when villains have handicaps, the things with which they surround themselves to overcompensate end up being obstacles for the hero to overcome.

Examples of villains with handicaps include:

- ***Enter the Dragon.*** Han loses his hand prior to the beginning of the film and uses this to his advantage by adding weapons in place of his hand, such as a steel fist to kill Williams and a claw and a row of knives to try to defeat Lee.
- ***Dreadnaught.*** White Tiger is a mad killer who goes crazy when he hears a metal jingling that reminds him of his dead wife.

Converting Handicaps into Assets

If the film starts out with the hero having a handicap, it is natural that the hero has to overcome this obstacle. First, the hero has to accept the handicap and where he currently stands with it. Then, he must find a way to operate with the handicap and not depend on others for help, while using other senses to compensate for his handicap. When his other senses come into play and become an active daily part of the hero's life, he is able to turn his handicap into an asset.

Examples of converting handicaps into assets include:

- ***Crippled Avengers* (aka *The Return of the 5 Deadly Venoms*).** A traveling salesman is blinded, the town blacksmith cannot speak and is now deaf, a poor man has both his legs cut off, and Wang Yi, a martial arts student, is reduced to the mentality of a child—all at the hands of a tyrannical Master Dao Tian-du. The four men all team up and learn martial arts from Wang Yi's master to get revenge on Dao. They learn to heighten their other assets to compensate for their handicaps with specialized training methods for each member.
- ***One-Armed Swordsman.*** Swordsman Fang Gang loses his right arm in a fight in the beginning of the film and decides to continue his training, but cannot because the normal length of the sword throws him off balance so he cannot fight. He then finds and uses his deceased father's broken sword, which only has half a blade but suits his center of gravity much better. He adjusts his fighting strategy by fighting in closer than others and is able to defend himself even more successfully than before. This is a prime example of a case in which the handicap turns into an asset.
- ***Cinderella Man.*** Jim Braddock breaks his right hand during a Depression-era fight and has to find work outside the ring in order to survive. He develops a strong left hand while working on the docks. Braddock comes back into the ring years later a better fighter because of his now-strong left hand and eventually wins the world heavyweight championship.

Time Bombs (Start and End)

Times bombs are usually external elements outside of the combatants' control that move the fight along much more quickly than the participants in the fight would like. The ending of the time bomb will endanger the lives of all the combatants. A time bomb places a definite end on the encounter and provides an additional element for the choreographer to add more tension and suspense to the fight. This can also divide the hero's attention by requiring him to multitask to "diffuse" the time bomb while still defending himself during the fight. Well-constructed time bombs can be great scenes in which you can effectively combine and integrate the elements of story and character with the fight scenes. The *Indiana Jones* trilogy is famous for giving us thrilling time bombs that take the audience on emotional rollercoaster rides.

Sometimes a distraction or multiple motivations can be misinterpreted as a time bomb. An example of a distraction is the fight on the subway train between Doc Ock and Spider-Man in *Spider-Man 2.* Doc Ock fights with Spider-Man on the moving subway and then yanks out the control lever of the train so no one can stop it. He then leaves the scene, while Spider-Man tries to stop the train by himself. The reason this is not a time bomb is because the fight between Doc Ock and Spider-Man is not still going on as the train barrels down the tracks out of control.

Following is a list (with definitions) of the elements that make up a time bomb:

1. **Recognizing and establishing the time bomb.** What will be used as a time bomb in the scene? Sometimes it might not be obvious what a time bomb will be until the fuse is "lit." A time bomb can be anything that, when lit, can cause damage to all involved in the physical confrontation. Until the time bomb is lit, the bomb is defined as *dormant.* For example, imagine a fight in which two combatants are fighting inside a car. The actual bomb is the car, although it is currently dormant.

2. **Lighting the fuse.** The starting of a time bomb can occur at any time during the script. It's important that the audience knows the time bomb exists, so it must be visually established in a scene. Audiences also need to know when the fuse is lit to start the time bomb. Whether the characters know a time bomb is lit depends on the film's storyline. For example, consider again the fight scene with two combatants fighting inside a car. One of them accidentally hits the emergency brake, and the car starts to roll down a steep street. The lit fuse is the car starting to roll down the street.

3. **Counting down to detonation.** The time bomb has been identified, and the fuse has been lit. Now even though a fight is going on, we need to see the fuse burn down to the end and detonate. What is involved here is knowing ahead of time what will detonate the time bomb. The characters are given a certain amount of time to finish up the fight before all will perish when the time bomb detonates. For example, suppose the combatants are still fighting in the car as it rolls down the street and manages to avoid oncoming cars and pedestrians. We know they have been lucky so far and that it's going to come to a nasty end because there is a razor-sharp hairpin turn ahead. If they don't make this turn, the car will fly off the rocky cliff and crash hundreds of feet below.

4. **Diffusing or detonating the time bomb.** One of two things can happen here:

   a. **Diffusing the bomb.** This is done by putting a stop to whatever the bomb is. Diffusing the bomb could be done in three ways (in combination or separately): accidentally, consciously, or by fate or acts of nature.

   Examples:

- **Accidentally.** As the car heads toward the cliff, one of the combatants kicks the emergency brake, and the car hangs on the edge of the cliff.
- **Consciously.** One of the combatants realizes the car is moving and is about to go off the cliff. He stops fighting and takes control of the wheel. The other senses something is wrong, looks around, realizes what is going on, and helps him control the car. They are able to pull off to the side of the road, just a hair short of falling off the cliff.
- **Fate or acts of nature.** The two combatants are oblivious that the car is out of control and heading for the cliff. The car spins and skids against the guard rail, which slows it down and cradles the car before it is able to fly off the cliff. The two combatants stop fighting to see what the noise was all about, and it takes them both a second to realize what just happened. They get nervous, tremble, and urinate in their pants.

b. **Detonating the bomb.** The bomb eventually takes its natural course and explodes, falls off the cliff, and so on. Is the hero able to get away before the bomb detonates? Do both fighters jump out just in the nick of time? Does the hero stop the detonation of the bomb?

There are also three different types of fuses:

- **Long fuse.** A long fuse is lit in one act and detonates in another act in the script. These are quite rare.
- **Medium fuse.** A medium fuse is lit in one act of a script and detonates or diffuses in that same act. These are more common.
- **Short fuse.** A short fuse is lit and detonates or diffuses in the same scene. These are extremely common.

Examples of time bombs include:

- ***Ultraman.*** In almost every episode of this 1966 Japanese TV series, Ultraman is in a Kaiju battle with a different monster intent on taking over or destroying the Earth. The light sensor on his chest is activated when the sun's rays have depleted his energy (lighting the short fuse). He needs to finish the battle before the light stops blinking, or else he will never be able to return to Earth again (countdown to detonation). This gives our intergalactic hero a sense of impending doom and shows that he does have a flaw or an Achilles' heel. Of course, Ultraman always wins his fights at the very last moment, so his time bomb does not detonate because that would be the end of his character and they would no longer have a show (diffusing the bomb).

- ***Raiders of the Lost Ark.*** A good example of a time bomb is in the fight with the big, bald German soldier and Indy, as a German-flown wing plane (use of environment) slowly circles around our hero, while the leaking stream of gas (the time bomb) from the fueling truck flows toward the barrels that are on fire (lighting the short fuse). Even though the flowing gasoline might be considered use of environment, it is much more of a time bomb because there is a definite end when the gas hits the flaming barrels (detonation of the bomb). The gasoline is a different element from the plane because it does not have a component of impending doom—it is more of an obstacle the combatants must be aware of and can avoid.

Bystander Investment and Reaction

Are there any characters who are helpless in the encounter and have to watch what is happening? This could be an audience member in the stands who has bet his life savings on the outcome of the fight, or it could be a captive family member who is tied up and held hostage, watching the hero do battle as he comes to the rescue. How do these characters affect the story of the fight? When the scene is done well, bystanders can reflect feelings and thoughts that might not be expressed by the fighters involved in the conflict. Bystanders can also be the voice—the ethical conscience—that can balance the presentation of the fight. The audience can also have an effect on the ego and/or feelings of the combatants in the fight.

Examples of bystander investment and reaction include:

- ***Way of the Dragon.*** The waiters are happy and relieved after Tang Lung first beats the Italian thugs in the alley.
- ***Ong-Bak.*** A good example is in the first fight in the fight club, when Ting arrives in Bangkok. Notice how the crowd is a part of the fight and reacts to the one-hit knockout as Ting drops his opponent with a single knee strike. They are loud and boisterous when the opponent is knocked out and then they are dead silent in awe as to what they have just witnessed. Also, this is the first time we see Ting fight, and we really didn't know how good he would be when meeting up with a live opponent.

Use of Surroundings and Environment

Depending on your story, the use of surroundings and environment is very important in making each fight scene unique and different from the next. Parts of this equation include the weather, the opponents, and their weapons (if any). The use of weather and/or an extreme landscape can show the fighters' ability or inability to adapt and change their strategy and approach due to inexperience, inferior training or ego.

The use of the environment and surrounding can also say a lot about the characters in the fight. Depending on the story, these elements can say any of the following about a character:

- The character is resourceful.
- The character is unaware of his surroundings.
- The character fights "dirty."
- The character does not have tunnel vision.
- The character is at a desperate and vulnerable point and feels that he needs to use the environment or surroundings to protect himself or to equalize or dominate the situation.

But more importantly, how a person uses the environment or surroundings can tell a lot about his character, personality, and emotions at that time.

Here are some questions to ask yourself when using the surroundings and environment in a fight scene:

- Do any of these environmental elements assist or hinder the characters?
- What do we learn about the character and reveal to the audience in this situation?
- If I need to adapt the character's strategy to the location, can I change it without altering the character's personality?

Examples of the use of surroundings and environment include:

- ***The Seven Samurai.*** The final battle is fought in the rain, making it tougher for both parties involved.
- ***Rapid Fire.*** In the fight in the kitchen between Jake and the FBI agents, Jake uses the kitchen utensils and the refrigerator door.
- ***Drive.*** In the fight in the hotel room between Toby and Vic's men, who are armed with Tasers, Toby uses rubber-soled boots on his hands to fight the men off.

- ***Predator.*** Dutch hides in the mud so the alien predator cannot use his heat-seeking vision to find him.
- ***Die Hard.*** Hans knows McClane is barefoot, so he gets his men to shoot out the glass walls to make it harder for McClane to run away. As a result, McClane severely cuts and damages his feet as he escapes. This scene is one of several payoffs that was set up in the first act.
- ***Lone Wolf and Cub: Sword of Vengeance.*** A good example is the duel to the death between Ogami Itto and a member of the Yagyu clan in the middle of a field. Due to the disadvantage of facing the sun, they both run toward each other. The sun is shining in Ogami's eyes, so he suddenly ducks his head to show Daigoro wearing a mirror on his forehead, which shines the sunlight in the Yagyu member's eyes and temporarily blinds him, giving Itto just enough time to decapitate him.
- ***Raging Bull.*** Martin Scorsese altered the size and look of the ring to show the emotion of Jake LaMotta for each fight.
- **Jackie Chan.** Chan has made the use of surroundings and environment pretty much a signature with his fight scenes. Following is a list of some of the films in which he provides excellent examples of use of surroundings and environment.

  Police Story. Every fight scene in this film provides an excellent example of environmental interaction, where items like chairs, tables, escalators, glass display cases, shelving units, and motorcycles are used as props, shields, or weapons.

  Police Story 2. The fights at the playground and the restaurant are good examples.

  First Strike. The fight in the shark tank shows how Chan can adapt to any situation and place.

  Armour of God II: Operation Condor. The fight over getting a handgun in the hotel room, the fights in the underground Nazi lair, and the fight in the wind tunnel are all excellent examples.

  Rumble in the Bronx. The fight in the grocery store and the gangster's hideaway are good examples, where Jackie uses items like shopping carts and refrigerator doors to help defeat his enemies.

Setting Up an Opponent

A setup is doing something (usually throwing a technique) to get your opponent to unsuspectingly give you an opening in his defense so you can take advantage of the opening and win, dominate, or stop the fight.

Setting up and capitalizing/taking control of the opponent shows a character's quick assessment skills of his opponent, as well as the character's ability to think on his feet and under pressure. If the opponent is able to nullify the setup, the combatant has to change his strategy to salvage the setup or come up with a different approach to defeat the opponent. A setup straddles both the narrative and physical elements because it has a non-verbal exchange between opponents, shows the character's intelligence, and has to be choreographed to tell a story. If the setup is planned before the fight begins (in the lead-up or earlier), it then becomes a *preplanned strategy*. A normal setup is conceived of and executed during the same fight.

A well-crafted setup and payoff do not let the audience in on the fact that a setup and payoff are occurring. If the audience *does* know it, then they will be looking for the payoff instead of concentrating on the rest of the story. It is important to keep ahead of the audience with setups and payoffs. You can do so by keeping the audience occupied with other story and character elements. Setups can turn into a chess game, especially between two evenly matched opponents. This occurs when each fighter is aware of the other fighter's intentions and nullifies these setups by changing and adapting his defense accordingly.

A real-life example of a setup is the Foreman-Ali fight in Zaire. Ali set up Foreman mentally by talking to him throughout the fight, saying things such as, "Is that all you've got?" This made Foreman question his own skills. Physically, Ali leaned up against the ropes and let Foreman punch away at him, eventually tiring himself out as Ali waited for the right moment to knock Foreman out in the seventh round to win the world heavyweight title for the second time.

Another example of a setup is when Keith Vitali fought Doug Smith with a rear leg sweep in a point-fighting match. Notice that Vitali got Smith to react the same way twice, using the same technique. Both times, Smith tried to jam Vitali's kick. The third time, Vitali went past Smith's jam and swept his rear leg with another technique.

Setups require the following skills in varying degrees, depending on the character:

- The ability to think and come up with a solution under pressure
- The ability to assess the opponent's strengths and weaknesses in order to avoid the strengths while attacking the weaknesses
- The ability to get the opponent to focus on another technique or become distracted while the fighter attacks the opening or weakness
- The ability to notice an opening when one is available
- The ability to choose the right technique to cause an opening in the defense

- An educated eye to recognize the opening to determine hand/foot speed and timing to throw the technique
- Self-confidence that the setup will work
- The ability to change the strategy if the setup does not work
- The ability to keep oneself protected from "reverse" setups

You see these examples all the time in Kung Fu movies and swashbuckler films, where the fights are extended rather than short.

Examples of setups include:

- ***Dragon Inn.*** In the 1966 King Hu version, the villain easily fights off three of the heroes of the film in the final fight scene—until he takes a pause to do an after-pose to show us that he is beginning to struggle with his breathing and that he has asthma. This is the setup. The heroes immediately recognize that he has a flaw and continue to attack him without giving him time to catch his breath. The payoff is when the heroes finally are able to wear the villain down and defeat him because of his asthma.
- ***Eastern Condors.*** A good example is in the fight on the catwalk atop the General's lair, between Ming-Sun Tung and one of the General's soldiers. During the middle of the fight, the soldier falls and sticks his foot out to jam any oncoming kicks. The soldier quickly stands up as Tung throws another kick, which is jammed by the soldier. Tung throws a fake as if he is going to kick. The soldier takes the bait and jams it, but Tung throws a punch to his head and knocks him down. Tung eventually defeats the soldier by breaking his back on the guardrail and throwing him down off the catwalk.

Preplanned Strategy

A preplanned strategy is a plan of action that is conceived, set up, and planned before the fight actually starts. This is different from a setup and payoff because it was consciously or unconsciously planned before the fight started.

Examples of preplanned strategy include:

- ***Rocky II.*** Mickey teaches Rocky to fight as a southpaw (right hand forward) during the training sequence in the second act. During the fight in the third act, Apollo is brutally beating Rocky. Mickey tells Rocky to be patient and wait for the right moment to switch. The payoff occurs when Apollo thinks he has Rocky in the corner and is ready to finish him off. Mickey tells Rocky to switch, and he switches his stance and hits Apollo as a southpaw. This naturally throws Apollo off his game. It is a conscious preplanning strategy.

- ***Enter the Dragon.*** Lee recalls the lesson he learned at the opening of the film with his sparring match at the Shaolin Temple. He starts to apply it to the fight with Han in the maze of mirrors by destroying the mirrors. This is an unconscious preplanned strategy because we were given the piece to the puzzle earlier, long before the fight between Han and Lee started.
- ***Coffy.*** When Coffy poses as Sir George's new prostitute, the other girls, led by Meg, are jealous of her. At a party, Meg "accidentally" spills a tray of drinks on Coffy. Coffy goes into the bathroom to change and put razorblades in her hair (the setup), then goes back out to start a fight with Meg. The other girls join in the fight as Coffy fights them all off. Frustrated, Meg grabs Coffy by the hair and, to her shock and surprise, Meg severely cuts her hands (the payoff).

Different Ranges in Emotion

A good fight shows different emotions in the fight that support and enhance the character and story. Showing different ranges of emotions during the fight also keeps the audience on their toes. Showing just a single emotion can get boring, especially if each fight has the same emotion attached to it. By just showing anger, you handicap yourself and are not able to tell a non-verbal story. Adding other emotions to support and enhance the anger will give the fight more emotional depth.

Adding emotions can be done using the following:

- Facial expressions
- Dialogue
- Body language
- Choice of technique
- Footwork
- A character's approach to an opponent
- Reveals during the fight to change the motivation of the characters

An example of a range of emotions shown in a fight scene is:

- ***The Fearless Hyena.*** The final fight scene with Shing Lung and Yen shows Shing going through different emotions taught to him in a form that he applies to the final fight with Yen. Notice the emotions of joy, anger, sorrow, and happiness are accompanied with techniques that complement each emotion. Also notice that each emotion and technique has a different approach and effect on Yen.

Overall Elements throughout the Fight

The following sections discuss elements that should be consistent throughout the three acts of a fight scene.

Ability to Maintain the Emotions of the Fight

The scene has to be well constructed to be able to maintain the proper emotions of the fight. This lies in the setup of all the characters and their motivations that led up to the fight. You will notice in some films that a fight scene cannot maintain the proper emotions because it is too long to justify the emotions of the characters to fight. The characters' reasons and emotions have to match or exceed the reason and length of the fight. Often, if a fight is too long and does not have a variety of emotions, you can easily lose the audience. A long fight should have some variety to hold an audience's attention.

Common Sense/Continuity

Common sense is a complex rule that is determined by how the world in the script is defined. Something you might be able to get away with in a science-fiction film might not be plausible in a period piece.

Common sense is a commonly ignored issue in many fight scenes. Common sense in fight scenes is developed through the story, the characters, and the abilities that have been established up to the point before the fight. The characters' world is constructed by the events that have occurred up to the point of the fight.

Continuity is also a commonly neglected issue in fight scenes. Effective continuity is achieved when there is smooth and logical visual flow between techniques and shots. Bad continuity is when that flow appears illogical or unnatural. For instance, in a poorly constructed fight scene you might see the hero pressed against a wall, blocking a barrage of punches from his opponent. Then the camera would cut to the face of the concerned girlfriend on the sidelines. Then, a half-second later, the camera would cut back to the fight scene where we'd see the hero kneeling on top of his opponent, hitting him with a baseball bat. How did he manage to switch positions and gain the upper hand during that half-second cutaway? Where and when did he get the baseball bat? Another common example is when two fighters are exchanging blows at close range and then the camera switches to a wider angle where, all of a sudden, one fighter is 10 feet away, running toward the other in order to throw a flying sidekick. We didn't see him move backward (or perhaps push his opponent forward), so the flow of the fight is not continuous or logical.

Following are some more hypothetical examples of films where continuity and common sense are not used.

- ***Film #1.*** At a particular time in the story, we do not know whether the hero knows how to fight. And, up to this point, he had a sidekick that did all his fighting for him, while the hero did the cerebral detective work. But the sidekick was killed a couple scenes earlier. The hero finally finds the villain in some old ruins, and they have a sword duel. The villain is dominating the fight. They get into a tight clinch, pressing their swords together. Finally, the hero breaks free and gets his distance from the villain. The villain's sword then turns into a nine-section steel whip chain that is able to destroy the large stone pillar behind which the hero is hiding. My question is: If the villain's sword is that tough, why couldn't it go through the hero's sword when they were in the clinch? It could destroy a huge stone pillar, but it could not go through the body of the hero and his thin sword? Also, the fight scene was distinctly Chinese in style and took place in medieval Europe, with no real explanation as to why this was so.
- ***Film #2.*** In the final fight scene, one of our two heroes has already been killed by the villain, and the other is hanging over a ledge, about to die. We don't see any possible way out for this hero. The villain up to this point has been incredible with his fights. He is faster and stronger than the two heroes in the film and he has posed a very formidable threat. The fights up to this point made the heroes take a defensive position—they were mainly in reactionary positions to the villain's extremely fast, razor-sharp timing and clean techniques. As the villain looks over our hero's impending death, the hero vaults himself up in the air, grabs his weapon, continues his forward momentum, flips over the head of the villain, and kills him with a single, telegraphed sword strike. This is all done as the villain stands there watching it all happen. Everything the villain had done up to this point was building up for a great ending, but it was wasted on that unjustified moment. Why did the villain's sharp and flawless fighting skills suddenly disappear? When you look at something like this that does not make any sense, it is a real emotional letdown for the audience.
- ***Film #3.*** There is an intense slugging-type brawl between two combatants that went down an abandoned stairwell. The villain has the hero up against the wall, tired and low on energy. The villain beats the hero with in-close, bruising shots and throws him up against the wall. The hero makes a final effort to lunge at the villain, who counters with a flashy and acrobatic Capoeira handstand kick to drive the hero back up against the wall for no reason. What the hell was that about? That kind of technique does not belong in a brawl-type of fight (unless it is part of the character and story) and it destroyed the tension that was already created with the fight so far.

> But unfortunately, the director wanted the technique in the fight because he had a severe case of "cool-move-itis"—a common disease among filmmakers who want to add into a fight scene a "cool move" that has nothing to do with the characters or anything that has been established or justified up to that point. Cool-move-itis destroys the emotion of the fight.

Unfortunately, these things happen all the time in films, but they really should not. These issues usually occur when a filmmaker is short on time and needs to come up with a quick ending other than what was originally planned. But these types of issues also show lack of common sense, understanding, and respect for the narrative elements that have been previously set up. These types of issues can also occur when the filmmaker has no understanding or no interest in what he set up and established in previous fight scenes, or they can be the result of simple negligence.

Non-Verbal Dialogue of Fight

Even though non-verbal dialogue is considered a physical element, the story aspect of the non-verbal dialogue of the fight should follow along with the narrative of the story. For the narrative, ask yourself what type of story you plan to tell with the characters involved in the fight.

Character Strategy

Each character's strategy and physical execution of the strategy should be a representation of that specific character's personality, background, training, emotions, and motivations for being in the fight. Questions to ask as you figure out the character's strategy include: What is the character's motivation for being in the fight? Is he willing to partake in the fight? Or is he thrown into it against his will? Whatever the strategy, it should be an extension of the character.

A good example of character strategy is:

- ***Rocky III.*** Having lost his title to Clubber Lang, Rocky gets a rematch with Lang. In the second fight, Rocky realizes that Lang is motivated by anger, so he aggravates Lang by taking shots and taunting him, saying things such as, "Is that all you got?" In short order, Lang is out of gas, and Rocky is able to knock him out. This is much like what Muhammad Ali did to George Foreman in their fight in Zaire in 1974.

9

Physical Elements of the Fight Scene

This chapter discusses the physical elements involved in putting together a fight scene. The choreographer should have all his information culled from the narrative elements in the previous chapter and be ready to apply it to the actual physical construction of the fight. You can review the narrative elements in terms of the rules and what justifies the moves and actions that make up the physical framework.

The Framework

Like writing a screenplay or composing music, know that you will have to revise the fight choreography several times before it becomes final. Don't think you will have a fully timed and running fight scene on your first stab at piecing together the action—it is too much pressure. Fine-tuning the basic fight and refining all the nuances and subtleties always takes several revisions to produce a truly polished fight.

Here's an example of what could happen:

- **First run.** This is where you establish a foundation to work from, setting out the basic building blocks with the fundamental techniques and your intent for those techniques. In this run, you see how the fight relates to and is a part of the environment. You should know exactly how the fight starts and ends, and you should start to fill in what happens between those points.

- **Second run.** This is when you replace some techniques with ones that better represent the emotion of the moment. It is also where you make the environment more a part of the fight.
- **Third run.** This is when you fine-tune intent to each technique in the fight, while introducing martial acting and the fighter's IQ into the mix.
- **Fourth run.** This is when you add the dramatic pauses and stutter beats, and you fine-tune martial acting moments. You also fine-tune the length of the fight.
- **Fifth run.** Now everything is in place. You do a dry run of the complete fight scene to see how the whole fight plays out with all the bells and whistles. Everyone is completely in synch with each other at this point.

Physical Elements Defined

This section provides the definitions of the physical elements of a choreographed fight.

Intent and Choice of Techniques

Using the information you culled from the narrative elements of the fight in the previous chapter, you should be able to choose the right technique for the character and the given situation. If you are having a hard time finding the type of techniques you want to use for the characters in the fight, try using an old acting exercise to help you along: Associate each character with the animal he would represent best in the animal kingdom.

When choosing the technique, also think about the character's intent behind it. Ask yourself what the character needs to say nonverbally with his technique for this particular scene. What is the mood of the fight? Is it playful? Is the character mad at the other characters, but does not want to seriously hurt them, or is he out to kill?

One other thing to remember is that a fight scene also has to maintain the emotional intent of the characters throughout the fight. It gets much more difficult to maintain the emotions when the fight is too long—the fight may run out of steam along the way.

Beats and Pauses

Consider the techniques used in a fight scene compared to a composed sheet of music. The techniques in the fight are the musical notes, and the blank spaces between the notes are the pauses between the techniques.

The actors involved in the fight are the musicians playing different instruments at varying levels of visibility (hero to thug) and importance, and the fight choreographer is the off-camera conductor who keeps the actors in time with each other. The song (fight) could be a duet (a duel, *mano a mano*), a band piece (a fight among several people), or an orchestral number (a big battle).

Rhythm

Still using the music analogy, rhythm for a song (and fight) is established by the use of the different musical notes (techniques) and the spaces between them (pauses). These are what comprise the rhythm of the song (or an exchange of techniques in the fight).

Repeating the same or similar types of notes (techniques) and having the same length of breaks (pauses) in between every technique will make the fight scene monotonous for the audience and can actually lull them to sleep. Good examples of this are found in the fight scenes from Hong Kong in the late '70s to early '80s. These fight scenes generally all had the same rhythm. They made up for this monotony by using spectacular techniques that were visually jaw-dropping and death-defying.

It is easy to forget about rhythm in a fight when you are too focused on technique. But remember, it is the rhythm of the fight that brings the scene to life.

Timing

Timing is essential for each person involved in a fight scene. Without it, fighters won't know when to come into the fight, throw techniques, react, and show the correct expression for the moment.

Cues

A cue is a specific, predetermined technique that the actor or stunt player responds to with either one or a combination of the following:

- A reaction to the hit
- A counter technique the attacker has to defend against or take a hit, thus changing the momentum of the fight for that moment
- A change to the style of the fight

A counter technique alters an attacker's momentum and requires him to change his attack. It forces him to immediately go into a defensive mode or change the style of fight. This is considered a cue. Blocking, dodging, or evading a technique is not considered a cue because it does not change the attacker's flow or momentum.

It is easy to notice a cue when someone is being attacked and can only block until he can see an opportunity to throw a technique, which is the cue for the attacker to either block and counter or take the hit and react to it.

Following are a few examples:

- ***Wheels on Meals.*** The final fight scene between Count Lobas' Thug (Benny "The Jet" Urquidez) and Thomas (Jackie Chan) starts with a series of cues in which they throw one technique, only to be countered (the cue) with something by the opponent. This goes back and forth in momentum to create a stalemate.
- ***Sha Po Lang* (aka *SPL*).** When Inspector Ma (Donnie Yen) first fights Wong Po (Sammo Hung) in the lobby of his penthouse, they are exchanging strikes. When Ma gets in closer and grabs the side of Po's jacket (cue), it changes the fight into a grappling match.

When you are choreographing a fight, it is important that a cue not be the same type of technique throughout the fight or the film. If the cue is the same type of technique throughout, the cadence and timing end up being too similar, and this affects the rhythm of the fight scene. The audience will pick up on the pattern and will anticipate the counter.

In many traditional martial arts systems, there is a practice called *one-step sparring*, in which two practitioners face off against each other. One person attacks with a right-handed lunge punch (a right-hand thrust punch with the right foot stepping forward), holds the punch out, and stops—he does not continue attacking. The other person defends against the attack of the punch with a set and preplanned technique, disposing of the attacker in a safe and controlled manner that does not injure the attacker, who is now a sitting target. This teaches the student distance, control, and timing against a limited moving opponent. This practice is often a staple of traditional styles and systems of martial arts. However, other systems also have an offshoot representation of this practice. If the choreographer is a traditional stylist, it can be difficult to break from this because of all the years of training to cue off of that one punch.

You will notice that in some movies, the fight choreographer is heavily influenced by a system that uses one-step sparring as one of the few tools to have a controlled and conditioned attack and response. This is great for live demonstrations, exhibitions, and tournaments, but can get extremely repetitive and boring for a two-hour film in which several fight scenes occur.

When you design a series of fight scenes that constantly cue off from a right-handed lunge punch, the fight choreographer can potentially have the following problems (depending on the style of fight you want to have):

- A fight scene can get boring when it uses the same cadence, timing, and rhythm.
- The fight can become very predictable, especially with people who are trained martial artists. Even though the viewer might not be aware of the cue, he can sense it by the rhythm that is set.
- The sense of reality can be diminished. You may be taking the fight scene into the unbelievable and just showing off the skill of the defender. First, no one in real life would really attack you like that (especially with the right hand and foot lunge). Second, an attacker would not sit there after the first strike and let you hit him.
- Fights are too short, especially if the attacker is disposed of after throwing one punch.
- The intelligence of the attacker is close to nil, and he does not pose much of a threat to the hero.

The beat of a lunge punch is a full beat. Rhythmically and visually, the cadence of the fight can get very boring to the audience without them consciously knowing it. Sure, the majority of the world is predominantly right-handed, but there has to be a variety of attacks to keep scenes fresh.

Often a choreographer will hide the right-handed cue by having the villain or thug throw a series of techniques as the hero ducks, dodges, or moves out of the way, but the fighter will finally react to the cue when he ends the flurry with a right-handed lunge punch. Sad to say, you will find this practice in action movies when the fight choreographer is limited by his own style. This is why fight choreographers need to be versed in other styles.

Length

There is a reason rollercoaster rides usually run fewer than three minutes. Riders can only experience such a high level of intensity for a short amount of time before they become exhausted. The same rule goes for a fight scene. The audience can only hold the same intense emotion for so long before they become exhausted and can no longer concentrate on the experience that is happening in front of them.

For this reason, it always is best to get to the point quickly regarding the content of the fight, and choose the content of your fight wisely, without too much fat or wasted movement. It is best to give the audience just enough action to satisfy their needs and allow them to release some steam, but you should leave them asking for more.

But the general rule of keeping your fight scenes short does not necessarily mean you *cannot* have a long fight scene. The key to having a long fight scene is to add small breaks and pauses so the audience does not get overwhelmed. They need a chance to take in what just occurred. Other important factors to long fight scenes are changing rhythm constantly; involving peripheral characters; changing locations, environment, and props; and changing the reason for the fight or the intensity of it. With long fight scenes, it is recommended that you add extended pauses and breaks (like "rounds" in a boxing match) so the audience can catch their collective breath and you can build up to the climax.

Following are some examples of long fight scenes with breaks; pauses; and changes in style, rhythm, and tempo.

- ***The Young Master.*** The final fight scene between Dragon (Jackie Chan) and Kam (Whang In Sik) is about 16 minutes long. However, the scene is broken up with "round" breaks, in which there is comic relief from Ah Suk (Feng Feng), who encourages Dragon to continue fighting with useless advice so he does not get beaten himself. Notice the fights are not the same with each round, and they have a different emphasis between each break even though the objective for each character is the same.
- ***Project A.*** Here, Jackie Chan strings together a series of action/fight sequences with short breaks in between so the audience can briefly take in and savor what just occurred. The specific scene I am referring to is when a group of thugs are after Dragon (Jackie Chan) and Fei (Sammo Hung), who sold rifles to them and cannot find where they originally placed them in a lumber yard and now the thugs are after the both of them. It starts with the thugs fighting Dragon and Fei, and then leads to a foot chase/fight after Dragon and Winnie. Then, the action moves to a bicycle chase/fight in the alleys, and then to a fight with Fei and Dragon against the thugs in a tea house. The action continues to move to a fight by the flagpole with Dragon and the thugs, and then to a fight inside the clock tower. The fight action finally ends with Dragon falling about five stories to the ground from the hands of the clock. This all ended up with a run time of a little less than 15 minutes. What made this work was that the villains were always nearby, about to get Dragon at any second and forcing him into impossible situations he had to get himself out of.

Environment

How does the fight scene blend in with the environment? By adding the environment into the fight scene, you start to individualize the scene for that particular fight. Adding the environment can mean using the terrain, such as having participants fight on uneven or wet ground, or it can mean something simple, such as a participant throwing dirt in his opponent's face if they are fighting in a field.

Stylization of Moves

Stylizing a technique for film means altering the technique so it has a cinematic visual impact that represents the actual technique, application, and impact. No matter how you see it, almost every move you show on screen has to be stylized in order for the camera to read it and the audience to see it. There are many techniques that might *be* quite effective in real life, but they might not always *look* effective, especially onscreen. A student, casual practitioner, professional, or master of a martial art or a combative sport will have a much deeper understanding of what is effective than the movie-going audience will. But remember that when you're choreographing fights for film, the majority of the audience will not be martial artists or professional athletes—they will be people who follow the action and live vicariously through the characters. Or, perhaps they're simply enjoying and appreciating what they see on the screen.

A great example of stylizing a technique is by using a side kick. A *side kick* is a linear technique that has a very short trajectory line to the opponent when thrown with the lead leg from a standing position. It is one of the strongest and most effective kicks in the martial arts, but when looking at a side kick on film, it has no real aesthetic visual quality to it. In fact, it looks rather short and choppy. But if you add a visual momentum to the side kick by having the actor take a couple of quick steps prior to throwing the kick, and chambering it for an extra beat, the kick will have a stronger visual impact.

An example of this technique is Bruce Lee in *Way of the Dragon.* During the practice session, he kicks the air shield and knocks a waiter (Wu Ngan) into a pile of boxes in back of the restaurant. Another good example is in *Enter the Dragon,* when Lee knocks Oharra out of the ring to win the match. A similar example is in *Best of the Best,* when Tommy Lee (Phillip Rhee) side kicks the air shield when he is trying out for the U.S. Tae Kwon Do team. When you see the technique being thrown in all these instances, you feel the impact of the technique by seeing the opponent's reaction while seeing the technique unfold before your eyes, complete with the over-exaggeration of the wind up and chamber and the extension of the kick.

The techniques you plan to use must be stylized in varying degrees, depending on the techniques used for the camera. This is necessary so the camera can pick up the technique and so audiences can see and appreciate it. The important thing is to have the technique look effective for the camera, while the stunt actor creates the proper reaction to the intent of that technique.

Some more great examples of stylization of arts and moves on film include:

- ***Above the Law.*** In Steven Seagal's first starring role, the art of Aikido was stylized to have practical application on the street.
- ***Prodigal Son.*** Sammo Hung's 1980s Kung Fu classic highlights the art of Wing Chun Kung Fu. Because Wing Chun is such an in-close art, the punches are stylized to look wider by altering and angling the body. The techniques are also stylized by overextending them to show commitment and power, and by making them more rhythmic in tempo so the audience can follow the action.
- ***Ong-Bak.*** Here, Panna Rittikrai and Panom Yeerum (fight choreographers) added elements of gymnastics, Wushu, and the elongated kicks of Tae Kwon Do into the mix to heighten the art/sport of Muay Thai (Thai boxing) for the screen. Notice that when the camera is wide, Tony Jaa throws punches that look like straight-armed haymakers. Would those punches be truly effective in a real fight? Nowhere close. But on camera they read better than a real punch because of how Jaa's arm sweeps across the screen and travels farther so the audience's eyes can recognize it right before it hits his opponent.

Stylization of moves also deals with the level of reality of the techniques and reactions. The degree of reality to fantasy comes into play here. For example, if you were going to have a gritty, realistic-looking street fight, you probably wouldn't incorporate flashy, high-flying Wushu techniques and fancy triple twisters as reactions.

When stylizing techniques for film, you will constantly juggle to get a balance between visual effectiveness (for the camera), stylization (visual aesthetics/level of reality), and fight strategy (practicality, believability, and character approach) that has been established for the film. While putting together the fight scene, ask yourself how visually successful the technique is when the camera cannot effectively pick up the technique and the audience cannot see it, feel the impact of the hit, and respond to it, in order to appreciate it. Ask yourself, "What can I do to change the technique to make it look as effective as possible on screen?" Visual and cinematic effectiveness of a technique that makes sense to the audience is the key to effective stylization of a technique or style.

Body Language

Body language and facial expressions are the major keys to martial acting, in which pantomime skills are heavily relied upon to convey feelings and emotions to the audience. To understand body language, one must understand the centerline theory, basic stances (and what they mean), facial expressions, and how they can be incorporated into the nonverbal narrative of the fight.

Centerline and the Centerline Theory

In the martial arts and combative sports, the centerline theory focuses on the fighter being in a position (in a stationary stance or moving) that enables him to be best suited to take action offensively and defensively at any given time. This is called being *centered* or, in layman's terms, *in control*. Each fighter has his own individual choice of how he likes to be centered, based on an accumulation of his training background, practical experience, intent, height, size, speed, power, injuries, assessment of the environment, and how he feels he initially wants to approach his opponent. Using this theory strategically in a fight, the goal of a combatant is to deliver to his opponent a technique in such a way that the defender has to compromise his own centerline. The fighter does this by having the opponent commit to a stimulus (either real or fake) that draws him into a position that limits his options. This also makes the opponent vulnerable and open to an attack. The combatant can take advantage of this vulnerability with a strike or throw before the opponent can recover his stability and balance in his centerline. This is called *seizing the centerline*. Fakes and leg sweeps are particularly effective ways of disrupting an opponent's centerline. Aiming a punch so that it knocks the opponent's centerline off is another way of making him lose his center.

However, it should be noted that if the combatant's stance or position of choice is one that plays into the opponent's strengths, then the combatant is in a vulnerable position where he can lose his center. In this case, the combatant must reassess and change his stance and/or approach.

Figure 9.1 shows an example of the centerline.

Figure 9.2 shows the centerline from the side, along with the major points that can affect the fighter's centerline.

Figure 9.3 shows a broken centerline when the fighter is bending at the waist.

A fighter's centerline is to be observed, assessed, and applied with a 360-degree perspective surrounding the fighter, as shown in Figures 9.1 through 9.3.

Figure 9.1

Centerline front view.

Figure 9.2

Centerline side view.

Figure 9.3

Centerline broken.

In martial acting, the centerline is used in a fight the same way as it is in real life—although in acting the use is stylized and more condensed. Fighters can also use the centerline as a way to express their feelings and emotions, as well as their intentions, strengths, and vulnerabilities.

Stances

Each stance has a purpose, strengths, and weaknesses. It is up to each fighter to know his weakness in that position and adjust when necessary so he doesn't lose his centerline. Cinematically, a stance and facial expressions can sum up where the fighter is at physically, emotionally, and mentally. Understanding the stances and how they work are the keys to making the stances communicate to the audience.

To a Westerner, watching a Kung Fu movie such as the *Once Upon a Time in China* trilogy might be fun and exciting, but when it comes to the fight scenes, the poses the fighters strike might not make sense to the audience simply because it is not a part of their culture. But the traditional stances actors use in period-piece Kung Fu movies do have a connection to the stances one might take in a modern-day fight.

Following are some examples of modern and classic stances.

> **Note**
>
> It is helpful to look at the centerline of each stance and find the similarities between the modern and classic stances. Look at the centerline of each fighter, as well as how their hand positions accentuate the position, and consider how the fighters might defend or attack from these stances.

Aggressive Offensive Stances

Notice how the stances lean forward and the body weight is front-heavy, ready to aggressively launch from the back foot into an attack (see Figure 9.4). The drawback to these stances is that the fighters have to shift their centerline weight to their back leg in order to retreat. This is much like a bull about to gore a matador or a ram about to butt heads with another ram. Another potential drawback of this type of stance is that most of the fighter's weight is on the front foot, so he is particularly susceptible to a front leg sweep.

Figure 9.4

Aggressive offensive stances.

Centered Stances

In Figure 9.5, notice that the fighters' centerlines are right in the middle, where they can choose to attack, counter, or retreat with little shifting compared to an offensive aggressive stance because in this case, his weight is distributed evenly between both feet. This stance shows a person who is well-balanced and ready for anything—not underestimating the opponent, but also sure of his own abilities.

Figure 9.5

Centered stances.

Defensive Stances

In Figure 9.6, notice that the body weight and centerline are now resting toward the back, and the fighters are ready to strike with the lead leg (which has no weight on it) or hand. The fighters can effectively strike with the lead leg or hand because they are the closest natural weapons to the fighter's opponent. This stance is much like a snake that is threatened, coiled, and ready to strike whatever is invading its space. An advantage to this stance is that a front leg sweep would be ineffective because all of the fighter's weight is supported by the rear leg.

Figure 9.6

Defensive stances.

Combination of Approaches

The different types of stances and approaches to the opponent can offer complex and deeper nonverbal dialogue that can show inner conflict with a fighter's feelings and the reason he is there. Figure 9.7 shows an offensive stance with defensive hand positions.

A hypothetical example for stances such as the one in Figure 9.7 might go something like this: The character knows he has to confront the opponent physically for what the opponent has done to a friend or family member, but the character is well aware of his opponent's skills and ability, and the fact that he has to stay on guard because anything can happen.

Figure 9.7

An offensive stance with defensive hand positions presents a good example of nonverbal dialogue between fighters.

When you put together stances in a confrontational situation, the body language of the stances can serve as the nonverbal dialogue and can tell the story without any actual words being spoken.

In Figures 9.8 and 9.9, Rick (left) attacks Robin (far right) as Garrik (center) protects her. Figure 9.8 shows a traditional stance, whereas Figure 9.9 shows the same confrontation using a modern stance. Notice the centerline for all three characters is much more obvious in the traditional stances and more subtle in the modern stances, but both stances have the same type of nonverbal dynamics.

Figure 9.8

Confrontation using traditional stances.

Figure 9.9

Confrontation using modern stances.

Camera Awareness

When choreographing and performing your fight scene, it is important to be aware of where the camera is at all times. If the camera is not in the right position, the move can look ineffective. Or, you might film the hit as a miss by being in the wrong position with the camera. Many film strikes are of course near misses, but choosing the right camera angles can effectively hide this cinematic sleight of hand. And further, if the camera is in the wrong position, you cannot see what is happening in the fight. As a stunt actor, you have to be aware of where you and the camera are to make your scene work.

A couple more useful definitions for you:

- **Hit.** This is a technique that crosses the camera line and obscures the intended part of the opponent's body, making it look through the lens of the camera like the technique made contact.
- **Miss.** This occurs when a fighter is throwing a technique and it does not cross the camera line, leaving space (or light) between the technique and the opponent's targeted body part. Even though the opponent reacts to the hit, it is not believable to the audience because it did not look like the technique made contact. Unfortunately, you see misses all the time, even on big-budget films for which they have more time to shoot the action correctly. There is no real excuse for having misses in the final product of a film—especially today, when you have video playback to see whether the take was good. Yet we still see misses. Oh well.

Collective Rhythm of the Fight

All the elements listed earlier in this chapter add up to the collected rhythm of the fight, which includes all nonverbal narrative elements put in place to tell the story. When you get to this point, you are now ready to have the scene lit for mood and effect and shot with the camera.

What Exactly Is Martial Acting?

In martial acting, an actor externalizes his character's emotions that occur right before, during, and immediately after a physical conflict. This functions as the emotional glue of the fight scene and aids in telling the narrative of the fight, holding it all together. Martial acting is one of the first things inexperienced filmmakers and actors usually neglect in their films. Without martial acting, you would not have a story to tell during the fight scene. When this is the case, you can easily lose the audience's attention no matter how good the action you choreographed is.

World-class cinematic fighters, such as Jackie Chan, Bruce Lee, Jet Li, and so on, perform their fight scenes onscreen with grace, style, and ease. They make it look so easy that you think you can do it yourself too, with a little practice. But in actuality, martial acting is much tougher than it looks, and it takes lots of practice to make it look so easy. Martial acting is a twofold process consisting of a martial aspect (the physical and technical aspects of the fight) and an acting aspect (the visual narrative during the fight).

The first part of this process, the martial aspect, requires a fighter to:

- Throw the techniques with believable speed and accuracy while not injuring the stunt actors
- Have the stamina to keep the scene fresh after multiple takes
- Remember all the moves he is going to perform
- Know the timing of all the opponents in the fight
- Always be aware of where the camera is
- Know everyone's cues, including his own

The second part of the process, the acting aspect, serves to:

- Create the illusion that the action scene is occurring right at that moment, even though the actors have rehearsed the choreographed scenes numerous times. To accomplish this, the actors must create genuine and honest acting moments in the fight scene.

- Express the desired emotion of the character and story through body language, facial expressions, and perhaps vocals.
- Constantly show different emotions in different stances while moving, throwing techniques, blocking, and taking reactions.
- Show the emotional content behind each technique thrown. This varies depending on the character's practical experience and level of expertise.

The fight can get much more difficult as skill level gets more advanced, timing between moves gets shorter, and reactions become more difficult and complex.

Good and Bad Martial Acting

To an untrained eye, it's sometimes tough to spot good martial acting because the viewer is enjoying or is too emotionally involved in the cinematic experience of the fight. But even an untrained eye will be subconsciously aware of bad or absent martial acting because the viewer will not experience any real emotional connection to the fight scene. To have good martial acting, the actors involved should consider the following in order to make their action scenes come alive:

- Find the emotional truth of the action scene.
- Understand the emotional content of the techniques the character is throwing, and also the ones that are used against the character.
- Make sure the character's presence and attitude match his physical ability.
- Don't exploit the moment by calling unnecessary attention to yourself.
- Find the appropriate emotions within yourself that match physical conflict, and then use your ability and experience to fully express them.
- Be comfortable exposing intimate, personal, and/or private feelings and emotions for the camera during a physical conflict.

In contrast, bad martial acting is very evident. There are several factors that can contribute to poor martial acting. Sometimes the actor may overact by over-expressing a particular moment. The actor might be so over the top with the moment that he ruins the scene by making it unnatural or worse yet, comedic. Another scenario occurs when the actor's emotion does not match the scene and the technique against which he is reacting. In this case, the scene will seem too big, and the reactions will not appear to be natural responses to the stimuli.

Bad martial acting or even no martial acting in a film can easily cause the film to lose an audience. The audience may lose interest or balk at the performance. There is a lot of bad martial acting out there that gives certain film genres a negative connotation. To go into a little more detail, the following list covers several issues that may cause bad martial acting:

- The actor did not match the proper emotion to the fight. This can happen if the actor is too over-the-top, if he underplays the scene, if he expresses an inappropriate emotion, or doesn't express any type of emotion at all. The audience senses something is amiss with the scene.
- The actor is not emotionally into the scene or is just aping the emotion.
- The actor might be inexperienced or undertrained, leaving him unable to get comfortably into the desired emotion. As a result, the actor may force the moment by creating an unauthentic or false acting moment.
- The script might be paper-thin as far as plot and character development go, and the actor might not have the experience to fully create his character from within himself.
- The actor might not be comfortable with feelings of vulnerability. He may not be open and intimate with his feelings, and this is required for his character. This usually happens when a martial artist is too arrogant or too aware of himself and his status. In these cases, the artist might use his art as something to hide behind instead of using it as a secure base from which to propel himself.

Martial Acting during a Fight

During the fight, the actor shows the character's intent; his reactions to the opponent's skills and techniques; his attempts to work through his own physical pain and emotional and/or mental blocks; his feelings; and his resolve for the act of hitting someone. Typically, the majority of martial acting is done without dialogue, and it expresses the character's initial intent for being in the fight. The actors follow through with this intent, along with the emotions they experience, by expressing the following during a fight sequence:

- **Body language and facial expressions.** These express:
    - Confidence—from weakness to ultra confidence
    - Feelings—from severe pain to elation
    - The current situation—from struggle to conquer

- **Strategy.** This shows the character's intelligence and how he might be able to adapt to and overcome the opponent's strategy.
- **Stances.** These show the character's external intent (even though this intent might conflict with his inner emotions).
- **Movement.** This can show a character's level of confidence and proficiency when compared to the opponent. Movement also includes footwork and how the character relates to the opponent. Here you can show a character being hesitant, cautious, assured, overconfident, and so on.
- **Technique.** The character's use of techniques can be expressed by the following:
    - The choice of techniques and how the combinations of techniques are put together are reflections of the character's personality, skills, and experience, and can also help to express the narrative of the story.
    - Characters can show levels of confidence with techniques, which can vary depending on a character's opponent.
    - Characters can apply what they learned in training in a high-pressured real-life situation or competition. How well integrated is the technique into the character's psyche? Does he have to think about it? Or is it a part of him that he doesn't have to consciously think about it (which slows down his reflexes when throwing the technique)?
    - How does the character react to a hit? This also says something about the character and the opponent throwing the technique; it delineates their relationship in terms of who is in control and is a better fighter.

Martial acting adds depth to a fight and, when done well, it can assist in the narrative of the story and the fight. Martial acting can emotionally link the audience with the characters and the fight by clueing them in on what the characters are feeling and experiencing at that moment. As a result, you get an emotionally complex fight scene. This is much like watching an old silent Chaplin or Keaton film, in which they had to project their thoughts, feelings, and emotions through facial expressions, movement, and body language.

As an example, you can show inner conflict and depth in a character when he is confronted and takes a defensive stance, has a confident body language, and yet his footwork is unsure as he closes the gap to meet his opponent. He throws a technique with the utmost confidence, only to have it easily blocked and countered with a strong, authoritative hit that sends him reeling back. The fighter is now shocked and impressed by the opponent's skills while he questions his own, and his martial acting should reflect this change in self confidence.

Following are some examples of good martial acting in a physical conflict:

- **Bruce Lee in *Enter the Dragon*.** A great example from this film is when Lee knocks the bottles out of Oharra's hands, kicks him to the floor, and stomps on him to finally kill him. Instead of seeing the actual move, we are shown a close-up of Lee as he crushes Oharra's chest. We see the change of emotions on Lee's face: They start with rage at Oharra for attacking him in unsportsmanlike conduct. There is anger at Oharra for forcing his hand to make Lee kill him. Then there is karmic revenge for the death of Lee's sister. There is sorrow for taking a man's life, and there is regret for breaking his passive Buddhist vows as a Shaolin monk of respecting all life. This very exact scene has been imitated many times by martial arts action film stars, and it ends up looking like a pale imitation and does not ring true because the actor is not being honest with the scene—rather, he is imitating and aping it.
- **Bruce Lee in *Way of the Dragon*.** A great example from this film is the end of the fight in the coliseum, when Tang Lung (Lee) finally has to kill Colt (Chuck Norris) by snapping his neck. All Tang Lung's fights that led up to the final fight have had varying playful to semi-serious tones to them. His opponents were badly injured, but no one died at his hands. But the last fight is more of a life-and-death situation, and it has a much more serious tone to it. The concluding moment is when the camera zooms in on Tang Lung's face as we see for the first time sorrow and regret for what he is about to do as he breaks Colt's neck.
- **Jackie Chan in *Project A*.** A great example here is the long foot-to-bicycle-chase-to-fight sequence between Jackie, the girl he's looking after, and the gang of thugs after them. We are along for the ride with Jackie due to his expressions and body language with regard to various dilemmas that cause stages of duress for him.

Martial Acting before and after a Fight

Depending on how a scene is set up and the choreography of the fight, martial acting not only takes place during a fight, but it can also take place before and after the fight.

If the character knows he is going to get into a fight beforehand, the actor can show the feelings, mental preparations, and resolve his experiences before it takes place. This is much like expressing an inner dialogue, while having the audience invade a private moment with that character. To use a baseball metaphor, this is like a batter in the on-deck circle as he mentally prepares for what is about to happen.

Immediately after the fight, you can show how the character handles the outcome of the physical confrontation mentally, such as how it might change his life or affect his beliefs about himself. You can also show how the character handles the outcome emotionally (the adrenaline rush and the harsh/forced intimacy of the physical encounter) and morally (violating or changing anything he might hold sacred). In addition, you can show how the character handles the outcome physically by showing the pain or injuries he has suffered. Something to ask yourself while putting together the fight is how violated or shaken up the characters might feel (even though they might have been victorious) from the skirmish.

Examples of Martial Acting before the Conflict

Following are examples of martial acting that takes place before the conflict.

- ***A Bittersweet Life.*** At the start of the film, a waiter at the hotel informs his manager, Sun-woo (Byung-hun Lee), who is finishing up his meal, that there is trouble that Sun-woo needs to take care of in one of the private conference rooms. Sun-woo tells him that he'll take care of it, then savors a last bite from his dessert. He claims his center and exercises his authority with the employees who know when he's there and immediately respond to his orders, as he walks down toward the conference room, aware of the little things in the hotel, before he confronts the men in the conference room.

- ***La Femme Nikita.*** When Nikita (Anne Parillaud) and Bob go out to a restaurant for the first time, there is shock and surprise on her face when she is given a gun as a present, told about her first real mission, and given three minutes to perform the assassination. Bob leaves Nikita by herself, and she wrestles with her emotions as she takes it all in, prepares emotionally and mentally, and then finally accepts what she is about to do. This draws the audience into her dilemma further.

- ***The Killer.*** John (Chow Yun Fat) is in his apartment by himself, waiting for Sydney to come pay him for his last hit. He comes to the realization, sadness, and resolve that Sydney, his best friend, has set him up on his last assignment to get him killed. This leads to the situation where Sydney takes John's gun and is about to kill him with his own gun, but there are no bullets in it. John's look of betrayal and sadness that his only friend is doing this to him is truly a genuine moment right before a gunfight starts between John and Johnny Weng's thugs.

Examples of Martial Acting after the Conflict

Following are examples of martial acting that takes place after the conflict.

- ***In the Line of Fire.*** John Malkovich plays former CIA assassin Mitch Leary. When he tests out his handmade gun in the woods, a couple of hunters close by want to try out his gun by shooting a resting duck in the lake. Mitch informs them that he needs the gun so he can shoot the president of the United States, and then he kills both of them with his gun. The camera still stays on Mitch after the hunters fall dead. Leary is somewhat indifferent after sinking a toy boat with his gun at the beginning of the scene. Then, when the hunters appear, there is a subtle hint of joy that appeals to the predator side of him. But after he shoots them, there is a certain hint of dissatisfaction on the surface, but with so much more depth and complexity beneath it. That year, Malkovich received nominations for Best Supporting Actor at the Oscars, BAFTAs, and Golden Globes for his portrayal of Leary in this film.
- ***Snake in the Eagle's Shadow.*** When we are first introduced to Chien Fu (Jackie Chan), Master Li torments him, and then beats him up in front of the class. Fu goes to the back of the school to dip his head in the bucket of water, and the camera closes in on his face to register the pain, hate, and sorrow on it. This moment is so convincing and believable that, from this point on, Chien Fu's character cannot do any wrong in the hearts and minds of the audience.
- ***Die Hard.*** John McClane (Bruce Willis) usually has a one-liner or a wisecrack after almost every conflict, commenting on what just happened.

Another prime example of solid performances in martial acting that take place before and after the fight is in *The Bride with White Hair*, starring Leslie Cheung and Brigitte Lin. I mention this film because Cheung and Lin were doubled extensively by stunt actors to perform all the action sequences, but what was great about their martial acting was that there were close-ups of both actors before and after the fight that were very convincing and matched the emotional content of the scene and the techniques thrown (by the stunt actors).

Ronny Yu, the director of *The Bride with White Hair* and *Freddy vs. Jason*, comments:

> *It's acting! It's pure good acting. Because they don't need to do the stunt. All they need to do is do the "before and after" the stunt. That calls for acting. To make it convincing after he does a fantastic move. That pose! That sort of moment is all in your eyes. In the look. That is acting. I chose Leslie Cheung to play this heroic guy in Bride. Of course everyone thought I was crazy. I said, "No, he's a very good actor. He doesn't need to do the stunts. Why should he?" But the acting alone will carry that and make it believable. Of course we had to find a stunt double which resembled him.*

> *But as long as the "before and after" looks convincing, that's it! We're home free! The same was with Chow Yun Fat [referring to the film he directed him in, The Postman Strikes Back]. As long as he got the "before and after!" That's why I feel [it would be very difficult for] some of the stuntmen to cross over and become action stars. They can be an action star, but minus the acting. They can't have more versatile roles to play. But an actor can be a fantastic action star. Like Bruce Willis. Hey listen, I don't think Bruce Willis knows martial arts or stunts. Same with Schwarzenegger or Stallone. But they can bring forth the emotion. The acting is convincing.*

Overall, martial acting before and after a fight shows an emotional ramping up (emotional preparation) and a coming down (realization and acceptance of what the character has just done) from the conflict. It also helps to humanize the characters, giving them more depth.

Reactions

Reactions to techniques are also considered a part of martial acting. If an actor does not react when he is hit, it will make the attacker and the technique lose their effectiveness, power, and impact. The recipient of the blow must act as if he does not anticipate the hit (unless it is in the storyline), and he must react accordingly as the blow crosses the line between the camera and the intended part of the recipient's body.

Timing between the person throwing the technique and the recipient is key in making the technique look believable. The intensity of the reaction has a direct and immediate correlation to the character throwing the technique because it shows the power of the technique and the prowess of that character. However, having the stunt actors always react hard (as opposed to light or moderate) to every hit gets boring quickly and makes the person throwing the technique appear indestructible or superhuman. Besides, the audience will already expect what's coming. Varying the type of reaction to the hits will keep audiences in the moment with what the character is doing.

As an example, one potential reaction to a hit, such as a punch to a stunt actor's face, might be for the recipient to take the hit and simply drop to his knee. But another option would be to have the stuntman take the reaction to the hit, and then perform something more spectacular and complicated , such as falling down a flight of steps or off a cliff, or doing a triple-twisting layout into a glass display case (such as in *Police Story*).

When watching action scenes, try to focus on the technique thrown and how it is related to the reaction to the hit. The relation between the actor throwing the hit and the one receiving it is integral in the nonverbal relationship between hero and opponent. It also shows the strength and struggles of the hero as an extension to the actor receiving the hit.

Following are some prime examples of reactions:

- ***Enter the Dragon.*** Bruce Lee's underground cavern fight with Han's guards is a standout as far as reactions to hits. Lee looked even greater when he used as stuntmen future Hong Kong and international film stars and fight choreographers Jackie Chan, Sammo Hung, Yuen Biao, Lam Ching Ying, Mang Hoi, Mars, Tung Wai, and Yuen Wah. The same holds true when Han's men attack Lee and Roper the next morning.
- ***Police Story.*** There are many scenes in this movie in which reactions are incredible examples. However, the standout one is the final brawl in the shopping mall. The hits, reactions, and stunts are plenty and varied in this scene.

Facial Expressions

Bruce Lee, Sammo Hung, Chow Yun Fat, Bruce Willis, Jet Li, Toshiro Mifune, Sylvester Stallone, Jackie Chan, and Arnold Schwarzenegger all have great facial expressions when they are in the middle of a physical conflict. As a result, they have all achieved international star status, even though other countries might not understand their culture or language. When you watch their action scenes in films such as *Drunken Master 2, Lethal Weapon 4,* and *Crouching Tiger, Hidden Dragon,* you do not need to understand a different language to comprehend how they are feeling in the midst of a conflict.

Facial expressions are usually the easiest and most efficient way to sell emotion or feeling to the audience. However, when body language does not match the facial expression, especially in a reaction shot, it does not work as a cohesive package.

Exercises

Here are a few exercises for you to try.

- Look for the definitions discussed in this chapter while watching a fight scene.
- Practice martial acting in front of the mirror or videotape it to study what you are doing well and what you aren't doing as well.
- Observe how and why the filmmakers assembled the fight scene the way they did.
- Ask yourself, "Is there anything I would do to make it better?"

10

The Technical Elements of a Fight

The technical aspects of fight choreography are often overlooked or not taken into account as integral parts of making a fight scene look effective onscreen. You might have put together a fight scene that would make Sammo Hung, Ching Siu-Tung, Tony Jaa, Jackie Chan, and Yuen Woo-Ping all tremble, but what happens if you can't see the fight because it was not correctly lit? What if the camera angles did not capture the true essence of the fight or you simply could not follow the action because the camera was too close or too wobbly to comprehend what happened? Then there's editing of the film. Are the editors going to understand the beats and nuances of the fight that you put together? In Asia, the fight choreographer/director usually guides the process through to the end. But in the West, you sit on pins and needles, wondering how it's going to turn out because editing and choreography are separate departments. That is to be respected. However, this experience is like giving birth. You wonder whether the baby you helped conceive will come out looking beautiful, will have some flaws or a defect, or will not even look anything like you? In the film world, what if your "baby" comes out looking nothing like what you choreographed?

If the film comes out great, you hold your head high and take in all the adulation and pats on the back for a job well done. But for you it's as relaxing and memorable as a Pepto-Bismol moment in church, especially if the film does not turn out as you had hoped. The crew does not say much because they are sensitive to your feelings and they are overly concerned with the scenes they worked on and how those scenes turned out. Chances are their fate won't be as bad as yours. You sink down in your seat and do your impersonation of Edvard Munch's "The Scream."

You join an anonymous fight choreographer's support group, which helps you deal with the ridicule of the fans and the critics who think it was all your fault for butchering the film. Every time your name is brought up, venom, boos, hisses, and colorful expletives that would make a sailor hide are uttered because the audience has been waiting years to see the film on the big screen, but now they are disappointed. For the rest of your career, when your name comes up, the initial response from fans is, "Oh, the guy who ruined the [*fill in name of animal or noun here*]-man movies." Those are the drastic highs and lows of a fight choreographer's career.

Cinematography

To state the obvious, cinematography is an extremely crucial factor in having an effective fight scene once you have finished choreographing your actors. A cinematographer is responsible for setting up and capturing the cinematic composition of the fight, which is essentially choosing the angles and frame speed and controlling the amount of light that goes through the lens and into the camera. You could have choreographed an incredible fight scene that would make Yuen Woo-Ping proud, but if the cameraman was inexperienced or unable to follow the action and get the right angles to make the fight scene effective, your hard work is all for naught. Unfortunately, the only people who know that you assembled a great fight scene were the members of the film crew who were there to witness it live. Shooting action is an art in itself, and not everyone can do it well or effectively.

Good cinematography for a fight scene is visually appealing, tells a non-verbal story, and conveys necessary information to the audience about the conflict so the audience can understand what is going on. Good cinematography effectively shows the conflict while still expressing the mood of the scene and the rest of the film.

On top of knowing how to put together an effective fight scene, a good fight choreographer has to know which angles are effective and which ones do not work for each technique. The choreographer must suggest to the cinematographer if he is shooting at an angle that might be ineffective.

The role of the cameraman is an integral part of the fight scene. When choreographing the fight scene, the choreographer should also keep in mind how the cameraman will be shooting the sequence. Try to see the cameraman as the last participant of the fight who is witnessing all the necessary information that is unfolding in front of him.

Rehearsing with the Cameraman

The cameraman is an important part of the physical choreography, and it should be set up so that the cameraman can walk through the action along with the actors so the shooting will go smoothly. The cameraman should also know the cues and what will be happening next in order to make all the necessary adjustments for following the action with his camera. It's also helpful and recommended that you explain to the director of photography what you have choreographed and some of the subtleties in the strategy and rhythm of the fight so he can begin to think about how he will visually compose what you put together through the camera.

If you are given time to do so, rehearsing the fight for the cameraman so he can follow the action is very helpful in getting the shoot to go smoothly. First, try doing it at half speed so he will recognize the cues. Then go through the fight again at three-quarters speed so he can get his rhythm down for following the action. Then take another pass at full speed to work out the timing and pace between the actors and the cameraman.

The following photos were taken at a recent shoot and demonstrate rehearsing with the cameraman.

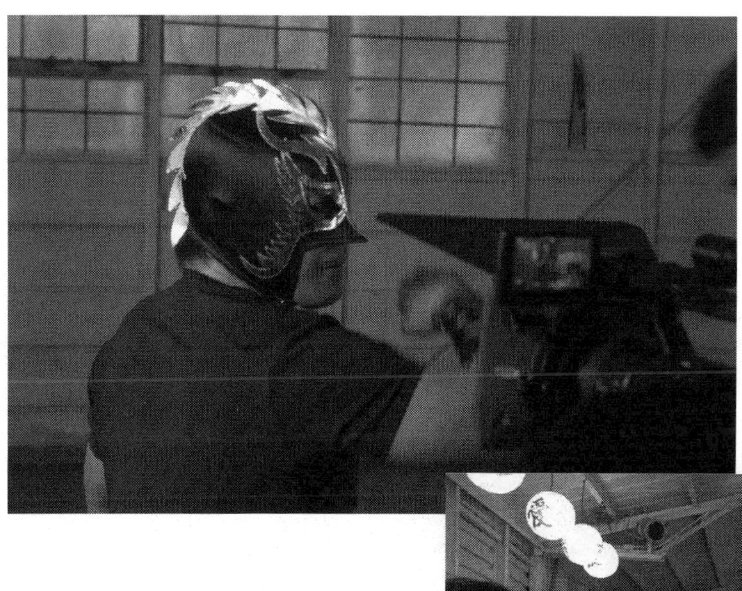

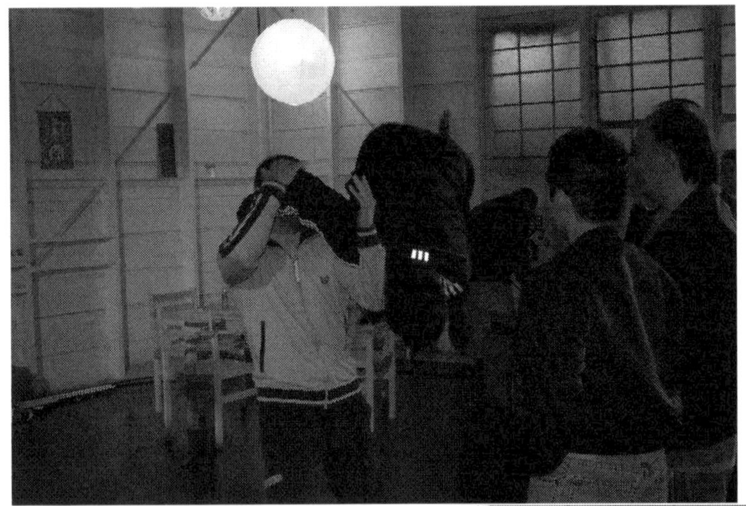

Effective Camera Angles

It is important for the person behind the camera to understand the correct angles in order to spot (and attempt to hide) the misses in the fight. Unfortunately, you often see these little glitches slip into Western films after they are released. What might be a few inches to the naked eye on the set may look on the big screen like 10 to 20 feet of space between the person throwing the strike and the actor performing the reaction. The angle of a technique can either heighten or minimize the impact for the audience.

There are basically three types of angles for how to capture the action:

- **Objective.** An objective angle is basically from the sidelines, as if the audience were a distant observer. This is a neutral point of view that does not take any side's point of view or emotional stance. This angle is great to show conflicting motives between the combatants and is commonly and effectively used right before the combatants are squaring off, ready to fight. Chinese filmmakers use this angle more often than Western filmmakers during fight scenes so the audience can see the action unfold and see active, changing relationships between the combatants throughout the fight. When using this angle, you are relying more on the story, character development, and acting skills that have led up to this point to get the audience emotionally involved.
- **Subjective.** This angle gives the audience a personal point of view of one of the combatants. The audience is placed into the conflict by taking the place of an active combatant or a character who is not intimately involved in the fight (but is still on a chosen side of the conflict). The camera acts as if it is a part of the action itself.
- **Point of view (POV).** This angle is a combination of subjective and objective angles. The camera is in the thick of the action (subjective) while taking in the action as it unfolds, but not from the POV of an actual participant. This filming technique is used to get the audience closer to the action while they can still see the conflict unfolding (objective), but without encouraging them to "choose sides."

A great fight scene is able to use all three types of angles (depending on the type of fight) to effectively tell the story and show the visual aesthetics of the fight.

Distance from the Fight

When shooting, the distance from the fight and the angles chosen are completely artistic choices on how you want your subjects to fill up the screen. However, a certain amount of information needs to be conveyed to the audience to make your fight scene effective.

Also remember that you are depicting a combative conflict that tells a story—you're not just capturing a fight on film. Ask yourself what type of story is being told with this fight.

The type of fight and the techniques involved in the mood and story you want to tell between the combatants should dictate the distance.

Here are some suggestions to think about as you are planning your shot:

- **Extreme long shot.** This shot shows the terrain, location, and environment and how the combatants plan to adapt, adjust, and relate to it, while depicting a vast area from a great distance away from the actors. These type of shots set up the scene that follows and put the audience in the proper mood, while providing them with the overall picture of where the characters are and how they relate to the environment. The environment can also include invested spectators to help tell the story. If the fight is a bare-knuckle brawl between two people, you can afford to get closer, as opposed to if the fight is between two warring clans of a thousand men on each side. Showing the environment or the terrain where the fight or battle will take place is an often overlooked element.
- **Long shot.** This shot is also known as the *master shot.* It establishes all the elements that will take place in the scene and gives the audience a frame of reference, so when things start to unfold during the scene, the audience will have their bearings as to the size and proportion of the room, the environment, and important props that might be used during the scene. In Hong Kong–style fight scenes, a long shot or master shot is used quite often because it allows the audience to see the action as it happens.
- **Medium shot.** In this shot, the actors are framed from just above the knee to the waist and above. This shot is usually used for dialogue scenes between actors. In one shot, you are able to capture subtle movements, reactions, and facial expressions clearly for the audience to see. For fights, the medium shot is used for medium- to close-range techniques, including grappling. If you're shooting the fight scene from a long shot, a medium shot can serve as an insert to show the actors' emotions, while still showing the actor in relation to his opponent.
- **Close up.** This usually is a shot composed from the shoulders and up, focusing on the head and face. In the fight scene, the close up is usually used for reaction to hits or for actually showing the hit.

Camera Height

The height of the camera, along with the angle, can add to, or take away from, the effectiveness of the technique and the actor's relationship with the opponent and the environment. If you were to have a character leap across the room and hit an opponent, having the camera hanging from the ceiling looking down would probably not be an effective angle because you would not be able to appreciate the spectacle of the technique from that angle. It would simply look like the character was quickly sliding across the room, as if he had skates on. It would not register to the audience, causing them to ask a *bad question*, because the technique was presented at an ineffective angle so the audience was not able to appreciate the technique and was not given proper information about what was happening in the fight.

If you were filming a huge battle sequence—such as something you'd see in *Braveheart* or *Saving Private Ryan*, where hundreds or thousands of people are fighting—and you want to capture everyone in battle from a master shot, you would have to find higher ground for the camera to capture the action and the terrain where it is taking place.

It is important to know how high to keep the camera in order to aid in the effectiveness of the technique. It is best to experiment with the height on various techniques and see for yourself how different heights can affect the same technique.

Usually the standard and safe height is the same height as the fighters' eyes or from below looking up, where you can see them clearly from either mid-length (waist up) to full length (toes to head). However, it all depends on the techniques and effect you wish to convey.

Here are some examples of effective camera height:

- ***Jackie Chan's Police Story.*** A good example is when Ka Kui tosses Carina into the pool from atop an apartment building. The angle is low (near the pool) as we see Carina fly down into the pool. This would not have a strong effect if the camera was high (such as atop the apartment building where Carina took off) because we would not get to visually appreciate Carina's descent.
- ***Fist of Fury* and *Fist of Legend.*** A good example is when Chen Zhen first goes to the Japanese school to challenge them. Notice the change in the height of the camera from high to low to mid-level.

Keeping It Visually Pure and Effective

So how are camera height, angle, and distance applied to a fight? Let's look at an example. Suppose you are filming the final fight scene with a high-flying/acrobatic screen fighter such as Tony Jaa, who has the bad guy in a daze after a series of techniques that were used to set up the finishing blow, which will kill off the bad guy to end the movie. The finishing technique is a spectacular flying kick that hits the bad guy in the head and kills him.

For the audience to appreciate the aesthetics of the move and for the move to have a spectacular and effective "wow factor," the following should be covered in the least amount of shots possible:

- **Height of the jump.** To accentuate the height of the jump and make it look higher, it would help to keep the camera at a very low angle (knee height or below).
- **Distance covered.** The distance covered should preferably be from one end of the screen to the other.
- **Visual spectacle of the technique.** Good visual spectacle is achieved by staying far enough away that the audience can appreciate the athleticism and aesthetics of the move, but still see the technique unfold before their eyes.
- **Visual relationship between hero and villain.** You should also stay far enough away that the audience can see the relationships between the combatants on the screen in one shot. This gives the audience an understanding of distance and space.
- **Emotions of the characters.** This is achieved by reinforcing to the audience the motive of the fight by showing the emotion of the characters (martial acting).
- **Selling the hit and reaction.** Showing the hit and reaction is much like placing the punctuation mark at the end of a sentence. It would be bad to end a strong sentence with a question mark; likewise, it would be bad to close a movie with an obscure ending because you are leaving the audience hanging. You've built them up to that moment and you don't give them a release if you don't show the actual hit and reaction.

If this can all be done in the least amount of different angles and cuts, the impact will be more effective and explosive to the audience. The audience will be able to see the events unfold before their eyes and know that they were not tricks in editing. They will appreciate the actor's athleticism. This has been done in Sammo Hung's *Warriors Two*, where Hua has Mo, the villain, reeling, and to finish him off, Hua leaps and does a spin kick over the large table and kicks Mo in the chest.

Inserts and Close-Ups

Inserts are used in action to show the emotions of the actors (martial acting) during a fight to inform the audience of the characters' feelings and thoughts.

An insert or close-up can be also used to illustrate the following:

- It can be used as a short break in the action so the audience can catch their collective breath and process the information about what they have just witnessed.
- It can also be used to change the direction of the fight. For example, in *Wheels on Meals*, in the middle of the fight between Thomas and Count Lobas' thug in the castle, Thomas takes the chair to keep the thug away and thinks about changing his approach to the fight. He loosens up by thinking it is a training session instead of a serious fight.
- It can be used to introduce and/or show characters who are about to take an active part in the conflict or a concerned bystander who is somehow emotionally invested in the outcome of the conflict.
- It can be used to show a technique that is pivotal in the momentum of a fight to one's favor. This also includes showing a hit.
- It can be used to show a short, in-close technique that might lose its effectiveness from a shot that is further away.
- It can be used to introduce any information that needs to be highlighted or introduced into the fight. An example would be a close-up of a knife that is just out of reach between two combatants—the knife is noticed by one of the combatants in the middle of the struggle.

Frame Composition

Frame composition is the choice of angles and how close or far you want to be from the conflict. Proper and effective frame composition should artistically and stylistically capture the narrative and physical elements of the fight so the audience can understand what is happening with the actors' performance of the conflict.

Composition is essentially how you choose to frame the fight scene through the lens of the camera and how you want the audience to see it.

The Issue of Getting in Too Close

In real life, if we had a chance to witness a fight unfold in front of our own eyes and the opportunity to get very close (hopefully without getting injured or involved), it would be an exciting and possibly hair-raising experience. That is the theory and current trend in a majority of Western cinema when it comes to fight scenes—to get in very close and aggressively fill up the screen so the action spills out, and to use a shaky handheld camera so the audience can feel the action as if they are right there.

In my humble opinion, this theory does not hold water. The fight ends up looking more like a Cubist representation of a conflict that you are asking the audience to piece together in their own heads.

Following are some factors that were neither addressed nor reasoned in this theory:

- **Depth perception.** A majority of humans have two eyes, which gives us depth perception so we can focus easily on the fight that is happening in front of us. The camera has only one eye that needs to be constantly adjusted manually. To see the strategy and subtleties, the camera has to focus in on it in some way.
- **Range of vision.** Our naked eyesight range is not just limited to what is focused in front of us, as a camera lens would be. We also have peripheral vision and a wider range of sight than a camera would. So if we were hovering a couple feet in the air over two combatants on the floor wrestling with each other, we would be able to see everything unfold from the legs up to the head by also using our peripheral vision. A camera lens does not have peripheral vision and is limited to what is seen through its lens.

  As a result, getting in close does not give us all the necessary information during a fight—in fact, it actually limits the information we get. We're watching two people fighting on the ground, grappling with one another as one of them tries to escape. The other is not letting go. If we are watching this with our own eyes and we are focused on the upper body (from the chest up), we can use our peripheral vision to see that the person trying to escape cannot because his legs are locked and he is trapped by his opponent's legs. But if we were looking through the camera, still focused on upper body and not moving the camera to show that the fighter cannot escape because of the leg lock, then we are not giving the audience vital information they need. As a result, they might have a different impression of the fight than what was originally choreographed and intended. This case is easily proven when you sit in a theater and look straight at the screen. The camera's limitations in vision are restricted to the image on the screen, but the audience member's vision extends beyond the screen.
- **Focus and visual stability.** Often when the camera gets in close, the cinematographer or editor might add some extreme wobbly camera movement to further blur the image we see onscreen. When our body shakes, our eyes are naturally able to adjust and stabilize our sight to a point. When we are watching a fight scene that is in constant motion while the camera shakes, we cannot stabilize the wobbling and gather our bearings because it is not happening in our own bodies. At worst, this can cause motion sickness for the audience.

At best, you may make the audience lose interest in the scene and emotionally detach from the movie because it is an unnecessary distraction for them to decipher what is happening onscreen. This scenario is much like what audiences experienced while watching *The Blair Witch Project*, which was, of course, perfectly appropriate in that case because the filmmakers specifically wanted the audience to feel confused and sick. But if visual clarity is your goal, keep this style of camera work to a minimum.

Sure, one of the main reasons for getting in close and obscuring an actor's technique originally was to hide the fact that the actor was not very adept in his film fighting skills. By going wide, filmmakers would have lost the audience's faith and belief in the character. Along with the magic of editing, you are able to tell a story and make the uncoordinated actor appear as if he could beat any and all comers. But this practice is happening all across the board and even to combative sports athletes and martial artists who are better at and have more notoriety for their athletic and combative skills than for their acting skills. In the end, you get a weak acting performance and you don't fully get to appreciate the fighter's athletic skills because you cannot see them—the camera is too close for the audience to register what the heck the fighter is doing. The audience thinks the acting is shallow and the action is unintelligible, which adds up to a viewing experience that is not satisfying to them.

Functionally, thematically, visually, and artistically, there are many problems with always getting in too close for action sequences to aggressively fill the screen (all depending on the type of fight scene being put together). This is because the audience:

- Does not get to visually see the fight unfold as it was choreographed; they only get a partial emotional representation of the fight.
- Cannot fully understand what is occurring in the conflict between the hero and his opponents. When you cut off vital information (non-verbal dialogue, body language, stances, and martial acting), the audience gets only part of the story. They have to fill in the blanks themselves and imagine what happened off screen.
- Does not get a visual reference of place and environment in relation to the actor when he is in the air performing a spectacular jump or aerial move. Therefore, the audience does not appreciate the physicality of the move.
- Does not get to fully see and appreciate the dedicated work from actors who have trained months (or sometimes years) for this moment to perform. It's hyped up in the interviews and PR for the film, but we don't get to really drink it in visually. So what is the point of training an actor for so many months when the audience doesn't get to see the end result?

- Cannot see and appreciate (depending on the type of fight) the aesthetic quality, mood, tempo, and rhythm of the fight.
- Does not get to see the three-act structure of the fight and the strategy of each opponent. Even though the audience might not consciously understand the strategy or reason a character is doing what he is doing, that does not mean we should not show it. Let the audience think about it and let them figure it out for themselves. The audience loves it when you give them pieces of information so they can discover the answers for themselves...even though technically you figured it out for them already.
- Does not get to see the full reaction to the hit taken by an opponent. This actually takes away from the hero because the audience does not see the prowess of their skills and impact directly from throwing the techniques.
- Does not see the combatants' relationship to each other and the adjustments they have to make for the environment.

As a result, the audience does not get a truly effective "wow factor" from all the tension built up to that point and they are usually let down when they don't get the emotional and visual release they want to have. Also, by getting in too close or giving a visual Cubist representation of the conflict, the audience misses out the most. They want to walk out of the theater knowing they witnessed and experienced the action that just happened onscreen. And by unnecessarily getting in too close with the camera, filmmakers are robbing the audience of that experience.

Getting in close does not usually happen as frequently in other aspects of the film (such as dialogue), but it always seems to happen with action sequences because many see this technique not as expositional, but as an artistic interpretation (when it actually is both). We also do not see getting too close occurring in other entertainment situations because if we did, people would stand up and take notice of it. Situation and case in point: Michael Jordan has the ball and faces a whole team geared to defend against him, but he's able maneuver past each opponent and score with a spectacular high-leaping dunk right as the final buzzer sounds to win the deciding shot that takes his team to the NBA finals.

How effective would the "wow factor" be to the viewers if the camera focused tightly on Jordan's face? Sure, you'll capture his emotions of intense determination, focus, and concentration to tell the story, but the audience would miss a much bigger picture—the whole non-verbal conflict and relationship between Jordan and his opponents. The audience would not be able to appreciate Jordan's incredible skill, grandeur, and graceful talent because they would not see who his opponents were. They wouldn't see how many opponents he was up against and what he had to do to get past the different strategies that were presented to him by each of the opponents. The audience also wouldn't get a sense of distance, space, and environment when Jordan makes the spectacular jump because they wouldn't know how high he was in relation to the floor and his opponents. But overall, it's not just Jordan's skills we are witnessing; it's the application of his skills in relation to his opponents that shows us his greatness and gets us to react to his moves.

Or how effective would it be to the audience if the cameraman decided to get creative with his artistic choice in composition by focusing on just the ball when Jordan drives to the basket? Sure, it might look interesting, but the audience would be missing vital information about the conflict between the teams. Angry viewers would expect to see the action unfold instead of seeing an artistic representation that covers the action in an abstract manner. This type of camera work draws too much attention to the cinematography and makes the scene more about the cameraman than the characters or the story being told onscreen. All these elements also apply to different expressions of dance or any other physical sport or activity in which physical movement and an opponent are involved.

Audiences want and expect to see action—they expect to see the hero kicking some ass, people getting hit, cars crashing, a villain getting his just desserts, and so on. Audiences get disenchanted when they get a vague visual representation of the action. They want to see world-class screen fighters such as Jet Li, Sammo Hung, Tony Jaa, Jackie Chan, and Bruce Lee; they watch these stars' movies to see them perform and creatively express themselves in a combative situation.

Like an athlete, there is a limited window of time in these stars' lives when they can perform these extraordinary skills. Eventually, their bodies will give out on them. The same also applies to the stunt actors fighting them, taking the hard-impact falls, and acting in response to the hero's hits. The audience appreciates actors' skills more because they get to see their magnificent skills unfold right in front of their eyes onscreen by seeing the actors dispatch opponents of varying skill levels. The audience also gets to see and visually drink in the aesthetic quality of these actors' skills; audience members can only dream of being so adept and graceful. All of this helps to forge a relationship and a bond between the screen fighter and the audience.

Showing Just Enough

Depending on the scene, the mood of the fight, the location, the film's proposed rating, and the skill of the actors involved, instead of showing the entire fight, you might be forced to show just enough of the scene to suggest there is a fight going on and/or compensate for the actor who can't fight. Be sure to also keep in mind that too much camera movement, coupled with the movement of the conflict, might cause the audience to experience varying degrees of vertigo or disorientation.

There are times when an actor or stunt actor might not be able to do a move that is required for the fight scene. This is when the choreographer and the cinematographer can get a little more creative, hiding the actor's weaknesses but still representing the fight effectively. For instance, if the actor is not flexible enough to throw a face kick, we might see a medium shot of him winding up and then a close up shot of a foot hitting the opponent's face.

Showing just enough should not be limited to actors who cannot fight. It should also be used to create tension, curiosity, and anxiousness with the audience. Following is a list of movies that showed just enough in the fight scene to get the audience more involved emotionally:

- ***A Bittersweet Life.*** The fight in the abandoned, rundown warehouse is a good example.
- ***Bloody Territories.*** Another good example is the final fight scene in the end, where the two combatants fight in the backyard and go through white bed sheets hanging out to dry.
- ***Twilight Samurai.*** The final fight in the house is a good representation of a fight scene in which you see only part of what is happening. From Seibei Iguchi's defensive stance and his opponent off screen, you have a very good idea what the opponent is doing.
- ***Battles Without Honor and Humanity.*** Another good example is the killing of a gangster in the shed.

Slowing Down or Speeding Up the Action

A 35mm film camera shoots film at 24 frames per second (fps) to capture movement at a normal pace. But when you speed up the fps on the camera, you are actually slowing down the action. When you see the film after it is developed, it looks like everyone is moving in slow motion with varying effect, depending on how fast you sped up the film and what type of techniques you used. When you do the opposite and lower the fps, the actors will appear to move faster than what you shot. Naturally, a scene shot in slow motion will take up more footage of film than a scene shot at normal speed.

A commonly overlooked issue with slow motion is that the execution of the technique and the reaction to it should be looked at more closely because a "miss" or a reaction to the technique that is slightly delayed is much more easily spotted by the audience. Also, try to be conservative about which sequences you decide to show in slow motion. If you look back and see that you have more action sequences in slow motion than you have at normal speeds, you have fallen too much in love with your work. The problem is that you are calling too much attention to the actor or the process of filmmaking, as opposed to telling the story.

The following sections describe some of the reasons why you might want to use a slow-motion sequence in your fight scenes.

To Highlight an Incredible Technique or a Move That Was Too Fast for the Normal Eye to Catch

This is probably the most commonly used application for slow motion as an effect, but it can easily and dangerously become an ego or vanity shot for the actor—his time to shine. The commonly overlooked issue when doing this is that the take should highlight the character's best techniques.

Great examples of use of slow motion to highlight incredible techniques include:

- ***Ong-Bak.*** There are many moves in this film that stun the audience so they can't believe what they have just seen. There are many times when the filmmakers have used slow motion to their advantage. One such scene is when Ting fights the villain and they throw each other out the window of the villain's office. Ting knees the opponent in the head as they fall through, which the audience would have missed if the shot been filmed at normal speed. Another such scene is when Ting is being chased by the gang down the city market streets and he does an aerial (no-handed cartwheel) between two plates of glass.
- ***Enter the Dragon.*** A great example is when Oharra grabs Lee's foot, and Lee does a standing half-pike while kicking Oharra as he flips over. This was such an outrageous technique at the time that it had to be shown in slow motion so the audience could fully absorb it. It is also interesting to note that this move was filmed from a single camera angle so the audience knows without question that Lee actually performed the entire stunt himself.

To Have the Audience Anticipate the Technique's Impact

This is usually done as a final technique that ends the fight or one that makes a dramatic turn in the momentum of where the fight is going.

An example is in *Warriors Two.* We see Hua jump over and across a huge table while doing a spin to kick the villain on the other side of the table.

To Emphasize or Build Up a Dramatic Moment

This should be done sparingly, with a certain amount of discretion, or else every moment may feel important and thus the whole movie would be in slow motion.

This technique can be used right before, during, or at the end of a fight. John Woo is popular for doing this for the dramatic moments in his action scenes. But his slow-motion sequences are mainly to emphasize dramatic moments that lead up to or occur during an action scene. Examples of this include:

- ***The Killer.*** A great example occurs when John walks away from the bar to kill his planned hit at the beginning of the film.
- ***Hard-Boiled.*** A great example from this film is when undercover cop Tony walks away immediately after he double-crosses and kills his own Triad brothers to show that he has allegiance to Johnny, his new boss. We see his tears and the complex emotions on his face as he wrestles with this betrayal that he must do to keep his cover.
- ***Enter the Dragon.*** In another good example, Lee crushes Oharra's chest and kills him. The close-up on Lee's face describes the conflicting emotions he goes through as he takes Oharra's life.
- ***Terminator 2: Judgment Day.*** Another example is when John Conner is in the hallway behind a mall and is running away from the cop/T-1000, who is after him. The Terminator shows up on the opposite side with nowhere for John to run. This scene is especially intense because it has not yet been revealed that the Terminator is actually the good guy in this film, rather than the villain, as he was in the prequel. The slow motion effect magnifies the tension of the scene, which occurs right before the two terminators fight and destroy the hallway, crushing the walls by throwing each other into them.

To Make the Audience Appreciate the Grace and Aesthetics of the Technique and/or Part of the Fight

This is reserved for performers who have grace and fluidity in their skills and techniques that can only truly be appreciated in slow motion. Doing this too often and for no real reason can result in too much of a vanity moment for the actor, or the feeling of a forced "style" by the cinematographer.

To Show a Strategy or a Turn in Momentum

This is used when a moment goes by much too fast for the audience to process it, lest they get lost in the action that follows it. This can also be overdone and should be used sparingly. When used too frequently, it suggests that the audience should pay closer attention to what is happening with this sequence. Doing this too often is considered very heavy-handed non-verbal storytelling.

Examples of this include:

- ***The Killer.*** This strategy is used when John escapes Inspector Li and beaches his boat. He notices a little girl playing in the sand. There are no words between them as she clues him in that there are people waiting for him. He takes off his sunglasses and sees the reflection of the sniper's scope on them.
- ***Warriors Two.*** Another example is the ambush of Leung Jan at the Inn. Notice the slow motion occurs twice during this fight (with the bear trap and then the table over his head that leads to the wine caddy being broken over his head and to his final death scene).

To Emphasize a Mood or Feeling in a Scene or Character

This does not necessarily mean showing a certain specific technique. Prime examples are:

- ***Rocky III.*** In the training sequence on the beach, Apollo is running at normal speed while scenes of Rocky running in slow motion are interspersed to visually express his emotional disconnection from everyone as a result of unresolved issues left by his recently and suddenly deceased trainer, Mickey.
- ***Vengeance.*** Another good example is when Yu-Lou is blinded and dies after a big fight at the gangster's house.

To Have the Audience Understand and Absorb the Visual Spectacle and Magnitude of the Fight or Stunt Unfolding in Front of Their Eyes

This applies to all types of stunts as well as fights. This is where distance and space usually need to be covered across the screen.

An example of this includes *Jackie Chan's Police Story*, when Ka Kui tosses Carina from the roof of an apartment building into the pool. Previously, we are set up with the view from atop the apartment and shown that the pool is in the next apartment building complex. The justification in the story is that she has to make the jump because the bad guys are about to knock down the door, ready to kill them both, and there is no other way to escape.

To Show Size and Mass of a Character

In many Kaiju films, they will shoot a creature (such as Godzilla) in semi-slow motion to give the character a feel of extreme mass and size, along with a miniature of a city (that usually gets destroyed in a battle) and sound effects to support the illusion.

The following sections describe some of the reasons why you might want to use fast-motion sequences in your fight scenes.

To Speed Up Action (aka "Under-Cranking")

Under-cranking is usually something that is associated with Chinese martial arts films in which you see actors fighting at super-human speeds that look almost comical. But Western filmmakers are also guilty of this trick in action films, from many silent films featuring Chaplin, Keaton, and the Keystone cops; to the black-and-white comedies of the Three Stooges, the Marx Brothers, and Red Skelton; to some of the John Wayne westerns (such as *Red River*).

One thing that will clue an audience into the fact that the film was sped up is looking at the background to see whether anything is moving unnaturally fast compared to the action in the foreground. Make sure everything in the background is stationary, does not move much, or moves at a speed that will not give any noticeable clues to the audience that the action is sped up.

To Create a Kinetic Rhythm, Look, and Feel to the Action

This increases the rhythm and pace of the fight and can give it a frenetic and more harried pace. This can also add the emotion of urgency to the fight.

To Make an Actor Look Faster than He Actually Is

There might be times when an actor is not able to perform the fight or a certain move at a speed that is convincing enough to make the audience believe in that character. This can happen for any number of reasons—for instance, the move might be beyond the actor's immediate skills and capacity. Slowing down the fps of the camera will make the actor look faster.

To Create Fewer Gaps in Timing between Opponents (aka Dead Pauses)

When putting together a fight scene, the rhythm between the opponents is also crucial in keeping the audience's attention. For example, the hero might have an opponent who is a little slow in reacting to a hit and then coming back at the hero. The gap between selling the reaction and countering might be too long for one reason or another, and you want to speed up the moment. By speeding up the scene, you will eliminate the dead pause that would have occurred if the scene was filmed at normal speed.

An example of this is found in *On Her Majesty's Secret Service.* The opening fight scene on the beach between Bond and an assailant is a perfect example.

To Create Cleaner Techniques

In some Kung Fu movies, you can see that the combatants are throwing techniques at each other incredibly quickly but also with incredible precision, snap, focus, accuracy, and control. This is sometimes achieved by having both combatants throw their techniques a little more slowly than usual, but with the same amount of intensity, focus, snap, power, and control. The speed at which all the combatants should be performing is the same as the speed of the slowest person in the fight; you should adjust the film speed to that person's speed.

To Show the Character's Superhuman Skills

Slowing the film speed can give the character superhuman skills against an opponent. Make sure that the person who is not being sped up is doing something sedentary, so they don't look like they are being sped up as well. The audience generally knows when something is being sped up, so it is best to have something or someone that is not moving at the same speed as the other object or person.

For example, consider *Superman II*, when Clark Kent meets up again with the trucker at the diner who harassed him earlier in the film when he had no super skills. This time, with his superhuman powers, Kent is able to beat the trucker.

To Have an Outrageous Comedic Moment

You see this in many of the old Three Stooges comedies and films that came before the Stooges in the silent era, and also in more recent comedies such as *Shaolin Soccer*. When you speed up the fight, the human eye knows that it was sped up, but the outrageous effect (an obvious strike and/or reaction) can be comedic to accentuate the speed of the film. By doing this, you can also remove the seriousness of the fight.

One Take: Continuous Action without Breaks

An important issue to keep in mind is to stay far back to appreciate the shot. Usually shots are done in masters because if the cameraman is shooting too close, you have a good chance of missing part of the action and would have to reset the piece and start over again. This type of scene should be considered and treated like a live sequence by the cameraman because it is truly unfolding right before him.

This is prepared and executed much like a stage play because there are no breaks or cuts in the action. All the actors involved must know their cues, and if they miss their cues, they should be given a certain limited freedom to improvise if possible to save the scene.

Every beat and cue needs to be rehearsed by the cast and crew involved with the scene.

The illusion is that the scene is really unfolding in front of your eyes, but also keep in mind that you can and should have crew members hidden off camera at various places (where the camera should know not to go) in order to assist in making the action sequence go smoothly. The more people involved, the more complicated the scene gets.

Here are some examples of scenes that go continuously without a break:

- ***Tom Yum Goong.*** A good example is the fight scene that goes up a circular ascending staircase, where Kham defeats a series of bad guys as he works his way up to the exotic animal restaurant at the top of the building.
- ***Oldboy.*** Another example is when Oh Dae-Su fights off a large group of men in the hallway of the hotel/prison (where he spent 15 years of his life) using only a hammer.
- ***Hard-Boiled.*** Another example is the gunfight in the hospital. The handheld camera follows them around from one floor into an elevator to another floor and down some floors. This scene reportedly took weeks to rehearse and to finally execute.
- ***Project A II.*** Think about the ballroom dance scene. Although it is not a fight scene, it was marvelously filmed and staged. The dance floor was full of people dancing, and as the camera cut across the floor, certain actors hit their marks and delivered their lines as the camera went by them. It is subtle and beautifully shot.
- ***Enter the Dragon.*** Remember the scene in which the guards attack Lee and Roper, before the underground prisoners join in on the big battle. Pay particular attention to the scene in which Lee is attacked by guards from all corners and is able to dispose of all the guards with kicks. Notice the camera stayed stationary and that there were no misses in that shot.

Editing

The process of editing the film is the making of the movie. Up to this point you have been shooting raw footage that will be assembled into the movie. A good editor can seamlessly put together scenes that do not make any logical sense—such as scenes from different times, time periods, and/or distances—and have the audience make sense of it all. A great editor also withholds information from the audience, making them feel as if they do not know what is going to happen next. This only empowers the storytelling. A good editor can make the difference between a good and a bad film.

The philosophy or approach toward editing is the manipulation or juxtaposition of two or more separate shots that are not related to one another. The audience's minds make a connection between the two separate shots when the shots are edited correctly.

Let's take a look at an example. Shot #1: A man walks down a street. He stops, and then starts running back in the direction from which he came. Shot #2: A woman yells for help from the top floor of an apartment building that is on fire. These two separate shots are not related at all, but when you edit these two shots together, with #2 in the beginning and then followed by (perhaps only the second half of) #1, the audience makes the connection that when the woman is yelling for help, the man hears her and starts running to her rescue.

Editing a fight scene can get really difficult depending on its complexity. A well-edited fight scene should include the basic principles of a fight scene. It should also enhance all the basic principles and tighten the pace, rhythm, and timing of the fight. A great editor can take out the unnecessary "dead air" in a fight scene, make it tighter, and give it more tension.

Different Styles of Editing

There are different types of editing in the West. The following list discusses the major schools of editing.

- **Western classic.** In this type of editing, the master shot matches the next edited shot, such as a close-up. It is so well done that you do not notice how good the editing is.
- **Western quick cuts.** This type of editing is usually associated with the MTV video type of edits we currently see in American action films. This type of editing can be effective as long as there is a flow that is natural to the type of action on display, as opposed to cuts that do not have any rhythm, flow, or natural progression to them. Senseless or arbitrary cuts that look like they've been tossed together to create a manic, jarring feeling, just for the sake of "style" will distract the audience from the narrative flow of the fight. For successful examples of this technique, look at the cuts made in the final gunfight in *The Wild Bunch* and in *Fighter in the Wind* when Choi fights the three different Japanese schools, intercut with a traditional dance sequence.
- **HK classic.** This type of editing is much like Western classic; it relies on a master with intercuts. It is what we usually saw in the 1970s and 1980s, with Bruce Lee and Jackie Chan. Slow motion was used to emphasize their techniques as well as the emotional moments of each scene. This style required more of the actor's movements to create the tension and drama. Camera movement was at a minimum, so the audience could see the action unfold right before their eyes. The same applies to editing—if you don't notice or realize the cuts, they flow seamlessly with the action.
- **HK new wave.** This type of editing is a more manic style of cutting together fight scenes. It was during this time that Tsui Hark, John Woo, and Wong Kar Wai came into prominence and changed how action was seen, with heavy cuts and speed that created an orgasmic style of cutting, but still had a lyrical flow to it. Logic was left out, but the emotion of the scene was more important. Fewer frames per cut were used, creating a more manic and kinetic type of flow to the action. Examples of this include *Hard-Boiled* and *The Killer.* Influences from European and American filmmakers got to HK mainstream filmmakers, such as John Woo and Tsui Hark. People such as Melville, Peckinpah, and Godard affected these Chinese filmmakers and created a manic blend of action, intercutting with fast- and slow-motion shots of the same scene.
- **HK modern.** The style of editing in Hong Kong is to cut between beats and show the hits. By doing this, filmmakers can increase the tempo of the fight or slow it down when necessary. Also, cutting between visual beats maintains, heightens, and/or intensifies the tempo and kinetic energy of the fight. HK style takes the best of classic and modern styles of editing to create its own kinetic energy and timing. We get to see the hits and the reactions to them. It is a combination of new wave and classic, but it is not as manic as new wave.

The Fight Choreographer's Dilemma

The writer has his script from which the story and dialogue are based. The actor has his performance to call his own. The cinematographer has his visual composition of the film. The director has his vision of how he wants the film to be. The editor has control of each frame of film and assists the director in making his vision come to fruition. They are all represented in the editing room by the script and the director. But for the fight choreographer, his work lies at the mercy of all these different departments to interpret it effectively.

The story justifies the type of fight. The actor has to physically make the fight convincing. The cinematographer visually composes what he thinks will look effective through the lens. The editor then has to edit the fight scene from the miles of raw footage that are given to him. At any given point through these departments, the interpretation of the choreographed fight can enhance or diminish its vision or purpose.

With the actor, you can show him the purpose and meaning of the fight for him to interpret and express. To the cinematographer, you can suggest and recommend effective angles from which to shoot that he might not be aware of. With the director, you show him the beats, rhythm, and non-verbal story behind the fight. But when it comes to editing, there is a very good chance that you will leave it entirely up to the editor to piece together the fight. Does he understand the principles of a cinematic fight? Does he understand some of the subtle nuances of a fight or strategy?

The fight choreographer's fight is not represented in the script except for maybe a vague description that is usually only a couple lines describing the action. The fight was assembled either a few days in advance or that same day and changed during the filming to adjust to unknown factors that might have occurred that day. So how is the editor supposed to know how to put together the fight when he has miles of film to cull through and no actual fight script to follow? Does the editor know the mechanics of what makes a cinematic fight work?

An editor can make the fight scene much better than what was filmed, but he can also destroy a fight scene. An editor is not a fight choreographer, nor do we expect him to know the nuances of a fight scene. But a fight choreographer is not fully represented in the editing room. The fight is usually left to the editor to use his instincts to piece it together. Speaking to many stunt coordinators and fight choreographers, often an editor does not understand the subtle nuances of a fight scene or an important move that has to do with the story. Even worse, the editor might piece together the fight scene backward.

The editor does not usually come onto the set and is therefore not emotionally involved in the day-to-day production woes and real-life drama that might occur on the set. As a result, the editor has a very objective view of what shots he can or cannot use by just seeing what is on film. The editor is then able to make tough critical decisions about material to which a director's judgment might be clouded from being too emotionally attached to the scene. There are very good reasons to keep an editor separate from the day-to-day shooting; it keeps his objective eye clear and ensures that he does not have any emotional attachments to any certain shot, setup, or scene. But this separation can often adversely affect the final version of a fight scene if the editor does not successfully maintain the clarity of the fight or effectively represent the choreographer's vision.

Mike Massa, stunt coordinator for the TV series *Angel* and stunt double for the show's star, David Boreanaz, comments on the process a stunt coordinator goes through:

> *You build your fight by reading the script. You make and create all this energy into the fight by having it a certain way. You shoot it that way, but out of sequence, because you've gotta shoot it one side first, then the reverse, and also get all of the actor's coverage, et cetera. But when it gets to the editing room, the editors don't give a damn about how you wrote out the story of the fight scene. They will change the fight. They'll put your ending techniques near the front and your starting moves near the ending. They put it together so that it does not make sense. You're looking at the fight that you put together and think to yourself, "What the hell is going on?" The editors don't look at it the same way you would look at it. They don't usually see your whole scenario. You'll shoot a master (if you're lucky), which shows the logical progression of the fight. But I've caught the editors putting the end of the fight at the beginning of the fight so many times. I'll tell them, "Guys, didn't you read the script? This guy can't be winning here; he's supposed to be losing."*
>
> *But they don't get it. They just put it together. It's just a rush to get it done. Everybody wants to put it together and get it out there. So a lot of times you can try to be really precise because it's your job. It's important. You should do exactly what the script asks you to do, unless you know the writers don't know how to do action, and they give you the permission and you can supplement. There are some scripts where it will read like, "The fight begins and we defer to Mike Massa [to put in whatever he wants]...then Angel gets hit...we defer to Mike Massa..." et cetera.*
>
> *In that case, which is fantastic, you can put your own stuff in. But otherwise you need to hold to the storyline because there might be something important to that storyline for the whole entire show. It's very important to do that, and hopefully the editors will stay on it and not swap things around, which they do a ton of. I've seen them change screen direction in the middle of the fight. They reverse the frame so instead of traveling to the left side of the frame, he'll travel to the right side. Guys, what are you doing? I'll go into post and take a look at the fight if I have time.*

I'll look at the edited fight and tell them, "He just got hit, and you threw him to the right side of the room. There's nobody over there, but he'll come back from the left side of the room to attack again. It doesn't make sense. How's that going to work?"

"Oh, they won't get that."

"The hell they won't get that! I just got it!"

It does happen. You have brand-new editors just like brand-new coordinators coming into the show. Some editors don't know how to edit action, just like some directors don't know how to shoot action. So if you have the time and they let you do it, sometimes it helps to go into the editing room and give them some of your creative juices without telling them what to do.

Solutions

In Hong Kong, the fight director goes into the editing room and advises the editor on what will make the fight scenes work. However, in the West, the roles are more departmentalized, and the fight choreographer has to be invited or asked by the editors to come into the editing room.

There are several things we can do to solve this issue if the editor is willing to listen. First, give the script supervisor copious notes on the fight scene and how it goes together, along with what were good in those takes. The other suggestion is to videotape the fight scene during rehearsal so the editor will know how the fight scene starts, what happens in the middle, and how it ends. Also, provide notes explaining what certain moves mean to the importance of the story.

Processing Information

The industry is torn between what is good and what is not. When it comes down to editing at a quick pace, they only get quick images of what represents a fight. Some say it is a result of the computer age, growing up on MTV, and the advances of videogames that makes kids today process information at a much quicker rate. This is true. The pace of storytelling has changed dramatically from what we saw in the 1950s to now. There is not as much dialogue as there was back then. I'm all for expressing yourself creatively in film; however, when you sacrifice story for cool-looking flash, who suffers in the end? We all do. Everyone from the filmmakers to the audience suffers. The audience is asked to "speed read" through a scene and they are not really given the chance to immerse themselves into the cinematic fantasy of the scene. There is a delicate balance of keeping the audience's attention while still being able to tell a story.

Some blame the influence of videogames and music videos. I beg to differ when it comes to videogames. The perspective of videogames changes, but the player still has a visual understanding of where he stands in respect to the environment a good majority of the time, partially because he controls the movement of the main character and therefore dictates the camera angles. In other words, the player becomes his own cinematographer. If the player did not know where his character was at all times, he would lose the interactive experience and the immersion of playing in the moment. This is especially true with first- and third-person games, such as *Tomb Raider*, *Resident Evil*, and *Doom*. The same applies to fighting games, such as the *Street Fighter* and *Mortal Kombat* series. The players get an emotional release of some sort when they achieve and/or see a hit.

Some blame fast-cutting of a movie on music videos. But the fast-cutting style has always been around, starting with the French new wave, in which they manipulated time with cuts that were not traditionally standard. There's nothing wrong with fast cuts as long as the images provide vital information about the scene that makes sense visually, as a narrative, and resonates emotionally about the scene. Take a look at the final gunfight in *The Wild Bunch* and the final ambush in *Bonnie and Clyde*. Look at *Fighter in the Wind*, when Choi Bae-dal first challenges and fights several fighters from the first three Japanese *dojos* after his self-imposed exile training in the woods. These scenes were all edited with fast cuts, manipulating time and space, and they made sense while still expressing the emotion of the experiences.

Nowadays, in a lot of Western films, we see a lot of bad editing of fight scenes (and sporting events), where the extremely quick images that are selected don't make any type of sense and don't provide any type of flow, rhythm, strategy, or narrative function—except for maybe a jarring experience for the audience to give them a simulated experience of the conflict. However, the style of manic cutting and meshing together images that don't flow together naturally robs the audience of a sense of what it's like to be in the fight. It is an inorganic, processed experience that has no natural rhythm or flow.

Fast edits during an action scene should be used sparingly and with discretion.

Western editors do not dwell on the nuances of the fight as much as Asian editors do. However, being more focused on the individual beats of a fight gives the fight depth.

The Pulse of a Fight Scene

Now that we've explored and explained all the aspects of a fight scene from narrative, physical, and technical elements, hopefully you can start to dissect a fight scene and find the strengths and weaknesses and what will make the fight scene better.

When looking at a fight scene, there might be something wrong that you cannot put your finger on; you may not be able to figure out what is missing from or wrong with the scene. Following are general descriptions of what you might encounter when putting together a fight scene. You can also use these definitions while watching films that are currently out in theaters or on home video.

What a fight choreographer should always strive to achieve is to have a believable and convincing fight scene. The definition of that is:

- **Perfect, on, or alive.** This occurs when the fight is technically exact and clean, has energy, has the timing and cues in sync, and holds convincing emotions throughout the conflict. Visually there are no misses, and cinematic composition and edits are such that the audience knows what is happening with each beat of the fight. The audience feels as if the fight is naturally unfolding right in front of their eyes because the martial acting is very convincing, supported by a solid story that justifies the action and the character's skill level.
- **Rooted or with substance.** This occurs with a fight scene that is strongly based on the story and character background and development. The actions are justified, and the reasons why the characters are fighting like they are make sense.

Here is a list of some of the things that might happen when you see a fight scene, but maybe you can't put your finger on exactly what might be wrong, off kilter, or missing:

- **Flashy.** A flashy fight contains a series of visually spectacular moves. This fight scene has only visual thrills and ignores the story; it can be called "all flash and no substance." (See the "No substance" bullet later in this list.)
- **Carrying the actor.** This occurs when in part of a fight scene (or in an entire fight scene), it is too obvious the attacker is catering to and adjusting his approach to the hero to make up for the hero's shortcomings in a valiant attempt to make the scene work. As a result, the audience is too far ahead of the film, having already anticipated the attack. By the time the attack *does* come, it is no longer exciting to the viewer.
- **Clash or bad fit.** This occurs when you are incorporating a style or technique that does not complement or work alongside the situation, character, and/or story.
- **Gratuitous violence.** This occurs with a fight scene or move that is used as a device to get a rise from the audience. For example, the use of excessive blood or gore to get a rise from the audience during a fight, especially if the other fight scenes in the movie were not like that.

- **Implausible or no steam.** This occurs with a fight scene that has no credibility or loses credibility right before or during the fight. As a result, the audience loses interest. The typical symptoms of this can be any or all of the following:
  - Martial acting that is unbelievable, false, or does not match the emotion of the character and/or fight scene
  - Flaws or weaknesses in the story or character development, so the character has no real justification for his fighting skills
  - Choice of style, skill level, and/or technique that does not match the story or personality of the character
  - Showing of technical flaws, such as misses, unflattering angles, off edits, poor lighting, and so on
- **"Cool-move-itis"** (pronounced *kool-moov-eye-tiss*). This is a serious (but curable) disease that impairs or blinds the fight choreographer's judgment skills and critical eye. The disease is putting in an unjustified "cool move"—a technique, style, or approach to fighting that is not justified by the mood, theme, character background, motivation, and/or story. This can also apply to a single move, technique, or moment in a fight scene that might not fit or blend in with the rest of the fight. It also can occur more noticeably when a martial artist turns into a "movie star" and feels the fight scene is his moment to shine in the spotlight and display his skills, while ignoring the principles of story and character development. The result of "cool-move-itis" can take the audience emotionally out of the scene so they lose faith and belief in the character's skills—or even worse, the complete movie-going experience.
- **No resonance.** This occurs with a fight scene that is emotionally false or nonexistent in martial acting and provides no emotional buildup and/or release. There is no real spirit or energy behind the actor's physical performance, which resonates to the audience.
- **No substance.** This occurs with a fight scene that has no real meaning or purpose behind it and/or is not connected to the story at all. The techniques used have no real meaning behind them.
- **Off.** This occurs when the timing of techniques and cues between actors are inaccurate and throw off the entire rhythm of the fight scene. Being "off" can also occur when the martial acting does not match the moment of conflict.

- **Oversold or too much.** This occurs when a fight scene (or parts of it) has too much energy (is over the top) and does not fit into the story and/or characters. This is easily noticed by audiences in martial acting because the scene (or parts of it) does not come across as genuine, honest, or sincere; rather, it calls and attracts unnecessary attention.
- **Posing.** This occurs when an actor is conscious of himself at any moment during the fight and poses in a fighting stance or a before or after pose for the camera. An actor can also be called a "poser," which means he is only there to fight and make himself look good for vanity and ego purposes.
- **Repetitious.** This occurs when a fight scene has the same repetitive rhythm throughout the fight. This also applies to repeating the same technique in a single fight or throughout other fights in a single film. The problem with being repetitive with a technique and rhythm is several-fold:
    - Strategically, it does not make any sense.
    - Mentally, the audience is already expecting it and they are already ahead of the fight.
    - Visually, it gets boring and lacks variety in the choreography.
    - Rhythmically, you can lull the audience to sleep, and it gets boring if the fight scene is long.

  A fight scene is much like dialogue in the script—it needs to progress at a steady pace. In comparison to real life, dialogue can get very tedious, cover the same issue over and over, and not really lead anywhere specific. A fight can easily be the same way if you are not aware of the different types of repetition.
- **Staged.** This occurs when the fight scene has a rehearsed and premeditated feel to it and it does not come across as organic or natural.
- **Stale or flat.** This occurs when there is no life or energy to the fight scene because the actors are not in the moment with the fight and they are not acting as if the fight is unfolding right there. A fight can also become stale or flat by having the same continuous rhythm and beat throughout. This can also happen by repetitiously using the same techniques over and over again, offering no real variety.
- **Stiff.** This occurs when the actors in the fight are too rigid and they are very conscious that they are in a choreographed fight. This is evident by the actors' ready anticipation of the next move—they know it is coming and they are not able to act/react/respond as if they do not know what the next move is. As a result, the fight looks rehearsed and has no real spontaneous energy because everyone is too conscious of the choreography.

- **Too aware.** This occurs when an actor breaks character and is too much aware that he is in a fight scene. The actor might appear just a little too excited to be in a fight scene and call unnecessary attention to himself because of this. The expression on his face might read, "Hey everyone! Look at me; I'm in a fight scene! Ain't it cool?"

Cinematography Exercises

Following are a few cinematography exercises for you to try:

- Watch the final fight scene in *Jackie Chan's Police Story*. How effective would that fight scene be if the camera was tight on Jackie Chan's character throughout the fight? Would the "wow factor" be as effective? Even though the camera was further away so you could see all the action (compared to what you would see in the West), you were still able to feel his emotional isolation. How were the filmmakers able to do that?
- Take a look at Kurosawa's *The Seven Samurai* and observe the choice in camera angles and how the filmmakers are able to get you involved in the fight. What angles are they using to get you emotionally involved? Then watch other films with fight/action scenes and see if and how the filmmakers used the camera to get you involved.
- Choreograph a simple fight scene in which you start off from long range, go to medium range, then move to in-close/grappling, and then back off to a medium or long range. Film the fight in pieces and play with the angles and distance needed to capture the techniques and reactions, which are the drama of the fight. Remember not to fall unconditionally in love with your work because you can never grow from it when you do.

Editing Exercises

Following are a few editing exercises for you to try:

- Pick various movies and break down how the fight scenes were edited. Ask yourself, "Is there anything different I would have done with the editing to make this fight scene more effective?"
- Study and break down the differences between Hong Kong and Western style edits. Learn to develop an eye for the rhythm and flow that is created by the edit.
- Shoot a fight scene. While editing the fight scene, play with the timing and rhythm of the fight, emphasizing different techniques and timing without calling attention to your editing to the point where a viewer would know that it was not a naturally timed fight scene.

11

Developing a Choreographer's Eye

I feel it is my responsibility to explain the method to my madness and how to watch and analyze a film or fight scene from an artist's perspective. You can no longer turn your logic off, watch a fight scene, and simply be entertained, because you are attempting to switch seats from being a receiver (passive moviegoer/consumer) to a creator (filmmaker/fight choreographer). You have to treat viewing a fight (real or choreographed, live or onscreen, or on TV) and films in general with a more educated, discerning, and critical eye. This also requires you to think differently by seeing places and situations anywhere you go (even when you are not working) as potential locales and opportunities for great fight scenes. You have to awaken that "fight choreographer mind" within you by developing, conditioning, exercising, and applying it to your craft.

It's easy to critique others' choreography and cast negative judgment on their work, but you have to get out there and do it yourself, even if the only camera to which you have access is an old VHS camcorder. Constantly study, learn, and apply to film everything you have seen and absorbed. Experiment, learn, and discover what works and what does not work on your own time so when it comes time for you to work on an actual production, you will be as prepared as possible. Spending valuable time trying to learn during the actual production of a film can prove to be costly and can easily result in you getting fired or not getting work afterward.

Developing an Eye for Action

Here are some tips so you can develop an eye for action and a deeper appreciation for action films. The important thing is to know that where you used to go for mere entertainment will now be a part of your lab and classroom for study. This does not mean that you should not be entertained while you are in the theater, but it is important to use your thoughts and feelings as a barometer as well. Start to look at things with a different perspective, from being a consumer (a passive and accepting frame of mind) to being a creator (an observing and application state of mind). This means understanding and seeing through all the smoke and mirrors used to disguise the flaws and cheat to keep the actors safe while creating the illusion of getting hurt. Does this mean you will not appreciate a fight scene once you know all the tricks? Yes and no. You will see fights that you might once have thought incredible, but now, after realizing the tricks of the trade, you will look at them as not very impressive at all. You will rediscover some that you never fully appreciated, but after learning about the fight game, you have grown to appreciate. Then there will be those fights that you thought were incredible, and after understanding the concepts, you will *still* feel they are incredible.

One of the important keys here is to be proactive in your journey. You can read every article, interview, book, and see every film out there, but if you have not assembled a crew or gotten together with some friends to put together a fight scene, you are not being proactive with what you have learned. It's very easy to stay too much in your head as you critique others' action sequences with your theories and ideas, without taking any type of action of your own. Try not to fall into that trap. Do your best to actively apply what you have learned to your craft as an artist. Keep a positive and healthy balance between living in your head and in your body. If you see an action sequence in a film that you think you could have choreographed better, prove it, by grabbing a camera and (safely) trying it out for yourself. Gaining practical experience on a film set is much different than having untested theories that you develop and keep in your head or on paper.

See Films in a Theater First

When possible, see all the action films that are out in theaters (first, if at all possible) and then on DVD (as a second choice—also see the "Starting a Video Reference Library" section later in this chapter for more info). This rule applies no matter what the film's genre or country of origin because (generally) films are made to be seen on the big screen first and on DVD second. The impact of seeing a film in a theater is much different and greater than the impact of seeing it on your TV. This is especially true for action films. It makes a greater impact when you see someone getting hit and flying across the length of 20 to 40 seats than when you see him fly only several inches on your TV screen. Most theater screens are made to encompass and fill our whole line of vision. This rule even applies to big-screen televisions because they still do not completely fill our line of sight as a theater screen would. Films are made to be larger than life. With certain action what sometimes appears obvious ends up coming across as subtle on TV. I have found this to be especially true with Hong Kong action films. What might seem subtle on TV might pack more of a punch in theaters.

When watching a DVD, you have the luxury of pause, rewind, and fast forward buttons, but filmmakers create their movies to be seen linearly and at a normal frame rate. Repeating sections, pausing for bathroom breaks, and fast-forwarding through the "slow" parts robs you of seeing a film the way the creator intended and can drastically alter its intended effect. Respect the filmmaker's vision by experiencing his creativity on the big screen whenever possible.

Sound quality is another issue. A majority of homes are built for us to live in and are not made to have optimum sound for a true theater feeling and experience. Besides, all of your neighbors would complain to the police if you had true cinema-quality sound and turned it up to the same level as a theater. Unless you retrofit your room to be soundproofed for quality sound, it is not possible for you to get the same feeling and experience you will get from a theater. What you get for the home theater is no comparison to the quality sound you get at a modern movie theater.

Also, there are many outside distractions at home that can quickly steal our attention so we are not focused on watching a film from beginning to end. These distractions break and can destroy our attention span. We can lose interest, miss an important moment, and/or forget what happened in the previous scene after several breaks from watching a film.

Impatience is a major killer while watching a film on DVD at home, whereas in a theater you are a captive audience member and your impatience is easily tempered. That's because the effort it took for you to get there makes you have more patience than when you're watching it at home. Also, you have more control over the elements at home (and, of course, you have a fast-forward button). I've noticed that I am much more impatient when renting a DVD and watching it on TV because the price I paid for the rental was pretty cheap compared to going to a theater.

Seeing movies on the big screen, you walk away mesmerized. Getting the DVD and watching it on your TV does not recreate the same viewing experience. Some of the best examples of this difference that I have noticed include *The Killer, Bullet in the Head, The Matrix, The Crow, Drunken Master II, Die Hard, Jackie Chan's Police Story, Jackie Chan's Project A, The Seven Samurai, Raiders of the Lost Ark, Kung Fu Hustle, Once upon a Time in the West,* and *Enter the Dragon.* So unless you have an actual theater with a theater-sized screen and projector, as well as a theater sound system and soundproofing in your home, then I suggest you first try to watch the movie in an actual theater before seeing it at home.

Study Audience Reactions

When seeing a film, you are also studying the audience's reactions. Even though it's not the best seat in the house, you can still see the movie and observe the audience's reactions. Going to a theater is no longer an entertainment event for you, but more like being in a classroom. This is easily done when you are sitting in the very back row. It is impossible to do this if you sit in the middle or near the front of the theater—you would have to look behind you to gauge the audience's reactions. Also know that each screening will get different reactions because of the general consensus of the audience, so it is always good to remember your emotions during the movie. To study the audience's reactions, don't just consider how they respond vocally to the scenes; you should also study their body language. Often audiences do not express their opinions verbally. But there is no mistaking how they feel if you pay attention to their body language. This was something I used to do when I was working professionally as a standup comedian, so I could gauge the emotions of the audience before I got onstage to perform.

If you have the time and money and you really liked a film and want to see it again, try going to another part of town to get a different response from the audience. A younger college or an urban audience will probably give you a response to a film that will be different than what you get from an older, more mature crowd. I noticed the crowd difference when I was a young kid watching Bruce Lee movies in the urban theaters in downtown Washington, D.C. The crowds would really get emotionally into the movie and react by yelling and heckling the bad guy on the screen. It was an event that vividly connected the audience to the screen. However, when I saw the same Bruce Lee movies in the suburbs of Maryland, you could almost hear a pin drop. This is not saying that one crowd got into it and one didn't, because, when I looked closer, the audience members were all reacting with only their body language and every once in a while verbally. But the suburban audience's reactions were much subtler and somewhat reserved in comparison. Both audiences reacted, but they had different ways of reacting to the same film.

Expand Your Tastes

Do not limit your movie-going experience by only going to the local cineplex or mall theaters, which usually show the most popular and heavily advertised studio films. Go to independent theaters, revival houses, and film festivals every once in a while. Take a chance on a foreign or a small independent film when the opportunity arises. Balance your film-watching diet by watching a healthy mix of studio, independent, and foreign films.

Independent films usually are smaller in scale and budget and are very personal in their message and story for various reasons. In general, they won't have the glossy high-production values, formulaic stories, and/or happy endings most of today's Hollywood studio films have. These films often have a message or deal with heavy subject matter that a big studio might not want to touch. Their action sequences might not be as spectacular or grand as a studio film, but usually will pack an emotional punch. Great examples of independent films that have effective fight scenes and gunplay are *Once Were Warriors* (domestic violence), *A Better Place* (teen violence), *Reservoir Dogs* (gunplay, challenge), and *Girlfight* (tournament fighting), to name a few.

Hollywood studio films are owned and run by big corporations who in turn own the film studios. As a result, they have a lot more money to put into their productions. However, the script has to be approved by various groups at the studios before a film can ever get made. This is so the studios can ensure the film can make a profit. This is good and bad. By the time it is ready to go into production, a story can lose its integrity and original appeal that made it unique as a result of too many "cooks" stirring the pot. On the other hand, studio films have the budget to afford big action set pieces that an independent film typically cannot. Hollywood has put together some of the grandest action and fight sequences. Some stellar classic examples are *Terminator 2*, the *Rocky* series, the James Bond franchise, *Butch Cassidy and the Sundance Kid*, the *Star Wars* series, the *Indiana Jones* series, the *Matrix* trilogy, and so on.

Foreign films are fun to watch because they often challenge the viewer to have a different point of view on life and as a result see things slightly differently than we do, but they are at times very universal, no matter what your belief system. Their way of expression in film is a result of a specific culture and belief system that can be much different than ours. Some of the greatest filmmakers are not from our shores. Some unforgettable films that have great action from other countries include *The Seven Samurai* (Japan), *La Femme Nikita* (France), *Crouching Tiger, Hidden Dragon* (Taiwan), *Once Were Warriors* (New Zealand), *City of God* (Brazil), *Ong-Bak* (Thailand), *Old Boy* (Korea), *The Good, the Bad, and the Ugly* (Italy), and the classic films of Jackie Chan, Sammo Hung, Yuen Woo-Ping, Shaw Brothers Studios, and Golden Harvest (Hong Kong). When watching a foreign film, look at the similarities more than the cultural differences and see how the filmmakers are able to transcend the language barrier with their works.

Revival houses are great places to catch classic movies that might be already available on DVD, but for which you might want to have a theater experience. You might be able to catch a Chaplin, Buster Keaton, or Harold Lloyd silent film, a spaghetti western, a swashbuckler, or a film that is no longer playing at your cineplex that you wanted to see but didn't have the time to when it was originally released. (See Figure 11.1.)

Figure 11.1

Seek out and support second-run theaters, art-house theaters, and revival houses that show classic, foreign, obscure, and forgotten films that the mainstream multiplexes ignore or discard. One such theater is the Beverly Theater in Los Angeles, California (shown here). Usually, each major city has a second-run theater or has a selected time when obscure and classic films are shown. If this isn't the case in your town, request it, start one yourself, or move to a city that has such places.

Film festivals are also great. Depending on what type of film festival it is, you might get to meet a new up-and-coming filmmaker whose work you might like. Also, going to a film festival exposes you to films you won't normally see released at the local cineplex or distributed on DVD for various reasons that might not have anything to do with the quality of the film.

Expand your tastes beyond the media-hyped "flavor of the month" films. Know the difference in viewing experience between an independent and a studio film.

Try Not to Prejudge a Movie

When going to see a movie, try your best to leave all critical judgments and preconceived expectations behind before you walk into the theater. This includes critics' and friends' opinions, preview trailers, media and PR hype, tabloid news, Internet rants and raves, and most importantly your own preconceived opinions. You are trying to develop your own sense of what works and what doesn't. By making a decision based on someone else's opinion of a film, you are taking on their judgments, limitations, and prejudices.

Have you ever really liked seeing a film on TV, video, or cable and you wished you saw it when it first came out? Today, we are inundated with so much advertising and sensationalist tabloid news that it can actually take away from the final product. Who cares if the movie went over budget, a lead actor's salary was more than enough to feed every Third World country, or the star threw a tantrum and burned his trailer down while having a wild orgy with a bunch of porn stars with DDD implants (and why wasn't I invited?!)?

The media loves to write sensational stories about the film industry and its money, whom the stars are dating and breaking up with, and the politics behind the scenes of Hollywood. This is because the film industry is the closest thing we have to royalty. But try your best to look past all that tabloid drama and focus on studying the craft of filmmaking. Was the movie experience worth the price of admission or rental? Was the film enjoyable to you? Did the actors do a believable and convincing job with their roles? Was the story well executed? Were the action sequences well performed, shot, and edited? Learn to separate the hype from the craft of cinematic storytelling.

Be Selective about Whose Reviews You Read

There is a delicate balance that needs to be established here. I'm not telling you to bury your head like an ostrich and not hear anything. What I'm suggesting is that you be discriminating about what you read or hear. There is always some kind of opinion attached to what films are out there each week, whether or not it is true. Too often, people take what they read in print as true or fact. Don't take one single person's opinion about a film as the law in your mind. Go out and establish your own boundaries as to your definition of effective cinema.

If you are going to read a critic's review on a film, try to read reviews where the critic comments on the art and craft of the film. You'll be surprised to see how many film critics on TV shows, newspaper columns, and the Internet focus on the gossip and rumors rather than the film itself, which might be topical news but is not the art and craft of filmmaking. I've also read quite a few reviews in which the critic has a personal vendetta against the actors involved or did not like the movie and just lambasted the choices actors made in their personal lives without really talking about the film. You will also read reviews in which a critic will call attention to himself by showing what a great writer he is, rather than actually reviewing the movie. Try to separate the craft from the B.S. It's okay for a critic to be opinionated and maybe biased, but he should explain why he has come to his conclusions. This is not high school (even though at times it really feels like it). Focus on the craft of filmmaking by reading columns by critics who actually review the craft.

If you are going to read a film review, read several of them and not just one. This helps to keep throwing your choice of seeing the film back in your court. Reviewers will tell you their opinion of the film. Some are very conservative in their views and some are not. Try to find the best ones that closely suit your views and likes. If four or five reviewers are of the consistent opinion that the film is not good, then don't say you weren't forewarned. But more importantly, look for critics who have the skill and are not afraid to break down the film and explain to you why they did not like it. Roger Ebert is a great example of a film critic who explains why he likes or dislikes a film. This in turn empowers you with regard to what elements you feel you like and don't like in a film. Remember that a film review is only an opinion; try to find a good film critic who feels responsible to his readers and is able to dissect the film and clearly explain to you why he did or did not like it. Remember, it's an opinion with which you do not necessarily have to agree.

Do Not Substitute Box-Office Gross for Aesthetics

Just because a movie made a gazillion dollars at the box office does not mean it is a good film. We are constantly bombarded in the news and commercials by information about how many millions a movie has made. We hear it so many times that it becomes something like an adult peer pressure—kind of like the peer pressure we experienced in high school. Unfortunately this makes a good majority of people into lemmings and gets them to think, "Well, if all these people went to see this movie and it made *X* millions on the first weekend, that must mean it is a good movie. I've gotta see this movie because everyone else in the world has seen it except for me."

Many different aspects come into play for a movie to make a lot of money. The box office race has been so much an obsession that it blinds the general audience to what is a good film. There are a lot of great films out there that do not have a powerful marketing team behind them, so they slip past our awareness. Deprogram yourself so you can think past the equation that a film with a huge box office equals a great film. Just because the fast food industry makes billions of dollars a year does not mean that their food is good for you. The same applies to the box office race. Just because a movie made millions, that does not mean it is a good movie; it only means that a lot of people were convinced one way or another (usually through the media) to see it. Learn to be aware of your impulses about what makes you go see a movie. There is no way to completely escape this type of thinking, but just be more aware of the types of movies you go see and what makes you go see them.

The word "success" for a film has different definitions.

- **Financially**. A film is a financial success when it does well, recoups the investment that was put into it, and eventually makes a profit. When a film does financially well, this helps the filmmakers' and the stars' next projects get made much more easily.
- **Critically.** A film is a critical success when it appeals to a majority of film critics, press, and media. Even though critics might adore a film, it does not necessarily mean the film will do well with audiences and at the box office.
- **Artistically.** A film is an artistic success when the director, actors, and writers are able to get the integrity of their message and the theme of the film across in the final product and it has some kind of an effect upon the audience.
- **Popularity.** A film is a popular success when the audience and/or critics like it.

Remember, the cost of admission to a film is always rising and is not a true indicator of the actual popularity of a particular film. How could a classic film such as *Gone with the Wind* compete with a film released today for the all-time box office champ when the price for admission in 1939 was around 25 to 50 cents? It's not fair to judge a film on box office receipts without an adjustment for inflation to even out the playing field. Next time you look at the top 10 highest-grossing films of all time, notice a good majority of the top 10 are less than five years old. This has a lot to do with the price of admission. Go to www.boxofficemojo.com for the all-time box office champions adjusted for inflation. You might be surprised to see how the standings turn out.

Learn to Read Subtitles

Watch the movie in its original language whenever possible. This requires you to multitask and be able to read subtitles while watching the film. However, a lot of Americans are "subtitle-phobic." There are several possible reasons for this.

- Perhaps certain viewers fear that they will miss a lot of the action if their eyes spend too much time at the bottom of the screen reading subtitles, rather than focusing on the middle of the screen where most of the really important visual stuff is happening.
- Perhaps it's due to a medical condition (like ADD) with which someone can't focus and process words quickly while paying attention to something visual on the screen.

- Perhaps there's an American-centric mentality in which the belief is, "If it ain't American, it ain't worth a damn." We tend to get seduced by the high production values that we have in U.S. productions, with which other countries might not be able to compete. However, this mentality will only limit and handicap our view of the world and our ability to take things into our creative psyche. Look beyond that and try to find the universal message of what a film can be. As artists, we get inspired by many different things in life if we let ourselves. To limit ourselves by manmade territorial borders and differences in customs and how we verbally communicate is a sad shame.
- Perhaps we don't associate reading with pleasure much anymore. Many feel reading is like eating hard-shelled crabs—too much work for little meat. When we go see a movie, we sit back, relax our minds, and expect to be entertained and not have to think—we just experience what we see onscreen emotionally. As a result, we are in a passive state of mind. However, reading requires us to be in more of an active state of mind. There is somewhat of a contradiction between what we want to experience and how many of us have been conditioned to watch a movie that takes us out of our viewing entertainment experience.

It used to be that when a movie had subtitles, it usually meant that the film would be released in an art house theater. It meant box-office death and a video release that would not get anyone's attention. A big change came when *Crouching Tiger, Hidden Dragon* was first released in the U.S. in 2000. At the time, subtitled films did not do spectacularly well in the U.S. Sure, films before this got critical acclaim, awards, and so on, but they never got an extremely bountiful box office, audience attention, and a wide release all over the country as *Crouching Tiger, Hidden Dragon* did. As a result, subsequent films such as *Hero*, *House of Flying Daggers*, and *Kung Fu Hustle* have been released in the U.S. with English subtitles and without dubbing. Even though foreign films are released in their original language with subtitles more often, studio executives still debate whether releasing a film dubbed or with subtitles will bring in a better box-office gross. Filmmakers are now not as afraid to use subtitles or to use other languages in their mainstream films. Some are creatively using subtitles as a part of the film, such as in *Man on Fire*.

The main reason I stress reading subtitles in foreign films is because you will get a better feeling of the emotions from the actors, even though you might not understand the language (which is what the subtitles are for). Often, while watching a film that is dubbed in English from another language, there is a good chance the actors doing the dubbing haven't gotten close to the emotions the real actors are conveying.

I have seen many martial arts films dubbed in English, and then seen the same films again in their original form with original language and subtitles. It is always a very different viewing experience. The story and characters are much deeper in the subtitled/original language versions. There is a certain amount of artistic integrity in the original presentation that makes the dubbed version come across as second-rate, cheap, and sloppy. How many times have you heard comedians make fun of those badly dubbed Kung Fu movies of the 1970s? This is because the dubbing actor was not close to capturing the emotional content of the moment, and that in turn does not match the stance and hand position the actor is using. Even when dubbing is done well, the actor doing the overdub is not close to the real actor who was in that scene. Dubbed movies cater to an audience that does not like to read and that just wants to be entertained. There is nothing wrong with that for the general consumer, but as a creator, you need to get close to the original version of the film.

Learn to read subtitles while watching what is happening onscreen and feel the emotion from the dialogue the actor is speaking in his native tongue. This is a skill that is developed over time after a lot of practice. Change your thinking from watching a movie as a passive experience to using a more active frame of mind. If you want to be a student of film, you are no longer considered part of the masses. You are coming from a point of creation and learning from other filmmakers who have preceded you. When you can do this, you will be able to have an experience that is much more fulfilling because there are some films that you'll watch and forget that you are reading the subtitles. A great example of this is when you are watching Akira Kurosawa's *The Seven Samurai*, which is in a film class of its own.

Know What to Ask Yourself after Seeing a Movie

After viewing a movie, replay it in your head and think about how you emotionally responded to it. The more vividly you are able to recall the film and your experience, the better. Ask yourself the following questions:

- Were you able to spot exactly where the first act ended?
- Were you able to spot exactly where the second act started and ended?
- Were you able to spot exactly where the third act started?
- Were you able to spot the major plot points?
- Was there any exposition in the dialogue? If so, was it done convincingly and as elegantly as possible?
- Did every fight scene tell a non-verbal story?
- Did each fight have three acts?

- How did you physically react to the fight scenes?
- Were the styles and techniques used in the fights fully integrated into the story?
- Was there a difference in the motivation, style, and emotion of the fights in each different act?
- Was the action an integral part of the story?
- Were the camera angles and editing helpful or detrimental to telling the story of the fight? In other words, were you visually able to see and comprehend what was happening in the fight scenes?
- Did you spot any misses during a fight scene?
- Were there any scenes in which any of the actors were obviously anticipating or expecting the next move?
- Did the tempo and rhythm change several times throughout a particular fight?
- Were the rhythm and tempo natural or forced?
- Were there any actors and/or stuntmen whose reactions were off time?
- Were you able to follow and see what the characters were doing with the fight?
- Were the actors' performances convincing in the fight sequences?
- Did any of the fight scenes take you out of the story, and why?
- Were there a variety of different styles of fights?
- Did the filmmakers use a variety of different techniques as opposed to doing the same thing over and over again?
- Were you able to spot any CGI enhancements in the fight scenes?
- Were you able to spot any wire gags?
- Were you able to spot the stunt doubles (if any)? If so, how did you notice them? Did you see their faces or could you tell because they moved differently?
- Was there anything with the fight scenes that you would change to make them more effective? If so, what would you have done differently?

Addressing these questions will help you develop an eye and a sense for fights by applying the principles shown in this book. You can choose to do this alone or with some of your friends who saw the movie with you—you can have a healthy debate with each question (but please, not during the film!). Answering these questions will surely spawn more questions, which is part of the growing process in developing an eye for seeing action.

Know Your Action Film History and the Contributors

I truly believe that if you do not know where you came from, you do not know where you are going. Knowing the people who have preceded you and their accomplishments is instrumental because you don't want to spend too much effort reinventing the wheel.

Here is a brief list of some filmmakers who work in the action genre and into whose filmography you should look deeper:

- Bob Anderson
- Bobby Bass
- James Cameron
- Jackie Chan
- Chang Cheh
- Ching Siu-Tung
- Charlie Chaplin
- Roger Corman
- Clint Eastwood
- Douglas Fairbanks
- John Ford
- King Hu
- Sammo Hung
- Buster Keaton
- Tsui Hark
- William Hobbs
- Shintarô Katsu
- Akira Kurosawa
- Bruce Lee
- Lau Kar Leung
- Sergio Leone
- Steve McQueen
- John McTiernan
- Kenji Misumi
- Sam Peckinpah
- Arnold Schwarzenegger
- Don Seigel
- Mack Sennett
- Steven Spielberg
- Sylvester Stallone
- John Sturges
- Paul Verhoeven
- Tomisaburo Wakayama
- John Wayne
- John Woo
- Cory Yuen Kwai
- Ng See-Yuen
- Yuen Woo-Ping

Start looking at the great cinematographers. Look at the works of Dean Cundey, James Wong Howe, John Alonzo, Lázló Kovács, Vilmos Zsigmond, Peter Pau, and Arthur Wong.

Also, look at the work of dance choreographers such as Gene Kelly, Michael Peters, Debbie Allen, Bob Fosse, Jerome Robbins, Fred Astaire, and Ginger Rogers. Analyze their non-verbal relationships when in movement, and look at film composition and camera movement. The *That's Entertainment* trilogy, *West Side Story*, *Singin' in the Rain*, and the documentary *Gene Kelly: Anatomy of a Dancer* are great places to start understanding movement in relation to the camera.

Learn to follow stunt coordinators and fight choreographers and their work. When watching U.S. films, stay for the end credits and look for the names of the stunt coordinator and the stuntmen on the film. It is much more difficult to spot the work of a U.S. stunt coordinator because films are more of a directors' medium in America, as opposed to Hong Kong/China, where the fight director is able to leave his creative mark on a film. As a result, it might be more difficult to pick out the stunt coordinator's style. A few suggestions are Terry Leonard, Vic Armstrong, and Jeff Imada. Their work is not as visible as their Hong Kong counterparts' work, but they are an integral part of the films. Go to the Internet Movie Database (www.imdb.com) online to get a scope of all their work. Remember that often a list is not complete because this is a user-supported website.

Don't forget that fight scenes are not limited to the action genre alone. There are some films that have fight scenes but are not heavily action-oriented. Examples are films such as *Once Were Warriors*, *Top Secret*, *Blazing Saddles*, *West Side Story*, *Fatal Attraction*, and *The Nightmare on Elm Street* series, to name a few.

Learn to Be Film Literate

The more knowledgeable you are about film, the more solid your foundation will be to create better action scenes. Being knowledgeable about film also helps you to be on the same page as other filmmakers on the set. Sometimes a director might not know what he wants, but he might tell you, "I'm trying to get the same mood here for the fight as in *Entrails of Vengeance*, when the black belt Ninja hooker finally walks into the brothel and confronts her peg-legged pimp for the final fight scene."

It is really helpful to watch a lot of movies and know who the contributors in the film industry are. Try to watch all types of films and be as well rounded in your knowledge as you can. This is especially true if you want to attempt something new and/or something that has never been done before because you have to know where you came from before you know where you are going.

Being film literate is an ongoing process throughout your career and is something you will not get in three easy lessons. The most obvious method is to simply watch and study a lot of films. I also suggest you get a book on the basics of world film history and, after getting a general understanding of the overall history of film, choose different eras to start studying more in depth. Of course there will be certain contributors and eras you won't like as much as others, so it is always best to first go with a time period, filmmaker, or genre in which you are interested. From there, start to expand and explore what preceded or followed it, or jump around to another genre or time that interests you. The more film literate you are, the bigger your palette will be because you are taking the experiences of filmmakers before you and using them to your advantage so you don't have to reinvent the wheel. Eventually, you should be able to tell which decade a film was made just by looking at the way the film was shot and by the film stock on which it was shot.

Know Whether the Film Was Made for You

When watching films that are from an older time period or another country, you might not initially grasp the message or understand why audiences responded so strongly. You might not understand the underlying feelings the filmmakers were trying to express because you were not a part of that culture and/or time period.

Also, there will be films that might not be morally or culturally acceptable in your region or country. A great example is Kinji Fukasaki's gritty Yakuza film, *Battles Without Honor and Humanity.* The opening title sequence shows the mushroom cloud from the atomic bomb on Hiroshima followed by the devastation of the city, and the film starts with a group of American G.I.s raping a Japanese woman, showing how people fought to survive after WWII and the birth of the modern-day Yakuza society. This would be uncomfortable for many Americans to see and accept because they would have to watch themselves in a bad-guy role. It is not something the American masses would probably flock to see. Nonetheless, it's still a great film that you should watch. Each country has its own point of view regarding world events. If you visit high schools in different countries, you will find that each country has its own version of world history. Who is right and who is wrong? It's all up to interpretation. As an artist, try to be open and see how different countries view life and events, especially with a filmmaker's expression on film.

Another example is the Korean action film, *Shiri.* When looking at it from an outsider's point of view, the film seems like your typical spy thriller and love story that deals with the reunification of North and South Korea. But if you were not up to date on Asian history and current events, you would probably think this was a formulaic "by the numbers" movie. You might think the filmmakers were imitating one or more of your typical Hollywood summer action films. But if you look beyond that and consider your knowledge of the general consciousness of the Korean population, you will notice that the film tugs on the general thoughts and emotions of the North and South Korean population. The film actually ended up breaking the Korean box-office record set by *Titanic.*

When you watch older films, know that they might appear dated in fashion, language, style, editing, camera angles, and technique. Understand the time and era when the film was shot and know that certain styles and techniques were not available at the time. Watching Jean-Luc Godard's 1960 classic *Breathless* with your eyes and mind today, you might feel that it is no big deal because, today, everyone is doing a handheld camera style of filmmaking and jump-cut editing. That style is seen everywhere, including in music videos and commercials. But Godard was the first to do this effectively, and that's one of the many reasons why this film is so unique and special.

Think about how people reacted when *The Great Train Robbery* first came out in 1903. This was a time when film was first introduced to the public. At the end of the film, the gunman shoots at the camera. Not frightening at all, right? But think about when it was first shown to audiences who did not know what film was. At that time, audiences were diving for cover at that scene.

Certain films might have been made because specific events were happening in real life; these films show the sign of the times. All these things I've discussed must be put into consideration before you harshly judge a film.

Pacing is another issue. Watching *A Touch of Zen* (1969) requires a little more patience than watching your typical Hong Kong action film today, due to its slower pacing. This applies to many different types of films from the past. The pacing on films has, in general, increased drastically over the decades. This is a good thing, a bad thing, or something between, depending on how you look at it. But try not to be in ADD mode when watching an epic or an older film; get into the pace of the film. Take it in as if you were drinking fine wine as opposed to guzzling ripple.

If you are watching a film from another country or time period, it would help you to try and learn a little about the country of the film's origin and whether the film has any significance to the people of that country. Try not to always watch a movie by coming from an American-centric and/or a present-time point of view. If the film is old, think about how the audience responded to it at the time and whether the connection would still work today. By doing this, you will begin to develop a worldview of human thought. Remember, you are not only being entertained, you are also learning world consciousness. We take into our psyche the things we experience in life, and as artists they end up being a part of our expression. Culture, morals, religious beliefs, and personal fears sometimes alter the experiences we encounter in life to make us different. But try to look beyond that for the human experience that is common to everyone. This is why films are universal.

Another reason why you are doing this is to learn about the powerful psychological connection between audiences and film. Remember, film is a series of celluloid images shot in sequence and projected onto a large screen. Ask yourself, how is cinema able to capture the imagination and psyche of people from all over the world?

Too Much Information to Handle?

I'm sure that's what you're thinking right now: "Man, that's just too much to think about. I can't do all that at the same time. That's impossible." With all the information you have read in this book, you will definitely see fight choreography differently than you did previously because you are shifting from the perspective of a consumer to the perspective of a creator…or at the very least, you are becoming a very aware consumer. Does this mean that you cannot still enjoy watching films? Of course not, but you will be much more discerning about how you see fight scenes from now on. But is it still possible to enjoy a movie while critiquing it at the same time? Yes.

The key to applying all the things to look for in a fight while still enjoying the film is to watch a film with both sides of your brain. If you can't do this, you should observe the audience's reactions while the movie is playing. How did the filmmakers get the audience to react this way? Experience the emotions of the movie with the right side of your brain (your creative and emotional side) while analyzing and gathering information with the left side of your brain (your logical and rational side). It will take some practice, but it is very necessary and rewarding when you are able to do it. And the more you do it, the better you will be at it.

Another method is to watch a film twice. One time as an analytical student, paying attention to techniques, styles, pacing, camera work, mistakes, etc, and the other time as a casual observer where you mentally switch off the analytical side of your brain and merely allow yourself to be entertained. Which one you do first is up to you.

Test Yourself

Are you able to identify an action sequence that was choreographed by Yuen Woo-Ping as opposed to one choreographed by Sammo Hung or Ching Siu-Tung without looking at the credits or finding out the answer beforehand? If you can, then describe to yourself what you see and feel are the differences between that choreographer and others. If you can't do that, ask yourself the following questions:

- What makes this choreographer special and sets him apart from other fight choreographers?
- What are his strengths?
- What are his weaknesses?
- Does he have a preferred genre in which he excels?
- Does he have any signature or trademark moves, stances, expressions, camera angles, and/or edits?

- What kinds of techniques does he prefer to use over others?
- How does he tell his non-verbal stories?
- What camera angles does he prefer for certain types of action?
- Are his editing pace and rhythm different?

Here's a test. In the movie *Kung Fu Hustle*, Sammo Hung shot and choreographed a fight scene before he was taken ill and was replaced by Yuen Woo-Ping. Can you tell the Sammo Hung fight scene from Woo-Ping's without using any outside resources—instead relying on your own eyes and senses?

One of the reasons why I mainly name Hong Kong fight choreographers is because they have more control of the camera angles and editing of their action as opposed to fight choreographers in the U.S. In Hong Kong, different fight choreographers are much easier to distinguish. So how do you develop an eye for differences and preferences? Watch enough of their movies back to back and often enough that you will begin to notice their preferences, styles, and approaches.

Daydream about Fight Scenes

No matter where you go during your everyday travels, think about how a fight scene would play out at that location. This exercises your mind and gets it into thinking about fight scenes more naturally. The more you do this, the easier it gets. Try to think of different scenarios, styles of fighting, and levels of practicality. Try to be as detailed as possible about the situation and the fight. Jackie Chan came up with the wind tunnel fight scene in *Armour of God II* (aka *Operation Condor* in the U.S.) while visiting the Mitsubishi car plant in Japan. "The idea was in my mind for a long time. I'm the image point man [spokesman] for Mitsubishi. I visited the Mitsubishi factory and I saw the wind tunnel. I see everything in my mind and thought, 'Ahh, that is going to be a good fighting scene!'" exclaims Jackie.

Design a Fight Scene Every Day

Training your mind to create action is the next step. Think up a fight scene each night before you go to sleep. Give yourself different scenarios, types of fighting genres, fighters' motivations, and number of fighters involved each time you do it. Use different ways of expressing yourself with a fight scene. Here are several ways to plan out your actions:

- **Illustrated storyboards.** Your storyboards do not have to look like works of art. All that matters is that you get the point across to others so they can understand what will happen in the fight.

- **Action figures.** This is a great way to experiment and visualize how the fight will appear. Because you are working on a three-dimensional form, you can experiment and visualize which angles will look the most effective. If you want to get creative, use a camera to record the moves as if it was the exact scene. For a great example of this, get the DVD for *Shanghai Noon* and watch the "videomatic" of a scene that did not make it on film. This videomatic is accessed when you play the quiz "Roy's Revenge" in the "Shanghai Surprise" section in the DVD's bonus material.
- **In screenplay form.** When writing your script, describe the initial emotional cause for the fight, the techniques thrown, the emotional responses, the beats, the cause and effect for each technique, and the ending emotion for the fight. Essentially, you should describe the three acts of the fight. Include dialogue when necessary.

Come up with a combination of these methods or your own way of mapping out a fight scene. The key with any of these methods is to convey your action scenes as simply and as quickly as possible. Like a muscle, your creative thinking skills need to be trained. Make your plan functional and practical, as well as easy to read and understand, and don't focus on making it a work of art. If you get good at it, try to create three variations of the same theme. When you get used to that, give yourself some more pressure and put yourself on a time limit. If you get stuck, pick a film and redo a fight scene from that movie the way you feel it should be done.

To get your creative juices going, look around anywhere and everywhere you go to figure out what places would make great fight scene locations. What everyday objects would make interesting weapons to fight with or obstacles to fight around? Think of a story and how the fight would revolve around the weapon and/or obstacle.

Learn, Observe, and Study Human Psychology

You have to understand the human psyche because then you will understand what makes a person fight or be violent. Try going to a bar and pick a spot where you can observe everything that's happening. It's best if you don't order alcohol so you can have a sober eye as you watch and study how others interact. If you've got the experience and the guts, get work as a bouncer in a club to see how you can prevent a fight from actually happening. You will soon notice that people often do not say what they really mean and are not usually direct in their approach to things. You will also notice that at times people's body language will not match what they are saying. Ask yourself, "How does that translate into a fight?"

Learn How the Human Body Moves and Works

Learn how the human body works and what its limitations are. How does gravity affect the human body when a person jumps? What are the limitations to the things a human body can do? Learning this will help you have a sense of how to make wire gags more realistic and natural. Watch and observe the human body in other physical disciplines, such as different types of dance and all sports. If you are able to, partake in as many of them as you can.

It is also a good idea to study human anatomy so that when your director requests a "solar plexus" punch, you'll aim for the right place, or when he wants the villain's knife held against the hostage's jugular, you'll know whether that vein is on the left or the right side of the neck.

Compare and Contrast

If you do not feel you have developed an eye for action just yet, one of the best things to do is to compare a good film to a bad one, watching them back to back. When doing so, try the best you can to keep the films in the same genre at first. When doing this exercise, you will notice story, character development, acting, and production-value issues, as well as quality of action. After you develop an eye for what's wrong, then mix and match genres.

There are many different ways to compare and contrast. Here are some recommendations to get you started:

- Watch a series of films by the same choreographer. This way you can start to get a feel for each choreographer's rhythm, choice of technique, emotion, and flow. Also try to mix and match genres by the same choreographer so you can understand the sensibilities of the choreographer on a deeper level. A good example is watching Woo-Ping's period piece *Iron Monkey* or *Once Upon a Time in China II* against his modern-day action films, such as *Tiger Cage 1–3* or *The Red Wolf.*
- After getting a good understanding and feel for each choreographer, mix and match choreographers' work so you can begin to see the differences, preferences, strengths, and weaknesses for each one.
- Compare and contrast action films of different action genres. This way you can get a feel for the parameters each genre has (with limitations to the story) to work with.
- Compare good and bad within each genre. This way you can appreciate what the choreographer has done, and it will be easier to see what the good artist is doing as opposed to the one in the bad film.

- Watch originals versus imitators. Watch a Bruce Lee movie, and then watch a Bruce Li (impersonator) movie. Remember, Bruce Lee only completed four movies in his adult life. He made a series of films as a kid and teenager, but none of them had any stylized martial arts fights that he was later known for. Make notes about what you see, feel, and notice after comparing the two. You can also do this with the Indiana Jones and James Bond films by watching the originals and then following them up with films in the same style and genre.
- Watch the same movie dubbed and in its original language with subtitles.

In order to start noticing the differences mentioned in the previous list, here are a few places to begin:

- What are the differences between a spaghetti western and a U.S.-made western made at the same time? What are the differences in their sensibilities? How do the gunfights differ?
- What were the differences in the tempo, mood, and angles of fight scenes between the first *Matrix* and the two sequels?
- What elements made the action scenes in the *Indiana Jones* trilogy memorable, exciting, and exceptional compared to the many copycat films that have followed?
- Watch the efforts of foreign talent on their home turf and then compare them to their efforts in the U.S. Look for quality of fight choreography with regard to camera angles, editing, pace, rhythm, as well as the impact and believability of strikes and falls. Also look for how they come across with story and character presence. For example:
    - For Jackie Chan, watch *Drunken Master II* or *Jackie Chan's Police Story* and then *Battle Creek Brawl* or *Rush Hour.*
    - For Jet Li, watch *Fist of Legend* or *My Father Is a Hero* and then *Romeo Must Die* or *Lethal Weapon 4.*
    - For Yuen Woo-Ping, watch *Iron Monkey* or *The Tai-Chi Master* and then *The Matrix Reloaded* or *Kill Bill: Vol. 1* or *2.*
    - For Toshirô Mifune, watch *The Seven Samurai, Yojimbo,* or *Sanjuro* and then watch *Red Sun* or *Shogun.*
    - For Chow Yun-Fat, watch *The Killer* or *A Better Tomorrow* and then watch *The Replacement Killers* or *The Corruptor.*

- How about remakes? Compare different remakes of *Cyrano de Bergerac* (Miguel Ferrer's versus Gérard Depardieu's), *The Count of Monte Cristo*, and *The Three Musketeers* and *The Four Musketeers.* Compare *La Femme Nikita* (France) with *Point of No Return* (U.S.), *Black Cat* (Hong Kong), and the TV show *La Femme Nikita.*
- Compare and contrast action films with women in the lead roles on TV and in film.
- Think about the difference in the quality of story and action sequences for an action film that goes straight to video as opposed to a film of the same genre that gets a theatrical release.
- Consider the differences in action and story with women in action films that go straight to video as opposed to *La Femme Nikita* (the movie), *The Long Kiss Goodnight*, *Buffy the Vampire Slayer* (TV), and *Alias.* Watch a good woman's action film against a sensationalistic one in which the sex, gore, and violence are played up to hide the almost nonexistent story.
- Think about the similarities and differences between *Ong-Bak* and any other kickboxing film out there.

Learn and Hear about the Creative Process

Another way of developing an eye is by hearing filmmakers talk about their process. Often hearing these filmmakers talk makes the filmmaking experience less daunting. This section describes some of the places that have helped me with my growth as an artist in the film industry because I've had a chance to ask my own questions of the sources themselves. Usually stunt coordinators and stunt players don't partake in Q&A, but it is still good to hear what the director's, actor's, and writer's thoughts were about the action.

And here's a word of advice: Ask educated questions when you meet these people. Don't ask simple filmmaking questions that can be answered in a basic filmmaking 101 book or geeky fan questions. I was at a comic-book convention where Jackie Chan was appearing to promote one of his upcoming films, and during the public Q&A, a geeky fan boy asked him the question, "If you were locked in a room with Bruce Lee and Jet Li and you had to fight to the death, who would win?" The response from the crowd was deafening as the collective audience groaned and booed at the person asking the question, while making Chan feel uncomfortable. Save the geek questions and theories for the Internet.

Another time, I was at a screening of *Sympathy for Mr. Vengeance*, and after the screening, the director (Chan-Wook Park) was there to field questions from the audience. An audience member asked him this question: "I've only seen a couple of movies from Korea and my question is, are all films from your country this depressing?" Again, the audience made a collective groan at the uneducated and stupid question.

I've seen this happen almost every time I've attended these Q&A sessions. There is a difference between giving an artist a challenging question and giving him a stupid one. Hopefully, you have the intelligence and common sense to know the difference. If you are not sure, then it's best to keep quiet and let someone else ask the questions. It really helps to do your homework before you go see the person—know his work and his contributions to the industry. Challenge him in a positive way by asking him well thought-out questions about his work that have not already been asked. The more educated you are when asking your questions, the better experience it will be for both you and the person you are meeting.

Here are some of the places where you might have the chance to ask questions of such industry people, as well as a few other resources where you might get some answers to your questions, albeit not in person:

- **Special screenings.** There are times when you will get a chance to go to a screening of a film (old or new) and you will get to talk with the people involved in the film.
- **Book and DVD signings.** This is another great place to meet filmmakers up close and personal. You also get a signed book by someone who is in a place you want to be eventually.
- **Shows and conventions.** There are many specialized shows and conventions to meet people in the industry. They might be signing autographs or just fans themselves. Comic book and movie memorabilia conventions are also good places to get hard-to-find DVDs, videos, and laserdiscs that you might not be able to find in your local area.
- **Filmmaking classes and seminars.** This is up for debate. Do filmmaking classes destroy the creativity of the artist by enforcing hard rules on students to turn out "cookie cutter" filmmakers? Or do the classes empower students by giving them the tools needed in order to be successful? I feel it is up to each individual to make the decision of what he feels he needs in order to be successful in the film industry. Of course, there are teachers and schools that are better than others, but going to film school does not necessarily guarantee you a job after you graduate. It is up to each individual to look at the school and the faculty where they wish to enroll and decide whether the relationship is feasible and beneficial for him.

- **DVD audio commentaries and special features.** Listening to an audio commentary from a filmmaker while the film is rolling is another way of continuing your education. Doing an audio commentary is an art in itself. There are some who are good at it and some who aren't. One of the most inspirational filmmaker commentaries I have come across is director Robert Rodriguez's commentary on *El Mariachi*, in which he describes shot for shot how he made his film. Special features on DVD can be fluff pieces, extremely detailed, or somewhere in between. Sometimes the filmmakers will show how they did a certain stunt for the film. I have found many such commentaries to be anywhere from poor to above average. This is because too many filmmakers simply don't understand action on a deeper level. Many of these special features still dwell on what is cool instead of the actual process. I feel the process deserves more attention than what is currently given.
- **Books.** There are many books on filmmaking that you can read to get a better understanding of the process and what is needed so you can express your action on film or video. I recommend you get books on screenwriting, directing, shooting with a camera, lighting, sound, and editing (see Chapter 12 for a list of suggestions). These are the tools you will need to have your action come across effectively when you are experimenting on your own films. Don't be intimidated; you might feel there is a lot to take in at first. Balance it out between reading and experimenting on your camera.

Go to the Creative Source

Pick a filmmaker who you admire, find out who his influences are, then look at their films and learn about them. For example, John Woo cites Jean-Pierre Melville and Sam Peckinpah as two of his influences. Jackie Chan always talks about Buster Keaton, Harold Lloyd, Gene Kelly, and Fred Astaire as his influences. Kurosawa cites John Ford as a director he has always respected. Quentin Tarantino has a virtual film encyclopedia in his mind that was developed from watching grindhouse films as a child, from Kung Fu movies to spaghetti westerns to blaxploitation, and so on. Watch some of their films and see how these filmmakers infuse another filmmaker's influence into their films. By doing this, you will see what the filmmakers have extracted from their influences and germinated to make their own art. Some might be really obvious and some might be subtle. Do this yourself with how you put together your action sequences. By doing so, you will learn that the creative process is not daunting, overwhelming, or completely impossible.

Attend Live Sporting Events in Which Physical Contact or Body Rhythm Is Involved

This is where art imitates life. You can find inspiration and ideas while watching a live sporting event. You can learn a lot from a flashy fighter who showboats, such as Roy Jones, Jr., or a no-nonsense "let's get to business" fighter, such as Mike Tyson. Also try to go and watch how a professional wrestler gets the audience involved in his matches. This is not easily seen on television; you are somewhat removed from the energy that is being created by the athletes because the camera chooses your perspective. As you would in a movie theater, sit farther back to observe the audience and their connection to the athletes. This is especially entertaining when watching a wrestling match. Think about what makes a person come to see the event. There is a strong connection between the athlete and the audience.

Watch other sports in which light to heavy contact is involved, such as basketball, football, rugby, arena football, soccer, Australian football, UFC, K-1, pride fighting, karate tournaments, and so on. There are more obscure sports you might want to look into, such as sepak takraw, a popular game in Asia that combines elements of soccer with volleyball. The team has to get a rattan ball over the net to fall in bounds on the opponent's side. The players cannot use their hands, but they can use their head, body, and legs. They usually serve the ball by kicking it over the net. They have a lot of authority, accuracy, and power in their kicks. Another little-known sport is the French urban art of Parkour. The art has been shown in the movies *Yamakasi*, *District 13*, and *Casino Royale*, as well as numerous commercials.

Watch Japanese Kabuki, Chinese Opera, and Filipino Singkil stick dances. Go to watch different types of dance movement—ballet, jazz, hip hop, tap, Irish, ballroom, and so on. Study their grace and flow and how it varies and is similar for each discipline. Find out why it varies. Watch how the dancers move together and how they tell a story with movements. Also, study the connection between the performers and the audience.

By watching these events you are definitely going to the source for inspiration. Think about how you can apply what you just saw to one of your action scenes. What alterations would you have to make if you had to choreograph an action sequence using that sport? This is definitely where art imitates life.

Learn Several Different Styles of Martial Arts

It is very important to know several different styles of martial arts. You must have a solid understanding of the techniques you are going to use on film. Try to learn a variety of different systems that are not similar or in the same family. For example, learn a long-distance kicking style such as Tae Kwon Do and then an in-close grappling style, such as Brazilian Jiu-Jitsu.

You'll soon learn that there is no such thing as the "ultimate" or "deadliest" style out there. Each style or system has a flaw or weakness to it. If an instructor tells you otherwise, run. Run fast and far because the instructor's ego is clouding what the actual martial art is about. Sure, on a rudimentary level it's about beating an opponent, but there's more to it than that. You will have your own experience regarding what you know works as opposed to what you *think* will work. Compete in a tournament and get the feeling of what it's like to face someone who does not care about you. If there are not many different schools in your area, another way of getting exposure to other arts is by taking seminars from martial artists who come by the area. Sometimes you might have to do a little traveling to train with these people. Legendary martial artists such as Dan Inosanto travel to cities all over the world almost every weekend to teach their seminars.

There is a certain amount of validity to getting a good foundation before you are exposed to other arts. Also, do not get involved in studio politics. This means catering to an instructor's ego or the school's inflated view of their prowess. There is no such thing as an ultimate school, style, or system. If an instructor tells you the system he is teaching is unbeatable, you should put on your shoes and walk away, far away. Nowadays, it's not the system that you should look for; the quality of instruction goes a longer way with the student. And you should also realize that, just because someone is a great martial artist, that does not mean he is a great instructor. How does the instructor relate to the class? Is he able to communicate his ideas to the students clearly? Does he have too big of an ego? Does he effectively show off his skills to the students in class or does he display them with arrogance? Can he get the point across to the students with words or does he have to constantly prove his own skills to get his point across? Is the teacher able to discuss the style's theories and finer points in an almost scholarly or intellectual manner?

The reason I bring this up is that there needs to be a balance with a good instructor. A certain level of trust needs to be established between student and instructor in order for the student to excel and become a better martial artist and person than when he first started taking classes. An instructor has to be a good role model to his students. He must be able to relate to each student's issues and individual needs when necessary, and he must be able to motivate the students physically as well as mentally.

Film Your Own Fights

After all the theory I've told you about in this book, the most important part is getting out there and filming fight scenes yourself. You can sit in a coffee shop and talk smack about the stunt coordinator for the last big action film he botched, but that's all talk. Talk is good, but having a working knowledge is the next logical progression to your growth as a fight choreographer. Do you think Yuen Woo-Ping and Jeff Imada got to where they are by merely studying, critiquing, and talking about people's work?

Get a cheap digital camera and start filming your own fight scenes. This is the only way you can develop and hone your skills and instincts as a fight choreographer—by doing it and doing it and doing it and doing it....

There are a lot of home editing programs out there for the PC and Mac. After getting good with some of the consumer home editing programs, you will probably notice the limitations of such systems and you will probably have to upgrade to a more professional editing system, such as Adobe Premiere Pro, Avid, or Final Cut for the Mac.

Regardless of which editing program you choose, there are some things to keep in mind when choreographing your own fights:

- Apply your storyboards, scripts, or videomatics that you designed and shoot them.
- Anyone can put together a series of moves that looks cool and exciting. But can you put together a fight scene that tells an effective non-verbal story that an unbiased viewer can understand? This is what separates the men from the boys.
- Don't be afraid to make mistakes. Consider this a major part of your education as you try to find out what works and what does not.
- Do not fall unconditionally in love with your own work. This is a crippling disease that newbies and even some professionals catch. Remember that you can't grow and develop as an artist if you think you are already great.
- Make your mistakes while experimenting with your own camera, not while working on a set. Thousands of dollars are lost each minute on a production. Don't be the reason a set is losing money.
- Learn to trust your instincts.
- Have fun while doing this.
- *Most importantly,* keep it safe for all people involved while making the fights *look* dangerous.

Learn to Take Criticism

Criticism is one of the hardest things to learn to accept, especially if you've labored over a project for months, only to have your spouse, loved one, or best friend have a lukewarm expression on his or her face after viewing the fight scene. Or even worse, you get a strong reaction such as, "That sucks!" The sting of that comment can last a lifetime and can hinder your expression as an artist if you don't know how to handle it. The most important thing is to not take it personally. I know this is very hard to do. But it is something you will have to learn to do in order to grow as an artist and as a fight choreographer. Any type of art (whether it be fine art or a commercial medium such as film or TV) is a very subjective medium, and everyone has an opinion on it. You have to develop a strong hide to survive, yet know when to be open to invite critiques and opinions in order to grow.

When receiving criticism from someone who struggles to find the right way to describe his thoughts, try to help him by being inquisitive yet open and light, without giving him the third degree. Because fight scenes show conflict in a physical and non-verbal manner, they affect audiences on a deeper emotional and instinctual level, and people might have a hard time explaining their reactions. I remember seeing *Once Were Warriors* and walking out of the theater with my knees shaking. I had to sit down and do some introspection to recall my thoughts and emotions throughout the film and to determine why it affected me so deeply.

There are people who might not be able to express themselves constructively and who just tell you that they did not like your film. The eventual goal of an artist is to take the criticism and filter the points that will make him a better artist. It's easy to choose a person who adores you, who has some sort of an emotional investment in you, who won't want to hurt your feelings because he or she cares about you, and who gives you a false sense of encouragement and builds up your ego. That might make you feel good about yourself, but it isn't going to make you a stronger or more mature artist and further you in the development process.

It is always best to seek out criticism from filmmakers and especially fight choreographers who are more experienced than you and who can give constructive criticism on how you can improve your work. Getting critiques from others who are more experienced than you will help you see things that you might not have seen or realized before.

You also have to accept the fact that not everybody is going to like, accept, embrace, or even appreciate your work. That comes with the territory of being an artist. When accepting critiques and criticism—negative, positive, and anywhere in between—the artist/creator should be open to what the person has to say. However, don't feel you have to stand there and take someone berating your work with the agenda of his own personal gain, stepping on you in order to divert the attention and have it focused on his selfish gain. When that starts to happen, simply thank them and walk away.

It is important not to defend your work, but rather to let it speak for itself. Your work has to have legs and be able to stand on its own. You cannot be at every screening to explain your actions. And if you feel like you have to do so, then you're not connecting with the audience and you're missing critical steps when leading your audience to where you want them to go. Defend your past mistakes by improving on them on your next efforts, rather than constantly explaining or dwelling on them.

I remember once giving a critique of a choreographer's fight scene when he asked for my opinion. I looked at it and gave him my honest opinion. I tried to be as positive and constructive as possible with my comments, giving him what I felt could help him along his way to getting future work if he could enhance his skills and presentation. In response, I got a sour-looking scowl because I was not in agreement with the choreographer's vision. The lesson to learn from this encounter is that when people ask you a question or for a critique, they usually are asking for one of two things from you—an agreement or an opinion. When someone asks for your opinion, but his underlying agenda is really to get an agreement, then unfortunately that person's insecure, sensitive (or perhaps over-inflated) ego is getting in his way of his growth as an artist. If an artist has healthy self-confidence mixed with an appropriate amount of humility, he knows it is not all about him and he is able to graciously accept all types of criticism and opinions, knowing that not everyone is going to like what he does.

If you are getting critiques that are generally consistent with other opinions, you should take note of them because they are a good indicator of the general consensus of how people are interpreting your work.

Getting great reviews and comments about your work can be very gratifying and well deserved after all the hard work you have done. But if your main agenda is seeking outside acceptance for your work, you will be clouding your vision by giving the audience what you feel they want, just to get that outer acceptance. There has to be a middle ground. Someone who is codependent on audience adulation is essentially an "acceptance whore." This type of person constantly seeks acceptance from others and is temperamental or moody when he does not get that acceptance or is not understood. To remedy this, it is important to accept yourself and where you truly stand in your life at this moment, along with your growth and progression from where you have come as an artist. Know that there is always more to learn and absorb no matter what level you are at, and there is always room to keep growing and evolving.

It is also important to remember that you are orchestrating "controlled violence" that functions as an interpretation of a narrative—the script, the story, and the end result that form the movie. People have different reactions to what they see as violence and action because of their past experiences, cultural upbringing, and religious or spiritual beliefs. Some will see what you do as glorifying the act of violence, and some will see what you do as an exhilarating rollercoaster ride.

Others will understand that you are choreographing non-verbal dialogue between characters. No matter what, you are going to get varied responses and interpretations about what you have done.

By the way, if you have any negative critiques or opinions on this book, you're wrong...so keep it to yourself! Just kidding.

Starting a Video Reference Library

It is important for a fight choreographer to have a DVD library because you have to see what is out there and you need to study the work of other choreographers. There are several reasons to have a DVD library, including the following:

- To continue your education in film literacy by listening to the filmmakers' audio commentary and bonus features
- To view different versions of films (such as director's cuts) that were not released theatrically
- To break down a film and/or action scene when necessary
- To stay current and know about action films and new styles and trends out there from all over the world
- To see a movie that might not have been released theatrically in your area
- To have a copy of certain titles that are no longer in print and/or are not available at your video store
- To use as an emotional and visual shorthand to get your idea across to producers or directors when preplanning or to show to actors and stunt players to show them the idea for a certain fight scene that you want to do.
- To have a lot of inspirational material handy. "Writer's block" (or the filmmaker's variation thereof) can often be cured by watching a few of your favorite movies or fight scenes. Doing this should help pump you up and rejuvenate your creative juices.
- To amaze and impress friends with your incredible DVD library

A Filmmaker's Artistic Integrity

Studios cut and edit films many times in order to appeal to a wider audience, to avoid offending certain groups, and/or to get more showings if the film is too long. Unfortunately, the filmmaker's artistic vision usually suffers. This constant struggle between art and commerce can get to be a vicious cycle. As a result, story, character development, and action get truncated to something other than what was originally planned. Often, this leaves the audience scratching their heads, wondering what the hell they just saw.

However, on DVD, the filmmaker has a second chance to appeal to the audience with the director's cut of the film. Often action scenes are cut or trimmed for various reasons. A good example of cutting down the effectiveness of a fight scene from a movie is in Corey Yuen's *The Transporter*, where they show the fight scene uncut in the bonus features on the DVD. Another example is seen in the director's cut DVD of *Daredevil*—the barroom fight is much clearer and easier to follow than what we saw in the theaters.

As a creative filmmaker, do your best to see a film the way the filmmakers intended it. This includes the correct aspect ratio at which the film was shot. Do your best to see a video or DVD in letterbox or widescreen format because if the image is cropped to fit your screen, you are missing from 1/4 to 2/3 of the image on the screen, where some important action might be taking place. This gets annoying and distracting when you are watching a fight scene because if the fight scene is shot wide (as in most Hong Kong action scenes), you will not fully appreciate the choreography.

Also, be aware of editing and censorship of films when you buy DVDs. Certain studios will buy the rights to a film and make drastic cuts to it. Hopefully they will include both versions of the film (cut and uncut) so the viewer can decide what he wants to see.

Video Stores

If you are heavily relying on video stores for your education on film, make sure their library of titles is varied and deep. Find a video store that has a variety of different, obscure, foreign, and out-of-print movies you've never heard of, as well as hard-to-find titles. Try to avoid going to the video store that only caters to the "casual" video renter/buyer and has only the standard collection and not anything in depth as far as classic, cult, and foreign films. Unfortunately, this is what you get with most video store chains. The way you can tell whether this is the case is that these sections hardly ever grow. Instead of expanding their foreign or obscure film library, they have 20 copies of the latest hit film and make room for the mainstream films that are coming out.

Quentin Tarantino was working at a video store and got very film literate because he saw almost every film there. If you have seen 80 percent of the films at your video store, it's time to move on. Find a video store that completely overwhelms you with the variety of titles they have in stock. When I say stock, it's not 20 copies of the latest hit that you'll forget about in a couple weeks.

All DVDs Are Not the Same

The quality of DVDs overall has been gradually improving over the ones first released in 1997. Quality is always suspect no matter what format of home video it is, even DVD. This all depends on what the creators used as a master resource in making the DVD. I have seen many DVDs for which they have used a VHS tape of the movie as the master source to make the DVD copy. The result is a below-average to poor picture quality on the DVD. It pays to read technical reviews of DVDs before you buy them.

Do not assume extra features, such as interviews or audio commentary on videotape or laserdisc, will be included in the DVD. The VHS copy of *The Crow* has the last interview with Brandon Lee, but the interview is missing on the special edition DVD in the U.S. (However, it is available on the Region 2 DVD.) John Woo's audio commentary for *Hard-Boiled* and *The Killer* for the Criterion and then for Fox Lorber has two different commentaries. DVDs from region to region will also vary in terms of extras features and film content because of varying views on censorship. For example, on *Kill Bill: Vol. 1*, the black-and-white fight sequence shown in the U.S. is in color on the Japanese DVD, along with other slight changes.

Do Not Limit Yourself to Viewing Only DVDs

Don't be too much of an elitist and think that if it is not on DVD, then it's not worth seeing. There are many titles that have not made (and probably will not make) the jump to DVD for one reason or another (usually some kind of ownership, legal, or copyright issue). Also, different versions were made in different video formats that were never transferred over to DVD. So don't throw away that VCR and do dust off that laserdisc player (if you've still got one).

Movies on VCD are another cheap way to expand your library without having to spend too much money. VCDs are extremely popular in Asia. They are playable on some DVD players and they are usually cheaper than DVDs, but they do not have any special features and the film is split onto two discs. If you've got the money, another way to put yourself more in debt is to buy and collect 16mm and 35mm prints of films, because there have been films that were never on any type of home video format.

Why Look for Imported DVDs?

There are several reasons to hunt for imported DVDs. A lot of the U.S. distributors don't think too highly of action films, let alone martial arts films. However, some are starting to wise up with some of the newer releases. Nevertheless, imported DVDs are your best bet for several reasons:

- **Unavailability of titles.** There are a lot of movies that won't be distributed in the U.S. anytime soon. A great example is the movie *Battle Royale*. Kinji Fukusaku's last film before he passed away will probably never see the light of day here due to teen violence, rights issues with the studios, MPAA ratings, and so on. Just because a film is not available here, that does not mean it is not worth seeing. More often than not, it has to do with money and politics more than art, theme, and subject matter. Some distributors will just hold onto a film title and not release it. A great example of this is Sammo Hung's classic *Pedicab Driver*, which is owned by Fox, but has not yet been released. Miramax owns the rights to one of Shintarô Katsu's *Zatôichi* films, which it was going to remake but to this date has not released. A studio might hold onto a movie for several years before releasing it or they might not release it at all, and it might not be available in your region.
- **Time lag.** Buying foreign films on DVD is very frustrating at times. It is very frustrating when you have to wait for the film to be released domestically because usually the film will not be released in a timely manner. Although some companies are starting to release films within a few months of when they are released on DVD overseas, a majority of companies release them six months to several years later than the original overseas release date. U.S. distributors need to pay closer attention to Asian release dates and release their DVDs closer to those dates. As a fight choreographer, you need to stay ahead of the curve and you cannot wait months or even several years for these films to be released here. Usually by the time a film is domestically released here, it is passé for a fight choreographer who is up to date with all the new things out there.
- **Censorship.** The other issue with domestically released DVDs of foreign films is censorship.
- **Alteration of storyline.** Scenes from films are sometimes cut or the story is sometimes altered due to poor subtitles or dubbing.
- **Special features.** Certain DVDs will have special editions in another country, but will have a no-frills edition here. The main reasoning from the marketing department is that if they feel they can make more money for that title by including extra features, then and only then they will include them. This is certainly true with many of the older Hong Kong action titles released here in the U.S. However, companies such as Tartan, Hong Kong Legends, and Premiere Asia in England release DVDs with an audio commentary and special features, which usually include interviews with the stars and other people who worked on the film. The Bruce Lee box set in the U.S. by Fox is pretty much a no-frills box set with only trailers as a "special feature." But Hong

Kong Legends' Bruce Lee box set is a six-disc set that has so much bonus material it would take about a week to look at it all! It was the top-selling DVD box set in Europe. Hong Kong Legends' reputation for quality and meaty extras is stellar. Another example is the film *Brotherhood of the Wolf.* The U.S. version is a single disc with a few extras. The Canadian version is a three-disc set with a ton of extras, behind-the-scenes documentaries, interviews, and so on. Both of these versions are Region 1 NTSC.

- **Picture quality and aspect ratio.** Picture quality and correct aspect ratio of the movie are two other reasons why you might have to go outside of your local region to get a DVD. Sometimes the best DVDs are from overseas, and this includes films that were produced here in the U.S. Overall, DVDs coming from Korea and Japan usually have the cleanest and sharpest picture—so much so that some other regions use these consumer DVDs as their masters.

How and Where to Find Rare, Obscure, and Imported DVDs

This section will provide you with information about how and where to find obscure and imported DVDs.

- **Comic book, movie memorabilia, and specialty conventions.** I have found these places to be great resources for hard-to-find titles. What is good about going to these conventions is that you can price-compare what different vendors have to offer. If at all possible, I recommend you inspect the quality of the DVD each time before you buy. A DVD might be cheaper than at the store, but it also might be a bootleg. Always check the quality before you buy.
- **Independent video stores and record shops.** I have found some independent stores have more variety than most corporate chain stores. Amoeba Music is an independent music store in Los Angeles that also sells new and used DVDs, laserdiscs, and VHS tapes. This place is much like a "video crack house" for me and many of my friends because of the different titles; the variety and depth of different types of films are perfect for film buffs like me. The video section takes up a majority of the second floor of a converted old warehouse. They broke the sections down into genre, then into filmmaker. You could easily spend a whole day there. I know because I've done it.
- **Online.** If there is not a place in your area to get imported or hard-to-find DVDs, the Internet is a good place to get them. Please look at Chapter 12 for websites that I have found to be good and reliable.

- **Chinatown, Koreatown, Thaitown, or Japantown.** These might seem intimidating at first because they might not be as easily accessible as a Circuit City or Best Buy in your town, but make it an adventure to go to these places. They will have stores that carry movies not readily available at huge chain stores. The reason is that they cater to their own community, and their library differs drastically from what you will see at your local store. These parts of town are also excellent places to visit in order to find typically inexpensive, multi-region DVD players to help accommodate your international film collection.

Tips on Going to a Video Store in Chinatown, Koreatown, and So On

Here are some tips on how to shop for videos in places that might not be in your normal routine. Going to places where you don't speak the language can be a little bit daunting, but don't give up after your first few times of going there. The more they see you coming to their stores, the more it will pay off for you.

- **Know what titles you are looking for.** If you don't know how to read the language, the clerk might not necessarily speak English well enough to understand the title you are looking for. This requires you to do your homework. I recommend that you do your research online, print the title of the film in its native language, then show the clerk the printed page so he can help you better.
- **Get the technical specifications before you buy.** Sometimes you will read a review of a film that you're simply dying to see. So you hustle down to Chinatown, buy it, and come home and put it in your DVD player. Several things could happen. It may not have any subtitles and you don't understand the language. Or the DVD might not play on your player because the player is not compatible with Region 3 (China/HK only) discs. In that case, you would have to get a DVD player that is compatible with that disc. Look carefully at the specifications of the disc before you buy it.
- **Know your film titles.** Understand that English titles for foreign films might not directly correspond to the title's name in its native language. If you walked up to a clerk at a Chinese video store and asked him for *Bullet in the Head* and he speaks some English, he might not know whether he has it. That's because the literal translation for that film from Chinese is *Bloodshed in the Streets.* This can get really confusing and frustrating for the consumer. However, this is a common practice with distributors, and you need to be prepared or you might buy the title twice without even knowing it. Also know that a lot of martial arts films will be released here under a different name and then have a completely different name when they come out on DVD. The changing of film titles also applies to U.S. films released overseas.

The change of titles happens constantly all over the world and is not just applicable to Asian titles that are imported to the West. An example is the French film *Danny the Dog*. When released in the U.S., the film's title was changed to *Unleashed*. But when the film reached Asia, it changed again. In China, it is impolite to call someone a dog (let alone one of their living treasures), so the title was changed to *The Tiger Is out of the Cage*. Meanwhile, Hong Kong changed the title to *The Immortal Dog*.

Table 11.1 presents some examples of film titles and how some change and some don't.

Table 11.1 Title Translations

Chinese Title	Literal Translation	English Title (Given by Chinese Studios)	Year Released (in Asia)	U.S. Title	Year Released (in the U.S.)	Other Titles
精武門	Doorway to Excellence in Martial Arts	Fist of Fury	1972	The Chinese Connection	1972	The Iron Hand
喋血雙雄	Bloodshed of Two Heroes	The Killer	1989	The Killer		Just Heroes (Australia)
龍兄虎弟	Elder Dragon Brother and Younger Tiger Brother	Armour of God	1987	Operation Condor 2: The Armour of the Gods		Operation Eagle, Superfly (Philippines)
飛鷹計劃	Operation Flying Condor	Armour of God II: Operation Condor	1991	Operation Condor	1994	
唐山大兄	China Mountain Big Brother	The Big Boss	1971	Fist of Fury	1971	
醉拳 I I	Drunken Fist II	Drunken Master II	1994	Legend of the Drunken Master	2000	
精武英雄	Hero of the Martial Elite	Fist of Legend	1994	Fist of Legend		
喋血街頭	Bloodshed in the Streets	Bullet in the Head	1990	Bullet in the Head	No domestic release on DVD or VHS. Only through imports.	
天下第一拳		King Boxer	1972	Five Fingers of Death	1972	

- **Don't judge DVD content by its cover and title alone.** Because you might not understand the language, do not judge a DVD's content by its cover. Some covers make it pretty obvious that they are action films, but there are many such films that do not have a sensational cover to attract you. Sometimes a DVD might have a deluxe slipcase that shows only the title of the film in its native language. How can you tell whether it's an action film if you do not know how to read the language and there is no one to help you? That's why it pays off to do your homework before you go to the store.

- **Be aware of film editing and censorship.** Know what version of the film to buy. In the long run it saves you time, money, and frustration. For example, in the film *Ong-Bak*, the Thai DVD is PAL, Region 3, and has no English subtitles. The Chinese version is NTSC and has English subtitles, but it is missing the leg break and arm break sequences at the end fight. For the longest time in England, all the *nunchaku* scenes in all of Bruce Lee's movies were deleted on video and theatrical screenings in that country. It wasn't until recently that Hong Kong Legends was able to release the films uncut, with the *nunchaku* scenes back in. Censorship laws vary from country to country. It pays to do your research and find out which version of a DVD to buy.

- **Don't be intimidated.** In the beginning, you might get intimidating or unwelcome looks from the shop owners that could make you feel like Jackie Robinson on his first day playing for the Dodgers. But the more you shop at the stores, the more the shop owners will remember you and eventually (hopefully) greet you with a smile. If possible, bring a friend who speaks the appropriate language on your first visits. Doing so may help you to become accepted by association. Another great way to break the ice is by knowing what to buy. When they know you've got good taste in films, they will appreciate you more for being brave and venturing where others were afraid to go.

  After a while you can transcend the language barrier because the shop owners will recognize that you have picked out a good title that they know. They will respect you for your film choices. Don't get frustrated the first time you feel uncomfortable or out of place. Keep showing up with titles you want, and over time they will respect you for your tastes. They will know what you will want to get whenever you come in and they will show you what is good and what they just got. To them, that's good "Kung Fu."

Be Aware of "Dubtitles"

When getting foreign films on DVD with subtitles from a company here in the U.S., often you will get subtitles that are a direct transcription off the English dub (when there are two different language tracks). The problem with this practice is that you are not getting the true translation of what the actors are saying. Many times when a film is dubbed into English, the story is usually changed drastically or you might get an abridged version of what is actually happening. The easiest way to find out whether a DVD has "dubtitles" is to watch the film with the English dub while reading the English subtitles on the bottom of the screen. If they match word for word, then you've got "dubtitles."

AnimEigo, Home Vision, Criterion, and Hong Kong Legends are some of the better companies who are doing proper translations. AnimEigo takes it a step further by supplying two different sets of subtitles. One has what the characters are saying; the second one translates what the characters are saying while also explaining what certain words mean. They also have different-colored subtitles when two or more characters are talking at once, so you will know exactly what each character is saying.

TV Size

It's best if you watch your DVDs on a screen of no less than 27 inches. This way you can easily read the subtitles and watch the film in its original widescreen format without making the characters look like tiny ants running across the screen.

PAL, NTSC, and SECAM

There are three different types of broadcast standards all over the world for television sets. In the U.S., South America, and certain parts of Asia, broadcast standards are NTSC (*National Television Systems Committee*), which is 525 lines of resolution on the screen and plays at 29.97 fps (*frames per second*). Parts of Europe, the Middle East, and certain areas of Asia use PAL (*Phase Alternating Line*), which has 625 lines of resolution and plays at 25 fps. SECAM is mainly used in France and also has 625 lines of resolution and 25 fps.

You need to be aware of what format the DVD you are watching is. If you have an NTSC DVD player and TV set, you cannot play a PAL DVD.

Watch an Action Scene without Any Sound

This is a great way to break down a film for the visuals, cuts, and techniques used. This way you will be able to see the action scenes and develop a more critical eye. You will not be easily swayed by sound effects and other tricks that can make you think you are seeing something that is not actually happening. You will be better able to see angles and edits with the sound off. You can also clearly see the misses in the shot. Also, see if you can sense, feel, and identify the actor's emotions during the fight scenes without the sound on. This is the mark of a great universal fight for which people from any country can understand what is happening with the scene.

Keep Your Movies in a Database

After a while you might have a lot of movies and you might not be able to keep track of them in your head. Make a simple Excel database or something similar that you can easily upgrade. It helps if you keep this on your PDA so when you do go out to the store, you can easily see whether or not you already have the titles you're considering.

For Those on a Budget

If you are on a limited budget, you can still start a library; you just have to be a little more resourceful and learn to curb your impulsive buying. Here are some tips that you might find helpful:

- **Know that DVDs are priced to be impulse buys.** Try to restrain yourself as best as you can to resist this temptation because it adds up quickly. You don't need to have anything so badly unless it's extremely rare or out of print. Know that the importance of adding a title to your library is only in your head. I know some friends who have ended up going broke simply because they convinced themselves that they really had to have a lot of things that they didn't *actually* need.
- **Price-compare.** It pays to know the average price of titles for each store in your area. For example, suppose Store A has *Boot to the Head* for $19.99 and *Entrails of Vengeance* for $14.99. Store B has *Boot to the Head* for $14.99 and *Entrails of Vengeance* for $19.99. So you buy the cheaper title at each store and save yourself $10. It really pays to price-compare if you want to save money. I've seen the price of the exact same DVD vary from store to store as much as $15!
- **Buy DVDs that are previously viewed.** There is nothing wrong with buying a used DVD as long as it still plays. DVDs are different than VHS because they do not wear down with each viewing.
- **Know what is on sale each week.** It pays to keep your ear to the ground so you know about sales and extra discounts. Getting the Sunday paper to see what will be on sale is a good way to save money and not pay full price when the sale goes off a week or so later.
- **Trade in the DVDs you no longer want for credit.** If you no longer watch a title or you don't feel it is important to have it anymore, trade it in for credit or cash toward something you really want.
- **Rent before you buy.** This is a safe and inexpensive way of continuing your education. And after viewing, you can decide whether you really want to have this title in your library.

- **Find a DVD haven.** A store such as Eddie Brandt's in North Hollywood is a haven for film students and aficionados alike. Their video and DVD rental library is pretty intimidating. Try to find a place that sells used DVDs because what is trash to one person is gold to another. If you are not in a major city and there are no places like this, try online services such as Netflix to rent, or try some of the sites I have recommended in Chapter 12.

Be Aware of "Double-Dipping"

A lot of video distributors like to release DVDs of a popular title several times over a certain period of time. Usually, the first time they release it, the disc won't have too much as far as special feature content—it is essentially a bare bones disc. Then, maybe six months to a year or so later (if the distributor feels they can make more money from it), they might release a more elaborate version of the movie with actor and filmmaker commentary, deleted scenes, interviews, behind-the-scenes documentary, and so on. The other justification they use is remastering older discs that were originally issued when DVD was first introduced in 1997, when the picture quality did not hold up quite as well as it does on a DVD released today.

Unfortunately, this is a common practice with most of the bigger studio-based video distributors. This can get really frustrating for the consumer because the distributors are making you buy the movie several times. This can get very frustrating especially if you are on a budget. The only thing you can do is trade in your older version of the DVD at a store that takes used discs for cash or trade-in value to absorb some of the costs of buying the newer version of the DVD.

12

Recommended Reading, Viewing, and Other Resources

This chapter contains a list of resources where you can further immerse yourself into the world of fight choreography...and then some. There are only a few specific references to the art of fight choreography because up to this point, this area has never really been explored or exposed in depth or critically. This is not by any means an ultimate list.

Further Reading

This section contains some books you may want to read to explore further areas related to fight choreography.

Stunt Related

Hobbs, William. *Fight Direction: For Stage and Screen.* Heineman, 1995.

Film Biography

Chan, Jackie and Jeff Yang. *I Am Jackie Chan: My Life in Action.* Ballantine, 1998.

Crowe, Cameron. *Conversations with Wilder.* Knopf, 1999.

Kurosawa, Akira. *Something Like An Autobiography.* Knopf, 1982.

Filmmaking: The Process

Katz, Steven D. *Film Directing Shot by Shot: Visualizing from Concept to Screen.* Michael Wiese Productions, 1991.

Katz, Steven D. *Film Directing: Cinematic Motion, Second Edition.* Michael Wiese Productions, 2004.

Rodriguez, Robert. *Rebel Without a Crew.* Faber and Faber, 1996.

Schmidt, Rick. *Feature Filmmaking at Used Car Prices.* 2nd edition revised. Penguin reissue, 2000.

Producing

Linson, Art. *A Pound of Flesh.* Grove Press, 1993.

Obst, Lynda. *Hello, He Lied.* Little, Brown & Co., 1996.

Steel, Dawn. *They Can Kill You But They Can't Eat You.* Pocket, 1993.

Film History

Logan, Bey. *Hong Kong Action Cinema.* Overlook TP, 1996.

Screenwriting

As fight choreographers, we are somewhat like screenwriters in that we are taking from a medium and adapting it into film. This section lists some books that might help you understand the process better.

Egri, Lajos. *The Art of Dramatic Writing: Its Basis in the Creative Interpretation of Human Motives.* Newly revised edition. Touchstone, 1972.

Goldman, William. *Adventures in the Screen Trade.* Warner Books, 1989.

Goldman, William. *Which Lie Did I Tell?: More Adventures of the Screen Trade.* Pantheon, 2000.

Hauge, Michael. *Writing Screenplays That Sell.* Reprint edition. Collins, 1991.

McKee, Robert. *Story: Substance, Structure, Style and the Principles of Screenwriting.* Regan Books, 1997.

Seger, Linda. *The Art of Adaptation: Turning Fact and Fiction into Film.* 1st edition. Owl Books, 1992.

Seger, Linda. *Creating Unforgettable Characters.* 1st edition. Owl Books, 1990.

Seger, Linda. *Making a Good Script Great.* 2nd edition. Samuel French, 1994.

Vogler, Christopher. *The Writer's Journey.* Revised edition. Pan, 1999.

Cinematography

Macelli, Joseph. *The 5 C's of Cinematography.* Cine/Grafic, 1973.

Van Sijll, Jennifer. *Cinematic Storytelling: The 100 Most Powerful Film Conventions Every Filmmaker Must Know.* Michael Wiese Productions, 2005.

Vineyard, Jeremy. *Setting Up Your Shots: Great Camera Moves Every Filmmaker Should Know.* Michael Wiese Productions, 2000.

Martial Arts

Anderson, Dan. *American Freestyle Karate: A Guide to Sparring.* Unique Publications, 1981. A great book on fighting strategy in competitive point fighting.

Draeger, Donn E. and Robert W. Smith. *Comprehensive Asian Fighting Arts* (formerly published as *Asian Fighting Arts*). Oxford University Press, 1981.

Deshimaru, Taisen. *The Zen Way to the Martial Arts.* EP Dutton, 1982.

Hyams, Joe. *Zen In the Martial Arts.* Reissue edition. Bantam, 1982.

Lee, Bruce. *Chinese Gung Fu: The Philosophical Art of Self-Defense.* 3rd edition. Ohara Publications, 1998.

Lee, Bruce. *The Tao of Gung Fu: A Study in the Way of Chinese Martial Arts.* Ed. John Little. 1st edition. Tuttle Publishing, 1997. This book fills in the gaps that were missing and helps make sense while reading the *Tao of Jeet Kune Do.*

Lee, Bruce. *Tao of Jeet Kune Do.* Reprint edition. Ohara Publications, 1993. Although this might be hard to comprehend for beginning martial artists, it is still a must-read to understand Bruce Lee's thoughts.

Musashi, Miyomoto. *The Book of Five Rings.* New edition. Shambhala, 2005. Miyomoto was one of the greatest swordsmen who lived in Japan. His philosophy and approach to fights are applied by modern Japanese society in their business dealings. This is required reading by business students at Harvard.

Tzu, Sun. *The Art of War.* Dover Publications, 2002.

Artists and Creative Issues

Becoming a working artist in the film industry is a very hard thing to achieve; not everyone can get there. Often we are our own worst enemy. Following are some books that will help you find that working artist inside you.

Cameron, Julia. *The Artist's Way.* 10th Anniversary edition. Tarcher, 2002.

Goldbert, Natalie. *Writing Down the Bones: Freeing the Writer Within.* Expanded edition. Shambhala, 2006.

Langer, Ellen J. *On Becoming an Artist.* Ballantine Books, 2005.

Suggested Viewing

This section contains a list of documentaries available on videotape and DVD to further your understanding and knowledge and expand your foundation.

Fight/Stunt Related

The Art of Action: Martial Arts in the Movies. Sony Pictures, 2002. Narrated by Samuel L. Jackson, the film explores the history of Hong Kong martial arts cinema and touches on all of the main contributors in Hong Kong cinema and their contributions to the genre. What this documentary does that others don't is trace the influence between East and West and how Hollywood has started incorporating the Hong Kong style of action into their films.

Cinema Hong Kong Documentary Series: Kung Fu and *Cinema Hong Kong Documentary Series: Sword Fighting.* Deltamac Entertainment, 2003. Two good documentaries on the history of Kung Fu, sword fighting, and the Wu Xia genre in Chinese cinema. Each documentary runs a brisk 50 minutes and explains how they edit a fight scene on camera, the evolution of King Hu's editing style, and what makes the Hong Kong style of fighting so unique. These DVDs contain interviews with Chor Yuen, Lau Kar Leung, and Gordon Liu, to name a few.

Double Dare. Capital Entertainment Enterprises, 2005. This documentary focuses on women in the stunt industry and what they go through to get work. The film focuses on veteran stuntwoman Jeannie Epper and a younger up-and-coming stunt performer, Zoe Bell.

Jackie Chan: My Stunts. Media Asia Group, 1999. Here Jackie Chan shows you how he does his stunts, from using cardboard boxes to brace his high falls, to using wires. The section titled "The Master Class" shows the subtle nuances of what Jackie feels makes a good and bad fight scene. That section alone is definitely worth the price of admission and deserves repeated viewing for future filmmakers, screen fighters, stuntmen, and fight choreographers; it should be studied and applied to their own fight scenes.

James Bond films (1962 to present). MGM. The James Bond films have always displayed jaw-dropping stunts and action. The DVDs that are available have plenty of supplemental extras that are very informative and explain how many of the stunts for each film were done.

Red Trousers: The Story of Hong Kong Stuntmen. Tai Seng, 2003. A rare and intimate look at what a Hong Kong stuntman goes through in filming a fight scene. They also go to the Beijing opera schools, where children train, and they discuss what they go through to succeed.

Filmmaking

The Cutting Edge: The Magic of Movie Editing. Warner Home Video, 2004. A documentary on the art and science of editing. The interesting section is the debate between filmmakers on the use of quick fast-paced editing and whether it is effective.

Visions of Light. Image Entertainment, 1992. A fascinating documentary on the history of cinematography and how it affects the audience and story.

Screenwriting/Storytelling

Joseph Campbell and the Power of Myth. Mystic Fire Video, 1988. In this six-part six-hour series, Bill Moyers talks with Joseph Campbell about how myth is a part of our psyche and is a universal and subconscious knowledge as humans that transcends one's race and religion. Campbell also explains how myth and the "hero's journey" plays a big part in the movies *Star Wars Episodes IV–VI.* After seeing this, you can easily see that Campbellian myth is sorely missing in Episodes I–III.

Film Biography

Buster Keaton: A Hard Act To Follow. Network DVD, 1987. An Emmy award-winning British documentary by David Gill and Kevin Brownlow. The documentary shows what made Keaton so special and shows the techniques and how he did some of his more spectacular stunts. Jackie Chan was inspired by Buster Keaton, and by watching this documentary, you will see why.

Gene Kelly: Anatomy of a Dancer. Warner Brothers, 2002. A chronicle of the life and career of American dancer and screen legend, Gene Kelly. This contains excerpts from his 1958 TV special "Dancing: A Man's Game," in which he explains that movements in sports and dancing are very much related to each other. Many of the principles of dance choreography for film are also either similar or the same in fight choreography.

Kurosawa. Well Spring, 2001. A good documentary that gives the viewer insight about the legendary filmmaker, who was born the son of a samurai. Although by no means complete (and if it was, it would run at least twice as long as its 215-minute running time), this documentary gives the viewer a very good introduction to who and what this director is about and his contributions to world cinema, influencing directors such as Steven Spielberg and George Lucas. After seeing this documentary, I urge anyone interested in knowing more about Kurosawa to seek out his films and books written on him.

Bruce Lee: A Warrior's Journey. Warner Home Video, 2002. A documentary on the late action star and martial artist, who introduced Kung Fu to the West. This DVD chronicles Lee's philosophy of the martial arts and film. The high point is the restored version of Lee's *Game of Death.* However, the obvious missing part of this documentary is the inclusion of an onscreen interview with Lee's protégé Dan Inosanto, who fought Lee in an episode of *The Green Hornet* and the movie *Game of Death.*

Martial Arts

The Art of High-Impact Kicking. Cav Distribution, 2003. An instructional video that shows all the basic to advanced Korean-style kicks and their applications demonstrated by the famous Hong Kong screen villain, Hwang Jang Lee. The instructional film was shot in the late 1970s, so the techniques are somewhat outdated compared to how techniques are thrown today. However, Master Lee executes each technique with ease, control, extreme confidence, and authority. He even executes many of the techniques in slow motion without the use of a slowed-down camera. This is a marvel to watch even to this day.

Budo: The Art of Killing. Synapse, 1982. Despite its exploitive title, this is a nicely filmed documentary on various Japanese and Okinawan styles of martial arts and weaponry. It uses very ingenious camera angles showing the uniqueness of the art of Aikido.

New Gladiators. Rising Sun Video, 2002. Funded by Elvis Presley with a music score by David Crosby and Graham Nash, this documentary follows some of the top American karate fighters in the mid 1970s, such as Benny "The Jet" Urquidez, Ed Parker, John Natividad, Ron Marchini, Roy Kurban, and Steve (Sanders) Muhammad, to name a few. It beautifully shows tournament point fighting in the "Golden Era," when control and clarity of technique were highly emphasized, right before the era of safety equipment was introduced.

Combative Sports

American Experience: The Fight. PBS Home Video, 2003. In the 1930s, the fights between Joe Louis and Max Schmeling became larger than life because of the mounting tensions between the U.S. and Nazi Germany, which eventually resulted in World War II. Schmeling studied Louis' fights on film and noticed he slightly dropped his guard when he threw his hook. Schmeling trained to evade the punch and counter when his guard dropped; he was able to capitalize on this by knocking out Louis for the first time in his career. But Louis came back in the second and third fights to assure himself that he was the superior fighter. The documentary delves into a volatile and sensitive time in the world, when race and national pride rested on the result of a boxing match.

Champions Forever: World Heavyweight Champions. Image Entertainment, 1989. What would happen if you gathered boxing legends Muhammad Ali, Joe Frazier, George Foreman, Ken Norton, and Larry Holmes all together in one room? Here you get a very interesting documentary as these fighters reflect about fighting each other at various times throughout their careers; what went on in their heads before, during, and after the fights; and how it affected them. Each fighter is profiled, and we get to see where each came from and what got him into boxing. Each fighter gets his moment to talk very candidly about his career. They also talk with each other about their fights and careers.

Choke. Manga Video, 1999. The documentary centers on Rickson Gracie, an undefeated MMA champion and a member of the legendary fighting Gracie family from Brazil, as he prepares for the 1995 Vale Tudo World Fighting Championship in Tokyo, Japan. The documentary also features two other fighters who will be competing against Gracie at the tournament—American heavyweight kickboxer Todd "Hollywood" Hays and Japanese shoot-fighting heavyweight champion Koichiro Kimura. Gracie intimately exposes his philosophy toward competitive combat as an art form by which he expresses himself. We also get an insightful look into the locker rooms before and after each fight and see how the fighters mentally and physically prepare for each match and how they handle their wins and losses.

On The Ropes. Fox Lorber, 2000. The award-winning and Oscar-nominated documentary that explores the life of three poor inner-city boxers and their trainer as they prepare for the golden gloves at their boxing gym in Bedford-Stuyvesant, New York. Their fight does not end in the ring or the gym; we see their struggle to have faith in themselves outside the gym in the Bronx and to have faith in overcoming their own personal adversity.

Shadow Boxers. Image Entertainment, 1999. An inside look into the world of women's boxing and what compels a woman to get into the ring. This centers around tough-as-nails kickboxer-turned-boxer, Lucia Rijker, who would later go on to star as the heavy in *Million Dollar Baby*, opposite Hilary Swank.

The Smashing Machine: The Life and Times of Extreme Fighter Mark Kerr. New Video Group, 2003. A fascinating personal look at a world-class MMA fighter who struggles with his demons for fame and money. The documentary delves into the life of freestyle-wrestler-turned-MMA fighter Mark Kerr. After a devastating loss (that was then overturned as no contest) to Ukrainian fighter Igor Vovchanchyn, Kerr overdoses and goes into rehab. His comeback to fight in the

2000 Pride Grand Prix is a tough uphill climb as his personal life outside the ring is extremely volatile. Also featured are his new trainer after rehab, the legendary Bas Rutten, and his close friend and fellow MMA competitor, Mark "The Hammer" Coleman, who previously lost his UFC title and then had a bad string of losses but is still in the game because he has a family to feed. The film is not a fast-paced, adrenaline-pumping documentary, but an intimate, somber, and probing film that does not need any narration; it makes the audience come up with their own conclusions.

The Ultimate Fighter: Season 1. Studio Works, 2005. It was a given that one day the marriage between combative sports and reality TV would occur. In this extremely colorful and dramatic DVD, eight middleweight and eight light heavyweight contenders are coached by UFC World Champions Randy Couture and Chuck Liddell in their quest for a contract to fight in the UFC. We see their training routines that are specific to cage fighting and what it takes to make it as an MMA fighter. The show runs 13 episodes, including the final in which a fighter is eliminated through competition each week. The final fight between Forrest Griffin and Stephan Bonnar is a great example of a fight filled with courage and undying willpower.

Unforgivable Blackness: The Rise and Fall of Jack Johnson. PBS Paramount, 2005. Directed and produced by the award-winning documentary filmmaker Ken Burns, this documentary is about Jack Johnson, the first African-American heavyweight boxing champion of the world. Johnson held the title from 1908 to 1915. The expansive documentary explores the life of the headstrong and defiant Johnson, who started from humble beginnings as the son of former slaves at a time in Jim Crow America when racism and segregation were blatant and prominent and when the world boxing title was exclusively reserved for Caucasians. The documentary shows how Johnson battled his way to the top of the boxing ranks while ignoring the color barrier by flaunting his money, driving expensive cars, and consorting with white women. Restored sections of Johnson's fights, as well as a documentary of the social conditions that surrounded the sport of boxing at the time, make this a very riveting documentary.

When We Were Kings. Universal Studios, 1997. The 1996 Academy Award–winning documentary that goes into detail about what led up to the "Rumble in the Jungle" in Zaire, Africa. In 1974, a 32-year-old Muhammad Ali was considered over the hill by everyone; it was thought that he could not beat George Foreman, the champion at the time—a younger and much stronger fighter who destroyed Ken Norton and Joe Frazier and who previously gave Ali his first two losses of his career. In the fight, Ali shows Foreman anything but respect as he hits the champ at will with his rear hand (the furthest hand to the opponent) as his initial technique. Ali also constantly talks to Foreman, asking him, "Is that all you got, George?"

This makes Foreman question his skills, eventually getting himself knocked out in the seventh round, giving Ali one of the greatest comebacks in modern sports history. Not only is this a great sports documentary, it also shows the differences in black culture in America and Africa. Including insights by Spike Lee, Norman Mailer, and George Plimpton, this documentary is one in which people who are not into sports, boxing, or Ali can easily become engrossed.

Sports Entertainment

Beyond the Mat: Directors Cut. Universal Studios, 2000. Director Barry Blaustein is very passionate about his love of pro wrestling since he was a kid, and it shows in this engaging documentary that goes behind the curtain and shows the real lives of several professional wrestlers and their families. We see the preparation and staging of the matches and meet Vince McMahon, the owner of the WWF (now WWE), who auditions Darrin Drozdov, an ex pro-football player and a promising upcoming wrestler whose gimmick is throwing up on cue. Then we visit a pro-wrestling school that teaches hopeful prospective wrestlers who are paying their dues by playing for small audiences for a measly $20 a night, but who come back for more, dreaming of the day they will make it to the big leagues. We come in on Paul Hayman and the then-fledgling ECW and its first PPV, and we have brief visits with Chyna and Jessie "The Body" Ventura.

But the documentary gets in depth with three wrestlers in different stages of their careers. One is Jake "The Snake" Roberts, who was a top wrestler in his day and is now dealing with the demons of his drug addiction, trying to make some kind of connection with his father, and trying to emotionally connect with his estranged daughter. Also included is veteran Terry Funk, who keeps wrestling beyond his years and against the orders of his physician and the wishes of his family. And then there's Mick Foley, the WWE world champ at the time, who performs extreme and dangerous matches every night. Here we see that what is happening is not fake at all, as his wife and kids sit ringside and cannot discern what is staged and what is real as they helplessly watch him get beaten while doing "a job" by giving up his title belt to The Rock.

Hitman Hart: Wrestling in the Shadows. Vidmark/Trimark, 1999. This explores the behind-the-scenes of the morality plays staged in the theatrical art of professional wrestling. The documentary follows the history and career of pro wrestler Bret "Hitman" Hart, his famed family, and his relationship with his father. Hart explains his inner monologue as a performer/wrestler and how he sees the audience from his point of view, along with the archetype of certain wrestlers, how they are to affect the audience, and how they can change when they are bored of a certain character. The documentary follows him from arena to arena and in the locker room, showing preparation before the matches, and concludes with the infamous "screw job" where Hart loses his title in a double-cross by owner Vince McMahon before leaving for the opposing competition, WCW, forever blurring the lines of reality and theatrics. To be fair, Vince McMahon states his opinions on the Bret Hart "screw job," in *McMahon* (WWE Video, 2006). See them both and decide who is right or wrong. At the time of this writing, this documentary is not available on DVD and is a highly coveted VHS tape.

Lipstick and Dynamite. Koch Lorber Films, 2004. A documentary that focuses on the first ladies of pro wrestling, who were pioneers paving the way for the women wrestlers of today. This documentary spotlights the lives of Gladys "Killem" Gillem, The Fabulous Moolah, The Great Mae Young, Ida Mae Martinez, and Penny Banner, and a few others. These salty ladies, now in their 70s and 80s, reflect on their past experiences, their struggles against sexism, and the dirty business that went on behind the scenes. These reflections are accompanied by archival footage of them wrestling.

MTV's WWE Tough Enough: The First Season. MTV, 2001. A reality TV show in which a group of aspiring wannabe wrestlers vie for a contract for the WWE. We see how hard the training is to become a professional wrestler, what it takes to be one, and that not everyone is able to make it. Pro wrestling stars Al Snow and Jacqueline are very passionate about their sport, and it shows in how they treat and train all the contestants. It's easy for us to look at a pro wrestler on TV and say that wrestling is fake, but seeing this reality series makes you realize and appreciate what it takes to be one of the chosen few in sports entertainment.

The Unreal Story of Pro Wrestling. A&E Home Video, 1999. An A&E documentary that shows the history of professional wrestling and how it became internationally regarded sports entertainment as we know it today.

Various WWE DVDs. The WWE puts out many titles that are specifically devoted to a certain wrestler, event, time, or other wrestling group. The documentaries are very well edited and informative. The annual Hall of Fame induction ceremonies are touching and at times humorous as the wrestlers being inducted reminisce and recall the wrestling business, what it did for them, and what they sacrificed each night in order to entertain the fans.

Other

They Drew Fire. Home Vision Entertainment, 1999. A documentary about the fine artists and illustrators in the military, who under the direct orders of General Eisenhower were to capture the emotion and situations experienced by American soldiers during WWII that were published in *Yank* magazine. The artists explain how they see the violence and conflict and then interpret and tell a story with what they saw in their paintings. The artists amazingly capture incredible moments of compassion, shock, misery, despair, and tenderness in the middle of the conflict. This is similar to what we do as fight choreographers, and it is a valuable tool to see how they capture what they saw and interpret it in their chosen medium. This is superbly directed by Pulitzer Prize–winning photojournalist Brian Lanker.

Frazetta: Painting with Fire. Razor Digital Entertainment, 2003. Frank Frazetta is arguably one of the most influential commercial artists/illustrators in the last half-century. He has captured the imagination of many people with his fantasy art of fierce warriors, fantastic creatures, and helpless damsels, spawning many imitators who might copy his style and technique but are not able to compose, tell a story, and create dynamic motion and dramatic tension like Frazetta can. This documentary shows Frazetta's best works and shows the man and his reason for painting.

Periodicals

Stunt-Related Periodicals

Inside Stunts (quarterly)
RI Media, LLC
11054 Ventura Blvd, Suite 288
Studio City, CA 91604
(323) 839-7840
info@insidestunts.com
www.insidestunts.com

Stunt Players Directory (annual)
www.stuntplayers.com

Screenwriting Periodicals

Creative Screenwriting
6404 Hollywood Blvd, Suite 415
Los Angeles, CA 90028
(800) 727-6978 or (323) 957-1405
Fax: (323) 957-1406
www.creativescreenwriting.com

Fade In
287 S. Robertson Blvd #467
Beverly Hills, CA 90211
(800) 646-3896 or (310) 275-0287
www.fadeinmag.com

Scr(i)pt
5638 Sweet Air Road
Baldwin, MD 21013-0007
(888) 245-2228 ext. 207
Fax: (410) 592-8062
www.scriptmag.com

Filmmaking Periodicals

American Cinematographer
1782 N. Orange Dr.
Hollywood, CA 90028
(800) 448-0145
(323) 969-4333
Fax: (323) 876-4973
www.theasc.com

Cinefex
PO Box 20027
Riverside, CA 92516
(951) 781-1917
Fax: (951) 788-1793
www.cinefex.com

Filmmaker magazine
104 W. 29th St., 12th floor
New York, NY 10001
(212) 563-0211
Fax: (212) 563-1933
www.filmmakermagazine.com

Movie Maker magazine
121 Fulton St., 5th floor
New York, NY 10038
(212) 766-4100
Fax: (212) 766-4102
www.moviemaker.com

Daily Entertainment Business Periodicals

Daily Variety
www.variety.com

Hollywood Reporter
www.hollywoodreporter.com

Action-Specific Entertainment Periodicals

Impact magazine (monthly)
MAI Publications, Revenue Chambers
St Peter's Street, Huddersfield, HD1 1DL
United Kingdom
Tel: (01484) 435011
Fax: (01484) 422177
www.impactmoviemagazine.co.uk/index.php

Screen Power / Jade Screen (bi-monthly)
PO Box 1989
Bath
BA2 2YE
United Kingdom
www.screen-power.com

General Film and Entertainment Reviews

Video Watchdog
www.videowatchdog.com

Martial Arts Periodicals

Black Belt magazine (monthly)
Aim Media
24900 Anza Drive, Unit E
Valencia, CA 91355
(661) 257-4066
www.blackbeltmag.com

Budo International
Budo International America
684 Britton Street Suite 4
Bronx, NY 10467
(718) 652-7100
(877) 592-3758
Fax: (718) 652-6800
america@budointernational.com
www.budointernational.com

Classical Fighting Arts (quarterly)
Dragon Associates, Inc.
PO Box 6039
Thousand Oaks, CA 91359
(800) 717-6288
Fax: (818) 879-0681
www.dragon-tsunami.org

Fighters Only
i 2 Media Ltd
6 Charlotte Square
Newcastle upon Tyne
Tyne and Wear
United Kingdom
NE1 4XF
Tel: +44 (0) 191 211 1947
info@chnmedia.co.uk
www.Fightersonlymag.com

Inside Kung Fu magazine (monthly)
APG Media
265 S. Anita Drive, Suite 120
Orange, CA 92868
(714) 939-9991
Fax: (714) 939-9909
www.insidekung-fu.com

Journal of Asian Martial Arts (quarterly)
Via Media Publishing Co.
941 Calle Mejia #822
Santa Fe, NM 87501
(505) 983-1919
info@goviamedia.com
www.goviamedia.com

Kung Fu Tai Chi magazine (bi-monthly)
Pacific Rim Publishing
40748 Encyclopedia Circle
Fremont, CA 94538
www.kungfumagazine.com

Martial Arts Illustrated
Martial Arts Limited, Revenue Chambers
St. Peter's Street, Huddersfield,
West Yorkshire
HD1 1DL
United Kingdom
Tel: 01484 435011
Fax: 01484 422177
martialartsltd@btconnect.com
www.martialartsltd.co.uk/mai

Tae Kwon Do Times
www.taekwondotimes.com

Combative Sports Periodicals

Boxing Digest
International Sports, Ltd.
8 West 38th St., Suite 200
New York, NY 10018
(212) 730-1374
www.boxingdigest.com

Tapout magazine (bi-monthly)
5252 Orange Ave., Suite 109
Cypress, CA 90603
(714) 226-0585
www.tapoutmagazine.com

Ultimate Grappling magazine
APG Media
PO Box 15159
North Hollywood, CA 91615-5159
(866) 368-5651
(818) 487-2077
Fax: (818) 487-4550
ultimategrappling@publicservice.com
www.ultimategrapplingmag.com

Pop Culture Periodicals

Giant Robot
PO Box 642053
Los Angeles, CA 90064
(310) 479-7311
www.giantrobot.com

Newtype USA
10114 W. Sam Houston Pkwy #200
Houston, Texas 77099
(800) 224-1348
subscriptions@newtype-usa.com
www.newtype-usa.com

Wizard
www.wizarduniverse.com

Professional Wrestling Periodicals

WWE magazine
Smackdown magazine
WWE Corporate Headquarters
Attention: (please include department)
1241 East Main Street
Stamford, CT 06902
(203) 352-8600
www.wwe.com

Inside Wrestling/The Wrestler
www.pwi-online.com

The Major Studios

Baa-Ram-Ewe
302/42-43 Ladprao 71
Wangthonglang, Bangkok 10300
Thailand
Tel: 66 2931 2701-2
Fax: 66 2931 2709
baabkk@yahoo.com

Buena Vista Home Video
Dimension Home Video
Walt Disney Home Entertainment
www.disneyvideos.disney.go.com

CJ Entertainment
www.cjent.co.kr

Fox Studios
www.fox.com
www.foxhome.com

Golden Harvest
The Peninsula Office Tower, 16th Flr
18 Middle Road
Tsim Sha Tsui
Kowloon, Hong Kong
Tel: 852-2352-8222
Fax: 852-2353-5989
www.goldenharvest.com

Lion's Gate Films
2700 Colorado Ave.
Santa Monica, CA 90404
(310) 449-9200
Fax: (310) 255-3870
www.lionsgate.com

MGM
www.mgm.com

Miramax
www.miramax.com

New Line Cinema
www.newline.com

Paramount Studios
5555 Melrose Avenue
Hollywood, CA 90038
(323) 956-5000
www.paramount.com

Sahamongkol Film Co., Ltd.
SP (IBM) Bldg., 338 Room 3B
Phaholyothin Rd., Phyathai
Bangkok 10400
Tel: 66 2273 0930-9
Fax: 66 2273 0596
www.sahamongkolfilm.com

Shochiku
4-1-1, Togeki Bldg. 12F
Tsukiji, Chuo-ku Tokyo, 104-8422
Japan
Tel: 81-3-5550-1623
Fax: 81-3-5550-1654
www.shochikufilms.com

Sony Pictures
10202 W. Washington Blvd.
Culver City, Ca. 90203
(310) 244-4000
www.sonypictures.com

Toho Pictures
Toho International Co., Ltd.
1-7-1 Yurakucho, Chiyoda-ku
Tokyo 100-0006, Japan
Tel: +81-3-3213-6821
Fax: +81-3-3213-6825
Los Angeles: (310) 277-1081; Fax: (310) 277-6351
New York: (212) 391-9058; Fax: (212) 840-2823
Hong Kong (Tel: +1-852-2523-6202; Fax: +852-2868-5975)
tohointl@toho.co.jp
www.toho.co.jp

Tsuburaya Productions
www.m-78.jp

Warner Bros. Studios
www.warnerbros.com

Additional Resources

Thai Cinema
www.thaicinema.org

This site gives all the names and numbers of all the studios, distributors, and production companies in Thailand.

DVD Distributors

Anchor Bay Entertainment
www.anchorbayentertainment.com

AnimEigo
P.O. Box 989
Wilmington, NC 28402-0989
(800) 24ANIME
In North Carolina: (910) 251-1850
Fax: (910) 763-2376
questions@animeigo.com
www.animeigo.com

Blue Underground
info@blue-underground.com
www.blue-underground.com

Celestial Pictures
www.celestialpictures.com

Central Park Media
US Manga Corps
www.centralparkmedia.com

The Criterion Collection
www.criterionco.com

Docurama
docurama.com

Dragon Dynasty
www.dragondynasty.com

FUNimation Entertainment
6851 NE Loop 820, Suite 247
Fort Worth, TX 76180
www.funimation.com

Geneon Animation
Geneon Entertainment
c/o The Right Stuf International
PO Box 680
Grimes, IA 50111
(800) 421-1621
info@rightstuf.com
www.geneonanimation.com

Hong Kong Legends
Freepost 29 ANG6618
London
W1W 8BR
United Kingdom
Tel: 0870 129 5039
enquiries@contendergroup.com
Fax: +44 (0)1462 420393
www.hongkonglegends.co.uk

Image Entertainment
Home Vision Entertainment
20525 Nordhoff Street, Suite 200
Chatsworth, CA 91311
www.image-entertainment.com

Mangpong Public Company Limited
59 Soi Lardprao 90 (Soi Parntipar)
Lardprao Road
Wangtonglarng Sub-District
Wangtonglarng District, Bangkok
10310
Tel : 02-514-7999
Fax : 02-514-5000
webmaster@mangpong.co.th

Manga Video
www.manga.com

Madman/Eastern Eye
www.madman.com.au

Media Blasters
Amime Works
Tokyo Shock
Shreik Show
Guilty Pleasures
519 8th Avenue, 14th Floor
New York, NY 10018
(212) 868-3315
info@media-blasters.com
www.media-blasters.com

Mei Ah Entertainment
www.meiah.com

Mondo Macabro
www.mondomacabrodvd.com

Network DVD
www.networkdvd.co.uk

Razor Digital Entertainment
www.razordigitalent.com

Rising Sun Productions
15808 Chase St.
North Hills, CA 91343-1133
(818) 891-1133
Fax: (818) 891-0332
www.risingsunproductions.net

Something Weird Video
www.somethingweird.com

Tai Seng Entertainment
170 So. Spruce Ave. Suite 200
So. San Francisco, CA 94080
Tel. (800) 888-3836
www.taiseng.com

Tartan Films USA
8322 Beverly Blvd. Suite 300
Los Angeles, CA 90048
(323) 655-9300
Fax: (323) 655-9301
www.tartanfilmsusa.com

Tartan Films & Tartan Video (UK)
Atlantic House
5 Wardour Street
London, W1D 6PB
Tel: 020 7494 1400
Fax: 020 7439 1922
www.tartanvideo.com

Independent DVD Dealers

Blue Laser
www.bluelaser.com

Cine East (Sells Asian films on DVD)
www.cine-east.com

Drunken Master
www.drunkenmaster.tv

DVD Asian
www.dvdasian.com

DVD Planet (Sells Region 1 DVDs)
www.dvdplanet.com

Five Star Laser (Sells imported Chinese DVDs)
www.fivestarlaser.com

Han Books
(Specializing in Korean films)
www.hanbooks.com

HK Flicks
www.hkflix.com

Nehaflix (Specializing in Bollywood films)
www.nehaflix.com

Poker Industries
www.pokerindustries.com

Sensasian
www.sensasian.com

Xploited Cinema (Specializes in cult, horror, art house, exploitation, and Erotic DVDs from all over the world)
www.xploitedcinema.com

YesAsia
www.yesasia.com

Organizations and Unions

American Cinema Editors (ACE)
100 Universal City Plaza
Verna Fields Bldg. 2282, Room 190
Universal City, CA 91608
(818) 777-2900
Fax: (818) 733-5023
www.ace-filmeditors.org

American Federation of Television and Radio Actors (AFTRA)
www.aftra.org

American Society of Cinematographers (ASC)
1782 North Orange Dr.
Hollywood, CA 90028
Mailing address: P.O. BOX 2230
Hollywood, CA 90078
(800) 448-0145
Outside US: (323) 969-4333
Fax: (323) 882-6391
www.theasc.com

British Society of Cinematographers
PO BOX 2587
Gerrards Cross
SL9 7WZ, UK
Tel: +44 (0)1753 888052
Fax: +44 (0)1753 891486
bscine@btconnect.com
www.bscine.com

Directors Guild of America
www.dga.org

Directors Guild of Great Britain
www.dggb.co.uk

Hong Kong Film Directors Guild, Ltd.
2/F, 35 Ho Man Tin Street
Kowloon
Tel: 2760 0331
Fax: 2713 2373
hkfdg@netvigator.com

Hong Kong Society of Cinematographers
Flat B, 19/F, Block A, Wylie Court 23
Wylie Path
Ho Man Tin, Kowloon
Tel: (+852) 9021 5449
Fax: +(852) 2358 3990

International Cinematographers Guild
National Office/Western Region
7755 Sunset Boulevard
Hollywood, CA 90046
(323) 876-0160
Fax: (323) 876-6383
www.cameraguild.com

Japanese Society of Cinematographers
1-25-14 5F Shinjyuku
Shinjyuku-ku
Tokyo 160-0022 Japan
Tel: +81-3-3356-7896
Fax: +81-3-3356-7897
info@jsc.or.jp
www.jsc.or.jp/en

Motion Picture Editors Guild
www.editorsguild.com

Producers Guild of America
(310) 358-9020
info@producersguild.org
www.producersguild.org

Screen Actors Guild (SAG)
5757 Wilshire Blvd.
Los Angeles, CA 90036-3600
(323) 954-1600

or

360 Madison Avenue 12th Floor
New York, New York 10017
(212) 944-1030
www.sag.org

Writers Guild of America, East
555 West 57th St., Suite 1230
New York, NY 10019
(212) 767-7800
Fax: (212) 582-1909
www.wgaeast.org

Writers Guild of America, West
7000 West Third Street
Los Angeles, CA 90048
(323) 951-4000
(800) 548-4532
Fax: (323) 782-4800
www.wga.org

Stunt Organizations

Brand X Action Specialists
(818) 701-9239
www.brandxstunts.org

Stuntmen's Association of Motion Pictures
10660 Riverside Dr., 2nd Floor, Suite E
Toluca Lake, CA 91602
(818) 766-4334
Fax: (818) 766-5943
info@stuntmen.com
www.stuntmen.com

Stunts Unlimited
7551 W. Sunset Blvd., Suite 203
Los Angeles, CA 90046
(323) 851-1970
Fax: (323) 851-7286
Media inquiries call:
(310) 300-0950 x232
info@stuntsunlimited.com
www.stuntsunlimited.com

Stuntwomen's Association of Motion Pictures, Inc.
(818) 762-0907
stuntwomen@stuntwomen.com
www.stuntwomen.com

Stuntwomen's Foundation
5699 Kanan Rd.
Agoura Hills, CA 91301
www.stuntwomensfoundation.org

V10 Stunts: Stuntwomen's Association
1028 Nowita Place
Venice, CA 90291
(818) 886-5413
www.v10stunts.com

Film Conservatories and Institutes

American Cinematheque
6712 Hollywood Boulevard
Hollywood, CA 90028
(323) 461-2020
Fax: (323) 461-9737
www.americancinematheque.com

American Film Institute
2021 N. Western Avenue
Los Angeles, CA 90027-1657
(323) 856-7600
Fax: (323) 467-4578
www.afi.com

British Film Institute
21 Stephen Street
London W1T 1LN
Tel: +44 (0)20 7255 1444
www.bfi.org.uk

Hong Kong Film Archive
www.lcsd.gov.hk/CE/CulturalService/HKFA

Sundance Institute
California Office
8530 Wilshire Blvd., 3rd Floor
Beverly Hills, CA 90211-3114
(310) 360-1981
Fax: (310) 360-1969
la@sundance.org

Utah Office
1825 Three Kings Dr.
Park City, UT 84060
Mailing Address
PO Box 684426
Park City, UT 84068
(801) 328-3456
Fax: (801) 575-5175
institute@sundance.org
www2.sundance.org

Tribeca Film Institute
(212) 941-3890
institute@tribecafilminstitute.org
www.tribecafilminstitute.org

From the Web site: Robert De Niro, Jane Rosenthal, and Craig Hatkoff founded the Tribeca Film Institute in the wake of September 11th to educate, entertain, and inspire filmmakers and film lovers alike. The Institute creates innovative programs that draw on the power of film to promote understanding, tolerance, and global awareness.

Women's Film Organizations

Women in Film
www.wif.org

New York Women in Film & Television
www.nywift.org

Women Make Movies
www.wmm.com

Women in Film & Video of Washington, DC
www.wifv.org

Women in Film Vancouver
www.womeninfilm.ca/index.php

Women in Film Seattle
www.womeninfilm-seattle.org

Women in Film Atlanta
www.wifa.org

Las Vegas Women in Film
www.wiflasvegas.org

Women in Film & Television Florida
www.womeninfilmfl.org

Women in Film & Video New England
www.wifvne.org/home.php

Women in Film & Television UK
http://www.wftv.org.uk

Critics Societies

Hong Kong International Film Festival Society Limited
United Chinese Bank Building
31-37 Des Voeux Rd.
Central Hong Kong
Tel: (852) 2970-3300
Fax: (852) 2970-3011
www.hkiff.org.hk

Hong Kong Film Critics Society
1/F., No. 30 Bowring Street, Jordan
Kowloon, Hong Kong
Tel: +852 2575 5149
Fax: +852 2891 2048
info@filmcritics.org.hk
www.filmcritics.org.hk/en

The International Federation of Film Critics
www.fipresci.org

Award Shows

This section lists awards shows that give out awards to action.

Academy of Television
Arts and Sciences
www.emmys.org
Category: Outstanding Stunt Coordination

Golden Horse Award
www.goldenhorse.org.tw
Category: Best Action Choreography

Hong Kong Film Awards
www.hkfaa.com
Category: Best Action Choreography

MTV Movie Awards
www.mtv.com/ontv/movieawards
Category: Best Fight

Taurus World Stunt Awards
US Office
Taurus World Stunt Awards
3940 Laurel Canyon Blvd. #236
Studio City, CA 91604
(323) 468-4011
Fax: (323) 468-4005
office@taurusworldstuntawards.com

Europe Office
Taurus World Stunt Awards
Spengergasse 37-39
A-1050 Vienna
Tel: +43-1-877 44 10
Fax: +43-1-8774410-33
office.europe@taurusworld-stuntawards.com

Foundation
3940 Laurel Canyon Blvd. #236
Studio City, CA 91604
(323) 468-4011
(323) 468-4005
www.worldstuntawards.com

Online Resources

Books

AsiaPac Books
www.asiapacbooks.com

Samuel French, Inc.
www.samuelfrench.com
A bookstore that caters to practically every aspect of the film and theater industry.

Celebrity Sites

Jackie Chan
www.jackiechan.com

Bret Hart
www.brethart.com

Sammo Hung
www.sammohung.com

Laurene Landon
www.laurenelandon.biz

Jet Li
www.jetli.com

Benny "The Jet" Urquidez
www.bennythejet.com

Rob Van Dam
www.robvandam.com

Keith Vitali
www.keithvitali.com

Daily Entertainment News (Subscription)

The following sites are online versions of daily periodicals dealing with the business aspects of the entertainment industry. No fluffy gossip on who is dating whom here to fill the pages.

The Hollywood Reporter
www.hollywoodreporter.com

Variety
www.variety.com

Screenwriting

Screenwriter's Utopia
www.screenwritersutopia.com

Screenwriting.Info
www.screenwriting.info

Wordplay
www.wordplayer.com
The site of A-list scribes Terry Rossio and Ted Elliot. They give out plenty of practical advice that you won't get in a classroom or book.

Writers Write
www.writerswrite.com/screenwriting

Movie News

Ain't It Cool News
www.aintitcool.com

Film Threat
www.filmthreat.com

Kaiju Shakedown
www.kaijushakedown.com

Kung Fu Cinema
www.kungfucinema.com
Run by Mark Pollard, the site has news stateside and internationally with links to other sites.

KFC Cinema
www.kfccinema.com

DVD Reviews and News

Most of these sites have links to other review sites I have not been able to mention, so you can get lost online for the rest of your life.

24 Frames Per Second
www.24framespersecond.net
For Asian, world, horror, and cult movie news.

The Asian DVD Guide
www.asiandvdguide.com
Posts all the DVDs that are coming out in Asia for a particular week.

Bad Movie Planet
www.badmovieplanet.com

Battle Royale Film
www.battleroyalefilm.net

Bright Lights Film Journal
www.brightlightsfilm.com

The Digital Bits
www.thedigitalbits.com
A site devoted to Region 1 DVD releases; it keeps you up to date with the latest on the digital media front and reviews of upcoming releases. Updated daily.

Dragon's Den
www.dragonsdenuk.com

DVD Beaver
www.dvdbeaver.com
DVD review site. The site has an in-depth comparison chart on selected DVDs from various regions.

DVDFile
www.dvdfile.com

DVD Reviewer
www.dvd.reviewer.co.uk

DVD Talk
www.dvdtalk.com
A review site that discusses and reviews films in current release and DVDs from all over the world, but primarily the U.S. and U.K.

DVD Times
www.dvdtimes.co.uk

Internet Movie Database (IMDb)
www.imdb.com
Need it be said, this is the biggest movie and TV database on the Internet. However, the information is not always accurate or complete because it is contributed by the public. It is nevertheless a Herculean effort online.

Jerry Beck's Cartoon Research
www.cartoonresearch.com

Koreanfilm.org
www.koreanfilm.org
Reviews and essays on Korean films.

Midnight Eye
www.midnighteye.com
Reviews and essays on Japanese film.

Rewind
www.dvdcompare.net
Has one of the most extensive DVD comparison sites online.

Roger Ebert
http://rogerebert.suntimes.com
The review site of the famed and noted film critic who also wrote *Beneath the Valley of the Ultra Vixens*, *Up*, and *Beyond the Valley of the Dolls* with cult director Russ Meyer. You gotta love the guy for admitting that one of his guilty pleasures is the film *Inframan.*

Toho Kingdom
www.tohokingdom.com
Site devoted to upcoming films from Toho.

Twitch
www.twitchfilm.net

Martial Arts Online References

International Sport Karate Association
www.iska.com

Martial Arts History Museum
http://www.mamuseum.com

PKA Kickboxing
www.pkakickboxing.com

Pro Karate Weekly
www.prokarateweekly.com

World Kickboxing Association (WKA)
www.wka.co.uk

Boxing Online References

The Boxing Times
www.boxingtimes.com

Fightnews.com
www.fightnews.com
Covers all aspects of competitive sport fighting.

HBO World Championship Boxing
www.hbo.com/boxing

International Boxing Federation
US Boxing Federation
www.ibf-usba-boxing.com

International Boxing Hall of Fame
www.ibhof.com

Showtime Championship Boxing
www.sho.com/site/boxing

Top Rank
www.toprank.com

World Boxing Association
www.wbaonline.com

World Boxing Council
www.wbcboxing.com

World Boxing Organization
www.wbo-int.com

Mixed Martial Arts Online References

Fight Resource
www.fightresource.com

Full Contact Fighter
www.fcfighter.com

International Fight League
www.ifl.tv

MMAFighting.com
www.mmafighting.com

Mixed Martial Arts Media
www.mixedmartialarts.com

MMA Weekly
www.mmaweekly.com

Pride Fighting Championships
www.pridefc.com

Sher Dog
www.sherdog.com

Ultimate Fighting Championships
www.ufc.com

World Fighting Alliance
www.wfa.tv

Pro Wrestling Online References

Highspots
www.highspots.com

The Mid-Atlantic Gateway
www.midatlanticgateway.com
History of Mid-Atlantic pro wrestling.

Obsessed With Wrestling
www.obsessedwithwrestling.com

Pro Wrestling Insider
www.pwinsider.com

Professional Wrestling Online Museum
www.wrestlingmuseum.com
A great online reference site of pro wrestlers from yesteryear to today; it tells you of their contributions to the game.

World Wrestling Entertainment
www.wwe.com

WrestleView.com
www.wrestleview.com

WrestlingInformer.net
www.wrestlinginformer.net

Wrestling Observer (David Meltzer)
www.wrestlingobserver.com
Also covers MMA events.

Pro Wrestling
www.prowrestling.com

Sports Wrestling Online References

Dan Gable
www.dangable.com

National Collegiate Wrestling Association
www.ncwa.net

National Wrestling Hall of Fame and Museum
www.wrestlinghalloffame.org

Real Pro Wrestling
www.realprowrestling.com

Rulon Gardner
www.rulongardner.com

TheMat.com
www.themat.com

Conventions and Festivals

Comic book conventions are no longer just places to get comic books. They are more pop culture conventions that have something for everybody. Here you will see and meet fans of any specific genre that range from casual and curious to hard-core. You can get rare books, posters, or movies that are extremely hard to find otherwise. A convention is also a way to meet a celebrity or filmmaker and ask him questions that might help you along with your own education, understanding, and career.

When shopping for DVDs, you can actually compare prices from each dealer and go for the one who has the best bargain. I recommend you bring a portable DVD player to see whether the DVD is playable. More than once, I have bought a title and found out that it was defective or the wrong title. Often the dealer will have a TV set and a DVD player to show you what you are buying. Ask to see it before you buy it if you are not sure of the quality of what you are buying and that the DVD is compatible with your player.

This is by no means a complete list of the conventions all over the country. There is usually one or several conventions occurring somewhere in the U.S. and around the world at any given time. For conventions in your area, I recommend you go to the Comic Book Conventions Web site listed below (www.comicbookconventions.com). The site is a great resource for current and upcoming convention info as well as reviews of past conventions and in-store signings.

Anime Expo

SPJA/Anime Expo
1733 S. Douglass Road, Suite G
Anaheim, CA 92806
(714) 937-2994
www.anime-expo.org

Anime Expo is a four-day convention, traditionally held on the Fourth of July weekend. It is a forum for enthusiasts and industry people involved in anime, manga, games, and culture of Japan. It is the largest convention of its kind in the U.S. The SPJA (or Society for the Promotion of Japanese Animation) is the non-profit organization that runs Anime Expo. The SPJA's mission is the promotion of anime and manga, as well as arts that influence or are influenced by them.

The Bruce and Brandon Lee Association

PO Box 25
Horsforth, Leeds
LS18 5TG, England
bbla@hotmail.co.uk
www.bbla.co.uk

This association holds an annual convention in England devoted to Bruce and Brandon Lee.

Capitol Legends Fan Fest

Mid Atlantic Wrestling Legends Fan Fest
NWA Legends Fan Fest
www.nwalegends.com

A convention for professional wrestling fans mainly held on the East coast. They also put together the NWA Legends Fan Fest and the Mid-Atlantic Wrestling Legends Fan Fest.

Comic Book Conventions

www.comicbookconventions.com

Provides the latest convention news and reports, along with in-store signings. It's a valuable resource.

Creation Entertainment

www.creationent.com

Traveling conventions of various themes and shows, such as horror, sci-fi, Xena, Star Trek, Terminator 2, Star Wars, Bruce Lee, Lord of the Rings, Stargate, and X-Files.

Dragon*Con

PO Box 16459
Atlanta, GA 30321-0459
(770) 909-0115
Fax: (770) 909-0112
dragoncon@dragoncon.org
www.dragoncon.org

An annual four-day convention held in Atlanta, Georgia, that has numerous themes and multimedia. Popular arts convention focusing on science fiction and fantasy, gaming, comics, literature, art, music, and film.

Los Angeles Comic Book and Science Fiction Convention

www.comicbookscifi.com

A bi-monthly one-day show put together by Bruce Schwartz. In the past, Bruce's guests have been Arnold Schwarzenegger, Jackie Chan (twice), Jet Li, John Woo (twice), Chow Yun Fat, Keanu Reeves and cast members from *The Matrix*, Vin Diesel, Michelle Yeoh, Sam Raimi, James Cameron, and Jean-Claude Van Damme, to name a few.

Comic-Con International: San Diego

Wonder Con 2007
Alternative Press Expo
Comic Con International
PO Box 128458
San Diego, CA 92112-8458
(619) 491-2475
Fax: (619) 414-1022
www.comic-con.org

The Comic-Con is the annual big daddy of all pop culture conventions. It lasts five days. It'll take you more than a full day to see everything this comic con has to offer. The Con has a great relationship with studios and filmmakers in Hollywood, and many stars come down to talk and show exclusive footage from their upcoming films. Comic-Con International also put together the Wonder-Con and Alternate Press Expo in San Francisco.

Super Mega Show

Heroes Unlimited
Box 453, Oradell, NJ 07649
(201) 261-4982
Fax: (201) 385-9291
heroes@optonline.net

or

Paradox Comics
269 Ridge Road
North Arlington, NJ 07031
(201) 998-1212
Paradoxcomics@aol.com
www.supermegashow.com

A comic book and autograph convention on the East coast.

Hollywood Collectors Show

Hollywood Collectors Show, Inc.
Ray and Sharon Courts
PO Box 5040
Spring Hill, FL 34611-5040
(818) 683-4203 or (352) 683-5110
Fax: (352) 688-8114
hcs@atlantic.net
www.hollywoodcollectorshow.com

Run by Ray and Sharon Court for 17 years, they have shows held quarterly in Hollywood/Burbank, California, and also in Orlando, Florida. Buy from dealers in different types of TV and movie memorabilia from all over the country and meet celebrities there to sign autographs for a fee. Past screen-fighter celebrities that have shown up are John Saxon, David Carradine, Rob Van Dam, and George Lazenby, to name a few.

Wizard World

www.wizarduniverse.com/conventions

A comic book convention that travels to different cities in the U.S. Put together by *Wizard* magazine, a pop culture monthly.

Festivals

Action on Film International Film Festival

(323) 878-5522
Info: info@aoffest.com
Submissions: submissions@aoffest.com
www.aoffest.com

A film competition and festival that honors and celebrates filmmakers and actors in the world of action. The festival showcases more than 200 projects from various independent and studio sources.

Black Belt Magazine's Festival of Martial Arts

www.blackbeltmag.com

Held and organized by Black Belt magazine, this is a martial arts consumer and trade show with one- to two-hour seminars by many of the leading martial artists today. A banquet inducting new members into the Black Belt Hall of Fame is one of the highlights of the festival.

Film Festivals Online Resource

www.filmfestivals.com

A Web site that lists and keeps up to date of all the film festivals occurring all over the world.

Slamdance Film Festival

http://www.slamdance.com

Sundance Film Festival

http://festival.sundance.org

Tribeca Film Festival

www.tribecafilmfestival.org

Index

A

Above the Law **(1988), 41, 61, 368**
action
  justifications of, 197–199, 214–215, 219–221
  vs. violence, 195–196
action figures, 435
action-adventure genre, 19–24
actors, 3–5
  learning styles, 181
  physical skills of, 179–180
  roles in films, 175
  and trainers, 178–179
  training of, 172–175
  understanding, 180–181
adjustment, 150
advanced fighter, 313
advanced forms, 246
Adventures of Ozzie and Harriet, The **(1952-1966), 12–13**
ageism, 58–59
aggressive stances, 371
"aha!" moments, 343–344
Alcott, John, 21
Ali **(2001), 23**
Ali, Muhammad, 149, 192–193
All the Marbles **(1981), 134**
Allen, Corey, 14
American Experience: The Fight **(2003), 462–463**
American Ninja **(1985), 40**
An Officer and a Gentleman **(1982), 40**
Anabasis**, 23**
ancient Greek dances, 2
Angel **(television series), 134**
AnimEigo, 453–454
Ano (ancient Greek sport), 99
antiheroes, 217–218
apprentice training sequences, 231–232
approaches, combination of, 373–374
Arbuckle, Roscoe, 8
Armour of God II **(1991), 354**
Art of Action, The: Martial Arts in the Movies **(2002), 460**
Art of High-Impact Kicking, The **(2003), 462**
Art of War, The **(book), 185, 194**
Artest, Ron, 126
Asian actors
  stereotypes, 68
  in Western films, 70–75
aspect ratio, 450
assistant directors, 16
Astaire, Fred, 15
Attack the Gas Station **(1999), 15**
attitude, 290
auditory learning, 181
Avildson, John, 40
award shows, 478–479

B

back story, 208–209, 276–277
Bad Boys **(1983), 15**
bad fit, 153, 412
Bale, Christian, 230
Bamboo House of Dolls **(1973), 20**
Bandwagon, The **(1953), 15**
barroom brawls, 10
Batman **(1989), 34**
Batman **(television series), 34**
Batman Begins **(2005), 230**
Battle Royale **(2000), 449**
Battlecreek Brawl **(1980), 38, 40, 71–72**
Battles Without Honor and Humanity **(1973), 431**
beats, 362–363
beginner fighter, 313
beginner forms, 245
Bell, Zoe, 66–67
Ben Hur **(1959), 18**
Bergman, Sandahl, 28

Best of the Best **(1989), 367**
Betamax, 27
Beverly Hills Cop **(1984), 29**
Beyond the Mat: Directors Cut **(2000), 465**
Big Boss, The **(1971), 43, 89–90, 305**
Big Brawl, The **(1980), 38, 40, 71–72**
Big Doll House, The (1971), 20
Big Trouble in Little China **(1986), 40**
Bigelow, Kathryn, 31
billing, 67
Billy Jack **(1971), 38, 198, 286, 329**
Bittersweet Life, A **(2005), 381**
Black, Jack, 130
Black Maria Studios, 3
Black Mask 2: City of Masks **(2002), 135**
Blackboard Jungle, The **(1955), 14**
Blade II **(2002), 65**
blaxploitation films, 20, 38
Blazing Saddles **(1974), 61**
blockbuster films, 24–25
Blood on the Sun **(1945), 35**
Bloodsport **(1992), 41**
bob, 141
body language, 378
Book of Five Rings, The **(book), 193**
book signings, 439
books, 457–460
- artists/creative issues, 459–460
- cinematography, 459
- film biography, 457
- film history, 458
- filmmaking, 458
- martial arts, 459
- producing, 458
- screenwriting, 458
- stunt-related, 457

Boorman, John, 70
Borgnine, Ernest, 22
Boston Strangler, The **(1968), 146, 247**
Bourne Identity, The **(2002), 36, 332**
Bourne Supremacy **(2004), 36**
Bourne Ultimatum **(2007), 36**
boxing websites, 482
Brando, Marlon, 13–14
brass knuckles, 13
Braveheart **(1995), 33–35**
brawlers, 140
brawls, 5–16
- *See also* fight scenes
- barroom, 10
- censorship of, 8–9
- in cliffhanger serials, 10
- in John Wayne films, 10–12
- origin of, 7–8
- philosophy of, 6
- rules in, 5–6
- and slug-fest, 6
- in teen films, 12–16

Brazilian Jiu-Jitsu, 100–101
Bride with White Hair, The **(1993), 382**
Bridget Jones' Diary **(2001), 333–334**
bridging the gap, 142
broadcast standards, 454
broken rhythm, 142
Bronson, Charles, 22
Brosnan, Pierce, 31, 33–36
Brotherhood of the Wolf **(2001), 450**
Brown, Clancy, 15
Brown, Garrett, 23
Bruce Lee: A Warrior's Journey **(2002), 461–462**
Bruckheimer, Jerry, 26
Budo: The Art of Killing **(1982), 462**
Buffy, The Vampire Slayer **(television series), 54**
buildup, 230–244
Bull Durham **(1988), 279**
Bullitt **(1968), 19**
bump, 150–153
Burning of the Red Lotus Monastery **(1928), 42**
Busey, Gary, 32
Buster Keaton: A Hard Act to Follow **(1987), 461**
bystander investment/reaction, 352

C

cable television, 26
Cage, Nicholas, 33
Cagney, James, 35
camera angles, 63, 390
camera awareness, 375
camera height, 392
cameraman, rehearsing with, 387–389
Campbell, Bruce, 247
Cannonball Run I **(1981), 71**
Cannonball Run II **(1984), 71**

Canutt, Yakima, 18
Capitol Wrestling Corporation (CWC), 121
***Captain Kronos: Vampire Hunter* (1974), 20**
Carpenter, John, 40
Carradine, David, 68
Carrey, Jim, 126
carrying the actor, 153, 412
***Casino Royale* (2006), 36**
caste system, 301
catalyst heroes, 218
Caucasian actors
in Asian films, 68
as Asians, 70
caught sleeping, 143
Cavens, Fred, 3–4
celebrity websites, 479
censorship, 8–9
centered stances, 372
centerline, 142, 369–371
chain of command, 51–53
chamber, 142
***Champions Forever: World Heavyweight Champions* (1989), 463**
Chan, Jackie
in *Battlecreek Brawl*, 40
break into American market, 71
in *Fearless Hyena*, 44
Kung Fu brawls, 45–47
martial acting by, 380
rhythm in fights, 169–170
in *Rush Hour*, 41
from stuntman to filmmaker, 66
time and preparation for fight scenes, 67
use of surroundings/environment by, 354
character arcs, 176–177, 209–211, 277–278, 293
character bible, 271–282
age/age range, 273
ambitions/desires, 276
back story, 276–277
beliefs/interests, 275–276
body image, 279–280
character arc, 277–278
character interactions, 281
comfort with surroundings, 282
definition of, 271
education, 275
emotional traits, 276
family relationships, 274
inner conflicts/contradictions, 281
interaction with other characters, 276
introvert/extrovert, 280–281
mental/mind games, 278–279
name, 272–273
occupation, 274–275
physical appearance, 273
self-sabotage, 280
senses, 281
social position, 274
where the character lives, 275
character strategy, 360
characters, 215–230
heroes, 215–221
mentors, 223–230
villains, 221–223
character/story inventory, 266–321
breakdown of script, 269–271
character bible, 271–282
fight charts/stats, 315–321
fighting IQ, 282–315
overview of, 266–269
Charisse, Cyd, 15
check, 142
Cheung Yan, Yuen, 73
***chi* (internal energy), 55, 58**
Chia, Tang, 44
Chiba, Shinichi, 38–39
***Chinatown Kid, The* (1977), 45**
***Chinese Connection, The* (1972), 198, 327–329**
Chinese film industry, 42–45
ageism, 58–59
art form vs. gimmick, 57
Asian talent in Western films, 70–75
billing/recognition, 67
camera angles, 63
chain of command, 51–53
choreographers, 64–65
code of ethics/conduct, 59
culture/religion, 55–56
editing, 62–63
emphasis of fight, 59–62
film genres, 68
length of fight, 62
mythology, 59
perception of action, 52–54
perception/stereotypes of foreigners, 68–70

Chinese film industry ***(continued)***
room for advancement vs. categorization, 66–67
sound, 65
special effects, 65
stories, 68
stuntmen, 63–64
time and preparation, 67–68
Ching Siu Tung, 44
Ching-Ying, Lam, 66
Choke **(1999), 463**
choreographers, 64–65, 184–185, 408–410
choreography training, 417–456
accepting criticisms, 443–445
action filmmakers, 429–430
avoiding to prejudge movies, 422–423
box-office gross vs. aesthetics, 424–425
compare/contrast films, 436–438
creative process, 438–440
creative sources, 440
daydreaming fight scenes, 434
design fight scenes, 434–435
expanding tastes in films, 420–422
film literacy, 430–431
filming own fights, 442–443
human body, 436
human psychology, 435
information processing, 433
learning different styles of martial arts, 441–442
live sporting events, 441
old/foreign films, 431–433
questions after viewing movies, 427–428
reading reviews, 423–424
reading subtitles, 425–427
self-tests, 433–434
studying audience reactions, 420
video reference library, 446–456
watching films in theaters, 418–420
Chui, Philip Kwok, 41
Cinderella Man **(2005), 349**
cinematography, 384–405
books on, 459
camera angles, 390
camera height, 392
close-ups, 394
continuous action without breaks, 404–405
distance from fight, 390–391, 394–398
frame composition, 394
inserts, 394
rehearsing with cameraman, 387–389
showing just enough fight scenes in, 398–399
slow-motion sequences, 399–402
under-cranking, 403–404
visual techniques, 393
Circle of Iron **(1978), 37**
City Heat **(1984), 26**
City Hunter **(1993), 137**
clash, 153
Class of 1984 **(1982), 15–16**
clean technique, 142
Cliffhanger **(1993), 33**
cliffhanger serials, 10, 19
climaxes, 261, 344–345
Clockwork Orange, A **(1971), 21–22**
closed stances, 142
closed tournaments, 105
close-range fights, 138
close-ups, 391, 394
closing the gap, 142
Coburn, James, 17, 22, 37
code of ethics/conduct, 59
Code of Silence **(1985), 41**
Coffy **(1973), 357**
Cohen, Rob, 41
combative sports, 96–97
See also mixed martial arts (MMA)
in fight choreography, 93–94
periodicals, 470
root of, 98
videos, 462–465
combination, 143
Come Drink with Me **(1966), 58**
comedic brawls, 12
comic book conventions, 484–487
comic book heroes, 34
commitment, 289
common man as hero, 31–33
common sense, 358–360
composure, 144
computer-generated imagery (CGI), 48, 65
Conan the Barbarian **(1982), 28**
Conan the Destroyer **(1984), 28**
conditioned fighter, 293–300
See also fighters
definition of, 293

falls, 295–296
hits, 296–297
with stick, 299–300
strikes, 298–299
conditioned reaction, 300–301
conditioned response, 300
Connery, Sean, 17
Conrad, Robert, 18
continuity, 358–360
continuous action, 404–405
conventions, 439, 484–487
coolmoveitis, 153, 412
***Copland* (1997), 33**
Coragus (Macedonian warrior), 99–100
counter-attackers, 138–139
Craig, Daniel, 36
Crane, Simon, 33
creative process, 438–440
creative sources, 440
***Crippled Avengers* (1978), 349**
Criterion Collection, 26
criticisms, 443–445
critics societies, 478
cross, 143
***Crouching Tiger, Hidden Dragon* (2000), 58, 75–77, 426**
***Crow, The* (1994), 30**
crowd, 147
***Crying Fist* (2005), 405**
cues, 363–365
culture and filmmaking, 55–56
Curtis, Tony, 146, 247
***Cutting Edge, The: The Magic of Movie Editing* (2004), 461**
cynical/wounded antihero, 217

D

Davis, Andrew, 41
Davis, Geena, 233
***Day After, The* (1983), 27**
Dean, James, 14
death, 310
defensive fighters, 138–139
defensive stances, 373
***Delicate Delinquent, The* (1957), 15**
DeNiro, Robert, 146, 247
Dennehy, Brian, 28–29
depth perception, 395
detective films, 19
dialogue, 285
***Die Another Day* (2002), 31, 36**
***Die Hard* (1988), 32**
climax, 261
death at hands of character in, 310
fight strategy in, 194
first act, 256
justifications for fighting skills in, 214
martial acting in, 382
pre-planned strategy, 335
second act, 258–259
setups/payoffs in, 213
third act, 261
use of surroundings/environment in, 354
villain in, 221
wise-crackin' hero in, 29
digital video discs (DVDs), 30
buying on budget, 455–456
commentaries/special features, 440
distributors, 472–474
dubtitles, 453–454
imported, 448–453
independent dealers, 474
online reviews, 481–482
quality of, 448
rare/obscure, 450–453
references, 460–467
reissues, 456
Dioxippus (Athenian fighter), 99–100
director, 51
director of photography, 51
***Dirty Harry* (1971), 19, 208, 314**
disengage, 143
Dobbins, Ben, 82
***Don't Give a Damn* (1995), 68**
***Double Dare* (2002), 460**
Douglas, Kirk, 18, 233
***Dr. No* (1962), 16**
Draeger, Donn, 35
***Dragon Inn* (1966), 356**
***Dragon Lord* (1982), 45**
***Dragon: The Bruce Lee Story* (1993), 41**
draw, 143
***Dreadnaught* (1981), 348**
***Drive* (1997), 353**

Drunken Master (1978), 224–225, 232, 236, 309, 314
Drunken Master II (1994), 67
dubtitles, 453–454
duck, 143
Dun, Dennis, 40
Duran, Roberto, 149

E

Eastern Condors (1986), 356
Eddie Brandt's (video store), 456
Edison, Thomas, 3
editing, 405–411
  Asian vs. Western films, 62–63
  fight choreographer's dilemma in, 408–410
  and information processing, 410–411
  solutions, 410
  styles of, 406–408
editor, 51
effective technique, 290–291
egos, 306–307
El Demonio Azul (The Blue Demon), 129–130
El Santo (The Saint), 129
El Senior Tormenta (1963), 130
elements of fights, 346
  bystander investment/reaction, 352
  changes in types of fight, 347
  character strategy, 360
  common sense/continuity, 358–360
  emotions of fight, 358
  exposition, 347
  handicaps, 347–349
  non-verbal dialogue, 360
  physical, 363–376
  pre-planned strategy, 356–357
  ranges in emotions, 357
  reveals, 346
  setup of opponents, 354–356
  surroundings/environment, 353–354
  time bombs, 349–352
emotional continuity changes, 320
emotional fighters, 141
emotions, 357
Emperor of the North (1973), 22
empty-handed fighting distance/range, 137–138
Enter the Dragon (1973), 71
  back story, 277
  changes in types of fight, 347
  climax, 345
  continuous action without breaks in, 405
  establishing characters in, 329
  fight scenes in, 61, 319
  fight strategy in, 88–89
  fighting styles in, 83
  justifying hero's actions in, 220–221
  martial acting in, 380
  pre-planned strategy in, 357
  previous story issues in, 331
  reactions, 384
  release after Bruce Lee's death, 38
  setups/payoffs in, 212–213
  slow-motion sequences in, 400–401
  stereotype Asian character in, 69
  stylization of moves in, 367
  villains with handicap in, 348
Enter the Ninja (1981), 40
entertainment news, 480
environment, 353–354, 367
epilogue, 345
E.T: The Extra Terrestrial (1982), 25
event films, 24–25
Evil Dead II (1987), 247
Excalibur (1981), 28
exchange, 150
exclamation point, 150
Executioners of Shaolin (1977), 55
exploitation films, 20–21
exposition, 209, 347
Extreme Championship Wrestling (ECW), 122–123
extreme long shot, 391

F

Face-Off (1997), 281, 344
facial expressions, 378, 384
Fairbanks, Douglas, Sr., 3
fake, 143
falling asleep, 143
falls, 294–296
false starts, 333–334
Fanning, Dakota, 197
Fastest Sword, The (1968), 273, 277, 293
Faulkner, Edward, 6
Faulkner, Ralph, 3–4
Fearless (2006), 135, 320–321
Fearless Hyena, The (1979), 348, 357

***feng shui*, 55**
festivals, 487–488
fifth run, 362
fight charts/stats, 315–321
audience learning about characters in, 319
characters involved, 317–318
charts, 315–316
classification of fights, 316
differences, 319
effect of fights, 320–321
justifications, 318–319
physical elements, 320–321
physical/emotional continuity changes, 319–320
results, 310
stats, 316–321
fight choreographers, 408–410
fight choreography, 176–177
in China/Hong Kong, 42–45
East vs. West differences in, 48–75
evolution of, 2–3
in 1960s, 16–18
in 1970s, 19–24
in 1980s, 24–29
in 1990-2000, 30–35
in ancient history, 2–3
birth of film in the United States, 3–5
brawls, 5–16
terminology, 150–153
***Fight Club* (1999), 57, 248**
fight coordinator, 31, 51
fight director, 51, 64–65, 410
fight scenes, 154
camera angles, 63
descriptions of, 153–156
designing, 434–435
editing, 62–63
elaborate vs. brief, 59–62
for first act, 262–263
length of, 62
physical elements of, 363–376
pulse of, 411–415
rhythm in, 168–171
staged vs. real, 157–167
structure of, 201–205, 324–357
elements of, 201–203
flexible elements, 346–357
lead-up, 326–335
physical fight/conflict, 336–345
physical vs. technical, 204–205
technical elements of, 385–415
time and preparation for, 67–68
***Fighter in the Wind* (2004), 242**
fighters, 157–167
as actors, 163–166
control, 164
frame of mind, 165–166
martial acting, 164
techniques, 163
vulnerability/ego, 164–165
conditioned vs. unconditioned, 293–300
falls, 294–296
hits, 296–297
with sticks, 299–300
strikes, 298–299
as fight choreographers, 166–167
screen, 167–168
styles of, 139–141
types of, 138–139
fighter's composure, 144
fighting distance, 302
fighting IQ, 282–315
acquisition of skills, 291–292
actions during events beyond control, 306
anger, 293
animal representation, 288
caste system, 301
categories of, 283
conditioned vs. unconditioned, 293–300
criteria, 282–283
effect of fights, 293
ego, 306–307
exposure to styles/disciplines, 290–291
fighting distance, 302
fighting spirit, 289–290
flashy vs. effective techniques, 290–291
flaws/weaknesses/strengths, 302
handicaps, 286
heightened intuition, 285–286
injury/death at hands of character, 310
interactions with skilled individuals, 314
inventory of skills, 305
issues about death, 310
justification of skills, 284–285
learning curve, 302
level of awareness, 291
morals/code of conduct, 305–306

fighting IQ ***(continued)***
motivation to fight, 302
number of fights, 284
personal carriage at rest, 308
pre-planned fights, 309
previous confrontations/fights, 303–304
proficiency level, 312–313
reaction/response, 300–301
reactions to difficult lessons, 309
relationship to mentor, 308
reputation, 314
respect for authority figures, 308
responsibilities, 292–293
result of each fight, 284
rituals, 303
signature moves, 311
signature weapons, 312
street sense, 304
symbols, 315
temperament, 289
things to avoid, 305
thinking process, 304–305
time period, 287
traditional vs. modern eclectic, 286–287
training, 308
transcendence to mental/spiritual/mythical aspects, 307
uncomfortable place/environment, 291
in uncomfortable situations, 308
fighting stance, 144
fighting terms, 141–150
film conservatories/institutes, 477
film festivals, 422, 487–488
film genres, 19–21, 68
film noir, 19
film studios, 471–472
film training, 172–175
filmmaking classes, 439
filmmaking, East vs. West differences in, 48–75
ageism, 58–59
art form vs. gimmick, 57
Asian talent in Western films, 70–75
billing/recognition, 67
camera angles, 63
chain of command, 51–53
choreographers, 64–65
code of ethics/conduct, 59
culture/religion, 55–56
editing, 62–63
emphasis of fight, 59–62
film genres, 68
length of fight, 62
mythology, 59
perception of action, 52–54
perception/stereotypes of foreigners, 68–70
room for advancement vs. categorization, 66–67
sound, 65
special effects, 65
stories, 68
stuntmen, 63–64
time and preparation, 67–68
films, birth of, 3–5
final reveal, 344
final straw, 335
final twist, 344
finishing technique, 144
first act, 254–258
First Blood **(1982), 28–29, 197, 306**
first run, 361–362
First Strike **(1994), 67, 354**
Fishburne, Lawrence, 42
Fist of Fury **(1972), 43, 83, 214, 327–328**
Fist of Legend **(1994), 61**
Fistful of Dollars **(1964), 194**
flashy fight scenes, 154, 412
flashy technique, 290–291
flat fight scenes, 154, 412
Fleischer, Richard, 70
Fleming, Ian, 16–17
focus, 395
follow-through, 144
follow-up, 144
footwork, 144
Ford, Glenn, 14
Ford, John, 18
foreign films, 421
foreigners in film, 68–70
Foreman, George, 58–59, 192–193
forms, 244–248
definition of, 145–146, 244–245
in films, 246–247
levels of, 244–247
advanced, 246
beginner, 245
use in combat, 247–248
formula films, 25, 145

Foul King, The (2000), 134
fourth run, 362
frame composition, 394
Fray Tormenta (Friar Storm), 130
Frazetta: Painting with Fire (2003), 466–467
free sparring, 104
From Russia With Love (1963), 16–17
front and center, 152
Fukasaku, Kinji, 70
fuses, 351

G

Game of Death (1978), 44, 78, 83, 137
gang war in films, 14
gangster films, 19
Gene Kelly: Anatomy of a Dancer (2002), 461
genres, 19–21
Gere, Richard, 40
Gibson, Mel, 31, 33–35
gladiators, 2, 18
going to sleep, 146
going wide, 153
Gold Dust Trio, 118–119
Goldeneye (1995), 31
Goldfinger (1964), 17
Good Guys Wear Black (1978), 39
Gordon, Tom, 122
Gossett, Louis, Jr., 40
Gotch, Frank, 117
Gracie, Carlos, 100
Gracie Challenge, 100–101
Gracie, Rorian, 100–101
Gracie, Royce, 30–31, 83–84, 101
grappling, 103
gratuitous fight scenes, 154, 412
Grave of the Vampire (1974), 20
Great Train Robbery, The (1979), 432
Green Hornet, The (television series), 37, 70, 81–82
grindhouse films, 20–21
Grindhouse: Planet Terror/Death Proof (2007), 20
ground and pound, 103
Gunfight at the O.K. Corral (1957), 194
Gunner, Robert, 17

H

Hackenschmidt, George, 117
Halley, Bull, 14
Hamill, Mark, 24–29
Hammer Studios, 20
handicaps, 347–349
Harakiri (1962), 311
hard fake, 146
Hard Target (1993), 41
Hard Times (1975), 22
Hard-Boiled (1992), 401, 405
Harding, Tonya, 126
Hatsumi, Masaaki, 35
Hays Code, 8–9, 14–15
Hays Commission, 8–9
Hays, Will, 8–9
Hell in the Pacific (1968), 70
Heremans, Jean, 3–4
hero of the piece, 152
heroes, 215–221
  agreements with mentors, 226–227
  with handicaps, 348
  justifications for actions of, 219–221
  and mentors, 240–241
  roles of, 215–216
  in training sequences, 238–239
  types of, 216–219
    antihero, 217–218
    catalyst, 218
    loner, 218
    superhero, 218–219
    underdog, 217
  and villains, 222
Heston, Charlton, 18
Hexum, John Eric, 26
Hidden Fortress (1958), 24
Higgins, Anthony, 230
high concept films, 25
High Noon (1952), 194
highly stylized, 146, 152
History of Violence, A (2005), 57, 320–321
Hitman Hart: Wrestling in the Shadows (1999), 465–466
hits, 152, 296–297
HK classic editing, 407
HK modern editing, 407
HK new wave editing, 407

Holyfield, Evander, 126
***Home Alone*, 194**
home videos, 25
hookers, 118
***Hooper* (1978), 29**
horror films, 20
horse operas, 10
human psychology, 435
***Hundra* (1983), 28**
Hung, Sammo, 44–47, 66, 247
Hunt, Peter, 17
***Huo Yun Chia* (2006), 135**

I

implausible fight scenes, 154, 412
***In Like Flint* (1967), 17–18**
in range, 146
***In the Line of Fire* (1993), 382**
inciting incidents, 258, 337
***Indiana Jones and the Last Crusade* (1989), 273**
***Indiana Jones and the Temple of Doom* (1984), 339**
initial emotion, 338
initial intentions, 338
initial strategies, 338–339
injuries, 183–185
inserts, 394
intellectual fighters, 141
intermediate fighter, 313

J

Jaa, Tony, 56
jab, 146
***Jackie Chan: My Stunts* (1999), 460**
Jackson, Phil, 193
jam, 147
James Bond films, 16–17, 27, 31, 36, 224
Jedis, 24
Johnson, Reginald Vel, 32
***Joseph Campbell and the Power of Myth* (1988), 461**
journeymen, 118
judo chop, 35
***Jurassic Park* (1993), 65**
juvenile delinquent films, 13–16

K

Kamen, Robert Mark, 40
Kane, Bob, 34
***Karate Kid, The* (1984), 40**
  back story, 209, 277
  character's reactions to lessons in, 309
  climax, 261
  first act, 255
  forms in, 146
  justification for actions in, 197
  pre-planned strategy, 335
  second act, 258
  signature moves in, 311
  training sequences, 232, 238
***Karate Kid, The, Part III* (1989), 274**
***kata*, 145, 244, 247**
Kato (ancient Greek sport), 99
Kaufman, Andy, 124–125
Keaton, Michael, 34
Kelly, Jim, 38
Kerrigan, Nancy, 126
***Kickboxer* (1989), 41**
***Kids from Shaolin* (1983), 46**
***Kill Zone* (2005), 135**
***Killer, The* (1989)**
  climax, 261
  death issues in, 311
  first act, 255–256
  inciting incidents, 258
  justification for actions in, 198
  martial acting in, 381
  resolution, 262
  second act, 260
  setups/payoffs in, 212
  slow-motion sequences in, 401
  third act, 261
Kimura, Masahiko, 131
kinesthetic learning, 181
***King Creole* (1958), 14**
King, Perry, 15
***Kiss of the Dragon* (2001), 73**
"kitchen sink" films, 16
klimax, 99
Kubrick, Stanley, 21–22
***kuen*, 145, 244**
Kumite, 103
***Kung Fu* (television series), 68, 210, 305**

Kung Fu brawl, 45–48
Kung Fu Instructor, The **(1979), 146**
Kurosawa **(2001), 461–462**
Kurosawa, Akira, 24, 70
Kwai, Cory Yuen, 44

L

***La Femme Nikita*, 236, 381**
labor unions, 474–476
LaRose, Guy, 124
laserdisc players, 26
Laughlin, Tom, 38
Lawler, Jerry "The King", 125–126
Lazenby, George, 17, 45
lead-up, 326–335
- environment/setting, 332–333
- establishing characters in, 328–329
- false starts, 333–334
- final straw, 335
- justifying physical conflict in, 327–328
- motivation to fight in, 329–331
- pre-planned strategy, 334–335
- previous story issues in, 331–332
- setting up physical conflict in, 326–327
- words/threats, 333

lean fight scenes, 154
learning curve, 302
Lee, Brandon, 30
Lee, Bruce, 77–89
- in *The Big Boss*, 43
- in *Enter the Dragon*, 22
- in *The Green Hornet*, 37
- lessons from, 77–89
  - cinematic vs. real fighting, 88
  - emotional content/impact of techniques, 82
  - fighting only when necessary, 89–90
  - fighting styles, 83–84
  - importance of stuntmen, 84–85
  - individualistic screen presence, 79–81
  - learning curve, 81–82
  - martial acting skills, 85–87
  - no noticeable misses/bad takes, 77–78
  - no trademark/signature move, 87
  - philosophy/fight strategy, 88–89
  - physique, 88
  - poses, 87
  - show of vulnerability, 84
  - simple/rarely repeated techniques, 78–79
  - timing/rhythm, 85
- martial acting by, 380
- in *The Orphan*, 15
- in *Way of the Dragon*, 90–92
- in Western film/TV productions, 69–71

Lee, Byung-hun, 381
Leech, George, 17
leg sweep, 147
Legion of Decency, 8
length of fights, 365–366
Leonard, Sugar Ray, 149
Leonard, Terry, 15
Lethal Weapon **(1987), 31, 277, 282, 292**
Lethal Weapon 4 **(1998), 42, 73**
Leung, Lau Kar, 44
Lewis, Ed "Strangler", 118–119
Lewis, Jerry, 15
Li, Jet, 42, 46, 72–73
License to Kill **(1989), 27**
Lincoln, Abraham, 116
Lipstick and Dynamite **(2004), 466**
Liston, Sonny, 149, 192
Living Daylights, The **(1987), 27**
Londos, Jim "Handsome", 119
Lone Wolf and Cub: Sword of Vengeance **(1972), 354**
loners, 218
long fuse, 351
Long Kiss Goodnight, The **(1996), 209–210, 232, 280**
long range, 137
long shot, 391
long-range fights, 137
looping punches, 11
Lopez, Gerry, 28
Lords of Flatbush **(1974), 15**
Lucas, George, 24, 55
Lucha Libre, 126–130
Ludlum, Robert, 36
Lutteroth, Salvador, 126

M

Macchio, Ralph, 146
Mad Max **(1979), 31**
Maeda, Mitsuyo, 99
Magnificent Butcher **(1979), 344**
Malkovich, John, 382
Man from Glengarry, The **(1922), 4**

***Man From Hong Kong, The* (1975), 45**
***Man on Fire* (2004), 197, 219, 331**
***Man on the Moon* (1999), 126**
***Man with No Name,* 273**
***Mark of Zorro, The* (1920), 4**
Marshall, Penny, 31
martial acting, 376–383
before/after fights, 380–383
definition of, 338
during fights, 378–380
good vs. bad, 377–378
training in, 164
martial artists, 97–98
martial arts, 95
books on, 459
definition of, 95
in fight choreography, 93–94
mixed, 98–100
periodicals, 469
videos, 462
websites, 482
martial arts films, 20
Asian influence on Western films, 35–42
globalization of, 75–77
***Martial Arts of Shaolin* (1986), 46**
Marvin, Lee, 14, 22, 70
***Massacre at Central High* (1976), 15**
master fighter, 313
***Master, The* (television series), 40**
Masuda, Toshio, 70
***Matrix, The* (1999), 42, 54**
Mazzola, Frank, 14
McCain, John, 102
McDowell, Malcolm, 18
McGraw, Charles, 18
***McLintock!* (1963), 6, 12**
***McMahon* (2006), 466**
McMahon, Vince, Jr., 30, 121–122
medium fuse, 351
medium shot, 391
mentors, 223–230
See also training sequences
agreements with heroes, 226–227
and heroes, 240–241
limitations of, 229
relationship to, 308
responsibilities of, 227–229
in training sequences, 239–240
as villains, 229–230
***Midnight Run* (1988), 61, 210, 276, 279**
mid-range fights, 138
Mifune, Toshiro, 70
Mil Máscaras (The Man of a Thousand Masks), 130
Miller, George, 31
***Million Dollar Baby* (2004), 274**
misses, 152
Mitchum, Robert, 38, 71
mixed martial arts (MMA), 98–103
Brazilian Jiu-Jitsu/Vale Tudo, 100–101
origin of, 98–100
pay-per-view events, 101–102
popularity of, 102–103
ranges of, 103
terminology, 141–150
websites, 483
modern eclectic fighter, 286–287
modern-day action-adventure genre, 19–24
mondo films, 20
Mondt, Joseph Raymond, 118–119
***Moonraker* (1979), 279**
Moore, Roger, 27
moral clauses, 8
Morales, Esai, 15
Morrow, Vic, 14, 26
Motion Picture Association of America (MPAA), 9
Motion Picture Producers and Distributors of America (MPPDA), 8
movements, 379
***MTV's WWE Tough Enough: The First Season* (2001), 466**
Murphy, Eddie, 29, 70, 247
Musashi, Miyamoto, 193
music videos, 26
musicals, 15
mythology, 59

N

***Nacho Libre* (2006), 130**
nailing a move, 152
names of characters, 272–273
National Television Systems Committee (NTSC), 454
Needham, Hal, 66
Neeson, Liam, 230
Nero, Franco, 40

neutral zone, 147
***New Gladiators* (2002), 462**
Nicholson, Jack, 34
nicknames of characters, 272
***Nightmare on Elm Street, A* (1984), 194, 334**
ninja films, 40
no resonance fight scenes, 154, 412
no steam fight scenes, 154, 412
no substance fight scenes, 154, 412
non-telegraphing, 147
non-verbal dialogue, 360
***Norbit* (2007), 70**
Norris, Chuck, 39, 41, 65
Norton, Edward, 247
NTSC (National Television Systems Committee), 454

O

objective camera angle, 390
occupation of characters, 285
***Octagon, The* (1980), 65**
***Octopussy* (1983), 27**
off fight scenes, 154, 412
offensive fighters, 138
offensive stances, 371
***Oldboy* (2003), 242, 405**
Olympic games, 98
***On Her Majesty's Secret Service* (1969), 17, 403**
***On The Ropes* (2000), 463**
***Once Upon a Time in China* (1991)**
 character arcs, 210
 morals/code of conduct, 305
 responsibility of character, 293
 signature moves, 311
 stylization of moves in, 152
 type of fight, 340
***Once Upon a Time in High School* (2004), 15**
***Once Upon a Time in the West* (1968), 194**
***One, The* (2001), 73**
***One-Armed Swordsman, The* (1967), 233, 242, 349**
one-man arm, 28
one-punch knockouts, 60–62
one-step sparring, 364
***Ong-Bak* (2003), 56**
 "aha!" moment in, 343
 bystander investment/reaction, 352
 fight scenes in, 60–61
 motivation in, 330
 slow-motion sequences in, 400
 stylization of moves in, 368
online references, 479–484
 books, 479
 boxing, 482
 celebrity sites, 479
 DVD reviews/news, 481–482
 entertainment news, 480
 martial arts, 482
 mixed martial arts, 483
 movie news, 480
 professional wrestling, 483
 screenwriting, 480
 sports wrestling, 484
on-set injuries, 183–185
***Open Range*, 194**
open stances, 147
open tournaments, 105
opening, 147
organic strategy, 188
organizations, 474–476
***Orphan, The* (1960), 15**
***Oscar* (1991), 33**
***Our Man Flint* (1966), 17**
out of range, 147
outer motivation, 338
outlaw biker films, 20
***Outsiders, The* (1983), 15**
oversold fight scenes, 154, 412

P

pace, 147
PAL (Phase Alternating Line), 454
Pankration (ancient Greek sport), 98–100
***Paradise Alley* (1978), 134**
Parillaud, Anne, 236, 381
***Passenger 57* (1992), 33**
pauses, 362–363
payoffs, 211–213
pay-per-view events, 101–102
***Pedicab Driver* (1989), 327, 449**
Pei-Pei, Cheng, 58
Penn, Sean, 15
perfect fight scenes, 154, 412

periodicals, 467–470
action-specific, 468
combative sports, 470
entertainment business, 468
film/entertainment reviews, 469
filmmaking, 468
martial arts, 469
pop culture, 470
professional wrestling, 470
screenwriting, 467
stunt-related, 467
Phase Alternating Line (PAL), 454
physical continuity changes, 320
physical elements, of fights
approaches, 373–374
beats/pauses, 362–363
body language, 369
camera awareness, 375
centerline, 369–371
cues, 363–365
environment, 367
intent/choice of techniques, 362
length, 365–366
rhythm, 363
stances, 371–373
stylization of moves, 367–368
timing, 363
physical fight/conflict, 336–345
See also fight scenes
environment/setting, 332–333
final twist, 344
heightened conflict, 340–342
changing/adjusting strategy, 341
exchanges in dominance/control, 342
increasing intensity/tension, 341
raising stakes, 342
intent and strategy, 336–339
emotional intensity, 340
inciting incident, 337
initial emotion, 338
initial intention, 338
initial strategy, 338–339
type of fight, 340
justifications of, 327–328
outcome, 343–345
"aha!" moments, 343–344
climax, 344–345
epilogue, 345
final reveal, 344
final twist, 344
next scene, 345
one final effort, 344
setting up, 326–327
picture quality, 450
Pioneer, 26
***plague*, 145, 244**
planned strategy, 187
***Point Break* (1991), 33**
point of view (POV), 390
***Police Story* (1985), 169, 331, 354, 384**
***Police Story 2* (1988), 354**
Pollack, Sydney, 38, 71
posers, 154, 412
posing, 154, 412
practical experience, 289
***Predator* (1987), 353**
pre-planned fights, 309
pre-planned strategy, 334–335, 356–357
Presley, Elvis, 14
previous story issues, 331–332
primal conditioned response, 147
***Princess Bride, The* (1987)**
death issues in, 311
false start in, 334
justification for actions in, 197, 221
mentor in, 226
reveal in, 346
wrestling elements in, 135
***Principal, The* (1987), 15**
***Prodigal Son* (1982), 368**
producer, 51
Production Code, 8–9
professional organizations, 474–476
professional wrestling, 108–109
brief history of, 116–121
Extreme Championship Wrestling (ECW), 122–123
as "fake"/worked sports, 110–111
vs. fight choreography, 111–116
differences, 112–116
similarities in choreography, 112–114
similarities in story, 111–112
on film and television, 133–135
hooking the audience to, 123–126
audience participation buildup, 124

blurred lines of reality and entertainment, 124–126
good vs. evil, 123
replication life events in, 124
outside America, 126–133
in Japan (Puroresu), 131–133
in Mexico (Lucha Libre), 126–130
periodicals, 470
popularity of, 30
as sports entertainment, 109
websites, 483
World Wrestling Entertainment (WWE), 121–122
proficiency level, 312–313
proficient fighter, 313
***Project A* (1983), 328, 365, 380**
***Project A II* (1987), 405**
***Promise, The* (2005), 65**
props, 285
***Protector, The* (1985), 71–72, 135**
Puroresu, 131–133
***Pyrrachia* (Greek dance), 2**

Q

Queen Elizabeth I, 3
***Quiet Man, The* (1952), 12**

R

***Raging Bull* (1980), 354**
***Raiders of the Lost Ark* (1981), 210, 212, 306, 351–352**
***Rambo: First Blood Part II* (1985), 29**
***Rambo III* (1988), 29**
range of vision, 395
ranks, 315
***Rapid Fire* (1992), 353**
reactions, 147, 300–301, 383–384
***Real World, The* (television series), 30**
reality television, 30
rebel teen films, 13–16
***Rebel Without A Cause* (1955), 14**
recall training sequences, 232–233
recognition, 67
***Red River* (1948), 12**
***Red Sun* (1971), 70**
***Red Trousers: The Story of Hong Kong Stuntmen* (2003), 461**
Reeves, Christopher, 34, 42
Reeves, Keanu, 33
references, 457–488
books, 457–460
conventions, 484–487
festivals, 487–488
online, 479–484
periodicals, 467–470
videos, 460–467
reissues, 456
religion and filmmaking, 55–56
remakes, 438
repetitious fight scenes, 154, 412
reputations of fighters, 314
resolution, 262
response, 148
responses, 300–301
restructure training sequences, 233–236
***Return of the 5 Deadly Venoms, The* (1978), 349**
***Return of the Dragon* (1972), 44, 84, 90–92**
reveals, 211, 346
reverse, 148
reverse punch, 143, 148
revival houses, 421
Reynolds, Burt, 29
Rhee, Philip, 367
rhythm, 168–171, 363
Richmond, Branscombe, 66
Rickman, Alan, 32
***Ricochet* (1991), 33**
***Rikidozan* (2004), 134**
Rikidozan (Japanese wrestler), 131
ring psychology, 124
rituals, 303
***River Wild, The* (1994), 33**
Robbins, Jerome, 15
Rocca, Antonio, 120
rock and roll music in films, 14
"Rock Around The Clock" (song), 14
***Rock, The* (1996), 33**
***Rocky* (1976), 23**
ambitions/desires in, 276
climax, 261
first act, 254–255
resolution, 262
second act, 259–260
setups/payoffs in, 212
training sequences, 242–243

***Rocky Balboa* (2006), 23**
***Rocky II* (1979), 194, 356–357**
***Rocky III* (1982)**
character strategy in, 360
events beyond character's control in, 306
hero with handicap in, 348
justification for actions in, 197
strategy in, 193
taunts in, 149
training sequences, 233, 236
words/threats in, 333
wrestling elements in, 135
***Rocky V* (1990), 135**
Rodman, Dennis, 126, 193
Rodriguez, Robert, 21
Rogers, Mic, 33
***Romeo Must Die* (2000), 68**
rooted fight scenes, 154, 412
"rope-a-dope" technique, 193
Rothrock, Cynthia, 68
Rowe, Nicholas, 230
***Rumble in the Bronx* (1995), 72, 354**
***Rundown, The* (2003), 149**
***Rush Hour* (1998), 41, 72**
Rush, Robert Lee, 15
Russel, Kurt, 40

S

Sakuraba, Kazushi, 132–133
Sandow, Billy, 118–119
***Sanjuro* (1962), 273**
***Saving Private Ryan* (1998), 33, 194, 261**
Scammell, Roy, 21
school training, 172–175
application of skills, 174–175
learning process, 173
length of classes, 173–174
purpose of, 172
techniques, 174
time for, 172–173
Schwarzenegger, Arnold, 28
Scorsese, Martin, 354
screen fighter, 167–168
screen presence, 80
script, 248–263
breakdown of, 269–271
climax, 261
and design of fight scenes, 435
first act, 254–258
first reading, 265–266
resolution, 262
second act, 258
second reading, 266
third act, 260–261
third reading, 266
and training of actors, 176–177
***Scum* (1979), 15**
Seagal, Steven, 41
SECAM standard, 454
second act, 256
second run, 362
second unit editor, 51
self-defense/combative system
definition of, 97
in fight choreography, 93–94
self-discipline, 289
sell, 152
seminars, 439
setups, 211–213, 354–356
***Seven Samurai, The* (1954)**
changes in types of fight, 347
comfort with surroundings in, 282
fight strategy in, 194
heightened intuition in, 286
preplanned strategy, 335
previous story issues in, 332
surroundings/environment, 353
sex exploitation films, 20
***Sha Po Lang* (2005), 135, 364**
***Shadow Boxers* (1999), 463**
shadow boxing, 148, 244–245
Shamock, Ken, 102
***Shanghai Noon* (2000), 275**
***Shaolin Temple, The* (1982), 46, 72**
Shaw, Robert, 17
Sheedy, Ally, 15
***Shiri* (1999), 56, 431**
shockfilms, 20
shooters, 118
short fuse, 351
showman, 141
shows, 439
sidekick, 367
signature moves, 148, 311

silent films, 3–5
***Silent Flute, The* (script), 37**
Silliphant, Stirling, 37
Simmons, Bob, 17
***sing sang* (mentor), 225**
"Singing in the Rain" (song), 21
Sin-Nak,Kim, 131
sleeper hold, 148
slow-motion sequences, 399–402
slug-fest, 6
***Smashing Machine, The: The Life and Times of Extreme Fighter Mark Kerr* (2003), 463–464**
***Smokey and the Bandit* (1977), 29**
***Snake in the Eagle's Shadow* (1978)**
- character arc, 278
- character's strengths/flaws in, 302
- handicaps, 287
- martial acting in, 382
- mentor in, 226
- training sequences, 238, 242

snapping, 144
Snipes, Wesley, 33
***Sons of Katie Elder, The* (1965), 12**
sound, 65
sources, 207–263
- buildup, 230–244
- characters, 215–230
- forms, 244–248
- script, 248–263
- story, 207–215

southpaw, 148
sparring match, 151
***Spartacus* (1960), 18, 233**
special effects, 65
special screenings, 439
***Speed* (1994), 33**
***Spider-Man* (2002), 281, 292, 319, 330**
***Spider-Man 2* (2004), 281, 349–350**
***Spooky Encounters* (1984), 248**
sporting events, 441
sports entertainment, 109, 465–466
sports wrestling websites, 484
spy films, 16–17, 36
square off, 148
stage presence, 80
***Stagecoach* (1939), 18**
staged fight scenes, 412
stale fight scenes, 154, 412
Stallone, Sylvester, 28–29, 33, 233
stances, 371–373
- centered, 372
- defensive, 373
- and martial acting, 379
- offensive, 371

***Star Wars Episode III: Revenge of the Sith* (2005), 346**
***Star Wars Episode IV: A New Hope* (1977), 24**
- back story, 208, 277
- climax, 261
- first act, 256
- mind games in, 279
- resolution, 262
- third act, 261
- training sequences, 238

***Star Wars Episode V: The Empire Strikes Back* (1980), 226, 236, 344, 346**
***Star Wars Episode VI: Return of the Jedi* (1983), 330–331, 333, 335, 345**
***Star Wars* films, 55, 231**
Steadicam camera, 23
stereotypes in Western films, 68–70
sticking a move, 152
stiff fight scenes, 154, 412
stiff jab, 148
***Stop! Or My Mom Will Shoot* (1992), 33**
stories, 68
***Storm Riders, The* (1998), 46, 65**
story, 207–215
- *See also* script
- back story, 208–209
- character arcs, 209–211
- exposition, 209
- justification for action scenes, 214–215
- payoffs, 211–213
- reveals, 211
- setups, 211–213

storyboards, 434
straight-to-video films, 25
strategy, 185–187
- and audience, 191–192
- and character/personality, 189–191
- on films, 194
- and martial acting, 379
- real-life strategists, 192–194
- types of, 187–188
- use of techniques with, 188–189

Streep, Meryl, 33

Street Fighter, The **(1974), 38–39**
street sense, 304
strikes, 298–299
striking, 103
Strode, Woody, 18
structure, 148
stunt coordinators, 16, 51, 183–184
stunt doubles, 175–176
stunt organizations, 476
stuntmen
  Asian vs. Western films, 63–64, 66–67
  importance of, 84–85
  roles of, 175–176
  and training of actors, 171
stylizing, 152
subjective camera angle, 390
submission, 103
submission hold, 148
subtitles, 425–427, 453–454
Sudden Attack! The Killing Fist **(1974), 38–39**
Sun Tzu, 194
superheroes, 218–219
Superman **(1978), 280**
Superman II **(1980), 280**
surroundings/environment, 353–354
swashbuckler films, 19
Sweet Sweetback's Baadasssss Song **(1971), 20**
switchblade, 13
sword and sorcery films, 28
symbols of fighters, 315

T

taboo films, 20
Tai, Robert, 44
Takakura, ken, 38
Takakura, Ken, 71
takedown, 149
tap out, 149
Tarantino, Quentin, 21, 39
Tarleton, Richard, 3
taunts, 149
Taxi Driver **(1976), 146, 247**
Taylor, Delores, 38
technical elements, 385–415
  cinematography, 384–405
  editing, 405–411
  pulse of fight scenes, 411–415
technicians, 139–140
techniques
  intent/choice of, 362
  and martial acting, 379
teen films, brawls in, 12–16
teen rebel films, 13–16
telegraphing, 149
temperament, 289
Terminator 2: Judgment Day **(1991), 262, 401**
Terminator, The **(1984), 256, 261**
They Drew Fire **(1999), 466–467**
They Live **(1988), 135**
third act, 260–261
third run, 362
Threads **(1984), 27**
threats, use of, 333
Three Musketeers, The **(1948), 4**
Three Stooges, 149
thriller, 19
throw down, 150
throwing in the towel, 149–150
thrust, 150
tight fight scenes, 154
time bombs, 349–352
timing, 150, 363
Titan in the Ring, A **(2002), 134**
titles, 451–452
Tom Yum Goong **(2005), 135, 405**
Tomorrow Never Dies **(1997), 31, 41**
too aware, 154, 415
too staged, 154, 415
Tora! Tora! Tora! **(1970), 70**
Touch of Zen, A **(1969), 432**
tournament fighting, 104
  blood and guts era, 105–106
  renaissance era, 106–108
  types of, 105
Trading Places **(1983), 247**
traditional Chinese medicine, 55
traditional fighter, 286–287
tragic/unlikable antihero, 218
trainers, 178–179
training, 178–185
  and actor's physical skills, 179–180
  actor-training relationship, 178–179
  horror stories, 183–185
  issues in, 181–182
  learning styles, 180–181

training sequences, 230–244
  acquisition of difficult skills in, 237–238
  and fighting IQ, 308
  fights in, 243
  heroes in, 238–239
  ineffective, 244
  and justification of skills, 285
  mentors in, 239–240
  overview, 230–231
  reasons for, 236–237
  self-seclusion/training alone, 241–243
  things to pass on during, 243–244
  types of, 230–236
    apprentice, 231–232
    recall, 232–233
    restructure, 233–236
  villains in, 241
trap, 150
***True Romance* (1993), 39**
Tucker, Chris, 41
TV size, 454
***Twilight Samurai, The* (2002), 281**
***Twilight Zone: The Movie* (1983), 26**
Tyson, Mike, 126, 140

U

***Ultimate Fighter, The: Season 1* (2005), 464**
Ultimate Fighting Championship (UFC), 30, 101–102
***Ultraman* (television series), 135, 351–352**
unconditioned fighter, 293–300
  See also fighters
  definition of, 294
  falls, 294–295
  hits, 297
  with stick, 299
  strikes, 298
unconditioned reaction, 301
***Under Siege* (1992), 33, 41**
under-cranking, 403–404
underdog, 217
***Unforgiven* (1992), 232, 242, 464**
uniforms, 315
unions, 474–476
***Unleashed* (2005), 73, 281, 292**
***Unreal Story of Pro Wrestling, The* (1999), 466**
Uyttenhove, Henry, 3–4

V

Vale Tudo, 100
Van Dam, Rob, 123
Van Damme, Jean-Claude, 41
Van Patten, Vince, 15
Van Pebble, Melvin, 20
***Vengeance* (1970), 45–48**
VHS video format, 27
video cassette recorders (VCRs), 30
video CDs, 448
video reference library, 446–456
  broadcast standards, 454
  on budget, 455–456
  database, 455
  finding video stores, 447
  imported DVDs, 448–453
  quality of DVDs, 448
  rare/obscure DVDs, 450–453
  TV size, 454
  video CDs, 448
video stores, 447, 451–452
videos, 460–466
  combative sports, 462–465
  fight/stunt-related, 460–461
  film biography, 461–462
  filmmaking, 461
  martial arts, 462
  screenwriting/storytelling, 461
  sports entertainment, 465–466
Vietnam veterans in films, 27–29
***View to a Kill, A* (1985), 27**
villains, 221–223
  See also heroes
  with handicaps, 348
  and heroes, 222
  mentors as, 229–230
  skills of, 223
  in training sequences, 241
violence
  vs. action, 195–196
  justifications of, 197–199
***Vision Quest* (1985), 285**
visual learning, 181
visual stability, 395
Vitali, Keith, 106–108, 140
Voyager Company, 26

W

Wachowski brothers, 42
Wagner, George "Gorgeous George", 119–120
Wallace, Bill "Superfoot", 140
Wanderers, The (1979), 13–15
war films, 19
War of the Roses, The (1989), 274
Warriors, The (1979), 22–23, 334
Warriors Two (1978), 224
Washington, Denzel, 33, 197
Waters, Chuck, 15
Way of the Dragon (1972), 90–92
  bystander investment/reaction, 352
  climax, 345
  fight choreography in, 44
  fight strategy in, 194
  forms, 248
  initial strategies, 339
  martial acting in, 380
  name of character in, 273
  stylization of moves in, 367
  vulnerability of character in, 84
  where the character lives in, 275
Wayne, John, 10–12
Wayne, Patrick, 6
weapons, 285, 312, 315
Weathers, Carl, 23, 233
weave, 150
West Side Story (1961), 15
Western brawls. *See* brawls
Western classic editing, 407
western films, 19
Western quick cuts, 407
Wheels on Meals (1984), 364, 394
When We Were Kings (1997), 464–465
wide, 153
Wild One, The (1953), 13–14
Wild Wild West, The (1965-1969), 18
will, 289
Williams, Van, 37, 82
Willis, Bruce, 29, 32, 382
Wing Chun, 83, 150
wise-crackin' heroes, 29
women in films, 31, 438
women in prison films, 20
women's film organizations, 477–478
Wong Fei Hung, 43
Woo, John, 41
Woodward, Edward, 33
Woo-Ping, Yuen, 42, 44, 66, 73
World Championship Wrestling (WCW), 30
words/threats, use of, 333
World Is Not Enough, The (1999), 31
World Wrestling Entertainment (WWE), 121–122
World Wrestling Federation (WWF), 30
wrestling, 30
Wu Shu, 46

X

X-Men (2000), 292
X-Men 2 (2003), 292

Y

Yakuza, The (1974), 38, 71
Yamazaki, Kiyoshi, 28
Yan, Yuen Cheung, 44
"yellowface" in movies, 70
Yeoh, Michell, 41
Yojimbo (1961), 194, 273, 275
You Only Live Twice (1967), 35
Young Master (1980), 365
Young Sherlock Holmes (1985), 230
Yu, Jimmy Wang, 45
Yu, Ronny, 382–383
Yun-Fat, Chow, 381

Z

Zatoichi (2003), 275, 286, 348, 449
Zuffa LLC, 31

50502568R00301

Made in the USA
Lexington, KY
18 March 2016